STUDIES IN
MEDIEVAL HISTORY

Oxford University Press, Amen House, London E.C.4

GLASGOW   NEW YORK   TORONTO   MELBOURNE   WELLINGTON
BOMBAY   CALCUTTA   MADRAS   CAPE TOWN

Geoffrey Cumberlege, Publisher to the University

F. M. Paricke.

STUDIES IN
MEDIEVAL HISTORY

PRESENTED TO

Frederick Maurice Powicke

Edited by

R. W. HUNT
W. A. PANTIN
R. W. SOUTHERN

OXFORD
AT THE CLARENDON PRESS
1948

To

SIR MAURICE POWICKE

We have sought an occasion to mark our affection for you and the debt which we owe you. During these years in Manchester and Oxford, we have been conscious in your presence and in your teaching of an influence above the hatreds and distractions of our present time. You have kept us to the study of men as they are beneath the destructiveness which scars the course of history, responding however faint-heartedly to the calls of friendship, practical idealism, and the love of God. We have learnt the value of quiet things. The images of life 'by the gentle waters of the Kennet', and of a mind at rest thinking of home in a strange land, the pieties which kept life sweet in a world of disappointments—these and many other things will be with us always. Under your guidance we have felt the deep influence of those lives which were the glory of their own time and still have power to invigorate us to-day. These are unforgettable experiences and it was with these things in mind that this book was planned and written. We wish it could have witnessed more adequately to your influence among us, but we offer it to you as an expression of our gratitude for all you have done in showing us the strength to be drawn from the past

TABLE OF CONTENTS

LIST OF PLATES

PLATE I. Fol. 85ᵛ shows one of the main hands of Tib. I. Note the different letter-forms used by the scribes in writing Latin and Old English, including the small differences in the forms of *e* and *h*. These distinctions were observed for more than a hundred years after the introduction of caroline minuscule for writing Latin in the middle of the tenth century. The method of showing an omission by crossed *d* in the text answering to crossed *h* in the margin, conforms with regular earlier Anglo-Saxon usage.

PLATE II. Fol. 121 shows hand (2) of Tib. II and alterations probably in hand (1), as follows: line 12 *modicam,* line 13 *eam* (interlined), line 19 *ab indigenis est,* line 20 *sita spo,* line 23 *loci,* line 24 *huius extitit. Hic fratrem,* line 25 *ui nimis diligebatur,* line 26 *a duobus regibus istius patrie.*

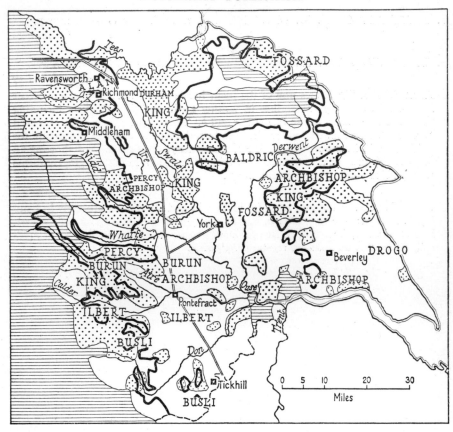

The thick line represents the 400-ft. contour.

Shading represents the areas apparently uninhabited in 1066.

Stippling represents the areas apparently depopulated in 1086.

The probable course of some Roman roads and the location of some of the greater tenants' estates are shown.

THE NORMAN SETTLEMENT OF YORKSHIRE

IN the Yorkshire section of Domesday, where the effects of devastations in 1069 and 1070 are conspicuous, there is evidence of subsequent migration and colonization on a very great scale, directed to economic and strategic ends by the first generation of post-Conquest lords.[1]

In 1066 the uninhabited parts of east Yorkshire were confined to large areas in the north Yorkshire moors and comparatively small areas of fenland round the lower Ouse. Most of the Yorkshire wolds were covered with large settlements; in some of the marshy areas on either side of the Ouse were settlements which must have been created and kept in existence by schemes of drainage; in the vale of Pickering and Holderness, in the basin of the Don and the lower Calder and Aire between the Nottinghamshire boundary and York, and in the wide vale between York and the Tees, about 1,200 settlements covered a plain as well suited as any part of England to medieval arable farming. About one-third of Yorkshire lies above and to the west of the 400-foot contour line bounding the continuously high ground of the Pennine Chain, where the climate and in many places the configuration of the land are unfavourable to arable farming. That large parts of this area, not confined to the principal dales, were also densely settled suggests that in Yorkshire as in other parts of the Danelaw there had been great pressure of population in the eleventh century. The typical Pennine settlement was small, valued at 10 or 15s., measuring three or four carucates, and containing two or three ploughlands; but the inhabitants of this part of

---

[1] The following works have been used: W. Farrer, 'Yorkshire Domesday', *V.C.H. Yorks.* ii, indexed in *V.C.H. Yorks.*, Index volume; C. W. Foster and T. Longley, *Lincolnshire Domesday* (Lincoln Record Society, xix); F. M. Stenton, 'Derbyshire Domesday' and 'Nottinghamshire Domesday', *V.C.H. Derby, V.C.H. Notts.*; R. W. Eyton, *Domesday Studies: Staffs.*; W. Farrer, *Early Yorkshire Charters*, i–iii; C. T. Clay, *Early Yorkshire Charters*, iv–vi; A. Le Prévost, *Orderic Vitalis*, ii; T. Arnold, *Symeon of Durham*, i, ii (Rolls Series. no. 75); Hodgson Hinde, *Symeon of Durham* (Surtees Soc., 1868); W. D. Macray, *Chronicon Abbatiae Evoshamensis* (Rolls Series, no. 29); B. Thorpe, *Anglo-Saxon Chronicle*, ii (Rolls Series, no. 23); L. Dudley Stamp, *East Riding*; S. W. Wooldridge, *North Riding*; S. H. Beaver, *West Riding* (Land Utilization Survey Report, parts 46, 48, 51); $\frac{1}{4}$-in. and $\frac{1}{2}$-in. maps of northern England, and 1-in., geological, and land-utilization maps and key plan of civil parishes of Yorkshire, published by the Ordnance Survey.

Yorkshire seem to have belonged to the same race and laid out their villages in the same manner as the inhabitants of the plain.[1]

In 1086 much of Yorkshire was waste. Of nearly 1,900 villages recorded in Domesday about 850 appear to have been entirely depopulated. In another 300 it is explicitly stated that there was some waste land. A further 400, in which waste was not recorded, were clearly underpopulated and understocked and had greatly declined in value since 1066. The value of Yorkshire had declined by about two-thirds. The surviving population was not uniformly distributed. Some of the villages in the north-east of the Yorkshire moors were depopulated; so was a block of fifty villages covering most of the wolds, and smaller groups in the marshy areas round the lower Ouse and Aire. Along the axis of the plain from York to the Tees there was a nearly continuous line of depopulated villages. But in the neighbourhood of Beverley and in the Derwent valley below Malton there were groups of villages in which little waste was recorded, and there was only sporadic waste in the plain south of the Aire, parts of which were densely populated. Merging in the south with this area, a belt ten or fifteen miles wide on the western margin of the Yorkshire plain was fairly densely populated, at least by contrast with the thinly populated area to the east. But the contrast was not only with the area to the east. To the west of this belt the extensive areas of Pennine settlement, between Sheffield and the Tees, were almost entirely depopulated. The condition of Yorkshire as a whole, for which the ravages of the Danes and Scots in 1069 and 1070 were partly responsible,[2] must be set down mainly to the methodical destruction carried out by the French in the winter of 1069–70; but if the condition of particular areas is assumed to be directly traceable to their operations, it must appear remarkable that William's army should have

[1] Craven seems to have been already uninhabited in 1066.

[2] The Danish fleet spent the winter in the Humber, according to most of the chronicles; according to one version of the *A.S. Chronicle*, 'between Ouse and Trent'—perhaps somewhere between the mouth of the Trent and a point below Selby where the Ouse lost its identity on entering an extensive delta. Whether they lay in the Humber proper, or in the less exposed station above Trent mouth, they probably ravaged the fenland villages round Howden and Snaith; less probably Holderness.

The Scots invaded north Yorkshire in 1070, and depopulated 'Cleveland' (i.e. the plain immediately south of Middlesbrough) and Teesdale (there is some evidence that this included upper Teesdale as well as the westward continuation of the Cleveland plain).

indulged in a no more than sporadic devastation of large parts of the plain, while carrying fire and sword to remote upland settlements.

That it was impossible for William to devastate the uplands in a winter campaign, that the campaign was not an attempt to hunt down dissident thanes in their Pennine fastnesses—these assertions cannot be made here, since proof, if they could be proved, would require a difficult and long discussion of the chronicles and of the native landowners named, but not always identifiable, in Domesday. But that the records of waste in Domesday do not represent the tracks of destroying armies can be demonstrated from the sporadic distribution of many waste areas, and from signs of recent colonization in populated ones. In all the large areas of generally dense population there were waste villages. And in at least a hundred villages containing densely populated estates there were estates which remained uncultivated. Such instances, it might be objected, do not show that isolated waste areas had not been devastated, but that they had, exceptionally, not been reoccupied. But, in subsequent discussion of some Yorkshire fees, it is the sporadic incidence of waste which will suggest that many places shown as uninhabited in the survey were not devastated in 1069 and 1070 but abandoned between 1070 and 1086. The local effects of the devastation are further obscured by the probability that many devastated villages and estates were reoccupied during the same period. Domesday statistics suggest that while some villages had been either continuously occupied since before the devastation, or reoccupied relatively early in the period 1070–86, others had been partly or wholly resettled after the devastation, and perhaps relatively late in the period 1070–86. About fifty villages[1] in the Yorkshire survey satisfy the following conditions: (1) They possessed a number of ploughs closely approximating to the number of ploughlands that they were estimated to contain. (2) The ratio of their inhabitants to their ploughlands was such as can be paralleled from Domesday in many parts of England unaffected by devastation. (3) Their values in 1086 closely approximated to their values in 1066. In these villages, then, a normal condition of things seems to have been maintained or restored. About fifty villages[2] contained denser populations and apparently superfluous ploughs; their values had in many cases risen. And in

[1] e.g. Harmby, Spennithorne, Seaton Hall.
[2] e.g. Fearby, Seamer (near Scarborough), Little Weighton.

about a hundred villages[1] where populations and ploughs were inadequate, the decline from pre-Conquest values was no more than in proportion. Of a majority of all these villages it is probable that the populations, dense or thin, were relatively long established, possibly survivors or descendants of pre-Conquest inhabitants. But of many more villages the catastrophic decline in value cannot be explained by deficiency of inhabitants and ploughs. In Handsworth 21 peasants and $8\frac{1}{2}$ ploughs were at work on land for 7 ploughs, but its value had declined from £8 in 1066 to 40s. in 1086. It cannot be that this decline in value measured a decline in population and ploughs, for in that case Handsworth would have been impossibly overpopulated and overstocked in 1066. It might be suggested that Handsworth had been severely but not totally devastated in 1070, and that the population had survived and resumed cultivation. But in that case they might be expected to have developed Handsworth in the course of sixteen years to something more than a quarter of its pre-Conquest value. It is probable that they had recently arrived and had not yet advanced far in clearing and cultivation. About 50 villages[2] were in this condition; 30 or 40 villages[3] had not been developed by denser populations and a much more than adequate number of ploughs to more than half their potential value; of about a hundred villages,[4] where men and ploughs were less than adequate, the values of 1086 were disproportionately less than those of 1066. It would, of course, be futile to attempt to establish from Domesday statistics a calculus for estimating dates of colonization; some of the factors which raised or lowered the values of 1086, and had perhaps raised or lowered those of 1066, were no doubt local and temporary. Of no one of these numerous villages can be stated with certainty what is nevertheless probably true of the majority of them: that their inhabitants were comparatively recent immigrants. Significance and added probability might be given to these speculations by plotting inhabited villages on a map of Yorkshire in symbols representing recent, and less recent, settlement; this, as will be shown, would be misleading, because it would neglect the most important factor in the resettlement of Yorkshire; but simply as an illustration it may be said that the rather thin population of much of Richmondshire seems

[1] e.g. Brompton on Swale, Kirk Ella, Newbald.
[2] e.g. Holme on Spalding Moor, Rotherham, Todwick.
[3] e.g. Hackness, Treeton, Whiston.
[4] e.g. Holmpton, Parlington, Tankersley.

to have been of long standing, and that among the deserted fen-land villages of the lower Don, Aire, and Ouse—where abnormal capital must have been required for drainage—a few large and well-equipped groups of colonists seem to have been established very shortly before the survey.[1] In some villages of the West Riding, where a shortage of ploughs could have been only local and temporary, large groups of peasants still had no ploughs or a quite inadequate number;[2] among possible inferences from this a probable one is that they were recent immigrants. About fifty villages[3] were clearly overpopulated and overstocked, at least in relation to Domesday estimates of ploughlands; men and ploughs in some of these may have found scope by extensive clearing and possibly by enlarging village boundaries to include additional pastures; but where surrounding villages were also densely populated,[4] or the property rights of more than one lord might have been affected by too extensive clearing,[5] it is possible that some superfluous men and ploughs were transient and would move on in a year or two to colonize waste villages. About 90 per cent. of the Yorkshire villages recorded in Domesday, whether as populated or as waste, have preserved their identities and appa-rently their approximate boundaries to the present day. Since this could scarcely have happened if many of them had remained waste for many years, it is probable that of the hundreds of villages which had not yet been reoccupied in 1086 some at least were on the point of being so.

Some parts of Yorkshire, it seems, must have been far more severely devastated than might appear from Domesday; others less severely devastated, or perhaps not devastated at all. An

---

[1] e.g. Adlingfleet, Arksey, Aughton (near Selby). The progress of reclamation on the fee of Ilbert de Lacy is illustrated in three villages situated where the ridge south of the River Went slopes down to the fenland between the lower Went and Don. Most of the territory of Campsall is on a well-drained slope rising to 200 feet; in 1086 it was normally populated and stocked, and had recovered or retained its value T.R.E. Norton, a mile to the north-east, lies mostly in the fenland; in 1086 it was densely populated and stocked, but had recovered only 70s. of its T.R.E. value of £6. Askern, one mile south-east of Norton, and still farther into the fen-land, was still waste and valueless. Arksey and Kirk Bramwith appear to be cases of colonization on the fee of Roger de Busli pushing northward into the marshes round the lower Don.

[2] e.g. North Milford. With a population three times normal this had regained its T.R.E. value of 10s. In numerous villages in the North and East Riding groups of peasants had no ploughs.

[3] e.g. Howden, Marton on the Forest, Riccall (East Riding); and cf. p. 3, note 2.

[4] e.g. round Bedale.

[5] e.g. in Bilham, Cowesby, East Ayton, and round Adwick upon Dearne and Welwick.

interpretation of the state of Domesday Yorkshire must account for devastated villages which had been colonized by 1086, and for non-devastated villages which had been abandoned; and not only for these; it will be incomplete unless it explains why other devastated villages had not been colonized, and why other villages immune from devastation had not been abandoned. And in a reconstruction of its agrarian history between 1070 and 1086 Yorkshire cannot be considered in isolation from the adjacent counties. What happened in Yorkshire was a colonizing movement of very wide if uncertain extent. The primary motive, in the years of famine and scarcity which followed the devastation, was undoubtedly that of reviving the most productive arable farming. Who the colonists were, whether any of them came from outside Yorkshire, how they were aided and equipped, and what the process of colonization was, are questions which must be answered; the first, in particular, by some less indefinite hypothesis than that of an internally reshuffled population. Postponing consideration of some of these questions, and recalling both the difficulties of mid-winter operations in the Pennine Chain and the waste condition of settlements in this and other hilly regions in 1086, I suggest that between 1070 and 1086 peasants migrated from less favourable conditions, especially in the uplands, to more favourable conditions, especially where devastation must have created opportunities for settlement in some of the most fertile parts of the plain.

It is certain that the available land was more than could be taken up, it is probable that the range of the medieval colonist was limited, and it is not to be assumed that his requirements were identical with those of the modern arable farmer. On these principles it is possible to reconstruct some movements of population within fairly limited areas: from a group of villages in the north-east of the Yorkshire moors to the neighbourhood of Whitby and the eastern end of the vale of Pickering, and from a block of fifty deserted villages on the wolds to the light soil and natural meadows of the Derwent valley below Malton. But it is in western Yorkshire that the tendency is most apparent: from Swaledale, Wensleydale, and their secondary dales to parts of the Richmondshire plain, and from the uplands west of Ripon and upper Wharfedale and Airedale into the lowland basin of the Wharfe, Aire, and Calder, which contains, in the triangle between Wetherby, Wakefield, and Snaith, what is reputed the best arable land in Yorkshire. Even in the extreme south of Yorkshire some of the upland villages near Sheffield had been evacuated by 1086, though part of the adjacent plain may, escaping devastation, have been itself a source of colonists, and part may have been colonized from northern Nottinghamshire. The notion of the Pennine Chain as something of a *réservoir d'hommes* might seem worth working out over the whole area of the nine northern counties which back on to it, and which had suffered by invasion, devastation, and political disturbance immediately before and after the conquest. But Northumberland and Durham had been invaded and devastated more recently than Yorkshire, and were not surveyed in 1086; their agrarian development remains obscure until the late twelfth century. Cumberland, Westmorland, and Lancashire were fought over until Cumberland was annexed by Rufus, and at least one colonizing movement in this area belongs to his reign. The Pennine region of Cheshire is at only one remove from the Welsh mountains, from another complicating source of political disturbance and—it may be—of immigrants and returned refugees. In the Staffordshire and Derbyshire surveys there are signs of a movement of population similar to that of Yorkshire. The Pennine region of north-east Staffordshire and north Derbyshire—an area as unattractive to the arable farmer as the Yorkshire uplands, and as unpropitious to military operations —was fairly densely settled in 1066, and was largely waste in 1086. If it was through Longdendale that William led his army in the descent on Cheshire, or along the ancient road from Sheffield to Manchester which joins Longdendale at its lower end, his passage might account for the flight or destruction of its inhabitants. But in the high country east of Stoke, in upper and lower Dovedale, in the country between Dovedale and the (Derbyshire) Derwent, and in the remote valleys which join the upper Derwent in the neighbourhood of the High Peak, the numerous villages which stand at heights of between 600 and 1,200 feet were probably not disturbed by William's operations, and were probably abandoned before 1086 because better land was now available elsewhere.

Nothing so far has shown that this movement was not a spontaneous one; that it was spontaneous is indeed suggested by the fact that except where it was marshy the best farming district of Yorkshire became relatively densely populated. But even within this district population was not at all evenly distributed; there were waste villages and waste estates; and in some thinly populated districts there were densely populated estates and villages. In 1086 one Yorkshire village in three was divided between two or more lords; and between the estates of different lords and of different sub-tenants in one village there was in many cases a wide difference in density of inhabitants and ploughs and, it would seem, in the extent to which each estate had been redeveloped. Thus in North Cave the archbishop's estate was waste except for one rent payer; on Nigel Fossard's there were 5 villeins and 3 ploughs, and it was worth 40s. in 1086 as in 1066; Robert Malet's 4 ploughlands were cultivated by 10 peasants and 3½ ploughs, but were worth only 13s.—they had been worth 70s. in 1086; Hugh Baldric's small estate was part of a manor which was densely populated and stocked and had increased in value from 40 to 50s. The simplest case of this difference is seen in about a hundred villages in each of which there was at least one estate containing some population and at least one estate recorded without ambiguity as waste. Thus in Hunsingore Ernegis de Burun had 4 carucates, 3 bovates where 2 ploughs could be, and he had there 1 demesne plough and 9 villeins and 3 bordars having 3 ploughs; his estate, with stock and population above average, had appreciated from 30s. in 1066 to 50s. in 1086. In the same village Richard Surdeval had 4 carucates where 2 ploughs could be; they had been worth 30s. in 1066, and in 1086 they were worth nothing, because they were waste. It might be suggested that the inhabitants of Hunsingore were indigenous survivors, who had been rounded up by Ernegis de Burun, as the first post-Conquest lord on the scene, and compelled to become his tenants. It is indeed possible that something of the kind occurred in the special circumstances, discussed below, where one part of a village belonged to Hugh fitz Baldric and another part to the king. But Surdeval's four carucates in Hunsingore stood for land which, in a village presumably suitable for resettlement, had for some reason not been taken up. And this anomaly, present in some form or other[1] in hundreds of Yorkshire villages, must suggest that in migrating to or remaining in the villages in which they were found in 1086 peasants were not acting entirely on their own volition, and were governed by some relationship to their lords. If the colonization of Yorkshire, between 1070 and 1086, had been mainly voluntary, medieval analogies (including analogies from the later history of Yorkshire) suggest that what-

---

[1] Various types of variations between estates can be seen in Wales, Walkington, Wath upon Dearne, Wawne, Welham, Willitoft, Wilton (Langbaurgh West wapentake), and Wombwell.

ever the social origins of the colonists they would have acquired
freedom. But 94 per cent. of the peasants enumerated in the
Yorkshire survey belonged to what must be provisionally termed
the unfree classes; and on the villeins and bordars of Yorkshire,
more or less as located in 1086, was founded the manorial
exploitation which, in a generally but not universally mitigated
form, subsisted for more than two centuries. It must therefore
be concluded that for the majority of the inhabitants of Yorkshire resettlement was compulsory. This supposes motive and
power in the compelling agents; and both were present. The
motive of a lord who settled peasants in district (*b*) may reasonably be supposed to have been agricultural profits. And the
power resided in his already existing control of them while
still in district (*a*). If the population of Yorkshire was largely
redistributed between 1070 and 1086—and further evidence will
be adduced to show that it was—this was not brought about by
a general and spontaneous movement of peasants from the worse
land to the better. It was, rather, the result of a number of movements, each initiated and controlled by some lord, and confined
by the limits of his fee.

Some illustrations may be found in a summary review of the
motives and opportunities of the principal Yorkshire tenants.
William de Warenne's soke of Conisbrough was confined to an
area of south Yorkshire probably not devastated in 1070. So
much is suggested, at least, by the survival in this area of the
only large groups of sokemen left in post-Conquest Yorkshire,
and by the high value of most of its inhabited villages. The dense
population of Conisbrough and its satellites in 1086 is not, of
course, simply explained by immunity from devastation; it is,
however, adequately explained by immunity from devastation
combined with the fact that William de Warenne had no other
land in Yorkshire. In the same area were some of Roger de
Busli's manors. It will be shown that he had a motive for retain-
ing a dense population on them; and they were in fact densely
populated in 1086. Colonists for what appear to have been
recently reoccupied manors in the north-west and north of his
fee were possibly derived from some of his manors, waste in 1086,
in the adjacent Pennine region near Sheffield; some of them may
have come from that portion of his fee which extended into north
Nottinghamshire. Colonists on the isolated fenland manor of
Geoffrey de la Wirce at Adlingfleet (almost certainly depopulated
in the winter of 1069–70) were no doubt derived from his estates

in an immediately adjacent part of Lincolnshire. But the Yorkshire fees which did not extend into the immediately adjacent
parts of Nottinghamshire and Lincolnshire had in most cases
only prospered in measure as they included sources of colonists
in regions of upland settlement. Among the more advantageously
placed lords were the archbishop, the canons of Beverley, William
de Percy, Berenger de Todeni, Ernegis de Burun, Odo Arbalaster,
Nigel Fossard, who held of the count of Mortain, and Gospatric,
who held of the king and of Count Alan. Their derelict estates
in the Yorkshire moors or the wolds or the Pennine area of the
West Riding account for their developed estates, not far distant,
in the vale of Pickering, on the middle Derwent, in Holderness,
or in the plain west of York and Selby. The great fee of Ilbert
de Lacy was almost equally divided between the Pennine region
and the Wharfe–Aire basin. In 1086, 90 per cent. of its population
were assembled in the eastern and lowland manors; the western
and upland manors were almost entirely abandoned. More
compact than the Lacy fee, and comparable with it in size and
population, Count Alan's castellate of Richmond was similarly
divided between nearly deserted western uplands and partly
inhabited eastern plain; the only part of the North Riding which
included a considerable number of depopulated upland villages,
it had recovered over 40 per cent. of its pre-Conquest value,
while the rest of the North Riding had recovered less than 15 per
cent. By 1086 two-thirds of Richmondshire was in the hands of
Count Alan's tenants; and the same antithesis existed on the fees
of those who can be identified as holding land both in the uplands
and the plain, including Bodin, Enisan, Ribald, Bernulf, Geoffrey,
and Gospatric. One of Count Alan's tenants, Robert de Musters,
had not been enfeoffed with any upland manors. His Yorkshire
fee consisted in ten estates all lying in the fertile plain between
the Swale and the Ure; nine of these were waste in 1086. Estates
mainly in the plains were held by the bishop of Durham, the
count of Mortain and his tenant Richard Surdeval, Robert Malet,
Ralph de Mortemer, and Ralph Paganel. Their estates were
under-developed and thinly populated, and had greatly declined
in value. As significantly if not so obviously under-developed
was the fee of Drogo de Bevrere, lying entirely in Holderness.
Few of his estates were totally waste; but on more than 500
ploughlands he had less than 600 men, and only about 160
ploughs; his fee—in contrast with the manors and berewicks of
the canons of Beverley and the archbishop, closely intermixed

with it—had declined to about 17 per cent. of its pre-Conquest value.

It is possible that William's confiscations, confirmations, and grants, after suppressing the rebellion, had put some of his Yorkshire tenants in possession of fees entirely devoid of inhabitants. But in 1086 every tenant-in-chief and every Norman and Breton subtenant possessed *some* inhabited and exploited estates. In this fact, I suggest, is to be found one of the special illustrations of William's feudal settlement which the Yorkshire survey affords. His grants had left the king still the greatest landowner in Yorkshire. His estates comprised one-fifth of its area and had in 1066 represented one-fifth of its value; they were, that is, a fair cross-section of the county. They were distributed in nearly every part of it, including some of the most fertile parts of the plain and many of the upland villages from which, as I believe, the plain was resettled. But in 1086 they represented only one-twenty-fifth of the value of Yorkshire at that date, and contained only one-twenty-fifth of its population. The derelict condition of the king's estates, alike in the uplands and the plain, contrasts particularly with the condition of one of the greater Yorkshire fees. Hugh fitz Baldric held few of the upland villages from which, it has been suggested, a post-Conquest lord might have drawn settlers; moreover on some of his manors on the fringes of the Yorkshire moors large populations were established or retained. But his fee had recovered more than 70 per cent. of its pre-Conquest value and was, by standards more general than those of Domesday Yorkshire, adequately populated and much more than adequately stocked.[1] An obvious inference is that as sheriff from 1069 to some time after 1080 Hugh had used his office to strip his master's estates of implements, cattle, and men. And clearly he had been no more backward than others among William's sheriffs in attending to his own interests. But it is probable that other tenants benefited by agricultural man-power drawn from the royal estates; probably it was the king's will that they should do so; for if, in the special conditions of Yorkshire, the object of the

[1] On 195 ploughlands he had 57.5 demesne ploughs and 465 villeins, 15 bordars, and 1 sokeman having 176.25 ploughs. Thus his peasants included an exceptionally high proportion of the class which normally owned most of the oxen. And his villeins, most of whom belonged to groups unmixed with bordars, had each on the average a larger number of oxen (3.1) than the average for Yorkshire (2.9), and much larger than the average (2.33) for the area (E. Riding and N. Riding excluding Richmondshire) in which his fee lay. These calculations have been suggested by Mr. R. W. Lennard's paper on 'The Economic Position of the Domesday Villani' (*Economic Journal*, lvi. 244).

feudal settlement was to be achieved, the economic recovery of the king's estates must be postponed, and grants of men without land must supplement grants of land without men. The same policy can be observed, one degree lower in the feudal scale, within the defensive bastion of north-west Yorkshire where sub-infeudation had farthest advanced. By 1086, grants to his Breton, Norman, and English followers had left Count Alan with demesne estates comprising one-third of Richmondshire; they contained only one-fifth of its population, and in agricultural value were no more than on a par with those of his tenant Enisan Musard.

But although in much of Yorkshire and England fighting power could be secured by endowing knights with agricultural profits, there were military necessities in the England of 1086 which required to be more directly met. Whether in organizing the predominantly military area of Richmondshire, or planting garrisons elsewhere among a disaffected population, or furthering the autonomous views and ambitions of barons and knights, groups of peasants were, it seems, sometimes located to provide food, labour, transport, and fuel to places chosen not for their agricultural but for their strategic value. The inhabitants of Richmondshire, brought down from the high dales, had not all been moved far into the plain.[1] At Melsonby and Newsham, where a high and exposed ridge carries a Roman road north-west from Scotch Corner towards the Tees, at Marske and Hipswell, at heights of 400 or 500 feet on the sides of lower Swaledale, at Spennithorne, nine miles above the lower end of Wensleydale, men and ploughs that might have developed potentially valuable manors in the plain had been assembled near Ravensworth, Richmond, and Middleham by Bodin, Enisan, and Ribald.[2] Elsewhere

[1] Thus Eastern Richmondshire remained generally uninhabited: and the adjacent plain of Allertonshire farther east was mainly held by the king, the count of Mortain, the bishop of Durham, and Robert Malet, who were, for various reasons discussed above, disadvantageously placed during the period of recovery. Hence the deep sector of continuous waste from the Tees to the vicinity of Thirsk.

[2] Cf. E. S. Armitage and D. H. Montgomerie, 'Ancient Earthworks', *V.C.H. Yorks.* ii. Whether the Norman castles in these places and the places subsequently named in the paragraph were in existence in 1086 does not affect the argument. But it may be suggested that the occasion of a colonizing movement was sometimes the necessity of assembling a labour force for construction, and that peasants who came to build remained to plough. Such may have been the origin of the villeins and gresmen found in the thirteenth century on the manor of Bowes. The earliest reference to Bowes Castle belongs to the twelfth century; but it is probable that the Roman camp of Lavatrae was adapted and garrisoned while the Scottish frontier was still on Stainmore. Cumberland was annexed by Rufus; the strategic motive in his colonization of the Carlisle area is evident.

in Yorkshire—at Kirkby Malzeard, Skelton, Whorlton—populations were established or retained where the first consideration could not have been agricultural profits. On high ground in north Derbyshire, mostly evacuated by 1086, Peverel's villeins, bordars, and demesne ploughs were at work in three manors near his castle of the Peak Forest. Between the Pennine uplands and the marshes south-west of the Isle of Axholme the gap which gave access to most of England north of the Trent was filled with the most densely populated and apparently longest established of Roger de Busli's manors, grouped round the strongpoints of Tickhill and Laughton en le Morthen. No doubt many of the motte and bailey castles of Yorkshire were intended simply for the local defence of manors colonized for their agricultural value. But within the best arable district of Yorkshire a strategic as well as an economic motive in organizing a working population may be inferred from the indications that this population was brought under a special discipline. In the thirteenth century peasants from surrounding villages worked on a central demesne at Tanshelf, which contained the capital of the Lacy honour.[1] Their labour services included week work; and this obligation—or the personal disabilities which had allowed it to be at some time imposed—had probably been inherited from the groups of unfree peasants that Domesday shows already concentrated in the villages round Tanshelf.[2] Week work was very uncommon in medieval Yorkshire;[3] its nearly unique occurrence at Tanshelf

[1] *Yorks. Inquisitions* (Yorks. Arch. Soc., Record Series), i. 50. Tanshelf in 1086 included the area of the castle and borough of Pontefract, not named in Domesday.

[2] I assume that such burdens as the medieval peasantry of Yorkshire endured were fastened on them between the years 1069 and at latest 1100: the period of a rebellion, a punitive expedition, entry into possession by a foreign military caste, social degradation of the inhabitants in comparison with those of the rest of the northern Danelaw, compulsory migration, and the creation of conditions antecedent to the manorial system in a mild form. It is possible that new obligations could have been imposed at particular times and places afterwards; a general presumption against this is created by the fact that most of the villages which were still uninhabited in 1086 were never afterwards manorialized.

In the Recapitulation of the Yorkshire Domesday Tanshelf appears as still belonging to the king; possibly, at the date of the survey, it had not long been granted to Ilbert de Lacy, and possibly its working population had been organized while it was still *terra regis*. If so, the activity of the king's agents in a place of strategic importance, contrasted with their neglect of his estates throughout most of Yorkshire, illustrates the predominance of strategic over economic motives. There is, however, some evidence that Ilbert de Lacy had been in effective possession for several years before 1086.

[3] The only other case was that of Buttercrambe (op. cit. i. 242), held by Hugh fitz Baldric in 1086.

must be considered to have been imposed by an exceptional effort of social and economic oppression, from a motive other than that of mere economic exploitation: a motive presented by the strategic importance of the Aire crossing in the vicinity of Pontefract.

T. A. M. BISHOP

THE REPORTS OF THE TRIAL ON PENENDEN HEATH

IN a short article lately published in the *English Historical Review*,[1] the writer sought to show that the trial on Penenden Heath could not be precisely dated on existing evidence in spite of the categorical statements of medieval documents and of modern historians; and, further, since the evidence is all in conflict on the point, that it is unlikely that a precise date ever will be established. The prophetic part of this thesis was challenged at once by the late Dr. Levison, who drew attention, on a postcard, to a late eleventh or early twelfth-century manuscript in the John Rylands Library[2] containing a report of the trial. Although this manuscript had been catalogued by M. R. James[3] and its contents duly noted, it seems to have escaped the notice of historians who have discussed the trial. It was disappointing to find, however, when it was examined, that this text was almost an exact duplicate of the report preserved in the Textus Roffensis, and was therefore unlikely to provide fresh evidence wherewith to date the trial.

The trial on Penenden Heath, whatever its exact date may be, has long been regarded as having some importance in the constitutional history of England for the indications it gives of William the Conqueror's attitude to English law and institutions and of their continuity through the Conquest. Lately Professor Douglas has found an added significance in the place it takes in the complicated process of settling the conflicting claims to property and jurisdiction in Kent during the years following the Conquest, a process which culminated, according to this view of the matter, in the Domesday Survey.[4] The texts upon which our knowledge of the trial is based are thus worthy of study. Two versions of a report of the trial had long been known (though the differences between them had not always been recognized) when

---

[1] *Eng. Hist. Rev.* lxi (1946), 378–88.
[2] MS. 109 (Latin), Crawford (126).
[3] M. R. James, *Descriptive Catalogue of the Latin Manuscripts in the John Rylands Library, Manchester*, 1 (1921), 193; 11, pl. 143.
[4] D. C. Douglas, 'Odo, Lanfranc and the Domesday Survey', *Historical Essays in Honour of James Tait*, ed. Edwards, Galbraith, and Jacob (Manchester 1933), pp. 47–57; *The Domesday Monachorum of Christ Church Canterbury* (Royal Historical Society, 1944), pp. 30–3.

Levison, in 1912, added a third.[1] Both he and Douglas have done much to sort out the relations between these reports, and the appearance of a fourth text encourages the attempt to take this process a step farther; but since it is impossible to reach any really satisfying conclusions about the trial without at the same time clearing up the whole of this pre-Domesday litigation in Kent (which has left many, though scattered, memorials), this essay does not attempt to do more than present a better text of the reports at present known, and to set out a hypothesis on their relations one with another.

These are the four texts:

A. John Rylands Library, Manchester, MS. 109 (Latin), Crawford (126), ff. 1 and 2. The book is a text of the Pauline Epistles, and is prefaced by two folios, forming a separate gathering, on which are written (*a*) the report of the Penenden Trial and (*b*) the first half of a charter of Henry I confirming the liberties of Christ Church, Canterbury.[2] The charter is addressed to Archbishop Ralph, and therefore cannot have been written earlier than 1114; but the handwriting of the charter is different from and clearly later than that of the Penenden report.

B. Rochester, Textus Roffensis, ff. 168–70.[3]

C. British Museum, MS. Cotton Vespasian A. xxii, ff. 120–1.[4] The book is a thirteenth-century volume containing chronicles and other historical matter relating to Rochester.

D. Library of the Dean and Chapter, Canterbury, Cartae Antiquae, A. 42. This is a thirteenth-century roll containing a fragment of a report of Penenden Heath. The roll has been described and the report printed by Levison.[5]

A may be assigned to the late eleventh or very early twelfth century;[6] B to the second quarter of the twelfth.[7] C and D both

[1] W. Levison, 'A Report on the Penenden Trial', *Eng. Hist. Rev.* xxvii (1912), 717–20.
[2] M. R. James, *Descriptive Catalogue*, i. 193; ii, pl. 143; cf. Dugdale, *Monasticon* i (1846), 109.
[3] The report is not printed in T. Hearne, *Textus Roffensis* (1720) (cf. p. 140), but is found in Wharton, *Anglia Sacra* i (1691), 334–6, in J. Thorpe, *Registrum Roffense* (1769), pp. 27–8, and elsewhere. See Douglas, 'Odo, Lanfranc . . .', p. 48.
[4] This text is printed in M. M. Bigelow, *Placita Anglo-Normannica* (London, 1879), pp. 5–9, and elsewhere. See Douglas, op. cit., pp. 48–9.
[5] *Eng. Hist. Rev.* xxvii. 717–20.
[6] This is the opinion of Mr. N. R. Ker, who kindly examined a photostat of the manuscript for me.
[7] Liebermann, 'Notes on the Textus Roffensis', *Archaeologia Cantiana*, xxiii. 103.

belong to the thirteenth century. The book in which A is now found is thought to have belonged to Rochester;[1] B, since it is included in the Textus Roffensis, clearly comes in its present form from Rochester; C is included in a Rochester book. But D belongs to Canterbury. A and B consist of a narrative of the trial in which some attempt was made to achieve a literary, almost a dramatic, effect, and these two texts are almost identical. The text of C is the same save for one passage in which the list of manors given as recovered by Lanfranc at the trial is very much longer than that given in A and B, and there is an additional note to the effect that three manors were subsequently transferred to Rochester, to which they rightfully belonged. D, on the other hand, has the appearance of a quasi-official record. In place of the introductory narrative of ABC, it opens with a formal dating clause; it is technical and concise and bears a strong resemblance in form—so far as it goes—to the document which embodies the Primacy Agreement of 1072, though whether it concluded in a similar manner with the attestation of witnesses cannot be determined, for we have only what appears to be the first half of the document. The manuscript breaks off abruptly in the middle of a line. We have, therefore, a narrative in two versions, a shorter (AB) and a longer (C), coming apparently from Rochester, and what seems to be a formal record from Canterbury (D).

The detailed correspondence of A with B is very remarkable. Substantially the two are identical, word for word; the punctuation is the same, and so, with one exception, is the spelling of proper names; both scribes put an open 'a' over the usual sign for 'prae', but sometimes they forget, and they forget on the same words. They differ only in the use of capital letters and of certain abbreviations and in this, that whereas A has no contemporary title (the title it now bears, 'Placitum apud Pinendam. 6 W:I. 1072',[2] is clearly much later), B is entitled 'De placito apud pinendenam inter lanfrancum archiepiscopum & odonem baiocensem episcopum', a title which is also found in C. On palaeographical considerations, there seems to be no doubt that A is the earlier of the two. Now B is contained in the Textus Roffensis, which was compiled on the initiative of Bishop Ernulf (1115–24) and drew much of

---

[1] This is what M. R. James thought, and Mr. N. R. Ker informs me that he has found evidence which makes it certain. I have to thank him for the trouble he has taken over this point.

[2] It would be very interesting to know whence the author of this title obtained his exact knowledge of the date of the trial, for it could not be deduced from this manuscript alone.

its material from Canterbury.[1] The trial concerns Canterbury much more directly than Rochester, and it is likely that the first reports of the trial would have been compiled there. It is tempting to think that A was written at Canterbury and was brought to Rochester to serve as copy for the Textus Roffensis, and there is one small piece of evidence for this. In the manuscript, the text of A is followed by a charter of Henry I confirming the rights and liberties of Canterbury, and the text of this charter, though the writing extends to the bottom of the page, is incomplete. This suggests that the first two folios of Rylands MS. 109 (Latin), a separate gathering it will be remembered, originally formed part of a collection of documents which included report A and the whole of the charter, which must have been completed on another folio. Subsequently this collection was broken up (in Rochester, presumably), and the two folios containing the Penenden report and the first part of the charter, which could not be separated from one another, were bound up with the Epistles. On general grounds, since it contained a Canterbury charter and the report of a trial which concerned Christ Church, Canterbury, more than any other monastery, it is not unlikely that this collection was made there.[2] It might be difficult to prove that B is a direct copy of A, but the two texts are strangely alike.

    The relation between C and AB is relatively simple. Apart from one long passage in C, most of which is not found in AB, it would seem that C is derived from AB. It has the same title as B; text and punctuation are the same; only the orthography differs in some respects, as one would expect. But since the passage which is peculiar to C gives a much longer list of the properties recovered by Lanfranc at Penenden, together with a note that three of them were subsequently handed over to Rochester, it is only natural to suspect C of being a later and less authentic edition of AB.[3] However, this longer list in C is clearly related to a statement of the properties recovered by Christ Church during the Conqueror's reign which is the substance of an obituary of the king in a twelfth-century Canterbury book;[4] and

---

[1] Lieberman, 'Notes on the Textus Roffensis', *Archaeologia Cantiana*, xxiii. 94 ff.
[2] By good fortune the page on which this argument is based was selected for illustration by M. R. James, see *Descriptive Catalogue*, ii, pl. 143. But it must be added that, in Mr. Ker's opinion, the handwriting of A seems to belong rather to Rochester than to Canterbury, and this opinion is a weighty argument against tracing A back to Canterbury.   [3] Douglas, 'Odo, Lanfranc . . .', p. 50.
[4] British Museum, MS. Cotton Claudius C. vi, f. 165*b*; cf. *Monasticon* (1846), i. 109, and B. W. Kissan, 'The Earliest Mention of Bow Church', *London and Middlesex Arch. Soc. Trans.*, N.S. vii (1937), pp. 436–44.

it certainly looks as though the compiler of C had obtained his
additional information from this or a common source, though
he has rearranged the sentences to some extent in order to fit
the matter into his copy of AB.[1] Now this obituary clearly
implies that the properties were recovered by Canterbury not on
one dramatic occasion, but during the whole course of William's
reign; and there can be little doubt that in this it correctly represents what took place.[2] If so, then the compiler of C has simply
attributed to the outstanding trial of the reign the results of
several less memorable lawsuits. Such a process is not unknown;
but since most of the properties that can be traced were in the
right hands by the time of the Domesday Survey,[3] it is unlikely
that the compiler of C has done more than this to confound the
historians.

There remains D, which in its present form is imperfect and
survives only in a late manuscript, so far as is known. If it is
compared with A it will be seen at once that they have much in
common; that nearly everything that is in D will be found in A,
apart from the initial dating clause, and that the matter which is
in A but not in D is mostly padding or corroborative detail. They
are in agreement on the facts, so far as D goes. It looks very
much as though A were a literary version of D; and if this is so
then the original of D must have been older even than A,[4] that is,
it must have been an eleventh-century document. Bearing in
mind the analogy between its initial dating clause and the similar
clause in the Primacy Agreement of 1072, it is not difficult to
accept Levison's view that D is indeed 'a kind of official Canterbury record of the litigation'.[5]

From all these guesses and suggestions, the following emerges
as a hypothesis. D represents a formal Canterbury record of the
trial on Penenden Heath. A is a 'literary' version of this record,
which conceivably may have been written at Canterbury and sent
to Rochester. B is a copy of this version made at Rochester. C
is an enlarged edition of AB in which the editor has inserted a
memorandum of properties recovered for Canterbury during the
whole of the Conqueror's reign in place of the much shorter list

---

[1] See notes to the text as set out below.
[2] Douglas, 'Odo, Lanfranc . . .', pp. 54 ff.; *Domesday Monachorum*, pp. 31–3.
[3] See notes to the text as set out below.
[4] On the argument that you can make a narrative from an 'official report', but
that it is difficult to concoct an 'official report' out of a literary narrative. Also
because A appears to be an inflated version of D.
[5] *Eng. Hist. Rev.* xxvii. 720.

that is found in AB. But it is this shorter list, since it is also found in D, which must represent the actual results of the Penenden Trial.

Apart from the *Acta Lanfranci*,[1] which supplies a date and a terse summary of one part of the proceedings at Penenden Heath and which, being almost contemporary, cannot be neglected, the references to the trial in the chronicles do not add much to our knowledge of it. One such reference, however, affords the opportunity for a final piece of speculation. If the account of the trial given by Eadmer in his *Historia Novorum*[2] is compared with A it will be seen at once that there must be some relationship between them, particularly in the opening narrative which describes Odo's depredations in Kent before Lanfranc's consecration. This, naturally, could be explained by saying that Eadmer based his account on some version of A, but it is possible that he was himself responsible for transforming the formal record represented now by D into the narrative which is represented by ABC. Certainly, this transformation is quite likely to have taken place at Canterbury.

In setting out the texts below, A, since it has not been printed before and because it is the earliest of the narrative texts, is set out in full. D, for purposes of comparison, is printed in a parallel column. B has been collated in detail with A; but C, since most of the smaller differences between it and A are due to the difference in age of the two manuscripts, has not been collated in such detail. The texts of A, B, and C are based upon photographs[3] of the manuscripts; D is a reprint of Levison's text.[4] The passage

---

[1] Earle and Plummer, *Two of the Saxon Chronicles Parallel*, i (1892–8), 289; cf. *Eng. Hist. Rev.* lxi. 378 ff.

[2] *Historia Novorum* (ed. Rule, Rolls Series, 1884), pp. 16–17. Other references to the trial will be found in Milo's 'Vita Lanfranci' (Migne, *Pat. Lat.* 105, cols. 46–7) and Gervase's 'Actus Pontificum' (*Historical Works of Gervase of Canterbury*, ed. Stubbs, Rolls Series, 1879–80, ii. 369). The story of a trial in which Lanfranc was greatly assisted by a vision of St. Dunstan seems to refer to some other occasion (see especially Eadmer, *Historia Novorum*, pp. 17–18). It originates, probably, in Osbern's 'Miracula Sancti Dunstani' (Stubbs, *Memorials of St. Dunstan*, Rolls Series, 1874, pp. 143–4), and is elaborated by Eadmer in his version of the 'Miracula' (ibid., pp. 238–9). William of Malmesbury seems to confuse the two (*Gesta Pontificum*, ed. N. E. S. A. Hamilton, Rolls Series, 1870, p. 70). Florence of Worcester's reference to a council of 'Pedreda', which has sometimes been confused with Penenden Heath, is concerned with something quite different (*Chronicon*, ed. Thorpe, 1848–9, ii. 7–8; cf. R. R. Darlington, *The Vita Wulfstani of William of Malmesbury* [Camden, 3rd series, xl, 1928], pp. xxix–xxxi).

[3] I have to acknowledge, with gratitude, the care and trouble taken by Mr. H. S. Wharton, Chapter Clerk of Rochester, to provide me with photographs of the relevant part of the Textus Roffensis.

[4] *Eng. Hist. Rev.*, xxvii. 719. I have to thank the Editor for his permission to

in C which marks the greatest difference between it and AB is printed at the end, with the Canterbury obituary printed side by side for comparison.

A and B are very tidy manuscripts. C when it was first written must have had several small gaps in it; and these have been filled and the text revised by a scribe to whom, in the notes to the text printed below, the name 'Corrector' has been given. Words written by him, either in the margin or in the body of the text, are enclosed in brackets.

A

John Rylands Library, MS. 109
(Latin)

Tempore[1] magni regis Willelmi[2] qui anglicum regnum armis conquisiuit. & suis ditionibus subiugauit; contigit Odonem[4] baiocensem episcopum & eiusdem regis fratrem multo citius quam Lanfrancum[5] archiepiscopum in angliam uenire. atque in comitatu de caent[6] cum magna potentia residere. ibique potestatem non modicam exercere. Et quia illis diebus in comitatu illo quisquam non erat qui tantę fortitudinis uiro resistere posset; propter magnam quam habuit potestatem terras complures de archiepiscopatu cantuarberię & consuetudines nonnullas sibi arripuit. atque usurpans suę dominationi ascripsit. Postea uero non multo tempore contigit pręfatum Lanfrancum[7] cadomensis ęcclesię abbatem iussu regis in angliam quoque uenire. atque in archiepiscopatu cantuarberię[8] deo disponente totius anglię regni primatem sullimatum esse. Vbi dum aliquandiu resideret. & antiquas ęcclesię suę terras multas sibi deesse[9]

D

Canterbury Cathedral, Cartae
Antiquae, A. 42

Anno[3] ab incarnacione domini nostri Iesu Christi MLXXII, pontificatus domini Alexandri pape undecimo, regni vero Willelmi regis sexto, presidente Lanfranco archiepiscopo ecclesie Cant*uariensi* pontificatus sui anno secundo,

reprint this text. Levison extended abbreviations and modernized punctuation and capitalization in his text. I have left it so. Professor C. R. Cheney very kindly checked the text for me while he was at Canterbury. Only one or two trifling corrections could be made.

[1] *A and D have no title. B and C bear the title:* De placito apud (aput C) pinendenam inter lanfrancum archiepiscopum & odonem baiocensem episcopum. *See above, p. 17.*

[2] uuillelmi *B.*   [3] *Initial letter lacking in manuscript.*   [4] odonem *B.*
[5] lanfrancum *B.*   [6] chent *C.*   [7] lanfrancum *B.*
[8] cant' *C.*   [9] *Written as two words in A and B.*

A

D

inueniret. & suorum neglegentia antecessorum illas distributas atque distractas fuisse repperisset; diligenter inquisita & bene cognita ueritate. regem quam citius potuit & non pigre inde requisiuit. Precepit ergo rex comitatum totum absque mora considere. & homines comitatus omnes francigenas & precipue anglos in antiquis legibus & consuetudinibus peritos in unum conuenire. Qui cum conuenerunt. apud pinendenam omnes pariter consederunt. Et quoniam multa placita de diratiocinationibus terrarum. & uerba de consuetudinibus legum inter archiepiscopum & prędictum baiocensem episcopum ibi surrexerunt. & etiam inter consuetudines regales & archiepiscopales quę prima die expediri non potuerunt; ea causa totus comitatus per tres dies fuit ibi detentus. In[4] illis tribus diebus diratiocinauit ibi Lanfrancus[5] archiepiscopus plures terras quas tunc tenuerunt homines ipsius episcopi. uidelicet herbertus filius iuonis. Turoldus de rouecestra.[6] Radulfus de curuaspina. & alii plures de hominibus suis. cum omnibus consuetudinibus & rebus quę ad easdem terras pertinebant super ipsum baiocensem episcopum & super ipsos prędictos homines illius & alios. scilicet. Detlinges. Estoces.[7] Prestetuna.[8] danituna. & multas alias minutas terras. Et super hugonem de monteforti diratiocinauit[9] hrocinges. & broc. & super radulfum de curuaspina. lx. solidatas de pastura in grean.[10] Et omnes illas terras & alias diratiocinauit ita liberas atque quietas. quod in illa

ex precepto predicti regis ad instanciam archiepiscopi iussum est totum comitatum absque mora considere et comitatus omnes Francigenas et precipue Anglos in antiquis legibus et consuetudinibus peritos convenire ad diracionandum libertates et consuetudines, quas ecclesia Christi in terras proprias habet atque in regias terras habere debeat. Qui cum convenirent apud Pynindenne, omnes consederunt, et quoniam multa placita de diraciocinacionibus terrarum et verba de consuedinibus[1] legum inter archiepiscopum et Odonem Baiocensem[2] episcopum, qui multas terras de archiepiscopatu sibi usurpaverat, ibi surexerunt[3] et etiam inter consuetudines regales et archiepiscopales, que prima die expediri non potuerunt, ea causa totus comitatus per tres dies ibi fuit detentus. In hiis tribus diebus diraciocinavit ibi Lanfrancus plures terras, quas homines ipsius episcopi tenuerunt

scilicet Detlinges, Estoce, Prestuna, Danintona; super Hugonem de Monteforti Horcinges et Broc, super Radulphum de Curva Spina LX solidatas de pastura in Grean. Omnes istas terras diracionavit ita

liberas atque quietas, ut nullus homo in toto regno esset, qui inde aliquid calumpniaretur. In eodem siquidem

---

[1] *Sic.*   [2] Baionencem *altered to* Baiocensem.   [3] *Sic.*

[4] *In C the passage corresponding to* In illis tribus diebus . . . Et in eodem placito *is quite different from A and B. It is printed below with the obituary from which it is presumably derived (pp. 24–6).*

[5] lanfrancus *B.*   [6] hrouecestra *B.*

[7] estoces *B.*   [8] prestetuna *B.*   [9] diracionauit *B.*

[10] *Both A and B have the words* insula est *written in small characters over* in grean; *and in A, B, and D* in grean *is written as one word. For the identification of these places see below.*

A

die qua ipsum placitum finitum fuit.
non remansit homo in toto regno
anglię qui aliquid inde calumniaretur.
neque super ipsas terras etiam paruum
quicquam clamaret. Et[1] in eodem
placito non solum istas pręnominatas
& alias terras. sed & omnes libertates
ęcclesię suę & omnes consuetudines
suas renouauit. & renouatas ibi diratiocinauit[3] soca. saca. toll. team. fly-
menafyrmthe. grithbrece.[4] foresteal.
haimfare. infangenne þeof. cum omnibus aliis consuetudinibus paribus istis
uel minoribus istis. in terris. & in
aquis. in siluis. in uiis. & in pratis.
& in omnibus aliis rebus. infra ciuitatem & extra. infra burgum[7] & extra.
& in omnibus aliis locis. Et[8] ab
omnibus illis probis & sapientibus
hominibus qui affuerunt. fuit ibi
diratiocinatum & etiam a toto comitatu
concordatum[9] atque iudicatum. quod
sicut ipse rex tenet suas terras liberas
& quietas in suo dominico; ita archiepiscopus cantuarberię[10] tenet suas

D

placito non solum istas prenominatas
terras, sed et omnes consuetudines
ecclesie sue et libertates renovavit et
renovatas ibi diraciocinavit, scilicet
soca and[2] saca, tol, team, flymena-
fyrmthe, grytbrece, forestal, haimfare,
infangeneþeof, cum omnibus aliis
consuetudinibus paribus istis vel minoribus istis, in terris et in aquis, in silvis,
in viis et in pratis et in omnibus rebus
et locis, scilicet infra civitatem et extra,
infra burgam[5] et extra. Et ab omnibus
sapientibus, qui affuerunt, fuit ibi
diracionatum atque iudicatum a[6]

(A cont.)

terras omnino liberas & quietas in suo dominico. Huic placito interfuerunt
Goisfridus[11] episcopus constantiensis qui in loco regis fuit. & iustitiam[12] illam
tenuit. Lanfrancus archiepiscopus qui ut dictum est placitauit & totum diratiocinauit.[13] Comes cantię. uidelicet prędictus Odo[14] baiocensis episcopus. Ernostus
episcopus de rouecestra.[15] Ægelricus episcopus de cicestra.[16] uir antiquissimus
& legum terrę sapientissimus. qui ex precepto regis aduectus fuit ad ipsas
antiquas legum consuetudines discutiendas & edocendas. in una quadriga.
Ricardus de tunebrigge.[17] Hugo de monteforti. Willelmus de arces. Haimo[18]
uicecomes. Et[19] alii multi barones regis & ipsius archiepiscopi. atque illorum
episcoporum homines multi. Et[20] alii aliorum comitatuum homines etiam cum
toto isto comitatu. multę & magnę auctoritatis uiri francigenę scilicet & angli.
In horum omnium pręsentia multis & apertissimis rationibus demonstratum

---

[1] & B. [2] Sic.

[3] C wrote dirationauit, adding ci above.

[4] grithbreche C. [5] Sic.

[6] At this point D breaks off abruptly in the middle of a line. The break was not due
either to lack of space or to subsequent mutilation of the manuscript.

[7] burgam altered to burgum C. [8] & B.

[9] C has recordatum with two or three letters erased between the e and the c.

[10] cant' C. [11] goisfridus B. [12] iusticiam B.

[13] C wrote dirationauit, adding ci above. [14] odo B.

[15] hrouecestra B; Rouec' C.

[16] In C the e of cicestra is written above an erasure.

[17] tunebregge C. [18] Haymo C.

[19] & (lower case) B. [20] & B.

fuit. quod rex anglorum nullas consuetudines habet in omnibus terris cantuariensis[1] ęcclesię. nisi solummodo tres. Et illę tres quas habet consuetudines.
hę sunt. Vna. si quis homo archiepiscopi effodit illam regalem uiam quę uadit
de ciuitate in ciuitatem. Altera. si quis arborem incidit iuxta regalem uiam. &
eam super ipsam uiam deiecerit. De istis duabus consuetudinibus qui culpabiles
inuenti fuerint. atque detenti dum talia faciunt. siue uadimonium ab eis
acceptum fuerit. siue non; tamen in secutione ministri regis & per uademonium.
emendabunt quę iuste emendanda sunt. Tertia[2] consuetudo talis est. Si quis in
ipsa regali uia sanguinem fuderit. aut homicidium. uel aliud aliquid fecerit
quod nullatenus fieri licet. si dum hoc facit deprehensus atque detentus fuerit;
regi emendabit. Si uero deprehensus ibi non fuerit. & inde absque uuade data
semel abierit; rex ab eo nichil iuste exigere poterit. Similiter fuit ostensum in
eodem placito. quod archiepiscopus cantuariensis[3] ęcclesię[4] in omnibus terris
regis & comitis debet multas consuetudines iuste habere. Etenim ab illo die quo
clauditur alleluia.[5] usque ad octauas paschę.[6] si quis sanguinem fuderit. archiepiscopo emendabit. Et in omni tempore tam extra quadragesimam quam infra
quicunque illam culpam fecerit quę cilduuite[7] uocatur. archiepiscopus aut totam[8]
aut dimidiam emendationis partem habebit. Infra quadragesimam quidem
totam. & extra; aut totam aut dimidiam emendationem. Habet etiam in eisdem
terris omnibus. quęcunque ad curam & salutem animarum uidentur pertinere.
Huius placiti[9] multis testibus multisque rationibus determinatum finem post-
quam rex audiuit; laudauit. laudans cum consensu omnium principum suorum
confirmauit. & ut deinceps incorruptus perseueraret firmiter precepit. Quod
propterea scriptum est hic. ut & futurę in ęternum memorię proficiat. & ipsi
futuri eiusdem ęcclesię Christi cantuarberię[10] successores sciant. quę & quanta
in dignitatibus ipsius ęcclesię a deo tenere. atque a regibus & principibus huius
regni ęterno iure debeant exigere.[11]

C.

[List of manors &c. peculiar to C.
See above, pp. 18, 22]

The Canterbury Obituary
(Cotton Claud. C. vi. f. 165 b)[12]

In illis tribus diebus dirationauit ibi
Lanfrancus archiepiscopus plures terras quas tunc ipse episcopus et homines
sui (tenuerunt)[13] videlicet. Herebertus
filius iuonis. Turoldus de Rouec'.
Radulfus de curua spina. Hugo de
monte forti. cum omnibus consuetudinibus et rebus (que) ad easdem
terras pertinebant. Scilicet Raculfe.[14]

Obiit WILLELMUS rex anglorum. Hic
reddidit ęcclesię Christi omnes fere
terras antiquis & modernis temporibus
a iure ipsius ęcclesię ablatas. Quarum
terrarum nomina hęc sunt. In cantia.

---

[1] cant' *C.*   [2] Tercia *B.*   [3] cant' *C.*   [4] ęcclesiae *B.*
[5] alleluya *C.*   [6] pascę *B*; pasce *C.*   [7] childwite *C.*
[8] *B adds a full stop after* totam.
[9] *In C the* a *of* placiti *is written over an* i *expunged.*   [10] cant' *C.*
[11] *The final stop in A is* ·,· *in B; and C, to fill up the line, has written* ex – I – ge –
R – E.   [12] *The text given in* Monasticon (1846), i. 109, *is unsatisfactory.*
[13] This word is written in the Corrector's hand.
[14] Reculver; *DM*, 80, 84; *DB*, i, f. 3b. (In the following notes, *DM* stands for
Douglas, *The Domesday Monachorum of Christ Church Canterbury.*)

Sandwic.[1] Rateburg.[2] Wdetune.[3] Monasterium de limminge[4] cum terris et consuetudinibus ad ipsum monasterium pertinentibus. Saltwde cum burgo hethe[5] ad saltwde pertinente. Langport.[6] Niwendenne.[7] Rokinge.[8] (Broche.)[9] detlinge.[10] prestetune.[11] Sunderherste.[12] Earhethe.[13] Orpintune.[14] Einesford.[15] Quatuor prebendas de niwentune.[16] (stokes.)[17] & denintune.[18] In Suthreia fauente rege Willelmo dirationauit ipse archiepiscopus. Murtelache.[19] In london'; Monasterium

Raculf. Sandwic. Rateburch. Wudetun. Monasterium de limminge cum terris & consuetudinibus ad ipsum monasterium pertinentibus. Saltwude cum burgo hethe ad saltwude pertinente. Langport. Niwendene. Rokinge. Detlinge. Prestentune non longe a fluuio medeweie sitam. Sunderherste. Earhethe. Orpentun. Ainesford. Denintun. Stocke. Quattuor prebendas de niwentune. & preter hęc omnia multas alias modicas terras tam in insulis quam extra insulas in

[1] Sandwich; *DM*, 89: 'quando archiepiscopus recuperauit'; *DB*, i, f. 3a.

[2] Richborough; cf. Douglas, 'Odo, Lanfranc . . .', p. 51.

[3] ? Wootton, Sussex; *DB*, i, f. 16b; cf. *Valor Ecclesiasticus*, i. 13; *Monasticon*, i. 88.

[4] Lyminge; cf. *V.C.H. Kent*, ii. 146. A document printed by H. Boehmer in *Die Fälschungen Erzbischof Lanfranks von Canterbury* (Leipzig, 1902), pp. 173–5, clearly implies that Lyminge, both church and village, were in Lanfranc's hands. I owe this reference to Mr. J. C. Dickinson.

[5] Saltwood and Hythe; *DM*, 31, 93; *DB*, i, f. 4b; Douglas, 'Odo, Lanfranc . . .', p. 52.

[6] Langport; *DM*, 92; *DB*, i, f. 4b; Douglas, 'Odo, Lanfranc . . .', p. 52.

[7] Newington; *DM*, 92 and note, 99; *DB*, i, f. 4a.

[8] Ruckinge; apparently this manor was still held by Hugh de Montfort at the time of the Domesday Survey—*DB*, i, f. 13b.

[9] Brook; *DM*, 81, 92. This word is written in the margin in the Corrector's hand, with a caret to indicate its position in the text. It has been misplaced in some printed texts—which may help to resolve the difficulty this passage presents: see Douglas, *DM*, 13, n. 8.

[10] Detling; *DM*, 50, 99.

[11] Preston; *DM*, 81, 93; *DB*, i, f. 5a.

[12] Sundridge; *DM*, 80, 87: 'Sunderhersce est manerium archiepiscopi quod Goduuinus tenuit tempore E. regis iniuste et archiepiscopus iste Lanfrancus explacitauit illud contra episcopum baiocensem iuste per concessum regis'; *DB*, i, f. 3a.

[13] Erith; *DM*, 86; *DB*, i, f. 3a.

[14] Orpington; *DM*, 94: 'Et in hoc eodem manerio tenet Malgerus ab archiepiscopo iii iuga terre . . . et hec iii iuga . . . sunt de explacitatione quam fecit archiepiscopus contra episcopum baiocensem per concessum regis'; *DB*, i, ff. 4a, 4b.

[15] Eynesford; *DM*, 88; *DB*, i, f. 4a.

[16] Newington; *DM*, 88, cf. 13, n. 8.

[17] Stoke; *DM*, 81, 98: 'Stocces est manerium episcopi rofensis quod Godwinus comes tenuit contra uoluntatem seruientium sancti Andree. Et archiepiscopus Lanfrancus diratiocinauit illum contra episcopum baiocensem iuste'; *DB*, i, f. 5b: 'Hoc manerium fuit et est de episcopatu rofensi, sed Goduinus comes T.R.E. emit illud de duobus hominibus qui eum tenebant de episcopo, et eo ignorante facta est haec uenditio. Postmodum uero regnante W. rege diratiocinauit illud Lanfrancus archiepiscopus contra baiocensem episcopum, et inde est modo saisita rofensis aecclesia.' The word *stokes* in C is written in the Corrector's hand, but in the main text.

[18] Denton; *DM*, 81, 97; *DB*, i, f. 5b.

[19] Mortlake, Surrey; *DB*, i, f. 30b.

Sancte Marie[1] cum terris et (domibus)
quas Liuing' presbiter et uxor illius
habuerunt. In Midelsexe. Herghas.[2]
Heisam.[3] In bochingehamsire. Rise-
bergam.[4] Haltune.[5] In oxenefordsire;
Niwentune.[6] In eastsexe. stistede.[7]
(In sutfolchia. frachenham.)[8] Item
super Radulfum de curuaspina. lx.
solidatas de pastura in grean.[9] Et[10]
omnes illas terras et alias dirationauit
(cum[11] omnibus consuetudinibus &
rebus que ad easdem terras pertinebant) ita liberas atque quietas. quod
in illa die qua ipsum placitum finitum
fuit. non remansit homo in toto regno
anglie qui aliquid inde calumniaretur.
neque super ipsas terras etiam paruum
quicquam clamaret. Stokes uero et
denintune (& frachenham)[12] reddidit
ecclesie sancti andree quia de iure
ipsius ecclesie antiquitus fuerunt. Et
in eodem placito . . . &c.

cantia sitas. Stocke uero & denentun
LANFRANCUS archiepiscopus reddidit
ęcclesię Sancti ANDREĘ. quia de iure
ipsius ęcclesię antiquitus fuerunt. In
suthrege. Murtelac. Lundonię monasterium Sanctę MARIĘ cum terris &
domibus quas Liuinguus presbiter &
uxor illius lundonię habuerunt. In
mildelsexum. Hergam. Heisam. In
buckingeham scire. Risbergam. Heal-
tun. In oxenaford scire. Niwentun.
In suthfolke. Frakenham. Hanc uil-
lam LANFRANCUS archiepiscopus reddidit ęcclesię Sancti ANDREĘ. quia
antiquitus ad ipsam ęcclesiam pertine-
bat. In eastsexum. Stistede. Stan-
brigge. Hęc omnia reddidit pro deo &
pro salute animę suę gratis & sine ullo
pretio.

[1] Possibly St. Mary Aldermary (W. Page, *London, its Origin and Early Develop-ment*, 1923, p. 160), but more probably St. Mary-le-Bow (B. W. Kissan, 'The Earliest Mention of Bow Church', *London and Middlesex Arch. Soc. Trans.*, N.S. vii, 1937, pp. 436–44).
[2] Harrow, Middlesex; *DB*, i, f. 127a; cf. *DM*, 99; Davis, *Regesta*, no. 265.
[3] Hayes, Middlesex; *DB*, i, f. 127a; cf. *DM*, 99.
[4] Monks Risborough, Bucks.; *DB*, i, f. 143b.
[5] Halton, Bucks.; *DB*, i, f. 143b.
[6] Newington, Oxon.; *DB*, i, f. 155a; cf. *DM*, 56.
[7] Stisted, Essex; *DB*, ii, f. 8a.
[8] Freckenham, Suffolk; *DB*, ii, f. 381a. This was one of the manors which Lanfranc restored to Rochester. Taking the colophon to Little Domesday at its word, this should have happened before 1086; but the charter which records the transfer is dated 1087 (Thorpe, *Registrum Roffense*, p. 359—taken from the same manuscript as Text C, Cotton Vespasian A. xxii).
[9] Isle of Grain, Kent.
[10] 'Et omnes illas terras . . . qui aliquid inde calumniaretur.' This passage, save for the words in brackets, is also found in Texts A and B.
[11] The words in brackets are written in the Corrector's hand in the margin. There is a sign in the main text which seems to indicate that this passage was intended to be inserted at this point.
[12] The words in brackets are written in the margin in the Corrector's hand, with a caret mark to indicate that they are to be inserted in the text at this point.

JOHN LE PATOUREL

LANFRANC OF BEC AND BERENGAR OF TOURS

I

THE two chief obstacles to the understanding of the thought
of the eleventh century are our ignorance of the scholastic
methods of the period and an inadequate biographical knowledge
of the masters who developed these methods. Between Gerbert,
whose methods of teaching have been sketched by his pupil
Richer, and the masters of the early twelfth century, the lecture-
rooms of Europe are only faintly illuminated. The sense of
familiarity and untroubled peace of St. Anselm's monastic
colloquies easily hides how little we know of the foundations of
those discussions to which he has given ideal form in his finished
works: a few scraps saved or snatched from his workshop by his
pupils alone remain to emphasize our ignorance.[1] The humanity
which clothes the utterances and inspired the pupils of Fulbert
of Chartres makes us forget that though his influence was of a
kind not to be tied down by any curriculum of studies, yet his
teaching was of arithmetic, astronomy, and grammar, and of this
only a few fragments remain in the form of rhymes for the use of
his pupils.[2] When the humanity of a Fulbert and the genius of
an Anselm are removed and we are left with the impersonal
records of teaching which must once have been brilliant, we
struggle with obscure technical terms and distinctions, of which
the significance if not also the plain meaning is often hidden.
Nor are we helped by there being any great abundance of such
material. The men of two generations later had so far outgrown
the scholars of the mid-eleventh century that they had little
interest in either preserving their work or understanding their
difficulties. John of Salisbury, in his confident command of a
logic harnessed to the service of practical life and sound learning, mocked at the logicians of a previous generation who had
strewn their sentences with the words *conveniens* and *inconveniens*,

[1] See especially the fragments published by F. S. Schmitt, *Ein neues unvollendetes
Werk des hl. Anselms v. Canterbury*, Beiträge z. Gesch. d. Phil. u. Theol. des
Mittelalters (Münster, 1936), xxxiii. 3. These pieces are jottings of arguments,
some of which are more fully developed elsewhere, rather than the remains of a
new unfinished work.

[2] Migne, *Pat. Lat.* 141, cols. 347–8 (carmen xvii); C. Pfister, *De Fulberti
Carnotensi Episcopi Vita et Operibus* (Nancy, 1885), pp. 35–8.

argumentum and *ratio*, and had multiplied their negatives to the obscurity of their meaning.[1] Yet, if he had looked back a little farther, he would have found it was not only blundering incompetents who wrote thus: the works of St. Anselm provide numerous illustrations of the characteristics of which he complains. Nor, unless they were marked out by some special sanctity, did the memory of the lives of the scholars of this generation outlive the recognition accorded to their thought. St. Bruno, the founder of the Carthusians, had a long career as a teacher at Rheims before he turned to the religious life, and his mortuary roll attests the extraordinary extent of his influence between 1055 and 1075. Men looked back over thirty years to record the debt which they owed to his teaching, but except for their testimony no further record of it remains.[2] If he had not been remembered for other reasons he might have shared the fate of the many masters whose praises are sung with perhaps extravagant praise in the verses of Baudri of Bourgueil, and who are now forgotten.[3]

Among the masters who were active between about 1050 and 1070 Lanfranc and Berengar stand out both by reason of the bulk of their surviving work and the comparative abundance of biographical material. But the interpretation of their lives and work suffers from the difficulties which beset the period as a whole. Both are famous for other reasons than for strictly scholastic ones, the lives of both have suffered from later misconstructions, and their thoughts present more difficulties when examined in detail than have often been realized. Miss Smalley has begun the work of revealing them in their true light as teachers and scholars outside the controversy which has made them famous.[4] In what follows I shall attempt to relate their controversial writings to the scholastic disciplines in which they excelled and to which, above all, they owed their fame in their own generation.

In England, when we think of Lanfranc before he became archbishop, the figure of the 'lawyer of Pavia' first rises to our mind: it is a picture which has been drawn by Maitland with vigorous

---

[1] *Metalogicon*, ed. C. C. J. Webb, p. 10 (*Pat. Lat.* 199, col. 829).

[2] *Pat. Lat.* 152, cols. 555–606; see especially the following titles for former pupils of Bruno: 3, 39, 45, 79, 156, 174, 176.

[3] Ph. Abrahams, *Œuvres poétiques de Baudri de Bourgueil* (Paris, 1926); see especially nos. lxiv–lxvi, xc–xcii, xcvii–ci, cix, cxxxvi, cxxxvii–cxxxix, clxi, ccxxxi.

[4] See the very suggestive pages in her *Study of the Bible in the Middle Ages* (Oxford, 1941), pp. 31–8; also 'La Glossa Ordinaria. Quelques prédécesseurs d'Anselme de Laon', *Recherches de Théologie ancienne et médiévale*, ix (1937), 365–400.

strokes.[1] Yet this was not how he appeared to his contemporaries. To them he was Lanfranc the dialectician. The mystery of his early years in Pavia has exercised on modern scholars a fascination out of all proportion to its importance. All that can be stated as almost certain is that his father was a 'lawman', as he would have been described in the England of the time, in the town of Pavia[2] and the young Lanfranc, who was to have succeeded to this position, must have been brought up from an early age to be familiar with the Lombard law. There is one striking piece of evidence of this familiarity in his later writings.[3] But he fled from the prospect of a lifetime spent in wrangling about the meaning of the barbarian laws of the Lombard kings and betook himself to the home of the rising arts of grammar and dialectic in northern France. It was not until Orderic Vitalis told a scarcely probable story of Lanfranc's early legal successes that this tradition began to filter into the literature of England and Normandy.[4] The position

[1] *History of English Law* (2nd ed.), i. 77–8.

[2] 'Vita Lanfranci', *Pat. Lat.* 150, col. 29: 'Pater eius de ordine illorum qui iura et leges civitatis asservabant fuit.' Cf. the description of a lawman in a document of 1106 from York: 'hereditario iure lagaman civitatis, quod latine potest dici legislator vel iudex' (quoted by Liebermann, *Gesetze d. Angelsachsen*, ii. 2, p. 565, col. 1).

[3] N. Tamassia examined the internal evidence for Lanfranc's legal knowledge in *Mélanges Fitting* (Montpellier, 1908), ii. 191–201. He analysed several passages in Lanfranc's 'Commentary on St. Paul' which make more or less definite allusions to legal doctrines. Most of these could have come from glossaries or from the ordinary handbooks of the day, but one of Tamassia's conjectures is entirely borne out by the manuscripts. In commenting on the word *Parentibus* in 1 Tim. v. 4, Lanfranc says: 'Parentes vocat quos superius filios et nepotes. Tota enim progenies *parentela* dicitur, unde et in mundana lege *parens parenti per gradum et parentelam succedere iubetur.*' (Vatican MS. lat. 143, f. 142ᵛ; the printed text makes nonsense of the words in italics.) Dr. F. Schulz has kindly examined for me the possible sources of this gloss and is satisfied that Lanfranc must have had in mind cap. 153 of the Edict of Rotheri, the earliest of the Lombard laws: 'Omnis parentilla usque in septimum geniculum nomeretur ut *parens parenti per gradum et parentillam* heres succedat' (*M.G.H. Leg.* iv. 35). I owe my thanks to Dr. Schulz for his advice on this point and to Miss Smalley for generously allowing me to use her photographs of Lanfranc's glosses on St. Paul.

[4] The fully developed Bec tradition about his early life is best represented by the 'Miracula S. Nicholai conscripta a monacho Beccensi' written after 1136 and printed in *Catalogus Cod. Hagiograph. Lat. in Bibl. Nat. Parisiensi* (Brussels, 1890), ii. 408–9. Neither this nor the first account of Lanfranc's youth in the 'Vita Lanfranci' ascribed to Milo Crispin (*Pat. Lat.* 150, col. 29) mentions his legal studies. Milo, however, gives also a second account unmistakably borrowed from Orderic Vitalis (*Hist. Eccl.*, ed. Le Prévost, ii. 209), containing the famous account of Lanfranc overcoming his adversaries in lawsuits. Robert of Torigni goes a step farther in describing Lanfranc as the colleague of Irnerius in the rediscovery of Roman Law: but he also, in the part of his chronicle which he wrote at Bec, has no reference to Lanfranc's legal studies; the legendary account which he later gives of these is among the additions made after he left Bec in 1154 (See R. Howlett, *Chronicles of the Reigns*

which he occupied in the estimation of his contemporaries was summed up by the anti-pope Clement III when he wrote to enlist his support, near the end of Lanfranc's life:

Blessed be God Almighty . . . who both made you a guide and light to lead the minds of the Latins into the study of the trivium and quadrivium, which had fallen into neglect and profound obscurity, and also, by his inestimable Providence, set you up as a master and most careful teacher of the Old and the New Testaments.[1]

Gilbert Crispin and Guitmund of Aversa tell the same story: he relit the light of the arts in the West. The account is so general that it becomes banal through much repetition. Only one point stands out which needs emphasis: great though he was in all the arts, he was greatest in dialectic. William of Malmesbury has, in his dramatic fashion, described the pupils of Lanfranc at Bec belching forth dialectic; Sigebert of Gembloux and the author of that important source for the early life of Lanfranc, the 'Miracles of St. Nicholas', have both singled out dialectic as his chief concern.[2]

We should know more exactly what they meant by this if we possessed two works—the 'Questiones Lanfranci' and 'Lantfrancus de dialectica'[3]—which were catalogued among the dialectical treatises in two contemporary collections. Unfortunately these are lost, but even so they emphasize the character of Lanfranc's work in his early and middle years of maturity.

of Stephen, Henry II and Richard I, Rolls Series, 1889, IV, pp. xliii–xlvii, 25–6.) If we are to believe that the Lanfranc of the 'Liber Papiensis' was our Lanfranc we must believe that the memory of the amazing young man was kept alive in Pavia for thirty or forty years by someone who followed his career from afar; in which case the casualness of the single reference to his identity would be hard to explain. Professor Stenton (Anglo-Saxon England [Oxford, 1943], p. 654 note) has recently pointed out the chronological difficulties involved in this identification; the silence of the Bec writers and the tendency of scribes and others to identify forgotten men with famous characters are other formidable objections. For the literature on this much-debated point, see J. H. Wigmore in Law Quarterly Review, lviii (1942), pp. 61–81 : like other writers on the subject he has not, however, noticed that Orderic and not Milo Crispin is the source of the account of Lanfranc's successes in Pavia.

[1] Printed by F. Liebermann, Eng. Hist. Rev. xvi (1901), p. 331; P. Kehr has given reasons for thinking that Clement was successful in his appeal and that England belonged for a time to the area of his obedience ('Zur Gesch. Wiberts v. Ravenna (Clemens III)', Sitzungsberichte d. Preuss. Akad. der Wissenschaften, 1921, pp. 359–60).

[2] Wm. Malms. Gesta Regum, ed. Stubbs (Rolls Series), ii. 150; Sigebert, 'Lib. de Script. Eccl.', Pat. Lat. 160, cols. 582–3; 'Mirac. S. Nicholai', loc. cit.: 'ipsa ars, scilicet dialectica, per eum reparata et renovata.'

[3] G. Becker, Catalogi Bibliothecarum Antiqui (Bonn, 1885), nos. 54 and 68.

To those who only know the archbishop, the brilliant and impulsive man of these years may appear strangely incongruous. But we must remember his adventurous career. He twice sacrificed an assured future for the hazards first of a scholar's life, when he had his way to make without friends or influence in the competitive world of free-lance teachers; then—no sooner rising to the reputation and fortune which teaching seems to have been able at that time to confer on outstanding men—he threw this up for life in an ill-established monastery. His teaching days, at least in the new way in which teaching was understood in the secular schools, seemed to be over; and probably they would have been but for the financial stringency of an impoverished foundation. The twenty years' teaching which made his name known throughout Europe began as the chance by-product of monastic poverty.

The only master of the time who could challenge Lanfranc's supremacy in the arts was his teacher and rival Berengar. Berengar has left his personality much more strongly impressed upon the records of the time than Lanfranc. One must not conclude from this that his teaching was therefore more original or impressive; he simply had tricks of style and behaviour which Lanfranc lacked. He was rich, liberal, pious; proud of his position as the leading master of his time and country and intellectually fastidious and arrogant. He had an unshakable confidence which made it impossible for him to see when he had been beaten; he regarded his opponents as a faction supported by a mob; he took for granted the support of those in high places and firmly believed that he was upholding tradition and orthodoxy.[1] Nor was he alone or wholly unjustified in this confidence. In his controversy with Lanfranc he was in many ways the conservative and Lanfranc the innovator. Provocative though he was in manner, yet cautious and conservative men might believe that his thought contained less novelty than that of his imperturbable opponent. Even in 1078 it would be rash to believe that he had fewer friends or found less favour in Rome than Lanfranc.[2] We must beware of thinking

[1] The contemporary characterization by Guitmund, later archbishop of Aversa, though hostile, contains some vivid and convincing detail (*Pat. Lat.* 149, col. 1429); there are some penetrating remarks on him by Dom G. Morin in *Rev. Bénédictine*, xliv (1932), pp. 220–6. But his own writings are the best revelation of his character: no other writer of the time conveys his own personality, with all its weaknesses, so vividly in what he writes.

[2] I am unable to accept the interpretation of Berengar's relations with Gregory VII given by C. Erdmann, 'Gregor VII und Berengar v. Tours', *Quellen und Forschungen aus ital. Archiv u. Bibliotheken*, xxviii (1937–8), pp. 48–74. The

that the judgements of the Councils of 1049, 1050, and 1059 compromised his position in the eyes of contemporaries very gravely. Everything conspired to delay the final irrevocable act of judgement; almost every judgement presented some loop-hole for escape. In particular the legality of the judgements of 1049 and 1050 was, on the grounds of Berengar's absence, not above criticism; and the formula of 1059 was framed in such terms that, whatever might be its essential orthodoxy, it was quietly abandoned by later councils. Throughout these years he remained in the eyes of Europe a great scholar and a great teacher.[1]

As a scholar he was, in the widest sense of the word, a grammarian.[2] 'He was', says Guitmund (who wrote as an enemy but with a personal knowledge which rings true), 'not an acute man in delving into the deeper secrets of philosophy, but delighted in new interpretations of words.'[3] He first appears in history as *grammaticus* and, far though he travelled from the simple tasks involved in this office, he remained a grammarian to the end: *in grammatica et philosophia clarissimus.*

It would be unwise to press too far the application of epithets which are used perhaps with no deep reflection on their technical meaning; nevertheless, the careless words of contemporaries or near-contemporaries probably touch truths which are missed by the considered statements of scholars writing at a distance of 900 years. In the general obscurity of the time, the slightest pointers are worth following, and these distinguish Lanfranc as above all a dialectician and Berengar as pre-eminently a grammarian.

II

If the ancient divisions of subjects had still provided an adequate guide to eleventh-century studies it would not have been difficult to draw a distinction between grammar and dialectic.

---

evidence for the relatively favourable attitude of Gregory VII towards Berengar is too strong to be explained away as he attempts to do; nor would I accept his severe judgement on Berengar's own account of the events of 1078–9 in Martène and Durand, *Thesaurus Novus Anecdotorum,* iv. 103–9. For the pope's growing irritation with Lanfranc, see his letter of 25 Mar. 1079 (*Reg.* vi. 30).

[1] See the letter printed in the Appendix, below, p. 48.

[2] See the testimonies collected by A. J. MacDonald, *Berengar and the Reform of Sacramental Doctrine* (London, 1930), pp. 27–9. Sigebert of Gembloux (*Pat. Lat.* 160, col. 582) forms an exception in characterizing him as *dialecticae peritia insignis.*

[3] *Pat. Lat.* 149, col. 1429.

Grammar is the art of writing and speaking correctly; dialectic is the art of argument. But all formal distinctions of this kind, which had never perhaps been more than school-room formulas, were upset by what was—apart from the contributions of individual genius—the most important event in the intellectual history of the century: the diffusion of that body of Boethius's translations, commentaries, and treatises which came to be known as the *Logica Vetus*. The material facts of this diffusion are now better known than before through the work of Mr. van de Vyver[1] and they invite reflection on the meaning of this diffusion in the obscure period with which we are dealing. The process by which these works of Boethius were collected together, arranged in a logical order, and multiplied in the libraries of Europe looks calm enough on the surface; a product, one might say, of the passage of time and the slow labour of copyists. But underneath these impersonal facts there are the traces of an upheaval and excitement no less disturbing or far-reaching than those which accompanied the philosophical innovations of the thirteenth century. The difficulty of these superficially repulsive works had condemned them to a long neglect—except so far as their ideas were transmitted in more elementary works and in popular handbooks—until the very eve of the eleventh century. From this neglect only the highest expectation of their importance could have saved them. The strength of the attraction exercised by these books on the minds of the men who brought them out of their honoured obscurity may be judged from the way in which their influence spilled over, as it were, from their proper field of dialectic into the neighbouring arts—into grammar in the first place, but also into rhetoric and even mathematics. They provided the starting-point of discussions about the 'squaring of the circle' and the angles of the triangle,[2] as well as about the types of valid argument and the forms of propositions.

It is difficult enough to understand the fascination which these books possessed, but it would be quite impossible if one did not take into account that they revealed an orderly view of the world which was urgently sought after. It was a view of the world which had never been quite forgotten. The Carolingian scholar who wrote in a glossary, among much similar matter, 'Ista sunt

[1] A. van de Vyver, 'Les Étapes du développement philosophique du haut moyen âge', *Revue belge de philologie et d'histoire*, viii (1929), 425–52; 'L'Évolution scientifique du haut moyen âge', *Archeion*, xix (1937), pp. 12–20.

[2] P. Tannery, 'Une Correspondance d'écolâtres du XIe siècle', *Notices et Extraits*, xxxvi (1901), 2, p. 487.

decem praedicamenta quibus constat universitas'[1] was perhaps attracted by the universality of Aristotle's teaching, though it can have had little relevance for his own thoughts. But the doctrines which became accessible in the eleventh century with a coherence and completeness unattainable since the sixth century, struck the scholars of this period with the force of a scientific revolution. If they did nothing immediately to encourage a scientific attitude towards natural phenomena, they taught habits of classification and arrangement which are the remote ancestors of modern science.

Even in the truncated Aristotle of the *Logica Vetus* there were many fields into which order was introduced, but above all— because having the appearance of objectivity and being therefore, in the early stages at least, outside the range of controversy—the description of the world in terms of substance and accidents, genera and species, took deep roots. A vast amount of labour and ingenuity was spent in the eleventh and succeeding centuries in elaborating the art of the syllogism, but though this may have been a whetstone to men's minds, its importance can easily be exaggerated. It was not in this, but in the idea of substance that dialectic imposed a profound modification on the thought of this period. Behind the world of appearances there were henceforth two worlds: the world of spiritual significances and the world of substance, genera, and species. They could exist and to some extent had long existed side by side. But the first had long been rich with meaning and the authority of great names at a time when the second had done little more than provide material for class-room exercises. Henceforth it was to be different: the vitality of new discovery and revolutionary effect belonged to the second. By the third quarter of the eleventh century, the bearing of the philosophic ideas contained in the *Logica Vetus* on long-established theological doctrines began to be a pressing problem: the Trinity, the Manhood of Christ, the Sacraments all invited and in part repelled the application to them of the idea of substance. The controversy between Lanfranc and Berengar was the first big-scale theological dispute to be fought out under the dominance of this idea.[2] It was not to be the last.

---

[1] E. Miller, 'Un Glossaire grec-latin de la Bibliothèque de Laon', *Notices et Extraits*, xxix (1880), 2, p. 181.

[2] As early as the last quarter of the tenth century Bishop Wolfgang of Regensburg had triumphantly silenced a doubter by applying the doctrine of substance and accidents to the problem of the Manhood of Christ, though only by way of similitude: 'Accidens est' inquit 'quadriforme: unum quod nec accedit nec

The extent of the influence of the books of the *Logica Vetus* on the neighbouring art of grammar is hard to define, but the cause of their influence is not hard to find.[1] Grammar is the most obsequious of subjects, the servant of the written word; but like a confidential servant it has ambitions. The words in which thought is expressed reflect in many ways the forms of thought itself, and it was not unreasonable for the grammarians to believe that books which analysed the forms of thought and argument with such unique completeness should also have something to tell them about the nature of the various parts of speech and the grammatical construction of the sentence. The grammarians were all the more willing to believe this because their view of the origin of language suggested that it reproduced the facts which it describes more faithfully than in fact it does. We shall see in Berengar how inseparably bound up the analysis of language became at this time with philosophical and even theological problems. In this he was not alone: the discussion of Boethius on the relation between the truth of future contingent propositions and free-will made a deep impression at this time;[2] and St. Anselm's argument about the existence of God is, in form at least, an attempt to apply the rules of language to prove the existence of the *Summum Esse*.

These are great problems and lead far away from the grammarian's everyday work of expounding texts: but just at this time the grammarian was raising his head above the texts and seeking new fields of speculation, being yet wholly uncertain of the limits within which grammar could help in the solution of the greatest problems. Dialecticians at this time were more than men who were skilled in the art of argument; they were men who were learning to think in terms of substance and accidents, genera and species. Grammarians, while not abandoning their texts, were bringing their own rather doctrinaire appreciation of words to the solution of the common problems.

---

recedit . . .; aliud quod accedit et recedit . . .; tertium quod non accedit et tamen recedit . . .; quartum quod accedit et non recedit. . . . Hac ergo similitudine Filius . . . induit quasi per inseparabile accidens humanitatem.' Othloni Vita S. Wolfkangi, *M.G.H. Scriptores*, iv. 538.

[1] For the whole subject of the development of grammar during this period see R. W. Hunt, 'Studies on Priscian in the Eleventh and Twelfth Centuries', *Mediaeval and Renaissance Studies*, i (1943), pp. 194–231.

[2] Cf. Peter Damian, *De divina omnipotentia*, c. 5, *Pat. Lat.* 145, cols. 602–4.

III

It was not an accident that the eucharistic controversy arose in the form in which it did in the middle of the eleventh century. But in the careers of the two chief protagonists it was an interruption and an incident in a life of teaching. Outside the range of public controversy both men were doing work which was helping to shape the future studies of Europe, and this work ran for the most part along similar lines. Of Lanfranc's work as a teacher we either have, or know of, his glosses on the Epistles of St. Paul, on the Psalms, on the Book of Job, on the *Collationes* of Cassian, on the *Rhetorica ad Herennium* of Cicero;[1] of Berengar's teaching work we either have, or know of, his glosses on the Epistles of St. Paul and the Psalms, and a Commentary on the Lord's Prayer.[2] This list gives a false impression if it suggests that Lanfranc covered a wider range of secular and ecclesiastical literature than Berengar. What we know is the merest fragment of the whole. One important point, however, emerges even from the inadequate information which we possess: they were both following the same plan in adapting the method of commentary, which had long been applied to secular texts, to the Bible. Whether they were doing anything new in this it is impossible to say. But there is at least a striking difference between their commentaries and those of the Carolingian scholars, with their wide expanses of accumulated learning and ancient authority and their comparatively superficial treatment of the text. Berengar and Lanfranc looked with keen eyes at the words in front of them; their notes are the remains of lecture-room material addressed to a generation eager for the facts; they cannot be read at ease but require—in the absence of the lecturer to enforce his meaning— much effort and constant reference to the biblical text to puzzle out the point. Yet, alike though they are, it is not impossible to see, even in their dry and precise notes, indications of differences in the approach of the two men to their texts.

The peculiarity of Lanfranc's work was marked by Sigebert of Gembloux: 'Lanfrancus dialecticus . . . Paulum apostolum exposuit et ubicumque opportunitas locorum occurrit secundum leges dialecticae proponit, assumit, concludit.'[3]   That is to

---

[1] *Pat. Lat.* 150, cols. 101 and 443; B. Smalley, *Recherches de théologie anc. et méd.* ix (1937), pp. 374–5; R. W. Hunt in *Mediaeval and Renaissance Studies*, i. 207.
[2] B. Smalley, op. cit., pp. 391–6, for the first two and, for the text of the third, V. Rose, *Verzeichniss der Lat.-HSS. der Königl. Bibl. zu Berlin*, 1893, i. 114–15.
[3] *Pat. Lat.* 160, cols. 582–3.

say—if we understand him rightly—he explained the argument, disentangled its branches, and put into proper logical form what the Apostle had left to be inferred from a few rapid sentences. 'The order of the argument is as follows. . . . This is a proof of the preceding verse. . . . This is an argument *a simili . . . a causa . . . a contrario.* . . . Here, by disproving one alternative, the Apostle proves, as his manner is, the other': these are phrases which often recur in Lanfranc's commentary.[1] Berengar, on the other hand, appears to be more interested in words and figures of speech than in arguments; he shines more in adducing parallels than in analysis. Our materials for judging this side of his work are so inadequate that it is difficult to be certain even of this, but in the one considerable fragment of a commentary which we possess—that on the Lord's Prayer—he was largely occupied in giving examples of the figure of speech called *parenthesis* and in proposing a novel interpretation of the force of the conjunction *et* in the phrase *et dimitte nobis debita nostra*.[2] One remembers the words of Guitmund,[3] and how Berengar's pupils made themselves conspicuous by introducing unaccustomed quantities into the familiar words of the church services,[4] and how Berengar himself had proposed a grammatical change in the liturgical texts of the Church.[5] His controversial works will provide many examples of this characteristic grammatical preoccupation.

Both men indeed retained to an extraordinary extent in their controversial works the habits which they had learnt in their lecture-rooms. It is one of the marks of this controversy that it shows so deeply in every way the marks of the scholastic disciplines which occasioned it. Not least is this shown in the external appearance of the two treatises which are its central documents.[6]

[1] Cf. the glosses on Rom. iii. 4 (ut justificeris); v. 19 (sicut enim); vii. 1 (An ignoratis, fratres); vii. 18 (Scio enim); viii. 23 (redemptionem corporis); 1 Cor. vii. 27 (noli quaerere uxorem); viii. 8 (abundabamus); x. 16 (Calix benedictionis); xv. 13 (Christus resurrexit). The character and extent of Lanfranc's commentary has often been misunderstood and the sense of Sigebert's comment lost owing to the form in which Lanfranc's glosses are printed in the edition of D'Achery, which is reproduced by Migne (*Pat. Lat.* 150, cols. 101–406); but, as Miss Smalley has explained, the edition of J. A. Giles, which in other respects is not superior to the earlier one, gives a more faithful picture of Lanfranc's work by omitting the quotations from Augustine, Ambrose, &c. (cf. B. Smalley, op. cit., p. 380).

[2] He argues: '. . . ut coniunctiva particula *et* non pendeat a superioribus sed pertrahatur ad sequens *et* tamquam dicat: "ad hoc valeat nobis panis ille noster qui de celo descendit, ut nulla omnino criminalia incurramus."' V. Rose, op. cit., p. 114.

[3] See *ante*, p. 32.   [4] MacDonald, *Berengar*, p. 29 note.

[5] Smalley, op. cit., p. 395.

[6] Lanfranc's 'Liber de Corpore et Sanguine Domini' is printed in *Pat. Lat.* 150,

Each treatise is written, for the most part, in the form of a detailed commentary on its predecessor: the text of Berengar's first treatise is only known because it is incorporated in Lanfranc's reply; if Lanfranc's reply were lost we should still have the greater part of it in Berengar's attack. The method led to much repetition and endless concern with details, to a good many merely debating points, and the use of abusive words on an unprecedented scale. If we compare them with the treatises written in the theological controversies of the ninth century, it is evident how greatly the conditions of debate have changed. The earlier controversies were conducted with the spaciousness of scholarly ease: the long placid stretches of exposition, into which the rough winds of debate broke only fitfully, betokened men whose habit it was to do their thinking and writing in the retirement of the study. But Berengar and Lanfranc, if they wrote in the study, never forgot the lecture-room and the keen debate.

In considering the differences in method and outlook which these treatises reveal, it is necessary at the outset to put into proper perspective one obvious difference which has often been taken to be fundamental. This is the difference in their attitude towards dialectic, or even towards reason itself. Lanfranc reproached Berengar for introducing dialectical questions into a sacred subject and Berengar defended himself in a passage of unusual eloquence:

Maxime plane cordis est, per omnia ad dialecticam confugere, quia confugere ad eam ad rationem est confugere, quo qui non confugit, cum secundum rationem sit factus ad imaginem Dei, suum honorem reliquit, nec potest renovari de die in diem ad imaginem Dei.[1]

These are striking phrases and a revelation of Berengar's temperament, but we must beware of attaching too much importance to what was partly a debating point and partly a

cols. 407–42; the reply of Berengar (which is incomplete at beginning and end) was first printed by A. F. and F. T. Vischer, *Berengarii Turonensis De Sacra Coena adversus Lanfrancum Liber posterior* (Berlin, 1834); it has recently been re-edited by W. H. Beckenkamp (The Hague, 1941). Modern scholars have ascribed the treatises to the most divergent dates. The most likely date for Lanfranc's treatise is that given by A. J. MacDonald in his *Lanfranc*, p. 51: 1059–62. His reasons for the later limiting date are not conclusive, but on all grounds a date in the early 1060's appears probable. Berengar's reply cannot be dated closely but it probably followed Lanfranc's attack without much delay. Beckenkamp, *De Avendmaalsleer van Berengarius van Tours* (The Hague, 1941), p. 10, dates it 1063–9. In what follows the references are to Vischer's edition, followed by the page-numbers of the manuscripts in brackets.

[1] *De S. C.* 101 (67).

commonplace. The debate, on both sides, was a debate about the meaning of texts. Both men applied to these texts, though in different ways, the results and methods of the same discipline; they both asserted that the interpretation given by the other was incompatible with the authorities quoted, and logically unsound. There is no need to question the sincerity of Lanfranc's reluctance to introduce the cut and thrust of dialectical debate into the discussion of a sacred subject, but he, like Berengar, was too deeply influenced by the ideas of the books which made up the *Logica Vetus* to forget them in a controversy in which these ideas were so plainly relevant. That was why in Berengar's eyes he was the chief enemy. He was the scholar, the man who understood what things meant, who nevertheless lent the weight of his learning to a delusion of the unlearned world: 'quod scribis, multum erat contra eruditionem tuam', is Berengar's constant refrain.[1] Even at the end, when many others had joined in the debate against him and Lanfranc had been silent on the subject for fifteen or more years, he remained the chief enemy, the offending view remained the *vulgi et Lanfranni vesania*. Cardinal Humbert, with his hot zeal and blunt speech, could be ignored; but Lanfranc was the scholar who had given the game away.

The simple question at issue was whether and in what way the doctrine of the Eucharist was affected by the philosophical doctrine of substance and accidents. In the ninth century, when the doctrine of the Eucharist had also been debated, this had not been a clear issue.[2] We shall take a wrong view of the dispute if we think that Lanfranc's view was at the time obviously more traditional and orthodox than that of Berengar. In truth he was allowing new science to give clarity and definition to a view which had been only adumbrated before. To understand Lanfranc's reticences it is necessary to see that he was allowing the new learning to guide him along a path which disclosed many new problems and of which the end was not in sight; and something of Berengar's lack of reticence was due to the fact that he was refusing to go along that path and was eager to give all the possible reasons for not doing so.

In reading the treatises, however, it is not immediately clear how far the two men were in possession of the philosophical idea

---

[1] *De S. C.* 142 (100); cf. also 113 (77), 163 (119), 181 (135), 192 (144), 280 (219).

[2] For the doctrinal background see J. Geiselmann, *Die Eucharistielehre der Vorscholastik* (Paderborn, 1926); Dom M. Cappuyns, *Jean Scot Érigène* (Louvain, 1933), pp. 86–91.

of substance, which was the new factor about the discussion on the Eucharist from this time on. It is well known that the word 'transubstantiation' does not appear until some time after this date, and when we get back to the 1060's and to the controversy of Lanfranc and Berengar the philosophical vocabulary is strikingly uncertain. The phrase which Lanfranc prefers in describing the change which he believes to take place in the consecrated elements are: *commutari secundum interiorem essentiam* (cap. 9), or *in pristinis essentiis* (cap. 5), or *in principalibus essentiis* (cap. 7), or *essentialiter* (cap. 16). Berengar equally avoids the word 'substance', except in describing the view of Cardinal Humbert. He prefers, in contrast to Lanfranc, to talk about the *corruptio subiecti* —'materiali, ut scribis, mutatione, quod ego malo secundum corruptionem subiecti scribere', and again, 'Scribis . . . de pane, ut verbis tuis utar, in essentia propria minime remanente, i.e. de pane per subiecti corruptionem absumpto'.[1]

Is this uncertainty of vocabulary an indication of uncertainty of ideas?

The truth rather is the opposite. They had good reason for avoiding the word *substantia*, not because it was too definite or too philosophical, but because it was not definite or philosophical enough. Of the two senses of the word to which common usage had accustomed them, one was that general indefinite sense of ordinary speech which talks about material *substances*; the other was in the formula of the Christian faith in which God was described as three Persons and one *Substance*.[2] Neither of these was the sense required in this context. It is one of the symptoms of the rapid infiltration of the ideas and language of the Boethian treatises and commentaries that, less than a generation later, the word was firmly established in its philosophical sense: the eucharistic formula of the Council of 1079 itself bears witness to the fact. But Lanfranc and Berengar chose to avoid a word whose meaning was at that time so indefinite.

The words which they used were evidently carefully chosen and consistently applied. Lanfranc in one place describes the view he is attacking as the assertion that the Bread and Wine remain after consecration *in principalibus essentiis*; he goes on to say that God made things *in principalibus ac secundis essentiis* and

---

[1] *De S. C.* 94 (61) and 96 (63).
[2] For the use of the word in the early Middle Ages down to the eleventh century, see J. de Ghellinck, 'L'Entrée d'*essentia, substantia* et autres mots apparentés, dans le latin médiéval', *Archivum Latinitatis Medii Aevi*, xvi (1942), 106–11.

disposed them as the cause of both true and false propositions.[1]
Now he is here translating into his own favourite terms the *prima*
and *secunda substantia* of Boethius,[2] and since the change which
was later known as transubstantiation is a change in what is here
called *prima substantia*, it follows that Lanfranc meant just this
by describing a change *in principalibus essentiis*. Berengar likewise had adopted a phrase from Boethius, though one might find
some significance in the fact that it came from the translation of
Porphyry and not Aristotle. Accidents are there defined as being
capable of being present or absent in a subject *praeter subiecti
corruptionem*;[3] it is not precisely stated but it can be inferred that
substance cannot be absent *praeter subiecti corruptionem*, and this
is the inference which Berengar made. In stating the case thus
he was leading up to a quasi-grammatical argument which will
be examined later: one can do no more than note a different trend
in the ideas of the two men, rooted though they were in the same
body of logic.

Whatever reluctance Lanfranc might express in introducing
dialectic into the discussion, his reluctance concerned the method
of argument rather than the set of ideas taught by the books of
dialectic: the latter he could not exclude. But even the manner
in which he expresses himself about the former reveals the dialectician:

> Et siquando materia disputandi talis est, ut huius artis regulis valeat
> enucleatius explicari, in quantum possum per aequipollentias proposi-
> tionum tego artem, ne videar magis arte, quam veritate sanctorumque
> patrum auctoritate confidere.[1]

At first sight it is far from clear what he means by this, though
there is an unmistakable note of pride in the technical mastery
which conceals art. What art can be hidden by the use of
equipollent propositions? The 'equipollency of propositions'
is a branch of logic which has a place in the manuals from
Abaelard to the present day:[4] but so far as I know the word *aequi-
pollentia* is not found earlier than Lanfranc. It was suggested,

---

[1] Cap. 8.
[2] Boethius, 'In Categorias Arist. Lib. II', *Pat. Lat.* 64, col. 181.
[3] Boethius, 'In Porphyrium Comm. Lib. IV', *Pat. Lat.* 64, cols. 132–4. See
also Martianus Capella, ed. A. Dick (Teubner, 1925), p. 166. Subiectum est prima
substantia.
[4] For Abaelard's use of the word and discussion of the subject see B. Geyer,
'Peter Abaelards Philosophische Schriften', *Beiträge zur Gesch. d. Phil. u. Theol.
des Mittelalters*, xxi (1933), pp. 498–502.

no doubt, to him or to whoever else first used it, by a small treatise on logic, ascribed to Apuleius, which was coming into common use in the eleventh century, alongside the other works of the *Logica Vetus*.[1] It is a word which only a man familiar with and practised in the discussion of these works could have used. Yet, even when one knows what the logicians mean by equi-pollency of propositions, it is still obscure what Lanfranc intends his remark to convey: skill in the detection of equivalent forms of propositions is generally held to be not an alternative, but a preparation for argument, and to proceed *per aequipollentias pro-positionum* suggests a man moving from one foot to another with-out going forward. But the mystery is cleared up by turning to the works of Lanfranc's pupil, St. Anselm: in these the manner of proceeding which he has in mind is abundantly illustrated. One of the most notable features of Anselm's works is his habit of arguing, not by means of formal syllogisms (even when these would be quite applicable to the matter in hand) but by the con-version of propositions by definition and expansion in such a way that the argument grows under the hands of both master and pupil. In his *De Veritate*, for example, there is this passage:

Magister: Ad quid facta est affirmatio?
Discipulus: Ad significandum esse quod est.
Magister: Hoc ergo debet.
Discipulus: Certum est.
Magister: Cum ergo significat esse quod est, significat quod debet.
Discipulus: Palam est.
Magister: At cum significat quod debet, recte significat.
Discipulus: Ita est.
Magister: Cum autem recte significat, recta est significatio.
Discipulus: Non est dubium.
Magister: Cum ergo significat esse quod est, recta est significatio.
Discipulus: Ita sequitur.
Magister: Item cum significat esse quod est, vera est significatio.
Discipulus: Vere et vera et recta est, cum significat esse quod est.
Magister: Idem igitur est illi et rectam et veram esse, id est significare
    esse quod est.
Discipulus: Vere idem.
Magister: Ergo non est illi aliud veritas quam rectitudo.[2]

[1] The phrase 'aequipollentes propositiones' (which is not in Boethius) is used several times in Ps.-Apuleius, περὶ ἑρμηνείας, ed. P. Thomas, *Apulei de Philosophia Libri* (Teubner, 1921), pp. 176–94. For the diffusion of this work see the manu-scripts cited in this edition and M. Manitius, *HSS. antiken Autoren in Mittelalt. Bibl. Katalogen* (Leipzig, 1935).
[2] 'De Veritate', cap. 2 (F. S. Schmitt, *S. Anselmi Opera Omnia*, i (1938), p. 178).

In the light of Lanfranc's statement it seems very likely that this was a method of arguing in theological subjects which was much practised in his school. It avoids the brilliant display of magistral syllogisms, it proceeds by definitions and a gradual enrichment of meaning. The argument is woven, as Lanfranc would say, *per aequipollentias propositionum*. Once Lanfranc is looked on as a logician rather than as a lawyer it is possible to begin to understand something of his influence on St. Anselm, and the contrast between the two men, which has always been re-marked, becomes less striking than the debt of the one to the other.

Taking together all the remains of Lanfranc's work in the period before he became archbishop the description of him as a dialectician seems to be very well justified. He was, of course, other things as well: he could not have got far without being also a grammarian, but he showed no tendency to indulge in those flights to which the higher grammar was aspiring in the eleventh century. With Berengar the case is quite different. We saw that the remains of his biblical commentaries provided only scanty evidence for testing the adequacy of the epithet 'grammarian' commonly applied to him by contemporaries or for investigating his reputed love of discovering new meanings in words. His long reply to Lanfranc abundantly supplies this deficiency. In the *De Sacra Coena* his arguments fall into two main classes: those which concern the *physical* impossibility of a change of substance taking place in an object without a change of accidents, and those which attempt to demonstrate the *verbal* difficulties and contra-dictions which are involved in such a conception. The first class of arguments show that he, like his opponent, was perfectly familiar with the commentaries and translations of Boethius. But more characteristic of Berengar's method are those arguments which he derives from grammar and in which he applies the doctrines of the grammarian to the explanation of his texts. Again and again he appeals to the conclusive force of some word in the text which has been overlooked: 'Ad hoc te cogit conjunctiva particula *tamen*. . . . Ad hoc te trahit, velis nolis, vis adversativae conjun-ctionis *sed*. . . . Attendenda erat etiam vis conclusivae dictionis quae est *ergo* . . .' and so on.[1] Most of these arguments are, to one way of thinking, hopelessly forced and misguided. They depended for their validity on theories about the significance of the various parts of speech which were much more crude than the language they set out to interpret. Hence, however important these theories

[1] *De S. C.* 121 (82), 133 (92), 187 (140), 220 (165), 230 (174), 241 (184).

were as a stage in the history of reflection about language, they could not be used as an instrument for the explanation of texts without doing violence to the sense. We have been told that, a century after this time, speculative grammatical doctrines, though they retained their place in works of theory, had no influence on the practical work of expounding texts.[1] Experience must have brought caution; but this was not a quality with which Berengar was blessed.

An example will illustrate his method. Of all his parts of speech, the pronoun was the one which most often arrested Berengar's attention.[2] In the light of the contemporary grammatical teaching about pronouns it is not difficult to see why the significance of this part of speech seemed specially relevant to the question at issue between him and Lanfranc. The grammarians of this period were developing a doctrine about pronouns which, though not new, had hitherto received little attention. They held that pronouns signified things in their substance only, and in this way were distinguished from nouns which signified both substance and accidents.[3] The success of this doctrine, after lying neglected since the time of Priscian, is itself a testimony to the profound interest which the distinction between substance and accidents aroused at this time: by the early twelfth century it had become a commonplace with grammarians and it passed into the main stream of medieval grammatical teaching. But however eagerly the doctrine might be accepted, its application to the exposition of texts, and above all of sacred texts, raised a delicate problem. What bearing, for instance, had it on the interpretation of the vital words *Hoc* [indicating the sacramental bread] *est Corpus meum*? It is not quite clear from the *De Sacra Coena* how far Berengar was prepared to go in pressing the theory of pronouns in his interpretations of this text—perhaps because it was in this case a double-edged weapon. His words are often obscure and do not suggest that he could refer confidently to a generally

[1] R. W. Hunt, 'Studies in Priscian', *Mediaeval and Renaissance Studies*, i (1943), p. 223.

[2] *De S. C.* 85 (53), 133 (93), 138 (97), 185 (139), 187 (140), 232 (176), 278 (217–18); Martène and Durand, *Thes. Nov. Anec.* iv. 105.

[3] The doctrine is found in Priscian (*Inst. gramm.* xvii. 37), where he is drawing on Apollonius Dyscolus, περὶ ἀντωνυμίας 33 B. It does not appear in later Latin grammarians before the mid-eleventh-century 'Ars Grammatica' of Papias (*Grammatici Latini, Supplementum*, ed. H. Hagen (Leipzig, 1870), p. clxxxii). For its appearance in grammatical works from the late eleventh century, see R. W. Hunt, op. cit., pp. 200–1. I am greatly indebted to Mr. D. J. Allan and to Mr. Hunt for help on this point.

accepted grammatical doctrine. But, without stating a general rule, he appealed on several occasions to the force of the pronoun in a text under discussion as proof that the object indicated was referred to in its substance and not merely *tropice* or in its accidents. Then, a few years later, Guitmund reported that Berengar was referring formally to this grammatical doctrine in commenting on some words of St. Augustine, 'Non hoc corpus quod videtis manducaturi estis':

. . . me audisse existimo quod Berengarius de pronomine *hoc* ad hunc modum ratiocinetur: '*Hoc*' inquit 'pronomen est; pronomina autem substantiam sine qualitatibus significant; cum igitur dicit "non hoc corpus" de substantia corporis, non de qualitatibus dicit.'[1]

Guitmund did not dispute the grammatical doctrine, which seems to indicate that it was widely accepted, but he sensibly objected that it would play havoc with the interpretation of texts if every writer of every pronoun were assumed to have the distinction between substance and accidents in mind.

The doctrine about pronouns was, we may believe, in process of development at the time of the controversy with Lanfranc, and its full possibilities may not have been realized. There was another argument, closely connected with it, on which Berengar pinned his faith. It was an argument of which he declared that if he were beaten here he was beaten everywhere—'hoc si subvertere posses, constans michi nichilum reliquisses.' This argument is not grammatical in the same strict sense as those arising out of the significance of the parts of speech, but it is an extension of the same line of thought exemplified in the treatment of pronouns. The argument was briefly this: no proposition, consisting as it does of subject and predicate, can stand if the subject is denied, destroyed, or contradicted by the predicate. In particular no sentence with the subject *hic panis* or the equivalent pronoun *hoc* can stand if it proceeds to deny the substantial existence of the subject of the sentence: hence *Hic panis* (or *hoc*) *est corpus Christi* (or *meum*) would be self-contradictory if it implied that the substance of the subject of the sentence ceased to exist. Whoever claims that this is implied 'ipse se subvertit, ipse sibi necessario contrarius existit'.[2] Thus Berengar, by a

[1] Guitmund, 'De corporis et sanguinis Christi veritate', *Pat. Lat.* 149, col. 1463.
[2] *De S. C.* 107 (72). For Berengar's first statement of this argument see Lanfranc, cap. 8. For his later statements see *De S. C.* 107–8 (72–3), 111 (75).
Lanfranc's reply to this argument has often been discussed (see references given by A. J. MacDonald, *Berengar and the Reform of Sacramental Doctrine* (London, 1930), pp. 292–3). This is Lanfranc's most obvious incursion into the field of

purely verbal argument, claimed to refute the assertion that a change of substance takes place in the Eucharist. In this argument we are once more brought to the border-line between eleventh-century grammar and dialectic. To us it is evident that in such an argument there is a confusion between words and things, between the *subiectum in quo accidentia sunt* and the *subiectum de quo accidentia praedicantur.*[1] But the distinction is in any age a baffling one and in the eleventh century it was new. The point of greatest interest which the argument presents is its close parallel with the far more famous argument of St. Anselm on the existence of God. Formally they are strictly analogous: they both, on the grounds of a pure verbal definition, argue that certain things cannot be because the propositions which would assert them are self-destructive. 'Non est Deus' and 'Panis et vinum, quae ponuntur in altari, sunt post consecrationem solummodo verum Christi corpus et sanguis' are both claimed to be statements of this kind. Anselm must have known Berengar's argument and he may have been struck by his method. It would be rash to speculate on this point. But St. Anselm combined in a unique way the disciplines of dialectic and grammar as they were then understood and, from a purely scholastic point of view, may be seen as the heir of both Lanfranc and Berengar.

Berengar remained to the end indefatigable in proposing 'new interpretations of words'. His last battle at the Lateran Council of 1079 proved that time had not changed him. The oath which he was obliged to swear at the conclusion of this debate bears witness to the persistence of his technique: he had to assent to the eucharistic formula approved by the council and to promise to interpret it in the sense in which it was understood by the council and not otherwise—'sicut in hoc breve continetur et ego legi *et vos intelligitis*'.[2] The story of a bitter struggle lies behind the last three words. Berengar had been proposing ingenious interpretations of the formula which would allow him to read the words of his opponents and find in them his own thoughts. But

dialectical discussion and as such has received attention. I have not thought it necessary to discuss it since it is clear that his reply, however justifiable according to the habits of debate then prevailing, touched only the form of words in which Berengar stated his argument and not the substance of it. In the passages cited above Berengar has improved his statement of the argument to meet Lanfranc's objection.

[1] Cf. Boethius, *Comm. in librum Aristotelis περὶ ἑρμηνείας*, ed. R. Peiper (Teubner, 1877), p. 58.

[2] Juramentum Berengarii in 'Gregorii VII Registrum', ed. E. Caspar (*M.G.H. Epp. Selectae*, ii, 1922–3), Lib. iii. 17a and vi. 17a.

the patience of the council was exhausted at last; his enemies rose up and demanded 'that I should confirm this also by oath, that I would henceforth interpret the writing which I held in my hand according to their interpretation'.[1] Berengar, abandoned by the Pope, to whom he looked for support, had to submit. His strength had lain in his power over words; shorn of this he was brought down at last, standing his ground as a grammarian to the end.

As for Lanfranc, he went another way, but it can scarcely be doubted that the subtlety and power of drawing distinctions which brought him so many successes as archbishop owed more to dialectic than to his recollections of the Lombard law which as a youth he had picked up in his father's house.

APPENDIX

WHEN all allowances have been made for flattery, the following letter preserves an interesting testimony to Berengar's position and reputation during the period after the condemnation of his doctrine on the Eucharist at the Council of 1059. It contains a description of a visit to Salerno by an unknown friend or pupil of Berengar. The bishop whose opinions it describes was Alphanus, bishop of Salerno (1058–85), a famous scholar of the day, a friend of the Reform party in the Church and the man with whom Gregory VII found refuge after being driven from Rome in 1084.[2] Alphanus was present at the Council of 1059 and it was probably here that he feared to differ from the opinion of the majority, which was against Berengar; if he said anything like what is here reported, his words cast a very curious light on the opinions of one important member of the council. In one respect the letter agrees well with what is known from other sources: Berengar's wealth and the favour which, as his enemies thought, he obtained thereby are mentioned by Lanfranc; William of Malmesbury describes the spread of his doctrines through the needy scholars whom he supported; and this wealth must have been the basis for the liberality for which he is praised by Hildebert. The date of the letter is impossible to fix at all exactly, but it would seem to be not very long after

---

[1] 'The words are taken from Berengar's own account of the council in Martène and Durand, *Thes. Nov. Anec.* iv. 105. C. Erdmann, who criticizes this account very severely (see *ante*, p. 31 n. 2) has failed to see that on this point Berengar's narrative is strikingly confirmed by the official text of his oath quoted above. A further recollection of Berengar's tortuous arguments at the council may be found in a poem addressed to him after 1079, in which are the following lines: Si pateat digne quod sis salvatus ab igne Quem tibi devota decrevit concio tota Pax mihi tunc tecum, sed fraus si vicerit equum Et tibi fallacem dederunt sophismata pacem Assumamus item Christo iudice litem. (The poem is in part printed by Ch. Fierville in *Notices et Extraits*, xxxi (1884), i. 138–9 and completed in *Revue belge de philologie et d'histoire*, xxii (1943), pp. 29–30.)

[2] See *Dict. d'hist. et de géog. eccl.* ii. 401–3; M. Manitius, *Gesch. d. lat. Lit. des Mittelalters* (Munich, 1923), ii. 618–37.

the council to which the bishop is reported to have referred so frankly. The name Smaragdus is not otherwise known among the doctors of Salerno at this time.

The text is taken from British Museum Harleian MS. 3023 which contains the collection of Berengar's correspóndence printed by E. Bishop in *Historisches Jahrbuch* (Görres-Gesellschaft), i (1880), pp. 272–80. For some reason, which is difficult to understand, Bishop thought it was a school-exercise, and neither printed it nor mentioned that it was addressed to Berengar; he dated the hand in which it is written later than that of the rest of the collection. I was unable to see any difference in the date of the hand-writing and the details given in the letter seem to exclude the hypothesis of a school-exercise. It is certainly written in an ambitious style, but that is not surprising in a letter to one of the leading grammarians of the day.

B.M. Harley 3023, fol. 65ᵛ

Domino B. E. salutem.

Cum venissem Salernum A. pontifex vir inprimis eruditus me liberaliter excepit. Cumque inter alia cuiatem me dicerem rogavisset, audivit Aquitanium. Tunc ille: 'Ego' inquit 'in partibus illis illustrem virum B. Turonensem amicissimum habeo et si quomodo se agit nosti, maxime velim referri.' Et ego: 'Ille' inquam 'obtime. Duo enim in diversis hominibus difficilia, in eodem fere impossibilia, elegantissimi philosophi et acerrimi principis munera ita exequitur ut miremur eum et etatem tranquillissimam agere et amplissimum gerere magistratum. Itaque complures ex diversis regionibus ad eum confluentes diligentissime instruit, potentibusque viris honore et milicia preclaris quomodo res maximas amministrent gravissima auctoritate prescribit et ne verbis prolixioribus tenearis, ille valetudine integer, refertus opibus, stipatus clientelis, dignitatibus pollens, ita fortune bonis expletur ut non tam ipsa illi benivolencia favere quam ille ipsi invite dominari videatur.' Hic pontifex hilariorem vultum exibens: 'Commode' ait 'de amico absente locutus es. Externa siquidem illius bona de quibus quia sunt cito variabilia dubitare poteram, rettulisti diffusius; interna vero vix tetigisti, que mihi iamdudum nota sunt et difficile moveri possunt. Nam ut illius in omni genere virtutum prestanciam quam nunquam satis predicarem preteream, illam eius constantiam novi, ut neque illum leticia gestientem nec egritudo faceret demissum. Doctrina vero ita probatur excultus ut communi arbitrio cuilibet peritissimo longe sit anteferendus. Et ut de ea sententia unde a quibusdam redarguitur loquar, licet ego a numerosiori parte removeri formidaverim, qualiter tamen ab eo dissenciam non intelligo si Augustino consentire velim. Hunc tantum virum, frater Aquitane, memento salutare, et si quid nostra tellus[1] ferat vel alia nobis mittat, quod ei placere sciam hoc eum habiturum pollicere.' Smaragdus omnibus Salernitanis in salute corporum prestancior te plurimum salutat et si quid muneris ei iniungas, in nullo imperium tuum recusat. Valete.   R. W. SOUTHERN

---

[1] nostra tellus n̄ra *cod.*

HEMMING'S CARTULARY

A DESCRIPTION OF THE TWO WORCESTER CARTULARIES IN COTTON TIBERIUS A. XIII

BRITISH Museum MS. Cotton Tiberius A. xiii has been called Hemming's cartulary at least since the year 1723, when Thomas Hearne published his edition, entitled *Hemingi Chartularium Ecclesiæ Wigorniensis*. An older and fuller title, 'Liber de Terris et redditibus Monasterii Sanctæ Mariæ in Wigorniæ Civitate, ab Hemingo . . . conscriptus',[1] was formerly to be found at the beginning of the manuscript, according to Hearne, who quoted and discussed it in his preface, pp. lxiv–lxix, and concluded that it was a sixteenth-century title and without authority. Nevertheless, from it Hearne took over the main assumption that the whole manuscript was Hemming's work. Hearne's greater contemporary, Humphrey Wanley, was more careful and ascribed to Hemming only the part of Tib. beginning on f. 119.[2] The title must have influenced him, however, as it has influenced later scholars through Hearne. I cannot otherwise account for his dating 'haud multo post Conquæstum Angliæ', which suggests that, in his opinion, the whole of Tib. was written at about the same time. Wolfgang Keller recognized, like Wanley, that there are two distinct manuscripts, ff. 1–118 (Tib. I) and ff. 119–200 (Tib. II), and that the second only is Hemming's cartulary. But he did not discuss the date of Tib. I.[3]

Anyone who compares the five main hands of the first part with the three main hands of the second part will see that the types of writing are quite different.[4] The hands of Tib. II are round and fairly large and belong to the period of transition from the flat and linear roundness usual in English manuscripts of the middle and the third quarter of the eleventh century to the more pointed

[1] Hemming is the proper form of the name. It is written so in Tib., ff. 131 and 134, and in the *Liber Vitæ* of Durham. The eighteenth-century transcript done for Richard Graves (Bodleian MS. Rawlinson B. 445), which Hearne used as the immediate basis of his text, has Heming. The form with one *m* was used by Maitland, by Round, and by Stevenson. Kingsford in his article on Hemming in *Dict. Nat. Biog.* (1891) seems to have been the first modern scholar to use the correct form.

[2] H. Wanley, *Catalogus librorum veterum septentrionalium* (part 2 of Hickes, *Thesaurus*, 1705), pp. 254–8.

[3] W. Keller, *Die literarischen Bestrebungen von Worcester in angelsächsischer Zeit*, 1906.

[4] See Pls. I and II.

roundness of the early twelfth century. They are just the sort of hands which we should expect to find in a manuscript which is datable from its contents in the last decade of the eleventh century. The hands of Tib. I are much smaller and do not give an impression of roundness. They suffer mostly from a lack of proportion in height between the ascenders and descenders and the letters on the line. Their affinities are with the hands employed in English manuscripts in the first half of the eleventh century.

The palaeography of the first half of the century, after the final breakdown of the insular hand about the year 1000, is not easy to understand. There is no single characteristic type of writing and no obvious course of development, until, in the early forties, as it seems, a round set hand of good proportions began to be used.[1] This hand rapidly became predominant in the main centres of writing from which our evidence comes, Worcester, Exeter, Canterbury, and Winchester. Five Worcester charters of this date belong to the years 1033–8, 1038, 1042, 1054–6, and 1058 (*Brit. Mus. Facs.* iv. 19, 22, 23, 32, and 38). The first three are in old styles of writing. The fifth is in the new.[2] The subsequent development of the new style at Worcester can be studied in the great collection of homilies and laws in the Bodleian, MSS. Hatton 113, 114, and Junius 121, all written, it seems, early in the sixties, and in a good many other manuscripts dating from the episcopate of St. Wulfstan.[3] The script of the first part of Tib. has no connexion with these manuscripts. It belongs to an earlier period, a period well before the Conquest.

For this earlier period palaeography is not much help. The evidence, such as it is, suggests that the set hand may have developed at Worcester rather later than at Winchester and Canterbury. How unstable Worcester writing was before this development, and how difficult to date, may be seen by comparing the six extant Worcester documents of the first half of the eleventh century.[4] Although they cover some thirty years or

---

[1] See for examples the Winchester charters of 1042 and 1045 (*Brit. Mus. Facs.* iv. 24, 31) and the Canterbury charters of 1042–4 and 1044 (*Brit. Mus. Facs.* iv. 25, 27).

[2] The charter of A.D. 1058 appears to have been written by the scribe who wrote most part of the great Worcester passional, Cotton MS. Nero E. i. The charter of A.D. 1054–6 (the dating is Sir Ivor Atkins's in *Antiquaries Journal*, xx (1940), 25) is altogether aberrant, since it is written in a rough imitation of tenth-century Anglo-Saxon minuscule.

[3] For a list of books which may have been written at Worcester in this period, see N. R. Ker, *Medieval Libraries of Great Britain*, 1941, p. xxi.

[4] *Brit. Mus. Facs.* iv. 13, 14, 15, 19, 22, 23. iv. 14, 15 are the Worcester portions

more, *c.* 1010–42, they show no regular progress and are not particularly like one another.[1] They make me feel that it is rash, in the present state of knowledge, to date Tib. I by its script more closely than within the wide limits of the first half of the century. The more helpful internal evidence for the date of Tib. I will be discussed later.

I. DESCRIPTION OF THE MANUSCRIPT

The damage caused to Tib. in the Cotton fire of 1733 was not serious. A few pages are hard to read and all the leaves have been burnt round the edges, occasionally with the loss of a word or two of the text. The nineteenth-century rebinding and separate mounting of each leaf was necessary to prevent further damage, but, as a result, the original quiring is not now easy to make out. In its present state the book consists of:

(Tib. I.) One hundred and seventeen leaves of a cartulary written at Worcester in the first half of the eleventh century. Now ff. 1–109, 111–18. The written space measures *c.* 190 × 100 mm. Twenty-six long lines on each page.

(Tib. II.) Eighty leaves written at Worcester in the last decade of the eleventh century. Now ff. 119–42, 144–52, 154–200. The written space measures *c.* 190 × 108 mm. Twenty-eight long lines usually on each page (27 on ff. 119–36, 177).

Three smaller pieces of parchment (ff. 110, 143, 153).

The original quiring of Tib. I can be reconstructed fairly certainly. Ff. 1–24, 31–102, 111–18 formed 13 regular quires, each of 8 leaves. The 7 leaves forming ff. 103–9 are probably a quire of 8 from which the last leaf, which was no doubt blank, has been removed. The 6 leaves forming ff. 25–30 are probably a complete quire of 3 sheets, for there is no sign that any text has been lost here. The collation is therefore 1–3^8, 4^6, 5–13^8, 14^8 (8, blank, missing after f. 109), 15^8.

The five main hands of Tib. I appear to be contemporary with one another. They occur as follows:

(i) ff. 1–8 (quire 1); ff. 47–62^v (quires 7, 8); ff. 98, line 18–99, line 24, and ff. 101–101^v, line 2 (parts of quire 13); ff. 111–13

of tripartite chirographs relating to lands in which Hereford and Evesham respectively had a main interest: it seems likely that both were drawn up at Worcester.

[1] Two of the hands (*Brit. Mus. Facs.* iv. 19, 23), A.D. 1033–8 and A.D. 1042, are large and handsome and rather strikingly like one of the hands which has written additions to Tib. I (below, C ii, G i, ii).

(quire 15). On ff. 1–8 this hand imitates features of ninth-century Anglo-Saxon minuscule, especially the angular form of *t*.

(ii) ff. 9–20, 22ᵛ–32ᵛ (quires 2–5).

(iii) ff. 39–44 (quire 6).

(iv) ff. 63–101 (quires 9–12 and the part of quire 13 which is not in hand i).

(v) ff. 103–9 (quire 14).

Tib. I consists of copies of charters (ff. 1–57 and 103–9) and of leases (ff. 57–101 and 111–13). The charters are grouped by shires, Worcestershire (A), Winchcombeshire (B), Oxfordshire (C), Gloucestershire (D), Warwickshire (E), and a sixth group relating mainly to Gloucestershire (F). Groups A, B, and C have occupied their present relative positions on quires 1–5 from the first. Groups D and E are on independent quires (D quire 6, E quire 14). Group F begins at the beginning of quire 7. I have assumed that group E containing the Warwickshire charters (ff. 103–9) is at present misplaced. The contents suggest that originally it was meant to come either before or after quire 6, but it has been in its present place since the time when the leaves were numbered in the fifteenth century. There is some evidence from another direction that in the eleventh century the quires were in the order 1–6, 14, 15, 7–13.[1] Blank spaces after groups A, C, and D, and at the end of quire 15, have been partly filled up in the eleventh and twelfth centuries.

A. Ff. 1–20. Headed 'INTO VVEOGERNA CESTRE'. Twenty-eight documents[2] printed by Hearne, pp. 1–46.[3] At the end the scribe left a blank space of four pages, which now contains:

(A i) ff. 20ᵛ–21. A grant of thirty hides at Ripple by King Oshere, A.D. 680, printed by Hearne, pp. 46–7 and *BCS*, no. 51. (A ii) ff. 21–21ᵛ. A grant of privileges to the 'monasterium' at Hanbury by King Wiglaf, A.D. 833, printed by Hearne, pp. 47–9, and from the single-sheet docu-

[1] See below, p. 66.

[2] I give the number of documents according to the layout in the cartulary, counting each separate text. This does not represent the number of single-sheet documents which came before the compiler of the cartulary: for example three texts on ff. 7ᵛ–9 are all derived from one document which was still in existence in the seventeenth century and was printed by Hickes, *Thesaurus*, 1705, pp. 171–2 (thence *BCS*, nos. 256, 308).

[3] Birch, *Cartularium saxonicum* (1885–93), nos. 357, 579, 295, 455, 701, 234, 608, 153, 256, 308, 76, 350, 368, 236, 430, 434, 575, 489, 163, 210, 183, 616, 561, 492, 171.

ment, Cotton Aug. II. 9, in *BCS*, no. 416. (A iii) f. 21ᵛ. An extract
from Domesday concerning the tax payable to the churches of Worcester
and Pershore at Martinmas (*ciricsceat*), printed by Hearne, pp. 49–50.
F. 22ʳ remains blank. (A i, ii) are in one eleventh-century hand which is
not much, if at all, later than the main hand of ff. 9–20. (A iii) is in a
hand of late xi c.

B. Ff. 22ᵛ–27. Headed 'INTO VVINCELCVMBE SCIRE'. Eight
documents printed by Hearne, pp. 50–8.[1] At the end the scribe
left a blank space of six lines.

C. Ff. 28–32ᵛ. Headed 'INTO OXENA FORDA SCIRE'. Eight documents printed by Hearne, pp. 59–71.[2] At the end the scribe left
six lines blank on f. 32ᵛ and then a blank space of twelve pages
(ff. 33–8ᵛ), running to the end of the quire. This now contains:

(C i) ff. 32ᵛ–33. Boundaries 'into readanoran' in Old English, printed
by Hearne, p. 71.[3] (C ii) f. 33. Boundaries 'of claceswadlande' in Old
English, printed by Hearne, pp. 71–2. (C iii) f. 33ᵛ. The introduction
to the survey of Oswaldslow, printed by Hearne, p. 72. This occurs
again in Tib. II, f. 137ᵛ. (C iv) ff. 34ᵛ–35ᵛ. A grant of land at Wick
Episcopi by King Offa and boundaries of Wick in Latin and Old English,
printed by Hearne, pp. 73–5, and *BCS*, no. 219. (C v) ff. 35ᵛ–36. An
agreement, drawn up *c.* 1086, between Bishop Wulfstan and Walter,
abbot of Evesham, by which the latter recognizes that lands in Hampton
and Bengeworth are part of Oswaldslow; printed by Hearne, pp. 75–6.
This also is in Tib. II, f. 136ᵛ. (C vi) ff. 36–7. Three documents relating to the Evesham dispute, printed by Hearne, pp. 77–9. (C vii) f. 37.
A writ of King William, demanding payment from the honour of
Worcester on the death of Bishop Wulfstan, A.D. 1095; printed by Hearne,
pp. 79–80: see also Round, *Feudal England*, pp. 308–13, and Ivor
Atkins in *Antiq. Journal*, xx (1940), 209. (C viii) ff. 37ᵛ–38. 'Com-
memoratio placiti' in the Evesham dispute, printed by Hearne, pp. 80–3.[4]
(C i) is in a hand of xi c. (C ii) is in a hand of xi c., which occurs
again in (G i, ii). The other additions are in various hands of xi/xii c.:
(C iv) in the second main hand of Tib. II and (C vii) in the same hand as
(C vi).

D. Ff. 39–44. Headed 'INTO GLEAWECESTRE SCIRE'. Seven
documents printed by Hearne, pp. 84–95.[5] At the end the scribe

---

[1] *BCS*, nos. 309, 246, 187, 156, 217, 283, 165, 540.
[2] *BCS*, nos. 221, 547, 509, 607, 666, 139, 436, 432.
[3] The name 'Readanora' died out early. The interlinear gloss 'id est pirit'' and
the marginal note 'To PERITVN', both xi c., identify the place with Pyrton, Oxon.
'Claceswadland' was adjacent to 'Readanora', as the boundaries show.
[4] On the Evesham documents see J. H. Round, *Domesday Studies*, ii. 542–5, and
V.C.H. Worcs. i. 254–6.
[5] *BCS*, nos. 166, 487, 580, 304, 226, 164, 574.

left a blank space of five pages (ff. 44ᵛ–46), up to the end of the sixth quire. This space now contains:

(D i) ff. 44ᵛ–45ᵛ. Grant by King Offa of fifty hides at Cropthorne, Hampton, Bengeworth, &c., A.D. 780; printed by Hearne, pp. 95–8, and in *BCS*, no. 235. (D ii) ff. 45ᵛ–46. A note of the annual rent in kind ('firma') due to the cellarer at Worcester, printed by Hearne, pp. 98–100.

(D i) is xi c., probably third quarter. (D ii) is xi/xii c., in a slightly current hand.

(D iii), added in the upper margin of f. 39, is a note of the number of hides, in all 116, formed by the vills of Bybury, Withington, Bishops Cleeve, and Westbury, printed by Hearne, pp. 83–4. Late xi c.

E. Ff. 103–9. Headed 'INTO WÆRINCG WICAN'. Seven documents printed by Hearne, pp. 218–31.[1] At the end part of f. 109 has been left blank. On the upper margin of the verso of this leaf is:

(E i) a note in Old English of rents due from tenants, xi c.; not printed by Hearne. Printed below, p. 74.

F. Ff. 47–57. No heading, but the first line was left blank. Fourteen documents, relating mainly to lands in Gloucestershire, printed by Hearne, pp. 100–21.[2]

G. At f. 57 there is no break in the text, but the scribe has written a heading, 'Her beneoðan synd þa genbec into gleawe-cesterscyre', and at this point the long series of leases begins. There are in all seventy-six leases, seventy-four of them granted by Bishop Oswald, one by Bishop Coenweald, A.D. 954, and one by Bishop Ealdwulf, A.D. 996. They occupy ff. 57–101ᵛ and ff. 111–13, and are printed by Hearne, pp. 121–217 and 232–40.[3] The heading 'þas génbéc hyrað into wincescumbe' is at f. 61ᵛ. At f. 92 a blank leaf before the lease of land 'æt clifforda' (Hearne, p. 197) marks the end of the series of forty-four leases in the hundred of Oswaldslow, which begins with Cotheridge on f. 63.

---

[1] *BCS*, nos. 157, 239, 450, 241, 123A, 123B, 533.

[2] *BCS*, nos. 379, 273, 313, 551, 218, 278, 274, 220, 665, 269, 231, 164, 559, 582.

[3] The leases are printed in chronological order, the earlier ones in *BCS* (which does not extend beyond 975) and the later ones by Kemble, *Codex Diplomaticus Ævi Saxonici* (1839–48), as follows: *BCS*, nos. 993, 1086–9, 1091, 1105–6, 1108–11, 1139, 1166, 1180–2, 1203, 1205–8, 1232–3, 1235–43, 1293, 1298–9; *KCD*, nos. 612–20, 623, 625, 627, 631, 634, 637, 644–7, 649, 651, 653, 660, 661, 666–71, 674–83, 695. The boundaries printed in *KCD*, no. 612, occur in Tib. II, f. 162ᵛ, and *not* in Tib. I. To the lease of Tiddington, *KCD*, no. 617, Kemble has attached the boundaries of Teddington derived from Tib. II, f. 164! The form *Tidingctun* listed in *Place-names of Worcestershire* (1927), p. 168, under Teddington, is a product of this confusion: it belongs really to Tiddington. *-d-* forms in place of older *-tt-* are not recorded for the name Teddington until after the Conquest.

The last leaf of quire 13 (f. 102) is blank, except for a later note in the margin, printed by Hearne, p. 217. The first part of quire 15 (ff. 111–13) contains six more leases, relating to outlying estates in Warwickshire and Gloucestershire, printed by Hearne, pp. 232–40. The first three lines on f. 111 were left blank, perhaps for a heading. The remaining leaves of this quire, at first left blank, contain:

(G i) f. 114. Boundaries of Withington, Glos., in Old English, printed by Hearne, p. 241, and *BCS*, no. 299. (G ii) f. 114ᵛ. A list of the bishops of Worcester from Bosel to Coenweald (929–57) and of the kings of Mercia from Penda to Æthelred, the successor of Ceolwulf II, printed by Hearne, p. 242. (G iii) ff. 115–16ᵛ. A homily in Old English beginning 'Adam se æresta man wæs gesceapen on neorxnawange', printed by Hearne, pp. 242–5, and by A. S. Napier, *Wulfstan*, 1883, p. 1. (G iv) f. 116ᵛ. Boundaries of Bishops Cleeve, in Old English, printed by Hearne, pp. 245–6. (G v) f. 117. Boundaries of Pensax, in Old English, printed by Hearne, p. 246. (G vi) f. 118ᵛ. A grant of land 'æt ofre' to the bishopric of St. David's by King Æthelred, A.D. 1005; partly illegible and so omitted by Hearne, who prints at p. 479 an abbreviated form of this document from Cotton Nero E. i. Printed below, p. 73. (G vii) f. 118ᵛ. A note of the descent of the land at Batsford after the lease by Bishop Oswald, not printed by Hearne.[1] Printed below, p. 74.

(G i, ii) are in the same hand as (C ii). (G iii, iv, vi, vii) are in other hands of xi c., not late. (G v) is in a hand of xii c.

Tib. II begins at f. 119 (Hearne, p. 248). This second part of the manuscript is more difficult to describe than the first part because the leaves were already bound up incorrectly at the time when the transcript was made for Richard Graves, and, therefore, the contents are printed in the wrong order by Hearne. To add to the confusion the pieces of parchment now numbered 110, 143, 153, were not numbered in Hearne's time, so that the foliation which he follows is first one, then two, and finally three behind that now in use.[2] Fortunately there is a late medieval foliation to keep us straight. This foliation is carried through from Tib. I and is proof that Tib. I and Tib. II were bound together in or before the fifteenth century. In Tib. I it runs from i to xcvi as at present, misses f. 97 by accident, and continues from xcvii to cviii on ff. 98–109 and from cix to cxvi on ff. 111–18. F. 119, the first leaf of Tib. II, is marked 'cxviii'. Thereafter not all the old numbers are legible, but there are only two which

---

[1] Oswald's lease of Batsford is not recorded in Tib.

[2] Thus Hearne's ff. '110–41' = manuscript ff. 111–42, Hearne's ff. '142–50' = manuscript ff. 144–52, and Hearne's ff. '151–97' = manuscript ff. 154–200.

cannot be found out, either from the table of contents (Hearne, pp. 363–8), which refers to these numbers, or because the sense is continuous from one leaf to the next. In the following comparative table of the old and new leaf-numbers of Tib. II, the old numbers which are not now legible are in square brackets. The page numbers in the third column show the order in which the texts should be read in Hearne's edition. The letters H–L are those which I have assigned to the five blocks of text which go to form Tib. II.

Old leaf-numbers	Present leaf-numbers	Pages in Hearne
cxviij–[cxlj]	119–42 (H, I)	248–316
cxl[iij]–[cl]	168–75 (J)	371–89
clj–[clvij]	194–200 (J)	434–50
[clviij]	176 (K)	391–2
clix–clxxx	144–52, 154–66 (K)	319–68
clxxx[j]–[clxxxxvj]	178–93 (L)	395–434

The numbers cxvii and cxlii of the old foliation do not occur in the above table. On the other hand four leaves of the present manuscript are not included there. Two of these four leaves, 143 and 153, form no original part of Tib.[1] The other two, ff. 167 and 177, must presumably be equated with the old 'cxvij' and 'cxlij'. 'cxvij' came between Tib. I and Tib. II. The contents of f. 177 (printed by Hearne, pp. 392–5) fit this position well, since they belong in date rather with the additions to Tib. I, made in the reign of the Conqueror, than with the additions to Tib. II, none of which is datable before the death of Bishop Wulfstan in 1095. F. 167 on the other hand belongs to Tib. II and is now in its proper place before f. 168, if, as seems quite likely, the words 'suprascriptarum uillarum' in the heading on f. 168 refer to the names of estates written on f. 167ᵛ.

Tib. II consisted evidently of ten quires. Six of them were certainly regular, that is of eight leaves each (ff. 119–42 = quires 1–3, ff. 168–75 = quire 7, ff. 178–93 = quires 8, 9). The other four quires consisted of ff. 144–52 and 154–66 (quires 4–6), ff. 194–200 (quire 10) and ff. 176, 177. Their exact collation is not certain, but it can be made out nearly enough for us to see that the texts in Tib. II, like those in Tib. I, were arranged in groups by quires, with a blank space at the end of each group running to the end of the quire. This is a point of capital importance for the understanding of the manuscript. Tib. II will be found to consist of five independent sections which can

[1] See above, p. 51.

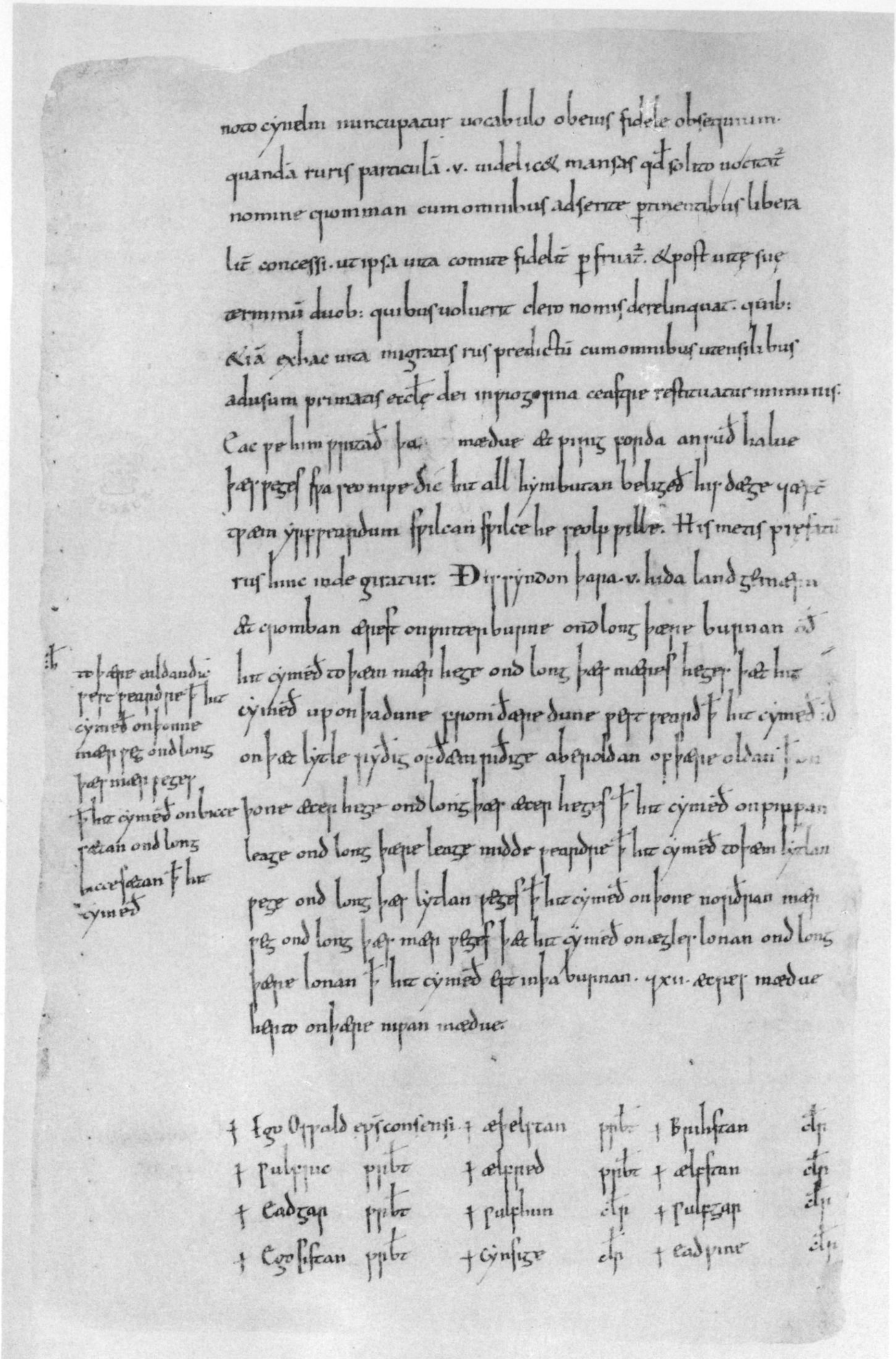

PLATE I

5

10

15

20

25

Cotton, Tiberius A. xiii, f. 85^v; see p. xiii
(*Slightly reduced*)

PLATE II

āne sabrinā sita ē. hanc ille q̃ aduix possidebat.
& p ea fidele seruitiū nob exhibebat. Morte ū sibi
sup ueniente illā nob restant. quā nos suscipien
tes ut ppā habere cepim̃. uerū n diu sub nr̄a dicione
tenere potuim̃. Instigante eni̅ diabulo fr̄ uicecomitis
ursonis RODBERTi nomine. nob abstraxe eū iniuste;
Nec solū illa sed & alias quā plures deb; nc loq̃ omitti
m̃ oportunis ii inlocis deipsis nullaten̄ tacebim̃.
Lt q̃dā ELFGARD uocabulo magnis
pollens diuitiis existebat. q̃ ENGITHE uenerande regi
ne camerarrā mahaldā nomine uxore ducebat.
huc sūmissa pce nos roganti. modicā uillā que clop
tun dr̄ cessim̃. p qua ipse tot annis quot habebat.
bene nob & fidelit seruiebat. Sed URSO uicecomes
eandē p modū sibimet adq̃siuit. tale seruitiū pea
se exibiturū pmittens. quale ille prius exhibuit.
Iure iurando illud pmisit. sed n du psoluere
uoluit;

Pro alia similit tra que ab indigenis est Ryn
MER LEHGE nominata iuxta duddanteto sita. spo
pondit se seruiturū esse. uerū p omia immemor
fact est promissionis sue;

Quidā diues sclaris ppositi nomine EARHWI loci
hui extitit. Hic frem sibi uehementr karū cui
uocabulu SPIRITUS habuit. Qui nimis diligebatur
a duobus regibus istius patrie. haroldo scili
INDECIUIT. Ipse aute atre suo sup dicto

Cotton, Tiberius A. xiii, f. 121; see p. xiii
(*Slightly reduced*)

be arranged in any order. There is no evidence that the order established in the fifteenth century is the right order, or that Tib. II is more than a bundle of incomplete sections, the fragments of a larger scheme.

The confusion in the order of the leaves which has taken place since the fifteenth century consists in the dislocation of the original fourth and fifth quires, which now stand seventh and tenth respectively.

The work of three main scribes can be distinguished in Tib. II, but I do not feel positive that only three were employed. The change of hand in the middle of f. 169, at the beginning of the 'Sture' charter (Hearne, p. 374), is very obvious.

1. Ff. 125^v–133, 135–41^v, 169 (from line 13)–175^v, 176^v,194–200. These leaves include the 'Prefatio istius libelli' (Hearne, p. 391) and the 'Enucleatio libelli' (Hearne, pp. 282–6), the two texts most intimately connected with Hemming. The hand is very like that of the Alveston charter issued by Bishop Wulfstan in A.D. 1089 and now preserved at Worcester.

2. Ff. 119–25. An addition to Tib. I (C iv), as well as additions to Tib. II (K i, ii, N i, ii, and part of M i), are in this hand, which wrote also the whole of Cambr. Univ. Libr. MS. Kk. 3. 18 (the Old English Bede), and parts of Corpus Christi College, Cambridge, MSS. 146 and 391, and of Bodleian MSS. Hatton 114 and Junius 121; also Harley Charter 83. A. 3 (*Brit. Mus. Facs.* iv. 43). The characteristic mark of punctuation, a triangle of dots above a comma, is reproduced by Hearne, e.g. p. 371. The hand is old-fashioned, compared with (1) and (3), and less professional looking. In vernacular writing the forms of round *d* and of the ligature *æ* are distinctive.

The original text on ff. 119–25, which contain Hemming's narrative, has been a good deal altered, probably by hand (1), and three paragraphs relating to Acton, to 'Ælfintun' and Sapey, and to Astley, are entirely in hand (1).[1]

3. Ff. 144–52, 154–63^v, 168, 169, lines 1–12, 178–89^v. This handsome hand is shown in the facsimile of f. 159 by W. Keller, *Angelsächsische Paleographie*, 1906, pl. xi. At least ff. 180^v–189 were written after the death of Bishop Wulfstan in 1095 (see Hearne, p. 404). Nearly all f. 178^v has been erased and rewritten, thirty-one lines being squeezed into the space for twenty. The overwriting is probably in hand (1). The original unerased text begins at the words 'Ego Eadwardus' (Hearne, p. 398).

[1] See Pl. II.

The three hands wrote the ten quires of Tib. II as follows:

Hand (1) wrote quires 2, 3, 10 (formerly II, III, V), follows hand (2) in quire 1 (formerly I), and follows hand (3) in quire 7 (formerly IV).

Hand (2) wrote most of quire 1.

Hand (3) wrote quires 4–6 (formerly VI–VIII), 8, 9 (formerly IX, X), and the first two leaves of quire 7 (formerly IV).

If the dislocations are allowed for, it will be seen that hand (1) wrote most of the first five quires and hand (3) most of the last five quires of Tib. II.

In describing the contents I have continued the series of letters used for Tib. I and refer to the five main independent blocks into which Tib. II falls by the letters H, I, J, K, L.

H. Ff. 119–34 (quires 1, 2). Hemming's account of the alienations of Worcester property, 'Codicellus possessionum huius ęcclesię . . .', followed by a paragraph about Oswaldslow; printed by Hearne, pp. 248–88. The last part of the 'Codicellus' is the well-known 'Enucleatio libelli' in which Hemming names himself and explains the measures which he and Bishop Wulfstan took to conserve the archives of the church of Worcester. The paragraph after the 'Enucleatio' consists of the Domesday 'testimonium' concerning Oswaldslow, with amplifications, followed by the famous statement that this testimony had been sworn before the Domesday commissioners and entered 'in autentica regis cartula'.[1] No doubt this is Hemming's composition; he writes once in the first person ('ut predixi').

The blank space at the end of quire 2 contains:

(H i) f. 134. A list of 'mansiones de dominico uictu monachorum', written in two hands, or at least in two inks, the second beginning at the words 'Has mansiones monachi tenent in burgo regis'; printed by Hearne, pp. 289–91, and by I. Atkins in *Antiq. Journal*, xx (1940), 210–11, and discussed by Round, *Domesday Studies*, ii. 545–6. Dated by Round *c.* 1100; the hand is contemporary. It begins very like the main hand, but becomes more current.

I. Ff. 135–42 (quire 3). Records connected with the Domesday survey: (*a*) ff. 135–6ᵛ. 'Indiculum libertatis de Oswaldeslawes hundred', printed by Hearne, pp. 292–6; (*b*) ff. 136ᵛ–137. The agreement between Bishop Wulfstan and Walter, abbot of

---

[1] One of the amplifications, the important words 'nec aliquis regalis seruitii exactor', is an addition in the margin. The actual Domesday version occurs below, f. 137ᵛ (Hearne, p. 298).

Evesham, concerning the disputed lands of Hampton and Bengeworth, printed by Hearne, pp. 296–7; (c) ff. 137ᵛ–141ᵛ. 'Descriptio
terrę episcopatus Wigornensis ecclesię secundum cartam regis
quę est in thesauro re[gali]', i.e. the Domesday survey so far as it
concerns the church of Worcester, in an abbreviated form; printed
by Hearne, pp. 298–313. There are two later additions to this
quire:

(I i) f. 137 in a small blank space. A writ of King Henry I addressed
to Walter de Beauchamp, sheriff of Worcester, printed by Hearne,
p. 298: see also Round, *Feudal England*, p. 170. Written in a contemporary hand.

(I ii) f. 142, in the blank space at the end of the quire. A list of the
lands held respectively by the bishop of Worcester, the monks, and the
barons in Oswaldslow and other Worcestershire hundreds; printed by
Hearne, pp. 313–6: discussed by Round in *Feudal England*, pp. 169–77,
and in *V.C.H. Worcs.* i. 324–7, and dated 1108–18. In a contemporary
hand.

J. Ff. 168–75, 194–200 (quires 7 and 10, formerly IV and V).
Twenty-one royal charters, printed by Hearne, pp. 371–89, 434–
50.[1] The heading in red capitals on f. 168 describes them as
'Testamentales schedulę testatorum ad confirmationem suprascriptarum uillarum'. The form of the mark of punctuation at
the end of the heading suggests that it is in hand (2). The charters
relate to estates in four counties outside Oswaldslow. They are
not arranged in any order. Twelve of them occur also in Tib. I.[2]

In the blank space at the end of quire 10 are notes (f. 200) of the dissolution of Worcester Priory in 31 Henry VIII and of the marriage of
John Alderford of Abbots Salford to Elizabeth Dormer, 6 July 1579;
printed by Hearne, p. 450. On f. 200ᵛ is the signature 'John Alderforde'.

K. Ff. 176, 144–52, 154–63 (quires 4–6, formerly VI–VIII).
This section consists partly of charters and partly of boundaries,
derived probably from leases.

(a) ff. 176ᵛ, 144–52, 154–7. Thirteen charters of lands 'quas
monachi de Wirecestra habent ad eorum propriam pertinentes
utilitatem', i.e. the demesne lands of the priory,[3] preceded on
f. 176ᵛ by a 'Prefatio istius libelli' and a table of the charters,
'Capituli [*sic*] istius codicelli'; printed by Hearne, pp. 391–2,

---

[1] *BCS*, nos. 1201, 351, 164, 163, 226, 359, 666, 357, 77, 239, 432, 221, 665, 487,
547, 700, 137, 216, 240, 313, 360.
[2] For a list see below, p. 68, n. 2.
[3] *BCS*, nos. 235, 204, 205, 537, 233, 307, 541, 937; *KCD*, no. 807; *BCS*, nos.
1006, 1007; *KCD*, no. 952; *BCS*, no. 428.

319–47. The charters begin on f. 144; they are written in hand (3). The two texts on f. 176^v are in two different hands, the 'prefatio' in hand (1) and the table in hand (2). These facts suggest that there need not be any original connexion between the 'prefatio' and the charters if, as seems likely, f. 176 was a single leaf on its own and not an integral part of the quire beginning on f. 144. The 'prefatio' does not read like a foreword to the charters, but like a general introduction to Hemming's work and a complement to the 'Enucleatio libelli' at the other end. Its present position appears to be the work of an arranger, who forged a link with the charters by setting out a table of them on the same page.

Boundaries, in Old English, are attached to most of the charters, but those of Shipston and Harvington are put in at the end of the series.

(b) ff. 157–63^v. A series of thirty boundaries in Old English, printed by Hearne, pp. 348–61. All the estates concerned are in Oswaldslow, except Salwarpe. The arrangement is roughly geographical, circling round Worcester. Twenty-two of the boundaries are in Tib. I also, attached to Oswald's leases.[1] Many of them refer to lands which are described by Hemming as having been alienated.

The recto of f. 176, originally blank, contains:

(K i) A list of bishops of Worcester from Seaxulf to Symon, 'cum terris quas ipsi monachis, hic deo et sanctę marię seruientibus, concesserunt', printed by Hearne, p. 390. Written in hand (2) in the time of Bishop Samson. The two names after Samson, Teoldus and Symon, were added in the xii c.

The blank space at the end of quire 6 contains:

(K ii) ff. 163^v–164. Boundaries, in Old English, of Acton Beauchamp, Tardebigge, and Teddington, printed by Hearne, pp. 361–3. The boundaries of Acton Beauchamp in the great Pershore charter of A.D. 972 (BCS, no. 1282; Brit. Mus. Facs. iii. 30) are the same as those given here. Written in hand (2).

(K iii) ff. 165–6. A table of contents of Tib. and Tib. II in a current fifteenth-century hand, printed by Hearne, pp. 363–8. The leaf-numbers in this table correspond with the medieval foliation of Tib.

---

[1] BCS, nos. 1087, 1106, 1108–9, 1208, 1235, 1240–2, 1298–9; KCD, nos. 614, 618–19, 627, 645, 649, 670, 680, 682–3: cf. above, p. 54, n. 3. The boundaries not in Tib. I are BCS, no. 362 (Salwarpe) and no. 1107 (Cotheridge), and KCD, no. 612 (Wolverton) and three, of Himbleton, Perry, and Wolverton (Hearne, pp. 356, 358, 360) which are not printed in the collections of Birch and Kemble. The boundaries of Perry are known also from Add. Ch. 19795, a lease by Archbishop Wulfstan, c. 1010 (Brit. Mus. Facs. iv. 13).

L. Ff. 178–89ᵛ (quires 8 and 9, formerly IX and X). A history of the estates obtained or regained for Worcester by Bishops Ealdred and Wulfstan (1047–95), including copies of thirteen charters ranging in date from 781 to 1093;[1] printed by Hearne, pp. 395–425. At least the portion from f. 180ᵛ was written after Wulfstan's death.

The originally blank space at the end of quire 9 contains seven additions.

(L i) f. 190. A paragraph containing a statement by Bishop Wulfstan, to the effect that 'ego supplex Wlstanus . . . elemosinas terrarum a cristicolis huc collatas in unum coaugmentare feci ne a succedentibus obliuioni tradantur', followed by his exhortation to all who love God 'quo nulla deo fauente a nobis coniuncta iniquo turbare audeant conamine' and a curse against all who do otherwise; printed by Hearne, p. 425. The heading is 'Excommunicatio cuncta supradicta concludens'. It is a very early addition to section (L).

Soon after Wulfstan's death an attempt was made to continue the collection of documents by writing the words 'EXPLICIT LIBER . IIII . INCIPIT LIBER V' at the end of the so-called 'excommunicatio' and entering copies of two texts:

(L ii) f. 190. A charter of Bishop Sampson, A.D. 1097, giving the church of Hartlebury 'ad uictum monachorum'; printed by Hearne, p. 426.

(L iii) ff. 190ᵛ–191ᵛ. The 'Priuilegium Fritherici', a list of the chapels, tithes, and land belonging to the church of St. Helen, Worcester, which the monks committed to the vicar, Fritheric, for life, 'post obitum episcopi Wlstani'; printed by Hearne, p. 427.

The attempt at a continuation failed. The remaining documents, added later, are only:

(L iv) ff. 191ᵛ–192. The notification of a grant by Prior Ralph (d. 1143) to Fulk of Horsley, with bounds in English, printed by Hearne, p. 429. In a contemporary hand.

(L v) ff. 192ᵛ–193. A copy of the survey of the Staffordshire lands held by the canons of Wolverhampton, as in Domesday, f. 247ᵛ, printed by Hearne, p. 430. The church of Wolverhampton was granted to Prior Thomas by Bishop Sampson (d. 1112). In a hand of xi/xii c.

(L vi) f. 193ᵛ. A fourteenth-century copy of the bounds of Cutsdean, agreeing with the bounds at f. 157ᵛ above, printed by Hearne, p. 433.

(L vii) f. 193ᵛ. Memorandum of an agreement between the prior and convent of Worcester and John Godard, A.D. 1336, printed by Hearne, p. 433. In a contemporary hand.

[1] KCD, nos. 805, 823; BCS, nos. 433, 223; KCD, no. 766; BCS, nos. 514, 240, 349, 462. Four documents relating to Cookley, Alveston, Westbury Church, and Tappenhall Mill are post-Conquest and not, therefore, included in Kemble's collection.

The whole of Tib. II is included in the sections H–L, except ff. 167 and 177.[1] I call the contents of these leaves M and N respectively.

(M i) f. 167. 'De regibus merciorum . . . et de terris quas huic monasterio dederunt', printed by Hearne, p. 369. The list of kings up to William II is in one hand: it is continued in two or three later hands to Edward I. The names of the estates are in hand (2).

(N i) f. 177. An addition sum in Old English, amounting to 192.

(N ii) f. 177. A list, in Old English, of taxes levied by King William on the valuables of the church of Worcester.

(N iii) f. 177ᵛ. A list of holders of the 999½ hides of geldable land in Worcestershire soon after the time of Domesday.

(N i–iii) are printed by Hearne, pp. 392–5, (N ii) also by Miss A. J. Robertson, *Anglo-Saxon Charters*, 1939, App. I, no. 6.

(N i, ii) are in hand (2). (N iii) is in a contemporary, or nearly contemporary, hand.

As noticed above, three pieces of parchment form no constituent part of Tib., into which they were probably inserted at quite an early date. I call the contents of these leaves O, P, and Q respectively.

(O) f. 110, inserted between quires 14 and 15 of Tib. I. A fragment of a leaf measuring 70 × 90 mm., containing, on the recto, eight names of witnesses to a lease (?), apparently of the early eleventh century. Not printed by Hearne. Printed below, p. 75. The dorse is blank.

(P) f. 143, inserted between quires 3 and 4 of Tib. II. A piece of parchment measuring 130 × 180 mm., containing a list of jurors 'ex parte episcopi' and 'ex parte prioris' and of witnesses in the time of Bishop John (of Pageham, 1151–8). At the foot, in pencil, is 'De Oswaldeslaw hundert'. Printed by Hearne, p. 291: in his time this leaf appears to have come between quires 2 and 3 of Tib. II. It has been folded in two. The verso is blank. The hand is contemporary.

(Q) f. 153. A slip of parchment measuring 58 × 180 mm., added to quire 5 of Tib. II and containing boundaries of Hallow in Old English, printed by Hearne, p. 339, with the reference 'Alia manu, inter folia'. As Grundy has pointed out, the copy of the grant of Hallow, Worcs., and of other lands to Bishop Deneberht by King Cenwulf of Mercia, A.D. 816 (ff. 152, 154), has attached to it, in the main hand, the boundaries of Hawling, Glos.[2] The insertion supplies the boundaries of Hallow itself in a hand of the twelfth century.

---

[1] See above, p. 56, where it is suggested that f. 177 belongs to Tib. I rather than to Tib. II.

[2] G. B. Grundy, *Saxon Charters of Gloucestershire*, 1935, p. 132.

II. DISCUSSION OF SOME PROBLEMS

An account of the contents of Tib., of its construction, and of the original order of the leaves is no more than preliminary scaffold-work to the real business of trying to understand what the manuscript is about. I wish to discuss here only three out of many problems: the relation of the statements in Hemming's 'Enucleatio libelli' to the facts as we know them, the relation between Tib. I and Tib. II, and the internal evidence for the date of Tib. I.

I. The 'Enucleatio libelli' contains four main statements of fact.

1. 'Hunc libellum de possessionibus huius nostri monasterii ego Hemmingus monachus . . . composui ut posteris nostris claresceret quę et quantę possessiones terrarum ditioni huius monasterii adiacere ad uictum dumtaxat seruorum dei monachorum uidelicet iure deberent quamque iniuste ui et dolis spoliati his caremus' (Hearne, p. 282).

The 'libellus' is the text on the twelve leaves immediately preceding the 'Enucleatio', in which Hemming surveys the lost possessions of the monastery. The limiting phrase 'ad uictum monachorum' is important. The term is applied to lands which were farmed directly for the benefit of the monks. Domesday, for example, distinguishes between the estates 'in dominio episcopi' and the estates held 'ad uictum monachorum' and the later survey contained in Tib. II makes the same distinction, using the terms 'episcopus tenet' and 'monachi tenent'. Hemming does not write like this in his 'libellus'. The burden of his story is 'sicque monasterium iniuste terram perdidit', 'tali modo hac terra caruimus,' 'sicque hec sancta ecclesia ius dominationis eiusdem uille iniuste perdidit', and other similar phrases meaning the same thing. Since the word 'monasterium' as used by Hemming and other writers is often a mere variant of 'ecclesia', meaning no more than church, it could be held that Hemming has failed to make the distinction which is made in the official surveys. The unambiguous sentence in the 'enucleatio' shows, however, that this is not so and that Hemming's story is really confined to the estates which ought, in his opinion, to have been contributing 'ad uictum monachorum'.

That it is confined to these estates may be seen also from the passage in which Hemming interrupts the regular geographical sequence of his narrative to describe how Abbot Æthelwig of Evesham obtained, 'ui uel fraude', Acton, Eastbury, Bengeworth,

Milcot, and Weston 'de uictu fratrum', and Evenlode and Daylesford 'de episcopatu'. The estates of the monks, except Weston, are duly referred to in their proper places, but Evenlode and Daylesford are not mentioned again.

With this limitation in mind, it is easier to reconcile Hemming's narrative, so far as it relates to Oswaldslow, with the facts recorded in Domesday. Hemming says nothing at all about the considerable lands held by the barons and others in the bishop's manors of Kempsey, Fladbury, Ripple, Blockley, and Tredington, and he deals with less than eighteen hides in the three other bishop's manors, Bredon, Wick, and Northwick, where the king and barons held nearly fifty hides. On the other hand he refers to all the alienated lands in the monks' manors of Hallow, Cropthorne, and Grimley, except for Hampton in Cropthorne and Knightwick in Grimley. The monks still held their other manors complete, Overbury, Sedgeberrow, Shipston, and Harvington.[1]

It is not easy to believe that Hemming is always right about the estates which had been held in the past 'ad uictum monachorum', but, unfortunately, almost nothing is known of their history in the earlier part of the eleventh century outside his pages. Just once, however, we are able to check what Hemming says by means of a legal document of good repute.[2] At the time of the Domesday survey Elmley in the manor of Cropthorne was held by Robert 'Dispensator'. Hemming tells us that Bishop Lyfing (1027–46) leased the land to one Ægelric, 'ea lege, ut, post obitum suum, ad monasterii dominationem redire deberet absque omni placito et contradictione, anathemate perpetuo ligans illum, qui amplius eam a monasterii iure retineret. Post cuius obitum, ad monasterium quidem rediit, et Withericus modo prepositus super eam fuit', but Robert took it away by force, 'sicque a nostra dominatione discessit' (Hearne, pp. 267–8). This can be set beside the actual lease by Bishop Lyfing, which was preserved at Worcester until the seventeenth century and is printed in Smith's *Baeda*, and thence in *KCD*, no. 764.[3] The lease, undated, is couched in the standard language of Bishop Lyfing's

---

[1] In the copy of Domesday in Tib. II the seven manors of the monks are described in one paragraph under the heading 'De terra monachorum'. The monks held also small estates, amounting in all to seven hides, in the bishop's manors of Bredon, Blockley, and Tredington.

[2] The charter of Hampnett, Glos., which comes in section (L) of Tib. II (Hearne, p. 398), is not to be relied on: see Ivor Atkins in *Antiq. Journal*, xx (1940), 33.

[3] J. Smith, *Baedae historia ecclesiastica latine et saxonice*, 1722, p. 780.

Latin leases, of which one survives in original (Brit. Mus. Add. Ch. 19798) and four are printed in the appendix to Smith's *Baeda* (pp. 779–81 = *KCD*, nos. 764, 765, 760, 777). It is made out to Ægelric for three lives, not for one life: there is no anathema and no use of the word 'monasterium': on the death of the second heir the estate was to be returned 'ad usum primatis æcclesiæ'. The relation between this lease and Hemming's narrative seems to me probably instructive for the interpretation of Hemming as a whole. It suggests that it is safer to trust to the main facts than to the details of his stories.

2. Secondly, the 'Enucleatio' records that Bishop Wulfstan II collected together the original charters (*primitiua testamenta et priuilegia*) and the leases (*cyrographa*) of Bishop Oswald and arranged them in two volumes (Hearne, p. 285).

This collection of original documents has long since been dispersed and lost, but one piece of evidence bears out Hemming's statement. A note of the name of the king by whom, or in whose reign, a charter or lease was granted is to be found, as an endorsement, on most of the existing original documents from Worcester. Thus, for example, Cotton Augustus II. 3, the oldest extant Worcester charter, is endorsed 'Æþelbald rex'. The endorsements are all by one hand of the later eleventh century. They are later than 1066, since Add. Ch. 19798 is marked 'Harald senior', and they may be later than 1089, for Hickes records that one of the lost documents which he printed was endorsed 'Willelm senior'.[1] In any case they prove that the archives were examined with care in the time of St. Wulfstan.

3. Hemming continues, 'Quibus ordinatis precepit cuncta eodem ordine in bibliotheca sanctę ecclesię scribi' (Hearne, p. 285).

I have noticed elsewhere,[2] following Sir Ivor Atkins, that the Bible of the church of Worcester here referred to was probably the great Offa Bible, and that fragments of a large-folio cartulary in the British Museum are likely to be the remains of the collection formed at Bishop Wulfstan's order and bound in with the Bible. Of this cartulary four leaves are in Cotton MS. Nero E. i, pt. 2, ff. 181–4, and one leaf and strips of another leaf in Add.

---

[1] Hickes, *Thesaurus*, pp. 175–6. Four other documents printed by Hickes (all now lost) were endorsed with the king's name. The endorsement 'Ægelredi regis', in the usual hand, on Cotton Ch. VIII. 37, shows that it is the Worcester portion of the tripartite chirograph.

[2] *Catalogus librorum manuscriptorum bibliothecae Wigorniensis*, ed. I. Atkins and N. R. Ker, 1944, pp. 77–9.

MS. 46204.[1] The remains are sufficient to show that this 'Nero' cartulary contained, or but for the carelessness of the scribe should have contained, exactly the same collection of documents as Tib. I, but in an abbreviated version.[2] The following table shows the correspondence between the two manuscripts.

Nero, f. 182	Tib. I, ff. 5ᵛ–9	Hearne, pp. 12–21
Add. 46204, f. 1	ff. 9–12ᵛ	pp. 21–8
Nero, f. 183	ff. 12ᵛ–17	pp. 28–38
Nero, f. 184	ff. 107, 109, 111–13ᵛ, 118ᵛ	pp. 227–40, 479
Nero, f. 181	ff. 114, 48–52	pp. 241, 100–9
Add. 46204, f. 2	ff. 57–61ᵛ	pp. 121–31

Comparison with Tib. I shows that the surviving leaves of Nero + Add. are the second, third, and fourth leaves of the first quire, followed, after a largish gap, by two adjacent leaves and a third leaf which was separated from the others by a gap of one.

The occurrence of the contents of f. 181 of Nero in two widely separated places in Tib. suggests that in the eleventh century the present quires 14 and 15 (ff. 102–9, 111–18) of Tib. I may have come immediately before quires 7–13 (ff. 47–101).[3] Otherwise the texts in Nero and in Tib. are arranged in exactly the same way, save that two documents, added early to quire 15 of Tib. I (G i, G vi), occur in Nero in the opposite order (G vi, G i). One leaf of Nero contains as much text as four or five leaves of Tib.

The texts in Nero are worthless. They are not merely abbreviated, but abbreviated very carelessly. For example, on f. 184 the scribe has left out the end of the first Shottery charter and the beginning of the second, and on f. 181 he skips straight from the preamble of a charter relating to Stoke Bishop to one relating to 'Huntenatun', omitting a whole charter in between.[4] His methods can be studied most conveniently when a charter exists not only in Nero and in Tib., but also in a single-sheet original. We can see then not only how Tib. and the original agree together

---

[1] Add. 46204 was bought from Lord Middleton in 1946: its contents are printed by W. H. Stevenson, *Report on the Manuscripts of Lord Middleton* (Hist. Manuscripts Commission, 1911), pp. 199–212.

[2] The only text not in Tib. is an addition to Nero, f. 184ᵛ. It is a list of the chief estates belonging to the church of Worcester, with the names of the kings who bestowed them, and is printed by Hearne, pp. 479–80, and in *BCS*, no. 1320. It is in a typical Worcester hand of the second half of the eleventh century.

[3] For other evidence that quire 14 of Tib. I is now in the wrong place see above, p. 52.

[4] See Hearne, pp. 227–8 and p. 108. For good specimens of more legitimate abbreviation, see Hearne, p. 230, and cf. *BCS*, nos. 1089 and 1090 and nos. 1166 and 1167.

against Nero, but also how Nero and Tib. occasionally share a bad reading which is not in the original.[1]

The bad character of Nero needs stressing, because it has been misdated in the late tenth or early eleventh century by W. H. Stevenson and others.[2] In fact this cartulary belongs palaeographically to the time of Bishop Wulfstan II. If we consider the relative dates of Tib. I and Nero, their agreement in contents and order, their common readings, and their common errors, we cannot doubt that Nero is a copy, and a very poor copy, of Tib. Does this conclusion show that Nero is *not* the collection of charters referred to in the 'Enucleatio'? I do not think that it does. It suggests, rather, that Wulfstan made use of Tib. I when he worked on the archives and that his scribe copied Tib. out in an abbreviated form for insertion into the Bible, instead of copying the original documents directly. This would be a quite reasonable proceeding, especially if Wulfstan used the older cartulary as a guide and arranged the two volumes of originals in the order of Tib. I. If he did so, Hemming's statement, 'precepit cuncta eodem ordine in bibliotheca sanctę ecclesię scribi', is exactly correct. It was not necessary for him to mention Tib. I, which was not his work, nor Wulfstan's, but simply an important archivist's tool.

4. Bishop Wulfstan 'precepit adhuc omnia priuilegia et cirographa terrarum, quę proprie ad uictum monachorum pertinent, separatim ex his congregari, eaque similiter in duobus uoluminibus eodem ordine adunari, quod in hoc codicello, eius, ut predixi, imperio, pro modulo meę paruitatis, studiosus lector fecisse me animaduertere potest' (Hearne, p. 286).

Part only of this obscure sentence can relate to anything now in Tib. II, for the manuscript contains no copies of chirographs. On the other hand ff. 144–52, 154–7 (section K) contain copies of thirteen charters of estates 'quas monachi dc Wirecestra habent ad eorum propriam pertinentes utilitatem et ad utilitatem suorum subditorum qui eis debita persoluunt seruitiorum'. Except for

---

[1] *BCS*, nos. 256, 308, 76 occur in Nero and in Tib. (Hearne, pp. 16–23) and also in copies by Hickes and Smith from single-sheet originals. The Old English piece in *BCS*, no. 308 (printed also by A. J. Robertson, *Anglo-Saxon Charters*, 1939, p. 6 (no. IV), and by Stevenson, op. cit., p. 206), is particularly instructive. The scribe of Nero modernizes the spellings common to Tib. and the original, writing, for example, 'witan' for 'weotan', 'come' for 'cuome', 'het' for 'heht', and substitutes the words 'ærendgewrit' and 'hired' for the older forms 'ærend (erend-) wreocan' and 'higan'. On the other hand he agrees with Tib. in the bad reading 'Bremergrafan' (Bromsgrove) and in adding the words 'beon mihte'.

[2] Stevenson, op. cit., pp. 197–8.

Crowle, all these estates belonged wholly or partly to Worcester and 'ad uictum monachorum' at the time of the Domesday survey. It may be, therefore, that we have here a copy by Hemming of one of the two volumes of monks' charters referred to in the 'Enucleatio'. No doubt the monks were well entitled to their estates, but the charters on which they based their claims are, as a group, untrustworthy. The Cropthorne charter, well known as a fabrication, occurs as an addition of the later eleventh century in Tib. I (D i). The others are not there. Other early charters of lands devoted 'ad uictum monachorum' are in section (L) of Tib. II.

II. Since Hemming is silent about the existence of Tib. I we would not expect to find that its contents were used in the compilation of Tib. II. The independence of the copies of *BCS*, no. 357, in Tib. I (Hearne, p. 1) and in Tib. II (Hearne, p. 381) is, indeed, abundantly clear. The restoration of the original readings of this charter by collating Tib. I with Tib. II is a pretty exercise in textual criticism which can be checked on Hickes's copy of the single-sheet original.[1] Now one copyist and now the other departs from the exact words of the original. The charter was witnessed by thirty persons. Only eighteen of the names were copied by the scribe of Tib. I and only nineteen by the scribe of Tib. II, but the selections are different, so that in all twenty-three out of the thirty names occur in one copy or in the other.

This example, helpful though it is to us, is unfair to the scribes of Tib. Collation of Brit. Mus. Add. Ch. 19789 and 19790 (*BSC*, nos. 187, 274) with the copies in Tib. I (Hearne, pp. 52, 109) and of *BCS*, no. 223, with the copy in Tib. II (Hearne, p. 401) shows that the scribes of both parts of the manuscript often faithfully reproduced the original documents and sometimes copied the names of witnesses in full. I suspect, therefore, that faithful copying, and not dependence, explains the rather close similarity between the texts of the documents which occur both in Tib. I and in Tib. II, and for which, unfortunately, no originals exist.[2]

III. The unsatisfactory nature of the palaeographical evidence for the date of Tib. I has been noticed above. The internal evidence for the date is, I think, more conclusive, and parti-

[1] Hickes, *Thesaurus*, p. 173.
[2] The following occur both in Tib. I and in Tib. II: *BCS*, nos. 163, 164, 221, 226, 239, 313, 357, 432, 547, 665, 666. In Tib. II they are all in section (J). I do not include the Cropthorne charter (*BCS*, no. 235) in the list, since it is a later addition to Tib. I.

cularly the evidence from the leases of Bishop Oswald. These leases are a valuable and perhaps nearly complete series for the years of Oswald's episcopate.[1] They are, however, only a particular series of the large number of leases for lives granted by the bishops of Worcester in the ninth, tenth, and eleventh centuries. This system of leasing for lives was already in use at Worcester well before the time of Bishop Wærfrith (915), as appears from *BCS*, nos. 304, 455, and 609. It was regulated as leasehold for three lives and employed on a large scale by Bishop Oswald and it was maintained by his successors. The last lease recorded in the main hand of Tib. I is of A.D. 996. Leases of later date than this are known to us only from such original documents as chance to survive either physically or in the pages of Hickes and Smith, and from the list of early documents at Worcester compiled by Dugdale in 1643.[2] From these sources we know that the archives of the cathedral contained in the seventeenth century five leases of Bishop Wulfstan I, two leases of Bishop Leofsige, a lease of Bishop Beorhtheah, fifteen leases of Bishop Lyfing, and five leases of Bishop Ealdred. The fact that we know, by chance, of as many as twenty-eight leases dated between 1016 and 1058 suggests that the total number issued in this period was probably not less than the number issued by Oswald.[3] Not only was new land let out, but from 1020 onwards, if not earlier, Oswald's leases must have been falling in at a good rate.[4] If Tib. I is much later than 1016 why does it ignore all the eleventh-century leases?

Good evidence, I think, that the date of Tib. I is not much, if at all, later than 1016 comes from certain notes to the leases. Nine of them, forming a run on ff. 68ᵛ–77 (Hearne, pp. 144–63), conclude with words which give the name of the original lessee and of his heir and once the name of the heir's heir also. These notes

[1] Of thirteen leases by Oswald known to us from other sources than Tib. I eleven are recorded there also. The two leases not in Tib. I are Brit. Mus. Add. Ch. 19794, A.D. 984, and Somers Ch. 14 (lost, but printed in Smith's *Baeda*), A.D. 969. The latter became out of date in 988, when the same land was leased again, as Tib. I records (Hearne, p. 173). For Oswald's lease of Batsford see below, p. 74.

[2] Dugdale's autograph manuscript is Bodleian MS. Dugdale 12 (*Sum. Cat.* 6502). The printed editions of the list by Hickes, *Institutiones Grammaticæ* (1689), pt. 2, p. 169, by Wanley, *Catalogus*, p. 299, and in Hearne's edition of Tib., pp. 579–85, are all derived from a faulty exemplar. For example, charter no. 28 is listed in the printed editions as 'H . . . Episc. de Penhylle'· MS. Dugdale 12 reads 'Carta Lyfingi Episcopi de Penhylle'.

[3] All the extant leases are for three lives, except two of the latest (A.D. 1049 and 1058), which are for one life only.

[4] For example, no. 23 in Dugdale's list is 'Wlstani Archiepiscopi de Tidelmetun'. Tidmington was leased by Oswald in 977 (Hearne, p. 192).

are in Old English and in the main hand. The wording is that of
a contemporary record, the original lessee is spoken of in the past
tense and the heir in the present tense; for example 'æþelnoð wæs
se forma man 7 leofwine his sunu is þe oðer', 'wulfgeat wæs se
forma man 7 wulfmær is þe oðer þe hit nu on honda stant', and
once 'Eadwig wæs se forma man 7 wulfgyuu wæs se oðer nu
hæft æþelsige hit to þan þe þu wyllt' (sic MS.; Hearne 'wylle').
Besides this nearly every lease on ff. 57–113 has written against
it in the margin a note, not in the main hand, of the name of the
original lessee, accompanied, usually, by the name of the heir and
sometimes by the name of the heir's heir. Judging from ff. 68ᵛ–77
the writer's information did not extend beyond that of the main
scribe. In nearly twenty cases, however, a later annotator has
added to the names in the margins and traced the descent further.
Thus of the lessees of Grimley (Hearne, p. 147) the main hand
records that 'Osulf wæs se forma man 7 æþelstan munuc is þe
oðer'. In the margin is 'Æt grimanlege 7 at moslege osulfe 7
æþelstane', to which another hand has added the words '7 ufede'.[1]
All this concern about the descent of the leases appears to me to
be strong evidence that Tib. I was copied and used at a period
not very remote from Bishop Oswald's time, when as a rule the
first heir of the original lessee was in possession.[2]

Another piece of evidence points to a date in or near the time
of Archbishop Wulfstan, the homilist, who died probably in 1023,
and from 1002 held jointly the sees of Worcester and York. A
writer of the eleventh century—not the man who annotated the
leases—has jotted down against many of the charters the name of
the place to which it refers.[3] The same man added words and

[1] Hearne prints these notes, but he does not indicate the later additions as such:
they are (p. 128) 'wulfric wulbyr', (p. 130) '7 ælfsige', (p. 131) '7 ælmære', (p. 132)
'7 ælfric 7 siric 7 ælfild', (p. 147) '7 ufede', (p. 153) '7 heora dohtor', (p. 165)
'7 wulfhelm 7 ælfnoð 7 godwine', (p. 173) '7 afæd 7 heora sunu', (p. 176) '7 godwine', (p. 183) '7 æþelwyn 7 æfod', (p. 192) '7 wulfware', (p. 193) '7 æþelric 7
leoftæt', (p. 197) '7 eadflæde', (p. 202) '7 æþelmære', (p. 203) '7 wulfrune', (p. 204)
'7 wulfrune'.

[2] The suggestion by Miss A. J. Robertson, Anglo-Saxon Charters, p. 363, that
the notes about the lessees have been copied from endorsements has nothing to
recommend it, since the extant original leases are not endorsed in this way and the
copies in Smith's Baeda of the leases recorded in Tib. ff. 70, 72ᵛ (Hearne, pp. 147,
153) do not contain the sentences beginning 'Osulf wæs se forma man' and 'Eadwig
wæs se forma man'. Nor is it likely that the notes in the margins were culled from
endorsements.

[3] The scribe of Rawlinson B. 445, whom Hearne followed, copied only a few of
these names, but sometimes he picked one out and used it as a heading, e.g.
BLOCCANLEAH (Hearne, p. 31). Of the names which he passed over the most
interesting is perhaps 'Ælfgyðecyrce' written against the three charters printed by

phrases to the Old English homily on ff. 115–116ᵛ (G iii). In the following sentence, for example, the words printed within carets are his additions: '7 swutule `eac´ mæg gecnawan be mistlican tacnan se þe wile soð witan. þæt þa habbað god lean `æfter heora liffæce´ þa ðe wisdomes gymað. `þa hwile þe hy libbað´ 7 þa ðe gode hyrað. 7 godes lage healdað. 7 soþes gelyfað 7 georne þæt smeageað'. This sentence and all the last part of the homily[1] is in the manner of Archbishop Wulfstan.[2]

The hand of these additions is unusual and very skilled. It is not so much a professional as a scholar's hand. The same hand has annotated the famous Worcester copy of the Old English translation of the *Pastoral Care*, Bodleian MS. Hatton 20 (*Sum. Cat.* 4113), as well as two other manuscripts from Worcester, Bodleian MS. Hatton 42 (*Sum. Cat.* 4117) and British Museum MS. Harley 55, ff. 1–4, and four manuscripts of unknown provenance which were written early in the eleventh century and are more or less closely connected with the activities of Archbishop Wulfstan as preacher and canon-lawyer.[3] Some of the notes, like those to the homily in Tib., are Wulfstanian in character and language. If they are not actually the archbishop's, they must at least proceed from his immediate circle and time.

Yet another thread of evidence leads us back to Archbishop Wulfstan. The main scribe, or a contemporary, wrote three lines of verse at the foot of f. 101ᵛ of Tib. I:

> Sit pariter lupo pax uita longa salusque
> Iungere gaudemus lapidem disiungere necne
> Lætatur pius his iunctis nostri memor et sit.

Hearne, pp. 8, 9, 12 (*BCS*, nos. 455, 701, 234). This, the proper form of the name Alvechurch, occurs again in a late xi c. text (*BCS*, no. 1320), which is misdated c. 1200 in *Place-names of Worcestershire*, p. 332. The forms of the names in these marginalia are consistently good.

[1] The first part of the homily is derived from Wærfrith's translation of Gregory's Dialogues.

[2] For Wulfstan's style (and his writings) see D. Whitelock, *Sermo Lupi ad Anglos*, pp. 15–16, and references there.

[3] For the Worcester provenance of Hatton 42, a ninth-century, continental collection of ecclesiastical canons, see Atkins and Ker, op. cit., pp. 48–9. Harley 55, ff. 1–4, containing laws of King Edgar, &c., was annotated later by the well-known 'tremulous' Worcester hand. The other manuscripts are: (1) Cotton Claudius A. iii, containing (ff. 32–5) the 'sinodalia decreta' drawn up by Archbishop Wulfstan for King Æthelred (Liebermann, *Gesetze der Angelsachsen*, p. 247); (2) Cotton Vespasian A. xiv, ff. 114–79, letters of Alcuin, &c., including verses in praise of Archbishop Wulfstan and a letter addressed to him; (3) Cotton Nero A. i, ff. 70–177, a volume of ecclesiastical canons and homilies, partly by Wulfstan; (4) Copenhagen, Gl. Kgl. Samml. 1595, 4to, a volume of ecclesiastical canons, including penitential letters issued by Wulfstan when bishop of London.

The name Wulfstan is here (*lupus–lapis*)—'Long live Wulfstan, and be mindful of us'. The hand is earlier than the time of St. Wulfstan. I do not think there is a more likely recipient of the greeting than his earlier namesake, the archbishop and homilist.[1]

Hemming's reputation, so far as it is based on the high quality of the texts in Tib. I, must suffer from this reassessment of the facts. But his claims to be the main author of Tib. II remain undisturbed. Sections (H) and (L), including the 'Enucleatio' and the life of Wulfstan, are his. No doubt, too, he assembled the charters in section (K), which includes, incidentally, one interesting piece of narrative.[2] As for sections (I) and (J) there is no evidence. The arrangement of the five sections of Tib. II can only be due to Hemming if he is identical with the scribe of ff. 119–25.[3] I have described above how this scribe seems to have connected Hemming's general preface on to section (K). He wrote the names of the estates in (M i) and the names of bishops and estates in (K i). The heading to section (J), with its reference back, is probably his,[4] and perhaps other headings as well. His hand occurs in an addition to Tib. I (C iv) and in other Worcester manuscripts. His personal interest in the claims of Worcester priory about the turn of the eleventh century is not in doubt. That this scribe is Hemming seems to me probable.

III. TEXTS NOT PRINTED BY HEARNE

Hearne was the most faithful of editors and his copy of MS. Rawlinson B. 445 is a true copy. It is our misfortune that he was not able to base his edition on the original Cotton manuscript. The scribe of Rawl. was not, indeed, incompetent, but he was not up to Hearne's standard.[5] He left out marginalia and texts

---

[1] The three lines are printed by Hearne, p. 217 (reading *Sic, laxatur* and *vinctis*). The six couplets in Cotton Vespasian A. xiv, f. 148ᵛ, are rather similar, e.g.

Floret in hoc opere pia mentio presulis archi
Wlfstani cui det dominus pia regna polorum

to which is added in the margin

Et sibi commissos tueatur ab hoste maligno.

These Vespasian verses are printed in *BCS*, no. 896, and by Stubbs, *Memorials of St. Dunstan* (Rolls Series 63, 1874), p. liv: Miss Whitelock has shown in *Eng. Hist. Rev.* lii (1937), 460, that they refer to Wulfstan, the homilist.

[2] The story of the monument of Wiferð and his wife Alta (Hearne, pp. 342–4).

[3] See above, p. 57.   [4] See above, pp. 56, 59.

[5] How very well Hearne could manage a difficult medieval text may be seen from the edition of the thirteenth-century library catalogue of Glastonbury, printed from Trinity College, Cambridge, MS. 724 at the end of Hearne's *John of Glastonbury* (1726).

which were difficult to read or, in his opinion, not worth copying, and he put in a few decorations of his own. His omissions and commissions became, perforce, Hearne's also.[1]

The chief omission, apart from the texts which were omitted deliberately, because they were already printed in the *Monasticon*,[2] is the grant of land 'æt ofre' (Tib. I, f. 118ᵛ).[3] This document is added at the end of the last quire of Tib. I in a hand of the first half of the eleventh century. It was omitted, because it was 'so much obliterated that it cannot be transcribed'. In a good light, and with help from the ultra-violet lamp, most of it can be made out. The first part of the document, fifteen lines, is complete in itself, apart from the names of witnesses:

Regnante in perpetuum domino nostro iesu cristo per | immensa quadriflui orbis clup⟨e⟩am (?). Anno | eiusdem incarnationis Millesimo Vᵒ ind*ictione* III Ego | æðelred rex anglorum cum consensu eiusdem | gentis Episcoporum uel principum. pro redemptione | animarum nostrarum Et pro sospitate necnon et | regni nostri quandam ruris portionem [hoc] est [. .] | manentium æt ofre ad episcopalem sedem que dicitur | deowiesstow plena mentis deuotione humiliter | perdonabo in sempiternam hereditatem. Pax ser[uantibus] | et custodientibus hanc nostram donationem [contra] | dicentibus uero sit dampnatio nisi ante [hic] | emenda[uerin]t.[4] Ego æþelred rex anglorum (?) | hanc meam elemosinam propria manu (?) | confirmabo.

This grant is followed, after a blank space of 2½ lines, by the words 'Ego .N. episcopus .N.', and, in another two lines, by 'ea ratione legis ut semper in seruitium sit illius | qui locum præfuit (?) episcopatus in loco .N. eclesię'.

In the margin, written sideways, is a further clause in four lines, much damaged: 'Ista autem conditione interposita ut ille semper sit in omnibus rebus humilis | et deuotus minister episcopo et familia eius et [. . . .] | coniungat et [. . . . .] post spatia [. . . . . . .]'.

The main piece here is a deed of gift of land 'æt ofre' to the bishopric of St. David's, without conditions and 'in sempiternam hereditatem'. The added clauses appear to contradict this by introducing the condition of service and, almost certainly, the condition of a lease for lives. The document is mysterious, the

---

[1] In Hearne's edition all the headings beginning with the word 'Carta' (e.g., p. 12), the words 'an. 904' on p. 13, the words in small type on p. 369, and the English sentences on pp. 247 and 451 are due to the scribe of Rawl.

[2] Hearne printed these texts from the *Monasticon* on pp. 451–75.

[3] See above, p. 55 (G. vi).

[4] For this formula cf. Hearne, p. 342 = *KCD*, no. 952.

more so as the place 'æt ofre' has not been identified. Possibly it, and the clauses added to it, are no more than formulary exercises. The scribe of the Nero cartulary, however, accepted them as matter of fact. In Nero, Æthelred's grant appears as a lease, with reversion after three lives to the church of Worcester, in the following words:

'Regnante in perpetuum domino nostro iesu cristo anno eiusdem incarnationis millesimo quinto ego æþelred rex anglorum cum consensu eiusdem gentis episcoporum et principum pro redemptione animę meę quandam ruris particulam æt ofre concedo ad episcopalem sedem æt dewiesstowe trium hominum spatio dierum. quibus decursis ad wigornen-sem restituatur ecclesiam ea tamen conditione tamen (sic) interposita. ut ille qui preest episcopatui predictę in omnibus subditus sit wigornensis ęcclesię pastori.'[1]

The three other texts not printed by Hearne are (E i), (G vii), and (O).[2] All are probably in hands of the first half of the eleventh century.

(E i) is in a small hand at the head of f. 109. The upper margin is damaged and a line or two has been lost at the beginning. '[. . . . . .] III or' 7 leofric I p'. Sæwine VI or' 7 heora andaga is half to nat' s' marie 7 half to alra halg[a]n. 7 [. . .] Eadwi ec (?) be gebir[de] half p' 7 wulfwi of upkota LX pen' to þam ilcan and' 7 leofric lirpanc half p' to michaeles tid'.
This gives us the names of five tenants, the amount of rent each paid, and the days on which the rent was due (andaga). 'p'' stands for 'pund'. If the ora was worth twenty pence, six oran are the equivalent of half a pound.

(G vii) follows the 'æt ofre' document immediately on f. 118[v], and, like it, is blurred. The first four lines record the descent of the lease of Batsford: 'Oswald b' bocode bæceoran ægelmære 7 ægelmær hit becwæð wulfgeate 7 wulfgeat hit sealde his wife to mornegife (? sic)'. The rest is difficult: I can make out only (line 5) he wæs os [. . . . . .], (line 6) Ð[. .]stan wæs eadwerdes [. . . .], (line 7) 7 ælfric (?) eadwerdes sunu (?), (line 8) [. . . .] þe hyre (?) to py[. . . . . . .]. There is no other record of the lease of Batsford in Tib.

(O) A torn leaf, f. 110, contains the end of a lease (?) of $1\frac{1}{4}$

---

[1] Nero E. i, pt. 2, f. 184[v], printed by Hearne, p. 479. Not in *KCD*.
[2] See above, pp. 54, 55, 62.

hides to one Ælfnoð: eight names of witnesses remain in two columns:

Ego æþeric abbas	Ego ægelric m[. . .]
Ego æua abbas	Ego alwald mi[. . .]
Ego eadric dux	Ego ægelsie deca[nus]
Ego god minister	Ego æþelstan sac[erdos]

Below the names is 'Ælfnoð. unam fidelicet [*sic*] mansam [*altered to* mansionem] et iiii^a p[. . .]'.

The names 'afa abbas' and 'eadric dux' occur as witnesses to Wulfstan's grant of Bentley, A.D. 1017 (*KCD*, no. 1313). Aua, abbot of Exeter, is in *KCD*, no. 729, *c.* 1019. The name is rare and probably fixes the date of the present document approximately. The hand is eleventh century, not late. The verso is blank.

N. R. KER

LONDON AND THE SUCCESSION TO THE CROWN DURING THE MIDDLE AGES

THE attention of historians has always been attracted by the singular claim, put forward by the citizens of London on the accession of Stephen, that it was their special privilege to elect the king. It is recognized that the action of London on that occasion was not without precedent: and students of the dynastic revolutions of the later Middle Ages are well aware that in each of these crises, too, London had an important part to play. It is hoped that a brief review of the claims and activities of the Londoners in regard to the question of the succession may serve some useful purpose, if only that of bringing together a certain amount of hitherto unrelated information. Such a review may make it possible to discover a certain consistency in the role allotted to or claimed by the city, even over a period of nearly 500 years.

London's claim to initiative in the election of kings may be traced back to the early years of the eleventh century. In his valiant struggle against Cnut, Edmund Ironside enjoyed the support of the London *burhware*:[1] and when Ethelred ended his unhappy reign on St. George's Day, 1016, the members of the Witan who were in London and the same *burhware* chose Edmund as king.[2] Twenty years later, on the death of Cnut, a gathering at Oxford which included Earl Leofric, almost all the thegns from the region north of the Thames and the *lithsmen* of London, named Harold as regent in the absence of his brother, Harthacnut, who was then in Denmark.[3] In 1042 Edward the Confessor seems to have been chosen king in London by some form of popular acclamation.[4] Inevitably, then, the Londoners played a prominent part in the national crisis that followed Harold's death at Hastings. Archbishop Aldred, with the Earls Edwin and Morcar, first tried to raise a party in the city to support the claim of Edgar the Ætheling. These Londoners are described in the Chronicle as the *burhwaru* of London, by Florence of Worcester

---

[1] Earle and Plummer, *Two Saxon Chronicles*, i. 147: 'hi hæfdon þære burh ware fultum of Lundene'.

[2] Ibid., pp. 148–9: 'ealle þa witan þe on Lundene wæron 7 se burhwaru gecuron Eadmund to cynge'.

[3] Ibid., p. 159: 'þa liðsmen on Lunden'.

[4] Ibid., p. 163: 'eall folc geceas Eadward to cynge on Lundene'.

as *cives et butsecarles*.[1] The scheme came to nothing, for the magnates soon decided to abandon a policy of resistance, but it may well have been the remnants of their party which made a last stand against the Conqueror as he approached the city.[2] At most they can have been only a remnant, for the leading Londoners had already joined the influential group which went out to Berkhamstead to offer William the crown.[3]

The bald record of these events which is all that remains to us leaves many problems unsolved. It is readily understandable that the position of London as the centre of the national resistance movement in the eleventh century should have entitled her citizens to a voice, even to a decisive voice, in matters of national importance; but the exact status of the *burhware, lithsmen, butsecarles*, and *betstan men* is not easily determined. Chadwick took the view that the *burhware* who elected Edmund were a garrison or body of troops and rejected the suggestion that 'the people' had a right to take part in the election of kings.[4] But the word *burhwaru* occurs in the English charters and writs of both Edward the Confessor and William I where the context seems to demand the rendering 'citizens'.[5] The references to *lithsmen* and *butsecarles* no doubt indicate the preponderant influence of the fleet which was based on London. It was the seamen of London who came to Oxford, presumably by arrangement, to join with the northern thegns in proclaiming Harold, following the example of the Danish sailors who had declared for Sweyn in 1013:[6] and seamen may well have preponderated among the *folc* who acclaimed Edward in 1042. They are hardly to be distinguished from the *butsecarles* who supported the Ætheling after Hastings. The 'best men' who went to meet William at Berkhamstead can hardly have been of this type but they may well have included some of the *burhthegns*, many of whom must have acquired their status by their enterprise as merchants, by having 'fared thrice over the wide sea' by their own means.[7] In short, London's claim

---

[1] Ibid., p. 199: *Flor. Wigorn.* ed. Thorpe (English Hist. Soc.), i. 228: 'cum civibus Londoniensibus et butsecarlis'.

[2] Stenton, *Anglo-Saxon England*, pp. 589–90.

[3] Earle and Plummer, op. cit., p. 200: 'ealle þa betstan men of Lundene'.

[4] Chadwick, *Anglo-Saxon Institutions*, p. 359.

[5] Kemble, *Codex Diplomaticus*, iv. 212; Dugdale, *Monasticon*, i. 111, no. xxxix; Liebermann, *Gesetze*, i. 486.

[6] Earle and Plummer (op. cit. ii. 210), draw attention to the Scandinavian origin of the word *liðsman* and believe that the *liðsmen* of 1036 represented 'the crews of the Danish ships, the standing naval force'.

[7] Cf. Stenton, *Norman London* (Historical Association Leaflet, no. 93).

to a voice in the election of kings seems to derive mainly from her position, in an age of sea-borne invasion, as a great naval base and the leading port of England.

Between 1066 and 1135 the claim to elect lay dormant. Rufus secured the throne through the influence of Lanfranc, and Henry I established himself by his seizure of the Treasury at Winchester and was elected by the Witan there assembled. Meanwhile, the post-Conquest years saw the steady infiltration of a wealthy Norman element into the old Saxon city: and it may well have been this element, inevitably hostile to the Angevin marriage of the empress, which turned the scales in favour of Stephen.[1] According to the well-known passage in the *Gesta Stephani*[2] it was the *majores natu* who agreed to elect Stephen as king, claiming it as 'their right and special privilege, when the throne was vacant by the king's death, to provide that another should take his place and follow in his steps'. Round sought to minimize the importance of this passage by his suggestion that what the Londoners were really claiming was 'not the right to elect a king of all England but to choose their own lord independently of the rest of the kingdom and to do so by a *separate negotiation* between himself and them', and that the agreement was in the nature of a bargain.[3] The author of the *Gesta* does indeed use the word *pactio* but the only 'terms' which he reports are that Stephen, in return for the support of the city, took oath that he would bend his whole energies to the pacification of the kingdom. In view of the part already taken by London in royal elections it seems improbable that the claim of her leading citizens in 1135 was limited as Round suggests. The wording of the *Gesta* clearly points to something much wider. The senior citizens, we are told, were assembled in council *utilia in commune providentes*. They said that the whole realm was exposed to danger when the source of order and justice failed, and that it was therefore of the utmost importance to choose a king 'qui ad communis utilitatis pacem reformandam et rebellibus regni armatus occurreret et legum instituta juste disponeret'.

The *Gesta Stephani* is our sole authority for this incident, but William of Malmesbury's independent account of the action of the Londoners at the Council of Winchester in 1141 affords con-

---

[1] This point was made by J. R. Green in a paper on 'London and her Election of Stephen' read at the London Congress of the British Archaeological Institute in July 1866.

[2] *Chronicles of Stephen, Henry II and Richard I*, iii. 5–6.

[3] Round, *Geoffrey de Mandeville*, pp. 247–9.

firmation of their predominant influence in this period. The Londoners appear to have been the only laymen present at the Winchester Council, and Malmesbury (an eye-witness) reports Henry of Blois as stating that they were summoned because from the importance of their city they were almost nobles—*quasi optimates pro magnitudine civitatis*.[1] When the deputation from London arrived, however, they made it clear that they were not prepared to enter into disputes on the succession question. 'They said that they were sent from their *communio*, as they called it, not to contend, but to entreat that their lord the king might be liberated.' This speech, which could be interpreted only as expressive of their determination to stand by their choice of Stephen, drew forth a sharp rebuke from the legate: but the Londoners were among the last to admit the claims of Matilda and within a few weeks of her arrival in the city they had driven her forth with ignominy.[2]

The significance of London's action in 1135 seems, then, to lie not in her imitation of the foreign practice of bargains between a commune and its chosen overlord but in an extension, in favourable circumstances, of an already established claim to take the initiative when the succession was in doubt. This is not to deny that the new communal aspirations of twelfth-century London may well have encouraged definition of a claim which in an earlier generation had derived less from political theory than from practical necessity.[3] London was now something more than a naval base, something more than a great port. She was rapidly becoming a self-conscious entity, she was *totius regionis regina, metropolis*.[4]

More than half a century was to elapse before the Londoners again found opportunity to exert their influence in the matter of the succession. In the crisis of 1191 Longchamp was the avowed champion of the claim of Arthur of Brittany to be Richard's heir. John, having set himself at the head of the opposition to the chancellor, was able to win from the Londoners, at the price of the grant of the commune, recognition of himself as heir-presumptive. 'The citizens of London made oath that they

[1] William of Malmesbury, *Historia Novella*, ii. 576.
[2] Henry of Huntingdon, p. 275; *Gesta Stephani*, p. 77.
[3] Cf. the well-known letter in which Hugh, archbishop of Rouen, thanks the illustrious senators, honoured citizens, and all the commune of London (*omnibus commune London*), for their fidelity to Stephen. Round, *Geoffrey de Mandeville*, p. 116.
[4] *Gesta Stephani*, p. 5.

would faithfully serve their lord, King Richard and his heir: and
if he should die without issue would receive Count John his
brother as their king and lord.'[1] Here, much more clearly than
in 1135, we see an example of a *pactio*, of London recognizing a
royal title in return for a highly valued privilege. Yet the bargain
could not be maintained, and there can be little doubt that the
power and prestige of the Angevin monarchy was tending to
strengthen the hereditary at the expense of the elective principle.[2]
Hubert Walter is alleged to have reaffirmed the elective basis of
the monarchy at the coronation of John, but his speech reflects
little more than a determination to support John's title against
that of his nephew Arthur.[3] It was John's own actions which
led to the revival of a moribund claim and drove a section of the
baronage, supported by the Londoners, to take the momentous
decision to expel the reigning king and elect a foreign prince in
his stead. Guala's excommunication of the rebel barons in 1216
included an interdict on the city of London. When Louis entered
London on 2 June he was received by the citizens with acclamation,[4] and, though there is no record of a formal process of
election, the Merton Chronicle refers to the performance of
ceremonial acts of homage, first at Westminster by the baronial
leaders and afterwards in St. Paul's Churchyard by the Londoners, headed by Fitz-Walter and the mayor, William Hardel.[5]
The initiative on this occasion clearly lay with the magnates: but
they welcomed the support of the Londoners, mainly on account
of the key position of the city, but partly, no doubt, because the
citizens could best supply the necessary element of *collaudatio*, or
acclamation.

Henry III is said to have been threatened with deposition:[6]
but the political atmosphere of the thirteenth century was increasingly unfavourable to the survival of ancient notions of
popular election and the changes in the coronation *ordo* of 1308
are indicative of their decline.[7] It was the crises of Edward II's

[1] Hoveden, iii. 141.
[2] Schramm, *History of the English Coronation*, p. 160.
[3] M. Paris, *Chronica Majora*, ii. 454: 'nullus praevia ratione alii succedere
habet in regnum, nisi ab universitate regni unanimiter invocata Spiritus gratia
electus.'
[4] *Histoire des Ducs de Normandie*, p. 171: 'li bourgois de la ville alerent encontre
lui, qui grant joie orent de sa venue.'
[5] Petit-Dutaillis, *Louis VIII*, p. 514: 'ipse eadem die recepit homagia civium
Londoniensium in cimiterio Sancti Pauli, Roberto filio Walteri primo illud faciente,
deinde Willelmo Hardel, maiore Londoniarum et multis aliis.'
[6] *Chronica Majora*, iii. 245.   [7] Schramm, op. cit., chap. iv and v.

last years which served to revive, in acute form, the whole question of the right of the nation to repudiate an unpopular king and to name his successor.

The detailed investigations undertaken by Miss Clarke and Mr. Wilkinson have done much to elucidate the obscure details of the revolution which overthrew Edward II, but, as neither of these scholars was primarily concerned with London, there seems to be room for a short postscript to their valuable essays.[1] It is possible that some influential London citizens may have had a hand in initiating the whole revolution. Such, at any rate, was the story that old men in London were telling their grandchildren at the close of the century. According to Froissart, it was the Londoners ('par lesquels tout le royaulme d'Angleterre se ordonne et gouverne'), who had suggested to Queen Isabella that if she were to land with a small force she would find the city of London, the majority of other towns, and the knights and esquires ready to welcome her and to put her in possession of the realm. The queen accepted the invitation and arrived with her party in England, 'sus le confort des Londriens, lesquels leur aidièrent leur fait à achiéver: car sans leur ayde et puissance ils ne fuissent jamais venus au dessus de leur emprise'.[2] There may well be some truth in this story. Edward II's high-handed actions had served to raise a party against him in the city: and when Mortimer escaped from the Tower in August 1323 he had done so with the connivance of two leading citizens, Richard de Bettoyne and John de Gisors.[3] Edward left London on hearing of Isabella's landing at Harwich, and one of the queen's first actions was to write to the city asking for assistance in destroying the enemies of the land. According to the French Chronicle, no answer was returned to this letter 'for fear of the King'.[4] About a fortnight later, on 6 October, another letter was sent asking particularly for the arrest of Despenser.[5] This letter was affixed to the Cross in Cheapside and copies of it were circulated elsewhere. The effects were inflammatory. On 15 October, the commonalty flocked to the Guildhall and forced the mayor, Hamo de Chigwell, to declare

[1] M. V. Clarke, *Medieval Representation and Consent*, chap. ix, 'Committees of Estates and the Deposition of Edward II'; B. Wilkinson, 'The Deposition of Richard II and the Accession of Henry IV', *Eng. Hist. Rev.* liv, 215–39.
[2] Froissart, *Chroniques*, ed. Kervyn de Lettenhove, xvi. 156 seq.
[3] *Chronicles of Edward I and Edward II*, i. 305, 318 n. (*Annales Paulini*); cf. M. Weinbaum, *London unter Eduard I. und II.*, i. 153–62.
[4] *French Chronicle of London*, p. 51.
[5] *Cal. Plea and Memoranda Rolls of the City of London, 1323–64*, pp. 41–2.

for the queen. On the same day, Bishop Stapledon of Exeter, who had been responsible for the publication of bulls of excommunication against the king's enemies, was brutally murdered by the mob.[1]

By this murder and the consequent disorder in the city London was virtually committed to the queen's cause. The election of the new mayor should have taken place on the feast of SS. Simon and Jude (28 October), but it was postponed until 15 November when the bishop of Winchester arrived with letters from the queen, permitting a free election. The choice of the citizens fell on Mortimer's partisan, Richard de Bettoyne.[2] By the end of the year, the Despensers had been executed, Edward II taken, and writs issued proroguing the parliament summoned for 14 December to 7 January. By a process of double election which, in Miss Clarke's view, reflects the disturbed condition of the city, London elected six persons, two of whom were to attend the parliament.[3]

When parliament met on the morrow of the Epiphany, the London mob crowded into Westminster Hall.[4] No doubt their presence was welcome to Mortimer and his friends as affording them the support of popular clamour. The proceedings of the opening days of the parliament are obscure. Miss Clarke accepts the testimony of the *Historia Roffensis* that the work of renouncing the father and acclaiming the son was put in hand at once, but Mr. Wilkinson thinks it inconceivable that such weighty business should have been hurried through in the first two days of a medieval parliament.[5] It seems clear, however, that during this week the magnates must have been negotiating with the city authorities the arrangements which were to secure the formal association of London with the coming revolution. On the Monday following (12 January), the mayor, aldermen, and commonalty sent a letter to the magnates asking whether they were willing to be in accord with the city, to swear to maintain the cause of Queen Isabella and her son, to crown the latter and to depose his father for his frequent offences against his oath and his Crown.[6] Miss Clarke calls this letter 'in fact an ultimatum' and suggests that by means of it 'the citizens of London forced the issue', but the promptitude of the magnates' response seems to make it

---

[1] *French Chronicle*, p. 52.
[2] Ibid., p. 55.   [3] *Parl. Writs*, II. ii. 359.
[4] *Historia Roffensis* in *Anglia Sacra*, i. 366–7.
[5] Wilkinson, op. cit., p. 225, n. 4.
[6] *Cal. Plea and Memoranda Rolls, 1323–64*, pp. 11–12.

incredible that they had no foreknowledge of de Bettoyne's plans.[1] The large and formal cavalcade, representative of all the estates of the realm, which set out for the Guildhall on the day following the dispatch of the letter cannot have been arranged overnight. The swearing-in took place 'in the presence of the Mayor, Aldermen and a great Commonalty'[2] and seems to have occupied at least three days. Propagandist speeches and sermons, addressed to London crowds, were useful adjuncts: but it was the proceedings at the Guildhall which secured the formal sanction of London for the deposition of the old king and the coronation of the new. As soon as the swearing-in had begun, the parliament at Westminster took steps to organize the deputation to Edward II at Kenilworth and appointed its members, among whom were at least three Londoners.[3] This deputation, like the deputation to the Guildhall, was to speak in the name, not of the estates of parliament, but of the estates of the realm.[4] The Londoners took their place in it as leading representatives of the estate of the commons or, if we accept the classification of the *Modus Tenendi Parliamentum*, of the citizens and burgesses. The rise of lesser towns and the frequent appearance of their representatives in parliament may have done something to modify the unique position accorded to London in an earlier generation. It is safe to assert that at no time would the architects of such a revolution have ventured to execute their plans without prior assurance of the support of the capital; but in the carefully chosen body, which conveys the decision of the nation to the king, the Londoners take their place with the representatives of other civic bodies. Such a scheme was probably in accord with their own wishes, for they, no less than the magnates, must have been anxious to secure the widest possible distribution of responsibility for a dangerous act.[5]

[1] Miss Clarke considered this possibility without committing herself to it, op. cit., pp. 180–1.

[2] *Cal. Plea and Memoranda Rolls, 1323–64*, p. 12.

[3] *Cal. Letter Book E*, p. 222.

[4] Neither Miss Clarke nor Mr. Wilkinson regards this deputation as a *parliamentary* committee of estates, Mr. Wilkinson because he does not believe the assembly then sitting at Westminster to have been a true parliament, Miss Clarke because she thinks that pressure of events prevented the plan outlined in the *Modus* from being put into effect. 'It was no time for scrupulous fulfilment of an academic design.' I suggest that we have here a foreshadowing of the distinction (explicitly recognized in the next century) between representatives of the estates of the realm *out of parliament* and of the estates of the realm *in parliament*.

[5] A sense of uneasiness is clearly manifest in the citizens' dealings with Reynolds and the bishops designed to gain them immunity from the consequences of Stapledon's murder. *Historia Roffensis*, p. 367.

The acts of 1399 were more dangerous still; and this is probably the main reason why their elucidation has proved a matter of such great difficulty. It is clear enough that towards the end of his reign Richard II had incurred great unpopularity in the city and that the 'London mob' became clamorous for his removal as soon as, if not before, they became aware of his capture by Henry of Lancaster. Londoners must have formed a preponderant element in the *populus* to whom the news of Richard's 'resignation' was conveyed by the archbishop of York in Westminster Hall, who heard the long list of *gravamina* and gave the *collaudatio* to Henry.[1] A few years after Henry IV's accession it was possible for the prior of St. Botolph's, Colchester, to say derisively that it was the London rabble who had elected him king.[2] In the dangerous opening years of the new reign it may well have seemed politic, both to the native chroniclers and to those responsible for the official version of the deposition, to pass lightly over London's share in what had been done. Froissart, who knew no such scruples, does not hesitate to ascribe to London the chief part in the whole drama. He suggests that it was the Londoners ('come chiefs du royaume d'Angleterre et puissans que ils sont')[3] who sent messengers to Henry in France urging his return and that, even before Richard was taken, they had struck a bargain in terms strongly reminiscent of the *pactio* of 1135. They had offered the crown to Henry and his heirs, had sealed a covenant to that effect, and had undertaken to secure the adherence of 'tout le demourant du royaulme d'Angleterre'. Froissart's narrative of the crisis is so notoriously inaccurate that we cannot well accept this tale as it stands:[4] yet confirmation of his suggestion of some kind of official overture to Lancaster from the citizens of London comes from two other, independent, sources. Usk (an

---

[1] *Rot. Parl.* iii. 417, 423. This would be true whether or not we agree with Mr. Wilkinson that the *populus* included the commons elected to parliament.

[2] Wylie, *Henry IV*, i. 420, quoting the deposition of the bailiff of Colchester in Exchequer Treasury of Receipt, $\frac{21a}{8}$ (6).

[3] *Chroniques*, xvi. 161.

[4] Froissart's version is very puzzling. It must have been composed almost contemporaneously with the events it describes; it is detailed and circumstantial; and at the time of its composition Froissart was enjoying the patronage of Albert of Bavaria, count of Hainault, and of his son, Count William of Ostrevant, who had offered hospitality to Henry during his exile and had sent him affectionate congratulations on his accession. Froissart's narrative must represent an old man's imperfect recollections of some verbal description of the crisis but, even so, it is hard to account for such flagrant errors as placing Henry's landing at Plymouth and making him visit London before his departure for the west. The whole story is marked by violent hostility to the Londoners.

eye-witness in Henry's train) states that when Henry reached Chester with Richard as his prisoner, three London aldermen and some fifty other citizens came to him 'sub sigillo communi ipsius civitatem sibi recommendando et regi Ricardo diffidenciam mittendo'.[1] The reference to the Common Seal certainly suggests an official deputation and is the more impressive because it comes from a Lancastrian source. Creton gives another and rather different version of what is plainly the same incident, a version which he admits reached him at second hand.[2] He places the meeting at Lichfield and describes the Londoners who made up the deputation as 'v ou vj des plus grans bourgois, gouverneurs de la dicte ville'. They are said to have begged Henry, 'on behalf of the commons of London', to execute Richard forthwith: to which Henry replied that such an act would eternally disgrace him, but that Richard should be brought to London and judged by the parliament. Thus, even if we regard Froissart with the scepticism which his inaccuracies warrant, we are justified in assuming that the responsible authorities of London, albeit outside the bounds of the city, signified their rejection of Richard and their acceptance of Henry in a way which made it safe for the latter to bring Richard to the Tower and to admit the populace to the assembly at Westminster which was to secure his deposition.

When the Yorkist party in their turn came to challenge the title of Lancaster, London once more proved an indispensable ally. Edward of York came up from the west towards the end of February 1461 and was received by the citizens, headed by the mayor and aldermen.[3] On the Sunday following his arrival there was a great gathering of soldiers and citizens in Clerkenwell Fields where William of Worcester heard the chancellor, George Neville, publish York's title and declare him to be the true king.[4] Hall adds that the crowd repudiated Henry VI, and, when asked if they would accept York as king, answered: 'Yea, yea, crieng, king Edward, with many great showtes and clappyng of handes.'[5] The support of the Londoners being thus assured, Edward's party held a council at Baynard's Castle where they laid their

---

[1] *Chronicon Adae de Usk*, p. 28.
[2] *Archaeologia*, xx. 176, 376. The *Chronique de la Traison et Mort* (p. 212) gives a dramatized and evidently derivative version of the incident which the author places at Coventry.
[3] *Registrum Abbatiae Johannis Whethamstede*, i. 404: 'ab omnibus, tam a Majore et a senatoribus, quam etiam a clero, ab omnique artificio totius urbis'.
[4] W. Worc., p. 777.
[5] Hall's *Chronicle* (1809), p. 253. Hall makes Lord Fauconberg the spokesman.

plans. On 4 March Edward was conducted to Westminster Abbey and there, *coram omni populo*, he again set forth his claim, ending with the question: 'Quid dicitis ad haec, vos populares, hic presentes?' To which the people answered with the *collaudatio*: 'Verus rex, Rex Edwardus: rectus rex, Rex Edwardus: justus, juridicus et legitimus rex, Rex Edwardus: cui omnes nos subjici volumus, suaeque humillime jugum admittere gubernationis.'[1] The Lancastrians were still in the field and the battle of Towton had yet to be won; but Edward's reign was held to date from the day when, in the words of a London chronicle, he took upon him the crown of England by the advice of the lords spiritual and temporal and by the election of the commons.[2]

Thus, in 1461, we see the Londoners assuming a new role. Even had Edward been willing to contemplate such a process, there could be no question of election by parliament, or by an assembly bearing the appearance of a parliament, for none was in session. Fabyan says, correctly, that Edward was 'electyd and chosen for Kyng of Englonde . . . by auctoryte of the sayde counceyll (i.e. of all the lords spiritual and temporal that were then available), and agrement of the comons there present'.[3] In other words, Edward had been chosen or, as he would have claimed, his legitimate title had been recognized, by the estates of the realm, out of parliament. London was solid in his support, the Lancastrians had retreated to the north, and the situation was probably less dangerous than in 1399. Partly for this reason and partly because circumstances offered little alternative, the Londoners took upon themselves the chief responsibility of speaking for the third estate, the estate of the commons. Even so, the official entry in the city records suggests that they had not altogether lost sight of the need to distribute responsibility. Edward is said to have assumed royal authority at Westminster 'diversis dominis magnatibus et proceribus ac immensa communitate *de diversis Regni partibus* ibidem interessentibus'.[4]

The precedent of 1461 was closely followed in 1483. As a preparation for a mass meeting in the Guildhall on 17 June a popular preacher named Ralph Shaa was put up by Gloucester's party to preach a sermon at Paul's Cross in defence of his title.[5] At the Guildhall, Buckingham and a number of other lords con-

---

[1] Whethamstede, i. 404–7.   [2] Gregory's *Chronicle*, p. 215.
[3] Fabyan, *New Chronicles of England and France* (1811), p. 639.
[4] Plea and Memoranda Roll, A. 85, m. 2. (I am indebted for this reference to the Deputy-Keeper of the City Records.)
[5] Polydore Vergil (Camden Society), p. 183.

fronted the mayor, sheriffs, aldermen, and other officers of the city with 'all the commons'.[1] Buckingham put the case for Richard, concluding with the suggestion that he be formally petitioned to take the crown, to which petition, it was urged, he would 'the more graciously encline yf ye, the worshipful citezens of this citee, being the chief citee of the realme, ioyne with us the nobles in our saied request'. The proposal was greeted with a disconcerting silence and it was only after repeated efforts that a little applause was whipped up. This could pass as a *collaudatio* and it gave the plotters what they wanted. They could now proceed with the formalities. Pressure must have been brought to bear upon the civic authorities, for on the day following the mayor, aldermen, and chief commoners, 'in their best maner appareled', met Buckingham and some nobles and clergy at Baynard's Castle and offered to the Protector a roll embodying a petition to take the crown. The sanctions underlying this offer were clearly set out in the first parliament of the new reign. The crown had been offered 'on the behalve and in the name of the thre Estates of this Reame of England, that is to wite, of the Lords Spiritualls and Temporalls, and of the Commons, by many and diverse Lords Sprituells and Temporalls, and other Nobles and notable persones of the Commons in grete multitude'. An exactly similar procedure had placed Edward IV on the throne, but whereas he had behind him the genuine enthusiasm of the people of London, Richard III's unpopularity had given rise to widespread murmurings at the irregularity of such arrangements.

'Forasmoch [the Parliament Roll continues] as neither the said three Estats, neither the said personnes, which in thair name presented . . . the said Rolle into oure said Souverain Lord the King, were assembled in fourme of Parliament; by occasion whereof, diverse doubts, questions and ambiguitees been moved and engendred in the myndes of diverse personnes, as it is said: Therfore . . . bee it ordeigned . . . that the tenour of the said Rolle . . . presented . . . to oure before said Souverain Lord the King, in the name and on the behalve of the said three Estates out of Parliament, now by the same three Estates assembled in this present Parliament, and by auctorite of the same, bee ratifyed, enrolled, recorded, approved and auctorized, into removyng the occasion of doubtes and ambiguitees . . . .'[2]

It seems, then, to have been widely recognized that the body which offered the crown to Richard purported to be representative of the three estates of the realm, and that the Londoners stood for the third estate. Mancini noted that the offer was made

---

[1] Hall's *Chronicle*, pp. 364 seq.   [2] *Rot. Parl.* vi. 240.

by the peers, the heads of the clergy, and the people of London and, for the benefit of his foreign patron, he added an explanatory comment: 'all important matters are deliberated and decrees made law by these three classes of men who they call the three estates'.[1] For nearly two centuries the claim to speak in the name of the estates of the realm, out of parliament, had proved a useful device to revolutionaries well aware of the difficulty of parliamentary action in such circumstances. In 1327, in 1399, and even in 1461, a case could be made for the deposing and electing bodies as in some sense representative of the estates of the realm: but when a party caucus of magnates, supported by some reluctant Londoners, took upon itself to speak for the estates, the cynicism of the device was self-evident and even a servile parliament had to admit its dubious character. No pretence of lip-service to a representative principle could serve to conceal the truth, succinctly stated by Polydore Vergil, that Richard III 'without assent of the commonaltie, by might and will of certaine noblemen of his faction, enjoyned the realme, contrary to the law of God and man'.[2]

Throughout the Middle Ages London takes a prominent part in every political crisis touching the succession. In Saxon times, and to some extent afterwards, this prominence derives from her position as England's first port, as the gateway to the continent of Europe. The post-Conquest period sees an immense development in the civic consciousness of the Londoners, leading them to emulate the privileges of foreign communes and to claim for themselves baronial rank. In the twelfth century London becomes, as never before, the true capital of England and her support proves indispensable to any pretender seeking recognition of his title. This position is never wholly lost: but as the urban population of the country increases and with it the concept of the nation as a congeries of 'estates', London's status tends to become rather that of *primus inter pares* than of *regina totius regionis*. She takes her place as a member, albeit a leading member, of the estate of the commons and a healthy caution prevents her responsible authorities from claiming in the fourteenth century the type of unique privilege which they were ready enough

[1] *Usurpation of Richard III*, ed. C. A. J. Armstrong, p. 119.

[2] Polydore Vergil, p. 187. At the time of writing this essay I was unfortunately unaware of the valuable material contained in Mr. C. A. J. Armstrong's paper on 'The Inauguration Ceremonies of the Yorkist Kings and their Title to the Throne', read to the Royal Historical Society on 10 May 1947. I am greatly indebted to Mr. Armstrong for his kindness in allowing me to read his paper in proof.

to assert in the twelfth. Only as the Middle Ages draw to their close and London, almost alone of English cities, increases and prospers despite the economic dislocation of the mid-fifteenth century, does she recover, for a time, something of her old ascendancy. In 1461 the pro-Yorkist sentiments of her citizens are strong enough for them to venture to speak for the Commons of England: but in 1483 they do so with reluctance and with such ill success that the experiment is unlikely to be repeated.

It seems that the Londoners have a dual role to play in these succession crises. The ancient idea of popular acclamation gradually loses its force after the Conquest, and in normal times it survives only in the formalized *collaudatio* of the Coronation Order. But when England is faced with a disputed succession, still more when she is faced with revolution, it is necessary to ensure that the acclamation shall have a spontaneous character. It is impossible to defer it till the king is crowned: his title must be popularly acknowledged at the earliest opportunity. By reason of their numbers, their notorious susceptibility to propaganda, and the geographical position of their city, the Londoners are those most evidently fitted to give the genuine *collaudatio*. The shouts of a London crowd, more than of any other single group, can convey the impression that the *populus* is clamouring for the removal of one ruler and the substitution of another. The impression may be most misleading, for the Londoners are often out of accord with the rest of the nation: but it gives the promoters of dynastic revolution the covering they need. Yet these astute and ruthless schemers were never content to put their whole trust in the plaudits of the mob. Their plans demanded some assurance that the wealth, power, and influence of the great city merchants would also be at their disposal. Thus in every such crisis we find that some kind of official recognition from the civic authorities is demanded and obtained. Without it no revolution could hope for success. Medieval England was primarily a land of rural communities and even her capital evinced little of the political vitality or civic independence of the great cities of the Continent. Yet those rulers who impinged too far on her 'liberties' seldom failed to regret their action: and, though the architects of successful revolution were undoubtedly the magnates, London was the foundation stone on which they found themselves constrained to build.

M. McKisack

RICHARD THE FIRST'S ALLIANCES
WITH THE GERMAN PRINCES IN 1194

THE alliances formed by Richard I with the German princes, and especially with the princes of the Low Countries after his release from captivity on 2 February 1194, are of fundamental importance in that phase of English foreign policy which ended disastrously at the battle of Bouvines in 1214. They were, of course, directed against France, but they had after 1197 another aim, closely connected with the first and scarcely less important to Richard—the promotion of his nephew Otto IV's candidature for the empire. The subject has been often and fully discussed,[1] and modern historians have unhesitatingly endorsed the judgement of contemporaries that Richard failed to honour the engagements into which he then entered. Evidence which has recently become available has, however, led me to adopt a more favourable view of the king's conduct.

Our information about these alliances comes from two reliable and well-informed chroniclers: the English historian, Roger of Hoveden,[2] who was singularly well acquainted with what was happening on the Continent, and Gilbert of Mons,[3] the chancellor of the count of Hainault. Both writers tell us that Richard entered into agreements with certain German princes who did homage and fealty in return for promises of annual rents. The lists of these princes are as follows:

Hoveden	*Gilbert of Mons*
Archbishop of Mainz	
Archbishop of Cologne	Archbishop of Cologne
Bishop-elect of Liége	Bishop-elect of Liége
Duke of Austria	
Duke of Louvain	Duke of Louvain
Marquis of Montferrat	
Duke of Limburg	Duke of Limburg
Duke of Swabia	
Count palatine of the Rhine	
Son of the count of Hainault	
Count of Holland	
'and many others'	

[1] It has been treated in the greatest detail by W. Kienast, *Die deutschen Fürsten im Dienste der Westmächte*, i (1924), 135 ff. For the general background see Sir Maurice Powicke's admirable survey in chap. iv of his *Loss of Normandy*, especially pp. 139–42. [2] *Chronica*, ed. Stubbs, iii. 234.
[3] *Chronicon Hanoniense*, ed. Vanderkindere, pp. 284–5.

Besides homage and fealty these princes were to give aid to Richard against the king of France in return for the promised annual rents; and Gilbert adds that Richard agreed to render help to the duke of Louvain in his war with the count of Flanders and Hainault and the marquis of Namur. 'These covenants', he then comments, 'were in no way observed; and no wonder, since the king of England never kept faith or pact with anyone, nor were all those named, with whom he confirmed treaties, accustomed to observe their covenants.' When in 1198 Richard, as a distinguished member of the empire (*sicut praecipuum membrum imperii*), was summoned to Germany to take part in the imperial election, he sent four representatives, fearing to go himself, as Hoveden says,[1] without a safe conduct. 'And no wonder; for he had not paid what he had promised to give to the magnates of the land for his release.' This, while in part corroborating the statement of Gilbert, suggests that some of these princes were to have received their money as rewards for their assistance in obtaining Richard's liberation. This is made more probable by the fact that no less than seven of the eleven princes, namely the archbishops of Mainz and Cologne, the bishop-elect of Liége, the dukes of Austria, Swabia, and Louvain, and the count palatine of the Rhine, rendered valuable service by acting as sureties that the terms of the release would be carried out.[2]

Recent historians, as I have said, have accepted without question the verdict of these contemporary chroniclers. Thus Alexander Cartellieri writes:[3] 'it was fortunate for Philip Augustus that Richard did not pay the money to the German princes', and Kienast comments[4] that the princes received not a penny from these covenants except the marquis of Montferrat. It is the purpose of this paper to show that these statements of contemporary and modern historians do less than justice to the good faith of King Richard, and that they are, at least in part, contradicted by the evidence of documents.

When Richard reached England in the spring of 1194, he and his justiciar, Hubert Walter, were faced with the task of raising the enormous sum of 150,000 marks for the ransom. All the resources of the kingdom had to be strained to the utmost to secure anything approaching the required amount. In these

---

[1] Hoveden, iv. 37–8.   [2] Ibid. iii. 232.
[3] *Philipp II August, König von Frankreich*, iii. 72, 174.
[4] Op. cit. i. 141. The latest writer who mentions the episode, Michel Sczaniecki, *Essai sur les Fiefs-Rentes* (1946), p. 134, merely cites the view of Kienast. On the marquis of Montferrat see below, p. 98.

circumstances it was obviously not possible for the king immediately to meet all his financial commitments. Similarly the allied princes on their side showed no inclination to fulfil their part of the bargain by active measures against France, as Gilbert of Mons admits. In the course of the next two or three years, moreover, several of the contracting princes were dead and the political situation so radically altered (especially by the sudden death of the Emperor Henry VI in 1197) that some readjustment of personal relationships became necessary. Nevertheless, in spite of all difficulties, the king took steps immediately to carry out at least some of his engagements.

Let us consider first the four princes mentioned both by Hoveden and by Gilbert of Mons—the archbishop of Cologne, the bishop-elect of Liége, and the dukes of Louvain and Limburg. The Emperor Henry VI was not unnaturally particularly anxious, as Gilbert observes,[1] that Richard should be on friendly terms with these four princes, who among them controlled the route between the coast and Germany, between Antwerp and Cologne, along which the ransom money would have to pass. A special importance, therefore, is attached to them.

Adolf of Altena, archbishop of Cologne, received his pension at once. It consisted of a rent of £38 per annum charged on the manor of Soham in Cambridgeshire. The rent for the half-year March to September 1194 is entered on the Pipe Roll of 6 Richard I[2] as paid to Adam the butler (*pincerna*) of the archbishop of Cologne, who continued to receive it on behalf of his master with fair regularity till March 1200.[3] Another rent of £20 a year charged on the manor of Brampton in Huntingdonshire is paid from the year 1194 to a certain Lambert of Cologne,[4] who, I am inclined to think, was also an agent of the archbishop; for on two occasions in 1195 and 1196 he receives the rent of Soham as well as that of Brampton,[5] and the payment of both rents ceases at approximately the same time.[6] He evidently belonged to the official rather than the commercial class, for he is called to warrant in a *mort d'ancestor* case concerning lands at Brampton,[7] and is

---

[1] p. 288.   [2] p. 76.
[3] *Pipe Roll 2 Jo.*, p. 163.
[4] *Pipe Roll 6 Ric. I*, p. 76.
[5] *Pipe Roll 7 Ric. I*, p. 119, and *8 Ric. I*, p. 275.
[6] The rent of Brampton ceases in December 1200 (*Pipe Roll 3 Jo.*, p. 120). The stoppage of payments was probably due to the clause in the treaty of Le Goulet (22 May 1200) by which John pledged himself to render no assistance to Otto IV. *Foedera* (Record Commission), i. 80.
[7] *Curia Regis Rolls*, i. 80.

associated with other officials such as John Lupus, the chamberlain of the emperor, and Conrad, the seneschal of Otto IV.[1] It therefore appears that the archbishop of Cologne for the years 1194–1200 was normally in receipt of a pension amounting to £58 a year.

Simon, bishop-elect of Liége, a boy of sixteen years old, was not destined to become bishop or personally to exercise any influence on the political situation. His election in October 1193 was the work of his father, the duke of Limburg, and of his cousin, the duke of Brabant; and it was only confirmed by the Emperor Henry VI in order to facilitate the passage of the ransom through the extensive territories attached to the see.[2] But on the appeal of his opponent Albert of Cuyk, the election was quashed in November 1194 by Pope Celestine III, who compensated the youth by making him a cardinal. He died, however, at Rome on 1 August 1195, and never had an opportunity to enter into Richard I's scheme of alliances.

Simon's father, Duke Henry III of Limburg, undoubtedly received a fief from Richard I. The evidence for this comes from a letter written by King John to the duke himself on 24 May 1212:

'We give thanks to you in that you have signified to us by the count of Boulogne that, if we should restore to you the fief which our brother the lord king Richard gave you, you would willingly come to our fealty and service and would do homage to us as to your liege lord for that fief against all men.'[3]

A safe-conduct for the duke and his escort was granted about the same time,[4] and in the following September he duly arrived in England where he spent four days (at Dunstable, St. Albans, and London[5]) and was paid a whole year in full of his fee of 400 marks.[6] When this was granted by Richard and when the payments ceased we have no means of knowing; but the business of the duke's messenger, who spent fifteen days in England in 1197–8, was doubtless connected with the payment of his master's pension.[7]

Henry I, duke of Brabant or, as he is always called in English

[1] Cf. *Pipe Roll 10 Ric. I*, p. 161; *Rot. Lit. Pat.*, p. 85 (1208). John Lupus had rents in the neighbouring manor of Alconbury (Hunts.).

[2] Gilbert of Mons, p. 288.

[3] *Foedera* (Record Commission), i. 106.

[4] *Rot. Lit. Pat.*, p. 92*b*.

[5] Seemingly 19–22 Sept. 1212. *Rot. Misae 14 Jo.*, ed. Cole, p. 242.

[6] 'Duci de Lamburg infeodato ibidem de feodo suo de anno integro . . . summa cccc m.' Ibid.

[7] *Pipe Roll 10 Ric. I*, p. 167.

records, duke of Louvain, was the most active and influential member of the group. He was on friendly terms with Richard, and, after the latter's release, accompanied him to Louvain and thence to Brussels; and it was from Antwerp in the duke's territory that Richard embarked for Swine on his way to England.[1] He received a prompt if trifling payment on account for his services. The sum of £13. 8s. ½d. was paid to Goscelin the seneschal of the duke of Louvain for the term of St. John (Easter to midsummer) 1194 from the rents of Kirton (Lincs.), Bampton (Oxon.), and Dunham (Notts.), manors of the great honour of Boulogne which was then in the king's hand.[2] To the lands of this honour the duke had certain pretensions which, according to Gilbert of Mons, Richard had agreed to recognize.[3] Renaud of Dammartin, count of Boulogne, and he had married respectively Ida and Matilda, the daughters and co-heiresses of Mary, the daughter of King Stephen, and Mathew, count of Boulogne, the younger brother of Philip of Alsace, count of Flanders.[4] But there were inevitable delays in bringing about a settlement of the claims of the two heiresses. Renaud, who had obtained possession of the county of Boulogne, was allied with Philip Augustus, and the duke of Louvain himself had not, it appears, openly broken off relations with the French king. Nevertheless, his representatives remained in England while negotiations proceeded. The expenses of one Reiner of Louvain[5] (who may perhaps be identified with Reiner de Werc the valet and messenger of the duke of Louvain in later years[6]) were paid on the account of 1194; and in the next two years small payments for clothes and other necessaries were made to Richard, clerk of the duke of Louvain.[7]

In the summer of 1197 the duke of Brabant departed on crusade, and when he returned a year later the political situation had been rendered more complicated by the unexpected death of the Emperor Henry VI (28 September 1197) and the election of rival

[1] G. Smets, *Henri I duc de Brabant* (1908), pp. 66–7.

[2] *Pipe Roll 6 Ric. I*, p. 7. He received £3. 8s. 4d. from the rent of Kirton, £6. os. 4½d. from Bampton, and £3. 19s. 4d. from Dunham. The full rent of these manors, respectively £200, £61, and £60, had been paid either to the count of Boulogne or to the count of Flanders during most of the reign of Henry II.

[3] 'et insuper duci Lovaniensi quandam terram in Anglia, quam Matheus comes Boloniensis, pater uxoris sue, reclamaverat, in feodo reddidit'. *Chron. Hanoniense*, p. 285.

[4] For the descent of the honour of Boulogne see J. H. Round, *Studies in Peerage and Family History*, chap. iii.

[5] *Pipe Roll 6 Ric. I*, p. 7.

[6] *Rot. Misae 14 Jo.*, ed. Cole, pp. 245, 259.

[7] *Pipe Roll 7 Ric. I*, p. 28; *8 Ric. I*, p. 20.

candidates for the imperial crown. Philip Augustus supported the Hohenstaufen, Philip of Swabia, while Richard I vigorously promoted the cause of his favourite nephew, Otto IV of Brunswick, whom he had recently (1196) created count of Poitou. The duke of Brabant was already committed to adopt the side of Otto. He had always been prone towards the English alliance, and, while he was still absent, his wife Matilda acting for him had betrothed their daughter Mary to Otto on the day of, or the day before, his coronation (12 July 1198).[1] It seems probable that it was also in his absence that the settlement of his claim to lands in England was determined; for in the course of this year the great honour of Eye in Suffolk, which was reckoned at 90½ knight's fees[2] and was valued at £131. 7s. 6d. per annum,[3] was granted to the duchess of Louvain. In the roll rendered at Michaelmas 1198 there is an entry for the farm of Eye for the half year *antequam daretur ducisse Luuanie.*[4] It would appear, therefore, that the grant took effect from Easter 1198. The duke regarded his new acquisition as of sufficient importance to be included among his titles. So in a charter contained in the cartulary of Wymondham Abbey he styles himself 'Henricus dei gracia dux Lotharingie marchio Romani imperii et dominus honoris Eye'.[5] A year's truce with France expired in September 1198, and it was doubtless before the renewal of hostilities that the duke with other nobles of France and the Low Countries formally broke off relations with Philip Augustus and joined the English alliance.[6]

Baldwin, son of the count of Hainault, is mentioned in Hove-

---

[1] Böhmer-Ficker, *Regesta Imperii*, v, no. 198 *i*; Winkelmann, *Philipp von Schwaben und Otto IV von Braunschweig*, i. 84; Smets, op. cit., p. 86. The bride was then seven years old. The marriage did not take place till 1214.

[2] The scutage on the honour, when assessed at 2 marks on the fee, was 181 marks (*Pipe Roll 1 Jo.*, p. 291; *3 Jo.*, p. 140). The statement in the *Book of Fees* (p. 138) that 'of that honour there are 80 knights' is therefore inaccurate.

[3] *Pipe Roll 7 Ric. I*, p. 79.

[4] *Pipe Roll 10 Ric. I*, p. 94. The editor of the roll (p. xvii) considers that the grant was made to the duchess rather than to the duke because it was in her that the hereditary claim lay. But it was the duke who was enfeoffed with the honour, who administered it, and was responsible for the scutage. It seems to me, therefore, that it was granted to the duchess because she was acting for her husband during his absence on crusade.

[5] British Museum, MS. Cotton Titus C. viii, f. 67*d*, cited ibid., p. xvii.

[6] Hoveden, iv. 54. The decisive event may well have been the treaty which Philip Augustus made with Philip of Swabia on 29 June 1198 (*M.G.H. Const.* ii. 1). The duke's brother-in-law, Renaud of Dammartin, count of Boulogne, joined the English alliance at the same time and was put into possession of the manors of Kirton, Bampton, and Dunham. He received the rents for the second half of the fiscal year 1197–8. *Pipe Roll 10 Ric. I*, pp. 44, 111, 189.

den's list of the princes who did homage to Richard I in 1194.[1] His father, the reigning count, Baldwin V of Hainault and VIII of Flanders, was a supporter of Philip Augustus and at bitter enmity with the Brabantine party in the Low Countries. Indeed the compact of 1194 between Richard and the duke of Brabant was, as Gilbert of Mons informs us,[2] particularly directed against the elder Baldwin. But in the summer of that year the duke was defeated and peace was made in May or June 1195 at Rupelmonde. This peace was negotiated by the younger Baldwin, who on the death of his mother, Margaret of Flanders, in the preceding autumn (15 November 1194) had in his own right become count of Flanders. By his father's death on 18 December 1195 he became count of Hainault as well.[3] By his action in 1194 he had shown himself favourably disposed towards England. Moreover, he bore a grudge against Philip Augustus, whose recent annexation of Artois was neither forgotten nor forgiven. Now that he was ruler of the united counties of Flanders and Hainault and at peace with his powerful neighbour, the duke of Brabant, we might reasonably expect him to throw his weight openly and energetically on the side of England. But on the contrary he remained on friendly terms with his French overlord, and in April 1196 even entered into a close alliance with him. This alliance, however, did not endure. The prosperity of the Flemish towns was being crippled by the economic pressure increasingly exerted by England during these years of hostility.[4] Their merchants had their goods confiscated[5] and some were themselves imprisoned;[6] an embargo was laid on the export of wool[7] and heavy amercements were imposed on those who ventured to send grain and other commodities to Flanders.[8] An embassy composed of William the Marshal and Peter des Préaux, who received 1,730 marks 'for carrying out the king's business in Flanders',[9] was dispatched in the summer of 1197, and the count was soon brought to terms. A treaty, which in the following September was solemnly

---

[1] Above, p. 90.   [2] p. 285.
[3] Cf. Cartellieri, *Philipp II. August*, iii. 147 ff.; Kienast, *Die deutschen Fürsten*, pp. 143 ff.
[4] For an excellent survey of the interrelations, political and economic, of England, France, and Flanders, see Gaston G. Dept, *Les Influences Anglaise et Française dans le Comté de Flandre au début du XIIIme Siècle* (1928).
[5] *Pipe Roll 7 Ric. I*, pp. 25, 81, 106; *10 Ric. I*, p. 183.
[6] *Pipe Roll 9 Ric. I*, p. 226. They were taken in the market of Lynn.
[7] *Chancellor's Roll 8 Ric. I*, p. 237.
[8] *Pipe Roll 10 Ric. I*, pp. 92, 137, 182, 209. Cf. Introd., p. xv.
[9] *Pipe Roll 10 Ric. I*, p. 172.

ratified in the presence of numerous and distinguished witnesses, was concluded whereby each party agreed to make no peace with the king of France without the consent of the other.[1] For this the count of Flanders was richly rewarded. He is said to have received 5,000 marks,[2] though the payment is not recorded in the accounts of the exchequer. But what is more interesting and more relevant to our present inquiry than the sum he obtained for his desertion of Philip Augustus is the fact that King Richard seems to have considered that something was due to him in respect of the original contract entered into in 1194. In the accounts for the financial year ending at Michaelmas 1197 there is the following entry: 'Et castellano de Gant et aliis nuntiis comitis Flandr' xliiii li. et x s. ad perficiendum ipsi comiti areragium feodi sui trium annorum. et comiti de Hano duorum annorum. per breve eiusdem.'[3] Siger, son Arnoul of Guines, was castellan of Ghent from 1190 to 1200,[4] and his expenses with those of other messengers and of the count himself in the settlement of this business were paid on the Norman account.[5] The curious expression 'for payment of the arrears of his fee to the count of Flanders for three years and to the count of Hainault for two years' can only be explained by the fact that, as already stated, Baldwin became count of Flanders in 1194 and count of Hainault a year later in 1195. It is evident, therefore, that as soon as the count fulfilled his side of the bargain, Richard redeemed the promise he had made in 1194 and paid up what was due to him.

No payment is recorded in the English accounts to Dietrich VII, count of Holland, the last member of the Low Country group mentioned by Hoveden. But he at least showed his leanings towards the Anglo-Welf party by giving his support to Otto IV at whose coronation he was present.[6]

The remaining princes may be dealt with very briefly. They were not greatly concerned in the struggle between England and France; and, as suggested above, the rewards promised by Richard I may have been in respect of their services in helping

---

[1] *Foedera* (Record Commission), i. 67. For the date (8 Sept. 1197) see Stapleton, *Rot. Scacc. Norm.*, II, p. lxxiii.

[2] Hoveden, iv. 20.

[3] *Pipe Roll 9 Ric. I*, p. 164. There is a further payment of 20 marks 'ad perficiendum areragium feodi comitis Flandr''. Ibid., p. 62.

[4] Gilbert of Mons, p. 266, n. 4.

[5] The count received £100 and his messengers £3. 14s. 7d. *Rot. Scacc. Norm.*, ii. 303, 307.

[6] Cf. O. Oppermann, *Untersuchungen zur Nordniederländischen Geschichte des 10. bis 13. Jahrhunderts*, Part II, pp. 36 ff.

to obtain his release. Three of them died very shortly after the agreement of February 1194 was made. Leopold II, duke of Austria, Richard's captor, received 4,000 marks of his share of the ransom before he died in the following December. Conrad of Rotenburg, duke of Swabia, the brother of the Emperor Henry VI, died in August 1196, and was succeeded by his younger brother Philip who, as marquis of Tuscany, was fully occupied with Italian affairs and had no dealings with England. Indeed, after his election to the empire in opposition to Otto IV in March 1198, he became England's official enemy. Conrad, the count palatine of the Rhine, was the brother of the Emperor Frederick Barbarossa. In the winter of 1193–4 his daughter and heiress married Henry of Saxony, the eldest surviving son of Henry the Lion (and thus nephew of Richard I) who was recognized as his successor; in fact he became count palatine on his father-in-law's death in 1195. Like his brothers, Otto IV and William, he had spent much time in his youth at the English court and remained on terms of intimate friendship with his uncle Richard. In 1197 he went on crusade, and on his return in 1198 was honourably received by Richard at Les Andelys.[1] It is doubtful whether the money fief and the lands which he later claimed in England relate to any previous transaction with Richard I. He visited England in 1209 and was granted 1,000 marks *de dono et de feodo suo*[2] and did homage to King John for certain lands which he claimed.[3] When he returned to Germany he left his son and namesake to be brought up in England.[4]

Boniface, marquis of Montferrat, who afterwards became famous as the leader of the fourth crusade, is included in Hoveden's list. It is difficult to understand why this north Italian magnate should enter into Richard's scheme of alliances. He does not appear as one of the princes who helped to obtain Richard's release, nor was he concerned in Richard's struggle with Philip Augustus. Yet he alone of these eleven princes is generally admitted by historians to have received his pension.[5] In 1198, when he was vigorously making war against a league of

[1] Hoveden, iv. 55; *Rot. Scacc. Norm.*, pp. 448, cxlix.

[2] *Rot. Lit. Pat.*, 89b. The payment of his pension (*de feodo suo*) for the year 1211–12 (500 marks) is entered on the *Misae Roll 14 Jo.*, ed. Cole, p. 238.

[3] 'Dux Saxoniae, Henricus, nepos regis Angliae, venit in Angliam, et facto homagio domino regi de quibusdam terris quas petiit . . . .' 'Annals of Worcester', *Annales monastici*, iv. 397.

[4] Ibid. The boy's personal expenses are entered on the *Misae Roll 11 Jo.*, ed. Duffus Hardy, *passim*.

[5] Powicke, *Loss of Normandy*, p. 141 n.; Kienast, op. cit., p. 141.

Lombard cities, he received from the Norman Exchequer £800 angevin *de feodo suo* besides a further gift of £26. 13*s*. 4*d*.[1] As the series of Norman Exchequer rolls is fragmentary, it is impossible to say whether Boniface received his fee before or again after that year.

Conrad of Wittelsbach, archbishop of Mainz, Hoveden properly places at the head of his list of German princes. He was the most influential, the most highly esteemed man of his time. 'There is no one after the pope either in the Roman church or in the Roman empire', Innocent III wrote to him, 'who has reached such a high position as you have done in both.'[2] He is the one man in those turbulent times who sought to do his duty as primate and statesman regardless of profit or self-interest. He went on crusade in 1197 and on his return did everything in his power to mediate in the German Civil War. He may well have used his influence at the meeting held in his city of Mainz from 2 to 4 February 1194 in order to bring about Richard's release; but it is extremely improbable that he would stoop to becoming one of Richard's pensioners.

AUSTIN L. POOLE

[1] *Rot. Scacc. Norm.*, p. 301. Stapleton, ibid., p. xiv, suggests that he was serving in Richard's army in France. But his activities in Italy at this time are abundantly recorded. See Böhmer-Ficker, *Regesta Imperii*, nos. 12136, 12147–8, 12150, 12152, 12159, 12161, 12174, 12182.

[2] *Registrum de negotio imperii* (Migne, *Pat. Lat.*, 216), no. 22.

THE ALLEGED DEPOSITION OF KING JOHN

THE protracted trial of strength between King John and Pope Innocent III has been so often studied that one might suppose that the events would have been clarified long since.[1] But just as, a few years ago, Dr. Knowles showed that the beginnings of this struggle are usually misrepresented,[2] so we find that its ending is still not clear. Modern historians generally agree that after John was excommunicated personally in November 1209, and after negotiations had broken down in the summer of 1211, the pope proceeded to release John's subjects from obedience and invited, or rather exhorted, Philip Augustus to come and take the English crown by force. Sometimes the release from obedience and the offer of the crown to Philip are represented as two distinct stages, sometimes the latter act is apparently deemed to include the former. The modern narratives do not agree in detail and often they are a trifle vague; but they mostly concur in telling us how Innocent III delivered a formal sentence of deposition in the winter of 1212–13 and bade Philip Augustus execute that sentence.[3] The dissentients among modern scholars are few,[4] but it is the object of this essay to amplify and justify their reasons for dissent.

---

[1] I am obliged to Professor V. H. Galbraith for reading this paper in manuscript and making valuable comments.

[2] 'The Canterbury Election of 1205–6', *Eng. Hist. Rev.* liii (1938), 211–20.

[3] Stubbs in *Memoriale fr. Walteri de Coventria* (Rolls series, 1872), II. lviii–lix; Paul Meyer in *Hist. de Guillaume le Maréchal* (Soc. Hist. France, 1891–1901), iii. 200, n. 3; C. Petit-Dutaillis, *Étude sur la vie et le règne de Louis VIII* (1894), pp. 35–7, and *La Monarchie féodale* (1933), p. 252; C. Bémont, *Chartes des libertés anglaises* ('Collection de textes . . .', 1892), p. xvii; Kate Norgate, *John Lackland* (1902), pp. 161, 167–8, 175; Else Gütschow, *Innocenz III und England* (1904), p. 164; G. B. Adams, *Hist. of England 1066–1216* (1905), p. 422; A. Luchaire, *Innocent III: les royautés vassales du s. siège* (1908), pp. 212–21; W. S. McKechnie, *Magna carta* (2nd ed., 1914), pp. 24–6; A. Cartellieri, *Philipp II. August*, iv (1921–2), 341–2; F. M. Powicke, *Stephen Langton* (1929), p. 78, and in *Camb. Med. Hist.* vi (1929), 317; S. Painter, *William Marshal* (1933), p. 175; W. E. Lunt, *Fin. relations of the Papacy with England to 1327* (1939), p. 134; J. Haller, *Das Papsttum*, II. ii (1939), 383.

[4] J. H. Ramsay, *The Angevin Empire* (1903), pp. 430–1, 436–9; H. W. C. Davis, *England under the Normans and Angevins* (7th ed., 1921), p. 367 (but cf. p. 369); H. Tillmann, *Die päpstl. Legaten in England* (1926), p. 96, n. 130. Professor Powicke implied some doubt about the version of events which he had accepted elsewhere, in reviewing volume v of Carlyle's *Med. Pol. Theory in the West* (*Eng. Hist. Rev.* xliv (1929), 299), when he wrote: 'Innocent III . . . threatened to depose John of England.'

We need not be surprised that historians say that John was deposed, for a mass of contemporary or sub-contemporary witnesses said so; but it is a little surprising that historians have not been more concerned about the difficulty of accepting this testimony. The evidence for John's deposition comes entirely from chroniclers, and they vary; no record material of any kind has been adduced in support. In reconsidering the matter we shall do best to let the chroniclers speak first, then note their inconsistencies, and finally confront them with the evidence of records.

No chronicler implies that, when sentence of excommunication on John was published in the churches of northern France, this specifically released his subjects from obedience or included any incitement to revolt.[1] Although the excommunication of a ruler in a Christian country would, strictly interpreted, make his position untenable and although canonists inferred that the pope's right to excommunicate kings gave him the right to depose them,[2] the canon law was careful to provide for occasions when it was expedient for the faithful to co-operate with excommunicates,[3] and cases in which a ruler was excommunicated without being deposed are too common to need enumeration. In condemning Otto IV, it is true, Innocent III speaks of excommunicate and tyrannical rulers as being unable lawfully to exercise jurisdiction;[4] but perhaps Otto's offence was greater than John's, for Otto had encroached on the Patrimony of St. Peter whereas John had not; and, as Innocent once told the king of Portugal, God particularly dislikes attacks on the rights of the Apostolic See.[5]

We may assume, then, that the pope did not, when he excom-

---

[1] Innocent's letter threatening John with excommunication, in Jan. 1209, does not state the temporal consequences of anathema, though we may find a veiled threat in the words: 'adhuc cum altissimi adiutorio contra te multipliciter processuri, si nec sic tuum corrigere festinaris errorem.' *Reg.*, lib. xi, ep. 211; Migne, *Pat. lat.* 215, col. 1528.

[2] See R. W. and A. J. Carlyle, *Med. Pol. Theory in the West*, i. 278–80, ii. 204–6, v. 161–2.

[3] Cf. Gregory VII in *Decretum*, ii. 11, 3, 103; Innocent III in *Decretales*, v. 39, 30.

[4] 'Cum tales legitime nequeant iurisdictionis officium exercere ab unitate fidelium separati.' *Reg.*, lib. xv, ep. 31; Migne, 216, col. 566. Cf. *Reg. super neg. imp.*, ep. 21 (Migne, 216, col. 1019): 'Unde iuxta sanctorum patrum canonicas sanctiones ei qui talis [i.e. excommunicatus] existit non obstante iuramento fidelitatis est obsequium subtrahendum', and Honorius III in *Decretales*, v. 37, 13. See also the letter threatening interdict on England. *Reg.*, lib. x, ep. 113; Migne, 215, col. 1209.

[5] 'Qui, etsi de aliarum ecclesiarum iniuriis graviter offendatur, tanto gravius adversus eos qui apostolicae sedis iura illicite detinent commovetur, quanto fortius peccare videntur qui eius quae caput est omnium et magistra non sine praesumptione sacrilega jura invadere non formidant.' *Reg.*, lib. i, ep. 448; Migne, 214, col. 425.

municated John, declare him to be deposed. Whether subsequently and in secret he advised the king's subjects to withdraw
allegiance or to depose John by a formal constitutional act[1] is a
question which cannot be answered; the question now under
discussion is whether the pope himself, by virtue of his plenitude
of power, ever passed sentence of deposition on John.

A papal sentence of deposition (as it may for convenience be
described) usually took the form of a statement that the pope
absolves the ruler's subjects from fealty and forbids them to obey
him.[2] Rarely was emphasis laid on the ruler's loss of office.[3] In
the political theory of the time there was doubtless a distinction
between release from obedience and deprivation of office;[4] but
if the two acts had different theoretic origins, they were both
designed to nullify the ruler's authority and were equally acts of
supreme papal power. After either act the pope withheld from
the ruler the title of his office.[5]

The earliest occasion on which, on any showing, Innocent III
deposed King John was when the nuncios Pandulf and Durand
met the king at Northampton on 29 or 30 August 1211.[6] Most of
our sources confine themselves to saying that negotiations broke
down, either because John refused to pay damages to the exiled
bishops or because he argued about his royal dignity. The *Annals
of Burton*, on the other hand, know all about it and are able to
give a verbatim report of the discussion between king and nuncio.[7]
A violent argument culminated in a declaration by Pandulf, of
which the crucial words are: 'We absolve, from to-day onwards,

---

[1] On the theoretical rights of the subjects in this respect see Carlyle, op. cit. v.
112–19 and F. Kern, *Kingship and Law* (trans. S. B. Chrimes, 1939), pp. 83, 86–8.
Langton's view is expressed in a letter of 1207: *Gervase of Canterbury*, ii, p. lxxxii,
and Powicke, *Stephen Langton*, p. 97.

[2] e.g. Alexander III on Frederick Barbarossa, 4 Apr. 1160 (Migne, 200, col. 90);
Innocent III on Otto IV, 22 Dec. 1210 (*Reg.*, lib. xiii, ep. 193; Migne, 216, col.
361, cf. P. Hinschius, *System des kath. Kirchenrechts*, v (1895), 46, n. 8); Gregory IX
on Frederick II, 20 Aug. 1228 (*M.G.H. Epp. saec. xiii*, i (1883), 399); Boniface VIII
on Philip IV, 8 Sept. 1303 (A. Baillet, *Hist. des démêlez du pape Boniface VIII avec
Philippe le Bel* (1718), p. 388).

[3] Gregory VII, passing sentence on Henry IV (1076), said: 'Heinrico . . . totius
regni Teutonicorum et Italiae gubernacula contradico' (*Registrum*, ed. E. Caspar, i.
270); Innocent IV, denouncing Frederick II (1245) said: 'memoratum principem . . .
ne regnet vel imperet, est abiectus' (*M.G.H. Leg.*, sect. iv, *Const.* ii. 512).

[4] Cf. Carlyle, op. cit. v. 116.

[5] See below, p. 112.

[6] Annales S. Albani (*Ungedruckte anglo-norm. Geschichtsquellen*, ed. F. Liebermann (1879), p. 169) say, 'iiii kl. Septembris', while the Waverley annals (*Annales
monastici* (Rolls Series), ii. 268) say: 'die Martis proxima post festum S. Bartho-
lomaei' (wrongly *s.a.* 1212, cf. ibid., p. 266).

[7] *Ann. mon.* i. 209–17.

the earls, barons, knights, clerks, and lay freemen and all Christians in the lands subject to you, from the fealty and homage by which they are bound to you. . . . The Lord pope proposes to send his army into England.' Different but obviously related versions of the dialogue occur in the chronicles of two Cistercian abbeys as far apart as Waverley (Hants)[1] and Meaux (E. Riding, Yorks.).[2] Another Cistercian chronicle, from Margam in south Wales, and a Benedictine chronicle from Durham, describe Pandulf's visit in terms which suggest knowledge of the dialogue.[3] But in all these narratives we have evidently to do with a common literary tradition and not a number of unconnected writers independently recording an event of common knowledge.

The next witness to be called is Roger of Wendover. He describes the visit of Pandulf and Durand in words borrowed from the earlier Annals of St. Albans and he knows nothing of any absolving from fealty by Pandulf.[4] But he, alone among the chroniclers, tell us that

'in the same year Pope Innocent, since the English king, John, had scorned to accept the warnings of his nuncios, and being amazed beyond measure at his manifold contumacy, absolved from fealty and subjection to the king those kings and all others, great and small, who owed obedience to the crown of England; and he ordered all and sundry, strictly and under pain of excommunication, to shun King John carefully at board and council and assembly.'[5]

This action by the pope must be dated very late in 1211.

The annalists provide more evidence *s.a.* 1212 to support Wendover's account. The *Brut y Tywysogion* (probably of Cistercian origin) says:

'That year, Pope Innocent absolved the three princes, namely Llywelyn, son of Iorwerth, and Gwenwynwyn, and Maelgwn son of Rhys, from the

---

[1] *Ann. mon.*, ii. 268–71. This would appear to be a later addition to are cension of the chronicle which had already recorded the nuncios' mission briefly in its proper context on the preceding folio (p. 266).

[2] *Chronica mon. de Melsa* (Rolls Series, i. 387–9).

[3] *Ann. mon.* i. 30–1; *Hist. dunelm. scriptores tres* (Surtees Soc., 1839), pp. 26–7 (Geoffrey of Coldingham). Stubbs (*Gervase of Canterbury*, ii. 107, n. 1) speaks of the 'best and oldest account' of the nuncios' visit as being contained in the Cotton MS. Tiberius A. ix. He is apparently referring to the version of the dialogue given on ff. 49ʳ–51ʳ, and not to the brief notice recorded by the Osney chronicler in the same volume at f. 58ᵛ (printed, *Ann. mon.* iv. 55). A version of the dialogue is said to be contained in the episcopal register of John Gynwell, bishop of Lincoln, 1347–62 (W. E. Lunt, *Financial Relations*, p. 135, n. 4).

[4] Wendover, *Flores historiarum* (Eng. Hist. Soc., 1841), iii. 235–6; Annales S. Albani (loc. cit.), p. 169.

[5] Wendover, iii. 237.

oath of fealty which they had given to the king of England. And he commanded them, for the pardon of their sins, to give a sincere pledge of
warring against the iniquity of the king. And the interdict, which he had
ordered five years previously in England and Wales, was remitted by the
pope to the three princes afore-mentioned within their dominions, and to
all who were united with them. And they, with one consent, rose against
the king and bravely wrested from him the midland district which he had
previously taken from Llywelyn son of Iorwerth.'[1]

The *Annals of Waverley* (also Cistercian) say that

'in this year Wales was absolved from interdict and from the yoke of servi-
tude to John, king of England, and also received an order to attack him
with all their might, as one who behaved not as a son of Holy Church, but
as her enemy, abrogating his predecessors' laws.'[2]

Precisely the same story is told by the Barnwell chronicler, who
also reports the rumour that at a meeting of English magnates
a letter absolving them from allegiance was read.[3] The Bury
annalist has the same report of a letter,[4] and Wendover speaks of
the rumour without mentioning the letter.[5] Matthew Paris, in
his *Gesta abbatum*, says that some of the nobles began to rebel
against the king (now the open enemy of the lord pope and the
Church) by command of Pope Innocent III.[6]

The final stage of John's condemnation is most fully described
by Wendover, in the following terms:

'About this time [end of 1212] Stephen, archbishop of Canterbury,
William, bishop of London, and Eustace, bishop of Ely, went to Rome . . .
and humbly besought the lord pope to deign, of his pious mercy, to help
the English Church, now reduced as it seemed to the last extremity. Then
the pope, . . . with the advice of the cardinals, bishops and other wise men,
definitively decreed (*sententialiter definivit*) that John, the English king,
should be deposed from the throne and another, deemed more worthy,
should with the pope's help succeed him. And for the execution of this
sentence, the lord pope wrote to the mighty king of France, Philip, to the
effect that he should undertake this task for the remission of all his sins and
that, once the English king had been expelled from the throne, he and his
successors should possess the kingdom of England lawfully and in per-

---

[1] *Brut y Tywysogion* (Rolls Series), p. 273. Similarly, *s.a.* 1211, the related
'Cronica de Wallia', *Bull. Board of Celtic Studies, Univ. Wales*, xii (1946), p. 34.
[2] *Ann. mon.* ii. 268. The (later) Osney annals also say that the Welsh were
incited to rebel by the pope's order (ibid. iv. 56).
[3] *Memoriale fr. Walteri de Coventria*, ii. 206–7.
[4] *Ungedr. anglo-norm. Geschichtsquellen*, p. 154.
[5] Wendover, iii. 239. The *Historia anglicana* of Matthew Paris is a little more
explicit (Rolls Series, ii. 128); cf. the Worcester annals (*Ann. mon.* iv. 400).
[6] *Gesta abbatum S. Albani* (Rolls Series), i. 228.

petuity. He wrote, moreover, to all the magnates, knights and other warriors of diverse nations, to take the Cross to overthrow the English king and, by following the French king as their leader in this expedition, strive to avenge the injury done to the Universal Church. He ordered, furthermore, that all those who gave money or aid towards overthrowing this contumacious king should, like pilgrims to the Holy Sepulchre, rest secure in the peace of the Church, both temporally and spiritually.

'This done, the lord pope sent the sub-deacon Pandulf as his representative to France with the above-named archbishop and bishops, so that he could carry out in his presence all that has been described above. But Pandulf, when he was about to leave the pope and the others were absent, in a private interview asked what the pope wished to be done if perchance the English king showed the fruits of repentance and wanted to satisfy God and the Roman Church and the persons concerned in this business. Then the pope declared clearly to Pandulf a form of peace by assent to which the king might win the favour of the Apostolic See.'

Wendover goes on to describe the arrival of Pandulf and the prelates in France in January 1213, and the calling of a council in which the papal sentence and mandate were solemnly published to the French king, bishops, clergy, and people. Philip's levying of an army of invasion, to assemble on 21 April, is described as a direct consequence of this. John was frightened into submitting to the pope on 13 May, and Philip's invasion was thereupon prohibited by Pandulf.[1]

No other contemporary tells of this definitive sentence issued by advice of the cardinals and others, or of the council held in January 1213 in France. But support for Wendover's statement that Innocent invited Philip to conquer England is found in the Winchester–Waverley group of annals and the *Annals of St. Davids*;[2] the statement is also made in a later London chronicle[3] and in an addition made by the Lanercost chronicler to the words of the Melrose chronicle.[4] Corroboration from the Continent is

[1] Wendover, iii. 241–3, 246–8, 256–7. The *Historia anglicana* (ii. 129) gives a brief account which, though couched in different terms, is probably derived from Wendover.

[2] Winchester annals (*Ann. mon.* ii. 82): 'Philippus rex Francorum promissione domini papae . . . .' The 'Winton–Waverley' annals (*Ungedr. a.-n. Geschichtsquellen*, p. 186) reads *permissione* and the Waverley annals (*Ann. mon.* ii. 274) *ex praecepto*. The Annales Meneviae (*M.G.H. Scriptores*, xxvii. 443, cf. *Annales Cambriae* (Rolls Series), p. 69) also reads *ex praecepto* and perhaps derives from the Waverley source.

[3] *Liber de antiquis legibus* (Camden Soc., 1846), p. 201: *ad monitionem praedicti papae*.

[4] 'Philippus rex Francorum *ex praecepto domini papae* [Melrose omits] haud dubium *et* [Melrose *quin*] divina dispositione adversus *regem Angliae excitatus* [Melrose *eum*] cum omni impetu exercitus sui [Melrose adds *insurgens etiam*]

perhaps even more noteworthy. This is provided by William, abbot of Andres, in the county of Guînes (dep. Pas-de-Calais), whose contemporary chronicle is specially valuable for the events of the Flemish border in the early thirteenth century. The abbot describes Philip Augustus's preparations for invasion and Pandulf's order to him to desist, after John had made submission to the Church:

'Then the French king, who had first been aroused to do this by the authority of the Roman Curia, being afterwards impeded by the nuncio of the said Curia, altered his plans and led his whole army into Flanders.'[1]

One other author remains to be cited. The Barnwell chronicler who, under the year 1212, described the release of the Welsh from their allegiance to John as a fact and the release of John's English subjects as a rumour, begins the year 1213 with the statement that the exiled English bishops persuaded the pope to put an end to their ills: the pope 'wrote to the French king Philip and the princes of those regions to say that unless the English king straightway recovered his senses (*nisi . . . resipisceret*), they should deliver England from him with armed force'.[2]

If we conflate all this testimony, we shall put the first sentence of deposition (i.e. the release from allegiance) into the mouth of Pandulf in summer 1211. It was confirmed by the pope at the end of that year and repeated solemnly by him a year later, when he also deprived John of his office. Then Innocent III, who had already urged John's subjects to rebel in the early part of 1212, summoned Philip Augustus to lead an attack on the deposed monarch. But it is to be noted that, excepting the last act, the chief papal pronouncements in this story are each vouched for by one source or group of sources, and never by more than one. Moreover, the Barnwell chronicler, one of the most judicious and best informed of contemporary writers, expresses the pope's invitation to Philip II as conditional upon John's continued resistance.

Let us take the incidents one by one: first, the John–Pandulf

usque ad mare anglicum pervenerat.' (*Chronicon de Lanercost* (Bannatyne Club, 1839), p. 11; cf. *Chronicle of Melrose* (ed. A. O. and M. O. Anderson, 1936), p. 58, f. 30ᵛ). The line in *L'histoire de Guillaume le Maréchal*: *Quer pormise li ert la terre* (14498), does not say that *the pope* promised Philip the land of England, and may refer to Philip's alleged negotiations with the English magnates.

[1] *Recueil des hist. de la France*, xviii. 575. This is repeated in slightly different words by Jean Le Long, abbot of St. Bertin in the fourteenth century, in a passage of his chronicle which is evidently taken from William of Andres (*M.G.H. Scriptores*, xxv. 829–30, cf. p. 739).

[2] Walter of Coventry, ii. 209.

dialogue. Not only is this dialogue suspicious in unessentials— it is surely odd to find an Italian, who had never been in England before, lecturing the English king on the wickedness of William the Conqueror's laws—it is incompatible with other chronicles on the matter of excommunication. For Pandulf is made to say:

'You may know that the lord pope has excommunicated you, but the sentence was suspended until our arrival in these regions subject to you. Henceforth, however, you may know that you are excommunicated and the sentence passed on you has effect.'

Now we are told by three apparently independent chroniclers that sentence of excommunication on John was published solemnly in churches of northern France in November 1209,[1] and this was presumably not known by the composer of the dialogue. If Pandulf declared sentence in this dramatic fashion it is surprising that Roger of Wendover, who is so fully informed of later events, knew nothing about it. There are, as we shall soon see, other good reasons for regarding the whole thing as pure fiction.[2] Proceeding for the moment to compare the two sentences decreed by the pope, according to Wendover, late in 1211 and late in 1212 respectively, we may find it hard to understand why a year should separate these two acts. Modern historians have apparently found some difficulty in this, and the former sentence is usually not mentioned. But those who reject and those who believe the story of the acts of 1211 nearly all accept and give a full account of the deposition declared in December 1212 and the consequent invitation to Philip Augustus. There is only one source for the whole of this episode: Roger of Wendover. One may read the story in the English of Kate Norgate, the French of Charles Petit-

---

[1] Powicke, *Stephen Langton*, p. 77, citing Jean Le Long. Cf. Dunstable annals (*Ann. mon.* iii. 32): *mense Novembri* and John of Oxenedes (*s.a.* 1210, *Chronica* (Rolls Series), p. 126): 'die dominica proxima post festum Omnium Sanctorum'. The pope's commission to the bishop of Arras and the abbot of St. Vaast to publish the sentence when requested by Archbishop Stephen, was probably dated 21 June 1209 (*Reg.*, lib. xii, ep. 57; Migne, 216, col. 64). The excommunication is mentioned by the continuator of Gervase of Canterbury and by Ralph of Coggeshall, and is implied by the annalists of Bury and Winchester. John's later absolution is recorded by the Merton-Southwark-Winchester-Waverley group and by the annalists of St. Albans and Tewkesbury.

[2] Sir James Ramsay offered reasons, mostly good, for rejecting the story *in toto* (*Angevin Empire*, p. 430). Stubbs (*Walter of Coventry*, II, p. lviii, n. 4) and Tout (*Dict. Nat. Biog.*, s.v. Pandulf) had already expressed grave doubts. Chroniclers who mention the unsuccessful mission of the nuncios, without any of the details contained in the dialogue, are Wendover, the continuator of Gervase of Canterbury, Thomas Wikes, the annalists of Osney, Worcester, Winchester, Southwark, Merton, and Bury.

Dutaillis, the German of Alexander Cartellieri, but it is always Wendover in translation.

There are episodes of medieval history which we can only reconstruct by piecing together the reports of various chroniclers who are complementary rather than corroboratory; each contributes something, sees events from an individual point of view, ignores one part of the story and illuminates another part.[1] But the historian's conflation of this sort of testimony is not altogether convincing if important chronicles make absolutely no contribution to the story. In this case the singularity of Wendover's account of the two papal sentences is highly significant; and both this and the other chroniclers' reports command less respect when the complete silence of other reputable writers is taken into account. Ralph, abbot of Coggeshall, had much to say about King John's misdeeds and was well placed to know about papal sentences upon him; but while he explicitly says that John was excommunicated, nowhere does he hint at deposition. So also Richard de Morins, prior of Dunstable (or whoever put together the Annals of Dunstable in their present form) and the continuator of Gervase of Canterbury. The omissions of the episode, in whole or in part, by some of the best narrative-writers of the time cannot be overlooked; they represent a real conflict of testimony. They do not in themselves invalidate the positive statements,[2] but they should make us treat these statements with extreme reserve.

Fortunately, we have other evidence as well, the evidence of official records, and they enable us to settle the matter. The difficulties of reconciling the story of deposition with the records seem insuperable. The papal registers of the thirteenth century provide ample material for observing by what procedure and with what effect the popes usually excommunicated ruling monarchs. The practice, after all, was not uncommon. In the winter of 1212–13 no less than four kings lay under the ban of the Church: the Emperor Otto IV, John of England, Alfonso II of Portugal, Leo II of Armenia; and Otto was deposed. We need not enter into the details of procedure, which naturally varied according to the exigencies of the case, but we ought to remember that it was elaborate, was conducted with careful attention to forms, and usually left abundant records. In the present case we know

---

[1] Cf. the remarks of F. M. Powicke, *Eng. Hist. Rev.* xxi (1906), 295, 630–3.

[2] Neither Ralph of Coggeshall nor the Dunstable annalist makes any mention at all of the nuncios' visit in 1211.

that John's excommunication was publicly pronounced in the churches of northern France in November 1209.

Extant papal letters arrange for the pronouncement and refer to John as excommunicate, but not one letter is known in which he is said to be, or to have been, deposed. The registers of Innocent III contain no document recording John's deposition in 1211 or 1212, no document freeing the Welsh from interdict and allegiance in 1212, no document inciting the English magnates to rebel,[1] or bidding Philip Augustus to act against John.

Stubbs was the first to account for this big gap by a letter which Innocent III directed to Nicholas of Tusculum in October 1213.[2] This is a mandate requiring the legate, after relaxing the interdict, to order the archbishop of Canterbury and his suffragans to hand over all the letters (both the former and the latter) which they had obtained from the pope against the king in case he should not accept the form of peace, and particularly those which begin with the words *Expectantes hactenus expectavimus*, which were to be sent (*destinandas*) to the archbishops and bishops throughout France, England, Scotland, and Ireland and the bishops of Liége and Utrecht. The legate was to have the letters chopped up small or burned. The ominous *incipit 'Expectantes'* and the intended distribution of the letter certainly suggest that it may have conveyed a sentence of deposition which was not to come into force unless John rejected the peace terms offered to him in the spring of 1213. But while this is a matter for conjecture, the terms of Innocent's mandate make it clear that the letters had not in fact been communicated to their addressees: they were still in the hands of Langton and his colleagues, from whom they were to be collected.[3] The mandate to Nicholas of

---

[1] Late in 1212 John obtained letters patent from magnates of England and Ireland proclaiming their loyalty to the king and expressing grief and surprise that the pope should propose to absolve the king's subjects from allegiance. (H. S. Sweetman, *Cal. Docts. relating to Ireland* (1875), i. 73; cf. *Ungedr. a.-n. Geschichtsquellen*, p. 155, and Norgate, *John Lackland*, pp. 172–3.) This, of course, only indicates that the pope had threatened deposition or that a rumour to this effect was abroad. The crucial words of the Irish magnates' letter are: 'sicut nuper accepimus dominus papa proposuit omnes fideles domini regis Angl' a sua absolvere fidelitate pro eo quod ipse restitit iniurie sibi illate super facto Cantuar' ecclesie' (Public Record Office, Red Book of the Exchequer, f. 180ᵛ). John probably obtained these letters to counteract rumour and to impress the pope with a picture of English solidarity when he sent his messengers to Rome in November 1212.

[2] *Reg.*, lib. xvi, ep. 133 (Migne, 216, col. 926) dated 31 Oct. 1213, and Rymer, *Foedera* (Rec. Com.), i. i. 116, wrongly dated 22 Oct. 1213. Cf. Stubbs, *Walter of Coventry*, ii, p. lviii, n. 4, and Powicke, *Loss of Normandy*, p. 475.

[3] As Ramsay hesitantly suggested (*Angevin Empire*, p. 431, n. 1). Langton and his fellow exiles were the natural bearers of such letters. Two of the letters may be

Tusculum, therefore, cannot be taken as evidence that an act of deposition was ever published, and the absence of any such act in itself justifies doubts about the chroniclers' stories.

We need not rely on arguments from silence. The letters which stand under the number 234, in the Register of Innocent III's fifteenth year, provide enough positive evidence to demolish a whole series of fictions.[1] The first of these letters is addressed to King John, beginning with the words: *Auditis verbis nuntiorum tuorum*. This has an appendix beginning: 'Exposiciones autem et explanaciones sunt iste',[2] and is terminated by the date: 'Dat' Laterani iii kal. Marcii pontificatus nostri anno xvi°' (27 February 1213). The first letter refers to the form of peace which had been transmitted to the king by Pandulf and Durand in August 1211 and this *forma* follows in the shape of the pope's original letter to Pandulf and Durand. It bears no date, but we know from an English copy of the original that it was dated 'xviii kal. Maii pont. nostri anno xiiii' (14 April 1211).[3] The form of the commission to the nuncios is particularly interesting because it destroys all faith in the John–Pandulf dialogue. As Ramsay pointed out: 'Pandulf and Durand had no authority to utter any sentence against John. They were directed if he proved obdurate to leave the prosecution of the struggle in the hands of Langton and

those issued late in February or early in March 1213 which stand at the end of Innocent III's register of the fifteenth year, nos. 238 and 239 (Migne, 216, cols. 781–2). The letter *Expectantes* is unfortunately not found with them; it may have started on the lines of Innocent III's letter 'Expectans expectavit diutius apostolica sedes', ordering the deposition of the archbishop of Bordeaux, addressed to the archbishop of Bourges and others on 31 Oct. 1205 (*Reg.*, lib. viii, ep. 150; Migne, 215, col. 725). Cf. a letter written about June–November 1214, which begins: 'Satis actenus expectavimus si forte duritia Narniensium per nostram posset patientiam emolliri' (ed. by K. Hampe, *Mittheilungen des Instituts für österreichische Geschichtsforschung*, xxiii (1902), 553). Cf. also Potthast, nos. 1753, 1769.

[1] Vatican Archives, Reg. Vat. 8, ff. 132ᵛ–133ᵛ. Whereas most of the registers of Innocent III are the originals, this volume, containing letters of the pontifical years thirteen to sixteen, is a copy made in the time of Urban V (cf. H. Denifle, in *Archiv für Literatur- und Kirchengesch. d. Mittelalters*, ii (1886), 21, 43, 74, n. 2). The earliest numeration of the letters (not original) attaches the numbers 232–4 to the three documents beginning respectively with the words *Auditis*, *Exposiciones*, and *Forma*. According to a later numeration (corresponding to the printed editions) all three are placed under the number 234. Printed in Baluze, *Epp. Innoc. libri undecim*, ii (1682), 727 and Migne, 216, col. 772. The undated text of the letter *Auditis verbis nuntiorum* preserved by the Burton annalist (*Ann. mon.* i. 217) gives the names of the six king's messengers, of whom only two are named in the papal register.

[2] The title *Pacis et reconciliationis leges* given in the printed editions of the register is not in Reg. Vat. 8.

[3] Gervase of Canterbury, ii, pp. cxiii–cxiv from Brit. Mus. Cotton MS. Cleop. E. i.

return to Rome.'[1] On the other hand Pandulf was authorized to absolve the king from excommunication if he were penitent, and this confirms our other information that excommunication had been published before this date.

Returning to the letter *Auditis verbis* and its appendix, we have first to note that although in 1635 the original editor François Bosquet gave the correct date, later editors have persistently misdated it *anno quintodecimo*;[2] although the book of the register in which it appears professes to concern the fifteenth year of Innocent III, this letter and the following six letters belong properly to the beginning of the sixteenth year.[3] Next, we see from its text that Innocent III has received John's representatives (who had been dispatched in November 1212)[4] and offers the king the choice of blessings or curses. The royal envoys have agreed provisionally to the terms which Pandulf and Durand had put forward in 1211; now it is for the king to confirm the agreement with pledges from his magnates. If he will not receive peace while he may, he will not be able to when he wishes and repentance will be useless once he is ruined. He is given until 1 June (1213) to ratify his envoys' agreement. It seems inconceivable that Innocent III should write in this strain to a king whom (if we believe Wendover) he had solemnly deposed some two months earlier. *Ruina* spells deposition. This letter contains a threat, and a threat of deposition, but only to take effect if John does not submit within three months.[5]

[1] Op. cit., p. 430.

[2] What is more, Achille Luchaire failed to note this fact in his critical analysis of Potthast ('Les Registres d'Innocent III et les *Regesta* de Potthast', *Troisièmes mélanges d'histoire du moyen âge*, Bibliothèque de la Fac. des lettres, Univ. de Paris, 1904, p. 77). W. H. Bliss (*Cal. of Papal Letters*, i (1893), 37, put the letter in its right place but did not indicate the terms of the dating clause in Reg. Vat. 8. The manuscript from which Bosquet took his text was probably the original register copied in Reg. Vat. 8 (cf. Luchaire, loc. cit., pp. 20–3).

[3] Innocent III's pontifical year began on 22 Feb. The correct date of 'Auditis verbis' has long been recognized (Stubbs, Walter of Coventry, II, p. lviii, n. 4) but the editors' misdating has been ascribed to the papal registrar (cf. preceding note). There is no need to dwell on the error, but it must be mentioned, since Rymer prints the letter with the date 'Kal. Mart. anno 15' (while setting it under A.D. 1213, *Foedera* (Rec. Com.), I. i. 108–9) and Potthast (*Regesta pontificum*, no. 4395) assigns it to 1 Mar. 1212. Luchaire falls into the trap (*Innocent III: les royautés vassales du saint-siège* (1908), p. 215) and Miss Gütschow tries to justify the date 28 Feb. 1212 (op. cit., pp. 164–5).

[4] *Rot. lit. clausarum* (ed. T. D. Hardy), i. 126; cf. Walter of Coventry, ii. 207.

[5] 'Alioquin, eius exemplo qui populum suum de servitute Pharaonis in manu valida liberavit, anglicanam ecclesiam in forti brachio de servitute tua studebimus liberare' (Migne, 216, col. 773). The phrase 'eritque inutilis penitentia post ruinam' (ibid.) is reminiscent of the threat in an earlier letter to the excommunicate

That Innocent did not regard John as already legally deposed is proved by the address and greeting of the letter: 'Johanni illustri regi Angliae spiritum consilii sanioris.' This is the address for an excommunicate but not for a man deposed from his office. The usual formula of apostolic benediction is withheld,[1] but the king is not denied his title. Both here and in a letter dated 7 March 1213[2] to Langton and his colleagues, John is *rex*. Another letter, probably of the same date, provides that if, after peace is made, the *king* does not make proper satisfaction, the *king* and *his* kingdom are to revert to the same state of interdict and excommunication in which they were before the peace.[3] It was not thus that the popes spoke of rulers who were deposed. Otto IV, once deposed, becomes 'dictus imperator, maledictus et excommunicatus'.[4] Frederick II becomes *quondam Romanorum imperator*, with various unpleasant epithets besides.[5] Nor was John

king, preserved only in an undated copy: 'quanquam tibi merito sit verendum ne sera sit penitentia post ruinam' (*Gervase of Canterbury*, ii, p. cxiii).

[1] While Innocent III observed in 1205 that his chancery might sometimes, in error or in ignorance of the facts, give the apostolic benediction to excommunicates (*Reg.*, lib. vii, ep. 224; Migne, 215, col. 542, and *Decretales*, v. 39, 41), the formula *spiritum consilii sanioris* was usual. The only other surviving letter of Innocent to John while the latter was excommunicate bears the same greeting; other examples are *Reg.*, lib. vi, epp. 38, 39, 149, 230; vii, ep. 18; ix, ep. 96; xv, ep. 122; xvi, epp. 22, 114 (Migne, 215, cols. 43, 44, 160, 260, 301, 911; 216, cols. 635, 810, 909), and *Foedera*, i. i. 136. Sometimes the pope took the trouble to explain why he wrote thus. On the very next day after writing to King John, he wrote to the excommunicate king of Armenia, saying: 'Inviti ac dolentes tibi negamus apostolicae salutationis et benedictionis alloquium, cui benedictionem et salutem aeternam in domino affectamus. Verum id exposcit tuorum excessuum magnitudo' (*Reg.*, lib. xvi, ep. 2; Migne, 216, col. 784). Cf. other letters of Innocent III (*Reg.*, lib. i, ep. 574; vi, epp. 39, 93; Migne, 214, col. 527; 215, cols. 44, 97), and the original of a letter of Alexander III to the Serbian prince Miroslav (1181), in which the usual 'Dilecto filio . . . salutem et apostolicam benedictionem' has been erased, and the following clause explains the reason (G. Battelli, *Acta pontificum* (Exempla scripturarum, fasc. iii, Vatican, 1933), pl. 9*b* and p. 11, n. 1). The papal chancery also coined formulas of greetings for infidels: see letters to the sultans of Aleppo and Damascus (*Reg.*, lib. xiv, ep. 69; Migne, 216, col. 434, and *Neues Archiv*, xxxi (1906), 592–3). The thirteenth-century writers on dictamen take account of these peculiar types of salutation: see L. von Rockinger, *Briefsteller und Formelbücher des XI. bis XIV. Jh.* (Quellen zur bayer. u. deut. Geschichte, ix, 1863–4), pp. 261, 366, 463, 731.

[2] *Reg.*, lib. xv, ep. 236; Migne, 216, col. 780. The 'Datum ut supra' (i.e. iii kal. Mart.) of Migne does not appear in Reg. Vat. 8, where no date is given. The copy, taken from the original by Nicholas of Tusculum, is dated 'nonis Martii anno xvi°' (i.e. 7 Mar. 1213. *Essays in History Pres. to R. L. Poole* (1927), pp. 280–1).

[3] *Reg.*, lib. xv, ep. 238; Migne, 216, col. 781.

[4] *Reg.*, lib. xiii, ep. 193; lib. xiv, epp. 78–9; Migne, 216, cols. 361, 439, 440.

[5] *Registres d'Innocent IV* (École franç. de Rome, 1884–1919), Index, p. 167 *passim*. Alexander III referred to Frederick Barbarossa consistently as *dictus*

denied his royal title by his enemies Philip Augustus and Frederick II when they made a treaty on 19 November 1212: they observe the formal distinction between 'Otto formerly called emperor and John king of England'.[1] Again, Prince Louis's pledge to his father, drawn up early in April 1213, speaks of John as king of England.[2] We can only conclude that when Innocent III directed *Auditis verbis* to John on 27 February 1213, he had not yet pronounced sentence of deposition and did not intend to do so before 1 June.

In the event, John submitted well within the time allowed. The documents connected with the submission nowhere suggest that the king had lost his royal title. It is, indeed, difficult to see how the transactions of 15 May 1213 could take place—how John could surrender the kingdom—if, according to the papal theory, he had no kingdom to surrender. Had John been deprived of his office some document must have recorded his reinstatement, but none survives; and of all the chroniclers who tell of his absolution, not one speaks of his restoration to the throne.

King John, then, was never formally deposed by the pope. But if that be so, what of the report that Philip Augustus prepared to invade England under papal auspices? The evidence of the English chroniclers must be discounted, since they have been discovered in error on the other point, and there is practically no other positive evidence.[3] French chroniclers are completely silent about the meeting in January 1213 which Wendover describes; and the Council of Soissons (early April) at which Philip Augustus

imperator from the time when he released Frederick's subjects from allegiance (April 1160) to the reconciliation in 1177 (e.g. Jaffé-Löwenfeld, *Regesta pont.*, nos. 10655, 10750, 11747, 12737). Supporters of the popes took their cue from the papal chancery. To John of Salisbury, Frederick I is *teutonicus tyrannus* and *ex-augustus* (cf. *Materials hist. Thomas Becket* (Rolls Series), vi, *passim*. Étienne de Gallardon, canon of Bourges, speaks scurrilously of Frederick II as 'Merdericum imperatorem, nominalem non realem' (*Bibl. de l'Éc. des Chartes*, lx (1899), 18).

[1] *M.G.H. Leg.*, sect. iv, *Const.* ii. 55.

[2] *Foedera*, I. i. 104. The date 'April 1212' is in modern terms April 1213; since the French chancery reckoned the year of grace from Easter, its year 1212 ran from 25 Mar. 1212 to 13 Apr. 1213.

[3] William, abbot of Andres (cf. p. 106 above), provides the only evidence from the Continent (if we exclude such a late and unreliable writer as Ptolemy of Lucca). William was well placed to pick up an English rumour. In 1211 he was at Paris, engaged in a lawsuit in which, out of three judges delegate, Richard Poore, dean of Salisbury, favoured William's cause (L. D'Achery, *Spicilegium*, ii (1723), 849; cf. *Innoc. III Reg.*, lib. xi, ep. 205; lib. xiv, ep. 19; Migne, 215, col. 1519; 216, col. 396). Some of the exiled English prelates may well have stopped at Andres during these years and may have passed that way on their return to England in July 1213.

formally announced his intentions, is reported at length by William le Breton in both his prose chronicle and his poem, without any suggestion that the pope was concerned. Philip, is indeed, represented as piously inclined to the invasion (*innata motus pietate*) and he poses as the defender and avenger of the Church, but the invasion is all his own idea (*mens mea proponit*).[1] If Pandulf had conveyed to Philip a formal commission to invade England, the French king could hardly fail to be aggrieved at the turn of events in May 1213. But there is no evidence of this worth having. In keeping with their account of Soissons, the French chroniclers report no recrimination by Philip Augustus against the pope when Innocent accepted John's submission: that was left for Wendover and the modern French historians who copy him. There is no official correspondence of Philip to suggest that he wanted or relied on papal backing; and when Innocent wrote to him on 5 July 1213, announcing the reconciliation of John to the Church, he wrote only a brief letter of credence for the legate[2] and not the sort of grandiloquent epistle with which this pope habitually justified his changes of policy. Again it proves impossible to reconcile Wendover's story with the evidence from other sources. We are under no obligation to believe that the pope behaved inconsistently at this juncture, treating with a deposed king, while he urged an enemy to dispossess him.

Maybe this verdict on the story of John's deposition and Philip's commission does not seriously alter our view of the events of 1211–13, but it tends to a toning down of the colours of the picture. It confirms the impression gained from other sources that the interdict and excommunication did not seriously impede royal government and that John's difficulties were of different origin, though they were aggravated by the displeasure of the Church. As the events of these years now appear, the pope was more of a statesman than he seemed when we believed in the various unheeded sentences of 1211, 1212, and 1213. He measured his words according to his means and did not declare deposition when he could not enforce it. On the other hand, this episode suggests that John was still strong enough in 1212 and 1213 to

[1] *Œuvres de Rigord et Guillaume le Breton* (Soc. Hist. France, 1882–5), i. 244–53, ii. 247–8, 255.

According to the *Histoire des ducs de Normandie et des rois d'Angleterre* (Soc. Hist. France, 1840), p. 120, the idea of invading England came suddenly to Philip early one morning, as he lay in bed!

[2] *Reg.*, lib. xvi, ep. 83; Migne, 216, col. 884–5.

choose the time and manner of his reconciliation with the Church. The pope was more anxious to pardon a prodigal than the king to solicit the forgiveness of his spiritual father. John's final acts of submission and homage were not the fruit of sudden desperation; they were the consequences of an embassy sent to Rome six months earlier. If it is true, and it may well be, that John acted on his own initiative when he made England and Ireland vassal states of the papacy, he made his intention known in Rome before Pandulf left for England; the formula of surrender shows that the act was premeditated. The terror-stricken tyrant and the domineering priest disappear from a story of well-calculated diplomacy by two men, each of whom had many qualities of greatness.

The inquiry has also a subsidiary interest. It has been concerned about a matter of fact: did Pope Innocent depose King John? The negative answer leaves us with a lot of bad evidence on our hands, which must be accounted for.[1]

The various chroniclers did not manufacture this evidence out of nothing. The truth seems to be that while the deposition of John was not a fact it was, in the years 1211, 1212, and 1213, a widespread and persistent rumour. The rumour flourished in the atmosphere of distrust which prevailed in an England labouring under tyrannical government and the shadow of four years' interdict. We know from various sources that the countryside was teeming with rumours, which set people's nerves on edge and probably worked powerfully on the imagination of the king.[2] It was widely known that John's nephew, the emperor, had been deposed as well as excommunicated and that a crusade was being directed by Simon de Montfort,[3] claimant to an English earldom, against the king's brother-in-law, Raymond VI of Toulouse. There were those in England and Wales who would use this information to start a 'whispering campaign' against the king. The failure of the nuncios' mission in 1211 encouraged a belief

[1] 'If every piece of news that reached an English abbey and is recorded could be traced to its source we should find their errors as natural and instructive as their accuracy.' F. M. Powicke, 'Roger of Wendover and the Coggeshall chronicle', *Eng. Hist. Rev.* xxi (1906), 295.

[2] See especially the Bury annals (*Ungedr. a.-n. Geschichtsquellen*), p. 153, and Walter of Coventry, ii. 206. The unsettled state of mind that prevailed in England in 1212 and early in 1213 is constantly remarked by the Barnwell chronicler (ibid. 207–11).

[3] According to the well-informed annalist of Dunstable, the rumours of conspiracy which reached John in August 1212 included the news that his barons had chosen Simon to be king of England (*Ann. mon.* iii. 33).

in deposition, the Welsh princes welcomed it as an excuse for throwing over a treaty very recently established, and finally, Philip's preparations for invasion were associated with the pope's calls to arms against enemies of the Church. Although the chroniclers cannot be trusted to tell us precisely what happened, they can therefore be trusted to report what the people of England (particularly in monasteries) felt and believed about current affairs. This at least is probably true of the Cistercian sources and the Barnwell chronicler: we must put the John–Pandulf dialogue[1] and Wendover's narrative in a class apart. As regards Wendover (and it is he whom modern historians have followed), the scrappy reports of other chroniclers seem to be not corroboration of his elaborate, circumstantial account, but the very material out of which he, or someone else, invented it. The rumours of 1212 may indeed have been magnified soon after John's submission if Langton let it be known that he had the letter 'Expectantes hactenus expectavimus' up his sleeve.[2] Be that as it may, the details of Wendover's narrative cannot be other than products of imagination. In the last few decades Wendover's work has come under close scrutiny and his reputation as an historian is sinking.[3] He had great opportunities at St. Albans to collect historical materials and he misused them, as he is reported to have misused the goods of Belvoir Priory. Inaccurate in small matters, when he tried to copy exactly, he seems to have been quite without the power of discriminating between true news and gossip. But if he is a poor historian, as a writer of dramatic narrative he shows very considerable ability. It is by his art that, in the history of this episode, fiction has successfully masqueraded as fact for more than 700 years.   C. R. Cheney

[1] I take this to be a literary exercise composed after John's submission and probably after his death.

[2] Cf. above, p. 109.

[3] Cf. V. H. Galbraith, *Roger Wendover and Matthew Paris* (David Murray Lecture, Glasgow, 1944). In 1903 Sir James Ramsay wrote: 'Wendover is a careless, inaccurate writer, on whom, however, we are dependent for a great mass of matter' (*Angevin Empire*, p. 524).

THE CHAMBER AND THE CASTLE
TREASURES UNDER KING JOHN

THE early thirteenth century, when the chancery rolls appear and give us a new insight into history, is a crucial time for monarchy. The king is as strong as ever but he has come to be isolated from the nobility. The growth of officials and officialdom has as yet hardly touched his power. Some parts of government are becoming specialized, but he has still an almost unchallenged right of intervention. The courts of law are not independent, for the king can deny judgement or reserve cases for his own hearing. He makes his appearance from time to time in the Exchequer.[1] Chancery has not yet gone out of court and is still his secretariate. The traditional check of baronial counsel acts only at critical intervals and often with much friction. King John, succeeding at this turning-point of history, has an intricate and powerful machine at his disposal and very little to control his predilections as to the driving of it.

All this is taken for granted by the king's subjects. Only one limit to royal power is yet seen with clarity and rouses any feeling—the king must not touch common right or privilege which is of long standing. Beyond this the critical capacity of the early thirteenth century scarcely goes. It is not, therefore, right to speak of any of the king's spheres of action as 'personal government', and our term 'prerogative' has no meaning. If we find him minimizing the functions of what are already ancient offices of state and encouraging those of newer and less highly organized offices which stand nearer to himself, or getting his revenue inventively by unusual means, he is hardly acting more 'personally', that is with a freer choice, than he might do by means of older conventions and institutions. No part of government is as yet a closed system against the king.

But, though we must refuse to make any contrast between personal and conventional or constitutional rule, because it would be an anachronism to do so, we can still find much that is individual in the way in which each king handles the fluid congeries of offices and officials, circles of government and their governors, that is at his disposal. One idiom of government arises from the temperament and character of John, another from that of his son, and,

[1] Publications of the Pipe Roll Society, New Series, XVIII, p. xi.

doubtless, if we had the means of detecting it, from those of each of his predecessors also. The reign is, in part, made by the king, not only in the personal drama of politics, but in the smaller and less easily detectable rivalry of departments and authorities. This is a passing phase in English history and a dangerous one. With John, the idiosyncrasy is strong and vivid enough to raise the friction of rival administrations into the foreground of history.

It would be hard to find a phrase for this quality though it marks every aspect of John's government as his own: nor, indeed, is what we know of earlier reigns enough to show how far he was breaking with the past. There is a strong military colour to his rule throughout: some of it is demonstrably a heritage from the years of war in which his apprenticeship was served. There is an adventurous experimentalism, a preference for the short way that brings immediate results, an indifference to ultimate consequences that may or may not be calculated. John will take his weapons where he finds them, and the greater wheels of Angevin government often grind idly while he is at work with new men and more direct methods.

The centre of this specifically royal activity was the household and, radiating from it, a favoured group of clerks, sheriffs, and castellans—the latter men with a training equally military and financial. From this centre John controlled almost all those parts of the state and its resources which served the upkeep and dignity of the king's court and person, together with those salaried forces that he retained as supplement or counterpoise to the feudal and national levies. If he should come to break with the conservative forces of society and government, this internal executive could be detached, as it was in 1215 and 1216, to form a self-sufficing military administration. At its upper levels the list of these faithful servants was not a large one. Throughout his reign in England the key points of John's power were held, turn and turn about, by a few Englishmen of exceptional trust and competence and by that formidable group of aliens who had accompanied or followed him from Poitou or Normandy. John was loyal to those who served him well and without question and upon whom his readily aroused suspicion did not fasten, and the names of some of those who still survived were upon the schedule of his evil counsellors in the Great Charter.

One plain component of John's complex nature was energy and tirelessness. In every medieval reign the crown and the household were itinerant, but he, above all his dynasty, was in motion ceaselessly, carrying his scrutiny into the west, and into the far north where kings seldom came: yearly, again and again, riding the great inner circuit of Angevin government that led through the southern counties to the March and circled back by Trent into the Midlands. In every journey the essentials of government, the *hospitium regis*—the chamber, the wardrobe, the butlery, dispensary, kitchen, marshalcy of the stables, the writers, the chapel, the reliquary, and the hunt—followed the court; a train of from ten to twenty carts and wagons, its equipment worn down to the bare necessities of effective action. Magnificent as he could be upon occasion a meagre state sufficed the daily majesty of the king.

The administration he did we should find it easy to enumerate but hard to summarize, since it was the work of omnicompetent authority working at its ease and picking its executants as they came. A fair and reasonably exhaustive account, taken from the rolls of any year, would show John paying or authorizing payment for the maintenance, harness, and transport of himself and the dozen or so *officia* of his household—for almost all the year away from London—the entertainment and expenses of foreign and domestic guests, and the prescribed hospitality of the great feasts; the pay and expenses of a corps of messengers and special representatives; the building, upkeep, and repair of the king's houses and castles so far as they did not depend upon allotted farms; the pay, allowance, and advances of such knights as were not already enfeoffed or borne upon the rolls of the exchequer and of an increasing swarm of serjeants and crossbowmen; the maintenance of the king's galleys and the pay of their masters, pilots, and seamen. This was the standing expenditure of the kingdom at peace. In time of war it became greatly expanded, for castles were to be hurried into defence, stored, and garrisoned, fleets enlisted and manned, and the roll of the enlisted knights and serjeants was vastly swollen.[1] With war in France, the 'treasure of England' was exported in a steady stream, and, when the king was abroad, the chamber, far more than the Exchequer of Caen, acted as an office for receipt and expenditure for the foreign revenue at large. It is with the financing of these civil and military undertakings, which together make up the practical government of the country, that this essay is concerned—the financing of that itinerant executive in which the king, working partly through his household and

[1] On one day in 1210, 1,000 marks were distributed *de prestito* to the knights and barons going on the Irish campaign (*Rot. de Praestito*, p. 203).

the provincial authorities most closely in touch with it, and partly in his own person, was constantly engaged.

Medieval revenue has been lavishly treated by historians, for it is part of that parliamentary background that has interested them most. But it has been barely recognized that the grant of aid and its collection was, in the age of John, only the beginning of a fresh problem. We are used to government concentrated at Westminster, with the ministries clustered about the Treasury, and we have a dozen ways of conveying the flow of money from head to members wherever these may be. But in the year 1200 money in the Exchequer was not money immediately accessible to the executive. The national store of treasure, the *Thesaurus Angliae*, was fixed already in the capital, but government was permanently on the road, and to get the king's money to the king's administration was a major undertaking upon which the whole safety and order of the nation must turn. The Exchequer provided a regular corps of couriers for the transport of treasure, but throughout the reign John and his associates were testing other, more satisfactory, ways of solving the problem. In the end, after their rough and ready fashion, they succeeded in solving it very thoroughly. The remedy could not, of course, be found in the Exchequer. Its traditionalism and fixity were the very restrictions to be overcome. But in the already strongly developed household, with its centre in the chamber, the means lay ready to hand.

The treasure that the chamber received and dispensed on progress must, in primitive times, have been drawn almost exclusively from Westminster or Winchester, itself acting only a derivative function. It continued to get its main supply thence for the first half of John's reign, until the summer of 1207, and some part of it for the rest of the reign also, drawing by the king's writ the supply of six weeks or a month, according as expenses went. The money came from London, in drafts of some thousands of marks at a time, in the only currency then obtainable, silver pennies, barrelled or in sacks of £100 each, and conveyed across the countryside by some principal servant of the treasurer, Robert de Winton or Peter de Ely, with two or occasionally more *servientes* in attendance.[1] For many years Peter and Robert held this charge, which the *Dialogus de Scaccario* allots to the *Clericus Thesaurarii*;

---

[1] Coin was stored in the London Treasury in *foruli* of £100 each (*Dialogus de Scaccario*, i. 3); cf. *Rot. Lit. Claus*. i. 116: 'Per manus Petri de Ely et Hugonis de Monasteriis et Elye de Chiltun decem et octo milia marcarum, scilicet sexties viginti saccos quorum quilibet continet centum libras'; see also *Rot. Lit. Pat.*, p. 148.

their lay companions, who were changed more frequently, correspond to the two knights of the chamberlains.[1] The passage of the treasure was protected by the sheriffs of the counties through which it was carried or by the military household.[2] When received in the chamber it was stored in the wardrobe and conveyed in the wardrobe carts.[3] As soon as it went into store it was known as the *denarii de garderoba*—in Richard's day it was the *thesaurus camerae*[4]—but it was still formally delivered into the chamber to Peter des Roches or to Philip de Lucy; after July 1207 we can say that it was delivered to the clerk of the chamber. Thenceforth it progressed with the court and was drawn upon for pay and expenses until it was exhausted. From time to time the Treasure of Ireland was also called upon, as well as the Treasure of England.[5]

But John was not satisfied with the service of the Exchequer, nor, indeed, could it supply the administration adequately. The Exchequer was often out of funds, so that the best that could be done was to order the money to be sent after the court as it came to hand. We hear of the king held up in the full course of his administrative progress: 'non habemus quid pacemus pro expensis nostris',[6] and it is not to the Exchequer but to one of the sheriffs that he turns. On this occasion the household was no further afield than Dorchester, but each year business carried it to Exeter, to Worcester, or to Nottingham, sometimes to York or beyond, and on two occasions into the almost impassable highlands of Cumberland and Lancashire. These furthest extensions of itinerant government a treasure at London could not supply or could only do so with risk and delay. The sources of revenue were in the countryside and the king might reasonably refuse to wait until it had been drawn to a centre in Westminster, only to take the backward road again into the provinces. Any prolonged stay in one of the provincial cities was likely, therefore, to be paid for in part by a combing of the district for such unpaid fines and outstanding profits as could be come by readily.[7] The *camera* was

---

[1] *Dialogus*, i. 3. A writ of 14 John (*Rot. Lit. Claus.* i. 122) describes the principal custodian as *Radulphus clericus Thesaurarii* and his two companions as *servientes camerariorum*.

[2] Cf. *Rot. Lit. Pat.*, p. 87; *Rot. de Liberate*, p. 102.

[3] Cf. *Rot. Misae*, pp. 238, 243, 249.

[4] T. Madox, *History and Antiquities of the Exchequer*, 1711, p. 181 n. *h*.

[5] *Rot. Lit. Claus*. i. 12.   [6] Ibid. i. 61.

[7] In February and March 1206 the king spent three weeks in the north, and Brian de Insula and Alexander de Dorset had to raise 150 marks from the fines and issues of the soke of Knaresborough and pay them into the chamber at Nottingham (*Rot. Lit. Claus.* i. 66).

to hand always, free to ignore or anticipate the Exchequer terms, taking up the king's debts where they fell due, a place of payment *ipsi domino Regi*, under the king's eye, where debtors could be more profitably dealt with than in the courtroom setting of the Exchequer under the restrictions of the *lex scaccarii*.[1]

The use of the chamber as a travelling treasury of receipt, collecting the king's profits, and withholding them from the Exchequer so that he might receive and spend them on progress, was not new—it was familiar to Richard fitz Neal. The writ *computate* sufficed to balance the treasurer's rolls and quit the debtor. The money was the king's, there was as yet no jealousy of 'prerogative', and not until 1258 was it to be established 'qe vengent totes les issue de la tere (al escheker) et en nule part ailurs'. Accordingly, we find that in every year a considerable though indeterminate revenue was taken up from fines, gifts, and promises paid immediately into the chamber, and that those great custodies which were maintained apart from the sheriffs' farm— the mints, the stannaries, and so forth—and the great wardships and escheats, were put in charge of such king's men as William de Wrotham, William and Reginald de Cornhill, and their revenues raided to the chamber's profit. At one moment it had seemed that John might overcome the financial contradictions of the time and place the whole problem of chamber revenue upon a logical footing. In May 1208 the enforcement of a whole range of clerical fines and debts from the northern province was committed to a single collector, Robert de Vipont, and a similar commission upon a smaller scale was given to John fitz Hugh in the south. All these profits—some of them debts outstanding for several years—enforced by a right of distraint wherever the debtors' lands lay, were to be delivered en bloc into the chamber, and the authority was explicitly set up under the privy seal: 'has litteras signari fecimus parvo sigillo nostro quia hec debita volumus reddi in cameram nostram, quas fecissemus signari majori sigillo nostro si ea ad scaccarium nostrum reddi vellemus.'[2] Here we have for the first time all the elements of a potential prerogative revenue: regional commissioners acting under the privy seal, the privy seal recognized as appropriated to the chamber, and the chamber itself as the place of receipt; but the parts essential to prerogative revenue are only momentarily exhibited together, the practice only applied locally, and on a single occasion.

[1] Cf. Madox, op. cit., pp. 180–2.
[2] *Rot. Lit. Claus.* i. 115.

The problem that it might have solved remained—to keep an itinerant administration in funds either from what it could glean as it went or through the slow channels of the Exchequer and its convoys laboriously finding their way to the distant, constantly moving court. It was solved at last, but not by the old methods, rather by a revolution in method, a drastic and, in general, a new solution which may best be called a system of provincial treasures. The treasure of London came to be dispersed and provincialized. At Bristol, at Devizes, Nottingham, Marlborough, Corfe, or Exeter, the king would henceforth have his treasure where he needed it, accessible at will.

The court was working towards new expedients during its first two years of war in France, beginning by throwing off the control of the Norman Exchequer, the inadequacy of which seems to have been established in the first months of the campaign. During the peace, from 1200 to 1202, the usual way of supplying the chamber was to bring coin from the *thesaurus Angliae* to Barfleur and thence to Caen, where it was absorbed into the Norman Exchequer and the Norman chamberlains, Abbot Samson of Caen and Ralf l'Abbé, acknowledged receipt.[1] It was then conveyed to its ultimate destination by Roger, a clerk of Ralf l'Abbé, and William Belet.[2] This service, the Norman equivalent of the London couriers, was maintained at least intermittently until October 1201 when the Norman Exchequer, for the last time, acknowledged the deposit of a sum—3,000 marks—from the London messengers, Peter de Ely, Hugh de Moustiers, and John de Cricklade.[3] On 27 May Robert de Winton delivered one sum of 2,700 marks and Peter de Ely another of 4,050, both to the king at Rouen.[4] From that time onwards all the English shipments were run through direct to the king or to some authority appointed by him to receive them. The Norman fiscal authority was thenceforth thrust aside from the line of supply from England, and other, more accessible centres took its place. For the future Caen dealt only with the Norman revenues, and its old monopoly as a general treasury was split up among a number of strategically disposed and defended castles at a distance from the old financial capital. By February 1203 John had given recognition to the separation of the two services by ordering Caen to make payments for him 'until our treasure of England shall come'.[5]

---

[1] *Rot. Normanniae*, pp. 28, 46, 51.　　　　[2] Ibid., pp. 36, 119.
[3] *Rot. de Liberate*, p. 33. This money was still being paid out in Jan. 1203 (ibid., p. 69).　　　　[4] Ibid., p. 37.　　　　[5] *Rot. Normanniae*, p. 75.

The Tower of Rouen and its constable were rivals to the Exchequer of Caen as early as the year 1200, and it was probably from this hoard that Robert de Vipont was paying large sums in the June of 1202.[1] For a period, at least, there were stores of coin at Loches and Chinon.[2] Angers and Poitiers, with their provincial exchequers,[3] could give the accessibility that the military administration demanded, and ease of access was guaranteed by the fact that the money was lodged in the hands of royal seneschals who were also constables. There does not seem to have been any reason in security for this detachment of the king's field treasure from the accounting office of the duchy, for the Norman Exchequer was able to continue receiving and paying from the purely Norman revenues, making block deliveries from the Norman tallage and from other profits as late as August 1203.[4] As late as October 1203 Caen was safe enough for part of the treasure of Ireland and £1,400 of that of England to be brought there—but even at Caen it was not to the Exchequer but to the chamber that it was consigned.[5]

The reason for this determined side-tracking of the established financial authorities cannot, therefore, have been fear of a French raid on Caen, but rather the convenience of a rapidly moving government with heavy and unpredictable calls upon its resources. The old system had been found wanting in the circumstances of war. There was, moreover, a trace of jealousy between the military and administrative entourage of John and the regular civil officials. Behind the stereotyped form of the writs we can detect the feeling of the king and his friends, and their satisfaction in getting treasure into their hands in bulk. Writing freely to his master, Jean de Préaux, bailiff of Rouen, reports the arrival of 2,000 marks, not to the Exchequer but direct to the castle of Rouen: 'and with this money', he says, 'you can do what you will, for it is in your own tower'.[6] What the army could do with money when it had uncontrolled possession we do, in fact, know. In later years, at least, they came to handle it as familiarly as any other kind of army stores, thinking of it not in terms of pounds, shillings, and pence, but in bulk, in the sack and the barrel. 'Pay the dealers for the horses out of the £700 cask from which £100

---

[1] *Rot. Normanniae*, pp. 54, 55, 59.   [2] Ibid., pp. 36, 64.
[3] F. M. Powicke, *The Loss of Normandy*, p. 42.
[4] At this date £2,300 (presumably pounds of Anjou) were paid into the chamber at Alençon (*Rot. Normanniae*, p. 102).
[5] *Rot. de Liberate*, pp. 66, 70.
[6] *Rot. de Oblatis*, p. 72.

has already been taken', writes John to Peter de Maulay, keeper
of his treasure at La Rochelle in 1214,[1] and, 'tell Brother Alan
how much you have taken out of the new sack'.[2]

These habits, acquired during the fighting in France, were not
such as favoured a return to traditional methods when the court
and the household were removed to England and conditions of
peace,[3] and the need for some more elastic system was still felt
almost as much as it had been during the war. The precedents of
Rouen, Loches, and the other castle treasures soon bore fruit in
John's policy at home.

In England there was already one provincial treasure, that of
Winchester, and much use was made of it when forces were being
assembled at Portsmouth for transport.[4] It has been questioned
whether the original Winchester treasure survived the secession of
treasurer and chamberlains to London. From the transactions
of John's middle years it would seem that it did survive, but at
the point of time for which the evidence of the Close Roll is
decisive, only as a dependency of Westminster. In the summer
of 1204 there was treasure stored at Winchester with appropriate
custodians, but there were no officials capable of acting upon a
writ of *Liberate*. For money to be delivered, the treasurer and
chamberlains—perhaps sufficient deputies would serve, but this
is not stated—were summoned from London and made the issue
in person.[5] We must, therefore, take it that, at this time at least,
Winchester was no more than a place of storage under effective
Westminster control, and its subordination is borne out by the
fact that the transport of the Winchester treasure was always in
the charge of the treasurer's clerk and chamberlain's knights of
London. There are no Winchester equivalents to Robert de
Winton and Peter de Ely.

---

[1] *Rot. Lit. Claus.* i. 168.   [2] Ibid., p. 169.

[3] When the king returned to England the Exchequer of Caen was used again
(*Rot. de Liberate*, p. 96).

[4] *Rot. Lit. Claus.* i. 4.

[5] Since this has been a crux in administrative history it may be useful to give
the evidence for the status of the Winchester treasure in the first half of John's
reign. That the presence of London officials was necessary is shown by several
writs, e.g. *Rot. Lit. Claus.* i. 6: 'Rex etc. W. Thesaurario et G. et R. Camerariis
salutem. Mandamus vobis quod statim visis istis litteris eatis usque Winton' et
capiatis de thesauro nostro qui ibi est 3000 marcas et illas deferatis London' et
liberetis eas sicut vobis mandabit venerabilis pater noster Cantuariensis Archiepiscopus per litteras suas patentes. Teste me ipso apud Oxon. IV die Augusti'
(1204); see also ibid., pp. 3, 5; *Pipe Roll 6 Jo.*, p. 88: 'Willemus Briwerre reddit
compotum de 1000 marcis de quibus commodate ei fuerunt de thesauro regis apud
Winton' *per Thesaurarium et Camerarios* 700 marcae.'

Winchester, however, did not provide the court and army with that unhampered access to treasure which they had had in France, nor was one provincial depot enough. The first move to set up similar deposits in England was made immediately after the court's return. In March 1204 the 'Treasure of Ireland' was brought across the Irish sea and lodged at Bristol, which thenceforth became a permanent safe-deposit for Irish and other revenues.[1] This new establishment at Bristol was a true rival of the London treasure, and was, in time, built up into a very great reserve—in 1213 it contained 120,000 marks.[2] For the moment it matters more to us that it was the first provincial treasure to gain and keep its independence, since, except that its outgoings from Irish revenue were, for a time, reported to the justiciar of Ireland,[3] it was neither retained under the jurisdiction of Dublin nor placed under that of Westminster. In contrast to Winchester, its custodians could comply with writs of *Liberate* without reference to any parent treasure.[4]

In France use had been made of the castles—the Tower of Rouen, Loches, Chinon, and others—treasure being stored there in charge of the constables and released on writs of *Liberate*.[5] This sort of receipt and payment must have needed a certain amount of experience and some machinery; at least the constables had clerks to help them. It is to be remembered, also, that the seneschals of the continental provinces were heads of ducal and comital exchequers, and this may have accustomed John to associate financial functions with the greater constableships. At least, when he set up his castle treasures in England it was to the men who had served as constables in France that he turned to staff them. At intervals, several of them began to make their appearance in England. The first, Robert de Vipont, came from Rouen to Nottingham in 1204, to begin his long career as an English castellan and sheriff. He was followed in 1207 by Gerard d'Athies,

---

[1] *Rot. Lit. Pat.*, p. 39: 'Rex etc. ducentibus thesaurum suum ab Hibernia salutem. Mandamus vobis quod thesaurum nostrum quem deferetis ad opus nostrum . . . liberetis Thome de Rochford Constabulario Bristollie.' Before 5 Oct. 1204 the committal to the constable was modified to a joint custody with Roger Cordewaner and a committee of Bristol citizens (*Rot. Lit. Claus.* i. 10).

[2] *Rot. Lit. Claus.* i. 153.

[3] *Rot. Lit. Claus.* i. 75: 'Rex etc. M. Filio Henrici Justiciario Hibernie etc. Sciatis quod Rogerus Cordewan' de Bristoll' pacavit nobis in camera nostra apud Winton' vigilia Natalis Domini anno etc. VIII⁰ CCC marcas ex parte vestra. Et ideo vobis mandamus quod idem Rogerus inde sit quietus' (26 Dec. 1206).

[4] Ibid., pp. 10, 36.

[5] *Rot. Normanniae*, pp. 28, 29, and *passim*.

Guido de Castellis, Peter des Chanceux, and others. At home John already had to his hand such tried servants as William Brewer, Hugh de Nevill, Reginald de Cornhill, and Thomas de Sandford.

The next few years reproduced some of the conditions of campaigning. The king made a prolonged visit to the north in 1205 and treasure went regularly into Poitou to carry on the war. Consequently we find some of the English castles used as stores for money which was taken out of the treasures of England or Ireland and accumulated at Exeter or Porchester preparatory to going across from Portsmouth or Dartmouth, or sent ahead of the king to be ready for his arrival on one of his longer progresses. By October 1204 Robert de Vipont had accumulated some of the coin for Poitou at Salisbury, of which he was *custos*, whence it was committed to a representative of the constable of Exeter, and finally to Andrew de Beauchamp and his colleagues, who were to take it overseas. Rather more than half of this was of the *Thesaurus Angliae*, the rest of that of Ireland.[1] At the same time, William Brewer was holding 2,000 marks at Exeter, *ad mittendum in Wasconiam*,[2] and from this the treasure of Exeter seems to have been built up as a forward depot for the western passage. In January 1206 William Brewer and Robert de Winton and his associates jointly dispatched 1,500 marks *de thesauro nostro apud Exoniam*,[3] and in January 1207, 'the custodians of our treasure at Exeter' were to take the whole of it to Savary de Mauleon and Robert de Turnham in Poitou.[4] During the progress into the north in February 1205, 4,000 marks were lodged at Northampton, the king taking only 1,000 with him for immediate use,[5] while the constable of Northampton was authorized to make essential payments by writ of *Liberate*.[6]

It does not seem that these treasures were either increased or diminished to any notable degree during the next two years. A beginning had been made but not developed, nor was it probable that it would be, so long as the comparatively lean financial harvests of the early years of the reign prevailed. A further deposit of 1,000 marks was made with Robert de Vipont at Nottingham in February 1205;[7] but as a rule the flow of treasure was still towards the south, where Salisbury[8] and Exeter[9] were

[1] *Rot. Lit. Claus.* i. 13. [2] Ibid., p. 2. [3] Ibid., p. 62.
[4] Ibid., p. 77. [5] Ibid., p. 20. [6] Ibid., p. 22.
[7] Ibid., p. 63. [8] Ibid., pp. 13, 97.
[9] Ibid., pp. 2, 34, 62, 63, 77.

halting-places for the export of coin for the new season's campaign in Poitou. The king's English expenses were habitually met by drafts from Westminster or from payments of fines and advances into the chamber as in the past. Those for his projected but abortive crossing from Portsmouth in the summer of 1205 were also financed for the most part in regular form, and the small sums recorded (in contrast with the very much greater ones that John got together, using his own new methods, for the wars of 1212–14), may suggest that poverty had as much to do with the failure of the expedition to sail as baronial reluctance.

Two things emerge from the history of the first half of this reign. In time of peace it was untrustworthy and cumbrous to finance the household by convoys from London and to look to what the chamber could pick up from provincial profits to bridge the gaps in their supply. For the purposes of war there was needed a larger reserve than could be got at any one time from the Exchequer. This John set himself to remedy. It was in the summer of 1207 that the plan of the castle treasures was consolidated: from that time half a dozen of them became permanent, standing reserves for the king's wars and journeys, and the size of the deposits there became enormously increased.

The reasons just given would, in themselves, have been sufficient for a change of system, but the change was, in fact, contemporary with certain alterations in the household, and followed upon an episode of friction between the Exchequer and the chamber. Without saying dogmatically that we have here cause and effect, the possibility of some connexion is strong enough to make it worth while giving the facts. Philip de Lucy had been receiver of the chamber for about two years, and part of that office had always been to present writs of *Liberate* at the Exchequer, usually for drafts of £200 at a time, for the payment of the king's expenses while in London, and to see the money collected or receive it in the chamber.[1] When the court was at Lambeth in January 1207 the treasurer and chamberlains refused and returned two of these writs in succession,[2] and the king had to order Geoffrey fitz Peter to override them with his authority as justiciar and to see that the payments were in fact made.[3] After this rebuff

---

[1] Cf. *Rot. Lit. Claus.* i. 76: 'Rex etc. W. Thesaurario et C. et R. Camerariis. Liberate de thesauro nostro in camera nostra cc libras ad pacaciones faciendas. Teste Ph. de Lucy apud Lamehethe. Die x Januarii. Per eundem' (1207).

[2] *Rot. Lit. Claus.* i. 75, 76. The writs, dated 8 and 10 Jan., are for £140. 18s. 10½d. and £55 respectively. They are noted as being cancelled *quia breve redditum fuit.*

[3] Ibid., p. 76: 'Rex etc. Galfrido filio Petri etc. Mandamus vobis quod si

Philip de Lucy was entrusted with the execution of this kind of writ on one other occasion only;[1] indeed, though his commission was allowed to run until St. Margaret's day,[2] he vanished from the receipt from that time forward and was superseded, first by one of Peter des Roches's personal interventions,[3] and, after 12 April, by the Bishop's confidential clerk, William de St. Maxence.[4] For the next three months the work of the receipt was done by a combination of the latter with Ralf Parmenter, *serviens camerae*, and a rising man in the household.[5] Finally, the most forceful of all the chamber's employees, Richard Marsh, was set at its head. We have our first formal record of his title as *Clericus Camerae* on 12 July 1207.[6]

The rolls, being already almost in common form, obscure rather than betray the crises of officialdom, but the recourse to the bishop of Winchester and his agent would alone vouch for some considerable disturbance. Whether or not the refusal of these particular writs was the cause alike of the fall of Philip de Lucy and the rise of Richard Marsh, Richard's appointment coincided with a change so calculated as to rid the court of its dependence upon the Exchequer and to place large sums at its disposal without the formality of writs of *Liberate* to the treasurer and chamberlains. This change took the form of the extinction of the subordinate treasure of Winchester and of a drastic clearance of treasure from Westminster and Westminster control. The money thus freed was lodged at Nottingham, Marlborough, Bristol, and Devizes, and intermittently in other centres. It was placed in the security of the castle towers and vaults and under the custody of the castellans, by whom no royal mandate, however worded, would be refused, and it is to be observed that at this very time John made most unusual efforts to bring to England not only Gerard d'Athies but Gerard's associates, Engelard de Cigogny and Andrew, Guy, and Peter des Chanceux.[7]

Thesaurarii et Camerarii nostri non fecerint habere dilecto nostro Philippo de Lucy 315 marcas sicut eis mandavimus vos ei illas habere faciatis ad pacaciones nostras faciendas et vos si fieri potest pacacionibus illis intersitis' (18 January 1207).

[1] On 13 Mar. 1207 (ibid., p. 79).
[2] *Rot. Lit. Pat.*, p. 74 (dated either 8 or 20 July 1207).
[3] Ibid., p. 70.   [4] *Rot. Lit. Claus.* i. 83, 87, and *passim*.
[5] Ibid., pp. 81, 82, and *passim*.
[6] *Rot. Lit. Pat.*, p. 74. He first warrants a receipt on 5 Aug. Until October Ralph Parmenter was occasionally associated with him.
[7] Provision was made for the whole group, Gerard, Engelard, and the three Chanceux brothers, in a kind of bachelors' quarters in the manor of Hurstbourne in Hampshire. This was in Mar. 1207 while Gerard was still a French prisoner. The king made a loan of 1,000 marks for his ransom in May and the Master of the

A beginning was made in July, when 20,000 marks were drawn and dispatched, 10,000 marks each, to Thomas de Sandford at Devizes and Hugh de Nevill at Marlborough.[1] This was on 7 July, and on the 19th 5,000 marks newly arrived at Winchester and 6,000 of old stock were taken.[2] The authority of the constable of Winchester was invoked to make this transfer, and the whole 11,000 was then taken into the chamber and dispatched to Nottingham to go into custody.[3] On the 29th a further 1,000 marks was sent to Reginald de Cornhill to form a treasure at Rochester,[4] and in August William Brewer carried 2,400 marks from Winchester to Exeter.[4] On this occasion livery was made by the constable alone, so that Exchequer control seems to have been at an end. Winchester must have been emptied by these withdrawals, and I cannot find that it was ever used again.

Withdrawals from Westminster continued throughout the autumn of 1207 and the spring of 1208: 10,000 marks to Exeter in October, 'Willelmo Briwerr . . . custodiendum quamdiu nobis placuerit apud Exoniam';[5] in November 4,500 to Salisbury,[6] and 2,000 more in January;[7] 2,000 to Exeter in March;[8] 17,000 to Bristol in April.[9] On 15 April it is ordered in general that revenue as it comes into the Exchequer is to be dispatched to Marlborough *ad ponendum ibi in thesauro*.[10] It is clear, then—and the fact will become increasingly clear as the reign goes on—that the castle treasures were no longer temporary resting-places for money going abroad, but had become the pivots of a new and permanent policy of decentralization. The principal Chancery rolls are lacking between 1208 and 1212, but the gap is to some extent filled by the rolls of the household expenses from Ascension 1209 to 1210, the Misae Rolls, which give us a different angle of approach. These show us that large intakes of revenue from the provinces passed through the chamber directly into the custody of the castellans, who were thus no longer solely dependent upon *Liberates* to the Exchequer for the maintenance of their stores.

Temple in France provided safe conduct to the coast for his wife and children (*Rot. Lit. Claus.* i. 79, 92; *Rot. Lit. Pat.*, p. 75).

[1] *Rot. Lit. Claus.* i. 86.   [2] Ibid., p. 88.

[3] Ibid., p. 88: 'Rex Thesaurario et W. et R. Camerariis etc. Sciatis quod recepimus in camera nostra apud Winton' die Beate Marie Magdalene anno regni nostri ix° per manus Lowici clerici et Petri de Ely et Willelmi Anglici 11,000 marcarum liberatas Roberto de Veteri Ponte ad ducendum usque Notingham per preceptum nostrum. Et ideo vobis mandamus quod vos et ipsi sitis quieti.'

[4] Ibid., p. 90.   [5] Ibid., pp. 95, 98.   [6] Ibid., p. 97.
[7] Ibid., p. 99.   [8] Ibid., p. 105.
[9] *Rot. Lit. Pat.*, p. 81.   [10] *Rot. Lit. Claus.* i. 111.

The profits of the ecclesiastical estates in the years of interdict flowed in large measure along these internal lines, £1,000—more than half of it from the *exitus* of the bishoprics of Durham, Ely, and Chester—went *ad custodiendum* to Ralf Parmenter at Corfe,[1] 100 marks of the fine of the archdeacon of Durham, 50 of that of the Durham monks,[2] and £300 from the archbishopric[3] were received by Reginald de Cornhill into Rochester. Rather later he took in £200 from the bishopric of Exeter and the canons of Newburgh.[4]

The practice, now well established, is for the chamber to receive point by point on its journeys as much of the great outstanding fines and profits as can conveniently be collected on the spot and to dispatch what it cannot use immediately into the nearest of the provincial treasures or to that which is most in need of funds.[5] Profits received in the south-east, when the court is in Kent, Surrey, or even in London, will in all probability be sent to Reginald de Cornhill at Rochester: from the middle west it will be committed to Thomas de Sandford at Devizes, to Corfe, or, most commonly, to the premier of all such centres in the south, to John's most favoured castle of Marlborough and its castellan Hugh de Nevill. Marlborough's counterpart in the north is Nottingham: at times Northampton comes into occasional use,[6] or, as in this year of 1209–10, when John is in Yorkshire and beyond, the furthest outpost of the chain, Brian de Insula's custody of Knaresborough. Thither went nearly 1,000 marks of the archdeacon of Durham's fine collected while the chamber was at York.[7]

Inevitably an exceptional group of officials arose to discharge the service of the provincial treasures. Unlike their purely military colleagues, they were kept for years at a time in the same castellanry; they had the aptitudes of the lay officials of the Exchequer and much the same kind of experience, though it was from the military household that most of them were chosen; they were men of substance and a high proportion of them foreigners. William Brewer and Hugh de Nevill, the first one of the leading financial experts of his day, whose intervention in all kinds of account was constantly sought, the second, as *custos* of the forests, the head of one of the largest financial administrations, hardly need to be characterized. William Brewer, accordingly, became

---

[1] *Rot. Misae*, p. 110.
[2] Ibid., p. 114.   [3] Ibid., p. 145.   [4] Ibid., p. 115.
[5] Ibid., p. 142 (£400 to Bristol), 152 (100 marks to Bristol), 147 (50 marks to Devizes).
[6] Ibid., p. 148.   [7] Ibid., p. 127.

constable of Exeter and its treasure from the day that it first came to be the base of supply for Poitou,[1] while Hugh de Nevill, acting sometimes through deputies, managed John's favourite stronghold of Marlborough till he surrendered it to Louis in 1216. Robert de Vipont, who had been *custos* of the treasure at Loches in 1202,[2] and of that of the Tower of Rouen in 1203, and gaoler of Prince Arthur, returned with John to England. In October 1204 he became castellan of Nottingham, then at the beginning of its history as a financial centre, and retained it until October 1208 when he was succeeded by Philip Mark.[2] Gerard d'Athies, as seneschal of Tours, had held an office which was partly financial. After his ransom from French imprisonment, he came to England in the spring of 1207, bringing with him his associates Engelard de Cigogny and Guy and Andrew and Peter des Chanceux. He was almost immediately sent to Gloucester with 1,000 marks to remain *in thesauro* there.[3] On 6 March 1208 he succeeded Robert de Roppsley in the castlery of Bristol.[4] He seems to have retained the charge of both treasures, for in April he took 17,000 marks of the treasure of Marlborough into Bristol, and in May received 1,500 marks of the servants of the Treasurer at Gloucester.[5] By 1212 Gerard d'Athies had been succeeded at Bristol by his follower Peter des Chanceux whom we find joint *custos* of the *thesaurus Bristollie* with Roger Cordewaner. Peter remained there until replaced by Philip d'Albigny on 20 July 1215.[6] At Devizes Thomas de Sandford, one of the fixed pillars of the reign, remained as constable throughout. From 1206 he had the Devizes treasure in custody,[7] and he was often busied in the transport and delivery of large sums of money to and from the chamber, his own castle, and those of other castellans.[8]

These men were the principal figures of the years before the Barons' War. The money that supplied the chamber and its provincial depots was carried by lesser, but still substantial, subordinates who took the place which the treasurer's clerk and his companions held in the Exchequer. Mainly they were members of the king's military and civil households or of those of the castellans. In 1213 and 1215 the principal of these couriers was

---

[1] *Rot. Lit. Pat.*, p. 11.
[2] *Rot. Lit. Pat.*, pp. 9, 26, 46, 86. Philip Mark retained the castle until the end of the reign, although the king was compelled to order him to surrender it in 1215.
[3] *Rot. Lit. Claus.* i. 99.   [4] Ibid., p. 105.
[5] *Rot. Lit. Pat.*, p. 81; *Rot. Lit. Claus.* i. 114.
[6] *Rot. Lit. Claus.* i. 221.   [7] Ibid., p. 61.
[8] Ibid., pp. 61, 71, 138, 153.

Master Ernulf de Auckland, among whose biggest undertakings was the transfer of the whole treasure of Bristol, on the same day, 26 December 1213, that Brian de Insula and Henry de Braybroke were dispatched to bring south the whole treasure of Nottingham.[1] In 1204 the head of the couriers for the channel crossing was Andrew de Beauchamp—who appears again in 1214.[2] About the same time Stephen de Turnham was employed, and at intervals during the reign, Robert de Barevill.[3] As soon as civil war broke out, the Templars Alan Martell and Emeric de St. Maure tend to replace the secular couriers.[4] The rolls give us glimpses of this or that man rather than the clear picture of a routine such as was borne by the London couriers, but the type of official employed, the household knight of the middle rank or the senior serjeant or yeoman, was constant, and, from time to time, the same individuals recur.

Until 1212 the financial map was clearly that of the civil administration, the treasures being so disposed as to serve the normal itineration of the court. Thus, in the eleventh year, for which we have the roll of the Misae, the full tale of the treasure castles was in active use: Reginald de Cornhill at Rochester, Brian de Insula at Knaresborough, Engelard de Cigogny at Gloucester,[5] Robert de Braybroke at Northampton,[6] as well those depots which had already become permanent, Bristol, Devizes, Corfe, Nottingham, and Marlborough.

War, on the other hand, emptied the castles more remote from the scene of action and concentrated money in the bases of the campaign. By 1212 it was already the castles and not the Exchequer that kept the army in the field, and war could have been fought without a penny from Westminster. When John was at Nottingham waiting for the assembly of the host that was summoned for 19 August 1212 to Chester, he received three small sums taken from the *denarii de scaccario*,[7] but there were none of the large Exchequer convoys of earlier days. From the castle treasures, on the other hand, coin was being delivered in bulk. The Close Rolls only resume on 6 May 1212: after this date

[1] *Rot. Lit. Pat.*, pp. 103, 104, 107, 108, 153.
[2] *Rot. Lit. Claus.* i. 13; *Rot. Lit. Pat.*, p. 107.
[3] *Rot. Lit. Claus.* i. 82, 89, 90; *Rot. Misae*, p. 236.
[4] *Rot. Lit. Pat.*, pp. 108, 117, and *passim*.
[5] *Rot. Misae*, p. 142.
[6] Ibid., p. 148.
[7] Three deliveries of rather less than £1,500 were made on 16, 17, and 18 Aug. by Ralph, the treasurer's clerk, Richard Scissor, and Walter Anglicus (*Rot. Lit. Claus.* i. 122).

48,000 marks were brought up from Bristol, while 4,000 were moved from Rochester to London to be forwarded by instalments, 'de tanto volumus accrescere thesaurum nostrum de Notingham'.[1] There must have been large transfers before the record begins, for after the dismissal of the host 120,000 marks were sent back to Bristol alone for redistribution in the western castles.[2]

In 1213 we have the Close, Patent, and Misae Rolls intact for the whole time of the preparation of the defensive war against the French. In May 1213, when John was watching the southern coasts against invasion, 10,000 marks were brought into Kent by the Templars, who now were coming to the fore as custodians of the king's treasure, and were received *in camera nostra apud Wingham*.[3] 10,000 were taken from Devizes and 30,000 from Nottingham at the same time.[4] A month later 20,000 were lodged in the New Temple to be drawn on by John fitz Hugh and Fawkes, 'nunc propter mille marcarum, nunc propter duo vel tria milia', for their embassy to the Low Countries.[5] 100,000 marks were moved eastward from Bristol into Corfe and Devizes, 50,000 for each castle, and in July Devizes provided 20,000 for Brian de Insula. 20,000 went from Bristol to the king at Canterbury.[6] The story of the campaign of 1214 in Poitou is much the same. John sailed in the second week of February, and six weeks before identical writs to Peter des Chanceux and Philip Mark emptied the treasures of Bristol and Nottingham in anticipation of his departure.[7] In October 1213 120,000 marks had been restored at Bristol, so that the sums drawn must have been very large.[8] A Close writ of the same day suggests that the treasure of Northampton was being brought south simultaneously under the convoy of its constable and Brian de Insula.[9] That of Corfe was moved to Portsmouth at the end of January.[10] Peter de Maulay was to be the *custos* of the king's treasure abroad with his headquarters at La Rochelle, and he took up 40,000 marks from the castle of Devizes by the livery of Thomas de Sandford at Portsmouth before he sailed.[11] No doubt this went across the Channel with him.

Again, as in 1213, the rolls show no signs of any substantial withdrawals from the Exchequer. Except for one draft of £500

[1] *Rot. Lit. Claus.* i. 123; *Rot. Misae*, p. 236.
[2] *Rot. Lit. Claus.* i. 153.   [3] Ibid., p. 134.
[4] *Rot. Lit. Pat.*, p. 99.   [5] *Rot. Lit. Claus.* i. 136.
[6] Ibid., p. 153.   [7] *Rot. Lit. Pat.*, p. 107.
[8] *Rot. Lit. Claus.* i. 153.   [9] Ibid., p. 158.
[10] Ibid., p. 162.   [11] *Rot. Lit. Pat.*, pp. 110, 112, 116.

in favour of the Chancellor, the provincial treasures, pooled at Portsmouth under Peter de Maulay, provided the coin with which John sailed for his last continental adventure. The surviving writs—it is to be doubted whether they tell us all the facts— show us, therefore, that over a period of years the provincial treasures were capable of providing a war chest of something like 200,000 marks at call. If John's methods were summary, he had at least found the secret of keeping a formidable financial machine in being and concentrating its power in emergency without delay. As one result it seems that the chamber became less ready to interfere with the flow of debts, fines, and other profits along their normal channels to the Exchequer than it had been before the provincial deposits were available. So much may go upon the credit side of the balance between routine and innovation.

The sums *in thesauro* from 1212 to 1214 were the accumulation of five years of reduced military effort, and it would seem that they were largely exhausted by the great campaign of 1214 with its army in Poitou and the subsidies sent to the cities and nobles of the Low Countries and the emperor. There would be many lean months before the treasures could be refilled, and during their convalescence John would inevitably revert to the normal impecuniousness of feudal kingship.

He returned to England in October 1214. In the ensuing eight months he was forced through a series of confrontations and concessions, utterly uncharacteristic of him, which ended in the temporary surrender of Runnymede. It is difficult to say how much of the unwonted enterprise of the baronage was due to a knowledge that the king was, for the time being at least, almost without money for a fresh war, but that fact is itself sufficient to explain his own hesitations and compliances and to reconcile us to the apparent contrast of his mood with his decisive handling of the treason of August 1212. Some of the treasures had been completely emptied and their stores carried to France or sent to Flanders: the rest must have been heavily depleted, and there is no evidence that they had been adequately restored. The strength of the years 1213 and 1214, with their steady flow of treasure along the financial arteries of the country, was now almost entirely lacking. We hear no more of convoys of tens of thousands of marks. The few mandates to the constables speak rather of scores and hundreds doled out in payment of mercenaries or for castle works.[1] The drafts made for the king's own use were similarly

[1] *Rot. Lit. Pat.*, pp. 126, 135, 136, 137, 142.

small.[1] Money was hard to come by from London also. Urgent payments were waiting for 'the next pence that shall come into the Exchequer'.[2] John was sending to Ypres and Ghent to recover his war subsidies,[3] begging *pro amore nostro et peticione* for release from the payment of the clergy's damages under the interdict settlement,[4] borrowing from the Templars the journey-money of his foreign knights, and lodging all his gold in the Temple because he could not repay them.[5]

There does not seem to have been much recovery before the Civil War wrested the whole system from its base. There was some treasure at the Tower under Peter des Roches,[6] perhaps what was left from his justiciarship, and also in Bristol, Devizes, Marlborough, Nottingham, and Corfe, the last three making payments mostly for local works and wages. In November 1214 4,200 marks were drafted into Marlborough.[7] Philip de Ulcote had money, perhaps at Durham, and the garrisons of the northern castles were being paid by him and also by Philip Mark from Nottingham.[8] But payments were small and local.

In the winter and spring of 1214–15 poverty threw the king back upon the Exchequer. What had been paid, in part at least, by the chamber, was now presented for the treasurer and chamberlains to pay in the form of comprehensive *Liberates* which covered the expenses of several weeks.[9] No doubt these took their turn to be honoured *de proximis denariis receptis*. For one matter, John could not afford to wait. It was vital that his foreign soldiers should have security for the payment of their fees; the chamber could no longer afford the wholesale advances which it had made in 1210 and 1212, and he, therefore, took the unprecedented step of breaking down the responsibility of the treasurer and chamberlains. For a period of about a month, in January and February 1215, Richard Marsh, chancellor since October, and still imbued with the principles of the *camera*, was imposed upon the Exchequer. For the payments of the *feoda Flandrensium*, *Liberates* took the strange form: 'Rex etc. Magistro Ricardo de Marisco Cancellario et W. Thesaurario et G. et R. Camerariis'.[10] The contemporary impression must have been violent and one may detect a proleptic echo of Peter des Roches's financial strategy of eighteen years later.

[1] *Rot. Lit. Claus.* i. 184.   [2] Ibid., p. 221.
[3] Ibid., p. 182; *Rot. Lit. Pat.*, pp. 122, 123.   [4] *Rot. Lit. Pat.*, p. 124.
[5] Ibid., pp. 135, 141.   [6] *Rot. Lit. Claus.* i. 192.
[7] Ibid., p. 176.   [8] Ibid., pp. 193, 214, 228, and *passim*.
[9] Ibid., p. 180.   [10] Ibid., pp. 185, 188.

The Exchequer had thus been under durance in the winter but, from 31 May 1215, London was in the hands of the barons, and as soon as the king took the field he lost all that London had and ceased to send his writs thither. From August 1215 the scene was one of increasing confusion in which our accustomed sources of record—*Liberate* and *Computate*—are discontinued or diverted. John had now to live on the country-side, taking up his ancient profits where he had peaceful control, and paying his English and foreign mercenaries partly by grants of *terrae inimicorum*, partly out of fines and tenseries wrested from the disloyal. In these last months the financial scheme was broken and contracted to the moving radius of the king's main army and to a few areas still in his power. Almost all the financial organization that remained came to be focused on the castles and their constables, especially Peter de Maulay, the paymaster of 1214, at Corfe, and Philip Mark at Nottingham; and inevitably these centres changed their character and began to do the double work of treasure and exchequer, each for so much of the north and south as lay within its range.

While John was subduing the northern rebels, Corfe remained the real financial centre for the south. By December 1215 it was able to send 10,000 marks to the king.[1] It paid garrisons as far away as Exeter, and threw large sums into Winchester, where William Brewer was organizing a defence.[2] Winchester thus accumulated nearly 20,000 marks by the spring of 1216.[3] As the campaign moved south again, John sent urgent demands for money, 'for the lack of which we may come into great peril'.[4] Nottingham, however, was more nearly the financial capital of the dismembered kingdom. John's winter and spring campaign was in the north and in East Anglia. It had been punitive and profitable, and when he turned south to meet Louis it fell to Philip Mark to exact and accumulate the great sums by which the northern rebels were still buying their peace. In so many words John ordered Philip to act in place of the lapsed Exchequer —*sicut dum scaccarium nostrum teneretur*—both for the new debts and for the customary farms of the Crown, and to store the profits in Nottingham castle; and he sent him the rolls in which the debts were recorded.[5] The commission was for Philip's sheriff-dom, but from February 1216 he was, in fact, receiving the fines, tenseries, and amercements from a much wider area; the fines of

---

[1] *Rot. Lit. Pat.*, p. 161. [2] Ibid., p. 155.
[3] Ibid., p. 173. [4] Ibid., p. 170. [5] Ibid., pp. 179, 183.

the cities of York, Lincoln, Newark, and Beverley, and such large individual compositions as William de Eynsford's 1,000 marks for his release, or the abbot of Peterborough's 1,220 marks for disafforestation.[1] As part of his settlement of the north midlands, John held court at Lincoln and Stamford on 24 and 28 February and received the submission of about twenty principal rebels, whose hostages and charters were committed to Nottingham and whose fines were paid into Philip's treasure *ad custodiendum*.[2] Of these the chief was Ralf de Normannville, who bought his own release and that of his knights for 525 marks, a sum so moderate as to bear out John's statement that 'he wanted the loyalty and not the money of his barons'.

Allowing for disorder and for the failure of normal revenue, we can say that John's system of provincial treasures served him well in 1215 and 1216. At least it kept an army in the field for a year after the Exchequer and the London treasure had ceased to exist as royal institutions. The story has been necessarily curtailed here and secondary matters have been omitted—Fawkes's short-lived treasure at Bedford, his custody of the chamber, and the gradual and intermittent supersession of the chamber by the wardrobe. It remains to outline the principles upon which the castle treasures worked and to bring home again their essential dependence upon the chamber.

The machinery of receipt and delivery by writ was designed at once to achieve security, to provide a quittance to those who had taken part in the transaction—primarily the couriers—and to determine the fact of the cessation of the Exchequer's responsibility and control. As a rule, mandates to the Treasurer to release coin into provincial custody were by letters close containing the term *liberate* or some equivalent form of words. Communications between the king and the constables were normally by letters patent, for they might have to be shown to a variety of authorities. Receipt would be acknowledged by the constable by his own letters patent and the king would then send a close writ to the treasurer and chamberlains, reporting that acknowledgement and declaring them and their couriers quit of liability for the sum transferred, 'quod tam vos quam ipsi servientes inde sitis quieti'. The warrantor of such writs of quittance, where warrant was given, was as a rule the clerk of the chamber.[3]

---

[1] *Rot. Lit. Claus.* i. 169, 174; *Rot. Lit. Pat.*, pp. 165, 192, 193.
[2] *Rot. de Finibus*, pp. 577–81.
[3] *Rot. Lit. Claus.* i. 90 (1207): 'Rex W. Thesaurario et C. et R. Camerariis etc.

The effect of these exchanges was to release the treasure into a new field in which the only authorities were those of the chamber and the constables, empowered to act by the king's writs. Without imagining rivalries and stresses which did not always exist, there was a sense in which, as Jean de Préaux remarked, 'the king can do what he will with this money'. He could have it where he would in the country and he could get at it by any kind of writ or by no writ, through any persons and under any forms of security that he cared to devise. Above all, he could have it in great stores, lying at the strategic points of the provinces against a sudden need or the normal calls of his working journeys.

The rules of deposit and custody are not so easy to determine. At Bristol the constable played a part in the custody, but the principal trustee, to whom writs of *Liberate* were addressed, and who, in virtue of his charge was immune from all legal action except before the king or the justiciar, was Roger Cordewaner, citizen and later mayor of Bristol, a strong west-country man of commerce.[1] He had with him as colleagues Nicholas and Peter la Werre, a commission which with little change continued in action until 1215. Something of the regulation of this Bristol treasure is known. It began, as has been said, with the *Thesaurus Hiberniae*, it was stored in the *vouta forinseca* of Bristol castle, and, if the usage of 1215 is to be taken as typical, it lay under the seals of the constable and the burgess custodians jointly and could not be opened without their joint authority, the constable having access to it on the king's writ in the presence of the burgesses.[2] Two other of the earliest founded depots may have had burgess custodians with somewhat similar functions, for we find three citizens associated with Robert de Bareville in receiving treasure from Exeter in 1207,[3] and at Gloucester, in 1208, Guido de Castellis

Sciatis nos recepisse litteras patentes Reginaldi de Cornhull testificantes quod in Octabis Apostolorum Petri et Pauli recepit mille marcarum de thesauro apud Roffam per manus Petri de Ely et Ricardi Terrici et Thome de Sebrichteswurth servientium vestrorum. Et ideo volumus quod tam vos quam ipsi servientes inde sitis quieti. Teste me ipso apud Rokingeham, x die Augusti. Per Ricardum de Marisco.'

[1] *Rot. Lit. Pat.*, p. 54.

[2] Ibid., p. 136: 'Rex Petro de Cancellis etc. Mandamus vobis, quod assumptis vobiscum Rogero Cordewan, Nicholao filio Nicholai, Philippo Longo et Petro la Werr accedatis ad thesaurum nostrum et per visum predictorum serruras infringi faciatis et iterum novas serruras apponatis et cum de thesauro illo ceperitis id quod capturi estis claves sub sigillis predictorum iiijor legalium hominum sigillari faciatis et illas in custodia vestra salvo custodiri faciatis. Teste ut supra. Mandatum est predictis iiijor hominibus quod intersint ad hoc faciendum ut predictum est.'

[3] *Rot. Lit. Claus.* i. 90.

took in ten sacks, presumably 1,500 marks, 'per visum burgensium Gloucestrie Ricardi Ruffi et Ricardi Burgensis'.[1]

In a fully constituted treasure, money *in thesauro* was packed in sealed *foruli*,[2] and by a practice known as *renovatio thesauri* computers and weighers could be sent from time to time to reckon and assay the coin.[3]

Matters changed after the war of 1214 during which cruder methods were employed under the direction of Peter de Maulay from his treasure at La Rochelle. In the days of civil war, variability and lack of fixed rule were inevitable and advantageous. After August 1215 there is in one sense an increase of precautions, but there is no longer any routine at all. The Templars, Alan Martell and Emeric de Saint Maure, with their comparative immunity, largely supersede the old official couriers. The Exchequer falls into abeyance. The constables are given a great responsibility. Peter des Chanceux—the burgess commissioners seem to have ceased to act—can draw upon the treasure of Bristol for the pay and expenses of his garrison.[4] Peter de Maulay at Corfe has an allowance *extra thesaurum* for the many concerns of the south-west that are in his hands.[5] Philip Mark at Nottingham seems at times to have free access to his treasure, and in the spring of 1216 he had a virtual monopoly of the king's financial concerns in the north.

But all this was in the bad days of war. Normally, the provincial treasure seems to be so much a part of chamber finance that one cannot be treated without the other. It is the chamber that controls the system and for which the system exists. A constant exchange is going on between the castles and the chamber. The chamber is involved directly or indirectly in most transactions. If coin in bulk is sent to build up the reserves of Marlborough or Devizes, Gloucester or Nottingham, it is not, as a rule, consigned from the Exchequer to the castellan. If it is reasonably possible it passes through the chamber. From the chamber, by warrant of its presiding clerk, the treasurer and chamberlains will get their quittance and the new custodian his authority. The Exchequer couriers and the recipient constable or his agent are brought together before the *Clericus Camerae* or other witness and the transfer is made in their presence and recorded. Thus,

---

[1] Ibid., p. 113.   [2] *Rot. Lit. Pat.*, p. 180.
[3] *Rot. Lit. Claus.* i. 180: 'Liberate ii computatoribus et i ponderatori euntibus apud Corf ad renovandum thesaurum xl solidos.'
[4] *Rot. Lit. Pat.*, pp. 137, 144.
[5] Ibid., pp. 154, 155, 161.

in June 1207, more treasure being needed for Marlborough and Devizes, the couriers under Peter de Ely presented 20,000 marks in the chamber at Winchester, and there, with the witness of the bishop of Winchester, delivered 10,000 to Hugh de Nevill and the other 10,000 to Thomas de Sandford, 'per preceptum nostrum eadem die et ibidem'.[1] Again, on 19 July the king, being at Devizes, ordered the servants of the treasurer at Winchester to deliver 11,000 marks to Robert de Vipont to be carried to Nottingham and arranged for the sheriff of Hampshire to provide transport.[2] From these two writs of the 19th it might be assumed that delivery had been sufficiently authorized and the transfer completed. But it was not so. The court moved in to Winchester on the 22nd, and it was not until Peter de Ely and William Anglicus had paid the treasure into the chamber on behalf of the Exchequer and it had been redelivered to Robert de Vipont that the 11,000 marks could start on their journey to the north.[3] Transfer of treasure from one constable to another would also, when possible, be made in the chamber.[4]

These drafts of treasure, therefore, passed out of the control of the treasurer and chamberlains into a provincial system of which the head was the itinerant *camera regis*, the limbs the castles of Marlborough, Bristol, Exeter, Devizes, Nottingham, and Corfe, and the hands William Brewer, Hugh de Nevill, Robert de Vipont, Reginald de Cornhill, Thomas de Sandford, Ralf Parmenter, Peter des Chanceux, Philip Mark, and Peter de Maulay. If the association of an office like the chamber with the great military charges of the constables seems wide and overstrained, that is largely because we have fallen into the habit of thinking of the household offices as civilian, domestic, and, in the modern sense, private. There is nothing public or private in the governing institutions of the early thirteenth century, and if the king be there all the power of the kingdom may be packed within the small compass of the *camera regis*. Under John, in practice and in temper, the greater part of executive government had in it the authoritarianism of military organization and borrowed easily from the precedents of war, and we can hardly exaggerate the extent to which the power and order of the kingdom was in this age a creation of the king. Where he did not infringe common right—and that is a large qualification—his strong executive government was an acting out of the full implications of king-

[1] *Rot. Lit. Claus.* i. 86.
[2] Ibid., p. 88.
[3] Ibid.
[4] *Rot. Lit. Pat.*, p. 81.

ship, partly as he had received it from his father and brother, partly as he himself remade it. That there was violence and abuse in his handling of the law the complainants of the Charter tell us, and we cannot question their verdict: but the general scope of John's kingship they accept in silence. They have known and can conceive no other. Law and exceptional affairs of state may come within the scope of a baronial *universitas*—*ideally* they may do so—but the executive is still the king's. It is there that we may look for the creativeness and strength of monarchy, and in doing so, understand that paradox of historians which speaks of John as 'the strongest of the Angevins'.

J. E. A. JOLLIFFE

THE DISPUTATION OF PETER OF CORNWALL AGAINST SYMON THE JEW

THE Augustinian Priory of Holy Trinity, Aldgate, in London, has disappeared without leaving any trace of its buildings.[1] It was one of the earliest houses of Augustinian canons to be founded in England. In the twelfth century it was a house with some reputation for learning. The first prior, Norman, was a pupil of Anselm of Laon, and the fifteenth-century chronicler of the house mentions the names of other scholars. His highest praise is reserved for the fourth prior, Peter of Cornwall (1197–1221), whom he calls the outstanding English doctor of his time.[2]

Peter tells us something about various members of his family in one of his works, the *Book of Visions*; but the little that we know about his own career has to be gleaned from indications in the prefaces to his various works. The four parts of one of them, the *Pantheologus*, were dedicated to Godfrey de Luci, bishop of Winchester, and two members of the Chapter of St. Paul's Cathedral, Ralph of Haute Rive and Master Henry of Northampton. Godfrey de Luci had been his fellow student in the schools,[3] and Master Henry of Northampton was apparently their master;[4] but whether the schools were those of St. Paul's we do not know. Peter represents Master Henry of Northampton as following with interest the literary work of his former pupil, now become a canon.[5]

---

[1] On the priory, see *V.C.H., London*, i. 465–74.

[2] 'Petrus de Cornubia prior quartus creatus est vii Id. Maii anno domini MCLXXXXVII, et obiit nonas Iulii anno domini MCCXXI, et sepultus est in medio capelle beate Marie virginis quam ipse edificavit. Qui quidem prior precipuus doctor inter omnes doctores Anglicos suo tempore floruit. Per triennium cum quodam Iudeo subtili disputans, ipsum convertens, concanonicum suum fecit. De sua disputacione diversos libros composuit, ac eciam Pantheologon, De reparacione lapsus, De duabus corrigiis predestinacionis et reprobacionis, et plures alios perutiles penes nos et alios habitos in diversis locis ad laudem Trinitatis.' The account of the house is prefixed to the cartulary, Glasgow Univ. Libr., Hunterian MS. U. 2. 6. I am indebted to Mr. J. C. Dickinson for a copy of this extract.

[3] This evidence of Godfrey's early training has not been noticed hitherto; cf. *Dict. Nat. Biog.* xii. 244. Peter says of him: 'Verumptamen quia maxima tibi est familiaritas cum literis, decet et famam nominis tui perpetuari per literas.' (Oxford, Lincoln Coll., MS. lat. 83, f. 1ʳb.)

[4] This is an inference from the way Peter refers to 'magister noster communis, qui adhuc superest' in the prologue of part IV (Lincoln Coll., MS. lat. 83, fol. 1ʳb), and his references to Mr. Henry of Northampton in the prologue of Part I (Oxford, Merton Coll., MS. 191, fol. 2ʳ).

[5] Part I, prologue, printed in *Trans. Royal Hist. Soc.*, 4th series, xix (1936), 38.

Master Ralph of Haute Rive, who was at one time master of the schools at St. Paul's, gave him money to hire scribes for copying the work.[1] We get a tantalizing glimpse of intellectual activity in the London of the second half of the twelfth century.

The date when Peter became a canon of Holy Trinity, Aldgate, cannot be ascertained precisely, but it was not before 1170. He remained there for the rest of his life, becoming prior in 1197. He died in 1221. He does not appear to have played any part in public affairs. The *Disputation*, which is the work to be discussed in this paper, was dedicated to Stephen Langton. It was finished in 1208, the year of the interdict, and it is of some interest to note that he was resting his hopes of the salvation of England on Stephen Langton.[2]

Peter was a voluminous writer. The first of his works was the *Pantheologus*, already mentioned, an enormous collection of *distinctiones* in four parts. It was finished about 1189.[3] In 1200 he was compiling a huge collection of visions, which has been analysed by M. R. James.[4] It is only known to survive in a single copy, 'which seems to have been transcribed under the eye of the author'. The *Disputation* against Symon the Jew was written in 1208. Two other works are referred to by the chronicler of Holy Trinity, Aldgate: *De reparatione lapsus generis humani* and *De duabus corrigiis predestinationis et reprobationis*. The former is dedicated to Gilbert Glanvill, bishop of Rochester.[5] It was written when Peter was prior, but earlier than the *Disputation*, which contains references to it. Its composition must therefore fall between 1197 and 1208. No manuscript of the latter has so far been identified.

Whether Peter was more than a compiler, and how far he was

---

[1] Part I, prol. preter rem, ibid., p. 33, n. 3.

[2] See the text printed below, p. 153. The text is unfortunately obscure.

[3] For a brief account of its genesis, see *Trans. Royal Hist. Soc.*, supra, p. 33 f. The second and third parts were the first to be finished. 'Hee due Pantheologi partes rudimenta operis mei erant.' (Oxford, Merton Coll., MS. 192, f. 1.) They were dedicated to Ralph of Haute Rive, who went on the Third Crusade in 1189 and was killed at Acre in 1191. In the prologue to the fourth part, dedicated to Godfrey de Luci, who became bishop of Winchester in 1189, Peter writes of Godfrey's promotion as a recent event: 'Honor denique episcopatus accessit tibi, si cogitetur etas, plus cicius quam tardius, si merita, plus tardius quam cicius . . . de cuius promocione datur amicis leticia, liuidis pena, posteris gloria.' (Oxford, Lincoln Coll., MS. lat. 83, f. 1rb.)

[4] *Descriptive Catalogue of the MSS. in the Library of Lambeth Palace*, Cambridge, 1930, pp. 71–85; cf. A. Wilmart, *Analecta Bollandiana*, lvi (1938), 15 f.

[5] A manuscript is briefly described in *Hist. MSS. Commission*, 6th Report, App., p. 344. I owe the reference to Mr. N. R. Ker. The references in the *Disputationes* are in MS. Eton Coll. 130, ff. 103ra, 121va, 214ra.

in touch with the newer theological learning of the schools in France,[1] an examination of the *De reparatione lapsus* may perhaps show. His reputation throughout the Middle Ages was maintained by the *Pantheologus*. References to it in the thirteenth century appear to be very few,[2] but in the fifteenth century it was regarded as an appropriate book for a learned library. There were copies of various parts in the University Library at Oxford,[3] and in Balliol (MS. 82), Lincoln (MS. lat. 83), Merton (MSS. 191–2),[4] and Oriel[5] Colleges. There was also a set at Syon Abbey (L 7–10). Most of the extant copies are of the first half of the thirteenth century.

Part of the *Disputation against Symon the Jew* is found in a fourteenth-century manuscript now at Eton College (no. 130),[6] where it follows the *Victoria contra Judeos*, written by Porchetus the Genoese Carthusian.[7] The manuscript was written in England, and it is noteworthy as showing that interest in the problem presented by the refusal of the Jews to accept Christ as the true Messiah continued after the Jews had been expelled from England. No other manuscript is at present known.[8] The opening words are: 'Ad probandum autem quod Messias iam venerit'. The work is cast in the form of a dialogue between Peter and a Jew called Symon, who was converted and became a canon of Holy Trinity, Aldgate. From the prologue we learn that the whole work was in two parts; the first, which is not known to survive, contained a collection of passages chiefly from the Old Testament, which refer to Christ, the true Messiah, and to His Church, and was called *Liber allegoriarum Petri contra Symonem Iudeum de confutatione Iudeorum*;[9] the second, which covers ff. 92–226ᵛ of the Eton manuscript, is divided into three books, and is called *Liber disputationum Petri contra Symonem Iudeum de confutatione*

---

[1] There is a general reference to the *Sentences* of Peter Lombard in the *Disputationes*, MS. Eton Coll. 130, f. 214ʳa.

[2] M. R. James noted that it was used in some manuscripts of the second family of manuscripts of the Bestiary (*The Bestiary*, Roxburghe Club, 1928, p. 14).

[3] *Epistolae academicae*, ed. Anstey (Oxford Hist. Soc. xxxv. 1898), p. 180.

[4] The missing volume of the set containing Part IV was cut up in the sixteenth century. Mr. N. R. Ker has discovered several leaves in the college library, which were used as wrappers or pastedowns. They are now collected in MS. E. 3. 5.

[5] Bale, *Index Britanniae Scriptorum*, ed. R. L. Poole and M. R. Bateson, Oxford, 1902, p. 321.

[6] I am much indebted to the Provost and Fellows of Eton College who have allowed me to use the manuscript in the Bodleian Library.

[7] This tract is not mentioned in the *Catalogue* by M. R. James (Cambridge, 1895). It fills ff. 3–91ᵛ.

[8] Bale noted a copy 'ex collegio Academiae, Oxon.', i.e. University College, *Index*, loc. cit.

[9] See below, pp. 154–5.

Iudeorum. In the first book of fifty-six chapters Peter sets out to prove that the Messiah has come and that He is the Christ; in the second book he attacks the Jewish method of literal interpretation of the Old Testament (chaps. 1–6), and then passes on to explain why certain Jewish rites and ceremonies were abolished after the advent of Christ (chaps. 7–14), and finally deals with objections against the view that Christ fulfilled the law and did not destroy it (chaps. 15–18); in the third book he goes through the proofs of the chief Christian dogmas from scripture and answers various objections raised by the Jews (chaps. 1–24), and in the last six chapters of the *Disputation* proper he amplifies remarks made earlier about God's call to the Jews and their rejection of it (chaps. 25–30). In the following chapter comes Symon's conversion (chap. 31). In four supplementary chapters Peter gives instruction to Symon, particularly on questions relating to the future state of man (chaps. 31–5).

Controversial literature directed against the Jews reappeared at the end of the eleventh century and was vigorously maintained throughout the twelfth, as the Jewish problem became more acute.[1] In England there appeared a series of tracts, beginning with Gilbert Crispin's *Disputatio Judaei cum Christiano*, dedicated to St. Anselm, one of the most widely known of all.[2] In the twelfth century we have the anonymous *Dialogus inter Christianum et Judaeum de fide catholica*, dedicated to Alexander, bishop of Lincoln (1123–48), the *Dialogus contra Judeos ad corrigendum et perficiendum destinatus*, addressed by Bartholomew, bishop of Exeter, to Baldwin, bishop of Worcester (1180–4) and later archbishop of Canterbury, and the *Invectiva contra perfidiam Judaeorum* by Peter of Blois.[3] In this list we should include the *Dialogi*

---

[1] For a survey of the printed texts, see A. Lukyn Williams, *Adversus Judaeos* (Cambridge, 1935), pp. 232–40, 365–407, to which I am more indebted than will appear from the following notes, and J. de Ghellinck, *L'Essor de la litt. latine au XIIᵉ siècle* (Brussels, 1946), i. 158–9 note, 161–8. I was not able to consult P. Brome, *Die Judenmission im Mittelalter und die Päpste* (Miscellanea hist. pontificiae, vi), Rome, 1942, in time to make use of it.

[2] See the list of manuscripts in J. A. Robinson, *Gilbert Crispin* (Cambridge, 1911), p. 61. I have noted three others: Brit. Mus., Harley 3021, saec. xii, written in Beneventan script, Oporto 34, and Zürich C. 121, f. 149, saec. xii.

[3] I have not included a brief anonymous tract, apparently not noticed hitherto, which is called in the catalogue of the library of Rochester Priory (1202) *Arma contra Iudeos*. A copy is in Oxford, Jesus Coll. 11, ff. 70ᵛ–76ʳ, saec. xii, where it is entitled: *Incipit disputatio contra incredulitatem Iudeorum excerpta ex libris prophetarum.* It begins: 'Dic igitur, o Iudee, qui dum trinitatem negas et unitatem consequenter ignoras.' The title in the Rochester catalogue is explained by the epilogue, in which the author writes: 'Quapropter dum nuda pene tibi scripturarum exempla proposui, velut sagittarum fasciculum in pharetra misi. Et quia ex verbis

cum Judaeo of Petrus Alphonsi, the converted Spanish Jew who migrated to England in the reign of Henry I, since it was widely known in England, at any rate from the second half of the century.[1] The writers of these treatises were men in touch with the schools, but not actually teachers.[2] They were concerned with a growing problem, both offensively and defensively. They set out to provide arguments to convince Jews, but often they were more anxious to arm Christians against attacks on their faith. An increasing bitterness of tone becomes evident. The courtesy and serenity that mark the *Disputatio* of Gilbert Crispin and the *Dialogi* of Petrus Alphonsi gives way to a bullying and threatening tone. Armitage Robinson has observed[3] that the anonymous author of the *Altercatio* 'is evidently dissatisfied with the leniency with which Gilbert treats his opponent. He is determined to secure the victory for his Christian opponent: he substitutes threatenings for arguments.' In the tracts of Bartholomew of Exeter and again in Peter of Blois[4] we find the sharpness combined with warnings against the dangers of open controversy with Jews. Bartholomew is worth quoting:[5]

'*Magister.* Nullus fidelium qui zelum dei habeat cum scientia eorum [*sc.* Iudeorum] calumnias seu blasfemias sine aliqua redarguitione sustinet, sed

---

contrariis suggeritur tibi copia respondendi, arma quidem prebui, quibus te in ictum effundere debeas, et quibus gladium stringere et clipeum circumvolvere, quia bella necdum imminent ad plenum docere non potui. Habes igitur coram posita que ad huiusmodi conflictum sunt necessaria. Utere paratis ut expedire decreveris. Omnipotens deus, dilectissime frater, ab invisibilium te insidiis hostium misericorditer protegat et immunem te de huius mundi certamine ad celestia regna perducat. Amen.' There are verbal parallels here with the epilogue of the *Invectiva* of Peter of Blois (*Pat. Lat.* 207, col. 870). The relationship between the two works requires further elucidation.

[1] On Petrus Alphonsi, see below, p. 151. The first reference which I have discovered is in the *Dialogus* of Bartholomew of Exeter (Oxford, Bodleian Library, MS. Bodley 482 (S.C. 2046), f. 22ʳb), where a passage beginning: 'Legi (Regi *cod.*) et ego expositionem cuiusdam de Iudaismo ad Christum conversi in hunc modum: Multi sunt termini . . .', which is taken from P. Alph., *Dial., Pat. Lat.* 157, col. 625. There are two twelfth-century manuscripts, Cambridge, St. John's Coll. 107, and Fitzwilliam Museum, McClean 120, a fine copy (see pl. 78 in the *Catalogue* of M. R. James). Other English manuscripts are Cambridge, C.C.C. 309, f. 37, saec. xiii in. (St. Mary's, York); St. John's Coll. 86, saec. xiii in. (Beauchief); Pembroke Coll. 244, saec. xiv in. (following Grosseteste's *De cessatione legalium*); Oxford, Bodleian Library, MS. Bodley 801 (S.C. 2659), f. 206 (Witham), Laud misc. 356; Merton Coll. 175, f. 281ᵛ, saec. xv, a fragment. There is an excerpt headed 'Petrus Alfonsus' in Oxford, Jesus Coll. 11, f. 21ᵛb = *Pat. Lat.* 157, col. 615*a*.

[2] De Ghellinck, op. cit., p. 161.

[3] Op. cit., p. 62.

[4] *Pat. Lat.* 207, col. 827*c*.

[5] Bodley 482, f. 1ᵛa.

nec cum ipsis coram infidelibus vel imperitis de fide contendit. Quotiens enim cum eis pro ipsorum etiam salute conferimus, inquietorum animalium more commune negotium semper impediunt, nolentes intelligere ut bene agant vel credant. Unde quantum salva caritate fieri potest, eorum non solum collationes, sed et colloquia universa declinare debemus, scientes quia corrumpunt bonos mores colloquia prava, et qui tetigerit picem inquinabitur ab ea.

Discipulus. Qualiter ergo discemus quid eis respondendum quidve sit obiciendum, cum opus fuerit, nisi conferendo cum ipsis?

Magister. Hoc a fidelibus disce qui maiorem habent utriusque testamenti peritiam quam Iudei.'

The source of all the writers whom we have mentioned is chiefly the Old Testament as interpreted by a long line of Christian commentators. Again Bartholomew is worth quoting:[1]

'*Discipulus.* In primis igitur quero que sit inter Iudeos et nos dissensionis causa principalis.

Magister. Causam principalem soli deo cognitam credo, cuius iudicio iustissimo quamvis occulto facta est ex maxima parte cecitas in Israel, ut plenitudo gentium intraret ad fidem. Quo facto Israel convertetur ad Christum. Causarum vero nobis cognitarum dissensionis inter nos et illos hec michi prima videtur quod illi omnem veteris instrumenti scripturam in qua literalem possunt sensum invenire, ad literam semper accipiunt, nisi manifestum Christo perhibeat testimonium. Tunc enim aut scripturam negant, dicentes hoc in Hebraica veritate, id est in suis libris, non haberi, vel ad aliud aliquid fabulose convertunt, vel ut nondum completum prestolantur, vel alia aliqua fraude serpentina, cum arctari se sentiunt, elabuntur. Allegoriam vero nunquam nisi cum alium non habent exitum recipere solent. Nos vero non solum scripturas sacras, sed et res factas et facta ipsa mistice interpretamur, ita tamen ut nec in rebus gestis historia, nec in scripturis competens intelligentia per allegorie libertatem aliquatenus evacuetur.'

The importance of Petrus Alphonsi is that he had first-hand knowledge of post-biblical Jewish writings, and thus could give Christians some insight into the viewpoint of their antagonists. The form chosen by the Christian writers we have mentioned was the dispute or dialogue, with the exception of Peter of Blois, whose work was cast in a rhetorical form. But it is to be noted that Bartholomew had already got away from this form of a dispute between Christian and Jew.

It is against this background of controversialist and apologetic writing that we must set the treatise of Peter of Cornwall. Even if he were not writing in a form fixed by a long tradition, we

[1] Bodley 482, f. 1ᵛb.

should not expect to find any great originality of treatment. The *Pantheologus* and the collection of visions show Peter as a tireless compiler, and what chiefly marks out his treatise is its great length. He says himself that he has disputed with Symon at greater length than any other Christian against any other Jew.[1] In the Eton manuscript there are 536 columns of approximately 64 lines. Text is piled upon text, example upon example, connected only by 'item'. For instance in the chapter proving that the Messiah has come and that he is Christ by the miracles and other wonderful works of the saints believing on Christ, a list of *opera miranda* performed by the saints fills a whole column.[2] In the preceding section he has gone through all the miracles performed by the Apostles one by one. He continues by saying that many other saints have performed miracles, and he gives a list of saints, which is worth reproducing. The saints are clearly those to which Peter had a special devotion:[3]

'Item. In nomine Christi non solum predicti sed etiam postea alii sancti et moderni multa miracula fecerunt et faciunt, velut beatus Nicholaus, Martinus, Bricius, Ieronimus, Gregorius, Augustinus, Laurentius, Vincentius, Ambrosius, Hilarius, Martialis, Apollinaris, Silvester, Dunstanus, Alphegus, Anselmus, Thomas Cantuarienses episcopi, Edmundus, Mellitus, Erkenwaldus, Edwardus, Albanus,Wlstanus et infiniti alii sancti per universum orbem constituti.'

Again, in his discussion of the credibility of the virgin birth as one of those events 'que . . . non fiunt contra naturam, sed secundum naturam que deo et non nobis cognita est',[4] he piles up alleged

---

[1] iii. 22, f. 214ra: 'Domine Iudee . . . tecum disputavi plus quam aliquis alius Christianus contra aliquem Iudeum umquam tractaverit vel disputaverit.'

[2] i. 26, f. 116ra–b: 'Per fidem enim vicerunt regna, operati sunt iusticiam . . . mortuos suos [Heb. xi. 33–5]. Quidam enim frondes silvestres mutaverunt in gemmas et postea easdem gemmas in propriam reformaverunt naturam. Sancti quoque venenum biberunt, et nichil eis nocuit. De ferventis olei dolio illesi exierunt. Super carbones ambulaverunt. Excruciati nichil senserunt. Montes et saxa mire magnitudinis transtulerunt', and so on. He ends: 'Quid plura? Non solummodo dies, sed etiam annus michi deficeret antequam percurrerem breviter narrando sanctorum opera miranda.'

[3] Ibid., f. 115va.

[4] iii. 3, f. 204rb–205ra. I give his preliminary division, since I have not found the source: 'Tripartita enim sunt opera dei, que tamen omnia fiunt secundum naturam et non contra naturam vel rationem. Quedam enim sunt ex ratione, quedam secundum rationem, quedam supra rationem. Nulla tamen contra rationem. ⟨Que ex ratione,⟩ sunt necessaria, ut Si est homo, non est lapis. Hoc enim rationi congruit. Que secundum rationem, credibilia sunt, ut Si pregnans est mulier, verisimile est quod cum viro concubuit. Hoc enim ratio exigit. Que vero supra rationem sunt, mirabilia sunt, quorum ratio deo nota est et angelis, sed nobis ignota est, ut de rubro [*leg.* rubo] ardente et non combusto et de trium puerorum camino et de partu virginis et de domini ianuis clausis introitu et de pluribus aliis.'

parallels from precious stones, plants, and the stars.[1] When Symon says he has had enough of these, Peter proceeds to give an astonishing list of *minuta animalia*, which apparently are generated contrary to the laws of nature.[2] The list is concluded with the legendary figures of the phoenix and the barnacle goose.[3]

Peter shows no knowledge of the interchange of ideas between Christians and Jews that had taken place in his lifetime, and which, through the influence of Andrew of St. Victor, profoundly influenced biblical exegesis. His treatment of the Old Testament prophecies follows traditional lines. He does not appear to have used any out-of-the-way sources. He quotes the *Logos stileos* of Hermes Trismegistus from Ps.-Augustine, *Adversus quinque hereses*.[4] His quotations of Vergil's *Eclogues* and the Sibylline prophecies[5] are found in other tracts against the Jews.[6]

To determine the extent of Peter's dependence on earlier writers against the Jews would require a more detailed investigation than is possible here,[7] but there is one debt, apparently unacknowledged, that deserves to be set out. There are a number of passages where Peter seems to show a knowledge of the Hebrew language and of Jewish literature. For instance:[8]

[1] They are drawn from Augustine, *De civ. dei*, xxi. 4–8, with some additions from Solinus and Isidore, *Etymol.*

[2] iii. 3, f. 204ᵛb: 'Vermes quidam sine semine nascuntur, ut verbi gratia, multipes de terra a multitudine pedum sic dictus et lymax ex limo et sanguisuga ex aqua et aranea ex aere ex quo nomen accepit et bombicines qui sericum procreant ex frondibus, et eruca ex oleribus que corrodit, et tinea ex vestimentis, et teredones ex lignis que terendo rodunt et perforant, et pediculi ex carne et pulices ex pulvere. Nec solum vermes sic nascuntur sed etiam quedam minuta volantia ut strabones (*leg.* scabrones) et stambones ex equis, fuci de mulis, vespe de asinis, cicade ex cuculorum sputo, apes ex boum cadaveribus.' He is drawing freely on Isidore, *Etymol.* xii. 5 and 8, §§ 2–4.

[3] Ibid.: 'Bernaces autem aves sunt que magnitudine equantur anseribus et in uno et de uno ligno infinite procreantur in mari occidentali et per rostra dependent a ligno, donec maiores facte separantur a ligno et natare incipiunt et ab hominibus nutriuntur.' The earliest references to the 'barnacles' by name are in G. Cambrensis, *Top. hibernica*, i. 15 (*Opera*, v. 47 f., Rolls Series), written 1188–9, and in A. Nequam, *De naturis rerum*, i. 48 (p. 99, Rolls Series), written between 1197 and 1204; cf. E. Heron-Allen, *Barnacles in Nature and in Myth* (London, 1928), pp. 10–12 and notes. Peter does not appear to depend on either.

[4] iii. 1, f. 194ʳa from c. 3, *Pat. Lat.* 42, cols. 1102–3. For other quotations of this passage see the edition of the *Asclepius* by A. D. Nock and A. J. Festugière (Paris, 1945), pp. 266–8, and the remarks of E. Gilson, *Rev. du moyen âge latin*, v (1947), 64.   [5] i. 7, f. 99ᵛa and i. 5, f. 99ʳa.

[6] e.g. Peter of Blois, *Contra perfid. Iudeorum*, *Pat. Lat.* 207, col. 870. There are other traces of apparent borrowings from this tract in i. 4, f. 99ʳa, from c. 23, col. 850; and in iii. 1, f. 195ᵛb, from c. 6, col. 834d.

[7] Apart from the instance given in the preceding note I have found that a passage on the representation of Christ (ii. 18, fol. 190ʳa) is copied from Gilbert Crispin, *Disput. Iudaei cum Christiano*, *Pat. Lat.* 159, cols. 1034a–b.   [8] i. 46, f. 137ᵛa.

'Symon. Illud scio ego quod *co* Hebraice Latine sic reddat, sed nusquam, puto, locum significat.

'Petrus. Facit utique in Exodo. Namque legitur de Moyse . . .'

On investigation this turns out to be taken from the *Dialogue* of Petrus Alphonsi against the Jews.[1] The only change is in the name of the Jewish interlocutor, Symon instead of Moses. The same holds good of all the passages where such knowledge is shown.[2] Peter appears to refer to Petrus Alphonsi only once by name, in the following passage:[3]

'Item. Est quidam liber apud Iudeos de quo Petrus Alphonsi in libro suo quem appellavit *Humanum proficuum* loquitur discipulo suo querenti ab eo que essent nomina angelorum illorum que invocata valerent ad mutandum ea que ex elementis fiunt in alia et metalla in alia, ita dicens: Hoc facillime potes scire si librum quem *Secreta secretorum* appellant valeas invenire, quem sapientes Iudei dicunt Seth filio Adam Rafielem angelum revelasse, atque angelorum nomina et dei precipua scripta esse.'

This is a quotation of some interest because the work of Petrus Alphonsi to which he refers is one that has not yet been identified.[4] It is included in the list of writings of Petrus Alphonsi in the *Catalogus librorum Anglie*, compiled in the thirteenth century,[5] and Boston of Bury gives a brief description of it in his *Catalogus*.[6]

We have noticed that there is an increasing bitterness of tone in the treatises against the Jews. It is to Peter's credit that he does not show this in an accentuated form. He can on occasion

---

[1] *Pat. Lat.* 157, col. 653c.

[2] i. 42, f. 131^{v}a = *Dial.*, col. 653; 45, f. 136^{r}a = *Dial.*, col. 650; 52, f. 152^{v}b; 53, f. 154^v = *Dial.*, cols. 581–93, 569–70; ii. 6, f. 170^{r-v} = *Dial.*, cols. 541–3, 549–50; 18, f. 191^{r}a = *Dial.*, col. 670c; iii. 1, f. 192^{v}a–b = *Dial.*, cols. 608–9; 2, f. 197^{v}a = *Dial.*, col. 615a. In some of these passages the text of the *Dialogus* is expanded or shortened.

[3] iii. 1, f. 193^{r}a.

[4] It is not clear whether it has any connexion with the *Epistola de studio artium liberalium precipue astronomie ad peripateticos aliosque philosophicos ubique per Franciam*, contained in Brit. Mus., MS. Arundel 270, ff. 40^v–44^v, which is briefly described by Lynn Thorndike, *Hist. of Magic and Experimental Science* (London, 1923), ii. 70–2.

[5] Oxford, Bodleian Library, MS. Tanner 165, f. 117^v.

[6] Cambridge, University Library, MS. Add. 3470, p. 116: 'Dialogorum libros 3, quorum primus de septem artibus, secundus de sec[re]tis legibus et credulitatibus, tertius liber sive tertia distinctio de humano proficuo. Principium: *Cum haberem discipulum*. Finis: *obfirmavit*.' Petrus Alphonsi is a writer who has had less than his due. For references to his works see G. Sarton, *Introd. to the Hist. of Science* (Washington, 1931), ii. 1, pp. 199–200; Manitius, *Gesch. d. lat. Lit. des Mittelalters* (1931), iii. 274–7; Haskins, *Studies in Medieval Science* (1927), pp. 114–19; L. Thorndike, loc. cit. I have not been able to consult J. M. Millas Vallicrosa, *Nuevas aportaciones para el estudio de la transmisión de la ciencia a Europa a través de España* (Barcelona, 1943).

be rather fierce with Symon and make offensive references to Jewish beliefs and customs; but the prologue printed below will show that he approached his task in a fairer spirit. In its phrasing we may catch what are probably intentional reminiscences of the calm reasonableness of Gilbert Crispin. Unlike Gilbert he had succeeded in converting his opponent, and he could no doubt afford to be generous. We will quote part of the passage on Symon's conversion:[1]

'Symon. . . . Volo igitur ut sine aliqua dubietate cordis tui scias, domine Petre, quod ego iam abiecta omni infidelitate et duritia Iudeorum fidelis sim Christianus, fidem Christianorum per omnia complectens. Gratias quoque immensas ago deo et tibi, domine Petre, quod per doctrinam sanam et disputationem tuam invincibilem et per misericordiam suam adduxit me deus ad id quod sum, per quem firmiter credo me debere salvari et genus etiam meum in fine seculi esse salvandum. Me igitur de cetero plene deo et tibi committo, et me servituti domini nostri Iesu Christi tueque obedientie plene subicio. Faciatque deus mecum secundum suam misericordiam et perficiat in me per te que adhuc desunt salvationi mee et perfectioni. *Nisi* enim *quis renatus fuerit ex aqua et spiritu sancto, non potest introire in regnum dei.*[2]

'Petrus. Et ego amodo, domine Symon, cum tali voluntate recipio te in meum, et gratias immensas ago ego deo meo quod non omnino vacuis manibus ad deum redibo cum te quasi manipulum, licet unum, tamen plenum spicis et granis virtutum et bonorum operum ad eum reportabo. Que autem tue saluti, ut dicis, desunt, deus, fili mi, in te perficiat, et ego gratanter ministerium et operam adhibebo ut omnia bene et perfecte in te compleantur que necessaria erunt corpori et anime tue. Vade, domine Symon, semper in Christo, qui sit tibi via, veritas et vita.'

Peter's treatise is the latest representative in England of the tradition revived by Gilbert Crispin, and it deserves fuller treatment in a wider context than has been possible here. Works of the same kind were written in many parts of Europe in the twelfth century—in France, Flanders, the Rhineland, Italy, Spain, Majorca—and the relationship between them has never been the subject of a comprehensive survey.

[1] iii. 31, ff. 223^{v}b–224^{r}a.   [2] John iii. 5.

APPENDIX

Prologue to Peter of Cornwall, 'Liber Disputationum contra Symonem Iudeum'

(MS. Eton College 130, f. 92ra)

DILECTISSIMO domino suo et patri in Christo Stephano dei gratia
Cantuariensi archiepiscopo et totius Anglie primati et sancte Romane
ecclesie cardinali Petrus servus eius devotus et prior sancte Trinitatis
Londonie dictus cum salute corporis et anime sinceram dilectionem et
debitum subiectionis famulatum. Aures sanctitatis vestre in cuius 5
sapienti eloquentia Gallia sapit et in religione quiescit et in utraque
spem salutis Anglia firmiter concepit, flosculis verborum Tulliane elo-
quentie onerare vel multis sermonibus epistole prolixioris pulsare
parvitas scientie mee timuit, erubuit, indignum iudicavit. Paucis igitur
et verbis simplicioribus sanctitatem vestram, cui presentem librum 10
disputationum contra Iudeos devovi, exoro quatenus manus cor-
rectionis emendet, explanet et feditates verborum et errores sententiarum detergat, et gratiam et auctoritatem quam in se libellus ille non
habet per vos plenissime recipere mereatur, et qui nunc latet sub modio
vel displicet per obscuritatem scriptoris fulgeat super candelabrum per 15
vitam et famam et doctrinam correctoris. Valeat sanctitas vestra in
evum pater venerande.

   Ego et quidam Iudeus in lege sua et in literis nostris adprime eruditus, nunc autem in ecclesia nostra fidelis Christianus et canonicus
effectus, sepe convenimus ut de lege sua et nostra disputaremus, 20
factumque est quod multis rationibus et sacre scripture testimoniis
sufficienter, ut estimo, probavi Messiam iam venisse et illum esse quem
nos Christiani dicimus Christum nostrum. Percurrens enim singulos
libros Veteris Testamenti manifeste ostendi illi qualiter omnes scripture
illius de Christo nostro et de eius tempore loquantur et illi soli con- 25
veniant. Ostendi enim quod ante adventum Christi totum Vetus Testa-
mentum clausum erat et septem sigillis signatum, id est obscuritatibus
et allegoriis et alienis parabolis et enigmatibus obvolutum et tectum, ut
a cognitione et intelligentia hominum preterquam admodum paucorum
remotum esset et alienum. Post adventum autem Christi nostri apertum 30
est et reseratum ut a multis intelligatur et ab omnibus operam dantibus
intelligi valeat, secundum tamen uniuscuiusque fidei mensuram. Ipse
enim Christus iam advenit de quo locutus est liber Veteris Testamenti
quem ipse aperuit, id est sensum eius prius obscuritatibus obvolutum
ad intelligentiam hominum eduxit. Qualiter enim sibi scripture libri 35
illius convenirent et sibi testimonium ferrent tripliciter aperiendo
monstravit, scilicet inspirando, docendo, operando; inspirando autem

---

11 manu *cod.*   13 et gratiam: at gratiam *cod.*   27 Apoc. v. 1.   31–2 Cf. Rom.
xii. 3.

quando primitus discipulis suis et postea aliis sacre scripture expositori-
bus aperuit sensum, ut intelligerent scripturas que de se et de ecclesia
sua loquebantur, quatinus ipsi que interius spiritu sancto docente ipsis
reserata fuerant alios docerent et aperirent; docendo autem illud idem
5 aperiendo monstravit quando aliquam scripturam pertractans exposuit
et ostendit sermone, qualiter sibi congrueret et de se loqueretur et sibi
testimonium ferret, sicut ubi ille ait: *Omnes vos scandalum patiemini in
me in ista nocte. Scriptum est enim: Percutiam pastorem et dispergentur
oves gregis* etc., et iterum ubi ait: *Sicut fuit Ionas in ventre ceti tribus*
10 *diebus et tribus noctibus, sic erit filius hominis in corde terre tribus diebus et*
tribus noctibus, et iterum ubi dicitur: *O stulti et tardi corde ad credendum*
in omnibus que locuti sunt prophete. Nonne hec oportuit pati Christum et
ita intrare gloriam suam? Et incipiens a Moyse et omnibus prophetis inter-
pretabatur illis in omnibus scripturis que de ipso erant, et infra, *Nonne cor*
15 *nostrum ardens erat in nobis dum loqueretur in via, et aperiret nobis*
scripturas? Et iterum ubi ipse ait: *Necesse est impleri omnia que scripta*
sunt in lege Moysi et prophetis et psalmis de me. Tunc aperuit illis sensum ut intelligerent scripturas; operando autem illud idem aperiendo
monstravit, quando aliquid operatus est per quod scripturam aliquam
20 que de illo obscure ante adventum suum loquebatur ad se pertinere et
de se loqui comprobavit, verbi gratia, hec scriptura: *Ecce virgo concipiet*
et pariet filium et vocabitur nomen eius Emanuel, quod est nobiscum
deus, valde clausa et obscura erat ante adventum Christi, nec umquam
intelligeretur, nisi Christus adveniret qui erat verus homo et vere
25 nobiscum deus, qui per operationem nativitatis sue ex virgine eam
aperuit et de se solo locutam fuisse, qui solus sic nasci potuit et solus
sic natus fuit, comprobavit. Similiter scriptura que dicit: *Ego dormivi et*
soporatus sum et exurexi etc., semper clausa remanet, nec umquam intelligi potuisset, nisi Christus adveniret qui eam operando, id est moriendo
30 et resurgendo, aperiret, et sic de se locutam fuisse opere ipso compro-
baret. Omnis enim dubietas tollitur et veritas declaratur, ubi non verbis
sed rebus ipsis veritas probatur.

Cum autem sepe ego et predictus Iudeus simul convenissemus nos
invicem colloquendo et disputando docentes, et iam finem et consum-
35 mationem studium et inquisitio nostra de vero Messia accepisset,
placuit sociis nostris ut in scriptum redigerem omnia que utiliter sive
colloquendo sive disputando disserueramus, sed quia perpendi omnia
non posse in unum librum coartari, nisi mediocritatem decentis quanti-
tatis liber excederet, ex utilioribus duos libros conscripsi, primum
40 scilicet in quo allegorias pro maxima parte totius Veteris Testamenti,
id est scripturas et auctoritates Veteris Testamenti que de Christo
nostro, vero scilicet Messia et eius ecclesia loquuntur, non tamen omnes,
sed utiliores et cognitioni necessariores inserui, prout eas sancti doctores
a Christo inspirati et edocti exposuerunt, et soli Christo nostro, tanquam

7–9 Matt. xxvi. 31.   9–11 Matt. xii. 40.   11–16 Luc. xxiv. 25–7, 32.
16–17 Luc. xxiv. 44.   21–2 Is. vii. 14.   27–8 Ps. iii. 6.

vero Messie, et eius ecclesie convenire manifeste ostenderunt. Secundum autem librum scilicet istum ex predictis in quo disputationes nostras de Messia et de fide nostra et lege veteri utili compendio disposui.

Et quia ego et qui mecum disserebat Iudeus Petrus et Symon dice- 5
bamur, placuit ut liber ille primus vocaretur liber allegoriarum Petri contra Symonem Iudeum de confutatione Iudeorum. Iste autem secundus liber [f. 92va] quia continet disputationes inter me et predictum Symonem factas simili modo placuit ut vocaretur liber disputationum Petri contra Symonem Iudeum de confutatione Iudeorum. 10

Modus autem tractandi et ordo disputationis nostre in hoc secundo libro disputacionis nostre talis est. In primis librum hunc secundum in tres partes sive in tres libros divisimus, in quorum primo multis rationibus multisque Veteris Testamenti probavimus scripturis verum Messiam et iam venisse et ipsum esse Christum nostrum et verum deum 15 et verum hominem et omnia illi et soli illi congruere que fides nostra de Christo nostro predicat. *Vicit* enim *leo de tribu Iuda, radix David, aperire librum* Veteris Testamenti *et solvere vii signacula eius.* Que autem sunt hec vii signacula libri Veteris Testamenti et qualiter ea solverit et aperuerit Christus noster, qui erat de tribu Iuda, et qualiter per 20 apertionem eorum, que fit per inspirationem, doctrinam et operationem, probentur omnia que de Christo nostro credimus, in eodem plenissime diximus, quamquam multa de his dixerimus in libro allegoriarum Petri contra Symonem de confutatione Iudeorum, et maxime de illa apertione libri signati que fit per inspirationem. In secunda autem parte, id est 25 in secundo libro huius libri disputationis Petri contra Symonem, plenissime invenientur digesta que pertinent ad confutationem literalis expositionis Iudeorum in Veteri Testamento, sive ad confutationem Sabbati et aliarum sollempnitatum illorum, sive ad confutationem circumcisionis, sive ad confutationem sacrificiorum et aliorum omnium 30 rituum legalium, sive ad Iudeorum reprobationem et Veteris Testamenti infirmationem, sive ad gentium vocationem et Novi Testamenti introductionem. In tertia autem parte, id est in tertio libro disputationis nostre, reperiuntur plura que pertinent ad fidem trinitatis et unitatis divine, sive ad miracula virginei partus, sive ad humanitatem 35 et divinitatem Christi, sive ad multa alia cognitu digna.

Sciendum est autem quod cum primo ad disputandum ego et predictus Iudeus convenissemus, convenit inter nos ut non contentiose nec clamose nec animo vincendi, sed cum omni pace et tranquillitate et tantum desiderio veritatem inquirendi simul tractaremus, et ut nec 40 ego sermonem suum nec ipse meum quamdiu loqui alterutri placeret interrumperemus, sed siquid questionis interim emergeret usque in finem sermonis illius silenter reservaremus. Postea autem aliud ab eo exigens adieci dicere: Tecum Iudee non disputabo nisi mecum agere

17–18 Apoc. v. 5.

volueris quasi essemus eodem tempore in quo Christus noster erat et
vidissemus et audissemus omnia que homines qui tunc fuerunt de eo
viderant et audierant et que tunc ipse predixerat vel fecerat et alia
multa que tunc historialiter contigerant. Si enim aliquod illorum negare
5 volueris, ut michi prescindas viam probandi que vera sunt, sicut semper
faciunt in disputationibus suis contra Christianos fratres vestri, videlicet Iudei iniqui et persecutores Christi, in vanum disputabo. Contra
enim veritatis inimicum et falsitatis defensorem, tutius michi videtur
silere quam disputare. Ad hec respondit michi predictus Iudeus
10 dicens, Verum quidem aliquando solet esse, domine Petre, quod dicis.
Sunt enim multi ex Iudeis nostris qui non sunt perscrutati interiora
legis, vel si perscrutati sunt, non omnia memoriter retinuerunt. Et
sunt multi qui pauca audierunt de hiis que historialiter contigerunt
tempore Christi vestri, et hii omnes ne superari videantur, impatienter
15 se habent, clamose disputant, vera sepe negant et falsa pro veris affir-
mant. Ego autem qui profunda et mistica legis nostre sepe rimatus sum,
et qui tecum ago tantum desiderio veritatem inquirendi et que ab antiquis patribus et predecessoribus nostris fere omnia que historialiter
contigerant tempore Christi vestri audivi, non sic. Patres enim nostri
20 qui tempore Christi erant enarraverunt filiis suis et etiam scripserunt
que tunc historialiter contigerant, et sic usque ad me et ad multos
maxime Iudeos qui nunc sunt, licet hec passim fateri noluerint, veritas
historie de Christo vestro pervenit. Reservatur quoque adhuc apud
quosdam Iudeos nostros ewangelium Mathei quod ipse Hebraice
25 scripsit, ex quo quidam assumpserunt que aliis enarraverunt et que sic
usque ad nos pervenerunt. Concedam igitur tibi, domine Petre, sine
omni ambiguitate omnia que de Christo vestro in scriptis nostris
secretis repperi et omnia que a patribus nostris audivi, dummodo tu
nullius scripture, preterquam legis nostre, testimonium contra me
30 inducas, quia nullum aliud recipiam. Tunc enim rite procedet inter
nos disputationis victoria cum quis nostrum convincitur lege propria.
Induc igitur, domine Petre, quecumque volueris testimonia scripturarum vestrarum que utique omnia concedam, si ea testimoniis legis
nostre, cum postulavero, vera esse probaveris, vel si ea a patribus
35 nostris audivi, vel in scriptis nostris secretis repperi. Cumque ego
respondissem iustum esse quod dixerat, adiecit ille: Et quia perinde
habeo vincere et vinci, dummodo veritatem inquiram per quam salvem
animam meam, expostulo a te, domine Petre, ut non solum scripturas
et rationes quas credis esse insuperabiles et necessarias contra me
40 inducas, sed etiam probabiles et persuasorias et verisimiles et pre-
sumptionem habentes. Tales enim forte plus movebunt animum meum
ad intentionem veritatis quam ille quas plus et fortius pro te facere
credis. Cum autem et hoc quod petebat ei concederem, benigno animo
et tranquillo et tantum veritatem inquirendi desiderio, ut postea patuit,
45 disputationem nostram exorsi sumus.   R. W. HUNT

5 prescidas *cod.*   17 desidero *cod.*

MAGNA CARTA, CLAUSE 34

MAGNA CARTA, clause 34, 'Breve quod vocatur Præcipe de cetero non fiat alicui de aliquo tenemento unde liber homo amittere possit curiam suam', was described by McKechnie as one of the most reactionary chapters in the Charter. The barons were refusing 'to be robbed of their right to determine, in their own courts baron, proprietary actions between their own tenants'.[1] This view rested, in part, on the belief that the barons were trying to check the use of the grand assize. But the attack on the writ *Praecipe* was not an attack on the grand assize, which lay in the option of the defendant whether the action was brought by writ of right in the lord's court or by a *Praecipe* in the king's. The barons, in fact, made no attempt to recover the large amount of business which was being lost to their courts through the grand and possessory assizes. It may be thought, however, that the writ *Praecipe* was being used to rob them of even those cases which remained, and that McKechnie was right in holding that the object of clause 34 was to prevent this. It will be suggested that this theory, even in this modified form, mistakes the purpose of the writ and attaches far too much importance to clause 34.

It is supposed that the feudal courts had originally enjoyed 'exclusive competence in proprietary actions';[2] that 'in pleas of disputed titles to land, feudal theory gave sole jurisdiction to the lord of the fief';[3] and that Henry II invented the writ *Praecipe* together with the writ of right and the assizes in order 'to draw into his own courts all pleas relating to land'.[4] Neither of these assumptions seems to be well founded. There seems to be no evidence to show that the English feudal courts were at any time competent to deal with all actions for land except those between tenants-in-chief. The 'exclusive competence of the feudal courts' clearly did not exist under Henry I, when the rule that actions in which the parties claimed to hold of different lords must go to the county court already held good, at least for certain types of proprietary action. This rule is stated later on by Glanvill in his discussion of the writ of right. The writ must be addressed to the lord from whom the demandant claims to hold the land, and not to anyone else.

[1] *Magna Carta*, 2nd edition, p. 349.
[2] Ibid., p. 350, quoting Pollock and Maitland, *History of English Law*, i. 151 2nd ed., p. 172).   [3] *Magna Carta*, p. 346.   [4] Ibid., p. 349.

'Sed quid erit si petens ipse de uno clamat tenere et tenens ipse de alio teneat? Et quidem in tali casu quia is cui breve dirigitur placitum illud tenere non potest, cum alium non possit de curia unde ipse saisiatus esse intellegitur iniuste et sine iudicio desaisiare, ex necessitate itur inde ad comitatum, et ibi procedet placitum vel in capitali curia. . . .'[1]

There is evidence to show that the writ of right was in use under Henry I, and there is some reason to think that the rule that no one need answer for his freehold without it was already in force.[2] Glanvill states that the rule is a customary one.[3] But if this rule applied under Henry I it seems likely that the corollary also applied, by which only the lord of whom both parties claimed to hold the land could deal with the action. In any case, it is known to have applied to certain types of proprietary action under Henry I, since it is expressly laid down in his 'Order for the holding of the Courts of the Hundred and the Shire' of 1109–11.[4] A plea 'de divisione terrarum vel de preoccupatione'[5] is to be determined in the king's court if the parties are his barons, in the court of their lord if both parties are vassals of one baron, but in the county court if they are vassals of different lords: 'Et si est inter vavasores duorum dominorum tractetur in comitatu.' This ruling seems definite enough. Yet Adams, who remarked upon it, set against it a clause in the *Leges Henrici Primi* which, he thought, stated the normal feudal rule, that such cases should be determined in the court of the defendant's lord.[6] This is clause 25, 2: 'Si est (placitum) inter homines duorum dominorum socnam habencium, respondeat accusatus in curia domini sui de causa communi.' The term *causa communis* may suggest the Common Bench pleas of the thirteenth century which consisted mainly of actions for land. But this is a later use of the

---

[1] *De Legibus*, lib. xii, cap. 8, ed. Woodbine, p. 152. The 'capitalis curia' is the Curia Regis, see below, p. 168.

[2] Cf. D. M. Stenton in *Camb. Med. Hist.* v. 586, and T. F. T. Plucknett, *A Concise History of the Common Law*, 3rd ed., p. 143.

[3] Lib. xii, cap. 25: 'Praeterea sciendum quod secundum consuetudinem regni nemo tenetur respondere in curia domini sui de aliquo libero tenemento suo sine praecepto domini regis vel eius capitalis iustitiae.'

[4] Stubbs, *Select Charters*, 9th ed., p. 122.

[5] Boundary disputes were sometimes determined, apparently by arbitration, in a boundary or march court. There are several references to such tribunals in the *Leges Henrici Primi*, cf. clauses 9, 4; 34, 1*a*; 57, 1; 57, 8. It does not appear that Henry I intended to put a stop to such arbitration. It was only if this failed that the parties had to go to the lord's court, if they held of the same lord, or to the hundred court, according to *Leg. Henr.*, cf. 57, 1*a*. 'Preoccupatio' would seem to cover most other types of land actions.

[6] *The Origin of the English Constitution*, p. 382.

term, and clause 25, 2, is not concerned with pleas of land. The compiler has been distinguishing between different types of *soc*, of judicial profits, arising in criminal causes. The *causa singularis* is one in which there is a special penalty, due to the king alone. The *causa communis* is one the penalty for which is the same, whether the recipient is the king or someone else, a local official or the culprit's lord. But this is still a pecuniary penalty for an offence and has nothing whatever to do with actions for land. The term *accusatus* itself suggests this. In fact the *Leges Henrici Primi* themselves state the rule whereby, if the parties claim to hold of different lords, boundary disputes (*querelae vicinorum*) go to a neutral court.[1] There is further evidence that this rule was in operation before Henry II's campaign against feudal jurisdiction is supposed to have been launched. The procedure of the assize *utrum* is laid down in the Constitutions of Clarendon, clause ix, where it is stated that if the assize finds that the land in dispute is lay fee, then the plea shall be heard in the royal court unless both parties hold of the same lord, 'nisi ambo de eodem episcopo vel barone advocaverint . . . sed si uterque advocaverit de feodo illo eundem episcopum vel baronem, erit placitum in curia ipsius'. The implication is plain that the lord's court is competent only in those cases where both parties claim to hold of him.[2]

In practice this rule must have imposed a very serious limitation on the jurisdiction of the feudal courts. Boundary disputes, for example, would not occur so frequently between the free tenants of one lord as between his villeins or between tenants of different lords, except in the rare honours, such as the 'county palatine' of Durham, where the fees held of the lord formed a continuous block of land. Normally, too, a vassal would hold lands of different lords and would marry a woman whose marriage portion would be held of yet another. When a man died, therefore, many disputes could arise which involved more than one

---

[1] See above, p. 158, n. 5. The suggestion that an action of this kind should go to the court of the defendant's lord conflicts with the evidence of the writ of right, which is addressed to the lord of whom the demandant claims to hold. *Leges Edwardi Confessoris*, clause 9, 2, may also seem to suggest that actions between tenants of different lords could be decided in the court of one of them, provided the king's justice was present, but from the context this again seems to relate to criminal matters. It certainly does not necessarily apply to land actions.

[2] There is a good example of the application of this rule in *Curia Regis Rolls*, iii. 272 (1205). William Revel seeks his court in a plea of land, but is not allowed it because the demandant is claiming to hold not of William, but of Aubrey de Vere, Earl of Oxford; see below, p. 171, n. 1, iv.

lord, e.g. his heir by his first wife might have occupied land held by the curtesy of England, but which had been the marriage portion of a second wife and should now have reverted to her heirs, holding of a different honour. Even more complex was the problem, when an elderly widow died, of assigning to the proper heirs the various parcels of dower land, accumulated on successive marriages. These lands might belong to many different honours and the problem of identifying the particular fees belonging to each after a separation of up to forty or fifty years might tax the resources of the king's court itself. The partitioning of a complex of estates among co-heiresses was another matter which must usually have involved more than one lord. Generally speaking the type of case which is appropriate to the feudal court is that which involves a dispute as to succession. The suitors of the court would probably be well able to determine such questions as which was the elder of two brothers. But when it came to the question whether a particular fee constituted part of a particular inheritance they might be at a loss. Such a problem might more appropriately be decided in a local court, such as the shire court, rather than in the central court of a widely scattered honour.

Some of these cases might, perhaps, in the Norman period be settled in the court of some common overlord. At any rate it was possible for certain cases between a mesne lord and his tenant to be heard in the court of the overlord.[1] The mesne lord might have to enlist the latter's aid in dealing with a contumacious tenant, or the tenant might appeal to him against an oppressive immediate lord. But cases of this type seem to have been uncommon, and at least by Glanvill's time it was not difficult for either party to appeal to the king's justices instead. Once the writ of right was devised, moreover, the overlord was ousted from this position in relation to pleas of land. Glanvill, in the passage part of which has already been quoted, insists that only the immediate lord to whom the writ is addressed is competent to hear the plea. The writ must not be addressed to anyone else, not even the chief lord: 'non ad alium nec etiam ad capitalem dominum', and if the immediate lord fails to do justice, then the sheriff is required, in accordance with the wording of the writ, to determine the action in the county court. If it is true that the

---

[1] *Leges Henrici Primi*, clause 56, 2, shows that a tenant in fee farm could be sued in the court of the lord of the fee even if he did not hold directly of him. Glanvill, lib. ix, cap. 13, shows that a mesne lord may sue his tenant in the court of his overlord if the tenant has made a purpresture, occupying land to which he is not entitled, and if he holds no other tenement of the mesne lord.

writ of right was introduced by Henry I rather than by Henry II, then the court of the honour must very quickly have lost cognizance of land actions between mesne tenants and their tenants, or between tenants' tenants. It is, of course, well known that by the thirteenth century the overlord could not lawfully take over an action on default in the court of his mesne tenant, or deal with complaints of false judgement there. This rule, too, seems to go back to the time of Henry I. The *Leges Henrici Primi* seem to state it clearly; in clause 10. 10, 1 the list of pleas *de iure regis* includes both *iniustum iudicium* and *defectus iusticie*. Clause 33, 1*a*, however, presents a difficulty, since it states: 'Defectus quippe iusticie et violenta recti eorum destitutio est, que causas protrahunt in ius regium vel in dicionem dominorum.'[1] The *Leges* are certainly not clear on this point, and it is possible that the rule was only just coming to be enforced at the time of their compilation. But this limitation on the competence of the overlord's court was sufficiently secured, so far as pleas of land were concerned, by the writ of right, which ordered the sheriff to do justice if the court of the immediate lord defaulted. With increasing subinfeudation and the commercialization of land these two rules would come into operation more and more frequently. Mesne tenants might well not have courts with enough suitors of sufficient standing to determine actions for free tenements.

It has been suggested, however, that the rule prohibiting the overlord from taking over a case on default in the court of the mesne tenant was not observed, since the barons petitioned for its enforcement in 1258.[2] The Provisions of Westminster (clause 16) and the Statute of Marlborough (clause 19), on the other hand, prohibit the overlord's dealing with pleas of false judgement, not default of justice. Perhaps this was thought to cover both. It is, however, dangerous to argue back from the petition for enforcement to the prevalence of the prohibited practice. There are, it is true, two cases in print of the overlord successfully claiming a case in the county court where it has come on default of justice in the mesne lord's court, but it is significant that in both these cases the overlord is the archbishop of Canterbury, and both are known

---

[1] Clause 59, 19, states that 'defectus iusticie ac violenta recti detencio . . . commune regis placitum est super omnes, sive soonam suam habeant sive non habeant'. But *commune regis placitum* can hardly have the same meaning as *causa communis* in clause 25. The meaning seems to be that the amount of the penalty is the same whether the culprit is a lord exercising *soc* or not. Anyone else guilty of *defectus iustitie* would presumably have to be an official.

[2] Petition of the Barons, cap. 29.

because the proceedings in his court were called in question.[1] The first case appears in the Curia Regis Rolls of 1199.[2] The original action, however, had been heard long before in the court of archbishop Thomas Becket, where it had ended in a final concord. This concord was now challenged, but evidently it was upheld by the Curia Regis, since in 1206 a second attempt was made to get it reversed.[3] On the former occasion, as the Curia Regis now records, the archbishop's court had brought the record of the proceedings there. The land in dispute had been sought by writ of right in the court of John de St. Clair; the demandant had afterwards gone to the county and complained that John's court had failed to do him right: 'et tunc venit senescallus domini Cantuariensis, scilicet Sancti Thome, et petiit inde curiam domini archiepiscopi, et habuit. . . .' The final concord made there was now upheld for the second time, but these two attempts to challenge it suggest that Becket's proceedings were unusual. Then in 1203 a similar case arose, the king's court inquiring into the proceedings of that of the archbishop, who had claimed and secured an action brought by writ of right in the court of his tenant, William de Ros, and removed on default there to the county court.[4] Again, the decision in the archbishop's court was upheld, and it seems likely either that the archbishops of Canterbury had a special privilege entitling them to take over actions in this way, or that Becket had established a precedent which the successors of Henry II did not care to override.[5] But the fact that each of these cases was reopened in the Curia Regis points to the general recognition of the rule that only the royal courts could take over cases from the county. The barons of 1258 may have been objecting, not to a practice which was common among

[1] For a similar but unsuccessful claim in the Curia Regis see below, p. 169, n. 1, v.

[2] *Rotuli Curiae Regis*, ed. Palgrave, i. 356–7.

[3] *Curia Regis Rolls*, iv. 264.

[4] Ibid. iii. 79.

[5] Eadmer mentions that matters which could not be settled in the hundred or county courts or even in the Curia Regis ought, according to the laws of the ancient kings, to be determined at the 'Suthdure' of Canterbury Cathedral, 'sicut in curia regis summi' ('Nova Opuscula', ed. A. Wilmart, *Revue des Sciences Religieuses*, 1935, p. 365; cf. *Gervase of Canterbury*, ed. Stubbs, Rolls Series, i. 8). This has been taken to imply an appellate jurisdiction, but is more likely to refer to the holding of the ordeal there in the most serious cases. That the archbishop held pleas of false judgement in the thirteenth century is shown by the agreement with the bishop of Rochester in 1259 (*Registrum Roffense*, pp. 82–4). Cases of false judgement in the bishop's principal court were to be determined 'die comitatus extra tamen comitatum, coram senescallo . . . archiepiscopi'.

themselves, but to one in which Boniface of Savoy was indulging as a privilege secured to his see by the activity of Becket and Hubert Walter.

Certain other types of action may have been reserved to the royal courts from a very early period. Under Henry II the action for dower *unde nihil habet* was reserved, and there seems to be no evidence of his introducing this rule. It is stated by Glanvill: 'Si tota dos alienata fuerit placitum ab initio erit in curia regis.'[1] Glanvill seems to imply, too, that all actions for advowson must be heard in the Curia Regis,[2] though his evidence on this point is not free from obscurity, for he quotes a final concord, involving an advowson, made in the court of Geoffrey FitzPeter.[3] But this final concord was afterwards 'recorded' in the king's court, and that this was necessary may well point to the fact that any matter touching an advowson was the king's concern. The writ of prohibition quoted in book iv, chapter 13, seems to be conclusive; 'Et quoniam lites de advocationibus ecclesiarum ad coronam et dignitatem meam pertinent, vobis prohibeo ne in causa illa procedatis. . . .' The first clause of the Constitutions of Clarendon also asserts that these cases belong to the Curia Regis, and though the point here, too, is to claim them as against the ecclesiastical courts, there is no hint of private courts having competence over them. Maitland took the view that pleas of advowson were reserved to the royal courts.[4] Another matter which was reserved to them, at least in the time of Henry II, was non-observance of a final concord made in the Curia Regis.[5] Since such concords could be made in any actions there, this rule might apply to disputes about land which was not held in chief of the Crown, and once the assizes had been introduced the number of cases which had to go to the king's court was increased by those involving a concord made after the summoning of a grand assize or an assize of *mort d'ancestor*.

The feudal courts, then, did not enjoy exclusive competence in proprietary actions until Henry II launched his supposed attack upon them. There were many actions which could only be determined in the public courts, and there was no reason why such actions should not be brought into the Curia Regis by the writ *Praecipe*. Glanvill's statement: 'Cum clamat quis domino regi

[1] *De Legibus*, capitula, lib. vi, ed. Woodbine, p. 32; cf. lib. i, cap. 3, p. 42; lib. vi, cap. 15, p. 94.

[2] Lib. i, cap. 3, p. 42.   [3] Lib. viii, cap. 3, pp. 117–18.

[4] *History of English Law*, 2nd ed. i. 148.

[5] Glanvill, lib. i, cap. 3.

aut eius iustitiis de feodo vel libero tenemento suo, si fuerit querela talis quod debeat vel dominus rex velit in curia sua deduci, tunc is qui queritur tale breve de summonitione habebit',[1] has been taken to show that the king used the writ *Praecipe* in an arbitrary way to draw actions away from the feudal courts. But the phrase *dominus rex velit* may mean no more than that the king is willing to deal with the action, and this passage itself shows that there are matters in which a *Praecipe ought* to be used. There is no reason, therefore, to suppose that the writ was originally devised as a weapon to be used in a royal campaign against the feudal courts.

An examination of the cases in which it is known to have been issued will show that it was not normally used to rob the feudal courts of their proper jurisdiction, though indirectly it may have deprived them of a few individual actions. Writs beginning with the word *Praecipe* were extremely common. The writ of right itself begins with this term, though it seems always to be referred to as the writ *de recto*. Magna Carta, clause 34, is thought to refer only to the writ *Praecipe quod reddat* in actions for land. But contemporary records use the term in a much more general way. Thus in examining the use of the writ *Praecipe quod reddat* in proprietary actions it is necessary to exclude many cases brought by a *Praecipe* of a different type. The Pipe Rolls of John's reign contain many entries of payments *pro habendo Praecipe* or *pro quodam Praecipe*. As Lady Stenton has shown,[2] it is possible in a number of cases to identify an action on the Plea Roll with one for which the purchase of a *Praecipe* is recorded on the Pipe Roll, and very occasionally the Plea Roll itself mentions the writ. The actions which can be identified in this way are extremely miscellaneous. Thus numerous cases of dower have been noticed,[3] but these are probably mainly actions of dower *unde nihil habet*, the writ for which begins *Praecipe . . . quod faciat*, and which are reserved to the royal courts in any case. Other entries relate to debt,[4] to advowson,[5] even to the assize of *mort d'ancestor*.[6] In

---

[1] Lib. i, cap. 5, p. 43.

[2] *Pipe Roll 6 Jo.* (Pipe Roll Society, N.S., vol. XVIII), pp. xxiii–xxxiii.

[3] Two of these are noted by Lady Stenton, ibid.

[4] e.g. Pipe Roll 2 Henry III, m. 8d: *Hugh son of Rob. Crumpe* v. *Auenell de Einesham*; cf. *Curia Regis Rolls*, VIII. xi.

[5] e.g. Pipe Roll 15 Jo., m. 16d: *Richard de Blevill* v. *abbot of Langley*; cf. *Curia Regis Rolls*, vii. 297, 315. Also ibid. ii. 311: *John de Rocheford* v. *Dodo Bard'*.

[6] e.g. Pipe Roll 11 Jo., m. 9: *Robert son of Yvo* v. *Laurence de Boueria*; cf. *Curia Regis Rolls*, vi. 46, and perhaps Pipe Roll 13 Jo., m. 5: *W. de Bec* v. *Eustace de Burn*; cf. *Curia Regis Rolls*, v. 288, vi. 221.

several instances the writ is used in disputes over wardship.[1]
In others it is a writ *de recipiendo homagio et rationabili relevio*,[2]
or is brought by the lord himself claiming customs and services.[3]
The writs of entry began *Praecipe quod reddat*, and many cases
prove to be of this type.[4] No reliable statistics can be obtained of
the extent to which the writ *Praecipe quod reddat* was being used as
an alternative to the writ of right. No case has been found of an
action in which the writ *Praecipe* is mentioned on the Plea Roll
coinciding with one in which the issue of a *Praecipe* is recorded
on the Pipe Roll. Thus neither source of information is complete.
Evidently only the writs bought on credit were entered on the
Pipe Roll, while many more proprietary actions recorded on the
Plea Rolls may have been brought to the royal courts by the writ
Praecipe than can be shown to have been brought by it. Such
records normally begin with the formula: 'A petit versus B x
virgatas terre', and there is nothing to indicate whether they have
been brought by a *Pone* or a *Praecipe*. But while no estimate can

[1] (i) *Pipe Roll 7 Jo.*, p. 274: *Nigel Pincebec and Alice his wife* v. *Robert de Tresgoz
and Sibilla his wife*; 'pro habendo quodam precipe de custodia terre et heredis
Walteri Biset versus Robertum de Tresgoz'.

(ii) *Pipe Roll 8 Jo.*, p. 103: Simon Brito, junior. Cf. *Curia Regis Rolls*, iv. 168;
Rot. de Oblatis, p. 352.

(iii) *Pipe Roll 9 Jo.*, p. 178: 'Rogerus de Sifeld debet ii m. pro habendo precipe
de c. solidatis terre quas habet in custodia cum herede Willelmi f. Ricardi de
Haletorp.'

(iv) *Rot. de Oblatis*, p. 390 (1207); *Robert son of Anketil* v. *Robert Maudut*.

(v) Pipe Roll 15 Jo., m. 3*d* (Surrey): Cecil de Grauene; cf. *Curia Regis Rolls*, vii.
262 (Surrey): Cecilia de Graveney claims wardship of land and heir of *Richard de
Graveney* v. *Geoffrey de Bulestrod*.

(vi) There is also a *Praecipe* in a case of warranty of wardship, Pipe Roll 15 Jo.,
m. 13*d*: *William Baucun* v. *Earl of Devon, de custodia terrarum*; cf. *Curia Regis Rolls*,
vii. 175.

[2] Pipe Roll 11 Jo., m. 4: 'Hugo fil. Ingelrami . . . pro habendo quodam precipe
v. priorem de Cokesford quod capiat homagium suum et rationabile relevium suum
de tenemento quod de eo tenet.'

[3] (i) *Pipe Roll 6 Jo.*, p. 76: *Hawisa de Houton'* v. *Ric. f. Joscelin and others*;
cf. *Curia Regis Rolls*, iii. 186, 220.

(ii) Pipe Roll 15 Jo., m. 2*d*: *abbot of Grestain* v. *J. de Montacute*; cf. *Curia Regis
Rolls*, vii. 146, 203, 232.

[4] (i) *Warin son of William* v. *Geoffrey de Cramaville, Curia Regis Rolls*, iii. 117,
125, 151; cf. *Pipe Roll 6 Jo.*, p. 32.

(ii) Robert son of Geoffrey, *Curia Regis Rolls*, iii. 93, 114, 125; cf. *Pipe Roll
7 Jo.*, p. 180.

(iii) *Adam de Mudiford* v. *Reginald de Frivill, Curia Regis Rolls*, iv. 268; v. 86;
cf. *Pipe Roll 8 Jo.*, p. 32.

(iv) *Matilda de Chandos* v. *Ralph Morin, Curia Regis Rolls*, vii. 36, 85, 122, 277,
282; cf. Pipe Roll 15 Jo., m. 9.

(v) See below, p. 174, n. 2.

See also *Rot. de Oblatis*, pp. 334–5, 347, 365, 378.

be made of the proportion brought by the latter, the cases identified throw some light on the problem of the use to which the writ was being put. Thus seven cases prove to be concerned with the action *de rationabili parte*,[1] and three with marriage portions.[2] In another the tenant asserts that the land is held as dower.[3] It has already been pointed out that actions of these types are likely to involve more than one lord, and therefore have to go to the county or the king's court. In five cases the land in dispute seems to have been held in chief of the Crown.[4] Several cases involve earlier proceedings in a royal court,[5] and such cases were, of course,

[1] (i) *Pipe Roll 6 Jo.*, p. 44: *Annota daughter of William son of William* v. *William Bardolf and Isabel his wife*; cf. *Curia Regis Rolls*, iii. 105, 116.

(ii) *Pipe Roll 6 Jo.*, p. 128: Roeisia daughter of Bartholomew (Rose Rastell); cf. *Curia Regis Rolls*, iv. 157.

(iii) *Pipe Roll 7 Jo.*, p. 235: William son of Estrild and Matilda his wife; cf. *Curia Regis Rolls*, iv. 175, 262.

(iv) Pipe Roll 11 Jo., m. 12d: *Alexander de Neuill* v. *Simon son of Walter and Sarra his wife*; cf. *Curia Regis Rolls*, vi. 49.

(v) Pipe Roll 11 Jo., m. 12d: *Herbert de S. Quintin and Agnes his wife* v. *Alice de Stuteuill*; cf. *Curia Regis Rolls*, vi. 76, &c.

(vi) Pipe Roll 11 Jo., m. 15d: *Matilda de Muntfichet* v. *Beatrice daughter of Henry*; cf. *Curia Regis Rolls*, vi. 201.

(vii) Pipe Roll 15 Jo., m. 10: *Walter son of Richard and wife* v. *Simon de Berton*; cf. *Curia Regis Rolls*, vii. 235, 298.

Not all of these cases involved two lords.

The action *de rationabili parte* was not in itself a reserved action. Glanvill gives the writ addressed to the lord which is appropriate in this action, lib. xii, cap. 5, p. 150.

[2] (i) *Pipe Roll 6 Jo.*, p. 112: *Rob. the Marshal* v. *Henry of Weston*; cf. *Curia Regis Rolls*, iii. 219; iv. 2, 76, 118, 271; v. 3.

(ii) *Pipe Roll 9 Jo.*, p. 100: *William de Tresgoz* v. *William de Coleuill*; cf. *Curia Regis Rolls*, v. 51, 137, &c.

(iii) *Rot. de Oblatis*, p. 347: *John de Auvill* v. *William de Mumbray*.

[3] Pipe Roll 11 Jo., m. 7d: *Gilbert de Gant* v. *Agnes de Rupe*; cf. *Curia Regis Rolls*, vi. 187, 288.

[4] (i) *Pipe Roll 7 Jo.*, p. 75: *Rob. de Aubenn'* v. *Geoffrey de la Mare*; cf. *Curia Regis Rolls*, iv. 41, 199, 270.

(ii) Pipe Roll 12 Jo., m. 2d: *Richard son of Osbert* v. *Richard de Sifrewast*; cf. *Curia Regis Rolls*, vi. 379; *Book of Fees*, i. 20.

(iii) Pipe Roll 15 Jo., m. 1: *John de Stanford* v. *James son of Peter*; cf. *Curia Regis Rolls*, vii. 307. The land concerned is in Stamford.

(iv) *Curia Regis Rolls*, v. 310: *William de Cantilupe* v. *prior of Dunstable*.

(v) Ibid. vi. 117: 'Robertus Bel offert dimidiam marcam pro habendo quodam precipe coram domino rege versus Hugonem le Bel fratrem suum de dimidio mesuagio in Notingham.'

[5] (i) *Pipe Roll 6 Jo.*, p. 86: *William de Tirant* v. *Godfrey de Porta*, to show why he brought an assize of novel disseisin against William for land which William had already recovered from him by the same assize.

(ii) Ibid., p. 128: *Yvo de Estroppes* v. *Herbert de Estroppes*; cf. *Curia Regis Rolls*, iii. 94, 106, 156, 164. This was an action for land deraigned in the king's court but not surrendered.

(iii) Pipe Roll 13 Jo., m. 16d (Lincs.): Josceus de Wastineis; cf. *Curia Regis Rolls*,

reserved. In other cases the action is against the lord himself. In Maitland's view a lord could not be sued in his own court. As Adams pointed out,[1] this does not seem to have been true in all cases, though it is difficult to discover precisely when it did apply. Glanvill, however, gives details of certain actions against a lord in the royal courts, and it seems clear that the lord might not deal with an action in which he was vouched or himself sued as warrantor. This is expressly stated in an action in the Curia Regis in 1221.[2] No fewer than seven entries on the Pipe Rolls relate to cases of warranty.[3] Another involves the difficult problem of the succession of one who would be both heir and lord.[4] This would certainly not seem to be a matter which could be settled in his own court. In one case it is clear that the lord's court has already defaulted.[5] Thus, in some thirty cases of the use of the writ *Praecipe* in actions of the writ of right type, there is likely to have been good reason for the action being brought into the king's court. In some cases which have been identified it is still impossible to determine the type of action. In ten instances it appears to be proprietary and the reason for its coming to the

vi. 142, 228, 308, 354 (Lincs.). It was asserted that homage had been taken for the land in dispute before the royal justices, whose record had to be obtained.

See also *Rot. de Oblatis*, pp. 356, 363, 537, 541.

[1] *Origin of the English Constitution*, pp. 94–6. There is evidence for the lord being sued in his own court in the thirteenth century also, e.g. *The Earliest Northants Assize Rolls*, ed. D. M. Stenton (Northants Record Soc., vol. v, no. 869): an assize of novel disseisin against Richard de Ofwod', who says: 'quod ipse nil clamat in terra illa nisi per Brienum nuncium qui presens est et dicit quod ipse terram illam dirationavit in curia prioris de Breset' versus ipsum priorem per judicium eiusdem curie et inde vocavit curiam.'

[2] *Curia Regis Rolls*, ix. 102: *Ralph de Alre* v. *abbot of Abingdon*, 'de placito quod warantizet ei v. hidas terre cum pertinentiis in Sudecot. . . .' The abbot is to be told not to hold the plea in his court, 'desicut ipsum abbatem vocavit ad warantum de eadem terra'. This is particularly significant as it comes from the period after Magna Carta.

[3] (i) *Pipe Roll 5 Jo.*, p. 100: *Robert de Trihanton* v. *Joscelin f. Payn*; cf. *Curia Regis Rolls*, ii. 136, 247, 280.

(ii) *Pipe Roll 8 Jo.*, p. 103: *Agnes de Amundeuill* v. *Nicholas de Amundeuill*, 'quod . . . warantizet ei feodum j militis'.

(iii) Pipe Roll 11 Jo., m. 4: *Ralph de Taterset* v. *William de Pinkini*; cf. *Curia Regis Rolls*, vi. 11, 70, &c.

(iv) Pipe Roll 11 Jo., m. 5d: *Alexander son of Alexander* v. *Matilda de Tarston, de Warantizacione*.

(v) Pipe Roll 15 Jo., m. 3: Susanna de Planez; cf. *Curia Regis Rolls*, vii. 272.

(vi) Pipe Roll 15 Jo., m. 7; *Robert de Wateruill* v. *Earl David*; cf. *Rot. de Oblatis*, p. 542.

(vii) See above, p. 165, n. 1, vi.

[4] *Pipe Roll 5 Jo.*, p. 213: *William de Bilton* v. *Theobald de Bilton and others*; cf. *Curia Regis Rolls*, iii. 185, 323–4, &c.; iv. 60, 76.

[5] See below, p. 169, n. 1, v.

royal court is not apparent, but in most of these few details are given, and there may have been an adequate reason. Since the writ could be used as an alternative to the writ *Pone* after the default of the lord's court had been proved, other cases may have come in this way.[1] Again, if a royal charter, even if only a charter of confirmation, was involved, then the feudal court was not competent to determine the action. No example of a *Praecipe* being used for this reason has been found under John, but there is a case in 1218.[2] It is possible, then, that the writ was used in preference to the writ of right in less than a quarter of the identified cases. This does not suggest that its main object was to bring actions into the royal courts when the lords' courts might have dealt with them.

Moreover, it is evident that the writ would have been ineffective if it had been designed to draw cases away from these courts, for the lord whose court was competent to deal with an action could claim that action in the royal court, and the claim might succeed, even if a *Praecipe* had been issued. This very significant fact seems to have been overlooked. Yet Glanvill describes the procedure in detail. If default by the lord's court has been solemnly established, he says, then the lord can never intervene or recover the action:

'Sin autem [he continues] priusquam curia aliqua praedicto modo probetur de recto defecisse, loquela aliqua ab ea ad superiorem curiam trahatur, poterit dominus illius curiae die placiti curiam suam ea ratione repetere, quod nondum probata fuerit de recto defecisse: et ita eam per iudicium retro habebit nisi ibi probetur eam de recto ut dictum est defecisse. Sciendum tamen quod si ad capitalem curiam domini regis ita tracta fuerit loquela aliqua, frustra vindicabit ibi quis die placiti curiam suam, nisi tertio die ante coram legalibus hominibus eam vindicaverit.'[3]

[1] Default was not necessarily due to negligence or unwillingness to deal with a case, or even to the action being outside the competence of the feudal courts. In a particular case the court might prove powerless to secure the presence of a warrantor, or some third party whose aid was sought by the tenant, e.g. a co-parcener. It might not even be able to secure the presence of the tenant himself, and to adjudge the land to the demandant on default by the tenant was a risky course, especially if summons and distraint could not be proved. To do this was to invite an action of novel disseisin in a royal court. Thus a great many actions found their way to the county court. References on the Plea Rolls to decisions there are frequent, and it is often stated that the tenant placed himself on the grand assize in the county, not in the feudal court; e.g. in the *Curia Regis Rolls*, i. 5–13, there are thirteen cases in which the tenant is said to have put himself on the grand assize in the lord's court, nine in which he did so in the county, and two in *Sudtridinga de Lindissei* (pp. 10, 11). But all these cases in the county courts could have been transferred to the Curia Regis by a *Praecipe* or a *Pone*.

[2] See below, p. 177.   [3] Lib. xii, cap. 7, p. 151.

This final proviso is doubly significant: it strongly suggests that the practice of claiming the lord's court is already familiar since detailed rules have already been worked out to meet problems arising out of it; and secondly it indicates a possible source of baronial grievance. The lords would resent not being allowed their courts if their claims were made too late, their jurisdiction being curtailed on account of a purely technical fault in making claims to actions which should properly have come direct to their courts. It is not clear from Glanvill's account that the lord could claim his court in this way if the action had been brought by the writ *Praecipe*. But fortunately there are six cases on the Plea Rolls which can be shown to have been brought by it and in which the lord comes and claims his court.[1] In the first of these six cases it is definitely stated that the lord is to have his court, and in the fourth and sixth it is very probable that he secured it. In the third case he may have obtained it, but found that he was

---

[1] These cases are as follows: (i) *Curia Regis Rolls*, i. 344: 'Alicia Basset petit versus Henricum de Puteaco villam de Iukeflet per breve de precipe: et testatum est quod baillivi episcopi Dulmiensis petierunt inde curiam episcopi ad horam et terminum. Et judicatum est quod episcopus habeat inde curiam suam: et Alicia habeat breve si voluerit ad prosequendum jus suum in curia domini episcopi Dulmiensis.' Cf. ibid., pp. 104, 272, 337. This is a Yorkshire case and the 'palatinate' powers of the bishop are not involved here. It comes from Michaelmas Term, 1200.

(ii) *Warin de Terefeld* (or Bradehoc) v. *abbot of Ramsey*, ibid. iii. 96; cf. *Pipe Roll 6 Jo.*, p. 33. The abbot himself claimed his court, but does not seem to have secured it; cf. *Curia Regis Rolls*, iii. 122, 141; iv. 30.

(iii) *Henry de Nevill* v. *William Arsic*, ibid. iii. 272; cf. *Pipe Roll 7 Jo.*, p. 212. Robert Arsic claimed his court, but it seems that he did not secure it, as the case was before the Curia Regis again; *Curia Regis Rolls*, iv. 252; v. 67, 157, 252; vi. 29. It is possible, however, that Robert's claim was allowed when it was made in Easter Term 1205, since the action does not reappear until Michaelmas Term 1206, when William Arsic vouches Robert to warranty. This vouching explains why the action could not be determined in Robert's court.

(iv) *Peter de Alto Bosco* v. *Eustace de Turgart'*, ibid. iv. 49; cf. *Pipe Roll 7 Jo.*, p. 236. The abbot of Hulme sought his court on the third day.

(v) *Ipolitus Pridias and Matilda his wife* v. *Clement de Turroc, Curia Regis Rolls*, v. 91; cf. *Pipe Roll 9 Jo.*, p. 100. The Templars sought their court but did not obtain it. The action had already been brought in the court of Clement himself and the court had defaulted. The Templars were, therefore, trying to secure the case after default in the court of a mesne tenant. Their failure was presumably due to the reservation of such cases to the public courts.

(vi) *William de Scoteny* v. *Alan de Chatterton, Curia Regis Rolls*, vi. 120; cf. Pipe Roll 13 Jo., m. 4. The steward of Simon de Kyme sought his court. As there are no further references to this action it is probable that the claim succeeded. There are also a few instances of *Praecipe* cases being claimed by boroughs which had the liberty whereby burgesses could not be impleaded save within the borough, and a similar claim was made by the sheriff of Kent on behalf of the royal manor of Milton (*Curia Regis Rolls*, iv. 61; cf. *Pipe Roll 7 Jo.*, p. 117). All these claims seem to have been successful.

not after all able to deal with the action as he himself was vouched to warranty. The reason why the claim failed in the fifth case was that the immediate lord's court had already defaulted, and in the second the failure was probably due to the fact that the lord himself was the defendant.

From an examination of these six cases it may be concluded that if the lord's court was in fact competent, and if his claim was made punctually, he would normally recover cognizance of the action even though it had been brought by a *Praecipe*.

The six cases considered so far are ones in which the action claimed is known to have been brought by the writ *Praecipe*, but it is probable that nearly all the land actions claimed by lords in the Curia Regis or at the Eyre had also been brought by this writ. The alternative writ, the *Pone*, would be likely to be used only in cases in which the default of the lord's court had already been proved.[1] It is worth while, therefore, to examine all these claims, the majority of which is likely to have been made in actions brought by a *Praecipe*. In any case their treatment will throw light on the problem of the royal policy towards the feudal courts. One of the earliest claims[2] is of particular interest, for it points to the strictly impartial treatment of the lords' claims at the beginning of John's reign. In this case two lords claimed their courts. It would seem obvious that the Curia Regis could very easily have refused them both, on the grounds that actions in which two lords were concerned could not be heard by either. But eventually one claim was conceded, presumably because it was found on investigation that both parties claimed to hold of this lord. Generally it is not possible to say definitely whether the claim was allowed or not. Apart from the *Praecipe* cases already mentioned, only eleven cases have been noted in John's reign in which the claim is stated to have been allowed,[3] and a

---

[1] Though it was used in at least one case which was claimed by a lord: see *Curia Regis Rolls*, v. 103: *William Gulafre and Matilda his wife* v. *Alice de Lundresford*; the abbot of Robertsbridge seeks his court; cf. *Pipe Roll 9 Jo.*, p. 41: 'Will. Gulafre et Matill. uxor ejus debent i m. pro habendo pone uersus Aliciam que fuit uxor Ricardi de Lundreford.'

[2] *Curia Regis Rolls*, i. 356, Michaelmas Term 1200: 'Elias de Ascell' ballivus Oliveri de Traci petiit tercio die ante placita curiam domini sui de loquela inter Robertum de Campell' et Willelmum de Campell' de placito terre. Rogerus de Punchardun petiit curiam suam de eodem'; cf. ii. 31, Michaelmas Term 1201: 'Robertus de Campell' recedit sine die a curia de loquela que fuit inter ipsum et Willelmum de Campell', quia Oliverus de Tracy habet curiam suam.'

[3] (i) *Rotuli Curiae Regis*, ed. Palgrave, ii. 118: 'Robertus de Boseuill recessit sine die versus Will. Flandr. et Matill. uxorem ejus de placito terre in Chirshamton quia Sibill. de Tingree domina feodi pet. inde curiam suam ad horam et habuit eam.'

dozen or so in which it seems clear that it was disallowed,[1] but

The entry relating to this action, *Curia Regis Rolls*, i. 131, probably belongs to an earlier stage of the proceedings.

(ii) Ibid. i. 164: *William Cokaine* v. *abbot of Faversham*. The abbot seeks his court and secures it. This is an important instance, as he is a party to the action. But William Cokaine seems to be identical with the William Fitz Ralph who also claimed land in Tring (see pp. 68 and 165, also *Rotuli Curiae Regis*, i. 272, 417; ii. 70). The abbot's claim to this action did not succeed, or perhaps was not pressed, as it appears that he did not hold the disputed land in demesne. The demandant was told to sue against the tenants if he wished.

(iii) *Curia Regis Rolls*, i. 337: *Roger de Pascarie* v. *John son of Edward and others*. The steward of Westminster seeks his court and has it. But this action reappears a year later, see ii. 86–7.

(iv) Ibid. i. 345: *Jukelinus de Smetheton'* v. *John Bec*, and *Walter Clerk* v. *John Bec*. The bishop of Durham sought his court *ad horam*, &c. 'Et ideo Jukelinus et Walterus eant inde sine die.' This is a Yorkshire case, not one from the palatinate.

(v) Ibid., p. 356, see preceding note.

(vi) Ibid., p. 370: *Herbert de Bolebec* v. *William de Turvill*. The earl of Leicester has his court.

(vii) Ibid. iv. 224: *Walter Nencumene and Eva his wife and Matilda her sister* v. *William Brule*; cf. p. 278: the parties are *sine die* because the abbot of Westminster sought his court *ad horam*.

(viii) Ibid. v. 149.

(ix) Ibid., p. 210.

(x) Ibid. vi. 241. For these three cases, see below, p. 176, n. 1.

(xi) Ibid. iii. 162: *John de Bassingeburn* v. *Hamelin de Andeuill*. In this case the claim is said to succeed by consent of the parties.

[1] (i) *Rotuli Curiae Regis*, ii. 46–7, 128, 281: *Richard de Garwinton* v. *Teobald de Tuitham*. But this seems to have been an assize and only a few of the greater franchises could deal with the assizes.

(ii) *Curia Regis Rolls*, i. 238, 329: *William de Lesnes* v. *prior of Christchurch, Canterbury*. Both the prior and the archbishop sought their courts, but apparently without success, since it is probable that this is the same action as in ii. 35, 181.

(iii) Ibid. iii. 197, 294: *Nigel de Luvetot* v. *Hubert de Bramford*. Nigel sought his court, but then the parties sought licence to agree and a final concord was eventually made in the Curia Regis, see iv. 203, 248, 256; v. 26, 198, 212, 271.

(iv) Ibid. iii. 272: *Roger de Burun* v. *Thomas de Herlaue*. William Revel claims his court but does not get it, because Roger claims to hold of the earl of Oxford.

(v) Ibid., p. 321: *Matthew de Gurnay* v. *Gilbert de Runhal'*. John Marshal seeks his court, but the action appears a year later, iv. 94, 204, 254; cf. v. 52, 137, 228.

(vi) Ibid. iv. 60, 123: *Geoffrey son of Richard* v. *Henry Ruffus*. The abbot of Messenden seeks his court, but apparently does not get it as this is a case of entry.

(vii) Ibid., p. 60 (Hilary Term 1206): *Ernald and Philip de Meissi* v. *Theobald de Valeines*. John de Bassingburn seeks the court of the heirs of Ralph de Mara, but the action is still in the Curia Regis in Trinity Term, see pp. 168–9.

(viii) Ibid. v. 1, 88, 196, 300 (cf. iv. 97, &c.): *William de Gimingham and Juliana his wife* v. *Hugh de Polsted and Hawisia his wife*. The countess of Perche seeks her court but evidently does not get it.

(ix) Ibid. v. 103, 207, 290. For this action see above, p. 170, n. 1. It is concerned with a marriage portion, and involves the question whether the land is held of the abbot of Robertsbridge who claims his court.

(x) Ibid. vi. 8, 12, 14–15, 80. See below, p. 176.

(xi) Ibid. vii. 128. See below, p. 175, n. 4. This is an action of dower.

(xii) See above, n. 3, no. ii.

(xiii) See below, p. 173, n. 3. Three other very dubious cases may be noticed:

in at least five of these the refusal was clearly justified (nos. i, iv, vi, ix, xiii); in others it may well have been so (nos. ii, iii, xi, xii). In some thirty cases the absence of further entries suggests that the lords secured their courts.[1] These figures certainly do not suggest that John was seeking every occasion to reduce the business of the feudal courts, and if many of these actions were in fact brought by the writ *Praecipe* it can hardly be asserted that he was encouraging litigants to secure the writ in order 'to draw into his own courts all pleas relating to land'. There would be no point in bringing an action in the royal court only to have it transferred to the feudal one.

But while the lord might recover his court it is possible that he did not always take advantage of this procedure, or if he made the claim it might fail on some technical count. It seems unlikely, however, that the lords often failed to take action. There was a good chance of success, and there was little likelihood of the action being heard in the royal court without the lord's knowledge. It was in the tenant's interest to employ any delaying tactics, such as warning the lord to put in his claim. Any lord who had the franchise of return of writs would automatically get to know of it. Some lords appointed attorneys to be present in the Curia Regis to claim actions pertaining to their courts as they arose. The earl of Leicester, for example, appointed an attorney in 1200, his function being 'quod ipse petat curiam suam et libertatem cum locus et necesse fuerit in curia domini regis'.[2] The number of claims mentioned may suggest that litigants were inclined to obtain the writ *Praecipe* in improper cases, even though they ran the risk of prolonging the proceedings if a

(xiv) *Curia Regis Rolls*, i. 249, 325, 464: *Peter de Brus* v. *William de Brus*. The bishop of Durham seeks his court. The parties have sought licence to agree, but the whole action is adjourned *coram rege* on account of the bishop's claim. He had already proved troublesome over this action, threatening to excommunicate the sheriff of Northumberland when the latter tried to summon William; see *Rotuli Curiae Regis*, ii. 178.

(xv) *Curia Regis Rolls*, ii. 131: *Achard* (*de Aldeham*) v. *Agnes and Nicholas*. Robert de Barevill claimed his court. The action reappears two years later, iii. 190, 203, 251, 310–11, when Nicholas puts himself on the grand assize. It is possible that the claim had been allowed and that Robert's court had defaulted in the interval.

(xvi) Ibid. iv. 274: *Ralph Brazur and Juliana his wife* v. *Walter Bolt*. The prior of Bermondsey sought his court. In the next term Ralph is *sine die*. This may be because the prior's claim is allowed; see v. 16.

[1] Where the court is stated to have been claimed *ad horam et terminum*, and there is no further reference to the action, it is highly probable that the claim was allowed.

[2] Ibid. i. 251.

successful claim could be made. But in fact the number of land actions claimed in any year was not very great—the largest number claimed in the Curia Regis Rolls[1] after 1200 is ten in 1206—and in the great majority of the identified *Praecipe* cases, as in the great majority of pleas of land in the royal courts, no claim was made. Normally, it would seem, a litigant secured the writ only if his lord's court was not competent, but in a dubious case he might obtain it, only to find that his lord was able to retrieve the action. Conversely, however, the lord might secure his court and then discover that the action after all transcended its competence, for cases successfully claimed sometimes reappear in the Curia Regis after a year or two. The business of claiming court must, however, have been a nuisance, and it is possible that the claim would not succeed if the action had reached a stage at which it was apparent that there would be little point in transferring it to the feudal court; for example, if the tenant had announced his intention of putting himself on the grand assize, or if the parties were ready to make a final concord.[2] The lords would have had a reasonable, if minor, grievance if particular actions brought by the writ *Praecipe* were being kept out of their courts in this way, or because of unpunctuality in making the claim.[3] But so long as they could claim their courts, the writ *Praecipe* did not constitute a threat to their normal jurisdiction. At the worst it might be responsible for the occasional loss of a case at an early stage of the proceedings, a case which very likely would have been lost anyhow at a later stage by the tenant's placing himself on the grand assize.

The object of Magna Carta, clause 34, cannot therefore have been to 'restore' the feudal courts' 'exclusive competence in proprietary actions', or even to reverse the process by which royal justice had been extended hitherto. Unless there was some change in policy just before 1215, the writ *Praecipe* did not con-

---

[1] Claims on the Eyre Rolls are very rare.

[2] e.g. this may be the reason why Roger Mortimer failed to obtain his court in *John de Bramton* v. *Margaret de Bocton, Rotuli Curiae Regis*, i. 291, 326; ii. 13, 32, 115.

[3] There is an example of the possible unfairness of this rule in 1206; *Curia Regis Rolls*, iv. 175. The demandants ask that the claim of Canterbury Cathedral Priory to its court should not be allowed, since it was not made *ad horam*. The monks pointed out that the king had seized all their possessions, and they had had no power to make the claim. But it is significant that the plaintiffs withdrew. If they wished to begin their action again they would have to do so in the monks' court, the right of which seems thus to be tacitly acknowledged, in spite of the lateness of their claim.

stitute a direct threat to feudal jurisdiction over land actions. It was the restriction of its competence by the various rules which have been discussed which mattered, not the writ *Praecipe*, which left it open for the lord to recover his court if none of these rules applied. But it is quite clear that clause 34 did not affect these restrictions. Bracton's account of the writ of right[1] shows them still in force. Nor were the various writs *Praecipe* which were not merely alternatives to the writ of right affected. The writs of entry, in particular, became extremely common after 1215.[2] Bracton speaks of the earlier, now unlawful, use of the writ *Praecipe* as an alternative to the writ of right,[3] and in the discussion of the new writ of cosinage in 1237 it was decided that this, although beginning *Praecipe*, did not infringe Magna Carta since it did not deprive anyone of his court in a case in which the writ of right might have been brought.[4] But for some years after 1215 the writ continued to be issued even as an alternative to the writ of right.[5] It would seem, therefore, that the barons were not attempting to prevent its use, but only to ensure that they did not thereby lose their courts in individual cases with which they were admittedly competent to deal. In short, *curia* in clause 34 does not stand for jurisdiction in general, but is used in the sense in which it is currently used on the Plea Rolls for cognizance of an individual action.

If the lords could still retrieve such actions by claiming their courts, the object of clause 34 can have been only to save them the trouble of making the claims, with the attendant risk of occasional failure. If, however, there was any change in royal policy by which claims of court were to be refused, then the barons may have feared that the writ would become more popular and the remaining business of their courts would be drained away. There is some evidence which may suggest a change in John's policy, or at any rate that the barons may have suspected such a change. But this evidence is by no means conclusive. The Pipe Roll of 1213 contains a large number of new entries *pro habendo Praecipe*, by far the largest number since 1204. From this it might

---

[1] See below, p. 178.
[2] There are many cases on the early Plea Rolls of Henry III; cf. Pipe Roll 9 Henry III, m. 5*d*. 'Abbas Sancti Ebrolfi . . . pro habendo precipe de ingressu versus plures.' Lady Stenton no longer holds that clause 34 was directed against the writs of entry; see *Pipe Roll 6 Jo.*, p. xxxii.
[3] *De Legibus*, ff. 105, 105*b*, ed. Woodbine, ii. 300.
[4] *Bracton's Note Book*, ed. Maitland, no. 1215.
[5] See below, p. 177.

seem that the writ was becoming more popular because it was found that the lords were no longer able to retrieve these actions. But this increase may be explained by the renewal of judicial activity at Westminster and the movement of the Curia Regis about the country. The entries still seem to be of a very miscellaneous character. Secondly, there is a decline in the number of claims of court in proprietary actions from 10 in 1206 and 6 in 1207 to 3 in 1208, 1 each in 1210 and 1211, and 2 in 1212. But this decline may well be explained by a probable decline in the total amount of judicial business during the Interdict, and the fact that far less is recorded. Moreover, in itself a decline in the number of claims would suggest that fewer cases were being brought in the royal courts when they should have gone to the feudal. It would be only if such a decline was found to coincide with an increase in the number of *Praecipes* issued in proprietary actions, or if a larger proportion of the claims was being refused, that it could be taken to indicate that the royal judges were seeking occasion to reject claims and so make the writ *Praecipe* more popular with litigants. Neither of these factors can be discovered. The number of *Praecipe* entries in the Pipe Rolls from 1205 to 1212 shows a marked decline after the peak year, 1204. Unfortunately, only one Curia Regis Roll has survived for the year 1213, in which there was a large increase in the recorded issue of the writ, and it is impossible to say whether fewer claims were made than usual. There is one claim of court on this roll, but it is unhelpful, since it is a claim by the bishop of Ely's steward to an assize of *darrein presentment*,[1] a matter with which only the greatest franchises could deal. The bishop, however, also appointed an attorney 'ad exigendum curias suas de loquelis que in curia domini regis movebuntur',[2] which suggests that no change in royal policy was expected. In 1214 he claimed a grand assize,[3] and Gilbert de Pleshey claimed an action for dower.[4] The latter claim did not succeed, probably because the action was for dower *unde nihil habet*. It would hardly have been made, however, if John had made clear his intention of disallowing claims of court. In general, moreover, the claims made in the latter part of the reign seem to have been fairly treated. The decline in the number made is not accompanied by an increase in the proportion which failed. Of the seven claims recorded between 1208 and 1212,

[1] *Curia Regis Rolls*, vii. 5.
[2] Ibid.
[3] Ibid., p. 129.
[4] Ibid., p. 128; cf. pp. 193, 208, 276.

three are definitely stated to have been allowed,[1] and two others were probably allowed.[2] On the other hand there are one or two cases which may have given rise to the suspicion that John was intending to use the writ *Praecipe* in a more aggressive way. During his quarrel with the Church one or two claims were refused and the reason for their refusal is not apparent. One of these claims, that of the abbess of Caen in Michaelmas Term 1207, was in an action between two brothers; but as it involved the summoning of recognitors this was probably not an ordinary writ of right case.[3] The other is a claim by the custodian of the bishopric of London in 1210 which also seems to have been refused.[4] But this was a complicated case, since a third party intervened, and this may account for the refusal. There is, then, nothing but the merest suggestion of a stricter policy towards claims on behalf of religious bodies during this period which might account for baronial suspicions. Until more evidence of this kind is discovered, it would be rash to conclude that there was any change in the treatment of claims of court, or any special inducement to litigants to obtain the writ *Praecipe*.

It is clear, then, that the barons were not trying to restore the feudal courts' jurisdiction over matters which had already been lost, and the evidence is insufficient to show that they were defending what remained of the business of these courts against a threatened royal attack. The explanation of clause 34 which remains is simply that they wished to obviate the necessity of claiming their courts, with the attendant risk of being deprived

---

[1] *Curia Regis Rolls*, v. 149 (Hilary Term 1208): *Ralph Parmenter* v. *Ralph de Cler.* Earl Warenne seeks his court, 'et habet curiam suam'. Ibid., p. 210 (Easter Term 1208): *Ralph de Brai* v. *William son of Ellis.* Henry de Oili seeks his court 'et habet'. But this action was back in the Curia Regis by the following Michaelmas Term, when William objected that he had not had reasonable summons. The sheriff's clerk confirmed this (ibid., p. 316). Ibid. vi. 241 (Easter Term 1212): *Richard of Brackley* v. *William, archdeacon of Buckingham.* The archdeacon sought his court, 'Et quia peciit illam ad horam, habeat eam. Et ideo sine die.' But this case, too, came back later, in Michaelmas Term 1213, when the archdeacon asserted that the land in dispute belonged to his prebend and that he could not reply without his bishop. No doubt it was for this reason that his court could not, after all, determine the action; see vii. 9–10.

[2] Ibid. vi. 120: *William de Scoteny* v. *Alan de Chatterton.* Simon de Kyme seeks his court. This is a *Praecipe* case, see above, p. 169, n. 1, vi.

Ibid., p. 282: *Adam Hasteng* v. *Roger de Cherlecot'.* Humphrey Hasteng seeks his court on the third day; cf. p. 265.

No later entries have been found dealing with these actions, and it is likely therefore that the claims succeeded. Cf. ibid. v. 210: *Gilbert Scot* v. *Lambert de Campis.* R. de Cornhill seeks his court in a *loquela*, probably a land action.

[3] Ibid. v. 111, 278, 292; vi. 38, 98.

[4] Ibid. vi. 8, 12, 14–15, 80.

of them in a few particular cases on some technical pretext, or at the least, to ensure that their claims succeeded. The onus of securing his court ought not to rest with the lord. It was for the demandant first to seek justice in his lord's court, however improbable it was that that court would be able to determine the cause. But only when its incompetence had been proved should he have recourse to the king's court. This, in fact, seems to be just what was ultimately effected by clause 34,[1] but if it was what the barons intended, the clause was not worded clearly enough. It did not expressly prohibit the issue of the writ as an alternative to the writ of right, and Chancery continued to issue it without, apparently, inquiring whether it was endangering the lord's court or not. Thus the entries *pro habendo Praecipe* still appear on the early Pipe Rolls of Henry III, especially in 1219; some of these are stated to be concerned with land actions,[2] and one or two cases on the Plea Rolls also show that proprietary actions were still being brought by it in the Curia Regis. One such case in 1218 is known from *Bracton's Note Book*,[3] its later history appearing in the Curia Regis Rolls of 1219.[4] Objection was taken to the writ by the tenant, but only on the grounds that he had not received proper summons. As a royal charter of confirmation was involved the case was one with which a feudal court could not deal. Then in 1220 there was a very significant case in which the writ *Praecipe* is not mentioned but was almost certainly used.[5]

[1] It may also have had the effect of enabling the defendant to get an action sent back to the county court. Thus in 1221, in an action *de divisis faciendis*, the defendant says that he has not been summoned *in comitatu*. 'Et ideo preceptum est vicecomiti quod secundum consuetudinem regni teneat in comitatu suo loquelam et non remaneat ea occasione quod posita fuit per preceptum domini regis apud Westmonasterium. . . .' *Curia Regis Rolls*, ix. 148.

[2] e.g. Pipe Roll 3 Henry III, m. 5: 'Willelmus filius Roberti . . . pro habendo Precipe de terra in Hugeden'; ibid.: 'Johannes de Mapedelham . . . pro habendo precipe apud Westmonasterium de terra in Wilie et Caldecot' contra Deodat. de Caldecot'; ibid., m. 6: 'Alina filia Stephani . . . pro habendo precipe versus Regin. Pichard. de terra in Bedesham.' (This may be a case of dower, as that of Hendina que fuit uxor Alard. de Sturem'e (ibid.) probably is); ibid.: 'Regin. de Huntindon . . . pro habendo Precipe versus Berenger. monachum de rationabili excambio duarum bovatarum terre in Gummecestr'; ibid., m. 8: 'Willelmus de Sutton. . . . pro habendo precipe de i molendino in Radeford'; ibid., m. 14: 'Margar' filia Alani de Dunhid . . . pro habendo precipe de i masagio in Dunhee versus Rad. de Mora'; ibid.: 'Adam de Gesemue . . . pro habendo Precipe de xii bovatis terre versus Gillebertum de Laval'; cf. Pipe Roll 2 Henry III, mm. 6, 7, 8, 8*d*. The total number of entries in 1219 is above the average for the later years of John's reign.   [3] Vol. ii, no. 10.   [4] viii. 17, 165, 352.

[5] *Curia Regis Rolls*, viii. 349. There are other instances of the use of the writ in actions which should have gone to borough courts, or to the court of a royal soke; see ibid., pp. 134, 202; but no objection was taken to the action for a messuage

Henry de Sacy comes and claims his court, saying that the land in dispute is held of him and the king has no demesne in the vill. This is admitted, and the parties are *sine die*. It seems evident that Henry's claim is based on clause 34, and that by now it is being maintained that the writ *Praecipe* should be used, in the first instance, apart from the reserved cases only for land held in chief of the Crown. The immediate effect of clause 34 had not been, then, to eliminate claims of court, but only to ensure their success in appropriate cases. But in the next year or two such claims in ordinary proprietary actions practically disappear.[1] This was probably due to the fact that it was no longer necessary for the lord to intervene, as he could now leave it to the tenant to except to the writ *Praecipe*. If the exception was allowed, the action would be quashed and the plaintiff would have to begin all over again by writ of right in the lord's court. Bracton emphasizes the tenant's right to except to the writ *Praecipe* in his section 'De Exceptionibus': 'Item cadit breve si impetratum fuerit contra ius et regni consuetudinem, et maxime contra cartam libertatis, sicut breve quod vocatur praecipe, per quod liber homo posset curiam amittere.'[2] Consequently it was no longer worth while for the demandant to secure a *Praecipe* as it was so easy for the tenant to get it quashed by invoking clause 34, and the issue of the writ seems to have become unusual. The entries on the Pipe Rolls dwindle away. Thus after a time this clause may have become only too effective, even the most dubious causes now being begun in the feudal courts, in order to avoid such delaying tactics by the tenant in the royal court. As Bracton remarks, the lord may be unwilling, or unable to hold the plea, or may not know how to do so, yet the case must first be brought to his court, and only transferred to the county when its default has been proved. It may then be transferred, if the king is willing, to his court; but this must not be done against the will of the lord, as it used to be done *per Praecipe*, except for these reasons, or when the lord voluntarily remits his court to the king.[3] This strict rule,

---

in Bridgnorth brought by a *Praecipe* at the Eyre of 1221; see *Rolls of the Justices in Eyre for Gloucestershire, Warwickshire and Staffordshire, 1221, 1222* (Selden Soc., vol. lix), no. 1175.

[1] There is a later claim, in 1222, Curia Regis Roll (P.R.O.) 82*a*, m. 17. But as this case was claimed for the court of the banleuca of St. Edmund's and the abbot's regalian franchises were stressed, it was probably one of the actions normally reserved to the Crown. Claims for other types of action continued, e.g. *Curia Regis Rolls*, ix. 283 (1222). The bishop of Ely claims his court in an action for customs and services within the Isle of Ely and obtains it.

[2] *De Legibus*, f. 414*b*, ed. Woodbine, iv. 289.   [3] Ibid., f. 105; ii. 300.

as he suggests later, must have led to many abortive attempts to get a writ of right action heard in a feudal court. The demandant, he says, may fail to get justice there because the tenant claims to hold of a different lord; or because the lord flatly refuses to do justice; or because there is no one in his court who can do right; or because the lord has not got a court. Nor, in such an impasse, may the demandant go to the court of his lord's lord, because the writ says that if so and so (the immediate lord) fails to do justice, the sheriff is immediately to take over. Bracton adds one or two more difficulties in the way of getting a decision in the feudal court, and concludes: *Et aliae sunt causae infinitae* for default of justice in the lord's court.[1] The writ *Praecipe* had provided a useful short cut to the king's court in cases where the lord's was likely to default. Magna Carta closed this short cut, so compelling the demandant to waste much time in trying to get his case heard by some feudal court which was really powerless to determine it. But though the demandant had now to take the long way round it seems likely, from what Bracton says, that he generally reached the royal court in the end. It is not surprising, however, to find litigants having recourse to new short cuts. Bracton mentions one of them, the voluntary remission of the lord's court. A special writ of right was devised, the 'breve de recto quia dominus remisit curiam'.[2] Armed with this the demandant might go straight to the king's court. Another device was to bring the writ *Praecipe in capite*, which since Magna Carta had been employed where the land in dispute was held in chief of the Crown, in actions for land not held in chief. The tenant could, of course, except to this writ on the grounds that the land was not held in chief, yet it seems to have come into very general use as the prospect of getting the matter settled in a feudal court became more and more remote. The effect of clause 34 was, then, to enable the defendant to except to a writ *Praecipe* in the royal court, so saving the lord the trouble of putting in an appearance in order to claim the action. While the intention of the barons seems to have been reasonable enough, the result was unfortunate; clause 34 established a rule which litigants were bound to find some means of evading, as it probably obstructed far more cases than it expedited. While it may have saved the lords some inconvenience, its effect on the volume of business determined in the feudal courts was probably negligible.   N. D. HURNARD

---

[1] Ibid., f. 329*b*; iv. 51–2.
[2] For an example of this procedure, see *Close Rolls, 1261–1264*, p. 109.

THE *SUMMA THEOLOGIAE* OF ROBERT GROSSETESTE

IT has often been asked whether Robert Grosseteste wrote a *Summa Theologiae*. In his rich catalogue of Grosseteste's writings Professor S. Harrison Thomson,[1] of the University of Colorado, lists 120 authentic works; but there is no mention of a *Summa*, or of a commentary on Peter Lombard's *Sentences*. Yet in his search he visited over 140 libraries and consulted about 2,500 manuscripts scattered over Europe.[2] We may, then, confidently be sure that there are no extant manuscripts of any such work. It is true that an entry in the *Index Bibliothecae Vaticanae* compiled in the time of Pope Sixtus IV refers to 'Linconiensis super Expositione Magistri Sententiarum'; but this codex, identified by Mgr. A. Pelzer[3] as MS. Vat. lat. 1101, contains the *Sentences* of Peter of Poitiers, not Grosseteste's.[4] Again, Bale,[5] followed by Pits,[6] attributed to Grosseteste a *Summa Theologiae* with the *incipit*, 'Spiritus Sanctus per os Salomonis', and Tanner[7] refers to the manuscript in which this work is preserved, MS. Bodl. Laud. E. 52, now MS. Laud. Misc. 374; we do not have here, however, a *Summa Theologiae*, but the *Dicta*. Further, the *Templum Domini* is described in the colophon of some manuscripts as a *Summa*: 'Explicit *Summa* quam Magister Robertus Grosseteste, quondam episcopus Lincolniensis, nunc vero sanctus, ad instructionem sacerdotum et ad salutem animarum salubriter composuit' (Bodleian Library, Oxford, MS. Rawl. A. 384, f. 106rb).[8]

Admittedly, it is not in itself extraordinary that Grosseteste wrote neither a *Summa Theologiae* nor a commentary on the

---

[1] S. Harrison Thomson, *The Writings of Robert Grosseteste, Bishop of Lincoln, 1235–1253* (Cambridge, 1940). Henceforth cited as *The Writings*.

[2] Thomson, op. cit., p. 1.

[3] A. Pelzer, *Codices Vaticani Latini*, ii, Pars Prior (Bibliotheca Vaticana, 1931), pp. 711–12.

[4] Professor Thomson rightly entered it under *spuria*, cf. op. cit., p. 260, n. 50.

[5] J. Bale, *Scriptorum Illustrium Maioris Britanniae Catalogus* (Basileae, 1557), p. 305.

[6] J. Pits, *Relationum Historicarum de Rebus Anglicis Tomus Primus* (Parisiis, 1619), p. 328.

[7] T. Tanner, *Bibliotheca Britannico-Hibernica* (Londini, 1748), pp. 349–50, n. *p*.

[8] The colophon in Merton College, Oxford, MS. 257 reads: '*Summa* magistri Roberti Lincoliensis episcopi de articulis fidei et de fide catholica et de omnibus rebus pertinentibus ad officium sacerdotale.' Cf. Thomson, *The Writings*, pp. 138–9.

Sentences. After all, very few masters did in fact compose such works. Moreover, in the early thirteenth century the custom of lecturing on the *Sentences* was by no means generally established. Nevertheless, the insistence with which the question is raised, and the fact that some of his writings are lost or still untraced, seem to have kept alive the hope that something of the sort might one day come to light.

A set of anonymous *quaestiones*, still unpublished, in the Library of Exeter College, Oxford, MS. 28, ff. 306ʳ–307ᵛ, have been attributed to Robert Grosseteste.[1] They deal with strictly theological subjects, *De scientia Dei, De voluntate Dei, De misericordia et iustitia Dei, De presentia Dei localiter*. Two incidental phrases in the *explicits* given by Thomson—'dicendum posterius in secundo, ubi dicetur de peccato'; and 'retribuendo et puniendo posterius dicetur in quarto per Dei gratiam'—suggested to me the idea that these *quaestiones* might well be fragments of a commentary on, or of a *Summa* written within the framework of, the Four Books of the *Sentences*. Undoubtedly the first phrase, 'dicetur posterius in *Secundo*, ubi dicetur de peccato', can refer only to Book II of the *Sentences*, where in dd. xxxiv–xliv Peter the Lombard treats of sin. Likewise, it is obvious that 'retribuendo et puniendo posterius dicetur in *Quarto*' can only mean Book IV, dist. xlvi, in which the problem of reward and punishment is discussed in connexion with the justice and mercy of God.

But before I say more about this conjecture, it will be well to examine at the outset a preliminary, though fundamental, problem, that is, the attribution of the *quuestiones* under discussion to Robert Grosseteste.

The Exeter manuscript is the only known copy of our *quaestiones*, and, as we have already pointed out, it bears no ascription. On the other hand, all bibliographers attribute them without any hesitation to Grosseteste. Boston of Bury[2] mentions at least three of them with their exact *incipits* and *explicits*: 'De scientia Dei. Pr. "Queritur", Fin. "recte"; De misericordia et iustitia. Pr. "Consequitur", Fin. "per Dei gratiam"; De locali presentia Dei. Pr. "Hic queritur", Fin. "filius" '. John Bale[3] reports four *quaestiones* with fuller *incipits* than Boston: 'De scientia et voluntate Dei, li. 1. "Queritur de scientia Dei, quomodo"; De

---

[1] See Thomson, *The Writings*, pp. 113–14.
[2] Boston of Bury *apud* Tanner, op. cit., p. xxxvii; and Thomson, ibid., p. 5.
[3] Bale, *Scriptorum*, p. 305; cf. also *J. Bale's Index of British and other Writers*, ed. R. L. Poole and M. Bateson (Oxford, 1902), pp. 375, 377.

Dei misericordia et iustitia, li. 1. "Consequenter tractatur de misericordia"; De locali Dei presentia, li. 1. "Hic queritur de locali presentia" .' Pits,[1] as usual, follows Bale, and Tanner[2] in his turn repeats the same account giving, in addition, MS. Br. Twin. Я 133 as his source.

Professor Thomson remarks that 'the matter of the authenticity of these *quaestiones* is complicated by the confusion in the information given us by the bibliographers'.[3] *Pace* Professor Thomson, this information would seem quite straightforward, although a few inaccuracies have unfortunately crept in. The real difficulty, in my opinion, lies in determining the origin of the information supplied by the bibliographers—whether it derives from Exeter College MS. 28, or from some other source. If the first alternative proves to be the right one, a further problem arises—on what grounds did the bibliographers ascribe these anonymous *quaestiones* to Robert Grosseteste?

According to Thomson we must 'posit the existence of a MS., now lost or unknown, which must be supposed to bear an ascription of these *quaestiones* to Grosseteste'.[4] There cannot be any doubt that it is possible that both Boston of Bury and Tanner saw a manuscript containing these *quaestiones* other than Exeter MS. 28. Yet on examination it would appear that their knowledge came mainly, if not exclusively, from the Exeter text. To render easier a comparison of the bibliographical data with the Exeter text I give the *incipits* and *explicits* of each *quaestio* in the latter document:

I. '*De Scientia Dei.* (i) De scientia Dei, quomodo scit singularia. Queritur de scientia Dei quomodo scit singularia ista . . . apud quem non est transmutatio, nec vicissitudinis obumbratio. In *Sententiis* est.'

   '(ii) Quomodo Deus scit ea que contingunt a casu vel a libera voluntate. Consequenter queritur qualiter Deus scit . . . et tamen non habet gratiam quia vult, sed ipsa gratia est eam volendi recte.'

II. '*De Voluntate Dei.* Consequenter queritur de voluntate Dei que distinguitur in beneplacitum et signum eius. (There are four points of inquiry) . . . ad voluntatem Dei dicendum posterius in *Secundo*, ubi dicetur de peccato.'

III. '*De Misericordia et Iustitia Dei.* Consequenter autem dicto de voluntate dicendum de misericordia et iustitia. Iustitia est voluntas . . . De effectu autem iustitie et misericordie Dei qui est in retribuendo et puniendo posterius dicetur in *Quarto* per Dei gratiam.'

---

[1] Pits, op. cit., pp. 329–30.
[2] Tanner, op. cit., p. 349, n. *p.*
[3] Thomson, *The Writings*, p. 114.
[4] Thomson, op. et loc. cit.

IV. '*De Presentia Dei localiter.* Hic queritur de locali presentia creatoris. Utrum sit ubique, et probatur quod sic . . . generat Pater et generatur Filius.'

It is plain that the *incipits* and *explicits* given by Boston of Bury agree with those of Q. I, *De scientia Dei*; Q. III, *De misericordia et iustitia*;[1] and of Q. IV, *De presentia Dei*; whereas Q. II, *De voluntate Dei*, is left out. The reason of this omission is unknown to us; but presumably it was caused through an oversight due to the repetition of the same word 'consequenter', a very common mistake. Bale, Pits, and Tanner undoubtedly included it under the title *De scientia et voluntate Dei*, thus joining together both *quaestiones*. We have it on Bale's own authority, from whom Pits and Tanner borrowed their information, that it is so. In fact, for his knowledge of the *De scientia et voluntate Dei*, Bale in his *Index* appeals directly to the Exeter text, *ex collegio Excestrensi, Oxon.*[2] Tanner refers also to MS. Br. Twin. ꝶ 133, which is now MS. Twyne 21 in the Bodleian Library; but there is nothing in that place except the bare mention of *De misericordia Dei* and *De locali praesentia Dei*, without indication of source. It is true that the *incipit* given by Bale for the *De misericordia et iustitia*, 'Consequenter tractatur de misericordia', is substantially different from that in the Exeter manuscript, 'Consequenter autem dicto de voluntate dicendum de misericordia'; but we are all aware from our own experience how very easily similar oversights creep in. Thomson himself, so exact and careful, gives as the *explicit* of his Q. i, 'ea que contingunt a casu vel a libera volunte', which in reality is the title of Q. ii in his list.

That Boston of Bury gives 'recte' as the *explicit* of the *De scientia Dei* does not prove the existence of a different source from the Exeter manuscript. As a matter of fact, there was no need at all for him to bring out *explicitly* Q. ii in Thomson's list, 'Quomodo Deus scit ea que contingunt a casu vel a libera volunte'. Quite rightly too he regarded 'the first two items as one', since they are not two separate *quaestiones*, but simply two points of inquiry within the same subject, *De scientia Dei*. Concerning God's knowledge the author considers a twofold aspect of the problem, (i) how God knows individual things, whether in their singularity,

---

[1] Boston's *Consequitur* is a manifest misreading of *consequenter*. Dr. R. W. Hunt tells me that similar misreadings occur frequently in the only extant manuscript of Boston of Bury, a transcript made by Tanner (Cambridge, Univ. Lib., MS. Add. 3478).

[2] *Bale's Index*, ed. cit., p. 377.

or only as contained in universal causes; (ii) how God knows contingent things which happen by chance or come from free will.

At all events, there seems to be no certain evidence that the bibliographers were in possession of other sources of information apart from Exeter College MS. 28.

On this assumption it remains to examine the other point at issue, how these *quaestiones* came to be attributed to Robert Grosseteste, though they are not specifically ascribed to him in the manuscript.

Perhaps the manuscript itself supplies a clue to the solution of the question. In the list of the contents, written on the fly-leaf in an almost contemporary hand, the *Quaestiones Theologicae* preceded by *item* are inserted among three of Grosseteste's treatises, the *De veritate, De libero arbitrio,* and *De libero arbitrio aliter quam prius,* which are all definitely ascribed to him. It is reasonable to suppose that the bibliographers, or rather Boston of Bury on whom the others depend, inferred from this that the *Quaestiones Theologicae* were also Grosseteste's own work. Obviously, the mere fact of their place in the Exeter manuscript between three indisputably authentic works does not necessarily argue oneness of authorship; nevertheless, their presence there provides a strong presumption in favour of this conclusion. This contention is further strengthened by the fact that the four items are written consecutively by the same scribe, and, as we have already learnt from the list of contents, that this manuscript formerly included the other recension of the *De libero arbitrio.*

In default of more explicit evidence in support of Grosseteste's authorship we may put to the proof the *Quaestiones Theologicae* themselves, and investigate whether there is anything at variance with his otherwise ascertained teaching, or contrariwise, whether they bear out any of his characteristic tenets.

It may be alleged that the terminology of the *Quaestiones* is to a certain extent different from Grosseteste's. Defining truth Grosseteste says both in the *De veritate* and in the *De veritate propositionis,* 'Veritas est *adaequatio* rei ad intellectum', or '*adaequatio* sermonis et rei';[1] whereas in the *Quaestiones* 'veritas est *coaequatio* rerum et intellectuum'.[2] Again, the author of the

---

[1] *De veritate,* ed. L. Baur, *Die philosophischen Werke des Robert Grosseteste, Bischofs von Lincoln,* Beitr. z. Gesch. d. Philosophie des Mittelalters, ix, 1912, p. 134; *De veritate propositionis,* p. 144. Henceforth cited as Baur.

[2] Cf. *infra,* p. 203, ll. 132–3.

Quaestiones discussing God's Knowledge or God's Will constantly distinguishes between the *causa* or *necessitas antecedens* and *causa* or *necessitas coniuncta*.[1] Now Grosseteste dealing with the same problems in the *De scientia Dei* and *De libero arbitrio* never uses, so far as I am aware, the word *coniuncta*, but *consequens, sequens*, or some other equivalent term.[2]

Yet it is unquestionable that there is nothing in these *Quaestiones* which is fundamentally inconsistent with Grosseteste's thought as expressed in his writings. The terminology may vary, but on the whole we notice a complete agreement both in the treatment of the subject-matter and in doctrine; especially if one takes into account that they are not a finished set of *quaestiones*, but rather what we should call a rough copy, doubtless meant to be revised, and, perhaps, altogether recast later. The trend of thought is Augustinian with a certain insistence on the theory of divine illumination. The 'new Aristotle' is completely absent. The use of *auctoritas* in introducing some of his quotations has rather an archaic flavour. The citations, including St. Augustine's, are taken from the Book of the *Sentences* with only a few exceptions, of which three are worth noting: one from Pseudo-Dionysius, another from St. John Damascene, and the third, here attributed to St. Augustine, made its appearance, attributed to various authors, towards the end of the twelfth century. A few instances brought forward by the author to illustrate his point are reminiscent of Grosseteste's leaning towards the natural sciences. The development of the *quaestio* and of the doctrine itself is to a certain extent elementary, and shows all the marks of that stage of scholasticism which preceded the golden period. In a word, the *Quaestiones* are representative of the late twelfth- and early thirteenth-century theological speculation that we have noticed in Grosseteste's biblical commentaries.[3]

To corroborate Grosseteste's authorship from internal evidence, an attempt should be made to detect in the Exeter text traces indicating oneness of author.

In Q. IV, *De praesentia Dei localiter*, it is explicitly stated that God is present everywhere and in all things not only as the efficient cause, but also as the formal cause and true form of every and each being: 'non solum sic est (Deus) presens ut causa

---

[1] Cf. *infra*, p. 196, ll. 8–11; p. 201, ll. 73–5.
[2] Cf. *De scientia Dei*, Baur, p. 146, ll. 9–10; *De libero arbitrio*, Baur, p. 158, l. 12; 159, ll. 12 ff.; 168, l. 24, &c.
[3] See D. A. Callus, 'The Oxford Career of Robert Grosseteste', *Oxoniensia*, x–xi (1945–6).

efficiens, sed etiam ut causa formalis et vera forma uniuscuiusque'.[1] Such a theory is based on the testimony of St. Augustine's
De libero arbitrio and of his comment on the words of Psalm cxlvii,
velociter currit sermo eius.

The conformity of this doctrine to Grosseteste's typical thesis
that God is *prima forma et forma omnium* need scarcely be stressed.
In reply to Master Adam Rufus, who asked his opinion in writing
about that problem, Grosseteste answered with deliberation that
it is true to posit that God is form, and form of all things; and,
since He is form, it necessarily follows that He should be the
first form, for nothing was before Him. He is the First and
the Last. To prove his contention Grosseteste brings forward 'the
great authority of the great Augustine', *magna magni Augustini
auctoritas*, and from the outset he cites Augustine's *De libero
arbitrio*, Book II.[2]

Likewise in the *De statu causarum* Grosseteste declares that in
God the efficient and formal causes are substantially one and the
same thing. He then goes on to say that there are many formal
causes or forms; one of these is that form which is the exemplar
in the artificer's mind, whereby things are. This form, which is
the exemplar whereby things are, is not united with the things,
but is simple in itself and separated from them. This is the first
form. Still it is difficult, he adds, to explain how all this is.[3]

Another piece of evidence leading to the same conclusion is
met with in Q. II, *De voluntate Dei*, where the description of
'white' is phrased in the same exact wording of Grosseteste's
De colore:

Album est ex incoruscatione lucis et claro et multitudine in perspicuo puro.[4]	Albedinis essentiam tria constituunt, scilicet lucis multitudo, eiusdemque claritas et perspicui puritas.[5]

Evidently, taken by itself this is a weak argument, since it may
well be that both authors have drawn from a common source;
yet, the verbal similarity has, it would seem, its significance.
Compared with the definition of 'whiteness' given, for instance,
by Albert the Great,[6] we see at once that, although substantially
the same, there is a difference in expression.

---

[1] Cf. *infra*, pp. 206–7, ll. 34–7.
[2] *De unica forma omnium*, Baur, pp. 106–11.
[3] *De statu causarum*, Baur, pp. 122, 124, 125.
[4] Cf. *infra*, p. 203, ll. 138–9.
[5] *De colore*, Baur, p. 78, ll. 23–5.
[6] 'In superficie clara porosa in qua multa lux potest diffundi, albedo est.'
Albertus Magnus, *Meteor.* iii, tr. iv, c. 10 (ed. Borgnet, iv. 678a).

A similar agreement between the Exeter text and Grosseteste's ascertained writings we notice in the definition of *causa antecedens*. God is the antecedent cause of a necessary thing inasmuch as He preordains that something happens out of necessity according to the natural course of things, as, for instance, the future eclipse of the sun and the moon. Now in the *De scientia Dei* we read that antecedent necessity forces a thing into being, . . . for the necessity of the solar and lunar motion forces the eclipse to come into being:

Dupliciter est Deus necessariorum causa: est enim causa antecedens, scilicet preordinans secundum cursum nature [ut] eveniat aliqua res de necessitate, ut quod futura est eclipsis solis et lune.[1]

Necessitas est duplex: una quae cogit rem ad esse, et est necessitas antecedens; . . . necessitas enim motus solaris et lunaris cogit eclipsim ad esse.[2]

Other indications may be traced in the Exeter text pointing to the same conclusion, such as the theory of knowledge by means of immaterial species.[3] The cumulative evidence, therefore, so far produced provides a well-founded argument of Grosseteste's authorship.

Among Grosseteste's philosophical works Professor L. Baur edited several tracts, such as *De ordine emanandi causatorum a Deo*,[4] *De veritate*,[5] *De veritate propositionis*,[6] and *De scientia Dei*,[7] which are closely related to each other. It is evident from the treatment of their subject-matter that they are theological rather than philosophical. Even a cursory inspection shows that these are not complete treatises, but rather mere fragments, or sections of a larger work. The *De ordine emanandi causatorum a Deo*, for instance, opens with a brief statement of the problem, namely, that certain untrained minds, full of fancies and corporeal imaginations, are greatly troubled by the Christian doctrine that in the Godhead the Son is without beginning and co-eternal with the Father, and, at the same time, that He proceeds from the Father. Grosseteste clearly proposed to examine several points of inquiry, as he goes on to say, 'Quare *primo* queritur'; but in reality he discusses one question only, and we look in vain for the second and ulterior questions. Here is a manifest sign that the tract in its present state is incomplete.

[1] See *infra*, p. 196, ll. 7–10.
[3] See *infra*, p. 194, ll. 12 ff.
[5] Baur, pp. 130–43.
[7] Baur, pp. 145–7.
[2] *De scientia Dei*, Baur, p. 146, ll. 9 ff.
[4] Baur, pp. 147–50.
[6] Baur, pp. 143–5.

Or again, let us take the *De veritate propositionis*, or *De scientia Dei*; there is no doubt that these are mere fragments. The former is obviously a continuation of the *De veritate*, whilst the latter is one single point of inquiry on God's knowledge of contingent things as exemplified in the proposition of the future coming of the Antichrist, a topic which greatly attracted the attention of the twelfth- and early thirteenth-century theologians, particularly since Abailard's time. The three tracts are in reality a threefold aspect of the same main question, the knowledge of God. It is possible that originally they formed one single tract with gaps in between. The fact that in the greater number of manuscripts they follow each other without interruption seems to strengthen this surmise.

The features of incompleteness, on the one hand, and of inter-relation, on the other, are even more apparent in the Exeter text. As we have it, it gives the impression of a set of notes jotted together in view of a further elaboration rather than a polished copy ready for publication. That the *Quaestiones Theologicae* are only fragments of a larger work is plainly shown from such expressions as 'ostensum est *prius* nullam rem posse cognosci', which implies that the theory of knowledge was discussed in a previous section, now lost or yet untraced. On the other hand, indications such as, '*consequenter* queritur qualiter Deus scit ea que contingunt a casu vel ex libera voluntate'; '*consequenter* queritur de voluntate Dei que distinguitur in beneplacitum et signum eius'; '*consequenter* autem dicto de voluntate *dicendum* de misericordia et iustitia', point to a systematic work well planned and already begun with these sections. But other phrases such as these, 'hoc *patebit* in principio *Secundi*'; 'quid autem sit veritas *posterius* perscrutabitur per Dei gratiam'; 'de contrarietate et oppositione nostre voluntatis ad voluntatem Dei dicendum *posterius* in *Secundo* ubi dicetur de peccato'; 'de effectu autem iustitie et misericordie Dei, qui est in retribuendo et puniendo, *posterius dicetur in Quarto* per Dei gratiam', are unmistakable hints that the work was not yet brought to completion.

We may take it for granted that the references in the *Quaestiones Theologicae*, twice to Book II—'in Secundo'—and once to Book IV—'in Quarto'—imply undoubtedly that Grosseteste's design was that his work would fall into four books. Naturally, a *Summa Theologiae*, or *Summa Sententiarum*, in four books pre-supposes a work according to the plan of Peter Lombard's *Libri Quatuor Sententiarum*. That this is so need hardly be proved. We have already suggested at the beginning of this paper[1] that the expressions, 'dicetur posterius in *Secundo*, ubi dicetur de peccato', and 'retribuendo et puniendo posterius dicetur in *Quarto*', can only be applied to Books II and IV of the *Sentences*. This becomes even clearer if both passages are read in their context. In the former Grosseteste speaks of the contrariety and opposition of our will to the will of God. Peter Lombard at the end of his treatise *De voluntate Dei* has a short chapter on the conformity or non-conformity of the human will to God's will (*I Sent.*, dist. xlviii, c. 1). But the main issue for Grosseteste was whether to oppose God's will is sinful or not; consequently he postponed the discussion to Book II, as to a more proper place, where the problem of sin is treated (*II Sent.*, dd. xxxiv–xliv). In the latter passage the point in dispute is whether reward and punishment of good or bad deeds in after-life is consistent with God's justice and mercy. Grosseteste thought it fitting to consider the matter in Book IV, *in Quarto*, since it is there (*IV Sent.*, dist. xlvi) that the question is raised and solved by the Lombard. The other reference to Book II, 'hoc patebit *in principio Secundi*', concerns the things created by God at the beginning of the world.[2] Now it is exactly at the opening of Book II, dist. i, that the 'Master of the Sentences' deals with creation.

Similar indications occur frequently in the *Quaestiones Theologicae*. Leaving aside the fact that the citations are for the greater part taken from the *Sentences* without acknowledgement, it is explicitly stated once at least, in introducing a quotation from St. Augustine, that its source is the book of the *Sentences*, 'in Sententiis est'.[3] Or again, in the question how God knows contingent things which happen by chance or come from free will, Grosseteste, following Peter Lombard step by step, first brings forward the opposite view of Origen, holding that God's knowledge of existing things is dependent on their existence, and of Augustine, maintaining on the contrary that God's knowledge is the cause of the existence of created beings, then proceeds: 'in *Sententiis* determinatur quod neutrum alterius causa'.[4] Moreover, the phrase, 'sicut scribitur in *Sententiis*', or its equivalent, turns up again and again in the Exeter text.[5] We cannot, therefore, escape the conclusion that Grosseteste had in sight all the time the book of the *Sentences*. Accordingly the *Quaestiones*

[1] Cf. *supra*, p. 181.   [2] See *infra*, p. 200, l. 30.
[3] See *infra*, p. 196, ll. 60–1.   [4] Cf. *infra*, p. 196, ll. 5–6; see also p. 197, ll. 28–9.
[5] See *infra*, e.g. p. 206, l. 25.

Theologicae are deliberately a section of a *Summa Theologiae*, or a *Summa Sententiarum*.

Other sections may also have been written. It is not unlikely that the *quaestiones* on the Trinity, which according to *Sentences*, Book I, would have preceded our *Quaestiones Theologicae*, were already completed. The *De ordine emanandi causatorum a Deo* in MS. Florence, Marucelliana, C. 163, bears the inscription, *De eternitate divinarum personarum*, and in MS. Prague, University Library, 1990, *De eternitate filii in divinis*.[1] It is evidently related to *I Sent.*, dist. ix, and may well have formed part of the treatise on the Trinity. The three tracts published by Baur, the *De veritate*, *De veritate propositionis*, and *De scientia Dei*, intimately connected with *I Sent.*, dd. xxxv–xxxvi, xxxviii–xli, in all probability were intended to be included in the whole work. If this is so, it is reasonable to infer that a good part, and perhaps the whole of Book I, although we possess only portions of it, was finished.

The result so far reached leads us to conclude that Grosseteste set himself to compose a *Summa Theologiae*, or *Summa Sententiarum*, within the framework of Peter Lombard's *Sentences*. The first book was very probably brought to completion, the greater part of which either perished or is not yet identified. The fragments still extant are:

(i) *De ordine emanandi causatorum a Deo*, corresponding to *I Sent.*, dist. ix.

(ii) *De scientia Dei* (I, II), *De veritate*, *De veritate propositionis*, dd. xxxv–xxxvi, xxxviii–xli.

(iii) *De voluntate Dei*, dd. xlv–xlviii.

(iv) *De misericordia et iustitia Dei*, dist. xli, c. 1.

(v) *De praesentia Dei localiter*, dist. xxxvii.

In this connexion it is perhaps worth noting that, following not the order of the 'Master of the Sentences' but the more logical sequence of Peter of Poitiers,[2] Grosseteste deals with the question of the mercy and justice of God immediately after the treatment of God's will.

Now arises the question whether Grosseteste did write the promised parts of his *Summa*, Books II–IV, or any sections of them. In the present state of our knowledge, it is not easy to give

---

[1] Cf. Thomson, *The Writings*, p. 111.

[2] Cf. *Sententiae Petri Pictaviensis*, ed. P. S. Moore and Marthe Dulong (Publications in Mediaeval Studies, vii). Notre Dame, Indiana, 1943, i, chap. xi, pp. 95–107.

a definite answer. Yet, some of his extant writings, and others mentioned by the bibliographers, although not in our possession, may prove of some help in solving, at least partially, the intricate problem.

The *De libero arbitrio* in the form in which we now have it suggests the technique of a treatise. Yet the structure of the arguments against and in favour of the thesis, and certain phrases scattered here and there, which are easily traced, such as 'alios autem audivi etiam respondentes';[1] 'istas tamen posterius quaestiones de ipso relinquimus determinandas';[2] 'diu de hac materia disputavimus',[3] may possibly hint at disputations. The earliest manuscript of the *De libero arbitrio* in the Laurentian Library, Florence, C. Plut. XVIII, dext. vii, of the middle of the thirteenth century and of English provenance,[4] bears the colophon, *Expliciunt questiones Roberti Grossetet*. That this treatise went through successive elaboration is shown by the two recensions printed by Baur.[5] The matter covered by this treatise, if we except the preliminary questions, corresponds to *II Sent.*, dist. xxiv, c. 3, and dist. xxv. The references to the *Sentences* occur frequently (cf. pp. 169–70, 174, 222, 233, &c.). It would seem that the *De libero arbitrio*, written originally in the form of *quaestiones*, grew out of the material gathered in the course of his theological teaching, which Grosseteste later arranged and set into a definite shape.

Boston of Bury attributes to Grosseteste a work on original sin, 'De Originali Peccato, li. 1, Pr. *Quocirca*'.[6] John Bale in his turn repeats the statement, but gives as its *incipit*, *Questio circa originale pecculum*.[7] (Boston's *Quocirca* is a manifest misreading of *questio circa*.) Such circumstantial description implies that they saw a manuscript, still unidentified, ascribed to Grosseteste. The question on original sin is discussed in the *Sentences*, Book II, dd. xxx–xxxiii. On the authority of the bibliographers we may accordingly assign another section of the *Summa*, Book II, to Robert Grosseteste. But whether he had also completed the treatises on creation and sin mentioned in the Exeter text we have at present no means of ascertaining.

There is nothing, so far as I am aware, to account for Book III. But a few sections of Book IV may well have been preserved. Professor Thomson lists a fragment, *De eucharistia*, extant in

[1] Baur, p. 161, l. 25.
[2] Baur, p. 240, ll. 29 30.
[3] Baur, p. 241, l. 17.
[4] Cf. Thomson, *The Writings*, p. 90.
[5] Baur, pp. 150–241.
[6] Boston of Bury, op. et loc. cit.
[7] Bale, *Scriptorum*, p. 305.

Trinity College, Cambridge, MS. B. 15. 20 (James's Cat., 356), cols. 519–20, and a treatise, *De dotibus*,[1] contained in two manuscripts, British Museum, MS. Cotton, Vesp. D. xxiii, and Cambridge, University Library, MS. Ii. i. 19. Further, Boston of Bury[2] and Bale[3] enter in their catalogues of Grosseteste's works a *De resurrectione*, without further detail. The subject-matter of all these tracts belongs to Book IV. The doctrine of the Eucharist is propounded in dd. viii–xiii; the resurrection of the dead is examined in dist. xliii, and *De dotibus*, as the second part of this treatise on the qualities of the risen came to be called, in dist. xliv. One may surmise that these tractates were parts of Book IV of Grosseteste's *Summa*. But as I have not seen these manuscripts I am hardly in a position to say more about this topic. Of the problem on reward and punishment after death, and how this is the effect of God's justice and mercy, announced in the *Quaestiones Theologicae*, there is so far no trace.

At all events, from the evidence at our disposal we may infer that Grosseteste planned to write a *Summa Theologiae*, or *Summa Sententiarum* in four books. A part of it was written, fragments of which are still extant. Other portions, intended to be included in the whole work, either were never written or have not come down to us. A corroboration of this is found in the fact that both the written parts and those still to be written tally perfectly well with the scheme of the *Sentences:*

Grosseteste	*Peter Lombard*
(i) De ordine emanandi causatorum a Deo.	*I Sent.*, dist. ix.
(ii) De scientia Dei (I, II), De veritate, De veritate propositionis.	*I Sent.*, dd. xxxv–xxxvi, xxxviii–xli.
(iii) De voluntate Dei.	*I Sent.*, dd. xlv–xlviii.
(iv) De misericordia et iustitia Dei.	*I Sent.*, dist. xli, c. 1.
(v) De praesentia Dei localiter.	*I Sent.*, dist. xxxvii.
(vi) De libero arbitrio.	*II Sent.*, d. xxiv, c. 3, d. xxv.
(vii) De creatione (promised).	*II Sent.*, dist. i.
(viii) De originali peccato (untraced).	*II Sent.*, dd. xxx–xxxiii.
(ix) De peccato (promised).	*II Sent.*, xxxiv–xliv.
(x) De eucharistia.[4]	*IV Sent.*, dd. viii–xiii.
(xi) De resurrectione (untraced).	*IV Sent.*, dist. xliii.
(xii) De dotibus.[4]	*IV Sent.*, dist. xliv.
(xiii) De retributione et punitione (promised).	*IV Sent.*, dist. xlvi.

---

[1] Thomson, *The Writings*, p. 130.   [2] Boston of Bury, ibid.
[3] *Bale's Index*, p. 375.
[4] I have not been able to examine these pieces.

It remains to say a word about the text and general character of the *Quaestiones Theologicae* in Exeter College MS. 28. The date of the manuscript is given by Professor Thomson as *c.* 1325. The scribe undoubtedly transcribed it from an imperfect copy. But he did his work carelessly and added not a few slips of his own. He wrote, to give one or two instances, *non* for *Deus*, *causalia* for *casualia*, and twice *Trinitas* for *veritas*; here and there a word is left out. I have attempted several corrections, but in one place the text seems to be beyond emendation. In Q. IV, *De praesentia Dei localiter*, Grosseteste proves, according to the *Sentences*, 'sicut scribitur in Sententiis', that God is present everywhere *potentialiter*, *praesentialiter*, and *essentialiter*; but then the text goes on: 'sed huic veritati propinqua est heresis que dicit...' (p. 207, ll. 37–8). This 'heresy' is no other than John Damascene's perfectly straightforward description of *Circumscriptibile* and *incircumscriptibile*. The manuscript has unmistakably *heresis*; expert palaeographers, Dr. R. W. Hunt, Mr. N. R. Ker, and Miss Marthe Dulong, have confirmed my reading. Here indeed John Damascene's name is written only in the margin and not in the text: 'Io. Dam. xiii capitulo, De Visione Dei.' And we may remember that Walter of St. Victor in his *Contra Quatuor Labyrinthos Franciae* does accuse St. John Damascene of heresy. But even so, I cannot for a moment consider that Robert Grosseteste would be guilty of such invective as the reactionary prior Walter. It suggests itself that the text is corrupt, and that the copyist must have omitted one or more lines. The last column is extremely bad (f. 307ᵛb), and contains extracts on the Trinity from St. Anselm's *Monologion* which are utterly out of place.

As for the general character of the *Quaestiones*, we have already remarked that they give the impression of a set of notes rather than of a finished work, and that they are representative of the late twelfth- and early thirteenth-century theological speculation. The main sources are the book of the *Sentences*—and only through it, I presume, the anonymous *Summa Sententiarum* and Hugh of St. Victor's *De sacramentis*—and the *Summa* of William of Auxerre, which Grosseteste faithfully follows in the order of the *quaestiones*, and often in the whole argument, although in an abridged form. The secondary sources are Abailard and the writings of his school, Peter of Poitiers, Simon of Tournai, and other Summists.[1]

---

[1] An unfortunate illness prevented me from pursuing more thoroughly the study of the sources. In particular I regret that I have not had an opportunity of examining the *Summa* of Simon of Tournai.

The *Quaestiones Theologicae* belong to Grosseteste's teaching career, and very probably to his early years. They corroborate the tradition of his pursuing his theological studies in Paris.

In conclusion we may say that we are justified in assuming that Grosseteste planned to write a *Summa Theologiae*, or *Summa Sententiarum*, in four parts on the model of the four books of the *Sentences*, of which we possess only fragments. If this great work was ever wholly written, either it did not come down to us, or it is still untraced. Nevertheless, until further evidence comes to light it is not safe to put forward more than a conjecture.

[QUAESTIONES THEOLOGICAE]

Exeter College, Oxford, MS. 28, ff. 306ʳ–7ᵛb.

f. 306ʳa [I] *De Scientia Dei*

(i) *De Scientia Dei, quomodo scit singularia.*

Queritur de scientia Dei quomodo scit singularia ista. Quidam enim dicunt quod Deus non scit singularia, quia
5 tantum novit seipsum. Alii vero dicunt quod in hoc quod novit seipsum novit omnia, cum ipse sit causa omnium. Sed dicunt quod non novit singula singulariter ut sunt singularia, sed in universali. Quorum utrumque falsum est: suum enim operari est suum intelligere; sed singulas substantias
10 ut singule operatus est Deus; ergo singulas novit substantias ut vere singule sunt. Quod patet hac ratione. Ostensum est prius nullam rem posse cognosci nisi per eius speciem immaterialiter genitam, vel immaterialem. Uniuscuiusque autem creature est duplex intellectus species immaterialis:
15 una que gignitur ex creatura sed per virtutem superioris; et alia que nullo modo dependet ex creatura, quia est eius causa, scilicet forma eius exemplaris per illam speciem [im]materialem que rem subsequitur. Cognoscitur res a rationali

17. Immaterialem: materialem *cod.*

17–22. 'Forma vero substantialis absolute dicta adhuc dicitur multipliciter. Dicitur enim uno modo exemplar separatum a re et non quo res est; et alio modo quo res est, ita quod sit coniunctum rei et non exemplar; tertio modo dicitur simul exemplar et quo res est. Exemplar dicitur solum forma illa, quae est in mente artificis, non forma illa quae est illud quo res est et non exemplar.' Grosseteste, *De statu causarum*, ed. Baur, p. 124, ll. 22–8. 'Forma vero, quae simul est exemplar et quo res est, non est coniuncta rei, sed abstracta, simplex et separata. Haec est forma prima.' Ibid., p. 125, ll. 23–5. Cf. P. Abaelardus, *Glossae super Porphyrium*, ed. B. Geyer, Beitr. z. Gesch. d. Philosophie des Mittelalters, xxi, 1919, pp. 22–3; *Theologia, Pat. Lat.* 178, col. 991a.

creatura vel intellectu vel sensu. Cum enim intelligimus
formam aliquam, intelligimus eam per speciem ex ea geni- 20
tam; et cum sentimus individuum, sentimus per species
accidentium susceptas in sensu sine materia. Per speciem
vero creature immaterialem, que est eius causa antecedens
et forma exemplaris, cognoscitur creatura solummodo a Deo.
Et quia ipsa species est ipse Deus cuius est primo ymago 25
genita, ideo verissimum est quod Deus intelligendo seipsum,
intelligit singulas substantias, et non aliter. Non enim
intelligit eas per species immateriales subsequentes; esset
enim tunc eius cognitio incompleta, quia huiuscemodi species
totam rem non exprimit; sed per speciem immaterialem que 30
est tota et sufficientissima causa substantie singularis, et ideo
per eam vere cognoscitur individuum; et hec species est una
omnium substantiarum, non sicut forma universalis, sed
verissime una. Et hoc est quod dicit beatus Dionysius in vii
de Divinis Nominibus: Deus 'non secundum visionem singulis 35
se immittit, sed secundum unam cause continentiam omnia
continens et sciens', quasi diceret, sua visio non est per species
subsequentes creaturas, singulis enim creaturis respondent
singule species.

Iam apparet qualiter Deus tantum novit se, et tamen 40
creaturas, quia ubi unum propter alterum utrobique tantum;
et etiam quod non novit eas in universali tantum, sed singulas
ut vere sunt quod sunt. Hoc est quod dicit beatus Augustinus
quod non aliter novit Deus res cum facte sunt quam novit eas
eternaliter antequam fierent per quam notionem facte sunt. 45

Abreviatio rationis talis est. Impossibile est [rem] cognosci
nisi per speciem. Licet enim aliqua res seipsa cognoscatur
non est hic nisi quia ipsa est sua species; et nihil est creature
nisi species duplex, scilicet species aliquo modo genita ex ea,

---

46. rem *supplevi iuxta* (p. 194, l. 12).   48. ipsa: ipsum *cod.*

34–7. Pseudo-Dionysius, *De divinis nominibus*, vii, *iuxta translationem Ioannis
Sarraceni. Translatio Roberti Grosseteste habet*: 'Non secundum ideam singulis
apponens, sed secundum unam cause continentiam omnia sciens et continens.' Cf.
Dionysiana, Paris, 1937, i. 398.

43–5. Augustinus, *De genesi ad litteram*: 'Haec igitur antequam fierent, non
erant. Quomodo ergo Deo nota erant quae non erant? Et rursus: Quomodo ea
faceret, quae sibi nota non erant? non enim quidquam fecit ignorans. Nota ergo
fecit, non facta cognovit. Proinde, antequam fierent, et erant, et non erant: erant
in Dei scientia, non erant in sua natura. . . . Ipsi autem Deo non audeo dicere
alio modo innotuisse, cum ea fecisset, quam illo quo ea noverat, ut faceret, *apud
quem non est transmutatio, nec vicissitudinis obumbratio.*' v. xviii, n. 36 (*Pat. Lat.*
34, col. 334). Cf. *I Sent.*, dist. xxxv, c. 9 (ed. Quaracchi, i. 223). See *infra*, ll. 56–60.

50 per quam est cognitio incompleta; et species antecedens,
scilicet forma eius exemplaris, que est tota causa et verissima
individui, et eadem una omnium. Igitur per eam est verissima cognitio uniuscuiusque individui, sed non est divisa
per singula, sed una est omnium et etiam unius tantum.
55 Igitur Deus, qui solus per hanc novit tantum se, novit et
tamen omnia et etiam singula verissime sicut sunt. Predicta
auctoritas (Augustinus *super Genesim*) hec est: 'Ipsi Deo non
audeo dicere aliter innotuisse, cum ea fecisset, quam illo
[modo] quo ea noverat, ut faceret, *apud quem non est trans-*
60 *mutatio, nec (f.* 306^r*b) vicissitudinis obumbratio.'* In *Sen-*
tentiis est.

(ii) *Quomodo Deus scit ea que contingunt a casu vel a libera voluntate.*

Consequenter queritur qualiter Deus scit ea que contingunt a casu vel ex libera voluntate. Dicit enim Origenes:
'Quia sunt, ideo novit ea Deus.' Et Augustinus e contra:
5 'Quia Deus novit, ideo sunt.' Et in *Sententiis* determinatur
quod neutrum alterius causa.

Ad hoc dicendum quod dupliciter est Deus esse necessariorum causa. Est enim causa antecedens, scilicet preordinans secundum cursum nature [ut] eveniat aliqua res de
10 necessitate, ut quod futura est eclipsis solis et lune; et est
causa coniuncta, scilicet ut cum sunt faciat ea esse. Nichil
enim fit quod eo agente non fiat. Primus modus non est
causa [rerum] futurarum contingentium. Deus enim pre-

---

59. modo *add. ex textu Augustini.*   9. ut *deest in cod.*   13. rerum *deest.*
Deus: non *cod.*

56–7. Predicta auctoritas, cf. *supra*, ll. 43–5.   59–60. *Iac.* i. 17.
60–1. Cf. *I Sent.*, dist. xxxv, c. 9 (223, n. 323).
3–4. Origenes, *Super Epistolam ad Romanos*, viii. 30 (*Pat. Gr.* 14, col. 1126);
cf. *I Sent.*, dist. xxxviii, c. 1 (242, n. 355).
4–5. Augustinus, *De trinitate*, xv. xiii, n. 22 (*Pat. Lat.* 42, col. 1076); cf. *I Sent.*,
ibid. (241, n. 354).
5–6. *I Sent.*, loc. cit.
7. Cf. *Disputationes Symonis Tornacensis*, ed. J. Warichez (Spicilegium Sacrum
Lovaniense, xii), Louvain, 1932, pp. 104, ll. 32–105, l. 29.
7–11. Cf. Grosseteste, *De scientia Dei*: 'Necessitas est duplex: una quae cogit
rem ad esse, et est necessitas antecedens; . . . necessitas enim motus solaris et
lunaris cogit eclipsim ad esse.' Baur, p. 146, ll. 9 ff.
10. eclipsis solis et lune: cf. Abaelardus, *Theologia*, iii. vii (*Pat. Lat.* 178,
col. 1109 c).
11. causa coniuncta: cf. *I Sent.*, ibid., c. 2, 'coniunctim' (244, n. 359); 'per con-
iunctionem', dist. xl, c. 1 (250, n. 368); 'ex adiunctione', *Sententiae Florianenses*,
ed. H. Ostlender (Florilegium Patristicum, xix), Bonnae, 1929, p. 12, ll. 11–13.

ordinavit ut per cursum nature eveniat ea de necessitate;
secundo e contra preordinat ab eterno ut hec a nulla causa 15
antecedente eveniant, sed a casu vel voluntate nostra.
Verumptamen secundo modo est ipse causa contingentium.
Cum enim ista casualia, non ex scientia Dei preordinante,
sed a casu vel voluntate contingunt, tamen non sunt vel fiunt
nisi eo efficiente, ipso tamen sciente non necesse est hoc fieri. 20
Primum modum considerans Origenes dixit, 'quia sunt, ideo
novit', et non e contrario; secundum modum considerans
Augustinus dixit e contrario: facere enim Dei et eius scire
idem est. Et non sequitur: scientia Dei, que est causa rei,
sicut loquitur Augustinus, est eterna; ergo est antecedens. 25
Antecedentia enim, de qua fit hic sermo, est eventus futuri
secundum cursum nature necessaria preordinatio. Quod
autem in *Sententiis* determinat Magister, quod neutrum
alterius causam, intelligit non primum modum quo loquitur
Origenes, quod res sit causa cognitionis divine sicut est causa 30
nostre cognitionis, sed intendit quamdam consequentiam
naturalem cum dicit, quia erit, ideo novit scire. Et hoc non
est aliud dictum quam si dicerem: quia erit, ideo erit, ut
dicit beatus Augustinus.

Tertio modo scit Deus mala quorum nullo modo causa est, 35
et quorum nulla est assimilatio Deo per formam exemplarem.
Per formam enim exemplarem boni scit Deus malum, quod
non est aliud quam boni privatio. Cum enim non possit
cognosci res nisi per speciem, malum autem non habet
speciem nisi bonum cuius est privatio, ipsum non cogno- 40
scetur nisi per bonum. Duplicem ergo comparationem habet
forma exemplaris, scilicet ad bonum cuius est forma per
intentionem, et ad malum cuius est species per accidens. Non
enim de intentione summi boni est ut ab eo recedat quid in

---

18. casualia: causalia *cod.*   20. sciente: ente *cod.*   21. considerans:
consideravit *cod. corr. iuxta 22.*   29. non: sed *cod.*

28. Cf. *I Sent., ut supra*, p. 196, ll. 5–6.
28–9. neutrum alterius causam: cf. *Ysagoge in Theologiam*, ed. A. Landgraf,
Écrits Théologiques de l'école d'Abélard (Spic. Sac. Lov. xiv), Louvain, 1934, p. 270:
'Dicamus ergo neutrum alterius causam esse. Sic ergo exponenda sunt verba
Origenis, ut in eis non notetur causa. Idem igitur est: quia futurum est, scitur a
Deo, et, quod futurum est, scitur a Deo.'
35–54. Cf. *I Sent.*, dist. xxxviii, c. 1 (?13); Guillelmus Altioo., *Summa aurea*, 1,
c. 9, f. 21ᵛ.
38–9. Cf. *supra*, pp. 194–5, ll. 11–34.—'Malum non est aliud quam boni privatio',
cf. Aug. *Enchiridion*, xi (*Pat. Lat.* 40, col. 236); *Contra adversarium Legis et Prophetarum*, v, n. 7 (*Pat. Lat.* 42, col 607).

45 quo sit malum; et ideo scientia boni dicitur approbatio, sed
    scientia mali non est. Et in hoc apparet, quod licet malum
    sit per se privatio boni, non tamen bonum est per se species
    mali; sicut per accidens essentialiter refertur ad per se, sed
    per se non ex intentione refertur [ad] per accidens. Iuxta
50 hunc dupplicem modum scientie divine currit duplex modus
    ordinationis eterne futurorum in tempore: predestinatio bono-
    rum finaliter et reprobatio malorum finaliter; vel conpro-
    portionaliter dictis modis sciendi erit predestinatio causa boni
    futuri, et reprobatio non erit causa mali futuri.
55   Et videtur quod predestinatio non sit causa boni futuri nisi
    sicut prescientia Dei est causa cuiuscumque contingentis.
    Deum enim predestinare hunc non est nisi Deum prescire
    ab eterno se daturum ei gratiam in tempore finaliter; et
    futurum quod potest non contingere, sicut est de aliis (*f.* 306^v*a*)
60 que sunt ad utrumlibet. Ad hoc dicendum quod secus est,
    hinc inde (?), quia in hiis que sunt a casu vel a nobis, non est
    voluntas Dei causa antecedens per intentionem, ut velit hoc
    esse vel illud, a sua scilicet voluntate immediate, sed vult hoc
    a nostra voluntate vel a casu fieri; et sic non est sua scientia
65 vel voluntas eorum causa, sicut dictum est. Gratie autem datio
    non est a nobis nec a casu, sed a voluntate divina immediate et
    per intentionem: nullum enim bonum ab eo est preter inten-
    tionem. Et ideo ab eterno disposuit se daturum huic gratiam.
       Ex hoc autem videtur quod datio gratie necessaria sit, cum
70 sit ex mera Dei voluntate immutabiliter, sicut esse angelorum
    et motus celi, et huiusmodi que immutabiliter sunt.—Ad hoc
    dicendum quod secus est; quia licet gratia detur a Deo im-
    mediate, tamen notandum quia non sic datio quod quodlibet
    donum, sed gratum facientem. Gratus autem nullus fit de
75 necessitate sed voluntarie consentiens gratie. Igitur licet
    Deus immediate det gratiam, et non a nobis, tamen gratia est
    que datur. Et ideo non necessaria sed ponens non esse. Hec
    est responsio dicte dubitationis.
       Post hoc notandum quod sicut reprobatio eterna nullo
80 modo est causa futuri mali, sic nec malus futurus est causa

49. ad *deest.*

45–6. Cf. *I Sent.*, dist. xxxvi, c. 2 (225–7).
53–4. Cf. ibid., dist. xli, c. 2 (257, n. 378).
55–65. Cf. ibid., dist. xl, c. 2 (251–3).   65. dictum est: cf. *supra*, ll. 15–20.
74. De differentia inter *datum* et *donum*, cf. *Disputationes Simonis Tornacensis*, disp. lxiv, p. 179, ll. 3 ff.
79–91. Cf. *I Sent.*, dist. xli, c. 1 (253–4).

reprobationis eterne. Prima pars patet quod nisi peccassemus originaliter, quod solum a nobis fuit, omnes predestinaremur et nullus reprobaretur, quia quantuncumque peccaverit quis actuali peccato in infinitum est maior Dei misericordia qua potest eius misereri si vult. Non est igitur in eo voluntas [85] miserendi propter merita; sed reprobare est nolle misereri, ut dicit Augustinus, quod indurare est non misereri, hoc est non apponere gratiam. Et dicit Augustinus quod homo non habet gratiam, non ideo quia Deus non dat, sed quia homo non vult accipere; et tamen non habet gratiam quia vult, sed [90] ipsa gratia est eam volendi recte.

[II] *De Voluntate Dei*

Consequenter queritur de voluntate Dei, que distinguitur in beneplacitum et signum eius.

Primo queritur de beneplacito, si ad ipsum de necessitate sequatur volitum; 2° in quo significetur signum beneplaciti; [5] 3° cuiusmodi signum est; 4° de numero signorum.

(i) De prima questione videtur quod cum voluntas Dei beneplacens sit sufficiens et tota causa eius quod vult fieri, ipsaque immutabilis, igitur volitum immutabile erit, id est, non poterit mutari quin eveniat; ergo necessario erit. Iuxta [10] illud videtur quod statim cum beneplacitum est necesse sit simul volitum esse.

Ad primum horum dicendum est quod duplicem effectum habet in creaturis Dei beneplacitum: quedam enim vult Deus fieri ex solo suo beneplacito, et hec necessario eveniunt; et [15] quedam vult ipse fieri ex altero assentiente beneplacito Dei; quod licet assentiat beneplacito, quia beneplacitum est, tamen potest non assentire: et hoc est Dei beneplacitum ut possit non assentire et quod illud quod ex ipso est assentiente possit non esse. Tale principium est materia et liberum [20] arbitrium. Non igitur manet hec voluntas Dei inexpleta,

---

85. *respicit ad Rom.* ix. 18.

87. Aug., *Ad Simplicianum*, I, q. ii, n. 15 (*Pat. Lat.* 40, col. 120); cf. *I Sent.*, loc. cit. (253, n. 372).

88. Aug., op. cit., n. 16 (*Pat. Lat.* 40, col. 121); cf. *I Sent.*, dist. xl, c. 2 (253, n. 371).

2–3. See *Sententiae Petri Pictaviensis*, ed. P. S. Moore et Marthe Dulong (Public. in Med. Studies, vii), Notre Dame, Indiana, 1943, i. 78, ll. 19–20. Cf. *I Sent.*, dist. xlv, c. 5–6 (274–6).

2–24. Cf. *Ysagoge in Theologiam*, iii (275).

21–5. Cf. *I Sent.*, dist. xlv, c. 5 (275); dist. xlvi, c. 1 (278).

quia evenit quod vult, sed non necessario. Ideo dicit Psalmus:
'Omnia quecumque voluit fecit'; non dicit: necessario fecit.
Apostolus ad Rom. ix: 'Vo(*f.* 306^v*b*)luntati eius quis resistit?';
25 et non dicit quod possibile est resistere. Sub primo membro
cadunt omnia que ordinata sunt sub necessario cursu nature,
que impediri possunt per corruptionem materie, sicut solem
oriri cras, et huiusmodi.

   Ad aliud dicendum quod quedam vult Deus simpliciter;
30 et hec statim fiunt, non tamen ab eterno, ut que creata sint
in principio. Hoc patebit in principio *Secundi*. Quedam
autem vult fieri non absolute, sed pro loco et tempore et
ceteris conditionibus creaturarum; hec non statim eveniunt
sed secundum exigentiam cursus nature.

35   (ii) De alia questione notandum quod signum beneplaciti, ut
in sacra reperitur Scriptura, quintuplex est, ut dicit hic versus:
       'Precipit et prohibet, permittit, consulit, implet'.
Et solet dici quod ista verba significant divinam essentiam, et
illud quod apponitur eis loco accusativi significat signum bene-
40 placiti. Quod falsum est. Non enim 'non furari' signum est
beneplaciti Dei. Sed preceptio Dei, licet sit divina essentia,
non tamen ex sua connotatione est voluntas beneplaciti ut fiat,
sed quod precipiatur; sed est voluntas qua vult illum obligari
ad mortem si non faciat. Et sic de aliis signis intelligendum.
45 Et hec voluntas Dei signum est voluntatis beneplaciti.

   (iii) De tertia questione queritur quomodo hec signa
dicuntur beneplaciti, utrum signa positiva, ut circulus vini,
vel naturalia. Non primo modo, ergo secundo. Sed signa
naturalia vel causantur a suis signatis, vel ipsa cum signatis
50 causantur ab eadem causa; sic ergo signum semper causatum
est. Sed hoc dupliciter: dicitur enim aliquando res causati
signum, et hoc non semper concordat rei; aliquando autem
totum causatum, et hoc semper concordat, exempla patent in
naturis. Ista autem non sunt signa secundo modo, quia bene-

---

37. permittit: promittit *cod.*

22–3. *Psalmus* cxiii. 11.   24. *Epist. ad Rom.* ix. 19.
29–34. Cf. *supra*, ll. 10–12.
31. patebit in principio *Secundi*: *i.e. II Sent., dist. i, ubi agitur de creatione.*
35–45. Cf. *I Sent.*, dist. xlv, c. 6 (275–6); Guillelmus Altiss., *Summa aurea*, i,
c. 13, f. 26^{v}b.
47. Cf. *Summa Simonis Tornacensis*: 'Positivorum vero quoddam nec est sacrum
nec sacre rei signum, ut circulus vini venalis. . .' cited by A. Landgraf, 'Sentenzen-
glossen des beginnenden 13. Jahrhunderts', *Recherches de Théologie ancienne et
médiévale*, x (1938), 45.

placitum Dei non habet causam. Erit ergo unumquodque 55
eorum vel causatum totaliter vel pars causati. Et dicitur communiter quod est pars causati, verbi gratia, quia Deus vult
istum salvari, non solum precipit sed implet. Ecce quod preceptum non est totum a beneplacito causatum, sed pars. Hoc
tamen videtur mihi falsum hoc argumento. Omne quod 60
singulariter intenditur, totaliter est intentum. Sed unumquodque istorum signorum singulariter intenditur a Deo.
Ergo totaliter est intentum. Minor patet. Precipit enim
quando non implet; sed in voluntariis quod est totaliter
intentum est totaliter causatum, et in naturalibus similiter. 65
Ergo unumquodque istorum est totaliter causatum a beneplacito Dei. Causatum autem non est sine causa; igitur nullum istorum signorum est sine beneplacito cuius est signum:
quod videtur falsum esse. Licet enim precipiat Deus ut fiat
aliquid, non tamen vult omnino ut fiat, et sic de aliis signis. 70
   Ad hoc dicendum quod Dei beneplacitum dupliciter ordinatur ad creaturas, vel creature dupliciter sunt subiecte illi,
sicut dictum est quod dupliciter est scientia Dei causa futurorum, scilicet antecedens vel coniuncta: similiter huiusmodi
beneplacitum antecedens vel coniunctum. Beneplacitum 75
antecedens dico cum beneplacet Deo ut fiat; beneplacitum
coniunctum non quod beneplacet ut fiat, sed quia beneplacet
si fit. Primo Deus solum vult predestinatos salvos fieri, et
huius beneplaciti coniunctum signorum signum est; quia
enim vult (*f.* 307^r*a*) ut salvi fiant, ideo implet dando gratiam. 80
Ecce qualiter signum causatum est a beneplacito cuius est
signum. Secundo modo vult omnes, etiam prescitos, salvos
fieri, id est, si salvi facti sint, beneplacet ei. Et intellige hoc
sane: non quod salvus sit causa beneplaciti, licet sic ponatur
in consequentia, sed e contrario. Beneplacitum autem est 85
causa salutis si est; ordinatur autem e contrario in consequentia, quia neutrum continget. Uterque istorum modorum intelligitur in isto Domini sermone: 'Volui congregare
filios tuos, et noluisti', id est, quosdam, scilicet predestinatos,
volui ut congregarentur, et ideo congregati sunt; alios vero, 90

---

63. totaliter: singulariter *cod.*

69–70. Cf. Hugo a S. Victore, *De sacramentis*, P. iv, c. 8 (*Pat. Lat.* 176, col. 237);
I Sent., dist. xlv, c. 7 (277, n. 412).
   73–4. Cf. *supra*, p. 196, ll. 7–12.
   82–3. omnes salvos fieri *respicit ad I Tim.* ii. 4.   90–1. Matt. xxiii. 37.
   82–91. Cf. *I Sent.*, dist. xlvi, cc. 1–2 (278–80); *Sent. Petri Pictaviensis*, i. 10 (91).

scilicet prescitos, si voluisses, placeret, et noluisti. Hoc patet
ex auctoritate Augustini fine capituli de scientia Dei.

Notandum autem quod aliquando non intenditur principaliter quod precipitur, sed quod preceptum concomitatur,
95 ut obedientia Abrahe, non immolatio Ysaac. Similiter de
prohibitione.

Sed de permissione dubium est qualiter ipsa sit ex beneplacito; neque enim placet ut fiat beneplacito antecedente,
neque beneplacet ei cum fit beneplacito coniuncto.

100   Ad hoc dicendum quod permissio est signum beneplaciti
Dei coniuncti. Non enim placet ut fiat quod permittitur,
quia non est causa mali, sed cum fit beneplacet propter bonum
universi. Nonne est ex placentia antecedente? nonne beneplacet Deo ut sit bonum universi? Igitur non sola impletio
105 est signum beneplaciti antecedentis sed etiam permissio.

Ad hoc dicendum quod absolute loquendo beneplacitum
Dei est causa antecedens boni universitatis. Sed quia idem
est Dei beneplacitum in bono universitatis et bono singu-
lorum, in universitate autem non est malum sed in singulis,
110 beneplacitum Dei, quod in universitate est indifferens, in
singularibus recipit differentiam, ut in bono singularis sit
beneplacitum antecedens in malo autem singularis non, sed
coniunctum; quia cum malum fit bene ordinatur in universo.

Unde dicit Augustinus quod omnipotens Deus non per-
115 mitteret malum fieri nisi ex malo bonum eliceret. Ergo quia
cum fit malum complacet ei in hoc malo bonum universi,
ideo permittit malum fieri. Idem tamen prohibet, quia si non
fieret beneplaceret ei in singulari et in universo.

Sed videtur quod mala fieri sit ex beneplacito Dei; quia
120 dicit Augustinus quod omne verum a veritate est. Veritas

101. permittitur: promittitur *cod.*   102. mali: nulli *cod.*   113. fit: sit *cod.*
120. veritate: trinitate *cod.*

91–2. Cf. *supra*, p. 199, l. 88.
93–5. Gen. xxii. 2 ff. Cf. *Sent. Hermanni*, c. 26 (*Pat. Lat.* 178, col. 1736 b–c);
I Sent., dist. xlvii, c. 3 (290); *Sent. P. Pictaviensis*, i. 9 (80–90); *Disp. Sim. Tornac.*,
pp. 151–2.   97. Cf. *I Sent.*, dist. xlvii, cc. 1–3 (287–90).
97. Cf. ibid., c. 2 (289–90); *Disp. Sim. Tornac.*, pp. 35–6.
101–18. Cf. *I Sent.*, dist. xlvi, cc. 3–5 (280–4); *Sent. P. Pict.*, i. 10 (92–4);
Sent. Rolandi, ed. A. M. Gietl (Freiburg i. Br., 1891), pp. 68–9.
108. Cf. *Ysagoge in Theologiam*, 276–9; *I Sent.*, dist. xlvi, c. 6 (284–5).
114. Cf. S. Aug., *Enchiridion*, 11, n. 3 (*Pat. Lat.* 40, col. 236).
119–35. Guillelmus Altiss., *Summa aurea*, i, c. 13, f. 27^{r}b.
120–3. Cf. *I Sent.*, dist. xlvi, c. 7 (286, n. 426); Gandulphus, *Sententiarum libri
quatuor*, ed. J. de Walter (Vindobonae, 1924), pp. 156–7.
120. S. Aug., *Liber lxxxiii Quaestionum*, qu. 1: 'Omne verum a veritate verum

autem Deus est. Ergo verum esse a Deo. Hoc argumentum
bonum est. Inde sit: omne verum a Deo est; sed malum fieri
est verum; ergo malum fieri est a Deo.

Ad hoc dicunt quidam quod veritas negationis negatio est,
et veritas propositionis significantis privationem esse privatio 125
est, et neutra istarum veritatum aliquid est, licet ea aliquid
sit verum; unde nec est a Deo. Sed veritas rerum naturalium
aliquid est; et hec sola est a Deo. Sed hii non noverunt quid
sit veritas. Credunt enim quod veritas sit res ipsa, quod manifeste falsum est. Deficiente enim re non deficit veritas. Quid 130
autem sit veritas posterius perscrutabitur per Dei gratiam.
Nunc autem supponamus quod veritas est coequatio rerum
et intellectuum. Quid autem sit hoc dictu non discutimus
modo nisi hoc tantum quod coequatio non est a re coequata,
sed a coequante, quicquid sit illud. Ergo in illo secundo argu- 135
mento est paralogismus ac(*f.* 307^r*b*)cidentis. Album est ex
incoruscatione lucis et claro et multitudine in perspicuo puro;
sed hoc corpus est album. Ergo hoc corpus est ex incoruscatione lucis etc.

(iv) Consequenter queritur de numero signorum, qui patet 140
hac ratione. Signa beneplaciti attenduntur in hiis solum que
sunt ex libero arbitrio consentiente voluntati Dei, vel dis-
sentiente. Hec autem sunt bonum sine quo non est salus, et
malum quod operatur mortem, et bonum perfectionis sine
quo est salus, et malum veniale quod mortem non operatur. 145
De bono sine quo non est salus duplex est Dei beneplacitum;
unde dupliciter exprimitur signum. Vel enim beneplacet ut
fiat hoc bonum, et ideo implet; vel beneplacet ei si fit, et ideo
precipit ut fiat. De malo autem mortali simpliciter duplex est

---

131. veritas: trinitas *cod.*   138–9. incoruscatione: incorporatione *cod.*

---

est; est autem veritas Deus; Deum igitur habet auctorem omne verum.' (*Pat. Lat.*
40, col. 11.) Cf. *I Sent.*, loc. cit.

132–3. 'Haec veritas (orationis enuntiativae), sicut dicit philosophus, non est aliud
quam ita esse in re signata sicut dicit sermo. Et hoc est quod aliqui dicunt veritatem esse "adaequationem sermonis et rei", et "adaequationem rei ad intellectum".
Sed cum verior sit sermo qui intus silet quam qui foris sonat, intellectus videlicet
conceptus per sermonem vocalem, magis erit veritas adaequatio sermonis interioris
et rei quam exterioris; quod si ipse sermo interior esset adaequatio sui ad rem, non
solum esset sermo verus, sed ipsa veritas.' Grosseteste, *De veritate* (Baur, p. 134).
'Veritas sermonis vel opinionis est adaequatio sermonis vel opinionis et rei. Haec
autem adaequatio nihil aliud est quam ita esse in re sicut sermo vel opinio dicit.'
Grosseteste, *De veritate Propositionis* (Baur, p. 144).

136–7. Cf. Grosseteste, *De colore*: 'Albedinis essentiam tria constituunt, scilicet
lucis multitudo, eiusdemque claritas et perspicui puritas.' (Baur, p. 78.)

150 beneplacitum, unde dupliciter exprimitur signum. Si enim
non fit, beneplacet quantum ad bonum universi et individui,
et ideo prohibet ne fiat; si vero fit, licet sit ad dampnationem
individui, tamen est ad bonum universi, et ideo permittit.
Prima divisio est secundum beneplacitum antecedens et
155 coniunctum; secunda secundum beneplacitum boni universalis et particularis et boni universalis tantum.

Nunc restat questio quare secundum bonum sine quo non
est salus et malum quod mortem non operatur non sunt duo
signa sicut in predictis preceptio et prohibitio, sed unum
160 tantum, scilicet consilium. Ad hoc dicendum, ut mihi videtur, quod bonum perfectionis est propria via vitandi veniale
quantum vitari potest in hac vita, et preter illud non est aliud;
et ideo non sicut preceptioni correspondet prohibitio ex opposito non sic consilio respondet aliud ex opposito.—De
165 contrarietate et oppositione nostre voluntatis ad voluntatem
Dei dicendum posterius in *Secundo* ubi dicetur de peccato.

[III] *De Misericordia et Iustitia Dei*

Consequenter autem dicto de voluntate dicendum de
misericordia et iustitia. Iustitia est voluntas reddendi unicui-
que quod suum est. Et misericordia est voluntas relevandi a
5 miseria; unde non est horum differentia nisi in effectu. Dicit
autem Cassiodorus quod omnia opera Dei sunt misericordie
et iustitie. Et huiusmodi est quod dicit *Psalmus*: 'Omnia
opera eius misericordia et veritas.'

Et tunc obicitur de operibus prime creationis, utrum sint
10 opera misericordie et iustitie. Quod non sint opera iustitie
videtur. Quia nulli in prima creatione reddebatur quod suum
fuit; non enim prius erat aliquid quod aliquid sibi debitum
exigeret, quia de nichilo creata sunt. Et potest dividi hoc
quod dico: *suum*, secundum exigentiam promissionis, vel
15 meriti, vel nature, et nullo istorum modorum in creatione

---

151. fit: sit *cod.*   154. et: est *cod.*   163. preceptioni: preceptio *cod.*
165. oppositione: operatione *cod.*   voluntatis: voluntate *cod.*   11–12. suum:
fuit *cod.*

164–6. *De contrarietate nostre voluntatis ad voluntatem Dei*, cf. *I Sent.*, dist.
xlviii, cc. 1–2 (291–2). *De peccato agitur in II Sent.*, dd. xxxiv–xliv.
1–17. *Fere ad literam apud* Guillelmum Altiss., *Summa aurea*, i, c. 15, f. 29ʳb.
3–4. Cf. *Ysagoge in Theologiam*, pp. 74–5.
5–7. Cassiodorus, *In Psalmum C*, 1 (*Pat. Lat.* 70, col. 700). Cf. *IV Sent.*, dist.
xlvi, c. 1 (1012, n. 414); c. 5 (1017); *Disp. Sim. Tornac.*, p. 164.
7–8. *Psalmus* xxiv. 10 (Vulgata): 'Universae viae Domini misericordia et veritas.'

prima reddebatur quod suum fuit alicui, ut videtur. Nec fuit ibi opus misericordie, quia non precessit miseria.

Ad hoc dicendum quod opus prime creationis fuit opus iustitie, scilicet promissionis. Promissio nichil aliud est quam expressio voluntatis plene creandi res. Ergo ab eterno promi- 20 sit, licet non esset creatura cui promitteretur. Ideo iustum fuit Deum solvere promissum, licet non esset iustum alicui creature solvi; sicut etiam in civilibus aliquando contingit quod iustum est aliquid dare, licet nulli dare sit iustum. Vel potest dici quod in opere explete promissionis non reperiun- 25 tur nisi tria, scilicet exigens, et promissio et solvens, quia opus talis iustitie non est nisi (*f. 307*^{v}*a*) solvere exigenti promissum. Hec tria per appropriationem reperiuntur in tribus personis, Patris, et Filii, et Spiritus Sancti. Filius enim qui est Sapientia genita, que sapientia est rationes omnium creaturarum, 30 exigit se rationes omnium exprimi in natura, sicut ars desiderat exprimi. Unde dicitur: 'Delicie mee est esse cum filiis hominum', propter quos est celi et terre creatio, et omnium que in eis sunt. Promissio vero, id est, expressio voluntatis plene, quid aliud quam processio Spiritus Sancti? Ex sua 35 enim ineffabili bonitate, que applicatur Spiritui Sancto, hoc voluit. Solvens autem Pater est a quo omnia. Et sic iustitia prime creationis in Trinitate completur. De effectu autem iustitie et misericordie Dei qui est in retribuendo et puniendo posterius dicetur in *Quarto* per Dei gratiam. 40

[IV] *De Presentia Dei localiter*

Hic queritur de locali presentia creatoris. Utrum sit ubique, et probatur quod sic. Nulli rei dum est potest deesse sua causa essentialis; sed essentialissima causa uniuscuiusque Deus; ergo Deus est ubique. Assumptum patet, quia nulla 5 est rei causa nisi participatione cause prime; unde et ipsa causa prima immediatissima est omnium causarum ad unumquodque causatum, sicut lux pertransiens vitrum coloratum colorat parietem obiectum, et immediatius splendet in pariete quam color vitri. 10

---

32. exprimi: expĺi *cod.*   36. applicatur: appellatur *cod.*

32–3. *Prov.* viii. 31.
38–40. Cf. *IV Sent.*, dist. xlvi (1011–17).
1. Cf. *I Sent.*, dist. xxxvii (229–40).
3–5. Cf. *Disp. Sim. Tornac.*, p. 306, ll. 7–9.

Item, virtus et potestas Dei nusquam deest; sed Deus idem est et sua virtus; ergo Deus ubique.

Sed notandum quod cum comparatur Deus ad hoc nullo modo comparatur locatum ad locum, dicente Augustino:
15 'Deus est in mundo non inclusus, extra mundum nec exclusus, supra mundum non elevatus, infra mundum non depressus.' Si est ibi aliqua proprietas et comparatio loci ad locatum, eo enim indigent omnia sicut proprio locante, ipse autem nullo indiget. Unde cum dicitur esse extra mundum, non dicitur
20 hoc quia ibi sit creatura vel locus qui ibi divine presentie subsistat, sed quia in se est qui in infinitum omnem creaturam excedit; quia ipse sibi stabilimentum est, et ideo ipse in seipso consistere dicitur.

Dicitur autem ubique tripliciter, scilicet potentialiter,
25 presentialiter, essentialiter, sicut scribitur in *Sententiis*. Potentialiter, quia illa virtus, ut dictum est, ad omnia se extendit; sed quia posset de eo credi, sicut de rege mortali, licet eius virtus sit in regno toto, non tamen ipse in propria presentia ubique est, quia non est ipse idem quod sua virtus,
30 ideo additur quod non solum potentialiter sed etiam presentialiter est Deus ubique. Et iterum [quia] in hoc quod dico potentialiter, presentialiter, intelligeret quis Deum solum esse causam efficientem omnium, ideo superadditur essentialiter, quia non solum sic est presens ut causa efficiens, sed etiam

31. quia *deest in cod.*

13–14. Cf. *Ysagoge in Theologiam*, p. 245; *I Sent.*, ibid., c. 5 (235–6).

15–16. *Fere ad literam habetur sub nomine* Augustini *apud* Guillelmum Altiss., *Summa Aurea*, i, c. 16, f. 31ᵛa; *sed locus est conflatus ex* Augustino, *De Genesi ad Literam*, viii. 26 (*Pat. Lat.* 34, col. 391), *et De praesentia Dei* (*Epist.* 187), c. iv, n. 14 (*Pat. Lat.* 33, col. 837); *ex* Gregorio Magno, *Moralium*, ii, c. 12, n. 20 (*Pat. Lat.* 75, col. 565), *et In Ezechielem, II, Homil. V*, 11 (*Pat. Lat.* 76, col. 991); *et ex* Isidoro Hispalensi, *Sententiarum*, i. 3: 'Immensitas divinae magnitudinis ita est, ut intelligamus eum intra omnia, sed non inclusum; extra omnia, sed non exclusum. Et ideo interiorem, ut omnia contineat; ideo exteriorem, ut incircumscripta magnitudinis suae immensitate omnia concludat.' (*Pat. Lat.* 83, col. 541b.) *Prima pars citatur ab* Alexandro Halensi, *Summa Theologica* (ed. Quaracchi, 1924, i. 68, cf. also n. 3); *et ab* Alberto Magno, *In I Sententiarum*, dist. xxxvii, a. 21 (ed. Borgnet, 26, 256 b). *In Summa vero Theologica*, pars I, tract. xviii, q. 70, *Albertus dicit:* 'Hoc est quod expresse dicit Gregorius (Lib. II Moralium, c. 12) quod "Deus est extra omnia non exclusus, et intra omnia non inclusus, et supra omnia per eminentiam non superatus, et infra omnia non depressus." ' (31, 729a.)

25. Cf. *I Sent.*, dist. xxxvii, c. 1 (229, n. 333; 231, n. 334).

26–31. *Fere ad literam apud* Guillelmum Altiss., *Summa Aurea*, i, c. 16, f. 31ʳa.

27–8. Cf. Abaelard., *Theologia*, iii. 6 (*Pat. Lat.* 178, col. 1106 a, b); *Sent. Parisienses*, pp. 15, 14–18.

34–5. *De Deo forma omnium*; cf. Grosseteste, *De unica forma omnium*, Baur, pp. 106–11.

ut causa formalis et vera forma uniuscuiusque, ut dicit Aug. 35
in primo libro *De libero arbitrio*, [et] super illum locum
Psalmi: *Velociter currit sermo eius*. Sed huic veritati propinqua est heresis que dicit, 'Circumscriptibile est quod
tempore vel comprehensione comprehenditur. Incircumscriptibile vero quod nullo modo horum continetur.' Intel- 40
ligibilis est Deus intelligentia. Sunt etiam scientiarum
spectamina plurima, tamen differunt. Nam terra visibilis est
et lux; sed terra nisi luce lustrata videri [non] potest. Similiter disciplinarum spectamina non possunt intelligi nisi ab
aliquo sole suo illustrentur. Quomodo vero in hoc sole tria 45
ad(*f.* 307ᵛ*b*)vertimus, scilicet quod est, quod fulget, quod
illuminat, sic et in secretissimo (?) Deo mihi (?) quidem quod
est, quod intelligit, et quod cetera facit intelligere. 'Utinam
ad vestiganda bona et mala omnes homines screnam mentis
aciem afferrent, ut possent videre summum bonum cui anima 50
rationalis perfecta et pura subiungitur. Hoc enim intellecto
et perspecto, simul vident omne illud quod summe est.'
Cassiodorus in libro de Anima sic ait: 'Ipse Deus omnipotens
solus lumen habitat inaccessibile quod super omnes claritates
sanitas mentis intelligat.' 55

36. et *deest*. 38. Circumscriptibile: circuminscriptibile *cod*. 43. non *deest*.

---

35. August., *De libero arbitrio*, ii. 16–17 (*Pat. Lat.* 32, cols. 1264 ff.); cf. *De unica forma omnium*, Baur, p. 107.

37. Psalm. cxlvii. 15. August.: 'Velocitas ipsa quid est, Fratres? Ubique est, non est in parte. Hoc pertinet ad Verbum Dei non esse in parte, ubique esse per seipsum Verbum, ex quo Dei Virtus et Dei Sapientia est, nondum assumpta carne. Si cogitemus Deum in forma Dei, Verbum aequale Patri: ipsa est sapientia Dei, de qua dictum est: "Attingit a fine usque ad finem fortiter." Quanta velocitas? Attingit a fine usque ad finem fortiter. Sed forte immobilitate attingit. Si immobilitate tamquam moles aliqua saxea impleat locum aliquem, dicitur quod attingit eiusdem loci a fine usque ad finem, non tamen motu. Quid ergo dicimus? Non habet motum Verbum illud et Sapientia illa stolida est? Et ubi est quod dicitur de sapientiae spiritu? Cum multa dicerentur: acutus, inquit, mobilis, certus, incoinquinatus. Sic utique sapientia Dei mobilis. Si ergo mobilis, quando hoc tangit, illud non tangit? Aut hoc tangit, illud deserit? Et ubi est velocitas? Hoc facit velocitas ut et ubique semper sit et nusquam inclusa teneatur.' *Enarrat. in Ps.* cxlvii, n. 22 (*Pat. Lat.* 37, col. 1931). Cf. *I Sent.*, dist. xxxvii, c. 9 (239, n. 350).

38. Cf. *I Sent.*, ibid., cc. 6, 8 (236–8).

38–40. *In marg. habetur*: Io. Dam. xiii. co. *De Visione Dei.* (*Pat. Gr.* 94, col. 854 b). *Translatio Burgundionis habet*: 'Circumscriptibile quidem est quod loco vel tempore vel comprehensione comprehenditur; incircumscriptibile vero est quod nullo horum continetur.' (MS. Bodl. E Museo 134, f. 379ʳa). *Translatio Roberti Grosseteste*: 'Circumscriptibile est quod loco vel tempore vel comprehensione comprehenditur; incircumscriptibile vero quod nullo horum continetur.' (MS. Ashmole 1526, f. 128ʳa.)

48–52. *In marg.*: August. in libro de moribus Ecc. (*Pat. Lat.* 32, col. 1345).

53–5. Cassiodorus, *De anima* (*Pat. Lat.* 70, col. 1288 b).

'Verbum summi Spiritus est omnino ex ipsius sola essentia, et sic singularis est ei simile, ut nulla proles sic sit omnino.' Idem in sequenti capitulo: 'Summi spiritus est verissime gignere, et Verbi eius verissime gigni.'

60 'Rem cuius memoriam habemus, hoc est mente eam dicere; verbum vero rei est ipsa cognitio ad eius similitudinem ex memoria formata.' Spiritum Sanctum appellat communionem et communem amorem Patris et Filii; et ideo sortitus est nomen Spiritus, quia hic fuit communis Patri et Filio, ut
65 infra lxii.

'Singulus quisque essentialiter est memoria, intelligentia, et amor.' 'Licet unusquisque seipsum omnes se invicem dicant, impossibile est tamen esse in summa essentia verbum aliud preter illud de quo iam constat, quod sic nascitur ex eo
70 cuius est verbum'; 'in eo quod seipsum dicit generat Pater et generatur Filius.'

---

56. *In marg.*: Anselmus.

56–71. *Sententiae ex Anselmi* Monologion *excerptae non videntur ad argumentum operis praecedentis pertinere.*

56–7. Anselmus, *Monologion*, c. xl (S. Anselmi Cantuariensis Archiepiscopi Opera Omnia, ad fidem codicum recensuit F. S. Schmitt. Edinburgi, 1946, i. 58).

58–9. Idem, ibid., c. xli (p. 58).

60–2. Idem, c. xlviii (p. 63).

62–5. Cf. c. xlix seq.

66–7. Ibid., c. lx (p. 71).

67–70. Ibid., c. lxiii (pp. 73–4).

70–1. Ibid., c. lxiv (p. 75).

D. A. CALLUS

THE *QUAESTIONES* OF SIMON OF HINTON

THE historian of the medieval schools 'must live in the valley and mix with the crowd before he follows the great teacher to the heights'.[1] Simon of Hinton is an authentic voice from the valley and he inhabits a spot which, from the historian's point of view, is thinly populated. We know so little about Oxford in the mid-thirteenth century that any information we can gain about methods and content of teaching is valuable.

Simon seems to have succeeded Richard Fishacre in the Dominican chair of theology after Richard's death in 1248. It is odd that not one of the medieval sources should allude to Simon as 'master', but since he lectured on Scripture he must be assumed to have had a master's degree. He became provincial in 1254. The general chapter of the Order of 1261 absolved him from his office, imposed a penance and sent him to teach at Cologne, or wherever the provincial of the German province should determine, because the ordinance of a former chapter concerning the support of friar students at the Dominican school at Oxford had not been observed. The diffinitors of the English province were also suspended and punished. In 1262 he was given permission to return to England and reassigned to the English province. We do not know what happened to him afterwards. His breach of regulations may have been due to an unwillingness to incur heavy expenses on inadequate resources and did not reflect on his personal character.[2]

His works are gradually being recovered. Of his commentaries on Scripture we now possess two: on the Twelve Prophets and on St. Matthew (the second in an incomplete copy), with a probable third, on the book of Job. The first two belong certainly, the third probably, to the Oxford period of Simon's career, 1248–54. We see the Dominican teacher continuing the English tradition of interest in natural science, an interest not merely bookish but alive and independent. As a lecturer Simon was given to anecdote; at least two *exempla* derived from his lectures were

[1] Sir Maurice Powicke, *Rashdall's Medieval Universities*, i (Oxford, 1936), p. xxxv.
[2] References and a few other details are given by J. C. Russell, 'A Dictionary of Writers of Thirteenth-century England', *Bulletin of the Institute of Historical Research*, Special Suppl. iii (1936), 152. The account of Simon's writings (ibid., pp. 151–2) needs some correction and has been supplemented by recent research. As usual, I have to thank Dr. D. Callus for his generous help in preparing this paper.

remembered and recorded. He also liked to illustrate his statements by topical allusions, particularly from the customs of magnates and princes and of their households, in a way that suggests first-hand experience.

His lectures are in the English medieval tradition of being long and discursive; but he could sometimes abbreviate. He produced two aids to study for the help of beginners, one scriptural, the other theological. The first is called in the manuscript *glosarium* and originally covered the whole of the Old Testament, apart from the Psalter, plus the prologues ascribed to St. Jerome. Judging from the one volume of the series that has survived, it consisted in excerpts from the *Gloss* to the Vulgate, arranged in a form which would be easier to handle than the big volumes which contained the full text and *Gloss*.[1] The second proved to be the most popular of Simon's works. His others survive in one or two copies each; this is known in some thirty manuscripts and in a set of excerpts with slight retouches. It has even been printed, among the works of John Gerson to whom it is falsely attributed.[2] As the preface states, it is a manual of theology, intended for beginners. Internal evidence fixes it in the years *c.* 1250–60. Probably it came after the biblical commentaries, since Simon quotes St. Albert on the *Sentences* in the manual, but not in the commentaries, even on theological points where it would have been relevant. It has been suggested that Simon came to know the work of St. Albert while teaching at Cologne, 1261–2, and that he finished the manual either during or soon after his stay there. This seems very plausible: continental theology was slow to penetrate the Oxford schools.

The most interesting part of the manual, from an historical, as distinct from a theological point of view, is the section on the Decalogue, where Simon discusses some day-to-day problems of casuistry. On the precept against stealing he raises the question of taxation: are princes and knights forbidden by this commandment to force excessive levies and tallages on their people?

---

[1] On Simon's scriptural works see B. Smalley, 'Two Biblical Commentaries of Simon of Hinton', *Rech. Théol. anc. méd.* xiii (1946), 57–85; 'Some More Exegetical Works of Simon of Hinton', ibid. xv (1948), forthcoming.

[2] John Gerson, *Opera*, ii (Paris, 1606), cols. 39–266, under the title *Compendium Theologiae*. The most important paper on the manual is by A. Dondaine, 'La Somme de Simon de Hinton', *Rech. Théol. anc. méd.* ix (1937), 5–22, 205–18. See also A. Walz, 'The "Exceptiones" from the "Summa" of Simon of Hinton', *Angelicum*, xiii (1936), 283–368; V. Burch, 'The "Exceptiones" from Simon of Heynton's "Summa"', *Medievalia et Humanistica*, iii (1945), 69–80, but this must be read with caution.

In reply he says that some distinguish according to the status of the taxpayer. The serf possesses nothing, save in his lord's name. Hence, it seems, the lord has a right to burden and tallage his serf at his will. If his oppression is excessive, then he does sin against the commandment, since it is against the interest of the commonwealth that a man should make bad use of his property: 'interest reipublice ne quis re sua male utatur'.[1] Another version of the text has: 'iustitia Dei exigit ut unusquisque re sua debite utatur'.[2] But this is not robbery, it is said, and the lord is not obliged to make restitution, though piety requires it. If the taxpayers are non-servile—Simon describes them as *coloni terre sive inhabitantes terram*—their consent must be obtained: 'taxanda est illarum talliarum seu exactionum acceptio'. The demand must be according to the expense which the lord incurs in defending the land they inhabit and in supporting his household and his dignity.[3] If he goes further than this it is robbery and is forbidden by the commandment.

There has been some discussion recently on the relationship between scholastic theory and contemporary practice.[4] This 'valley' opinion is more specific than that of St. Thomas on the same theme. Three points emerge from Simon's discussion: the rightlessness of the serf, whose only protection is the moral sense of his lord, though there is a hint that the State may be interested in the use the lord makes of his belongings; the contrasting right of free men to be consulted and their corresponding duty to grant necessary taxes; the general nature of the obligation to ask consent from free men. Simon is not, it seems, referring especially to national taxation. The authority levying the tax may be local, a knight just as well as a prince. He brings us fresh proof of how widespread the idea of consent to taxation was in thirteenth-century England.

The remaining work of Simon, his *Quaestiones*, has not so far been studied, although it is contained in a much-discussed manuscript, Brit. Mus., MS. Royal 9 E xiv, and although G. Lacombe

---

[1] Oxford, Bodleian Library, MS. Laud misc. 2, ff. 86ᵛ–87; MS. Laud misc. 397, ff. 120ᵛ–121 has: 'interest qualiter unusquisque re sua utatur'.

[2] Printed text, col. 60.

[3] Both manuscripts have the reading: 'secundum expensas quas necesse est facere bonas secundum principis familiam et honestatem'; the printed text reads: 'secundum expensas quas necesse est principi vel militi facere secundum suam moderatam et honestam familiam.' Apart from these two passages the printed text agrees with the two manuscripts. A critical study of the text would be desirable.

[4] See, for instance, H. Rothwell, 'The Confirmation of the Charters, 1297', *Eng. Hist. Rev.* lx (1945), 18 et seq.

published a list of the questions from the titles written in the margin.[1] The *Quaestiones* are written in hands of about the middle of the thirteenth century, ff. 117ᵛ–133. They break off unfinished; most of the second column of f. 133 is blank. In the top margin of f. 123 a different but roughly contemporary hand has written: 'questiones fratris Symonis de Hentune et quinque folia precedentia et dimidium.' The incipit is: 'Rom. ii: *Et cum gentes.* . . . Ex hoc patet quod lex divina . . .', the explicit: '. . . non habendo oculum ad iustitiam.'

The original form of the *Quaestiones* must remain an unsolved problem unless further evidence should come to light. Perhaps they represent part of a *summa*. The arrangement is systematic: Simon discusses first natural law, then divine law and the Decalogue. The fourteenth-century catalogue of Ramsey Abbey lists an item: 'Quaestiones fratris Symonis de Hentone de peccato originali cum aliis.'[2] This seems to indicate that the original work, even if it were never finished, at least included a whole section which has now disappeared. On the other hand, the section that we possess shows signs of having been planned as a self-contained unit. Simon says that divine law will be considered in only one of its aspects: 'Secundo de ipsa lege divina, non omni, sed (ea) que continetur in decalogo, discutiendum est' (f. 117ᵛa). It sounds rather as though he were restricting himself to the Decalogue, after writing an introduction on natural law and its relationship to divine law.

The text as we have it breaks off in the section on perjury, arising out of the third commandment. We know that Simon intended to go straight through the precepts. Near the beginning, when he is discussing the difference between the Old Law and the Gospel, he says that a certain point will be treated more fully in connexion with the precept against fornication (f. 120ᵛa). He makes references to the *Quaestiones* in his commentary on St. Matthew which prove that he carried out his project. One reference can be verified in the existing section; commenting on Matt. xviii. 15–16, he sends his students to a fuller treatment of the text *in questionibus de iuramento*.[3] It is, in fact, quoted, with

[1] G. Lacombe, 'La *Summa Abendonensis*', *Mélanges Mandonnet* (Bibl. Thomiste, xiv), ii. 161–81. For subsequent discussion of the manuscript see F. Pelster, 'Die Quaestionen des Alexander von Hales', *Gregorianum*, xiv (1933), 401–22, 501–20; P. Glorieux, 'Autour de la "Summa Abendonensis"', *Rech. Théol. anc. méd.* vi (1934), 80–4.

[2] W. D. Macray, *Chron. Abbat. Rames.* (Rolls Series), p. 363.

[3] MS. Bodl. e Mus. 29 (S.C. 3505), f. 98; see B. Smalley, op. cit. xiii. 60.

other examples from Scripture, to prove the lawfulness of taking oaths for lawful purposes (f. 128ᵛb). There are two references to questions on scandal:[1] 'Dictum est in questione de scandalo ...'; 'Quid autem sit scandalum et quotiens sit, quid pro scandalo vitando faciendum vel omittendum, patet in questione de scandalo, secundum modum nostrum plene dictum.' A discussion of scandal came normally in that part of medieval works on the Decalogue which dealt with man's duty towards his neighbour. Simon must, therefore, have come near to finishing his account of the precepts. One can only say that if he did plan the *Quaestiones* as part of a *summa*, and if he intended the whole to be on the same exhaustive lines as the section before us, *secundum modum nostrum plene dictum*, it was a colossal enterprise. It is a pity that the questions on the precept against stealing are missing; they may well have included a fuller inquiry into the morality of taxation.

Simon refers occasionally to the *Sentences* of Peter Lombard, but he is not writing a commentary on them. His two principal sources are the *Summa aurea* of William of Auxerre[2] and the *Summa de penitentia* of Raymond of Pennafort.[3] He quotes verbatim from both, more particularly from William of Auxerre, from whom entire *quaestiones* have been lifted. He will sometimes disagree with them and sometimes carry the argument farther. We have an exact parallel in his biblical commentaries. For the theological parts of these he also relies on William and Raymond. In both *Quaestiones* and commentaries he refers several times to William of Auxerre by name, *ut dicit Altissiodorensis*, though more often he quotes without acknowledgement. His quotations from Raymond are never acknowledged. Both authors found especial favour with the Dominican Order;[4] Simon's use of them is typical. The commentaries make use of Alexander Nequam's *Corrogationes Promethei*. There is one reference to Alexander

[1] MS. Bodl. e Mus. 29, ff. 98, 95ᵛ.

[2] Ed. Paris, 1500. I collated the section dealing with natural and divine law, ff. 153–5ᵛ, and the section on oaths and perjury, ff. 218–21, with Simon's *Quaestiones*.

[3] I used the copy in MS. Selden Supra 48 of the Bodleian Library. The most important borrowings come from the section on divination and magical practices and on oaths and perjury, ff. A 28–B 6 (the manuscript still has its medieval foliation).

[4] See A. Dondaine, op. cit., p. 14, on Raymond of Pennafort and the Dominicans. Of the secular masters of the early thirteenth century, William of Auxerre seems to have influenced the Dominicans, Philip the Chancellor the Franciscans. See O. Lottin, *Psychologie et morale aux XIIᵉ et XIIIᵉ siècles* (Louvain, 1942), pp. 219–20; 'L'influence littéraire du chancelier Philippe sur les théologiens préthomistes', *Rech. Théol. anc. méd.* ii (1930), 326.

Nequam in the *Quaestiones* which I have not been able to identify.[1] Commentaries and *Quaestiones* alike are dotted with references to the canons, over and above what Simon has taken at second hand from his sources. He seems to have been particularly interested in canon law.

The manual differs from both the commentaries and the *Quaestiones* in its use of sources in two ways. Here Simon's principal authorities in theology are St. Albert on book iv of the *Sentences* and Richard Fishacre on the *Sentences*; he does not use them in the commentaries and I have not found any trace of them in the *Quaestiones* either. In the manual Simon quotes Raymond of Pennafort by name, not anonymously as in his other works. He also quotes other leading canonists by their names.[2] All this goes to show that the *Quaestiones* and the commentaries belong to an earlier stage in Simon's teaching career than the manual. He evidently found time for study, kept up with the current output on his subject and enlarged his range of knowledge. He was not one of those writers who constantly reproduce their own works. The manual does not draw on the commentaries or on the *Quaestiones*. The commentary on St. Matthew, as we have seen, refers back to the *Quaestiones*; but he does not quote himself in the commentaries, even when he discusses the same subject. Three passages in the commentaries deal with oaths and perjury,[3] and one with the question, arising from the story of Jonah, whether it is permissible to cast lots.[4] A comparison with parallel passages in the *Quaestiones* shows Simon using much the same authorities from Scripture and the canons, and reaching the same conclusions, but organizing his material quite differently.

Lacombe dated the whole manuscript before 1240. Neither his arguments from the contents nor his dating of the hands has been generally accepted. The *Quaestiones* contain no precise indication of date, though it is possible that a meticulous study of Simon's canon law sources might bring us nearer. At present we have only the composition of his lectures on St. Matthew as a *terminus ad quem*. This was not the first of Simon's biblical works;

[1] On the question of revenge in the Old Testament Simon quotes the text 'Non facies cum eis pacem etc.' (Deut. xxiii. 6) and continues: 'Libri Regum et Iudicum idem docent per opera que ibi leguntur et dicit magister Alexander Nequam quod licuit eis persequi inimicos etiam causa vindicte, quod non credo. . . .' (f. 120ᵛa). This does not come from the *Corrogationes Promethei* on Deuteronomy, Kings, or Judges.

[2] A. Dondaine, op. cit., p. 14.

[3] Oxford MS. New College 45, ff. 6, 168; MS. e Mus. 29, f. 10ʳ and ᵛ.

[4] Ibid., f. 329.

a commentary on St. John's Gospel, which is still lost, but which probably also originated in a lecture course, preceded it.[1] So the lectures on St. Matthew were not given at the very beginning of his teaching period in 1248. But we cannot take 1248 as a *terminus post quem* for the *Quaestiones*, since Simon may have written them before he held his chair at Oxford.

At least we have one piece of evidence to show that the date *c.* 1240–50 is not wildly out. Simon devotes one of his longest *quaestiones* to the duty of a debtor whose creditor has been excommunicated: ought he to wait until the creditor has been absolved, or to pay a member of the family, if one can be found who has not also incurred the sentence, or to hand over the sum to a third party to be held in trust until the sentence has been lifted? All these possibilities are discussed. Many counsels and opinions are given. The problem seems to bristle with difficulties and Simon hesitates. He had taken the question from Raymond of Pennafort but evidently did not feel satisfied with Raymond's brief and allusive answer. Eventually he decides that the debtor is not bound to repay until the sentence has been raised; but he gives as his opinion that a simple-minded person, who does repay, for fear of offending God by perjury, not understanding the ill consequences which may follow and ignorant of the Church's prohibition, either does not sin or has much excuse.[2] The question became urgent in high politics when Urban IV excommunicated the Ghibelline bankers of Siena and Florence in 1262.[3] The faithful were commanded to pay their debts to receivers appointed by the pope and those who persisted in repaying directly were also excommunicated. The most simple-minded debtor could hardly have pleaded ignorance of his duty after this. A theologian writing after 1262 would surely have mentioned the occurrence. Simon's whole attitude puts his work before 1262.

Simon shows the same personal traits in the *Quaestiones* as he does in the commentaries and manual. Kings and courts interest him. If one of the king's knights were to be mistaken for the royal person and honoured as such, the king would be pleased and would regard it as an honour paid to himself. The valet, *garcio*, of the king is honoured for the sake of his master. The royal standard is carried before the king to announce his coming and the herald calls out that the king has passed.[4] Simon's

---

[1] B. Smalley, op. cit., p. 61.   [2] f. 130^{r}a–b.
[3] See E. Jordan, *Les origines de la domination angevine en Italie* (Paris, 1909), p. 339 seq.   [4] ff. 123^{v}b–124^{r}a; 124^{r}b; 125^{r}a.

preoccupation with the literal and mystical senses of Scripture cannot be repressed, even when he is supposed to be engaged on a strictly theological work. A comparison between the ten commandments and the ten plagues of Egypt, in their mystical sense, still lingered on in *summas* of the early thirteenth century as a legacy of the period when theology and exegesis had been taught together without differentiation; it is found, for instance, in William of Auxerre. Simon works out the comparison with loving detail and ends by an appeal to St. Augustine, from whom the comparison has been taken, lest, as he says, it might be regarded as unnecessary.[1] He considers at length the question, which I cannot find in his sources, as to how the commandments were disposed on the tables of the Law. According to Augustine they were inscribed three on the first table and seven on the second. Chrysostom, on the contrary, says five on one and five on the other. The Jews and Josephus agree with this opinion. Josephus states that he has seen the two tables, each having two and a half commandments written on its outer and inner side. Peter Comestor in the *Historia Scholastica* is also consulted. Simon thinks that God must have observed the requirements of proportion and symmetry in disposing his commandments; hence they must either have been divided into the three longer and the seven shorter, or else, if they were five and five, the first three were written without their commentary and explanation.[2] Simon always wanted to know what things looked like.

Another trait comes out in the *Quaestiones*. He is very ready to give his own opinion. Only twice does he refuse to commit himself because he has no guidance from his elders.[3] On one occasion he rejects a patristic authority, without attempting to 'interpret it' and with only the saving clause that he may not have understood it correctly.[4] His additions and subtractions are sometimes illuminating. William of Auxerre raises the question of the pope's power to dispense subjects from their oath of fealty to the

---

[1] 'Ne autem videatur hec adaptatio in vanum quesita, attendamus quod dicit Augustinus in libello de decem plagis unde hec tractata est coaptatio. Non est, inquid, sine causa, dilectissimi ...' (f. 123ʳa). The reference is to Pseudo-Augustine, Migne, *Pat. Lat.* 46, cols. 946–54. The quotation is not verbally exact and it seems that Simon was using a very different text from that printed in Migne.

[2] f. 119ʳb.

[3] ff. 117ᵛb, 130ʳa.

[4] f. 129ʳb: 'Ad argumentum Crisostomi dicendum est quod probabiliter arguit, non tamen necessario, nisi aliud sit quam ego videam. Propositiones autem vere sunt quas dicit ... sed tunc insufficiens est divisio, salva tamen auctoritate sancti, quem forte non intelligo.'

ruler, instancing the action of Innocent III in releasing the German princes from their oath to the Emperor Otto IV;[1] Richard Fishacre borrows from William in this connexion.[2] Simon was following William closely in this part of the *Summa aurea*; he mentions the oath of fealty in his list of permissible and lawful oaths, as William does; but he omits altogether the question of dispensation. Perhaps he did not want to encourage rebellion. Raymond of Pennafort asks whether, if a corporate body, such as a city or a college, has bound itself by oath, the obligation passes to the successors of those who took the oath after their death. He replies that the successors are not guilty of perjury if they default, although they are bound by the oath, because the obligation incurred by the oath is personal and is not passed on.[3] Simon thinks this position illogical. How can the successors be bound by the oath if neither the obligation to fulfil nor the guilt of perjury in case of default is transmitted to them? He replies that the obligation is sometimes transmitted and sometimes not. When the goods of one man pass to another by way of succession the obligation pertinent to the goods passes with them, as far as they extend, otherwise not. What is transmitted, however, does not pass on by reason of the oath or the promise, but by reason of a rationally founded human institution.[4] The criticism of Raymond is significant. Simon has taken the argument a stage further, probably with the help of some other legal text which he had in mind. Unfortunately his reply is compressed and he does not give any example to clarify his meaning.

---

[1] *Summa aurea*, op. cit., ff. 220ᵛ–221.

[2] Oxford MS. Balliol College 57, f. 221ᵛ.

[3] MS. Selden Supra 48, f. B 2ᵛ: 'Dico quod non sunt periuri; obligatio enim iuramenti personalis est et non transit ad successores quantum ad periculum periurii; tenentur tamen implere.'

[4] f. 132ʳa: 'Si civitas vel congregatio aliqua obligavit se iuramento ad aliquid, mortuis iuratoribus, queritur an successores sint periuri si transgrediantur. Videtur quod sic, quia omnes obligationes antecessorum transeunt ad successores. . . . Contra: qui non iurat non periurat [peierat *cod.*]. Successores nunquam iuraverunt, ergo nec transgrediendo periuri esse possunt. Si dicatur quod obligatio transit, sed non iuramentum, quia iurare est actio personalis, contra quero qua ratione successores obligantur. Si dicatur quod ratione iuramenti, hoc nullo modo esse potest, nisi transeat in eos aliquo modo iuramentum, quia nusquam potest esse effectus nisi ubi est causa eius aliquo modo. Si dicatur quod ratione promissionis, contra: promissio est actio personalis, sicut et iuratio.

'Respondeo: quandoque transit obligatio, quandoque non. Quando enim bona alicuius transeunt ad alium post modum successionis, transit ad eundem obligatio que contingit huius bona, quantum bona illa se extendunt, alioquin non. Quod autem transit non est ratione iuramenti vel promissionis sed ratione constitutionis humane, rationabiliter condite.'

It will be asked whether the *Quaestiones* ought to be edited. I hope that these few extracts will have shown that they deserve to be studied. There are some interesting things, particularly in the sections on sorcery and divination and on perjury. I doubt whether it would be worth while to undertake the formidable task of editing them *en bloc*. The section on natural and divine law at the beginning, on the other hand, comes into a different class. It touches on some of the fundamental questions of contemporary theology. This brief analysis of its content will, it may be hoped, stir up some scholar to give us an edition.

The outlines of medieval teaching on natural law, in St. Thomas Aquinas and his predecessors, have been clearly described by Dom O. Lottin.[1] Simon fits easily into the framework. He starts from the position of William of Auxerre and does not challenge William's main contentions. William distinguishes three definitions of natural law: the laws which are common to the universal order of nature, the instincts which are common to the whole animal kingdom, the dictates of natural reason, which is proper to man. He prefers the third and confines himself to it in his discussion. Simon adopts this third definition, barely considering the other two. He takes from William of Auxerre the two precepts of natural reason: to love God above all things and to love one's neighbour as oneself. He does not, however, adopt William's differentiation between the precepts of natural reason and the Decalogue. William holds that they differ according to their end: the precepts of natural reason help us to acquire the moral or 'political' virtues, the Decalogue to acquire the theological; the Decalogue is directed towards enabling man to reach his supernatural end. Hugh of Saint Cher distinguishes between acts which are bad in themselves and recognized as such by natural reason, and acts which are bad because forbidden, as the eating of the forbidden fruit in paradise. Simon seems anxious to minimize the difference between natural law on the one hand and what he calls *preceptum discipline*, as the forbidding of the fruit to Adam, on the other hand. Both precepts of nature and precepts of discipline are dictated by natural reason, the former directly, in itself, the latter by deduction. In the second sense every command of God is also a precept of nature, because nature tells us to obey our superior. Here, typically, Simon adduces and enlarges on an argument from natural science: if we consider

---

[1] *Le droit naturel chez Saint Thomas d'Aquin et ses prédécesseurs*, 2nd ed. (Bruges, 1931). My references are all taken from here.

nature by herself, from inanimate nature in the elements up to rational nature, we see that the lower things are always governed by their superiors. The elements, for instance, are governed by a celestial body or by its influence, while in man, before sin corrupted his nature, the lower forces were wholly subject to reason. Since, therefore, God and God alone is man's natural superior, natural reason dictates that he is to be obeyed in all things. But, Simon adds, this does not apply to human precepts; by nature all men are equal; there would have been no human 'prelacies' but for the fall, just as there will be none in heaven.[1]

This last concept had reached the early scholastics from the Roman lawyers via the Fathers, together with the view that in 'the state of nature' before the fall men had possessed the earth in common, private property, like state authority, having been introduced as a consequence of sin. St. Thomas seems to have been the first of the scholastics to break with the view that natural, uncorrupted reason dictated communism and to describe appropriation as a dictate of natural reason. The early scholastics had, therefore, to answer the question: whether, if communism is a dictate of natural reason, man sins in appropriating and in holding private property. They replied by explaining that the fall had created a new situation in which appropriation was right and necessary, with certain safeguards. Simon poses the question and comes to the usual conclusion; but the question seems to have had an unusual interest for him. He brings forward nine objections, none of them taken directly from William of Auxerre, in favour of communism, and even in replying to them he elaborates the reason why communism was natural and necessary in the state of nature.

The reason he says, was both human and divine in its origin: divine, because God gave all in common to all, commanding his creatures to increase and multiply; human if we consider

---

[1] f. 117^{v}a: 'Respondeo: natura(m) dictare aliquid faciendum est dupliciter, vel in se vel ex consequenti. Primo modo non est omne preceptum Dei naturale sed secundo. Dictat enim natura obediendum esse superiori; unde et ubi est sola natura, ut in elementis et ceteris, usque ad rationalem naturam, reguntur semper inferiora a superioribus, ut elementa et elementata [eiata *cod.*] a corpore celesti vel spiritu coniuncto; unde etiam ante peccatum, quod naturam corrupit, fuerunt vires inferiores omnino subdite rationi. Cum sit ergo Deus et solus ille per naturam superior, sic rationali natura dictat rationalis ei per omnia obediendum esse. Non sic autem in preceptis humanis, quia nemo per naturam est alio superior, quippe cum sint omnes pares natura; unde, si mansisset natura in sua integritate sine corruptione peccati, non fuissent in homines prelatie, sicut nec erunt in patria, ubi erit plena libertas a corruptione et culpa.'

man in his relation to God and in his relation to the inferior creatures. Man was made in God's image and likeness; he is called the son of God and was like God in his nature; 'but if son, heir also'.[1] As son and heir of God, he had a right in the things of God. Moreover, he was one spirit with God. Simon refers to the text: 'Know you not that he who is joined to a harlot is made one body? "For they shall be", saith he, "two in one flesh." But he who is joined to the Lord is one spirit' (1 Cor. vi. 16, 17). If the physical union of man and woman in one body in marriage makes all things common between them, much more does the union (of man with God) in one spirit, since this is stronger and more sublime. Simon clinches his point with a metaphysical argument: the more abstract things are, the greater is their capacity for union; the philosopher says that the intellect and its object (intelligible things) are more truly united than are matter and form.[2] The 'philosopher' is Averroes on the *De anima*.[3] It is interesting to find Simon quoting from Averroes, and still more in this context, when he wants to stress the initial union of man with God.

He goes on to a less subtle argument. The reason for communism in the state of nature arose also from man's relation to inferior creatures. Men worked together in common as they found convenient, and they used in common only necessary things (as distinct from superfluities).

Simon gives the current explanation as to why man came to appropriate possessions after the fall. He lost his dominion over

[1] From Rom. vii. 17.

[2] f. 118^{r}a: 'Ad secundum dicendum quod ante peccatum erant omnia communia tripliciter: quoad dominii possessionem et usum, cuius ratio fuit et a parte Dei et a parte hominis: a parte Dei quia communiter omnibus omnia dedit, Gen. i: *Crescite et multiplicamini* etc. Ex parte hominis comparati ad Deum et ad inferiora: ad Deum *in imaginem et similitudinem*; unde imago, inde filius Dei. Filius enim dicitur quia fit ut ille, precipue in naturalibus; imago autem in materia est. Unde vero filius Dei, inde ius habuit in hiis que Dei sunt. Si enim filius, et heres, Rom. viii. Hoc dico nisi demeruerunt, quod vero non (fecit) homo ante peccatum. Unde quidem similitudo, inde unus spiritus cum Deo, Cor. vi: *Qui adhesit* . . . Si ergo coniunctio carnalis eius reperitur [*sic*, facta?] inter membra in corpore uno viri et mulieris in coniugio facit omnia esse communia, multo fortius coniunctio in spiritu uno, cum sit fortior et sublimior. Quanto enim aliqua sunt maioris abstractionis, tanto sunt maioris unionis; unde dicit philosophus quod verius uniuntur intelligibile et intellectus quam materia et forma.' My summary hardly does justice to this closely packed argument.

[3] Averroes, *Comm. de anima*, III, textu 5° (chap. iv): 'Est manifestum quod materia et forma copulentur ad invicem ita quod congregatum ex eis sit unicum, et maxime intellectus materialis et intentio intellecta in actu: quod enim componitur ex eis non est aliquid tertium aliud ab eis, sicut est de aliis compositis ex materia et forma.'

inferior creatures. God granted him the right to make use of them, but at the price of work. Greed brings with it a desire for superfluities, and since men's capacity for work is unequal the obligation to communism ceases. Simon was ever on the watch for a practical application. He now states his opinion that, nevertheless, infidels and bad men have no true dominion over anything, since they are enemies of God, to whom all things belong, and from whom all dominion over men is derived. He quickly counteracts the dangerous consequences of his position by adding that God sometimes allows the use of dominion to bad men, either to reward them in this life for some good that they do or on account of the sins of those they rule over.[1] Many examples from Scripture follow.

The practical side of things occupies Simon's attention throughout. He discusses in detail the restrictions on man's right to appropriate and to make use of private possessions without committing sin. Later, in considering the implications of the precept to love one's neighbour as oneself, he goes fully into the morality of the death sentence which was passed on robbers. He justifies it, as his predecessors had done, but with a personal qualification: 'if the judge could be sure that the robber would turn over a new leaf and that others would not be emboldened to evil doing, I do not think that he should be hanged on any account, but rather let go with a penalty suitable to his guilt.'[2]

One of the *Quaestiones* touches on a philosophical problem. The question of how natural law is written in men's hearts, as the Apostle says (Rom. ii. 15), involves a theory of cognition and a consideration of the part played by sensory perception in the formation of ideas. Simon could have found the question in

[1] f. 118[r]a, [r]b: 'A parte hominis comparati ad inferiora, tum quia communiter prout eis conveniebat operabantur, tum quia communiter solis necessariis utebantur.

Peccante autem homine, quia fuit inobediens Deo, unde similitudo amissa est et imago deformata, amisit ius dominii in ea que per naturam infra ipsum facta sunt; unde et repugnare ceperunt contra eum; usum autem concessit Deus homini ex misericordia ad necessitatem, sed cum erumpna et labore suo, Gen. iii: . . .

Quia ergo post peccatum plus requirit concupiscentia quam appetat natura et labor apud homines inequalis est, cessat obligatio possidendi et utendi omnibus equaliter. Estimo autem quod apud infideles vel quoscumque malos nullius rei residet verum dominium, cum sint hostes Dei cuius sunt omnia et a quo omne dominium derivatur in homines. . . . Non dico quin aliquando Deus concedat malis [malum *cod.*] usum dominii, sive propter aliqua bona que faciunt ut in presenti remunerentur, sive propter peccata eorum quibus preficiuntur. . . .'

[2] f. 118[v]b: 'Utrum tamen si posset constare iudici de correctione latronis in posterum et quod aliis audacia maleficiendi non prestaretur, non credo aliqua ratione quod suspendi deberet, sed potius dimitti cum pena condigna culpe precedentis.'

William of Auxerre. He answers it quite differently. The passage in the *Quaestiones* is rather obscure and requires a much fuller treatment than it can be given in this paper. It is one of the two instances where Simon refuses to commit himself. Fr. Pelster writes of the 'Augustinismus eines Richard Fishacre und Simon von Henton'.[1] Simon approaches this crucial problem by quoting at length from St. Augustine's *De Trinitate* (lib. xiv. *c.* 15 and lib. xii. *c.* 3).[2] He holds the Augustinian view of illumination very strongly. William of Auxerre had confronted St. Augustine with Aristotle, preferring St. Augustine, but trying to harmonize them.[3] Simon has omitted the Aristotelian theory of knowledge altogether.

We know from the commentary on St. Matthew that Simon held a doctrine, derived from, though not actually taught by Avicenna, that God is the *intellectus agens*. He mentions this very controversial point without discussion and almost as though it were axiomatic to him.[4] The *Quaestiones*, I think, suggest a deeply Augustinian outlook. But they strengthen the impression of Simon that one forms from his commentaries. He was not primarily a speculative theologian. He preferred the particular and the concrete. The scholastic façade of the *Quaestiones* can barely conceal the biblical scholar and the preacher.

B. SMALLEY

[1] *Thomas von Sutton und das Correctorium 'Quare detraxisti', Mélanges Auguste Pelzer* (Louvain, 1947), p. 465.

[2] f. 117ᵛb: 'Tertio modo: quod scriptura hec intelligatur illustratio superioris partis rationis ab ipsa luce prima qua [quam *cod.*] conversa anima videt regulas quibus instruitur quid faciendum, quid non. Unde Augustinus, *De trinitate*, lib. xiv, c. 15: Domini sui mens reminiscitur. . . . Non solum hoc in moribus dicit Augustinus, sed etiam cum ratio iudicat de sensibus. . . .'

[3] O. Lottin, op. cit., pp. 34–5.

[4] B. Smalley, op. cit., pp. 76–7.

THE MISE OF AMIENS, 23 JANUARY 1264

T HE drastic terms of the Mise of Amiens of 23 January 1264[1] appear to make a clean sweep of the English political situation, voiding all that had gone before since the parliament of Oxford in 1258, and forcing the contending parties to make a new start in their struggle on a new and changed basis. It has therefore seemed temptingly easy to isolate the Mise from the confused and kaleidoscopic struggle of the preceding year, especially as until recently little has been known of the detailed course of the conflict and of the changes in the strength and position of the two parties during the months of flux and crisis which led up to the award.[2] But by thus taking the Mise out of its detailed context, and reading it in isolation from the crowded background of events which form its essential setting, we have seriously misinterpreted the award, misjudging the nature of the attempt and failing to understand the response of the rival parties and the effect on the course of the struggle as a whole. The present paper attempts, with the aid of newly discovered evidence, to see by what means Louis came to his decision, and also, by restoring the Mise to its necessary context, to reinterpret the reactions of the two parties in the light of their hopes and expectations.

The project of arbitration by Louis IX on the embittered constitutional conflict in England was not the resort of two equally matched forces doubtful of the issue of an appeal to force or worn down to compromise by months of indecisive struggle. Nor was it the desperate attempt of a dwindling radical rump to save some part of their aims, and even their very lives, from total obliteration at the hands of an overwhelming royalist majority with victory in its grasp. The Mise of Amiens was the outcome of an offer made, and a limitation self-imposed, by Simon de Montfort and his allies at the very peak of their triumph in July 1263, when there seemed to be no power in England able and willing to compel any fraction of abatement of their terms. Helpless in face of the swift, well-organized campaign of Simon and the

[1] The full text of Louis' award, with the letters of compromise from both parties in the arbitration, is printed in Rymer's *Foedera* (Rec. Com., 1816), I. i. 433. The terms themselves, omitting the letters of compromise, are given in Stubbs, *Select Charters* (9th ed., 1913), pp. 395–7.

[2] For detailed accounts of the events of 1263 see R. F. Treharne, *The Baronial Plan of Reform, 1258–63* (1932), pp. 299–342, and more recently, Sir F. M. Powicke, *King Henry III and the Lord Edward*, ii (1947), 431–55.

western barons, Henry III had, without a show of fight, surrendered on Simon's terms. He had agreed to the immediate
restoration of the Provisions of Oxford of 1258 and to the system
of government instituted thereby and developed subsequently by
the Council of Fifteen; but, to meet the complaints which Henry
had made in 1260 and again in 1261, and to place the restored
Provisional Government upon a basis of lawful consent, Simon,
in the very hour of total victory, had offered to submit to impartial
arbitration upon 'whatever in the Provisions might seem harmful to the King or to the realm'.[1] It was from this offer, delayed
though the outcome was until the vastly different circumstances
of six months later, that the Mise of Amiens came.

The importance which Simon attached to the idea of impartial
arbitration as a means of placing the Provisional Government on
a legal basis of mutual consent can be seen from the persistence
with which, alike in good times and in bad, he pursued this aim.
It is vital to our understanding of the man; it is essential to our
comprehension of his policy and his actions. Profoundly religious
and austerely idealistic, the friend of Robert Grosseteste, Adam
Marsh and Walter Cantilupe, and the sharer in the great bishop
of Lincoln's obscure 'great design',[2] Earl Simon was too civilized
to believe in violence as the solution of political problems. There
were, indeed, worse things even than civil war, and his strength
lay in the fact that he combined a hatred of force with a resolute
determination not to surrender his fundamental ideals, and if
necessary to fight to the death to save them. Such men make un-
comfortable politicians, for they cannot compromise upon essentials, but insist on maintaining first principles even when they
show almost infinite patience in negotiation upon detail: but without them ordinary men lose their way in compromise and adjust-
ment, and politics suffer degeneration in consequence. Simon
was willing to go to almost any lengths to avoid open rebellion,
provided he could maintain unimpaired the fundamental principle
of limiting Henry's power, for the rest of his reign, by an elected
council working along the general lines laid down by the Provisions of Oxford. He had, therefore, set himself the task of reconciling Henry and Edward to the principle of the Provisions, and
to do this he was willing to accept any modification in detail
which would leave the principle of control untouched. It was an
impossible task, for although in 1260 and in 1261 Henry had

---

[1] Treharne, op. cit., p. 307.
[2] Bémont, *Simon de Montfort* (trans. E. F. Jacob, 1930), pp. 42-7.

stated his objections to the Provisions in terms of detail, it was the very principle of limited monarchy to which Henry objected and to which he could never resign himself.

It is easy to say that Simon should have seen what is obvious to us, that no arbitration, however just and wise, could reconcile Henry's ideas of government with his. But Simon was seeking to establish his ideal of government on something more durable than force, and to draw from impartial arbitration either a genuine foundation of mutual consent, or, that failing, a legal and moral basis so secure that should Henry, having once sworn to accept it, ever seek to revoke his oath, he would from the outset be fatally discredited in the eyes of all honourable and law-abiding men. Such an attempt did not accord ill with the temper of the age, the age of Bracton, Beaumanoir and Aquinas, an age when law was deeply rooted in the minds of men of education and political experience, and when arbitration was more readily employed, both in public and in private affairs, than in any other period before the close of the nineteenth century. Whatever Justinian's Code or Henry's conception of divine right might maintain, neither feudal practice nor English political custom, nor even the political philosophy of the great Schoolmen, could admit the idea of untrammelled royal absolutism which in fact underlay Henry's rejection of advice and control. Revolutionary innovator though he might seem, Simon might justly have contended that he sought only to give definite form and explicit sanction to the indefinite and implicit medieval limitations upon royal authority, and that he was justified in his aim by Henry's refusal to recognize those limitations as long as they remained indefinite and implicit.

Simon sought, then, to achieve this fundamental aim by arbitration, though he was prepared to fight rather than forgo it. How keenly he desired to avoid civil war can be seen in the skilful strategy of his campaign early in the summer of 1263, when, with no less political than military genius, he isolated Henry and compelled his surrender by a plan designed to avoid conflict with any force commanded either by Henry or by Edward.[1] How far he was prepared to go and how much he was prepared to risk to achieve the desired settlement by mutual consent can be seen from his acceptance—perhaps even his own proposal—of Louis IX as arbiter and his readiness to place the whole question before Louis, relying upon the justice of his case and the impartial

[1] Treharne, op. cit., pp. 303–8.

reputation of the arbiter. The first steps in proposing French arbitration are obscure: an agent from Louis had been at Henry's court in June, and it may have been through him that the first suggestions were made, though on whose initiative we do not know. The beginning must have been made soon after Simon came to power in mid-July, for by 16 August Henry is found replying—of course, under control by the revived Council—to an invitation to come to France 'to have Louis' counsel and aid for the amelioration of the King's estate, and to talk about other things as with his lord'. The council, while demanding certain guarantees from Henry and from Louis to avoid a repetition of the intrigues of the early months of 1260,[1] were willing to let Henry go to France and to send a strong delegation with him in the hope of obtaining the much-desired settlement. Unfortunately for their hopes, this attempt failed, for although a conference was arranged to meet at Boulogne at Michaelmas, Louis' impolitic partiality ruined its prospects from the start. Unduly persuaded, it was said, by papal representations, family pressure and the clamour of refugees from England gathered at his court, Louis attempted to turn the conference into a formal trial in his court as king of France, of Simon and his allies for rebellion against their overlord King Henry, Louis' vassal. Such a process was far from the impartial arbitration which Simon sought, and he and his fellow proctors firmly repudiated Louis' claim of jurisdiction, saying that they 'were not bound to answer for their actions in the court of the King of France, but that they should be judged in the court of the King of England, by their peers and by faithful men upon oath'.[2]

It is the measure of Simon's eagerness to put the Provisions on to a legal basis of mutual consent that, despite Louis' display of partiality and prejudice, and despite the ominous ill-feeling and hostility shown to the English envoys before the conference, Simon persisted in his efforts to secure the French king's arbitration. The political situation in England, already beginning to turn against him in September, was growing now rapidly worse, adding a new force to the argument for settlement by negotiation lest the realm fall into civil war and the plan of reform be utterly overthrown. The violent forcing tactics employed by Edward, and the Marchers' change of sides early in October enabled Henry to reassert his independence of Simon and his dwindling band of

[1] Treharne, pp. 217–35; Powicke, op. cit., pp. 411–16.
[2] Treharne, op. cit., pp. 319–22.

supporters on 16 October, while the young earl of Gloucester and several other magnates appear, for the time, to have withdrawn from Simon's side without, however, joining the king. It was probably this uncertain element which prevented Henry from putting his support to the test and forcing the issue, for when, about 22 October, Simon sent the bishops of Worcester, London and Exeter to Windsor to persuade Henry to negotiate, Henry prudently replied on 25 October that he was willing to treat for peace, and sent his brother King Richard with other negotiators to London to discuss terms. Agreement was speedily reached 'to compromise in Louis, King of France, touching all contentions and discords between the King and the nobles of the realm on account of the Provisions of Oxford or other cause', and on 28 October Richard informed his brother 'that firm peace was likely to be made very soon'. Accordingly, Henry appointed two proctors to swear, in his name, that he would observe whatever Louis should ordain, and the imminent danger of civil war receded a little.[1]

The completion of the arrangements for Louis' arbitration required another six weeks: his consent to undertake the duty under the new conditions had to be obtained, exact terms of reference agreed upon and adopted by both sides, and time and place had to be settled. Envoys passed across the Straits and messengers went to and fro, though we catch no glimpse of their instructions. Henry, who had resumed control of the administration on 2 November, did not regard the truce as prohibiting him from raising a great force at Windsor and seeking to compel the baronial custodians of Dover Castle to surrender their charge. Nor, when that failed, did he scruple to plot with his sympathizers in London to entrap Simon and his friends in Southwark and to force them to fight under hopeless conditions or to surrender: but Simon's London allies foiled that act of treachery too. Despite these gross breaches of the truce and other open—and partly successful—attempts by Henry to strengthen his hold on the country, Simon did not waver in his resolve to accept arbitration, even though Henry's conduct indicated that he regarded Simon and his allies as rebels with whom no faith need be kept. Louis' envoys, bearing his proposals for the final arrangements for arbitration, reached Dover even while Henry was closing the trap round Simon at Southwark, but on 13 December Simon and his allies sealed their solemn consent to Louis' arbitration,

[1] Ibid., pp. 322–9; Powicke, op. cit., pp. 450–1.

and on the 16th Henry and his chief supporters followed suit.[1] The quarrel was now committed to Louis' arbitration, and though the circumstances were changed beyond any expectation, Simon's promise of July was at last to be fulfilled.

By identical letters, the two parties accepted Louis' arbitration 'on all provisions, ordinances, statutes and obligations of Oxford, and on all contentions and discords arising from the said provisions' up to 13 December,[2] the date when the baronial letters were sealed. Both sides promised, by the most solemn oaths, 'to observe in good faith whatever the king of France should ordain on all or any of these matters, in great as in small', provided only that Louis should declare his award before Whitsuntide next. Both parties were to appear before Louis at Amiens on 8 January to present their cases and in due course to hear Louis' award.[3]

A document recently discovered in the Archives Nationales in Paris by Professor É. Perroy[4] enables us both to understand the procedure followed before Louis at Amiens, and to see the objections which Henry asserted to the system of government under which his opponents sought to place him and his kingdom: it also helps us to understand how Louis reached the decision embodied in his Mise. The document is a record of Henry's complaints (*gravamina*) against his barons, followed by a formal petition for compensation and relief in the manner of a *petitio libelli* according to French legal form. The record is written on a sheet of parchment ten inches long by six inches wide. One hand records, item by item, the seven paragraphs under which Henry's *gravamina* are listed, with an eighth stating generally that further grievances will be presented at the proper time and place. After an erasure of one line, another hand records the *petitio* for heavy monetary damages and for relief from the wrong, in the form of the total cassation of the Provisions and of all that had followed from them: this portion of the record runs over on to the dorse of the sheet. The large number of interlineations, deletions and erasures, altering sense and substance as well as correcting grammatical errors or changing construction and word order, indicates that the document is a draft, though it was probably, in its heavily

[1] Treharne, op. cit., pp. 329–33; Powicke, op. cit., p. 451.

[2] The text of Henry's letter, with the assent of his chief supporters, is printed in W. W. Shirley, *Royal Letters* (Rolls Series, 1866), ii. 250–1; Louis published both letters with his award (*Foedera*, I. i. 433).

[3] Treharne, op. cit., p. 334.

[4] Professor Perroy kindly informed me of this letter and sent me a transcript of it, with his generous permission to use it as I saw fit.

altered form, the version from which Henry's clerks transcribed
the fair copy for use as the *petitio libelli* in the arbitration.

The form of the document is important. Borrowed by French
lawyers, probably through the medium of procedure in the Courts
Christian, from the elaborate libellary process of late Roman law,
it had become a normal and established form of procedure in
French customary courts by this time. Beaumanoir, for instance,
cited it to show how the customary courts, in taking over Roman
forms, had translated Roman technicalities into the vernacular.
The French version of this procedure, allowing each party to
plead in bar once only, after which issue must be joined on
questions of fact, was much simpler than the Roman and canon
law forms, which allowed duplications and triplications of the
defendant's *exceptiones* to the plaintiff's *petitio libelli*, and of the
plaintiff's *replicationes* to the defendant's *exceptiones*.[1] While
the English courts had not copied this procedure, the several
types of 'bills' familiar in English legal practice from the late
thirteenth century onwards, bear a general resemblance in form
to the *petitio libelli*, and may have derived their name from the
French *libelle*.[2] The unwritten *querela* of the English courts,
virtually formless and apparently of great antiquity,[3] has been
suggested as the possible origin of the 'bill in eyre':[4] it may, not
unreasonably, be represented as an embryonic expression of the
fundamental principle underlying the fully developed Roman
petitio libelli. It was the principle, going back on the English side
to primitive Germanic custom, that a free man has a right to
justice, and that he may come into court to state his case in his
own way and to demand that justice be done—a principle not
wholly submerged by the necessary rise of formal procedure even
in primitive times, and still standing out from the spreading tide
of writs and other set forms of action even in thirteenth-century
England.

The French procedure of the *demande*, or *petitio libelli*, and the
somewhat analogous English practices of *querela* and bill in eyre

[1] Sir P. Vinogradoff, *Roman Law in Medieval Europe* (1909), pp. 73–4.

[2] W. C. Bolland, *Select Bills in Eyre* (Selden Soc., xxx, 1914), pp. xi–xv, and
Sir F. M. Powicke's discussion of the point in his notice of this work (*Eng. Hist.
Rev.* xxx. 334). See also Sir W. Holdsworth, *History of English Law*, ii (1936), 339.

[3] T. F. T. Plucknett, *A Concise History of the Common Law* (3rd ed. 1940),
pp. 330–2; G. B. Adams, *Council and Courts in Anglo-Norman England* (1926),
pp. 348–52; E. F. Jacob, *Studies in the Period of Baronial Reform and Rebellion*,
pp. 65–70.

[4] Miss H. M. Cam, *Studies in the Hundred Rolls* (in Oxford Studies in Social and
Legal History, ed. Sir P. Vinogradoff, vi, Pt. I), pp. 133–8.

were, however, lawsuits brought before courts of law, where one party as plaintiff prosecuted another as defendant, and the court had powers of jurisdiction enabling it to compel the defendant to appear, and to enforce its award. The Mise of Amiens was, on the other hand, a voluntary act of arbitration in a political dispute where the two parties, to avoid civil strife, agreed to submit to the award of a presumedly impartial referee, who had no power to hear a complaint from either side, to compel appearance of either party, or to enforce whatever award he might make. What relevance had the form of legal procedure to the act of arbitration?

The answer to this question lies in the political sense of the English baronage and in the spirit of the age. Simon and his friends sought, as long as the faintest glimmer of hope remained, to solve their political problem without recourse to anarchy, and they naturally thought of politics in terms of law. The subject-matter of the conflict was political, and not properly susceptible of solution by law, quite apart from the absence of any competent jurisdiction. Nevertheless, alike to Louis IX and to the rival parties, there seemed to be no reason to distinguish between the principles of political arbitration and those of a legal process: they sought naturally to decide their political disputes by the familiar processes and known principles of law. Our own present search for legal principles and processes to govern the settlement of international disputes should enable us to sympathize with them, even though they did not admit that the differences between the determined champions of the idea of a limited monarchy and the no less resolute supporters of traditionally unlimited monarchy could not be resolved to the satisfaction of both sides by any tribunal or upon any legal principles known to that, or any other age.

Granted the conception of deciding arbitration by a process borrowed from legal procedure, and on the principles of known law, what was the form of procedure to be used? In the absence of formal jurisdiction, nothing resembling procedure by writ was possible, but the *petitio libelli* offered a solution. It was appropriate to the circumstances, it was familiar to Louis and his advisers, and to the English, king and barons alike, the *querelae* which the reformers themselves had developed so rapidly and widely in 1258 and 1259[1] had doubtless made this form of approach seem reasonable and warranted. We do not know what procedure had been adopted in the various earlier arbitrations,

[1] Treharne, *The Baronial Plan of Reform*, pp. 111–15, 137–9, 147–55.

save in the case of that of March 1261 between the king and the council. The record of that arbitration shows that the *petitio libelli* had been followed, at least in that Henry had stated his *demande* in the form of a list of specific *gravamina* set out in writing, and the council had replied in the form of a *libellus responsionis*, making its *exceptiones* point by point in answer to the king's complaints.[1] Exactly the same form had been followed when Henry had arraigned Simon de Montfort before a committee of six bishops in the summer of 1260.[2] In neither case does the surviving record include a formal demand for damages, penalties and relief, like that which concludes the document now under discussion; but this may be because the surviving records of the affairs of 1260 and 1261 were documents drawn up, during the hearings, to set each point of the king's *gravamina* against the corresponding point of the *responsio* of the earl or of the council, omitting the final *petitio* for damages and relief as irrelevant to the examination of the issues of fact.

Thus there was adequate precedent in 1264 for treating Louis' arbitration as a matter suitable for procedure by *petitio libelli*, and our document shows that this was in fact done. While we can easily see why all concerned adopted this procedure, we can also see that certain fatal consequences were likely to ensue. The *petitio libelli* was a form of legal procedure: it made Henry a plaintiff, his barons defendants, and Louis a judge. Since neither customary nor positive law could be applied, Louis could judge only by natural law. To Louis, with his religious conception and idealization of kingship, natural law could give only one answer in a dispute between a lawfully annointed king, demanding undiminished restoration of the royal power and rights which he held immediately of God, to whom alone he was responsible, and his barons seeking to control that divine right through a committee of subjects according to a constitution devised by men. The very form of the procedure encouraged him to give this answer. Political arbitration normally means compromise, a halfway settlement giving something and denying something to each side, so that both, however reluctantly, may reasonably be expected to acquiesce. In a lawsuit the decision is quite different. The judge pronounces which of two parties has the better right; a half-way decision is rarely appropriate, and the judge normally and properly pronounces wholly for one side or the other. In

[1] Ibid., pp. 253-6; E. F. Jacob, in *Eng. Hist. Rev.* xli. 559-71.
[2] Treharne, op. cit., pp. 238-41.

this way the form of procedure adopted for Louis' arbitration helped to prejudge the issue and to ensure an award which the barons could never accept.

Henry pressed his advantage to the full. In England his military and political position seemed overwhelmingly strong:[1] at Amiens, with his fellow monarch, brother-in-law and friend, as judge, with papal exhortations urging his cause in the name of Christian religion and justice, and with the swarm of embittered refugees poisoning the air with their unscrupulous propaganda, Henry must have felt that the game was in his hands.[2] One final stroke, delivered with the immense moral authority of King Louis, must surely end for ever the pretensions of the terrible earl, and obliterate all but the bare memory of the hated Provisions. In the contrast between the thin querulous tone of the *gravamina* of 1261 and the determined ring of his claims at Amiens we can feel the measure of Henry's exultant expectation. Then he had strung together a long list of charges great and small, significant and trivial, without ever challenging the principle of the Provisions: he complained against the working, not the existence of the Provisional Government.[3] How different his *demande* of January 1264! Sure of his strength and in full cry for final victory, he takes his stand squarely on the principle of untrammelled monarchy, appealing to tradition and to Louis' sense of the fitness of things, and demands the utter abrogation of the Provisions and of all that had followed from them. *Il fallait en finir!*

Seven brief paragraphs state his case. Under the Provisions the justiciar is elected by the councillors appointed by the barons, whereas Henry and his ancestors have been wont to appoint and to remove justiciars at will as need arose: no justiciar was needed when the king was in his kingdom, and the justiciar was burdensome and expensive to the king. The chancellor and the treasurer, who ought especially to safeguard royal rights, and whose positions enabled them easily to subvert those rights at will for the profit of others, were similarly appointed by the councillors, whereas the king ought and had always been wont to choose for these offices men whom he himself knew to be most apt and trustworthy. The sheriffs, who should specially safeguard his rights in their shires, and with whose connivance the magnates and others could encroach upon and usurp those rights, were also

---

[1] Treharne, p. 335; Powicke, op. cit., pp. 443–50.
[2] Treharne, op. cit., pp. 337–9; Powicke, op. cit., pp. 453–5.
[3] Treharne, op. cit., pp. 253–6.

appointed by the councillors, though Henry and his ancestors had been accustomed to appoint and dismiss them at will. The lesser justices, who in their judgements should do right to the king and to all others of his realm, are appointed by the councillors, whereas the king had always created and removed them at pleasure. The royal castles are committed by the councillors, whereas the king himself, for his own security and that of his realm, had always committed them to men whom he thought best for himself and the realm. The stewards and other ministers of his household, too, were appointed by the councillors, though the king had always chosen and dismissed them at pleasure. The king's powers of overseeing and correcting the actions of justiciar, chancellor, treasurer and the other officers of the realm the barons have committed to the councillors, thus withdrawing them from the king. Lastly, his castles and those of Edward and of his other faithful followers in Wales and elsewhere have been seized and demolished; his goods, and those of his queen, his children, and others faithful to his cause, both clerks and laymen, have been plundered, and countless enormities inflicted on ecclesiastical persons and goods; all of which, with many other evils, spring from that enforced oath that all who opposed the barons' constitutions were to be held as mortal enemies by all in the realm. Other grievances would be stated at the proper time and place, concerning which, together with the matters rehearsed, contention and discord had arisen between the king and his barons. Such were the *gravamina*: they did not specifically propose the dissolution of the council, but they denounced every shred of administrative authority which it exercised, and they attributed all the evils and disorders of recent years to the universal oath of support for its decrees.

Henry went on from this indictment to demand that the barons be condemned to pay him £300,000 sterling for damage done to his interests, and 200,000 marks for the injury to his dignity, for he would not willingly have suffered such wrong for that sum. Finally, he asks that Louis shall declare null and void the provisions, ordinances, statutes and obligations on which his adversaries rely, with all that has followed from them, and that he shall declare the king of England no longer bound to their observance, but restored to that state in which he was before the Provisions were made, especially as these restraints have all been annulled and voided by papal authority, and all who observe them excommunicated, and especially also because Henry cannot grant or permit these things against his coronation oath, nor can his subjects take upon themselves or intermeddle with these matters in defiance of their oath of fealty sworn to him.

There was nothing more that Henry could ask. He based his case on the rejection of the Provisions in principle, expressly refraining at this stage from any complaint against the working of the system or the action of the barons in detail. It would be interesting indeed to see the *exceptiones* of the baronial *libellus responsionis*. Thomas Cantilupe, the principal expert baronial proctor at Amiens, had studied civil law at Orleans and canon law at Paris, and had lectured at Oxford on the latter branch[1]: he was thus familiar with the procedure adopted and doubtless argued the baronial case with expert skill. The *petitio* suggests that the barons relied on Henry's oath of 1258, repeated in 1263, that he accepted the Provisions and all subsequent reforms arising therefrom: this had been their reply in 1261 and Simon's defence in 1260, and it was almost certainly Thomas's case at Amiens.

Whatever the defence, Louis clearly followed the procedure indicated by Henry's statement, for his award when published, not only accepted Henry's case as presented, but echoed the arguments and even the very words of the royal *demande*. Louis states that he had heard the arguments put forward by both sides, 'et etiam defensionibus ac rationibus partium plenius intellectis', a form of words suggesting the libellary procedure, with its *responsiones*, *exceptiones*, and *replicationes*. The award, like the *petitio*, uses the form 'provisiones, ordinationes, statuta et obligationes . . . et quicquid ex eis vel occasione eorum subsecutum est'.[2] Louis' sentence, 'attendentes . . . juri et honori regio plurimum fuisse detractum, regni turbationem, ecclesiarum depressionem et depraedationem, et aliis personis ipsius regni, ecclesiasticis et saecularibus . . . gravissima dispendia provenisse' echoes Henry's argument and paraphrases his words. In annulling the Provisions he says, *cassamus et irritamus*, where Henry had asked for them 'cassari et irritari seu cassa et irrita nunciari'. The special reason fortifying his own decision he announces almost in Henry's own words, 'maxime cum appareat summum pontificem eas per litteras suas cassas et irritas nunciasse'.[3] As Henry asked, he expressly invalidated the universal oath binding

[1] *Dict. Nat. Biog.*: Cantilupe, Thomas de.
[2] *Petitio*: 'et quicquid ex eis et ob eas . . . .'
[3] *Petitio*: 'maxime cum premissa sunt auctoritate apostolica cassata et irritata'.

all men to hold as mortal enemies all opponents of the Provisions. Recapitulating Henry's officers in the titles and order in which the *petitio* had named them, in Henry's own words he declares that he may appoint, dismiss and remove them *pro suae libito voluntatis*. These and other verbal quotations and substantial parallels suggest strongly that, in drafting Louis' award, his clerks had Henry's *petitio* before them. The wheel had once more come full circle: if legal process and solemn arbitration availed anything, Henry was restored to untrammelled power on terms devised by himself.

The Mise was a dead letter from the day of its publication. The quarrel was too deep for law, which is valid only when men agree on fundamentals. For Simon, acceptance of the Mise meant the ruin of his ideals and work: thereafter he could only depart, dishonoured and forsworn, into exile. So long as England held enough men of like mind to himself to put the matter to the ultimate test of battle, he could not abandon them or desert his trust. And for many in England, the Provisions of Oxford, despite all that Henry alleged against them, had stood for something very big—for an ideal of justice and good government, of reform in law and in administration, not to be forsaken at the bidding of a foreign king, however saintly, or however upheld by papal exhortation. The publication of the Mise in England was met with widespread hostility. Simon and his friends rejected it outright. Gloucester, Giffard and several other waverers came over to Simon's side, and some who had been with Henry in December withdrew their support from his forces. We can never know precisely the effect of the Mise on the party divisions, but whereas in December Simon's cause had seemed almost hopeless, when the fighting began in April the barons and knights under Simon's banners outnumbered those who fought for the king.[1] Never had any arbitration more surely precipitated the very struggle it was designed to avoid.

The question remains whether Simon and his friends perjured themselves in rejecting the Mise, or whether Louis' award exceeded the powers entrusted to him and so justified the repudiation. On the evidence of the letters of compromise of 13 and 16 December, no reservations or limitations had been placed

[1] I hope to establish this in a forthcoming work on 'The Barons' War, 1264–68', by a full list of those who fought or worked on either side, so far as the surviving materials allow the party groupings to be discerned. Meanwhile, the point is sufficiently confirmed by reference to C. H. Pearson's remarkable lists in W. H. Blaauw, *The Barons' War* (2nd ed. 1871), pp. 364–80.

upon the scope of Louis' arbitration either implicitly or explicitly. Both sides had bound themselves in advance to accept Louis' award in all matters, 'great and small', touching the Provisions and all that had arisen from them. The wording of these letters, standing alone, would render Simon guilty of perjury. Yet it is a curious fact that both at the time and subsequently, the royalists, whether in proclamations or in chronicles, never used the charge of perjury in this matter either to weaken Simon's cause or to blacken his memory. The Dunstaple chronicler and a few others went so far as to accuse Louis of exceeding his powers.[1] In face of the letters of compromise, it is difficult to maintain this charge on any formal grounds, and yet the silence of the royalist writers on the point must count for something. Even Wykes, who misses no chance of imputing dishonour to the Montforts, says only that Louis acted 'with less wisdom and foresight than were necessary'.[2] The political truth of his comment needs no underlining.

To see the matter as it appeared to contemporaries, we must put the Mise back into its context. It was not merely the outcome of the letters of compromise of December; its source lies far back through the truce of October and the abortive Boulogne conference of September to Simon's undertaking in July. At the height of his triumph he had offered to submit to impartial arbitration 'whatever in the Provisions might seem harmful to the King or to the realm'. It was an offer of arbitration on the details of the Provisions while keeping the principles intact; a reasonable and even generous offer in the circumstances. Subsequent events, and especially the history of Simon's attempts after Lewes to obtain French arbitration within limits reserving the principles of the Provisions, show that this was Simon's declared policy and the means by which he hoped to legalize his position. It is impossible in the light of his behaviour either before or after the Mise to suppose that he contemplated any award which destroyed all that he had hitherto sought to save. In submitting to voluntary arbitration, he was relying on an impartial judgement upon the detailed arrangements by which Henry should be restrained and controlled by his barons; he was not risking the principles of the Provisions themselves. Arbitration meant com-

[1] 'Annales Prioratus de Dunstaplia' (*Ann. Mon.* iii, ed. H. R. Luard, Rolls Series, 1866), p. 226; *Gervase of Canterbury (Continuator)*, ed. W. Stubbs (Rolls Series, 1880), ii. 232.
[2] 'Chronicon Thomae Wykes' (*Ann. Mon.* iv, 1869), p. 139.

promise within the framework of the Provisions, not an examination of their essential validity.[1]   Admittedly, none of these reservations appears in the letters of compromise, but probably, in the uncertain position of mid-December, the wording of these letters was deliberately left undefined, since neither side would have tolerated a definition acceptable to the other.[2]   As late as 20 December, Henry, in a proclamation reassuring his people, had felt it politic to deny that he intended to repudiate the Provisions and had declared that he was and would always be ready to observe them.[3]   He did not dare to disclose in England the case he was preparing for Amiens.

Agreements which have diametrically opposite meanings to mutually hostile parties are familiar in politics at all times.   The least that we can say is that, in the absence of any royalist outcry of perjury, and in view of the comments of the chroniclers, Englishmen of the time, both royalist and rebel, felt that Louis had gone too far and that the Mise of Amiens commanded no acceptance of its ill-advised terms.

APPENDIX

The gravamina *of Henry III against his Barons, and his* petitio *to the king of France for the Mise of Amiens (December 1263).*

Paris, Arch. Nat., J. 654, no. 29 *bis*.
   Per ista subscripta grauatur Rex Anglie.[a]

   1. Quod scilicet (per) constitutiones Baronum fit capitalis Justiciarius per eleccionem consiliorum [*sic*] quos posuerunt Barones in consilio Regis, cum tamen dominus Rex et eius antecessores capitalem Justiciarium cum opus esset pro sua voluntate preficere consueuerunt (et amouere), et etiam cum opus non sit huiusmodi Justiciario dum rex egerit in regno.   Et preterea onus eiusdem Justiciarii graue est et sumptuosum eidem domino Regi.

   2. Item quod etiam Cancellarius et Thesaurarius qui jura Regis specialiter conseruare debent, et qui Iura ipsius leuiter subuertere pro voluntate seu commodo aliorum possunt, ponuntur per eosdem consiliarios, cum Rex ipse eos eligere et ponere debeat et semper consueuerit quatenus eos sibi meliores nouisset et fideliores.   Quod etiam vicecomites qui iura Regis

---

[a] The paragraphs are not numbered in the manuscript.   Interlineations in the manuscript are printed in brackets.

[1] See Powicke, op. cit., pp. 451, 453; Treharne, op. cit., pp. 340–2.
[2] Powicke, op. cit., p. 453, n. 1.
[3] Treharne, op. cit., pp. 334–5.

externis in suis Balliuiis specialiter conseruare debent et quorum permissione[b] poterunt magnates et alii iura Regis subtrahere et sibi ipsis appropriare, ponuntur per eosdem consiliarios, cum tamen Rex ipse et sui antecessores eos semper ponere et deponere consueuerunt pro voluntate sua.

3. Item quod etiam Justiciarii minores qui ius reddere debent tam Regi quam aliis omnibus de regno in iudiciis suis, ponuntur per eosdem consiliarios cum dominus Rex eos ponere consueuerit (et amouere) ad (voluntatem)[c] suam.

4. Item quod castra Regis committuntur per eosdem consiliarios cum tamen Rex ipse, pro sua et regni sui securitate, ea libere committere consueuit[d] quibus sibi et regno suo viderit expediri.

5. Item quod senescallus et alii ministri hospicii Regis ponuntur per eosdem (consiliarios) cum tamen Rex eos[d] semper posuerit et deposuerit pro sue libito voluntatis.

6. Item quod potestatem Regis quam habet et habere debet cognoscendi et corrigendi facta Justiciarii, Cancellarii et Thesaurarii atque aliorum ministrorum regni, commiserunt eisdem (consiliariis) et eam per consequens Regi subtraxerunt.

7. Item per hoc quod castra sua et domini Edwardi filii sui et aliorum fidelium suorum in partibus Wallie et alibi capta fuerunt et diruta et depredaciones facte bonorum suorum, Regine et liberorum suorum ac aliorum tam clericorum quam laicorum Regi adherencium et in personis et rebus ecclesiasticis enormia quamplurima perpetrata, quibus omnibus et aliis malis infinitis occasionem dedit (statutum) Juramenti[e] illius[f] (scilicet) quod omnes qui eorum constitucionibus obuiarent ab omnibus de regno inimici capitales haberentur.

8. Sunt etiam alia grauamina suo loco et tempore proponenda, de quibus et supradictis sunt et fuerunt contentiones et discordia inter dominum Regem et Barones suos.

g

[h]Vnde petit Rex Anglie predictos Barones ad interesse suum quod estimat[i] (CCC) milia[j] libr' sterling. sibi condempnari, et pro iniuriis sibi factis per eosdem in ducentis milibus marc', pro quibus dictas iniurias sustinuisse noluisset.

Petit eciam predictas prouisiones quibus nititur pars aduersa, ordinaciones, statuta et obligaciones, et quicquid ex eis et ob eas secutum est per vestrum arbitrium et ordinacionem, domine Rex Francie, cassari et irritari seu cassa et irrita nunciari, et pronunciari ipsum Regem Anglie non teneri

---

[b] 'm' erased at end of *permissione*.
[c] *voluntatem* interlineated above *eleccionem* erased.
[d] The rest of this sentence is written over an erasure.
[e] Altered in manuscript from *juramentum*.
[f] Altered in manuscript from *illud*.
[g] A line erased.
[h] The *petitio* is written in another hand.
[i] *centum* deleted.
[j] Altered in manuscript from *milibus*.

ad obseruacionem ipsorum et dictum Regem per vestrum arbitrium (et) ordinacionem in eum statum reduci in quo erat dictus Rex ante statuta, obligaciones et ordinaciones predictas, maxime cum premissa sunt auctoritate apostolica cassata et irritata et singuli excommunicati qui premissa obseruant. Hec dicit saluo jure suo in aliis.

(*dorse*).

Maxime cum[k] dominus[l] Rex contra iuramentum suum quod prestitit in coronacione sua premissa facere vel concedere non potuit, nec[m] sui subditi vice versa contra iuramentum fidelitatis quod eidem domino Regi preffecerunt predicta in se suscipere vel de illis intromittere.

[k] *Rex in coronacione sua iurauerit* deleted.
[l] *in sua coronacione* deleted.
[m] *vi* deleted.

R. F. TREHARNE

THE TOURNAMENT IN THE THIRTEENTH CENTURY

I

IT is impossible to be chivalrous without a horse. Homeric combats were fought on foot, and though the Anglo-Saxon rode to battle he dismounted to fight. The mounted warrior was a Norman innovation, made possible by the Frankish invention of the stirrup.[1] At first the war-horse was light and fleet, but with the development of armour for man and beast, a heavier type was used. This development had profound social effects. The gradual encasement of the feudal knight in heavy plate armour made war expensive, involving a considerable outlay of capital, and when this came about, as it did during the thirteenth century, the day of the knight-errant was over. One result was that knights became fewer, another that tournaments became less dangerous and more picturesque. It was difficult in the later Middle Ages to unhorse a man who rode in a high cowboy saddle with boot-like stirrups, difficult even to hit him fair and square on his rounded and polished armour as he trotted ponderously past on the other side of the lists that separated the combatants. Such, however, was fifteenth-century tilting, in which the riders approached each other along opposite sides of a barrier (the 'lists' were originally a stretched cloth), and, riding left arm to left arm, could only poke at each other at an angle. There was nothing like a head-on collision in this later medieval jousting, and the risk of serious injury was minimized.

We must dismiss such pictures from our mind in thinking of the tournament from A.D. 1150 to 1350. It is for the most part not a matter of individual jousting, but a mass-meeting of side against side, resulting in a mêlée which differed little from real war. The tournament during those two centuries had an importance that no modern sport can parallel. It was training for war, and recognized as such, and so a tournament, like military manœuvres, could have a deep political significance.[2]

[1] R. W. Moore, in a letter to *The Times* newspaper of 20 Mar. 1947, pointed out that the stirrup and horse-armour were used in Alexander the Great's army, but forgotten by the Romans, and possibly—on R. G. Collingwood's theory—reintroduced in the last years of Roman Britain by Arthur as a Roman cavalry leader. In this paper, however, I deal only with a later period.

[2] The 'training-for-war' aspect of tournaments is illustrated by two facts:

The habit of holding tournaments helped to develop in the baronage that political cohesion which is more obvious in the thirteenth century than at any other time. They could be, and especially in the first half of the thirteenth century they were, a focus for baronial discontent. For until the Lord Edward came to manhood it was the barons and not the king who organized and enjoyed these assemblies, they were social gatherings of earls, barons, and knights, without any royal summons, in the absence of the king and often against his express command. They therefore emphasized an existing cleavage between the barons and a court composed of the friends and foreign relatives of Henry III, and so justified a policy of restriction, which it is proposed to trace.

The thirteenth century is the best period of the tournament. Its popularity was at its height; there was some degree of organization; but the sting had not yet been taken out of the fighting. The 'lists' were still in the distant future, when the war-game, fought by teams, was replaced by the futile but highly stylized and ornamental pageants of the fifteenth century.

The origin of tournaments is obscure,[1] but when they were legalized in England in 1194, the institution and its rules, such as they were, came from France,[2] and it will be well to see what stage its development had reached before dealing with its history in this country.[3]

(1) John XXII in reallowing the tournament in 1316 (*infra*, p. 243) explains that it was difficult to get sufficient numbers of the right kind of person (i.e. trained soldiers) for the Crusade without tournaments, and (2) for tournaments the baronial household is put upon a war footing. The retinue is doubled, as in the earl of Hereford's contract of 11 Edw. II with Sir Peter de Ouvedale, Kt., to serve him for life, as given by Dugdale (*Baronage*, i. 183–4, 'ex ipso Autog. penes Thomam Comitem Elginiae, 1659'), 'and to receive Livery of Robe . . . as his other Batchelours; as also bouche of Court; with Hay and Oats for four Horses; and Wages for four Groomes in time of peace, whenever he should come to Court by his command. But *in times of War and for Tourney*, Hay and Oats for eight Horses, and Wages for eight Groomes; with satisfaction for such Horses and Arms as he should lose in War in his service.'

[1] A sixteenth-century Bavarian herald, George Rüxner, is responsible for the mythical tournament in 936 at Magdeburg. The anonymous Chron. Turonense under 1066 credits Godfrey de Preuilly, who died in that year, with inventing tournaments. They undoubtedly developed rapidly in France and Flanders in the twelfth century and spread with equal rapidity to other lands. A tournament is reported at Würzburg in 1127 by Otto of Freising, and one at Antioch in 1156. Three years after the Würzburg meeting came the first papal prohibition. On the whole subject of tournaments on the Continent see A. Schultz, *Das höfische Leben zur Zeit der Minnesinger*, ii (Leipzig, 1889), 106–50.

[2] Ralph of Dis, about A.D. 1200, in a phrase often attributed to Matthew Paris, calls them *Conflictus Gallici* (see *Chron. Maj*. ii. 309, 650 where Mat. Par. is copying from Dis, whose phrase he glosses). Cf. *Hist. Angl., s.a.* 1179.

[3] On the French tournament the basic work must always be *L'Estoire de*

In the twelfth-century French tournament there was great variety. Sometimes everything was arranged beforehand, even the price of the ransoms. At times the vanquished lost all they possessed. The sport, which ended at nightfall, consisted of a general mêlée between perhaps thirty or forty a side. The combatants could roam all over the countryside, and had refuges where they could arm and disarm. Occasionally infantry as well as knights were employed. The knights fought with lances until they were unhorsed and then continued the battle on foot with swords if they could. In his second tournament William Marshal unseated one of his opponents with his lance, but before he could complete his capture, William was attacked by five others. Count Philip of Flanders used to hold aloof from the fighting until the combatants were thoroughly exhausted. He would then charge into the fray at the head of his men and take many prisoners at small risk. A favourite and apparently successful device of William Marshal and the young Henry was to pretend that they were taking no part in the tournament and then charge in when everybody was occupied. They fought till dusk and then gathered together to award the prize and raise money to ransom their friends. Some of these were international tournaments, but most were local affairs for local men. An energetic knight-errant had the opportunity of attending about one a fortnight. The Marshal and a friend did a systematic tour lasting two years, which proved a great commercial success. In ten months the partners captured 103 knights. At one gathering at a castle in the Seine valley they reached the field before their opponents. There they found the countess of Joigni and her ladies—the only French tournament of the period at which the presence of ladies is mentioned—who had come to watch the sport. To while away the time the knights and ladies danced to a song sung by William. When he had finished a young minstrel who had just been made a herald sang a song of his own composition, of which the refrain was 'Marshal, give me a good horse'. Just at that moment the first knight of the opposing party arrived on the field. William left the dancers,

Guillaume le Maréchal, ed. P. Meyer (Paris, 1901), vol. iii. This Anglo-Norman poem describes in great detail the life of a landless knight-errant, the fourth son of a small baron, who won renown by his physical prowess and became eventually earl of Pembroke and regent of England. William Marshal had already made his reputation as a fighter when he was appointed to take the young Prince Henry, son of Henry II, to France to complete his military education there in a series of tournaments. Lines 2471–5094 are devoted to the marshal's tournaments, and see the Introduction, pp. xxxv ff.

mounted his charger, dismounted the newcomer, and gave his horse to the minstrel. There is more than a touch in this of the romantic, courtly, and chivalrous ideals which were then finding their way northwards from the south. William is the perfect example of the landless knight becoming a great man through his physical prowess. He was still a knight-errant, with no landed estate, when he quarrelled with Henry II and sought another lord. The count of Flanders and the duke of Burgundy each offered him £500 a year for his services. In the romances men like this would also rescue beautiful ladies from wicked men or savage dragons, but though William won 500 tournaments and was 15 years a knight-errant, there is no evidence that he was affected by the softer side of chivalry.

The attitude of the Papacy was uncompromising from 1130 to 1316. Innocent II had condemned tournaments in the well-known ninth canon of the Council of Clermont in 1130, regarding 'detestabiles illas nundinas vel ferias quas vulgo torneamenta vocant', and the prohibition was frequently repeated[1] until John XXII, in a much less well-known edict, decided to allow tournaments, at the instigation of Philip IV of France. This decision was incorporated in the *Extravagantes* under the heading *De torneamentis*.[2] The period during which the Papacy set its face against tournaments was of course the age in which they cost men's lives. The mortally wounded at a tournament was not to be refused the viaticum, but he might not have ecclesiastical burial—in theory.

Thus papal prohibitions on this subject were neither new nor strange when Celestine III in 1192 ordered the bishops and Richard I to forbid tournaments owing to the wretched state of the Holy Land.[3] Richard I's writ licensing tournaments in England came almost on top of this, in the form of a writ to the archbishop of Canterbury. It seems to have been merely a temporary measure, a licence *pro hac vice*,[4] for meetings at five places in open country. These places were conveniently placed to cover the needs of the whole of England—one south of Thames

---

[1] Hefele-Leclercq, *Histoire des Conciles*, v. i. 688, 729; ii. 1103, for 1139, 1148, 1179, and cf. *Ann. Burt.* 271 for Council of Lyons (1245).

[2] Friedberg, ii, col. 1215 (*Quia in futurorum*, 16 Kal. Oct. 1316).

[3] *Foedera*, i. 56.

[4] The writ was issued on 22 Aug. 1194 from Bresle near Beauvais (Norgate, *Richard the Lion Heart*, p. 299). It is printed in R. Diceto, II. lxxx, lxxxi from a Lambeth manuscript, but the *Foedera* text (i. 65) from B.M. Cotton MS. Claud. C. iv. f. 233 is slightly the better of the two.

(near Salisbury), two for the Midlands (one between Warwick and Kenilworth; the other at Brackley), one in East Anglia (at Stamford in Suffolk not far from Thetford and Bury, *not* Stamford in Lincolnshire); and one for the north (Blyth, in Nottinghamshire—the most popular of them all). The later history of the tournament largely revolves round these places, but instead of being *between* Warwick and Kenilworth they will be *at* Warwick or Kenilworth.

The occasion of this ordinance is not obvious unless William of Newburgh is right, that Richard I was impressed with the greater efficiency of the French knights.[1] It seems much more likely that there had been an outbreak of tourneying after the Civil War of 1193, just as there was after the Barons' War in 1267, and that Richard I's ordinance is, therefore, parallel to the ordinance which in this paper is attributed to 1267. This 'licensing-system' of 1194 imposed heavy but graded entrance fees—20 marks for an earl, 10 marks for a baron, 4 marks for a landed knight, 2 marks for a landless knight. It established a rudimentary court of control, comprised of William, earl of Salisbury, with Clare and Warenne, and laid down that two clerks and two knights were to take the oath from earls and barons that they would keep the peace and pay their fees in advance.[2] We do not know whether this system worked for long, or at all, but if it did, a meeting of thirty a side would bring in say 200 marks. Richard's ordinance is never directly referred to in later documents concerning tournaments.[3] Other clauses of this ordinance are obscure,[4] and neither they nor the comments of Howden or William of Newburgh tell us anything of the way tournaments were fought in England in 1194.

Tournaments had existed in some form in Henry II's reign, possibly also under Stephen,[5] but at the time that they were

---

[1] *Infra*, n. 5.
[2] Cf. Howden, iii. 268.
[3] The story in *Mem. St. Edmunds* (Rolls Series), ii. 260 seems to be given as a comment on it.
[4] They are forbidden to take food or forfeits on the road (*Curia Regis Rolls*, viii. 50, 158 provide illustrative material). This is clear enough, but the document continues 'Et si aliquis torneator foedera alii debeat . . .' he is to give him a truce in the tournament as well as in coming and going. This I cannot interpret.
[5] William of Newburgh, ii. 422 (*s.a.* 1194): 'Sane hujusmodi, nullo interveniente odio, sed pro solo exercitio atque ostentatione virium concertatio militaris nunquam in Anglia fuisse noscitur nisi in diebus regis Stephani, cum per ejus indecentem mollitiem nullus esset publice vigor discipline.' He also tells us that under Henry II tournaments had been prohibited, so that those who wanted this kind of sport had to go abroad for it. Richard I, he continues, seeing that the French knights were

licensed they were still sufficiently foreign to require explanation by the chroniclers—by Ralph of Dis as *Conflictus Gallici*, by Coggeshall as contests *more Francorum*. From this time onwards they might be expected to come into fuller view. But Richard I's reign provides hardly more than the vivid story from Bury St. Edmunds,[1] and a fine from Roger Mortimer for tourneying without a licence,[2] while the records of the eminently unchivalrous King John are bare of tournaments between 1200[3] and 1215.

The downfall of John marks an era in the history of the tournament in England. From 1215 to the rise of the Lord Edward the tournament is primarily a baronial affair. The king is interested only to delay or prohibit meetings, which are often thinly veiled pretexts for baronial conspiracy or war, as may be seen in 1215 after Runnymede,[4] in 1219 at Brackley,[5] in 1228 at Chepstow,[6] each being associated with the initiation or furtherance of factional interests. At the very time that this is becoming obvious the mock tournament with blunted weapons and light armour is found. The first known occurrence of this, in 1216, saw also the death of Geoffrey de Mandeville, earl of Essex.[7]

Henry III's policy towards tournaments was to prohibit each one as it was arranged. This was also the policy of his ministers and that of the Church. Only very rarely as in 1232, 1245, or 1256 were tournaments arranged with his express sanction. But they were very frequently held against express royal prohibitions,

more skilful than the English, introduced the tournament into England. On the whole passage see Paul Meyer's comments (III. xxxv–xliv). The greater efficiency of the French knights was generally admitted (ibid., ii and note 1, cf. Wendover, on the last fight of Richard Marshal in Ireland).

[1] *Supra*, p. 244, n. 3.

[2] *Rot. Cur. Reg.* i. 87.

[3] In 1200 the chamberlain of Tankerville and Hugh de Ferrers were in mercy for attending a tournament, which may have been in Normandy. (*Rot. de Obl. et Fin., 1199–1216*, ed. Hardy, p. 75.) In the same year Ralph Fitz-Stephen rendered account of 100 marks 'pro libertate habenda de periurio de torniamento' (*Pipe Roll 2 Jo.*, p. 81).

[4] Kate Norgate, *John Lackland*, p. 239 for details. The prize, presented by a lady, was to be a bear. In the same year Prince Louis of France and his knights held tournaments among themselves in the south of England, under threat of excommunication (*Ann. Dunst.*, p. 51); cf. Walt. Cov. (*s.a.* 1217), ii. 40: 'adhuc enim quasdam discordiarum reliquias in frequentibus exercuere torneamentis.'

[5] *Infra*, p. 246.   [6] *Infra*, p. 247.

[7] Mat. Par. *Chron. Maj.* ii. 650: 'Ad equestrem ludum (quod hastiludium vel torneamentum dicitur) cum hastis tantum et lineis armaturis.' This is Wendover's description with Paris's gloss in brackets. That the weapons would be blunted seems a legitimate deduction from the fact that the armour was light. Note the absence of swords.

about 100 of which were enrolled between 1216 and 1274. Up to 1233 these writs are usually addressed to 'the Earls, barons, and knights who' &c. In and after 1234 they are sent to one or two heads of nearby religious houses, who are to go in person and prevent the tournament. But though they are issued with a full knowledge of what is planned to happen, they are so timed that there is no possibility of cancelling the meeting. Often they can only have arrived the day before the tournament, sometimes on the very day itself, but this was not always so. The writs assume not merely that the tournament has been arranged, but that the competitors are coming and will be found at the place named in the writ. The writs cannot always have been expected to have much effect: some are genuine, others purely formal. It was generally understood that those who disregarded the prohibition were in the king's mercy, but except on the few occasions specified below we do not know what action was taken upon them. Their chief value is as a witness to the magnitude of the problem and for the light they throw on government policy.

During the legation of Pandulf,[1] and afterwards until the death of Stephen Langton in 1228, the full co-operation of the Church was secured in the suppression of tournaments. All who attended the count of Aumale's tournament at Brackley in November 1219 were excommunicated, for he had refused to surrender Rockingham and Sauvey Castles and the combatants were regarded as his supporters.[2] Thus was nipped in the bud—secular measures were also taken—the first of Aumale's rather half-hearted risings. In August 1220 Pandulf issued a general prohibition,[3] to bring English policy into line with that of the Papacy, but presumably with little effect, as the series of prohibitions had to continue.[4] One in 1223 is of interest because though ineffectual it was

---

[1] Two prohibitions were issued in 1217 and 1218 on account of the insecure state of the realm (*Pat. Rolls*, pp. 116, 174). Pandulf threatened to excommunicate those who had arranged to tourney at Northampton in July 1219 (*Pat. Rolls*, p. 194: 26 June for 1 July; cf. p. 198: 23 July for Staines on 24 July).

[2] *Royal Letters*, i. 56; *Curia Regis Rolls*, i. 158. Cf. the important letter in *Rot. Lit. Claus.* i. 434 b; *Pat. Rolls*, p. 257.

[3] *Foedera*, i. 162; cf. *Ann. Dunst.*, p. 60. The king's messenger Adam le Rutier was paid 22d. for taking Pandulf's prohibition to the bishop of Lincoln (*Rot. Lit. Claus.* i. 440). He also received 6d. on 11 Oct. 1222 for having taken a prohibition to Thetford (ibid. i. 512).

[4] *Pat. Rolls*, p. 295: 4 July for Brackley 6 July 1221; p. 358: for all Ireland, 1222; p. 388: 21 Oct. for Brackley 23 Oct. 1223; p. 405: 1 Mar. for Blyth 6 Mar. 1223. A letter to the archbishop of Dublin as justiciar of Ireland, 23 Feb. 1223, orders him to take into the king's hand the lands of anyone who presumes to tourney in Ireland (*Rot. Lit. Claus.* i. 536).

followed up by strong measures. After the tournament at Blyth on 6 March, fifteen barons, headed by Richard de Munfichet, had their lands taken into the king's hands.[1] We do not know if they were fined in addition, but they lost their lands for a month and in some cases ten weeks.[2] This perhaps reflects Hubert de Burgh's increased confidence after the publication of the papal bull declaring Henry III of age. It is noteworthy that Pandulf's threats were not implemented, and this is the more remarkable as Stephen Langton's famous *sententia* of excommunication against all disturbers of the peace had only recently been issued at the Council of Oxford. Its wide implications seem to have been forgotten until 1228.

In 1225 government policy began to weaken, becoming more and more embarrassed and self-contradictory, as Hubert de Burgh lost ground, until 1232. A series of ingenious but often naïve excuses gave substance to irresolute prohibitions of tourneying *ad presens*,[3] with the threat of excommunication included almost as an afterthought. It is clear from them that not only earls and barons but even knights[4] were arranging tournaments at will, and it will appear from what follows that supporters of the Government were allowed to do this. Many of the writs were no doubt directed against their opponents.

The political motive appears strongly in 1227. After the abortive rising of the eight earls at Stamford, the disappointed barons went off with the earl marshal to his castle of Chepstow, nominally for a tournament, but they were faced with a writ that had a surprisingly Edwardian ring. The meeting was forbidden on the ground that although not within the county, Chepstow was

---

[1] The writs were sent to the sheriffs of nine counties, tested at Nottingham. The prohibition had been dated 1 Mar. for 6 Mar. (*supra*, p. 246, n. 4). The king was at Sawley in Derbyshire on 2 Mar. and Shrewsbury on 9 Mar., thereafter coming south again (*Pat. Rolls, 1216–1225*, p. 391). The writs were sent out as follows: Richard de Muntfichet; Bucks. for Robert de Ferrers; Leics. for William de Ferrers; Gloucs., Warw., and Leics. for Hugh de Gurnay; Oxford and Warwick for Thomas de Arderne; Kent for Ralph de Normanville and Thomas his brother; Derby for Matthew de Havereseche; Notts. for William de Bucles, Lomi de Malvoers, Geoffrey Giun, Simon de Hedon; Devon for Henry le Tyes; Leics. for Henry de Tibetot, Robert de Campania; Derby for Peter de Coudray. The names from the distant counties of Kent, Essex, Bucks., Devon, are of more interest than the rest, as presumably only serious competitors would travel so far for a tournament (other things being equal).

[2] *Rot. Lit. Claus.* i. 539 *b*, 545, 547. Orders dated between 4 Apr. and 17 May for the lands to be repledged.

[3] This occurs in five writs (1225–8) in *Pat. Rolls*, i. 506; ii. 71, 118, 125, 202.

[4] *Pat. Rolls*, p. 71, 18 Nov. 1225 for Worcester, the only tournament mentioned during the Gascon expedition.

nevertheless within the kingdom.[1] This is Hubert de Burgh claiming to override Marcher privilege on grounds of public policy. The publication on 27 February 1228 of Gregory IX's bull prohibiting tournaments in England because they promoted *conventiculas, conjurationes, colligationes, et conspirationes*,[2] was obviously inspired by a request from England arising out of these events. An attempt was at once made to act upon this, when in May 1228 the sheriffs of Norfolk-Suffolk and Essex were ordered to seize the horses and equipment of persons coming to Suffolk (no doubt to Stamford) to seek chance encounters (*casus fortuitos*) and thus to tourney in secret.[3] The bishops of Norwich and Ely were to excommunicate them. This is one of the few occasions on which the records allude to actual knights-errant and almost the last on which there is any question of excommunication. Almost in the next breath the Government admitted that tournaments were being arranged by their supporters and in their presence. A letter of 26 July 1228 did not prohibit but prorogued a meeting arranged for Stamford on 9 September to Northampton in October.[4] But it was suddenly found inappropriate because of an urgent expedition against the Welsh,[5] so Stephen Langton's convenient *sententia* was invoked and meanwhile the king would ask the pope if they could lawfully tourney in England in future. Nothing, however, was done for four years. Then, as part perhaps of Hubert de Burgh's last bid to save himself, tournaments were granted in 1232 at Dunstable, Stamford, Brackley, and Blyth.[6] But no sooner had royal policy reached the point of grudgingly allowing tournaments at the accustomed places than the earl of Chester's illness was made an excuse for cancelling a meeting at Northampton in May.[7] In July a Round Table, not a tournament, was forbidden at an unspecified place on account of a Welsh expedition.[8] This is the first Round Table in the Public Records, as opposed to literary sources, and it antedates the famous occasion

---

[1] 8 Sept. 1227 (two writs).   [2] *Foedera*, i. 189.

[3] *Close Rolls, 1227–1231*, p. 106.   [4] Ibid., p. 113.

[5] *Pat. Rolls*, ii. 202–3.

[6] For further prohibition in 1228–30 see *Pat. Rolls*, ii. 230, 316, 321. Late in 1231 Hubert de Burgh wrote from Brittany that on his return to England the king would provide by his common council where the barons might tourney (ibid., p. 452). This promise was repeated in Jan. (ibid., pp. 457, 459) and Feb. 1232 (ibid., p. 463). The actual grant seems to survive only by allusion in *Ann. Dunst.*, 130.

[7] *Pat. Rolls*, ii. 473.

[8] Ibid., p. 492 = *Foedera*, i. 205: 'Rex omnibus fidelibus suis qui conventuri sunt ad rotundam tabulam salutem . . . nullatenus ad predictam rotundam tabulam convenientes turneare presumatis.'

usually taken by writers on the tournament to be the earliest by just twenty years. The writ, which does not distinguish it from any other kind of tournament, also contains a general prohibition against 'tournaments in our realm in future'. Not a whit embarrassed by this statement, the Government six weeks later prorogued a tournament from Blyth to Northampton, because Chester, Cornwall, the Marshal, Ferrers, and Lacy could not attend by reason of the Welsh war.[1]

During the period of Henry III's personal rule, his treatment of tournaments displays just that degree of whim and caprice that we have come to expect of him. He was never afraid of contradicting himself, but there is a thread of purpose running through all his doings. Although the lay power is increasingly invoked and excommunication ceases to be mentioned, the actual delivery of the writs from 1234 to 1274 is invariably entrusted to the nearest abbots or priors. It will be noted that the years 1270-4 show an administrative unity not broken by the death of Henry III in 1272.

In this period the tournament is not simply legalized war, nor is it purely decorative. In spite of the Church, it had a real function to perform—training for war. But, as these years showed beyond doubt, neither Henry III nor Richard of Cornwall his brother had any military aptitude, and the problem therefore became one of controlling meetings which might in their absence merely serve to foment discontent among barons already too remote from the court. The history of the tournament during the reign of Henry III illustrates as well as any isolated series of events can do the problem of the medieval king who was not a warrior.

When the problem became acute it was, as Henry's letters of 1230-2 have shown, properly regarded as a matter which concerned the *universitas*. It was dealt with by Provision (and not simply by *ad hoc* prohibitions) in 1233. Just as in 1232 the *Commune Consilium* had given permission, so in 1233 at Oxford, just before the outbreak of Richard Marshal's rebellion, it prohibited them. The Provision had little success, for in 1234 alone nine prohibitions were necessary. Even the squires were *behourding*.[2]

---

[1] *Pat. Rolls*, pp. 498, 499; *Close Rolls*, p. 131.

[2] The Latin *burdicium* or *buhurdicium* = O.Fr. *behourd, behours*, from *bourdis*, a lance. Wace (*c.* 1150) uses the phrase *les uns alerent bohorder*. The *buhurdicium* of 1234 was between the esquires of two barons, William de Clifford and H. fitz Matthew. Geoffrey le Baker (ed. E. M. Thompson, p. 75) tells us that Edward III licensed a *bourdis* at Northampton in 1341. This he distinguishes from the *solempne*

The fact that tournaments are a fit subject for Provisions is to be borne in mind in considering the origin of the Statute of 1292 concerning them.

During the years when Henry III was settling into the saddle, and particularly before and after Richard Marshal's rebellion, there were many prohibitions—forty-two between 1232 and 1241, even though from 1239 to 1240 the Chancery rolls are missing. The ensuing eighteen years (1242–59) yield only thirty-one. This is a remarkable drop. But those eighteen years are also the 'peak years' for tournaments as described by Matthew Paris, who apart from the Dunstable annalist is almost alone amongst the chronicles in his interest in tournaments. There may have been some relaxation of policy, but apart from 1232, only in 1248, 1256, and 1267 are tournaments known to have been held with government approval. The drop in prohibitions is not, then, indicative of any change in policy, but they were less necessary because it was more closely recognized that unlicensed tournaments were a breach of the peace, and consequently it was the duty of the sheriff to forbid them, as laid down in the series of Watch and Ward ordinances.[1]

Until after the Marshal's rebellion the same delaying tactics were used, i.e. prohibitions *pro hac vice* with a promise that tourneying would soon be permitted.[2] But in September 1234, after Richard Marshal's death, there was another attempt at enforcement,[3] and in the 'forties policy for a while grew much stronger, reaching its peak in 1245 with the establishment of a

---

hastiludium held at Dunstable the same year. The instance given below (p. 262) of squires 'behourding' shows that the *bourdis* does not refer merely to tilting between individuals, but is, like *hastiludium*, applied to tourneying between teams. The *behourd* was probably a less highly organized form of tourneying.

[1] The Watch and Ward ordinances of 1233, 1242, 1253, and 1255 expressly forbade tournaments, but (as Edward I was at home) they are not mentioned in the Statute of Winchester.

[2] An Oxford Provision of July 1233—the last on which the threat of excommunication was used—was to last until November (*C.P.R.*, p. 20; *Close Rolls*, p. 318). Three years later it was to run from May till Michaelmas 'so that the King may take counsel' (*C.P.R.*, p. 148), and the year after that from June till Michaelmas 'and the King will then take counsel how they can best tourney' (ibid., p. 188).

[3] In Sept. 1234 mandates were addressed to seven earls and ten barons concerning tournaments arranged for Northampton and Cambridge (both on 15 Sept.) warning them not to go there or to any other tournament without the king's licence (*C.P.R.*, pp. 67–8; cf. *Close Rolls*, p. 159 of 28 Dec. 1234 for Chepstow which was the occasion for a writ to all sheriffs). The Cambridge writs gave thirteen days' notice but two barons (John de Burgh and Gerard de Furnivall) made fine for tourneying there and William de Say had his lands restored because he did not take part (*Close Rolls*, pp. 210, 212: Nov. 1235).

committee of three earls—the king's brother, the steward, and the marshal, to deal with those who tourneyed against the prohibitions.[1]

We hear nothing further of these sanctions until in May 1261 a number of well-known knights met at Pontefract and tourneyed against the prohibition. Their lands were taken into the king's hands, but within a few days they were pardoned.[2] The barons themselves when they came into power in June 1258, instead of seizure of lands, proposed as a penalty service with the king for one year at the combatants' own cost. This, which was equivalent at least to a fine of £50, was announced when a tournament was arranged at Brackley in October.[3]

In prohibiting tournaments the Government uses a variety of words and phrases, but if different kinds of tournament are meant, it is impossible to distinguish between them. All are forbidden indiscriminately. But despite this the tournament can be seen to be changing as the century wears on. The rout of Rochester in 1251 was almost the last, perhaps, of its kind, for the develop-

[1] When Henry was in Gascony in June 1243 it was necessary to forbid a tournament at York, or anywhere else while the king was out of the realm, upon pain of being visited so grievously that they should feel it all the days of their life and their heirs after them (*C.P.R. 1266–1272*, App., p. 722). The cancellation of a tournament at Blyth in 1255 on the ground that the Lord Edward was in grave danger in Gascony was accompanied by no such threats, as it had originally been sanctioned by the king (*C.P.R. 1247–1258*, p. 432, addressed to Gloucester and forty other magnates). Economic sanctions were tried in 1241 by prohibiting the sale of food to tourneyors at Blyth (*C.P.R.*, p. 266) and in 1244 by taking the names not only of tourneyors but of those whose inns were taken for tourneying at Landwaz by York (*C.P.R.*, p. 424). In 1245 eleven barons had their lands seized and had to 'put themselves on the ordinance' of the three earls (*Close Rolls, 1242–1247*, pp. 361–3); the names were James of Audeley, Ralph Camoys, Peter de Montfort, Warin Fitz-Gerald, William Blund, Simon Pecché, Robert de Wendeval, Urianus (? Brian) de S. Petro, Roger de Paveli, Baldwin de Rossay, and William de Beauchamp of Eton.

[2] *Close Rolls, 1261*, pp. 475, 477. Robert de Ros of Belvoir and Alexander de Kirketon his knight were pardoned. Others present, whose fate we do not know, were: Peter de Ros, William and Alexander his brother, Hugh de Eure, William de Percy, Robert Fitz-Brian, Robert Pikot, William Fitz-Ralph, Walter Gwen, William de Goldingham, Marmaduke de Tweng, Richard de Tweng, William de Rosel', John de Sethill, William de Steyngrave, Walter de Grindale, Hugh de Nevile. Cf. *C.P.R.*, p. 150 (26 Apr. 1261) for the writ of prohibition. In 1262 all sheriffs south of Trent and some of the Marchers were warned not to permit tourneying while the king was abroad and in particular not to hold a tournament arranged for Salisbury in September. The barons named were: John Gifford, Hamo le Strange, Peter de Montfort, junior, James de Audley, Roger de Clifford, and Roger Leyburn. (*Close Rolls*, 25 Aug. 1262, p. 133; *C.P.R. 1258–1266*, p. 227; cf. Treharne, *The Baronial Plan of Reform*, p. 286.)

[3] *C.P.R. 1247–1258*, p. 665; cf. ibid. *1258–1266*, p. 5 (15 Nov. 1258 for Dunstable prohibited because Llewelyn proposed to break the truce).

ment of heavy cavalry broke the old habit of dashing wildly all over the country-side and imposed a new *tempo* upon all the proceedings. It led to the tournament's becoming more static, and a softening of manners led to its becoming more of a social occasion. Not, however, till Edward I came home from crusade did it become a fully fledged social institution, officially recognized and formally attended by the court. This was due to Edward himself and it was he who gave it its rudimentary organization.

The little that we know about how tournaments were conducted in England in Edward's youth comes entirely from the *Chronica Majora* of Matthew Paris.[1] Seven meetings are described by Matthew, held between 1237 and 1257, at Newbury, Hertford, Brackley, Rochester, Walden, and Blyth.[2] The first five are of the old-fashioned kind—of north against south, or Englishmen against aliens. These were always liable to develop into real battles, and show no advance at all on the kind of meeting attended eighty years before by William Marshal and the Young Henry. They were important, nevertheless, in a number of ways. The 'venture' at Hertford in June 1241[3] had important political repercussions in that the leading baron of England was killed. Gilbert, earl of Pembroke, was the third of the four ill-fated sons of the great marshal. He had been intended for the Church and, though not properly trained for war, had proposed to lead the English at a recently forbidden meeting at Northampton. On this occasion he was riding an Italian charger when the bridle broke and he was thrown and killed. He received the viaticum and a Christian burial, but Henry III refused to give his younger brother his inheritance on the ground that the tournament had been pro-

---

[1] The Dunstable annalist mentions a large number of tournaments after 1232, because Dunstable was a great place for tournaments, but he tells us nothing about them.

[2] At Blyth in 1237 much good work recently done by the Legate Otho was nearly undone (Mat. Par. iii. 404). At Northampton a meeting *quasi hostile* was proposed by Peter of Savoy, John Biset, and Gilbert Basset, for Englishmen against aliens. They were at first encouraged but finally forbidden by Henry III, who sent John the Templar, his almoner, to stop them (iv. 88). The writ dated 13 Apr. 1241 is in *C.P.R.*, p. 249.

[3] Mat. Par. iv. 135, 157. The prohibition has not been found. There is some temptation to confine the phrase 'to seek adventures' to knight-errants hunting singly or in couples, but Matthew Paris twice ironically plays with the baronial description of their meeting as a 'venture'. It is quite clear from this and from five writs of prohibition that it usually refers to the chances sought and found in general combat. Cf. 'Neither under the name of a tournament nor of an adventure' (1233), 'not to meet in quest of adventures, or go armed in the king's land' (1236), 'to seek adventures' (1237, 1262), *C.P.R. 1232–1237*, pp. 20, 62, 148, 188; ibid., *1258–1266*, p. 227. Cf. *casus fortuitos* in 1228, *supra*, p. 248.

hibited. On the marshal's death the meeting degenerated into a mêlée, in which Robert de Saye, one of his retinue, was killed, and many other knights and squires were seriously wounded. The marshal's retinue dispersed intent on booty and what had been a mass-defence became a rout. This double calamity of 1234 and 1241 was, of course, a vital factor in the relations of king and baronage. It may also have had a sobering effect on the promoters of illegal tournaments, thus helping to account for the sharp contrast between the periods before and after this fatal day.

Paris's third assembly at Newbury on 4 March 1248 is remarkable because it was held with the king's permission and marked the début of William de Valence, who, though later famous as a jouster, was on this occasion thoroughly 'beaten up' (*egregie baculatus*).[1] The fourth, at Brackley, was won by Valence and the aliens with the help of the fickle Richard de Clare, 'to his great dishonour'. They ill-used many knights 'who like to be called bachelors',[2] but in the next, near Rochester (8 December 1251), the English had their revenge and the aliens on their flight to Rochester, after being routed on the field, were well hammered by the squires with sticks and clubs.[3] The growing number of squires and their unruly behaviour was a problem which had arisen since the marshal's day, and was in part due to the development of heavy armour. It became the subject of a special ordinance or statute at a later date.

The last two meetings recorded by Matthew Paris were different in kind from these mêlées, though no less disastrous in their results. The first was the famous Round Table at Walden in 1252. It is the only description of a thirteenth-century Round Table which tells us how the combatants fought. Matthew Paris is careful to distinguish it from the *torneamentum quasi hostile* which was fought with sharpened weapons. In the jousting at the Round Table only rebated weapons were used. This is very

---

[1] 'Tiro novellus, ut titulos militie sibi famosus adquireret' (Mat. Par., *Chron. Maj.* v. 17–18). Next year, still described as a beginner, he urged the barons to hold a tournament at Northampton on 19 Feb. This won him much popularity, but the snowy weather made it impossible to tourney (ibid., pp. 54–5). Valence was also well hammered with Richard de Clare in France in 1253 (ibid. v. 367, when the pair are described as *juvenes calamistrati et delicati*). Under 1247 are mentioned challenges by Guy de Lusignan and Richard de Clare, both of which were forbidden by the king (ibid. iv. 633, 649).

[2] 'Ubi multi de militibus universitatis regni qui se volunt bachelarios appellari sunt contriti.' William de Odingesseles was one of the ill-treated bachelors (Mat. Par. v. 83).

[3] Mat. Par., *Chron. Maj.* v. 265; *Hist. Angl.* iii.

important, but it is wrong to deduce, as most writers have done, that the Round Table was itself a form of tournament. It was, as we shall see, a social occasion accompanied by various games, of which jousting with blunted weapons was one. Only two other Round Tables are recorded in Henry III's reign (1252, 1257) and only three in the reign of his son (1279, 1281, 1284), and these tell us nothing of the way in which the combatants fought. The mock-tournament had been known in England from at least 1216, and the jousting that took place at the Round Table was thus a special form of it. The writ of 1232 forbidding the first Round Table known to have been arranged implies some degree of familiarity and sympathy with the Arthurian legends in the English baronage. Its occurrence is a welcome link between the Walden meeting of 1252 and the Round Table of King Arthur's knights, which had been introduced to the English literary world about 1150. As an element of the Arthurian romances the Round Table is not found in Geoffrey of Monmouth, but is alluded to by Wace as if his readers would be familiar with what he meant. In origin it may have derived from the circular form of table used in Celtic (especially Irish) mead-halls to avoid disputes over precedence, and a feast so arranged would be a suitable prelude, as the Annals of Worcester seems to suggest, to a form of tournament in which all accredited knights might take part without regard for rank.[1] Matthew Paris in striving after clarity as to the manner of fighting has misled modern writers into thinking that it was itself properly a *form of tournament*. But it was obviously and necessarily more.[2] As the Worcester Annals show, it *sat* at

[1] The literary aspect of this matter is clearly put in the *Cambridge History of English Literature*, i. 265, by Mr. W. Lewis Jones. It is Wace who says that the Round Table was made by Arthur to settle all disputes about precedence among his knights (ll. 9,994–10,007). Layamon's *Brut* (ll. 22,910 seqq.) adds to Wace a description of the actual making and properties of the table, made for Arthur by a man from overseas whom he met in Cornwall: 'a board, wondrous fair, at which sixteen hundred men and more might sit' (op. cit., pp. 234, 235). This Round Table material is England's contribution to the Arthurian legend prior to the fourteenth century. The prevalence of the term by 1232 (if it was prevalent) may be due to the diffusion of Layamon's *Brut* as much as any other written source. I regret that *Geoffrey of Monmouth and the later Latin Chroniclers, 1300–1500* (Berkeley, Univ. of California Press, 1946), by Laura Keeler, was not available when I wrote this paper, and that I did not see the valuable article on 'The Influence of Romances on Tournaments of the Middle Ages' in *Speculum*, 1945, by Ruth H. Cline, until too late to make use of it.

[2] See for the festivities and games associated with the Round Table by c. 1303 the prefatory matter to R. Mannyng of Brunne's *Handlying Sinne*, ed. J. Furnivall for the Roxburghe Club, 1862. Furnivall, unfortunately, did not reprint this valuable material in his edition for the E.E.T.S. (1903).

Warwick in 1257.[1] Nothing else is said. A Round Table is essentially a session of knights and the tourneying is incidental. Hence it is unnecessary to postulate a 'mimetic element' in order to drag in the Arthurian cult.[2] The Arthurian part came before the jousting began. That the Arthurian cult flourished at Richard Cœur de Lion's court is evident from his gift (on 6 March 1191) of King Arthur's sword Caliburnus to Tancred of Sicily.[3] But this fact, convincing as it is, stands almost alone. The Arthurian background for tournaments in the reign of Henry III cannot yet be fully displayed, because like his father (though for very different reasons) the king himself was no more interested in Arthur than he was in tournaments. The cult was kept alive by the baronage and flourished again, as we shall see, under Edward I.

I put it tentatively and merely as an expression of opinion that at the Round Table individual jousting prevailed to the exclusion of the general mêlée. It seems to me that it would be quite inappropriate to describe a match of north against south, or England against the aliens as a Round Table, or indeed any meeting at which a leader with his troop held the field against all comers. Such a meeting could hardly be logically accommodated at less than two Round Tables. To Matthew Paris it is a *ludus*, and the jousting began after two days' great festivity.[4] The gathering was specifically prohibited by writ of 6 September 1252 as a Round Table, but the writ continued as if that were by no means the end of the matter, 'ad torneandum vel ad justas faciendas', which is the first occurrence of jousting in these writs.[5] The jousting, which may have been individual and not an incident in a mêlée, was fatal, but though someone was later charged with murder, we hear of no excommunications, fines, taking of lands, or imprisonment. What happened was that Arnold de Muntinni,[6] a knight of the royal household, was caught between helmet and breastplate—he lacked a collar—by Roger de Leyburne, later a

---

[1] *Ann. Wigorn.*, p. 445.

[2] E. K. Chambers, *Arthur of Britain* (1927), p. 127: 'It may be presumed that it had a mimetic element, with champions fighting as Arthur's knights.' The mimetic element in the thirteenth century occurs only at Boston Fair, but this was in no way Arthurian. It was not uncommon in the fourteenth century (see J. Tait, *Chronicle of John of Reading*, p. 41, and Index, s.v. tournaments), but not as part of an Arthurian tradition.

[3] Benedict of Peterborough, *Gesta Regum* (Rolls Series), ii. 159.

[4] See further J. Furnivall, loc. cit.

[5] *Close Rolls*, p. 251; cf. *C.P.R. 1247–1258*, p. 157 for Warwick (15 Apr. 1252).

[6] On the family see W. O. Hassall in the *Genealogist*, x, no. 15 (1946), pp. 21–3.

friend of Edward I, whose lance was exceedingly sharp.[1] Roger was suspect because his lance should have been blunted and he had had his leg broken by the same adversary in a previous tournament.[2] This very important passage, a primary authority for the nature of the Round Table, is the only mention of jousting in Matthew Paris. It coincides with the first jousts mentioned in the chancery rolls, and so gives some ground for the belief that jousting was only now becoming popular in England. This, too, would obviously be facilitated by the development of armour. It is to be noted that Arnold was not refused burial in Walden Abbey, and that the ecclesiastical agents sent to prohibit the tournament should have reminded the participants that they incurred the danger of excommunication.

The last meeting described by Matthew Paris marked Edward I's début at the age of seventeen. It was held at Blyth on 4 June 1256 *secundum legem et disciplinam militarem*, and was presumably sanctioned by the king. The young Edward fought in cloth-armour with light arms *ut militaribus legibus informaretur*. But the sport grew rougher and many were laid low, beaten, and trampled on. William Longespée, Roger Bigod, the Earl Marshal, Roger de Quinci, earl of Winchester, and two judges, Alan de Watsand and John of Lexington, never fully recovered. 'All of these', says Matthew, 'had distinguished themselves at the tournament at Blie and exerted themselves beyond their strength to such a degree that their muscles were torn and they never afterwards recovered their health.'[3]

[1] It is a tribute to the tremendous influence of the St. Albans school of history that Roger's name should be persistently corrupted as Lemburne in most modern accounts of this tournament, following Matthew Paris. *Ann. Theok.*, p. 150, gives the correct form, though it misplaces the tournament at Blyth. A grant of the king's peace and protection and mandate to all not to molest Roger de Leyburne on account of the death of Arnulf de Munteny, lately killed by accident at a Round Table, is dated 20 Oct. 1252 in *C.P.R.*, p. 154 (for 'Ernulf' cf. *Close Rolls, 1248*, p. 119, which shows him as a king's knight).

[2] Mat. Par. v. 318–19: 'De quodam hastiludio quod milites tabulam rotundam vocant. . . .' Although a *hastiludium* it was not the kind commonly called a tournament 'sed in illo ludo qui mensa rotunda dicitur'. For the first two days the English knights 'strenue nimis et delectabiliter . . . jocabantur', and then started jousting. Jousting is a general word used, under 1141, by William of Malmesbury: 'tentavere primo regii proludium pugnae facere, quod justam vocant.' It is derived from Latin *juxtare* and is in all the Romance languages. A general prohibition of Nov.–Dec. 1255 specified three kinds of jousting, in a mandate to all sheriffs, in these words: '. . . torneare vel ad papilionem, carrum, aut pavonem vel alio modo justeare seu arma militaria portare in predicto regno vel potestate regis presumant sine licencia regis speciali.' Tilting at a flag or peacock may be understood as a variant of the ancient sport of the quintain, which was tilting at a mannikin, generally a Saracen. See Cripps Day, *The Tournament* (1918), p. 19.   [3] Mat. Par. v. 557, 609.

II

I turn now to the *Statuta Armorum* in the *Statutes of the Realm*. The texts are corrupt. My thesis is that the old printed version, which gives it as a Petition, not yet a Statute, is the best, and that this is fundamentally a document of 1267. The Statute is undated, and each text has been tampered with in an attempt to bring it up to date. But the Parliament Roll, which all writers have ignored, shows that there was such a Statute at the beginning of 1292. When the probability that this Statute was based upon a Provision of 1267 has been established we may resume the story of the tournament.

The behaviour of squires at tournaments was the subject of regulation by one of the so-called 'Statutes of Uncertain Date', which has been very generally accepted as a document of about 1292. By this 'Statute' a committee of four or five earls was set up to administer the rules of the tourney. Mr. Cripps Day has summed up what appears to be the general view of the matter by saying: 'historians have fixed the date not later than 1295, because among other reasons, the Earl of Gloucester died in that year; William de Valence, Earl of Pembroke, died in 1296, and was the last of that name; Edmund Crouchback, Earl of Lancaster, died in 1296; all of whom are mentioned in the Statute'.[1] A reference to the Rolls of Parliament would have shown that a statute about tournaments was made in the session that opened on 5 January 1292,[2] but a reference to the texts as printed shows that the three known sources give three varying committees, no one of which as it stands will fit 1292, or any other year at all.

This necessitates a closer scrutiny of the texts. There are three available in print, and it is clear from these that we have to deal with two quite distinct questions. What the *Statutes of the Realm* calls the 'Printed Copies' (primarily Ruffhead's *Statutes at Large* and Cay) depend upon an unknown manuscript. But for us it is the most important, for what it prints is an Anglo-Norman

---

[1] Op. cit., p. 38; cf. Oswald Barron in *Encycl. Britannica*, 11th ed., s.v. Tournaments, and A. R. Wagner, *Heralds and Heraldry* (Oxford, 1939), p. 26.

[2] The petition begins: 'To our lord the king pray and request the earls and barons and the chivalry of England, that they are agreed that he might wish to command and confirm a statute of arms that . . .' The answer in parliament refers to a petition containing a Provision made by the chivalry of England (*milites arma in regno isto exercentes*) and confirmed by the seals of the earls and barons who presented it to the king for confirmation as a statute. This the king granted clause by clause (without, unfortunately, reciting them) asking the sheriffs, constables of castles, and wardens of prisons to receive those committed to them by the wardens (*custodes*) of the Provision named within it. The Provision is referred to as *de Valettis ad tornamenta venientibus et adire volentibus*.

petition asking that a Statute be made.   The other two sources are
MS. Rawl. C. 820 (*olim* MS. Rawl. 277), which professes to be
in the form of a Statute ('a la requeste . . . ordine est e par
nostre Seignur le Rey comaunde'), and *Liber Horn* which says
that the contents were provided and confirmed by Statute.   This
difference in the preamble of the three sources sets Ruffhead's
petition in a class apart from the other two, which profess to be,
and perhaps are Statutes.

Returning now to the committee as set up by these texts, the
alternatives are:

1. 'Mouns. Edward fiz le Roy, e Mouns. Emoun frere le Roy,
   le Counte de Gloucestre e du [*sic*] Counte de Nichole.'
   Liber Horn.
2. 'Sire Edward fiz le Rey E., Sire Eumond frere le Rey, e
   Sire Willeme de Valence, e sire Gilbert de Clare, e le Cunte
   de Nichole.' *Rawl. MS.*
3. 'Sire Edward nostre Seignur fitz le Roy e Sire Edmund son
   frere e Sire Willame de Valence e Sire Gilbert de Clare e
   le Counte de Nichole.' Ruffhead's *Statutes at Large*, x,
   p. 26 f. 'ex perantiquo MS.'

The first two are from the *Statutes of the Realm*, pp. 230–1, which
also states that (John) Cay (*Statutes at Large*, pub. 1758) printed
Sir Edmund son frere from 'some antient MS. not specified'.   I
have had no opportunity of using Cay.   His manuscript may have
been the same as Ruffhead's.

These lists associate an *Edward fiz le Roy* with an Edmund
who is variously described as *frere le Roy* and *son frere*.   The
Edward in question cannot be Edward II, who was only eight
years old in 1292.   He was therefore only twelve in 1296 and after
that Clare and Valence were dead.   Moreover, he was only
knighted in 1306, for he was no soldier.   The Edward meant is,
therefore, Edward I.   But this 'Statute' is actually in the form of
an Anglo-Norman petition of the earls, barons, and chivalry of
England to the king to confirm what they have done in making
rules for tournaments, with penalties for breaches of the rules,
and a committee to enforce them.   It is plain that a committee
containing the king would not petition the king, and that the
reference is therefore to Edward (I) before he became king,
Edmund (of Lancaster) his brother, with the young earls Gilbert
de Clare and William de Valence.   This is very nearly what
Ruffhead's Petition would have us read, and this gives a very

different picture. Instead of three men well advanced in years and one child fresh from the nursery, we have four young men in the prime of life. The date will therefore be some time before 1272 when Edward became king, and before August 1270 if we remember that he then went on crusade. It will clearly be after Edmund came of age in 1266, and no one of this committee is likely to have thought of tourneying till the settlement of 1267. Now it was precisely in that year after the harvest that the great flood of tournaments mentioned by the chronicler Wykes began, and it was specifically under the auspices of Edward and Edmund, according to the same writer, that the revival took place. Of tourneys, he says, which had previously been hindered by royal prohibitions, more were held in 1267 than for ten years or more, so that once two were held simultaneously, at Brackley and Warwick, within a day's ride of each other.[1] There is a total absence of prohibitions from the autumn of 1267 to August 1270, and it is to this period that the original Provision must be assigned. It is natural then to suppose that it came at the beginning rather than at any other point in the period, and that it is to be associated with the permission to tourney which was tacitly or explicitly given at that time. The Lord Edward had had eleven years' experience of tourneys in France and England as well as much hard fighting and was fully qualified to codify the rules of the sport that he loved above all others.[2] The Provision in its original

[1] After the harvest (in any case after 26 July—fall of Isle of Ely), 'cooperantibus duobus regis Angliae filiis, nec non illustris Romanorum regis primogenito [i.e. Henry of Almain murdered at Viterbo 1271], *edicto publico preconizabantur praeliorum preludia*, que vulgari nuncupatione torneamenta consuevarant appellari.' (Wykes, p. 212.) The phrase *edicto publico preconizare* is normal for 'to herald' or 'proclaim' a tournament, but it is just possible that by this rather inflated alliterative jingle Wykes meant to allude to the Provision of 1267–70. Hardly anything is known about this flood of tournaments. It was perhaps at this time that the Lord Edward asked the convent of Durham to receive the body of Sir John de Vaux, killed in the tournament of 'Treek' (which Mr. Barlow identifies as Thirsk: Surtees Soc., 1945, p. 96).

[2] Edward went to France to tourney in 1260;
    And hauntede torniamens with ful noble route,
    With Gascoine that was his, and gode kni3tes adde,
    As Sir Warin of Bassinbourne, that him about ladde,
    And Sir Hamond the strange, and Sir Gemes of Audele,
    Sir Roger of Clifford and othere (*Robert of Gloucs.*, ed. Hearne, ii. 534).
He appears to have been gloriously defeated: 'Qui cum omnibus suis, in multis locis male tractatus, et multa mala in corpora perpessus, equos et arma, et alia que ibi detulerat, plane perdiderat.' (*Ann. Dunst.*, pp. 216–17.) Under June 1260 a tournament at Dunstable is reported, and it is noted that Edward was wounded while tourneying abroad. Cf. *Gerv. Cant.* ii. 211 (1260): 'In omnibus torneamentis bene se habuit.'

form may therefore be assigned with some confidence to the period of the Statute of Marlborough. It marks the complete reconciliation with Gloucester after his rising on behalf of the Disinherited in the summer of 1267. When Edward came to the throne in 1272 he would be replaced on the committee by his friend Henry de Lacy, whom he made earl of Lincoln in that year. There was no earl of Lincoln between 1258 and 1272, thus leaving our original committee with Edward, Edmund, Gloucester, and Valence. It will be remembered that Valence, like Edward, had worked his passage in the matter of tournaments.

The presence of Lincoln's name in our texts may perhaps be explained in the following way. It is reasonably clear that our committee of four belongs to 1267 or not long after, but it is equally clear that something very similar was presented to Edward I as a Petition and granted by him in 1292. This revival induced scribes who could not obtain a modern text to modify their copy, which, as we have seen, they did not do very skilfully.[1] So the text as we have it is neither that of 1267 nor of 1292, but a modification of the former to bring it up to date. How far it has been modified other than by the corruption or insertion of names and titles we do not know and have no means of telling. But as the only change on the committee is the substitution of the stolid Henry de Lacy for Edward, it is not difficult to believe that the committee found the fundamental rules which applied in their youth to be good enough for their declining years. They may have modified them in some points, but the rules as a whole form a harsh code for a savage age and do not sound as if they were modernized in 1292. The names of the committee are, at any rate, grammatically and logically bound up with the document in which their functions are described.

To understand this Statute we must be clear as to its aim. It is not concerned with the single combat known as jousting in which individuals tilted at one another with spears. Neither tilting, nor the use of the lance, nor the Round Table is mentioned. The Statute is concerned with the old team-game, or mass-tournament, which was popular far into the fourteenth century. This was fought with blunted swords. Spears would have been little use in a mass-tournament after the first impact. With heavy cavalry it was hit or miss; you could not manipulate a spear for

---

[1] For revision of early Statutes to bring them into conformity with a later issue see H. G. Richardson and G. Sayles, 'The Early Statutes', in *Law Quarterly Review* (1934), 541.

more than one shot in one course. The Statute does not admit the tournament *à outrance*, as it was later called, but only *à plaisance*, using arms of courtesy. Perhaps we owe it to this Provision that, though there were no prohibitions in 1267–70 or from 1274 to 1299, that is while Edward I was at home and not too busy with the Scots, few deaths at tournaments are recorded. It is pleasant to think that Edwardian legislation really begins with the Provision concerning squires coming to tournaments in 1267, instead of the customs duties in 1275. Edward never forgot, and it is very typical that it should receive his final blessing in 1292.

The chief problem that the Provision attempts to solve is that of the turbulent squire. At Rochester in 1251, as at the Little Battle of Châlon in 1273 or, an extreme example, Boston Fair in 1288, it was not so much the knights as the squires, footmen, and spectators who got out of hand. Of knights who break the rules it is merely said that they shall lie in jail at the will of the committee and lose their equipment. The squires are the subject of four clauses, and give the Statute its title. There are twelve clauses in all, which may be analysed as follows: (i) no earl, baron, or knight shall have more than three esquires, (ii) each of whom shall wear the device (*chapel des arms*) of the lord whom he serves for the day; (iii) no knight or squire is to carry pointed sword or knife, or stick or club, but only a broad-sword for tourneying; (iv) standard-bearers (*baneours*) are to be armed with defensive armour only—knee-caps, thigh-pieces, and shoulder-pieces of cane; (v) all are to obey the committee (who are here named) and knights who do not are to lie in prison at the will of the committee and lose their equipment; (vi) squires to lose horse and arms and lie three years in jail; (vii) no one is to assist a fallen knight except his own squires—penalty three years in jail; (viii) a cadet is only to be armed with knee-caps and thigh-pieces on pain of losing the horse he is riding for the day and three years in jail; (ix) spectators are not to wear any kind of armour and to be penalized like squires; (x) no groom or footman is to carry pointed sword, pointed knife, club, stick, or stone on pain of lying seven years in jail; (xi) if any great lord holds a feast he is not to admit any squires except those who carve for their lord; (xii)[1] heralds and marshals are to carry no concealed arms save

---

[1] Wagner, pp. 26, 130, follows the *Statutes of the Realm* in reading 'No king of heralds or *minstrels*', but, as shown above, Ruffhead prints the better text and Cay has the same.

their blunted swords and the kings of heralds are to wear their mantles of arms and no more.

In one point of language the correlation of Petition and Answer brings to light the real social problem which lies behind. The Petition speaks of *squiers* which the Answer latinizes as *Valetti*. One might have expected *armigeri* or *scutiferi*, but these words have regard only to the more obvious functions performed by the *valet*, who is essentially a personal attendant of superior status, and looking after equipment may be foreign to his work. Hence, to speak of the king's *valetti* as his 'yeomen' (e.g. of the chamber, the buttery, or the guard) is permissible and technical, but yeoman in the fourteenth century also becomes technical for a small independent farmer and there is no idea of this in the *valetti* of the thirteenth century. It is therefore misleading to use the Public Record Office translation of *valetti* by 'yeomen' at the date of this statute unless we are quite clear that the king's household is in question. We are liable to be misunderstood if we speak of a baron's *valetti* as his 'yeomen' when we really mean his squires or his household clerks, for both *valettus* and 'yeoman' are at this date undifferentiated; either may be a soldier, clerk, layman. It appears then that this Edwardian Statute is using a much wider word than *squiers*, perhaps to cover the behaviour of others mentioned in the Provision who came in the guise of footmen or spectators. But since 1267 the 'squier' had hardened somewhat and slightly raised, perhaps, his status. By 1292, if not before, he was clearly above the 'valet' in the royal household. Consequently the use of 'squier' in the Petition where the Parliament Roll uses 'valet' may be taken as another slight indication that the Petition is appreciably earlier in date.[1]

If we reflect upon the Statute it may seem that the man with more than three squires is really the baron with a band of retainers. The Provision of 1267 is a reply to such behaviour as that of the squires at Rochester in 1251 who hammered the fleeing knights with sticks and clubs. The problem of the turbulent squire was clearly a pressing one for many years. They held their own *behourds*, as at Boston Fair in 1288, when, with one side dressed as monks and the other as canons, the fair was sacked and part of the town burnt. For this the ringleader was hanged, but he would not betray any of his fellows.[2] This was while Edward

---

[1] On this verbal usage see J. H. Johnson in *The English Government at Work*, p. 208, n. 2, and H. Johnstone, ibid., p. 283.

[2] *Flor. Wig. cont.* ii. 240; Hemingb. ii. 17. For the *behourd* see *supra*, p. 249.

was abroad, and, as we shall see, the problem of armed violence was becoming wider than that of tournaments.

From 1267[1] until 10 August 1270 when Edward went on crusade there are no prohibitions, and this may be taken as a clear indication of government policy, somewhat obscurely alluded to by Wykes. The lack of writs and the lack of interest on the part of the monastic chroniclers prevent us from describing this period of efflorescence, and so we pass paradoxically to the period 1270–4 when, since they were again forbidden, they again come to light. Ten days before Edward sailed proclamation was made that none should tourney or 'seek adventures' while he was abroad.[2] The writs to enforce this prohibition show about the usual degree of activity, but at some unusual places—Leicester, Beverley, Kingston (three), as well as Stamford, Chepstow, Nottingham, Blyth (two), and Warwick (three). It is rather more explicitly stated than had been usual that the penalty for tourneying without special licence is loss of lands. It will be noticed that now that tournaments were less mobile it was less necessary to hold them in the open country between two towns. There are in all twelve writs during these four years, plus a general protection for the university of Cambridge that no tournament should be held within five miles of the town.[3]

While tourneying was merely surreptitious at home, reputations were being made abroad. Edward had been an amateur of the tournament for eighteen years and his prestige had been enhanced by a crusade when he was challenged in Burgundy by the count of Châlon. He was now thirty-five and it may have been his last tournament. It is not known if there was any expostulation by Pope Gregory, who next year wrote exhorting Edward not to attend a tournament in France, assuring him that if men were not killed at tournaments one could call them childish games.[4] On being challenged, Edward sent to England for reinforcements proclaiming that he and his crusaders would hold the field

---

[1] For the years before 1267 we have the abortive challenges exchanged between Simon de Montfort's sons and the de Clares in 1265 for tournaments at Dunstable (17 Feb.) and Northampton (20 Apr.). The first was prevented by Simon de Montfort in person and the second fell through because of Gilbert de Clare's withdrawal to Wales. (Rishanger, de Bellis, p. 42; Ann. Dunst., p. 238; cf. C.P.R., p. 479; Wykes, p. 162; Ann. Lond. i. 67.)

[2] The proclamation of 10 Aug. 1270 is alluded to in C.P.R., p. 611. Edward sailed on 20 Aug.

[3] C.P.R. 1266–1272, pp. 446–7 (24 July 1270). The other writs alluded to are indexed in this and the next volume.

[4] Foedera, i. 512 (15 May 1274).

against all comers.[1] The well-known story of the count's failure to observe the conventions, by seizing the infuriated king round the neck at what developed into the Little Battle of Châlon, has only the interest of the old-fashioned mass-attack degenerating into a mêlée, with footmen fighting in earnest, and unarmed bystanders who had come to watch and plunder being slaughtered, with great bloodshed on both sides. It was precisely this that Edward's rules of 1267 were designed to check. The point of technical interest is that the opposing teams attacked one another with swords.[2] There is no mention of lances at all.

With Edward in the saddle the thirty years after 1267 are likely to have been the golden age of the tournament in England, but as neither his Chancery nor the monks had any interest in the matter it is difficult to know much about them, or, unless the committee continued to function, to tell how they were regulated. But it is impossible to doubt that the patronage and presence of the king, no less than the rules with which he was associated, had a moderating influence on later thirteenth-century tournaments, and help to explain the fact that the only recorded calamity is the collapse of the dance-floor at Nefyn. Apart from six tournaments held at Dunstable,[3] only five meetings between 1274 and 1299 were sufficiently famous to have been recorded. Four were in England and one in Wales. At the royal tourney at Windsor Park in 1278, the swords—no spears are mentioned—were made of whalebone. Roger de Trumpington, famous for the brass of 1289 in which he is pictured—the earliest surviving ecclesiastical brass in England—was one of the thirty-eight knights who took part.[4] Next year, at Michaelmas, Edward I was present at a Round Table given by his friend Roger Mortimer at Kenilworth, where a very large crowd of knights and ladies assembled.[5] Edward was particularly interested in Round Tables about this

---

[1] Hemingb. i. 338–40.

[2] Rishanger, *Chronica* (Rolls Series), p. 79; *Flores*, iii. 30, 31. For conflicting modern versions see Tout's *Edward I*, p. 87, and Ramsay, *Dawn of the Constitution*, p. 306.

[3] *Ann. Dunst.*, pp. 280 (1279), 283 (1280), 286 (1281), 354 (1289), 373 (1292), and 376 (1293). The last is assigned to 1293 (Ash Wednesday, 19 Feb.) as a matter of probability because Thomas and Henry of Lancaster who were both there stayed with Edward of Carnarvon on the way home in February of that year (H. Johnstone, *Edw. of Carnarvon*, p. 17, n. 5). Though the Dunstable annalist is assiduous in recording tournaments he does not mention them all. I have noted one at Dunstable in the Clare Receiver's account between Michaelmas 1273 and Michaelmas 1274.

[4] *Archaeologia*, xvii. 297.

[5] Wykes, p. 281; *Ann. Dunst.*, p. 281; *Ann. Wigorn.*, p. 477 (gives 'Warwick').

time, as he had had Arthur's tomb at Glastonbury opened the year before, and his interest was maintained to the end of his life. It is usually assumed that ladies were present at Round Tables, but they are not mentioned by Matthew Paris and this is the first occasion on which we can prove that they were there. Except for the lady who presented a bear in 1215 the ladies at Kenilworth are the first heard of in connexion with English tournaments. Men tourney for love in the *Ancren Riwle* (*c.* 1225) and in the romances, but England was not a great place for courtly love and thirteenth-century romances are few. The most helpful for us is that of *Fulk FitzWarin*. The hero was a real person who lived in the reign of King John, and the romance is thought to have been written in verse about 1258.[1] It shows what contemporaries would have liked to happen, and may be taken as a somewhat idealized picture of an Edwardian tournament. The presence of the ladies is assumed, but there is no special accommodation for them. They ascended a high tower to watch the sport. The men tourneyed for some time and then a joust was proclaimed in which Fulk was three times successful. The heroine, Melette de la Tour Blanche, at that point (seeing, I suppose, that Fulk was likely to win) sent Fulk her glove and asked him to defend it. They are specifically stated to have tourneyed for love (*pur amurs*). We have no actual records of this in thirteenth-century England: it is full-blown courtly love of the Provençal and southern French type. Afterwards the heralds and *diseurs* co-operate with the magnates in awarding the prize. The knights of FitzWarin's party then go off to their tents in the forest and make great joy, but apparently without the ladies.[2]

There is Arthurian influence[3] in *Fulk FitzWarin* but no mention of the Round Table. The next recorded in England was 'sumptuously held' at Warwick in 1281.[4] The third and last at present known to us was held by Edward I in 1284, to celebrate his victory over Llewelyn, at Nefyn on the Carnarvonshire coast.[5]

---

[1] See J. Vising, *Anglo-Norman Language and Literature* (Oxford, 1923), p. 60 f.

[2] *The Romance of Fulk Fitz-Warin* (Rolls Series), pp. 290–3. Jousting is also mentioned (p. 365).

[3] Op. cit., p. 313.

[4] Hemingb. ii. 8.

[5] *Ann. Wav.*, p. 402 ('about 1 August'). It is also mentioned without date in *Peniarth MS. 20* (ed. T. Jones for the Welsh University Press), p. 229. For the midsummer celebration arranged by the king at Nefyn see *Various Chancery Rolls*, p. 293, and cf. *Littere Wallie*, ed. J. G. Edwards (1940), no. 1328. I am indebted to the late Sir John Lloyd for these references. The tournament was about the second week of July. The King's Almoner's roll for 1284 (P.R.O., E. 101. 351/15) has,

The festivities included dancing in an upper chamber which caused the building where it was taking place to collapse, so that everybody fell through the floor.[1] Many English and foreign magnates were there. About the same time the body of Constantine the Great's father and the crown of King Arthur were discovered. Of the presentation of the latter to Edward the Waverley annalist remarks: 'Thus the glory of Wales was transferred to the English.'[2] Edward was evidently prepared to carry the cult of Arthur to the same sort of extremes that his father had accorded to the Confessor's memory. This is the explanation of the Feast of the Swans in 1306 when he knighted his eldest son and vowed on the Swans to reconquer Scotland,[3] for by that time the legend of the Swan Knight in at least one form had become interwoven with the quest of the Grail in the Parsival legend. The story never seems to have achieved wide popularity in England, and we do not know the exact form in which it came to Edward.

The bestowal of the symbolic crown at Nefyn marks for us the end of the story of Edwardian Round Tables. Before he went to Gascony in 1286 Edward forbade armed gatherings of any kind, and this could be held to include tournaments. During the king's absence there were recurrent prohibitions (1288–9) against riding in arms, and though general in their terms these were clearly linked with the private war between Gloucester and Hereford. But the first was issued only a few weeks after the sack of Boston and was sent, not merely to the most important Marcher barons, but to all the sheriffs of England.[4] However, it was thought better

under mid-July, the following entry: 'In pascendis fratribus de Monte Carm' Cestrie celebrantibus missas pro militibus euntibus apud Neuyn ad torniand' per 9 dies 45s.', and similarly to the Friars of the Sack 13s. 6d., the Franciscans 73s. 4d., and the Dominicans £4. 7s. 6d.

[1] Ann. Wigorn., p. 489. For a similar calamity in 1331 see Chronicon G. le Baker, ed. M. Thompson, pp. 48, 230.

[2] Ann. Wav. Peckham wrote a formal letter—he cannot have hoped for any success—to the bishop of Bangor ordering him to forbid 'quoddam militaris exercitii spectaculum apud Neuyn' shortly to be held. But he also wrote in a quite friendly way to Edward the next day advising him to order the Welsh to live in towns, to work hard, and to send their children to England to be educated (3 and 4 July 1284: Registrum, ii. 775–6). The fourth tournament in England was at Croydon on 15 Dec. 1285, where William de Warenne, the earl of Surrey's heir, was killed. He had only just been knighted (see G.E.C., old ed., vol. S–T, p. 328, and D.N.B., s.v. Warenne, p. 824).

[3] He might have founded an Order of the Swans as his grandson nearly founded an Arthurian order, but when it came in 1348 it was established as the Order of the Garter, and this perhaps killed the Round Table in England.

[4] 'Boston Fair' was in July 1288 and the first general proclamation of 22–25 Aug.

to regulate tournaments by statute rather than to prohibit them entirely and in any case they continued to be held. The 'nineties saw no tournaments of importance, so nothing is known of the effect of the Statute of 1292, save that no more routs are reported.

In 1299 we enter the last period of the reign, a time of general prohibitions, no longer addressed to churchmen but sent out to all sheriffs, to forbid all 'tourneying, tilting (*bordeare*), jousting, seeking adventures, or otherwise going with arms without the king's special licence', for the duration of his war with the Scots. The first of these writs was dated 30 December 1299, at Berwick,[1] and they continued until the great drive against Scotland in 1306 when the jails were opened and men made knights at the king's expense. Forfeiture of everything that a man can forfeit was threatened,[2] but with as little effect as anything that Henry III or Pandulf had attempted. Tournaments were arranged at Warwick (November 1300 and 1302),[3] Braintree (1301),[4] and Doncaster.[5] After the fourth warning Giles of Argentine, who had already been imprisoned for contempt and freed to fight the Scots, deserted and made jousts at Byfleet in Surrey with six other barons. They were to have their lands seized, to be imprisoned, and to be had before parliament.[6] But the wicked Giles was irrepressible, and as 'King of the Greenwood' he held the field against all comers at Stepney in 1308.[7]

Even after his threat to destroy them utterly in 1306, Edward

contains the phrases 'quidam magnates et alii de regno nostro preparant se ad arma hiis diebus unde murmur magnum fit in populo nostro', 'si congregaciones seu conventicula armatorum et incidencium . . . posset ex hoc majoris et gravioris dissensionis et turbacionis materia suboriri'. It was sent to the more important Marchers, including Gloucester, but *not* Hereford who was the complainant, at any rate a little later (*Foedera*, i. 685). It was also sent, three days later, to all sheriffs (ibid.) and repeated almost verbatim on 24 May 1289 (*Foedera*, i. 709). On 26 June 1289 Edmund of Cornwall sent a similar writ *Cum Rex . . . pluries* on the complaint of the earl of Hereford that de Clare was building a castle on his land, commanding the latter to suspend operations until the king's arrival (*Foedera*, i. 710). Ten days after he had landed Edward ordered all sheriffs to take the names of those who had been guilty of riding in arms and to report personally at the next parliament at Westminster (*Foedera*, i. 711). Sir James Ramsay seems to associate these events with an outbreak of tourneying during Edward's absence, but there is no evidence of tournaments other than those mentioned in the text.

[1] *Cal. Close Rolls, 1296–1302*, p. 373; cf. pp. 408 (25 Sept. 1300), 588 (16 July 1302).   [2] Ibid., *1302–1307*, p. 433 (6 Apr. 1306).

[3] Ibid., *1296–1302*, pp. 411, 583 (after Trinity).

[4] *Abbrev. Plac.*, p. 243 (Easter 29 Ed. I).

[5] *Cal. Close Rolls, 1296–1302*, p. 411.

[6] Ibid., *1302–1307*, p. 66. The others were: Henry de Leyburn, Robert de Monte Alto, Robert de Tony, William de Creye, John Joce.

[7] *Ann. Lond.* i. 157; *Ann. Paulin.* i. 267 (28 May).

had to admit that 'certain of his subjects make and purpose to make tournaments and to proclaim other deeds of arms',[1] and so it continued to the very end, the last writ being directed against a tournament in June 1307 at Colchester.[2] But even these fulminations were not to be taken, if one was a king's man, *au pied de la lettre*. On 26 February 1307 it was ordained at Lanercost that Gaveston should be banished and that he must be ready to cross the sea at Dover *immediately after three weeks from the next tournament*. A very human touch, for Gaveston excelled at tournaments.[3]

N. DENHOLM-YOUNG

[1] *Cal. Close Rolls, 1302–1307*, p. 459 (24 Sept. 1306); cf. p. 210 (June 1304). A man was imprisoned in 1306 for going abroad to tourney (*Cal. Fine Rolls*, p. 544). The charter to Cambridge (*supra*, p. 263) was renewed on 7 Nov. 1305 and ten persons, half of them barons, sent to prison for tourneying there in spite of it. They were: Thomas Pecché, Roger 'Tamory', Nicholas Bath, Robert Houell, Philip Coleville, Warin de Bassingburn, John de Exning, Walter de Orewell, John de Hunton, and Henry Chaumberleys de Bek (*Foedera*, i. 976, 977). Oxford received similar protection on 12 Nov. 1305 and 20 Jan. 1306 (ibid. i. 977).

[2] *Cal. Close Rolls, 1302–1307*, pp. 535–6.

[3] Ibid., pp. 526–7, and in *Foedera*.

ARCHBISHOP PECHAM'S SERMONS AND COLLATIONS

LIKE most friars Archbishop Pecham attached an excessive importance to sermons, even going so far as to assert that preaching was the principal duty of a bishop.[1] None of the sermons delivered during his thirteen years' metropolitanship has, however, survived, although he must have preached frequently at state ceremonies and at visitations as well as on less formal occasions. On one of his visits to Lewes, a house for which he had a warm affection because of kindnesses received during his boyhood,[2] the chronicler relates that at the end of his sermon he had the different causes of excommunication read in English to the people and then appealed to them to avoid such acts in future, giving them at the same time absolution for their past sins.[3] This is the only description of his preaching which has survived, and his reputation must, therefore, rest on the sermons and collations of his Franciscan period.

As a disciple of St. Bonaventura, Pecham had as a model one of the greatest preachers of the period. The training of their pupils in the art of sermon-making was one of the duties of the masters of theology. As regent master first at Paris and then at Oxford, and as Franciscan lector at both places and afterwards as provincial of England, he must have played a considerable part in the instruction of the young friars. His *Commentary on Lamentations* composed during his Paris regency[4] contains two suggested themes for sermons, one on the Passion and the other on the conversion of St. Paul.[5] He had already a strong sense of the pre-eminent holiness of the preacher's vocation which the allegorical method of interpretation gave him an opportunity to express. When commenting on the text 'Their horses were swifter than the eagles of the sky', he interprets eagles as preachers, since the great master of all preaching, St. John, was represented by this symbol.[6] Even at this time preaching was regarded by him as an important part of the episcopal office, for he describes prelates

---

[1] *Reg.* (Rolls Series), ii. 696.   [2] *Reg.* iii. 902.

[3] Ed. W. H. Blaauw, 'The Early History of Lewes and its Seals', *Sussex Archaeo-logical Collections*, ii. 33–4.

[4] *Expositio Threnorum.* Edited as a work of St. Bonaventura in *Opera Omnia* (Quaracchi), vii. 607–51.

[5] pp. 620, 621.   [6] p. 651. Ier. iv. 13.

as the doors through whose instructions the people outside are admitted to the mysteries within the Temple.[1] In spite of his interest in sermons and belief in their supreme importance none of the innumerable manuals on the technique of sermon-making has ever been ascribed to him.[2] His theories on the subject are, however, to be found in two of his other works, the *Divinarum Sententiarum Librorum Biblie*[3] and the *Expositio super Regulam Fratrum Minorum*.[4] In the first of these, a useful collection of suitable texts for sermons on various themes and for the different festivals of the Christian year, he devotes sections to preaching and to good and bad preachers, comparing the former to the sun, moon, and stars created by God to give light to the world.[5] His views on preaching are given in the form of texts with the appropriate explanations. For instance, 'Quando congregandus est populus simplex tubarum clangor erit' and the words of Balaam to the messengers of Balak, 'If Balak would give me his house full of gold and silver, I cannot go beyond the word of the Lord my God to do less or more', are preceded by the rubrics, 'De predicatione quod sit simplex', and 'Quod predicatio non sit de falsis et fabulis'.[6] Sometimes the texts suggested as suitable for sermons on the art of preaching are too obvious to need comment, as for example, 'Hide not thy wisdom in thine eloquence',[7] but it requires some ingenuity to see the connexion between 'Samgar the son of Anath, which slew the Philistines, six hundred men with an ox-goad' and the necessity of simplicity in sermons.[8] Similar views are put forward much more directly in the chapter on preaching in the *Expositio* which was probably composed during Pecham's short provincialship. Here, whilst insisting that preaching was for edification and that the preacher should not despise the poor and ignorant or use his sermon as a means of displaying his own learning,[9] he also stresses the need for a thorough training in the art of sermon-composition. No one must

---

[1] Op. cit., p. 630.
[2] On these cf. P. Charland, *Les Auteurs d'artes praedicandi au XIIIe siècle d'après les manuscrits*, Études d'Histoire Littéraire et Doctrinale au XIIIe siècle, i (Ottawa, 1932), p. 41 f.
[3] Printed Paris, 1513–14; Cologne, 1541.
[4] St. Bonaventura, *Opera Omnia* (Quaracchi), viii. 391–437.
[5] f. 73^v, cf. Gen. i. 14–19.
[6] f. 72^v, Num. x. 7; f. 73^r, Num. xxii. 18.
[7] f. 72^v, Eccli. iv. 28.
[8] f. 72^v, Judic. iii. 31.
[9] 'Ne predicent se ipsos ut suam philosophiam ostendant et fimbrias magnificant', p. 430.

be permitted to preach unless he knows how to arrange his material;[1] and since St. Francis had intended that his friars should preach he must also have wished them to study, for otherwise they would not be able to use words with precision and accuracy.[2] Pecham's own experience as a preacher comes out in his admirable advice that sermons should be short and pithy and that all involved sentences and verbal subtilties should be avoided, since prolixity caused boredom and led to small congregations.[3] It is to be hoped, however, that for the sake of their audiences the young friars did not accept his suggestion that all jokes and humorous anecdotes should be carefully omitted.[4] Like the Spirituals Pecham was an advocate of the simple eloquence of St. Francis, not realizing that his insistence on form would have destroyed its directness and spontaneity.

Most of Pecham's theories are the commonplaces of medieval sermon-manuals, but in his case his extant sermons show a complete correspondence between theory and practice. The biggest collection of these is in two Bodleian manuscripts, MS. Laud Misc. 85, ff. 1–31^{r}a, and MS. Rawlinson C. 116, ff. 30^{r}a–39^{v}a, the former of which contains his collations on the epistles and gospels for Sunday and the latter only those on the gospels.[5] There are also a few isolated sermons, a Christmas one preached during his regency at Paris which is little more than a scheme,[6] a sermon and a collation for the fourth Sunday in Advent, both obviously delivered to a university audience,[7] and one with the incipit *Qui audit me non confundetur*, which, however, is merely a fragment.[8] A sermon for Holy Saturday in a manuscript in the

[1] 'Nullus debeat predicare, nisi sciat ipse sermonem facere et sufficienter disponere', p. 430.
[2] 'Sine studio non possunt verba modo debito examinare', p. 431.
[3] 'Brevitas excludit verborum ambages et sententias involutas.' 'Prolixitas, generando fastidium, auditores retrahit pluries ab auditu', p. 430.
[4] 'Haec autem castitas excludit corruptionem falsitatis et immixtionem non solum enormitatis, immo etiam omnis vanitatis seu verbi risum provocantis', p. 430.
[5] Both manuscripts are mutilated, for MS. Laud Misc. 85 begins with the collation for the third Sunday in Advent, and the Rawlinson manuscript with the one for the gospel for the first Sunday after Epiphany. It contains only the last few lines of the collation for the fourth Sunday in Advent.
[6] Milan, Bibl. Ambrosiana, Cod. A. 11 supp. (n. 94), ff. 28^v–29^v.
[7] Venice, Bibl. Marciana, Cod. Lat. 92 (vi. 36), ff. 203^{v}b–206^{r}a; and ff. 206^{r}a–207^{v}a. These and the sermon for Christmas have been edited by P. G. Melani, O.F.M., 'La Predicazione di Giovanni Pecham, O.F.M.', *Studi Francescani*, xxxviii (1941), 197–220.
[8] Angers, Cod. 250, f. 285^v. I owe this information to the late Dr. A. G. Little who examined this manuscript.

Bibliothèque Nationale at Paris is ascribed both to him and to a certain 'Fr. Rogerius', so that his authorship is doubtful.[1]

The most striking characteristic of Pecham's collations and the two Paris sermons on which his reputation as a preacher rests are their extreme conciseness and simplicity. He avoids the multiplicity of subdivisions and the elaborate analogies and metaphors which confuse readers unfamiliar with medieval sermon technique, and although he uses the allegorical method of interpretation, his types would have been well known to any educated medieval audience. In the collations, for instance, Joseph feeding his brethren in Egypt, David, Cyrus, and Ahasuerus were all figures of our Lord,[2] Raphael freeing Tobias from the demon was a symbol of the divine providence,[3] Rebecca at the well represented penitence,[4] and Zacchaeus on the sycamore contemplation.[5] More obvious types were the leper, the sick of the palsy, and the dumb man possessed of the devil who represented the sinner,[6] whilst the bringing of the foal of the ass to Christ represented the conversion of the sinner.[7] The pool of Siloam was a symbol of baptism, Judah of confession, and the ship from which the disciples saw Christ walking on the water was a figure of the Church.[8] Natural objects also had an allegorical significance, salt meaning discretion, the feet the feelings,[9] and shoes human foresight, a quality which Pecham as a good Franciscan regarded as a form of avarice.[10] The head naturally represented the mind, and the story of Samson and Delilah was an example of what occurred if the reason, being put to sleep, ceased to control the other faculties.[11] Like most of his contemporaries Pecham was fascinated by

[1] Cod. Lat. 15956, f. 226va. Cf. P. Glorieux, *Répertoire des maîtres en théologie de Paris au XIIIe siècle*, ii (Paris, 1934), 91.

[2] Collation on the gospel for the seventh Sunday after Trinity, MS. Laud Misc. 85, f. 26ra; collation on the epistle for the third Sunday after Easter, f. 8ra; collation on the gospel for the seventh Sunday after Trinity, f. 26ra; first Sunday after Trinity (gospel), f. 24rb. All references are to MS. Laud Misc. 85.

[3] Fourteenth Sunday after Pentecost (epistle), f. 12rb.

[4] Eleventh Sunday after Trinity (gospel), f. 27rb.

[5] Eighth Sunday after Trinity (gospel), f. 26rb.

[6] Fourteenth Sunday after Trinity (gospel), f. 27vb; Nineteenth Sunday after Trinity (gospel), f. 29rb; Third Sunday in Lent (gospel), f. 19va.

[7] 'Per solutionem pulli asine qui est animal stollidum peccatorem designans ad Christum conversum.' Palm Sunday (gospel), f. 20ra.

[8] Fifth Sunday after Trinity (gospel), f. 25rb: 'Judas enim confitens vel confessio interpretatur'; eleventh Sunday after Trinity (gospel), f. 27rb; twenty-second Sunday after Pentecost (epistle), f. 14rb.

[9] Tenth Sunday after Pentecost (epistle), f. 11va; Sexagesima (gospel), f. 18va.

[10] 'Calceamentum est provisio humana, que provenit ex avaritia.' Palm Sunday (gospel), f. 20rb.   [11] Second Sunday in Advent (gospel), f. 15va. Cf. Judic. xvi.

the interpretations of Hebrew names, drawing his information from such well-known sources as St. Jerome's *Liber de Nominibus Hebraicis*[1] and St. Isidore's *Etymologiae*.[2] Thus Amon, which meant a barn, stood for the body and its lusts, whilst Jabesh-gilead where Saul defeated the Ammonites signified sorrow, and stood for the spirit struggling against the enticements of the flesh, and Saul himself represented the penitent imploring the divine mercy.[3] Again, the Israelites were delivered from Egypt, the place of torment, by Moses, whose rescue from the Nile by Pharaoh's daughter was a symbol of baptism.[4] Lebanon, which meant whiteness, signified the cleansing from sin and the beginning of a new life.[5] The best example of his typically medieval preference for the spiritual interpretation of the scriptures is the sermon and collation for the fourth Sunday in Advent given at Paris where the fourfold sense forms the basis of the whole scheme. In the former Pecham takes as his text 'the peace of God which passeth all understanding',[6] and begins by considering it in connexion with the coming of Christ. Peace could be interpreted anagogically as the enjoyment of Christ through preservation from evil and the gift of grace, for which reason all true prayer consisted of the two elements of praise and petition. Allegorically, it implied the redemption of humanity ruined by the sin of Adam, through the destruction of the power of the devil and the reconciliation of each individual with God, with himself and his neighbour. Thus the inchoate matter of the human personality received its proper form which was Christ, or, to use a more modern terminology, was reshaped into the image of the God-man. Then he considers peace in itself, using the fourfold classification. It signified anagogically the eternal peace of God and the harmony between the three persons of the Trinity, allegorically the peace of the Church, considered as the whole company of the redeemed, morally, the peace of the individual, now reconciled to himself and to God through his victory over the world, the flesh, and the devil. Peace with God was secured by obedience, with the world by fortitude, with the flesh by penance, and with the devil by steadfastness in resisting temptation. In regard to the literal meaning of peace, goodwill between man and man, Pecham has little to say except that it

[1] *Pat. Lat.* 23, cols. 771–859.   [2] Ibid. 82.
[3] Sunday after the Ascension (epistle), f. 8ᵛb. Cf. 1 Sam. xi.
[4] Fourth Sunday after Pentecost (epistle), ff. 9ᵛb–10ʳa. Cf. Exod. ii.
[5] Third Sunday after Epiphany (gospel), f. 17ᵛa.
[6] Phil. iv. 7.

was dependent on unselfishness and mutual forbearance. Just as in nature the different elements could not combine to create the higher forms without losing some of their individuality, so without a mutual union of wills there could be no harmony between man and man. The exposition of the four senses is less elaborate in the collation. Here Pecham takes for the *thema* the text 'There standeth in the midst of you one whom ye know not',[1] and for the *prothema*, 'the voice of one crying in the wilderness'.[2] The crier is the preacher and the wilderness the world; Advent implied the coming of God to those who made His paths straight by preparing their hearts to receive Him, through obedience to His word. Christ's standing in the midst could be interpreted in three senses, historically, by the fact of His life on earth, allegorically, by His role as a mediator between God and man, and tropologically, by His indwelling in the soul through grace.[3] He only, however, develops the first meaning, showing how Christ by His appearance in the world had conferred a threefold benefit on men by illuminating their understanding, by kindling and inflaming their affections, and by reforming them in His own likeness. Through Christ's life and miracles His divinity was made manifest and the ignorance which had resulted from sin was destroyed and man's love was gained, by one who came not as God surrounded by angels, but as brother, friend, and comrade.[4] The sermon ends with a fine description of the tenderness of Christ who had come to minister, leaving us an example that we might follow in His footsteps. The eagle encouraged its little ones to fly and if they were too weak carried them on its own wings. The two wings on which Christ supported men were mercy and love. Augustine had written that man's answer to God's exhortation to hasten to attain to eternal glory was 'I cannot'; but Christ would not accept this excuse for lukewarmness, replying, 'Yet run, for if ye are unable to press forward alone, I will be with you and bring you to my glory'.[5]

[1] Joh. i. 26.   [2] Isa. xl. 3.

[3] 'Hoc verbum tripliciter exponitur. Christus stetit *medius* vestrum per humilem conversationem, vel *medius*, scilicet pro hominibus, inter Deum et hominem, vel *medius*, scilicet in cordibus, qui inhabitat per gratiam. Prima expositio pertinet ad sensum historicum, secunda ad sensum allegoricum, tertia ad sensum tropologicum.' Melani, op. cit., p. 217.

[4] 'Potuit enim, si voluisset, in aere in angelis magnifice apparere, sed ad inflammandum homines ad sui amorem, voluit humiliter venire ad homines et in eis humiliter conversari. . . . Cum enim apparuit in terris hominibus conversatus est inter eos, ut frater, ut socius et ut amicus', p. 219.

[5] 'Cum pulli aquile non possunt volare, aquila supportat eos, sic Christus

The collations on the epistles and gospels are structurally less elaborate. There is no *prothema* and the *thema* generally consists of two words, each of which, after being explained in the introduction, is briefly developed in a separate division. Three points are made in regard to each, and these are impressed on the minds of the audience by the citation of three different texts. The sermon concludes with the usual prayer that both preacher and hearers might have grace to carry out the lessons suggested by the text, or with an exhortation to carry these out. A very good example of Pecham's technique is his collation on the text *Ambulate in spiritu* from the epistle for the thirteenth Sunday after Trinity.[1] An arresting beginning in the form of a citation from St. Bernard to the effect that in the spiritual life failure to advance towards perfection was to retreat from it, is followed by the declaration that *Ambulate* was an invitation to action.[2] *In spiritu* defined the purpose of all action, the imitation of Christ, under whose leadership we should effectively advance from strength to strength until we shall see the God of gods in Sion.[3] The just walked in the light of faith and were unflagging in good works, for their whole being was concentrated on the One who had neither end nor beginning. Of them it could truly be said, as of the apostle, 'we walk by faith and not by sight',[4] or as of the One spoken of by the prophet, 'he walked before me in peace and justice for ever'.[5] Such a life was, however, impossible without the assistance of the divine power and the guidance and protection of the divine wisdom and mercy. Under this support and governance we could live in virtue and in security, for it was written in the Book of Wisdom: 'How could anything have endured, if it had not been Thy will?'[6] The archangel Raphael, when he freed Tobias from the demon, had said: 'By the will of our God I came, that I might free thy son from hostile assaults and lead him wisely on his way.'[7] May He therefore lead us in

---

supportat alis suis homines qui non possunt volare. Ale quibus Christus supportat homines sunt due: id est misericordia et charitas . . . Augustinus' (Sermo clxiv, §4–6, *Pat. Lat.* 38, col. 897 seq.). ' "Currite, currite." "Non possum." "Curram ego, feram te, perducam te", dominus dicit, "currite ad gloriam meam." Et piger, qui non curat benefacere, dicit, "Non possum." Et dominus dicit iterum "Curre, et si non potes currere per te, ego feram te et perducam te ad gloriam meam" ', p. 220.

[1] Gal. v. 16, f. 12ʳa–ʳb.
[2] *De Purificatione beatae Mariae*, Sermo ii, *Pat. Lat.* 183, col. 961.
[3] Ps. lxxxiii. 8.   [4] 2 Cor. v. 7.
[5] Mal. ii. 6.   [6] Sap. xi. 26.
[7] Tob. xii. 18.

His mercy to His eternal glory where among the elect we may repeat in thanksgiving the words of the Psalmist: 'Thou hast holden me by my right hand and hast led me by Thy will and hast received me into Thy glory.'[1] The whole collation is exceedingly short, covering less than a column of a medium-sized manuscript, and most of the others are about this length.

The collation was a literary form which exactly suited Pecham. Although his lectures are diffuse owing to the disproportionate space devoted to the discussion of the different points raised in the objections, his treatises suggest that he was naturally a concise writer. The rigid structural scheme imposed on him a discipline he badly needed, for works like the *Tractatus de Paupertate Evangelica*, in spite of some beautiful and poetical passages, are somewhat lacking in form. St. Bonaventura was obviously his model, but he had also carefully studied the rhetorical rules laid down in such manuals as the *Ars Concionandi*.[2] For instance, when he makes his three points in each division an active or passive verb in the first clause is always followed by one in the same voice, mood, and tense in the two others. The same rule is observed in regard to participles and gerundives. The three texts quoted in each division generally either have one key word, a common rhetorical device to impress them on the memory of the audience, or repeat the words already spoken by the preacher. The result of these studied combinations, especially when accompanied, as it was in Pecham's case, with great clarity and simplicity of diction and considerable poetic gifts, was not monotony or preciousness, but the grave cadences of the 'Imitation' and of the great Latin hymns. The effect can best be judged by the conclusion to his last collation, preached on the text *Congregabunt electi*. God's purpose for those whom he predestined to salvation was a threefold one: 'Ad fragrandum suaviter per sanctitatem internam, ad fructificandum viriliter per caritatem fraternam, ad inhabitandum feliciter civitatem supernam.' These three ends necessitated a triple reorientation through the life of grace of man's relation to God, to himself and to his fellows: 'Interna sanctitate homo in se perficiatur, fraterna caritate proximus eruatur, in civitate superna Deus videatur'.[3]

---

[1] Ps. lxxii. 24.

[2] The *Ars Concionandi* is printed in St. Bonaventura, *Opera Omnia*, ix. 9 seqq. It is anonymous and Pecham follows it very closely. Gilson draws much of the material used in his 'Michel Menot et la technique du sermon médiéval' (*Les Idées et les lettres*, Paris, 1932), from it.

[3] Mat. xxiv. 31. Twenty-fifth Sunday after Trinity (gospel), f. 30ᵛb–31ʳb.

In his sermons and collations Pecham certainly carried out his advice to avoid any parade of learning. Apart from the Bible which he cites constantly,[1] his quotations from any authority, even the Fathers, are singularly few. In the collations there is hardly any use of philosophical terminology. He could not, however, free himself from his long association with the Schools and the author most frequently cited by him is Aristotle.[2] He was also fond of the works of the Pseudo-Dionysius, making use of a commentary on the 'Hierarchies' which I have not managed to identify.[3] The collations must, therefore, have been intended for an educated audience, and it is probable that they were given to the Oxford Franciscans, or to the friars at some other important friary, during Pecham's lectorship or provincialship. There are naturally no citations from romances or popular poetry, and very few of those delightful references to contemporary custom which make many medieval sermons a quarry for the social historian. There are, however, one or two vivid little descriptions, such as that of the songs, illuminations, and feasts which accompanied the visit of an earthly ruler to his capital, in one of the Advent collations.[4] The Paris sermon and collation also contain some topical allusions. In the former he complains of the bad behaviour of the students at inaugural lectures,[5] and in the latter his description of the three types of infidel as those who deny the existence of God, those who deny His interest in the world, and those who declare that He neither rewards nor punishes, is certainly a hit at the Averroists.[6]

A set of sermons is naturally a better guide to a man's religious philosophy than an isolated one, and the collations are an excellent background to the intense Christo-centric piety which is so apparent in the *Canticum Pauperis* and the *Philomena*. The chief characteristic of Pecham's religious experience was a sense of

[1] The average number of texts in each collation is ten.

[2] There are 7 citations from Aristotle, 3 from the *Ethics*, 1 from the *De Anima*, and 3 for which he gives no source and which I have failed to identify.

[3] Cf. f. 1ʳa and f. 23ᵛb. The two passages are as follows: 'Est enim gaudium cum diffusione, ut dicit Commentator super Angelicam Ierarchiam, cap. 7', f. 1ʳa; 'Amor est rex per se sola gaudiosa [*sic* MS.] et delectabilis, sicut ait Commentator super Angelicam I(er)archiam', f. 23ᵛb. Dr. Callus has kindly examined these passages and tells me that they are not from Grosseteste's commentary.

[4] 'Sciendum est quod alicui magno ad suam civitatem venienti, triplex preparatio, videlicet in lucernarum radiositate, in cantelenarum suavitate, et epularum copiositate.' Third Saturday in Advent (gospel), f. 15ᵛa–b.

[5] 'Sed heu, modo non est disciplina Christi in clericis, sed disciplina histrionum, quod patet in principiis magistrorum quando scholares diversificant se', Melani, p. 212.

[6] Ibid., p. 218.

the utter generosity of God as manifested in the creation and redemption of mankind. One magnificent phrase is worthy of St. Francis himself: 'I say He has loved courteously, expecting no return.'[1] Man's relation to God should be a combination of reverence, adoration, and gratitude. In his teaching on prayer, whilst not ignoring petition and insisting that men should pray with humility, confidence, and assiduity, he laid much more stress on praise and thanksgiving. His description of it as 'penetrating the clouds by its fervour, delighting the angels by its fragrance, and winning for the suppliant his desire'[2] shows that to him the true goal of the Christian life was contemplation, for which, however, careful preparation was needed. The four requisites for the friendship of God were purity of heart, compassion, humility, and obedience, and these were only achieved through the way of purgation which was the preliminary to the higher path. 'Thou who hast attained to the friendship of God through the way of purgation, ascend now to please him by the sweetness of contemplation.'[3] This, however, was merely the last stage in the long ascent up which the soul was drawn by the cord of love 'royal, joyous, free and altogether lovely', destructive of even venial sin as fire consumes water, until in the end the loving heart by the sweetness and fervour of its devotion attained to the radiance of the beatific vision.[4]

Man's own contribution to his ultimate salvation was, however, negligible, for Pecham's conception of redemption which is the central theme of his collations is almost Pauline. His final Advent sermon is devoted to the mediatorship of Christ, not only as man but also as God.[5] His relationship with the other persons of the Trinity was that of an intermediary, for He was Himself begotten of the Father and their mutual love had resulted in the production of the Holy Ghost.[6] As the Word of God He was the medium

---

[1] 'Dilexit, inquam, curialiter, nullam remunerationem expectando.' Pentecost (epistle), f. 9^{r}b.

[2] 'Nubes penetrat suo fervore . . . supernos delectat suo fragore . . . optata impetrat suo postulatore.' Tenth Sunday after Trinity (gospel), *Domus mea domus orationis est*, Luc. xix. 46, f. 27^{r}a.

[3] 'Tu ergo qui amicitiam Dei adquisivisti puritate mundicie, ascende ad placandum Deum per suavitatem contemplationis.' Seventeenth Sunday after Trinity (gospel), *Amice ascende*, Luc. xiv. 10, f. 29^{r}a.

[4] 'Amor est rex per se sola gaudiosa [*sic* MS.] et delectabilis.' Pentecost (gospel), f. 23^{v}b. 'Sicut enim ignis consumit guttam aque, sic ardor delectionis peccatum veniale.' Fifth Sunday after Trinity (gospel), f. 25^{r}b.

[5] Collation on *Medius vester stetit*. Joh. i. 26, f. 16^{r}b–^{v}a.

[6] 'Nullum enim magis medium esse debet quam persona que producit et producitur que etiam est media trium personarum, Christus Iesus', f. 16^{r}b.

and cause of all creation, the light of the understanding, and the goal of the soul.[1] This divine light through which all other objects were known was in itself inapprehensible, just as Moses had seen the burning bush but not the fire which should have consumed it, save for the miracle which caused him to realize God's presence.[2] Christ as man was the advocate who represented and took the place of His client in the courts, and thus through His work of creation and redemption became the source of all life whether on a natural or a supernatural level.[3] The incident of the burning bush is used with even greater effect in the collation for Passion Sunday. God's description of Himself to Moses as 'I am'[4] is here applied to Christ in His twofold capacity of God and Saviour, 'the light of Heaven, the ruler of the world and the despoiler of Hell, illuminating the angels by his unchanging radiance, governing the universe by his wisdom, and snatching its prey from the kingdom of darkness by his victory'.[5] The words also indicated the consummate excellence of our Redeemer who being God was pure act, eternal, unchanging, and ever-lasting.[6] In another collation the Cross is compared to the great tree in Daniel's vision, and the birds nesting in its branches to the different types of souls flying heavenwards, the active, the contemplative, and the martyr, all of whom found in it the satis-faction of their deepest need, the first rest, the second a means of ascent, and the third exultation.[7] The fruits of this tree which had been watered by the blood of Christ were justification,

[1] 'Inquantum igitur in illo est ratio intelligendi, similis est medio logicali quo cetera lucide declarantur, inquantum vero est ordo vivendi, similis est medio morali quo spiritus in finem ordinantur, inquantum vero est in illo causa subsistendi, similis est medio naturali cuius efficacia cetera in esse conservantur', f. 16^{v}a.

[2] 'Locutus est dominus Moysi de medio ignis. Per ignem que invisibilis nobis est in puritate sua et videtur tamen in materia aliena congrue lux eterna', ibid.

[3] 'Officium vero advocati est stare et pro cliente suo que expediunt proponere, sicut docet civilis doctrina. . . . Stetit, inquam, ad reconciliandum impios . . . quod interpellando fecit patrem. . . . Stetit etiam Christus tanquam medium naturale cetera in esse supportans', ibid.

[4] Exod. iii. 14, f. 20^{r}a.

[5] 'Ego, scilicet supernorum illustrator, terrenorum gubernator, infernorum depredator, ego, inquam, qui illustro celicolas lumine indefectibili, guberno terrigenas prudentia mirabili, expolio infernales excubias triumpho nobili', ibid.

[6] 'Deus est actus purus, ideo subditur nostri reparatoris actualis excellentia, ibi "Sum", inquam, ante tempora initialis, in tempore invariabilis, post tempora interminabilis', ibid.

[7] 'Signanter dicitur arbor bona quia ipsa est electis materia quiescendi, ascen-dendi et congaudendi . . . quiescendi laborantibus, ascendendi contemplantibus, congaudendi triumphantibus. . . . Hec enim tipice est arbor magna et fortis in cuius ramis aves, id est anime, avolantes ad celestia morantur.' Cf. Dan. iv. Eighth Sunday after Trinity (gospel), f. 26^{r}a–^{r}b.

sanctification, and salvation, and under its shade the elect rested tranquilly, freed from sin.[1]

Redemption was not, however, a mere mechanical process but involved the reintegration of the whole personality, through the action of the three theological virtues on the different faculties of the soul, the rational or intellectual being reformed by faith, and the irascible and concupiscible, or repulsion and desire, the two faculties of the will, by hope and charity.[2] Thus the natural trinity composed of the three faculties of memory, intellect, and will which through the Fall had been changed into an evil trinity, consisting of the desire of the flesh, the desire of the eyes, and the pride of life, was once more restored, but on a higher level, and the soul through the infusion of the life of grace became a true image of God.[3] The new relationship created between Man and God was due to a special unsolicited act of redeeming love on the part of Christ in which man had been incapable of participating. Pecham takes the rich man in the parable of the unjust steward as a type of Christ, all powerful, all wise, and utterly generous,[4] and contrasts him with man in his fallen state, helpless, ignorant, and avaricious, for whom the best figures are the leper and the sick of the palsy.[5] Conversion was, however, no sudden change, but the work of a lifetime, finding its expression, not merely in sincere repentance, humble confession, and atonement, but also in bodily penance, almsgiving, and works of practical charity.[6] Zacharias the publican who had received Christ with joy into his house and given half of his wealth to the poor was a type of the penitent sinner,[7] and the best antidote to venial sin was brotherly love, which destroyed it as fire consumed water drops.[8] Conversion involved a rectification

---

[1] 'Crux itaque Christi sanguine irrigata sub qua electi quiescunt suaviter, facit fructus bonos per culpe remissionem', f. 26ʳb.

[2] 'Fidei splendor rationalem illuminat, spei vigor irascibilem comfortat, caritatis ardor concupiscibilem inflammat.' Ninth Sunday after Pentecost (epistle), f. 11ʳa.

[3] Trinity Sunday (gospel), f. 24ʳa.

[4] Luc. xvi. 1. Ninth Sunday after Trinity (gospel), f. 26ʳb–ᵛa.

[5] 'Sed contra illud triplex incomodum homo iste (scilicet Christus) triplex habet privilegium. Est enim contra impotentiam potentissimus, contra ignorantiam sapientissimus, contra avaritiam liberalissimus', ibid.

[6] 'Triplex est lotio per quam malum eliminatur et anima aspirante spiritus sancti gratia emundatur iuxta omni [?] quod triplex malum hominem inquinat et deformat, scilicet peccatum originale, actuale et veniale, triplicem requirit absolutionem, scilicet baptismalem, penetentialem, et dilectionem fraternalem', f. 25ʳb.

[7] Luc. xix. 5–8, ibid.

[8] 'Sicut enim ignis consumit guttam aque, sic ardor dilectionis peccatum veniale', ibid.

of man's relation to himself and his neighbour as well as to God. In a fine sermon on the text 'We are the sons of God'[1] Pecham declared that sonship implied imitation. This was attained through the reception of the wisdom from on high and peace with one's brethren through the exercise of the three virtues of charity, gentleness, and forbearance.[2] God's friendship was purchased through the fulfilment of the obligations of each relationship, to God was due humility and obedience, to oneself repentance and purity from sin and all uncleanness, and to one's fellow Christian mercy and compassion.[3] In a collation on the merciless servant, pity is described as 'fruitful, gracious, and glorious, these qualities being displayed in the instruction of the ignorant, the forgiveness of injuries and the succour of the needy'.[4] Friendship was not a specifically Christian virtue for man in his natural state was a rational being, and thus amenable to prudence and discipline and adapted to living in society.[5] Pecham's insistence that conversion should be accompanied by the sur-render of temporal possessions,[6] and his use of the traditional division of the elect into beginners, proficients, and perfect certainly suggests that his collations were intended for the mem-bers of a religious order.[7] Nevertheless, the ideal they represent of contemplation bearing fruit in action makes them equally applicable to those who, whilst remaining in the world, desire to live a life of active charity in the service of God and of their fellows. In spite of the slightness of man's part in the process of conversion, the Christian life was not one of negation or passivity,

[1] Rom. viii. 16. Eighth Sunday after Pentecost (epistle), f. 10ᵛb–11ʳa.

[2] 'Ista filiatio paternam importans imitationem ex tribus . . . scilicet ex pacis fraterne conversatione, ex eruditionis superne perceptione et ex flagellationis fraterne sustentatione', ibid.

[3] 'Homo in hac progressione fruatur familiaritate divine amicitie . . . triplici conditione scilicet puritate mundicie, largitate misericordie, humilitate obedientie. Vite enim puritate homo in se venustatur, misericordie largitate proximus adiuvatur, obedientie humilitate Deus honoratur.' Collation for the seventeenth Sunday after Trinity (gospel), on the text *Amice ascende* (Luc. xiv. 10), f. 28ᵛb.

[4] 'Pietatis officium est fructuosum, gratiosum, et gloriosum . . . fructuosum in ignorantium informatione . . . gratiosum in iniuriarum condonatione . . . gloriosum in indigentium sublevatione.' Twenty-second Sunday after Trinity (gospel), Mat. xviii. 33, f. 30ʳa.

[5] 'Est enim homo animal rationale, et ita prudentia vigens et disciplinabilis; est animal mansuetum natura et ita debet mitis esse et humilis; est tandem animal sociale et per consequens debet esse ad convivendum humilis.' First Sunday in Lent (gospel), f. 19ʳa.

[6] Fifth Sunday after Trinity (gospel), f. 25ʳa–b.

[7] Palm Sunday (gospel), f. 20ᵛa; second Sunday after Easter (gospel), f. 22ʳa; eighth Sunday after Trinity (gospel), f. 26ʳb.

but of heroic struggle against the world, the flesh, and the devil. According to Pecham the best armour for this combat was the threefold vow of poverty, chastity, and obedience.[1] The exhortation with which he began his collation on this subject, 'My son, when entering upon the service of God, stand fast in righteousness and prepare thy soul to meet temptation',[2] was equally applicable to every Christian.

Pecham's sermons and collations, although not great literature, are more readable than those of many of his contemporaries, because they represent the permanent and not the transient values of the Christian civilization of the Middle Ages. They also reflect a side of his own personality which has been ignored. The historical Pecham is the doughty fighter and champion of a conservative school of philosophy, the conscientious and energetic archbishop who frequently spoiled his case by a failure to distinguish principles from personal prejudices. The other Pecham is the Franciscan poet who, if not himself a contemplative, could appreciate and aspire to the mystic's vision of reality.

DECIMA DOUIE

---

[1] 'Armatura spiritualis triplex contra triplicem hostem est assumenda, contra carnem continentia, contra mundum paupertas voluntaria, et contra dyabolum humilis obedientia.' Twenty-first Sunday after Pentecost (epistle), f. 13^{v}b–14^{r}a.

[2] Eccli. ii. 1.

THE DEATH OF A CHAMPION (1287)

IN 1287 John de Creke, Ralph Berners, and Godfrey Beaumont as co-heirs of Nesta de Cockfield sought by writ of right to recover from the abbey of St. Edmunds the manors of Semer and Groton in Suffolk. As tenant in the action the abbot had the choice of two procedures: he could either put himself upon the verdict of a jury or he could stake his cause on trial by battle. He chose the latter course and—his champion being killed in the fight—lost his suit. At this time the *duellum* was rapidly giving ground in England. 'We doubt whether in Bracton's day the annual average of battles exceeded twenty',[1] and this was thirty years later. Why then should a great ecclesiastic at so late a date have made this barbarous choice and gone through with it to the bitter end? To this question, on which the narrative of the plea roll (printed below) throws no light, an unprinted entry in the contemporary Bury chronicle supplies the answer and thereby sheds a ray of light on the last days of the civil duel in England.

The dispute about Semer and Groton is a long story.[2] Both manors were immemorial possessions of the abbey of St. Edmunds, for which there were no title-deeds. The monks believed that a 'certain noble lady' (*inclita matrona*) had given them Semer *sine carta*: as for Groton, when a list of the abbey benefactors was drawn up,[3] there was not even a tradition left regarding the donor. In the troubled reign of Stephen, the abbey, anxious about the safety of these remote possessions, leased both manors for life to Adam de Cockfield, who from his own stronghold at Lindsey could best defend them against neighbouring castellans. In due course they passed to his son, but no charter was granted in either case and Robert recognized before Abbot Samson and many witnesses that he had no claim by hereditary right to either. His son Adam married Rohais; and on Adam's death, by a judgement of the King's Court (1201),[4] the manors were awarded to his only daughter Nesta, then under age, as of fee-farm. Nesta in due course married Thomas, brother of Hubert de Burgh, and in 3 Henry III Rohais released to Thomas and Nesta her dower lands

---

[1] Pollock and Maitland, *History of English Law*, ii. 633. A cursory examination of the rolls, with the assistance of Mr. H. C. Johnson and Mr. Hector, suggests that by 1287 the award of the duel was very rare.

[2] *Chronica Jocelini de Brakelonda* (Camden Soc., 1840), pp. 91, 140.

[3] *Pinchbeck Register* (ed. Lord Francis Hervey), ii. 292, 294.

[4] *Curia Regis Rolls*, i. 430, where Adam's daughter is called Margaret.

in Cockfield, Semer, and Groton, other lands being assigned to
her. After the death of Thomas, Nesta successively married John
de Beauchamp and Matthew de Leyham: and in 26 Henry III
the abbot of St. Edmunds, in return for a grant of lands in
Cockfield from Nesta and the third husband, renounced all claims
on their lands in Semer, Groton, and certain other places. Finally,
about 1248, Nesta died without issue, leaving as co-heirs the
three demandants in the action mentioned above. While Nesta
was actually *in extremis*, they asserted, the abbot of St. Edmunds
unlawfully gained seisin of Semer and Groton under cover of a
lease made by Nesta's last husband, but without her knowledge,
to John de Cramaville. A writ on the close roll of 1248[1] records
the case of the co-heirs, but the abbot was still seised of the
manors when in 14 Edward I they sought by writ of right to
recover them.

At this point the plea roll takes up the story, setting out the
descent of the three co-heirs from Nesta[2] and the particulars of
their claim: the denial of the abbot and his offer to defend his
cause by the 'body of his freeman Roger, son of Robert de
Mutford'; the proffer by the three claimants of *their* freeman
Robert, son of William Le Bret; the award of the duel; the giving
of pledges; the delay due to the abbot who essoined himself, and
the final encounter on Tuesday, 14 October, at London: 'quo die
venerunt partes et similiter servientes armati et fuit duellum inter
eos armatum et percussum et serviens predicti abbatis devictus
et interfectus.' Judgement followed for the plaintiffs.

Between this evidence and that of the chronicle[3] there is a
perfect correspondence. Dates, times, and places all agree, but
its peculiar value lies in a single clause: 'and at length after discussion of the case, since we were doubtful about the countryside
(*patriam*), as friendly with (*familiarem*) and akin to (*affinem*) our
enemies, we decided that our right was to be defended by the
duel. . . .' It is not difficult to imagine the anxious consideration
that preceded this decision. The mere fact that the story is
recorded suggests that the choice of the duel was now unusual,
though, clearly, still decent; while the simplicity of the chronicler
illustrates the motives which perpetuated an old abuse and delayed
the final triumph of the jury procedure. Nor is it a long step from
considerations of this kind to the admirable prudence of the prior

[1] *Close Rolls, 1248*, p. 120.
[2] The full pedigree is printed by Gage, op. cit., p. 144.
[3] Infra, p. 293.

of Barnwell,[1] when the justices came on circuit, or the plain bribery with which Mr. Denholm-Young has familiarized us.[2] The local feeling of the countryside, the monks feared, was against them. They therefore took a chance on the duel, but every effort was made to reduce this to a minimum. No expense was spared. A champion was found from Lincolnshire, familiarly and perhaps affectionately known as 'Roger the Clerk', who received 20 marks in cash, with the promise of a further 30 marks to be paid after the battle. In addition, both he and his trainer (*magister*) were entertained by the abbey for at least six months before the meeting.

That this was the market price[3] for a good champion, and that payment was normally made in two instalments, is shown by another contract,[4] between the Chapter of Southwell and a champion called Roger of Malton. The same sum—50 marks— was payable in two moieties—25 on the day battle was waged, and 25, which were entrusted to the chief justice who presided, after the fight. If, after all, no duel took place, or if only the formal blows (*ictus regis*)[5] were struck, the deposit was to be given back to the Chapter or their attorney. In addition there were certain 'extras'—40 shillings for being present on the day, a shilling a day for the period of waiting, 10 pounds for the trainer and so on— which we may set off as roughly equivalent to the hospitality

---

[1] *Liber Memorandorum Ecclesie de Bernewelle* (ed. J. W. Clark), p. 171. In the whole of this eyre the House was only once amerced owing to the wise expenditure of quite small sums—all recorded—and some further payments in kind—bread, beer, wine, &c.

[2] *Seignorial Administration in England*, pp. 110–11.

[3] A generation earlier it was 20 marks. See the case of Henry of Fernbureg, known as 'the marshal', who was hired by the abbot of Glastonbury in 1258. Here again the payment was in two instalments, and there is mention of 5 marks paid on his being shaven (*in tonsione mea*) (Neilson, *Trial by Combat*, p. 53). The full text of the deed, with a picture of the seal, is printed in the notes (p. 36) to Nicholas Upton, *De Militari Officio*, printed by E. Bysshe (1654). The champion states that he has done his homage to the abbot and church of Glastonbury and holds himself bound by his charter to wage and fight the duel against the church of Wells on behalf of the right of the church of Glastonbury in certain lands named and the advowsons of certain churches (London, 28 April, 42 Henry III). The seal depicts a champion with square shield and baton, as in the well-known drawing on the plea rolls. Another seal of a champion is reproduced in *Yorkshire Archaeological Journal* cited in n. 4 *infra*.

[4] William Brown, 'Trial by Combat', *Yorkshire Archaeological Journal*, 1915, pp. 304–7. The contract is enrolled on Assize Roll no. 1092 of 21 Edward I. For this reference and for other valuable help in preparing this paper I am indebted to the encyclopaedic knowledge of my colleague Mr. L. F. Salzman.

[5] Mr. Charles Johnson suggests that the *ictus regis* were the equivalent of the 'engage and disengage' of the beginning of a fencing competition.

enjoyed by Roger the Clerk and his *magister* during their six months of waiting. The editor of this curious document calculates that, if the duel took place, it must have cost the Chapter of Southwell 46 pounds *plus* an indeterminate sum for 'daily wages'.

By the second half of the thirteenth century, to which period surviving records of these elaborate contracts belong, the legal theory of the 'civil' duel for land had undergone great developments. In early days the plaintiff was required to employ as champion one of his freemen, who must also be a witness ready to swear to the truth of the cause he defended. As late as Glanville's time the tenant might either fight in person or employ an unobjectionable witness-champion or (after Henry II's Grand Assize) decline the duel altogether in favour of a verdict of neighbours. Hired fighters were forbidden, and cases are recorded of objection to a champion on the ground that he was a hireling and a professional.[1] By Bracton's day both sides must use champions, and in 1275 the statute which abolished the material words in the champion's oath in effect freed him from the obligation of acting as a witness. It is tempting, but probably incorrect, to suppose that the rise of the professional champion moved *pari passu* with these changes in the law, and so to postulate a sort of golden age when a system of witness-champions really worked. The professional hired champion, however, is no late development; he goes back to the first half of the twelfth century, and probably even earlier. It would appear that the lawyers, by the thirteenth century, while in practice they had severely limited the occasions on which the *duellum* was, in fact, employed, had ceased even to pretend that the champion was also a witness. Theory, in short, now squared with the facts, and public opinion having reached this stage, it became respectable and even prudent to record such contracts or, as in the Bury case before us, the motives for declining the Assize. In this connexion it is significant that our first explicit evidence of champions permanently 'retained' by religious houses—who surely belong to the earliest days of the *duellum*—only dates from the second half of the thirteenth century. A well-known example is that of Thomas Cantilupe,[2] bishop of

---

[1] e.g. *The Earliest Lincolnshire Assize Rolls* (ed. D. M. Stenton, Lincoln Rec. Soc.), no. 260, of the year 1202, *campionem conducticium*; cf. Introduction, p. lxviii. See also Sir Cyril Flower's analysis of the record evidence in his *Introduction to the Curia Regis Rolls* (Selden Soc. lxii, 1943), p. 120.

[2] Coulton, *Medieval Garner*, p. 433, with a picture; but such champions were not confined to religious houses. Between 1229 and 1242 the earl of Warwick granted land to John Archer, *pugili meo*. (Bodleian Lib. MS. Dugdale 17 p. 26.)

Hereford, who in 1276 agreed to pay Thomas of Brydges, or Bruges, half a mark yearly 'so long as the said Thomas is able to do the work of a champion'. He was to fight against Gilbert, earl of Gloucester, and Hereford or any other man, 'those lords only excepted to whom he was bound before the making of this present deed'. The words of the agreement seem to reach back to an age that was fast passing away, and it is worth noting that in spite of his dangerous trade Brydges was still annually drawing his half mark thirteen years later. Our other examples are even later: for instance, the famous monumental brass of Bishop Wyvil and his champion which belongs to the fourteenth century when the duel was all but extinct.[1] Where the evidence is so late, we are bound to suppose that the employment of hired champions under contracts long antedates the records of them in the thirteenth century. They may well be as old as the introduction of the *duellum* into England.

This, as is well known, was very late; not, in fact, until the Norman Conquest; and its absence from England, the home of expanding law in the Dark Ages, is perhaps the most striking fact in the whole history of trial by battle. Authorities are unanimous in describing the *duellum* as a true form of the 'ordeal', the *iudicium dei*: but it is really more profitable to stress how fundamentally it differed, at least in Christian times, from the use of hot iron or the cauldron. That 'God is on the side of the big battalions', and that 'a good big 'un will always beat a good little 'un', are maxims as old as our race, and the doubts of common men about the justice of the duel must be at least as old as King Gundobad of Burgundy, who it appears 'first tempted his subjects into court by a kind of compromise'.[2] For, after all, the duel was barbarous and anti-Christian, as well as the very negation of law, and was denounced by Christian thinkers from a date coeval with the first record of its existence. Maitland suggested that its

[1] Coulton, loc. cit. Evidence as to the exact procedure when the champions met is later still. See *Year Book*, 1 Henry VI (1422), ed. C. H. Williams, Selden Soc., pp. 95-6. By this time it was only a memory and there were doubts as to how it should be conducted, e.g. whether the baston should have a knob on the end, 'as the baston of an approver or an appellor has'. They also decided (wrongly perhaps) that the champions should not be shaved. They were dressed in red leather; five pennies were put in the glove of each champion, &c.

[2] Pollock and Maitland, *History of English Law*, i. 39, n. 7, and p. 50. The first of these references which denies the statement that 'trial by battle was only private war under regulations' seems to me to be flatly contradicted by the second. For a general survey of 'wager of battle' see H. C. Lea, *Superstition and Force*, which brings together a large collection of miscellaneous evidence. George Neilson's *Trial by Combat* (1890) is concerned only with Scotland and England.

absence from Anglo-Saxon procedure was due 'to the persistence of extra-judicial fighting', but few would care to maintain to-day that there was more of this in England than abroad in the Dark Ages. It is more likely that to the best medieval minds the duel was something to be ashamed of, but something from which they were unable to escape. In the following tale[1] taken from the ninth-century *Miracles of St. Benedict* it already appears as a last resort when rival legal systems were in hopeless conflict:

'Not long afterwards another controversy arose between the patrons (*advocati*) of Fleury and St. Denis. A great body of masters of the laws and judges was brought together by both sides; and there were present besides as royal *missi*, Jonas, bishop of Orleans and Donatus, Count of Melun. Since, however, the judges of the Salic law were unable to decide a religious dispute governed by Roman law, the royal *missi* saw fit to move the plea to Orleans. Arrived there, the masters and judges on both sides disputed keenly, for there were present doctors of the laws both from the province of Orleans and from the Gâtinais. At length, when neither side would yield any ground to the other, the court gave judgement that a witness from each side should go out, and after the taking of an oath, should settle the controversy by battle with shields and staves. All present had approved this decision when a doctor of law from the Gâtinais, christened, almost providentially, with the name of a beast instead of a man, who had been bribed to act for St. Denis and feared lest in a single combat their witness should fail, gave as his judgement that it would not be right for the witnesses to settle a dispute about church property by battle: rather should the two patrons make division of the property (*mancipia*) between them. With him the vicomte Genesius agreed, and turned the whole council to his view. But St. Benedict was in no wise forgetful of that judge and legislator who first cunningly and, according to his name, bestially, suggested partition. For as soon as the division was made, he was so smitten by the just judgement of God that his tongue refused its office and he lost the power of speech.'

Of this story, which comes, as it were, from another world, the end is easily guessed. Rushed by his servants to the shrine of the saint whom he had so grievously offended, the unhappy man by prayers and repentance slowly regained his power of speech, though never so far as to be able to utter the blessed name of St. Benedict. M. Philip Wolff suggests that the doctor, 'cui, quodam presagio, bestiale nomen pro humano indictum erat', was none other than Servatus Lupus, Loup de Ferrières as the French call

[1] *Miracula Sancti Benedicti*, ed. E. de Certain (Soc. de l'histoire de France, 1858), p. 56. I have to thank Mr. Southern for calling my attention to this remarkable case.

him; and if we could be sure of this the identification would both add point to the story and, as it were, authenticate it. If indeed the notion of partition came from the greatest scholar of the age, the story has a place in the history of thought. It is clear that the objection to settling disputes between ecclesiastics by the duel persisted and even increased in the eleventh century, though, oddly enough, as Maitland pointed out, English ecclesiastics had no deep dislike for the duel in later times. However that may be, the interest of this story lies above all in the conflict of ideas. The writer, Adrevald, could see no virtue in compromise, preferring even the ordeal of battle, where simple justice was unobtainable: but already in the ninth century the best opinion was against him. In England the clash of rival codes was largely absent, owing to the dominating influence of the Church on legal development; and no doubt this difference is bound up with the absence of the duel from our early law.

The steps by which first in Glanville and then in Bracton we trace the rise of a working alternative to fighting are momentous advances in civilization, but in England at least there are few indications that the *duellum* as such either 'developed' or 'declined'. It arrived with the Normans as already an old abuse, so notorious that William's English subjects were specifically allowed to refuse it; and, almost at once, the towns strove to secure similar exemption. We must, of course, distinguish the 'civil' from both the criminal and the personal duel or duel of honour, the last of which had still centuries of life before it. Yet the differences even here are merely of degree, and it is not clear that the traditional requirement regarding witness-champions in the civil duel on writ of right meant much more than the idea of the *iustum pretium* in the sphere of economics. In favour of this view is the marked disinclination at all stages of these witness-champions—like the Italian *condottieri*—to proceed to extremes. Even Glanville,[1] praising the Grand Assize because it saves men's lives, feels bound to add in effect, 'or at any rate (*vel saltem*) saves the vanquished from the disgrace of having to cry "Craven" '.

The casualties were not very high in the civil duel: but it was extremely costly. Glanville himself points out that the Grand Assize was much cheaper for poor men, and when we reach

---

[1] Ed. Woodbine, p. 63: 'Ac per hoc contingit insperatae et praematurae mortis ultimum evadere supplicium, vel saltem perennis infamiae opprobrium illius infesti et inverecundi verbi quod in ore victi turpiter sonat consecutivum.' The defeated champion confessed himself a 'recreant', and fines for *recreantisa* are recorded on the Pipe Rolls.

written records in the thirteenth century, not only is the hired champion a most expensive luxury, but it is already common form to pay him by instalments to ensure an honest performance of his contract. 'There was much talk of fighting', says Maitland, 'but it generally came to nothing.' In spite of innumerable offers to defend civil suits by fighting, the duel was only awarded in a small number of cases. Pledges were then given, the duel was formerly wagered (*vadiatum*), and Heaven help the man, we are told, who failed to present his champion on the day appointed, for there was no further legal remedy for such a one in this world. Yet blood-curdling as this sounds, we find that even when the champions met and the duel was *armatum*, it could still be composed by a *concordia per finem duelli*. Nay, even when blows had been struck (*duellum percussum*), it was still not too late for friends to interpose and induce a compromise. Altogether not very many men seem to have perished in the civil duel, even on the evidence of the Curia Regis rolls. As for the chronicles, they are full of stories like that told in the St. Frideswide cartulary, wherein the two champions were so frightened of each other that they just sat down and refused to fight:[1] or the instructive narrative in the Meaux chronicle[2] of two duels in a single suit—each *vadiatum, armatum et percussum*—which came to nothing. For the second of these the abbey retained at very great expense seven young warriors (*tirones*) together with their horses and servants. Like the more famous Abdul and Ivan Skivinski Skivar, the two champions fought from morning till night, and even then the abbey's man was only beginning to weaken (*paulatim succumbente*), when Roger Thurkelby the Justice (called 'our friend' by the chronicler) brought the parties comfortably together. Nor was the civil duel any more fierce when waged in private courts: witness the curious story in the Rievaulx cartulary[3] (*c.* 1170) when, with royal officers present at the court of Roger de Mowbray to see fair play between Alan of Rydale and the convent, 'congredientibus illis (i.e. the champions) tandem post multos assultus et ictus, compellentibus amicis', the dispute was sensibly settled by a *concordia per finem duelli*. This interference of friends or armed attendants often went too far. Some time before 1239,[4]

---

[1] Ed. Wigram (Oxford Hist. Soc.), ii. 325–6: 'utrisque sedentibus, cum neuter eorum alium esset ausus aggredi, formata fuit pax etc.' This duel, which I owe to Professor Cronne, is dated by the editor *c.* 1147.

[2] Ed. Bond (Rolls Series), ii. 97–102, about 1250.

[3] Surtees Soc., p. 111.

[4] *Calendar of Papal Registers*, i. 179–80; cf. Flower, op. cit., p. 117. The abbot

for instance, Sir Robert Marmion claimed the manor of Wat in the diocese of York against the abbot and convent of Mont St. Michel:

'The predecessor of the present abbot was summoned before the King's court, where the said knight offered to prove by duel that the manor was his, which challenge, although he had other defence, the late abbot indiscreetly accepted. The combatants fought in a place appointed by the king, the knight bringing a multitude of armed men, and the knight's champion was more than once brought to the ground, on which the knight's party interfered to rescue him, and threatened death to the abbot and his champion, so that the abbot, fearing that death would ensue, came to the spot and renounced his right.'

This story which comes to us from a papal letter confirms the impression left by nearer records that the civil duel in England was an outworn and sordid procedure which even the participants seemed to feel defeated the ends of law.

In the Curia Regis rolls and Bracton's *Note-Book* the civil duel presents an imposing front; but the layman is in danger of taking the lawyers more seriously, or at least more literally, than they took themselves. Their formal evidence requires to be checked at every point against the scanty but crucial testimony of the chronicles. Here we meet a double difficulty, for the age of abundant literary record arrives only in the thirteenth century; and, apart from this, the fiction of the witness-champion drawn from the plaintiff's feudal men was long sustained by society to render respectable a procedure already suspect when it arrived in England. The Church had long condemned it and William the Conqueror himself interposed to prevent a duel between the champions of St. Wandrille's abbey and William count of Évreux, 'ne causa ecclesiae determinaretur humano sanguine'.[1] The substitution of a better alternative, the use of the jury, can be followed across two centuries, and the Bury duel of 1287, here examined, illustrates perhaps better than any that has yet come to light how to the very last this transition was impeded by vested interests and particular motives.

'And so', writes the chronicler, 'our champion having been

and convent have appealed to the Pope, claiming that the renunciation is invalid. The archbishop of York is to make an inquiry and the parties are ordered to appear before the pope either personally or by proctors. A conflict of royal and papal jurisdiction might well have arisen from this inquiry: but nothing more is heard of the case. The papal letter is printed in the *Register of Archbishop Gray* (Surtees Soc., 1872), pp. 182–3.

[1] *Neustria Pia*, p. 168 (A.D. 1074). Cf. Pollock and Maitland, *Hist. of English Law*, I. 74.

slain in the duel at London we lost our manors of Semer and Groton without any hope of getting them back.' Yet he was wrong, and wrong just because he *was* contemporary, for, in fact, the monks recovered both manors. Beaten in the courts, the abbot turned again to private bargaining; and after complicated negotiations, in 1290 bought out Ralph Berners, who now owned two parts of the manors:

'*Memorandum*,[1] that Ralph de Berners, Knight, came into the King's Court at Westminster, on Wednesday before St. Peter in Cathedra, and granted and released to the abbot and convent of St. Edmunds two parts of the manors of Semere and Grotene, which the said Ralph and John de Creyk lately deraigned against the abbot in the king's court at Westminster by duel waged between them. The King granted licence to Ralph to grant the aforesaid two parts to the abbot and convent, and to the abbot and convent licence to enter the two parts together with the remaining third of the manor, notwithstanding the Statute of Mortmain. For this recognizance the abbot paid Ralph 400 marks—the bishop of Ely, the Treasurer, received the acknowledgement.'

The remaining part, held by the Beaumont family, was apparently acquired by charter about the same time, though the licence to retain it in Mortmain was only granted in 1297. A man was killed, in fact, in a vain attempt to save the abbey of St. Edmunds rather more than 400 marks: but the safer moral for the historian is perhaps that neither records nor chronicles are fully trustworthy when studied in isolation.

---

[1] *Cal. Close Rolls, 1288–1296*, p. 126. The three successful claimants apparently fell out after their successful action against the abbot. A writ of 4 July 16 Edward I orders the taking of an assize of Novel Disseisin to decide whether Godfrey de Beaumont, Robert le Bret, and others disseised John de Creyk and Ralph de Berners of two parts of the manor of Semer (cf. Assize Roll 1282, m. 6d). See also Rye, *Cal. of Feet of Fines, Suffolk*, p. 94 (18 Edward I). For the remainder of the manors see *Cal. Close Rolls, 1288–1296*, p. 361: *Cal. Pat. Rolls, 1281–1292*, p. 414; *1292–1301*, p. 230.

APPENDIX

I

College of Arms, MS. Arundel XXX

f. 173^v [*Florence of Worcester*, ii. 236,[1] after 'Devonia', l. 21 : 1286.]

Facta est itineracio iusticiariorum in comitatu Norfolch' in crastino sancti Hyllarii sub iusticiariis dominis Salamon de Roff', Roberto Fultone, Ricardo de Boylund, Waltero de Styrchele, Waltero de Hopeton', Thoma de Sudend' et aliis.

f. 174^v [Ibid., p. 237, after 'terruerunt', last line but one: 1287.]

In crastino sancti Hyllarii sederunt apud Catishale iusticiarii itinerantes qui supra: in quo quidem itinere implacitaverunt nos domini J. de Creyk, Godefridus de Beaumund', Radulfus de Berners de maneriis nostris de Semere et Groten. Cuius quidem cause facta discussione tandem patriam habentes suspectam utpote adversariis nostris familiarem et affinem, ius nostrum per duellum decrevimus esse defendendum. Die igitur a die Pasche in unum mensem ad Bancum apud Westmonasterium partibus assignata, sic saltem eo tempore negocium est protelatum. Cuidam pugili de partibus Lincoll' qui dicebatur Rogerus clericus contulit abbas de proprio pre manibus XX marcas XXX^a marcas post duellum recepturas ab eodem. Idem vero pugil toto expectacionis tempore una cum magistro suo apud nos quamvis sub calumpnia est commoratus.

[Ibid., p. 238, after 'Severini', fifth line from the bottom.]

Die sancti Kalixti [14 October] prevalentibus adversariis nostris pugilique nostro in duello Londoniis interfecto maneria nostra de Semere et Grotene amisimus sine aliqua spe rehabendi.

II

Placita de Banco: 15 and 16 Edward I [C.P. 40/69 m. 8 d.][2]

Suffolk   Johannes de Crek Radulfus de Berners et Godefridus de Bello Monte petierunt coram Salamone de Roff' et sociis suis iusticiariis itinerantibus apud Cateshull' in comitatu Suffolk versus abbatem de sancto Edmundo manerium de Semere cum pertinentiis, exceptis quinquaginta et septem acris terre, sexaginta et duodecim

---

[1] The St. Edmundsbury chronicle has been published as a continuation of *Florence of Worcester* (ed. Thorpe, 2 vols., English Historical Society, 1848–9) from Corpus Christi College, Cambridge, MS. 92, a Peterborough manuscript. The editor overlooked the original Bury manuscript, preserved in the College of Arms (Arundel xxx), which contains a large number of domestic entries omitted in the later Peterborough copy. The entries printed above are taken from this Arundel manuscript, and references are added to the printed text, to show where they occur. I hope in due course to publish the full text of the chronicle with a translation.

[2] I have to thank Mr. S. C. Ratcliff for unearthing these proceedings.

perticatis pasture in longitudine et una perticata pasture et dimidia
in latitudine, et advocatione ecclesie eiusdem manerii. Et manerium de Grotene cum pertinentiis, exceptis viginti et duabus acris
terre et advocatione ecclesie eiusdem manerii ut ius suum etc.
per precipe in capite. Et unde dicit quod quedam Nesta antecessor
etc. tempore pacis tempore domini Henrici regis patris domini
regis nunc fuit inde in seisina in dominico suo ut de feodo et iure
capiendo inde expleta ad valentiam etc. Et de ipsa Nesta quia
obiit sine herede se resorciebatur ius etc. quibusdam Alicie
Beatrici et Gunnore ut amitis et heredibus. Et de predicta Alicia
descendit ius propartis sue cuidam Roberto ut filio et heredi.
Et de ipso Roberto cuidam Bartholomeo ut filio et heredi. Et de
ipso Bartholomeo cuidam Roberto ut filio et heredi. Et de ipso
Roberto quia obiit sine herede de se descendit ius etc. cuidam
Galfrido ut fratri et heredi. Et de ipso Galfrido quia obiit sine
herede de se descendit ius etc. isti Johanni qui nunc petit ut frater
et heres. Et de ipsa Beatrice descendit ius propartis sue cuidam
Radulfo ut filio et heredi. Et de ipso Radulfo cuidam Willelmo ut
filio et heredi. Et de ipso Willelmo quia obiit sine herede de se
descendit ius etc. cuidam Radulfo ut fratri et heredi. Et de ipso
Radulfo isti Radulfo qui nunc petit ut filius et heres. Et de ipsa
Gunnora descendit ius propartis sue quibusdam Alicie et Agneti
ut filiabus et heredibus. Et de predicta Agnete quia obiit sine
herede de se descendit ius propartis sue predicte Alicie ut sorori
et heredi. Et de ipsa Alicia descendit ius etc. cuidam Willelmo ut
filio et heredi. Et de ipso Willelmo isti Godefrido qui nunc petit
simul etc. ut filius et heres. Et quod tale sit ius suum offerunt etc.

Et abbas venit et defendit ius suum quando etc. et seisinam predicte Neste antecessoris etc. ut de feodo et iure. Et totum etc. Et
hoc paratus est defendere per corpus liberi hominis sui Rogeri
filii Roberti de Mutford qui presens est et hoc offert defendere
per corpus suum vel qualitercumque curia considerauerit etc.
Et si de eo etc. per alium etc.

Et Johannes Radulfus et Godefridus dicunt quod predictus
abbas iniuste defendit ius suum et seisinam predicte Neste antecessoris etc. ut de feodo et iure quia dicunt quod eadem Nesta fuit
inde in seisina . . . [as above] . . . Et quod tale sit ius suum offerunt
disracionare per corpus liberi hominis sui Roberti filii Willelmi le
Bret qui presens est et hoc offert disracionare per corpus suum vel
qualitercumque curia considerauerit. Et si de eo etc. per alium etc.
Et ideo consideratum est quod duellum sit inter eos. Et quod
predictus Rogerus det vadium defendendi. Et predictus Robertus
det vadium difforciandi: plegii predicti Rogeri Robertus Bardolf
et Ricardus de Weylaund: plegii predicti Roberti Johannes de
Bello Monte et Johannes de Rameseye etc. Dies datus est eis hic

die Lune proxima post mensem Pasche. Et tunc veniunt servientes armati etc. Ad quem diem predictus abbas fuit essoniatus et
datus fuit eis dies die Martis proxima post quindenam sancti
Michelis hoc anno quo die venerunt partes et similiter seruientes

Duellum armati et fuit duellum inter eos armatum et percussum et serviens
predicti abbatis devictus et interfectus. Ideo consideratum est
quod predicti Johannes Radulfus et Godefridus recuperent seisinam suam de predictis tenementis versus predictum abbatem

Miseri- tenendis sibi et heredibus suis quiete de predicto abbate et suc-
cordia[1]
Baro cessoribus suis imperpetuum. Et abbas in misericordia etc.

V. H. GALBRAITH

---

[1] *Misericordia* has been struck through and *Baro* written below. The explanation
of this is supplied by the *Tilliol* v. *Percy* case cited above (*Year Book*, 1 Henry VI,
ed. Williams, pp. 97–8) where it is laid down that 'because the earl is a peer of the
realm he will be amerced by his peers according to the Statute and for this reason
we do not specify the amercement', &c.

THE TREASON OF
THOMAS TURBERVILLE, 1295

IN discussing the history of treason in England prior to the statute of treasons of 1352, Maitland has remarked that during the thirteenth century 'such stories as have come down to us do not entitle us to say that many persons, except the Jewish money-clippers, suffered for it'.[1] Apart from the wholesale executions of these Jewish money-clippers as traitors in 1278, he lists hardly a dozen instances between 1196 and 1305. There was, in fact, at least one case of some importance which he does not mention—that of the Welsh prince Rhys ap Maredudd, who was executed for treason in 1292, and whose sentence is entered on the Close Roll of that year.[2] One of the cases to which Maitland does make just a passing reference, in the course of discussing the punishment of treason, is that of Thomas Turberville in 1295.[3] This was in its day a *cause célèbre*. It is mentioned, at greater or less length, by most of the chroniclers, and it was the subject of a contemporary 'political song'.[4] In the eventful year 1295 it seems to have excited as much general interest in England as did the treason of Roger Casement in 1916.

The circumstances were these. In 1294 open war had broken out between England and France. In the autumn, Edward I had

---

[1] Pollock and Maitland, *Hist. Eng. Law* (2nd ed.), ii. 506.

[2] Close Roll 109 (20 Ed. I), schedule to m. 5d: 'Deliberacio gaole regis de Eboraco facta de Rees Amereduk in crastino sancte Trinitatis anno regni regis nunc vicesimo per speciale preceptum eiusdem regis coram Petro de Campania, Johanne de Lythegreynes, Johanne de Melsa, et Willelmo de S. Quintino, justiciariis ad hoc assignatis. Qui quidem Rees ibidem coram prefatis justiciariis ductus fuit et convictus de seductione domino regi facta, homicidiis combustionibus roberiis et latrociniis contra pacem eiusdem domini regis factis, et castellis eiusdem regis prostratis. Adjudicatus est quod pro seductione domino regi facta detractetur, et pro dictis homicidiis combustionibus roberiis et latrociniis et castellis prostratis suspendatur.' He was hanged on the same day (2 June 1292) on Knavesmire, and left hanging for three days and nights; *Chron. Lanercost* (ed. Stevenson, 1839), p. 145; see also *Place-Names of the East Riding of Yorkshire and York* (E.P.N.S. xiv), p. 292.

[3] Op. cit. ii. 500, n. 6. By an obvious misprint, the date is given as 1293.

[4] Printed in *Roman d'Eustache le Moine* (ed. Fr. Michel, 1834), pp. xlviii–l; in *Chron. Lanercost*, pp. 484–7; and in *Croniques de London* (ed. Aungier, 1844), pp. 100–3. The piece is interesting, not for its facts (which are closely parallel to those recorded by the chroniclers) but for its 'national' spirit: thus it ends by warning the French king (who is called 'Charles' throughout the poem) of the futility of warring against England, and points the moral by recalling the failure of 'Duke Louis' in 1217.

sent a force under the command of John of Brittany, to carry on
the struggle in Gascony while he himself dealt with the Welsh
revolt which had broken out in September 1294. Among those
who accompanied John of Brittany was Thomas Turberville.
On this occasion Turberville is known to have had a retinue
consisting of at least nine persons,[1] and he was clearly a man of
some standing and experience. He was a knight, and had been a
member of the king's household.[2] In that capacity he had served
as one of Edward's captains in the Welsh wars of 1277 and 1282,[3]
and had accompanied the king on his journey to Gascony in
1286.[4] John of Brittany's expedition of 1294 came to an inglorious
end. He landed at Rions and garrisoned it. In the spring of 1295
the French laid siege to the town, and in less than a fortnight the
garrison surrendered. This was on 7 April 1295.[5] Turberville
was among those who were taken prisoner. With his departure
into captivity, he disappears from view for almost exactly four
months. When he reappears at the beginning of August he is
back again in London, moving in court circles, and busied in his
treasonable enterprise. Subsequent events were to show that he
had undertaken this mission while a prisoner of war in French
hands, and that he had been released by his captors for the
express purpose of pursuing it.

The chroniclers who give the longest account of the whole
business are Hemingburgh and Bartholomew Cotton,[6] and
Cotton's account is especially valuable because it includes the
text of two documents which are not actually quoted elsewhere,
though there are indications that several of the chroniclers knew
of them. One of these documents was a capital exhibit in the
case. Turberville was ultimately, as one of the London chroniclers
expresses it, 'drawn and hanged because of letters of treason',[7]
and it is the most important of these letters that Cotton has

[1] *Rôles Gascons*, iii (ed. Bémont, 1906), nos. 2286, 2288, 2352, 2546, 2597, 2759,
2828, 3370, 3449 (96): the nine persons were Hugh of Pembridge, Vincent son of
Philip le Spicer of Gloucester, Gilbert of Clayhanger, and six Welshmen.
[2] 'Miles de familia regis'; Ann. Worcester in *Ann. Mon.* (ed. Luard, Rolls Series,
1864-9), iv. 520: 'domesticus et praecipue domini regis Angliae familiaris'; John of
Eversden (of Bury St. Edmunds) in Thorpe's ed. of *Florence of Worcester* (Eng.
Hist. Soc. 1848-9), ii. 278.
[3] Morris, *Welsh Wars of Ed. I*, pp. 174, 198.
[4] *Cal. Pat. Rolls, 1281-1291*, p. 240.
[5] *Chron. Walteri de Hemingburgh* (ed. Hamilton, 1849), ii. 46 52.
[6] Ibid. ii. 60-3; Cotton, *Hist. Anglicana* (ed. Luard, Rolls Series, 1859), pp.
304-6.
[7] *Croniques de London*, p. 24.

preserved. It was addressed to the provost of Paris in the following terms:

'A noble beer e seynur, provost de Paris, syre duz, le seon home lige de ses meyns al boys de Viciens, saluz.

'Cher syre, sachez ke jo suy venuz seyn et hete a la curt le rey de Engletere, e si trovay le rey a Lundres,[1] et muz de noveles me demaunda, dount jo ly diseye le meuz ke jo savoye. E sachez ke jo trovay terre de pes en Guales, dunt jo ne osay bayler la chose ke vus bien savez a Morgan. E sachez ke le rey ad byen grante pes et trowes,[2] mes bien vous gardez et avisez ke nules trues ne pernez si ne seyt a vostre grant prou; et sachez si nules trues ne feysez, grant prou vus avendreyt: et ceo poez dire a luy haut seignur.[3] E sachez ke jo trovay sire Johan le fiz Thomas a la curt le rey pur treter pes entre luy et le cunte de Nichole [sic] del cunte de Ulvester,[4] mes jeo ne saveye mie uncore coment la bosoyne se prendreyt, kar cete lettre fu fete le jur apres ke les cardinaus furent respunduz, dunt jo ne oseye ren tucher de les bosoynes ke vus tuchent.[5] E sachez ke poy de garde jad vers le su de la mer. E sachez ke Ille de Wycht est saunz garde.[6] E sachez ke le rey maunde en Alemayne ii cuntes ii eveskes et ii baruns pur parler et cunseyler al rey de Alemayne de ceste guerre.[7] Et sachez ke le rey maunde en Gascoyne xx neefs charges de blee et de aveyne et de autre vitalie e graunt fuysun de argent; e sire Edmun frere al rey i ira e le cunte de Nichole, sire Hue le Despenser, le cunte de Warwyk et muz des autres bone gens[8]: et ceo poez dire a luy haut seygnur. E sachez ke nus quidoms aver assez a fere ver ceus de Escoce; e si ceus de Escoce se relevent contre le rey de Engletere, le Gualeys se releverunt autresi: e ceo ay jeo ben fest, et Morgan me ad ceo ben encovenaunte. Dunt jeo vous conseyl ke vus

[1] A parliament had been summoned to meet at Westminster on 1 Aug. 1295 'vel saltem infra tercium diem subsequentem ad ultimum'; Palgrave, *Parl. Writs*, i. 28. Edward was at Worcester, en route from North Wales, on 20 and 21 July; *Ann. Mon.* iv. 521. His itinerary shows that he was in the neighbourhood of High Wycombe on 29 July. So he had quite probably reached London by 1 Aug.

[2] In deference to the cardinals' request, Edward agreed to a suspension of hostilities until 1 Nov., provided that the French king concurred; Hemingburgh, ii. 68; Rymer, *Foedera* (Rec. Comm. ed.), i. ii. 824–5.

[3] i.e. Philip IV of France.

[4] For the documents concerning this case, which came before the parliament on 16 Aug. 1295, see *Rot. Parl.* i. 135–7. The dispute was between two Irish magnates, John Fitz Thomas of Kildare and Richard de Burgh earl of Ulster. (The 'Nichole' of Turberville's letter is doubtless a transcriber's error for 'Ulton'.) On the whole dispute see Orpen, *Ireland under the Normans*, iv. 116–19.

[5] Turberville and his French employers would be interested in the Irish dispute because it might seem to open up promising possibilities of disaffection in Ireland, as well as in Wales and Scotland.

[6] For measures to strengthen the defences in these regions at the end of August and in October and November see Palgrave, *Parl. Writs*, i. 268–75.

[7] The statement that the king was sending an embassy to Germany is correct, though it was not eventually constituted as Turberville here reports; Hemingburgh, ii. 68; *Foedera*, i. ii. 824.

[8] For Earl Edmund's projected expedition to Gascony see *Parl. Writs*, i. 269–70.

hastivement maundez granz genz en Escoce, kar si lenz poez entrer, a tuz
jurs gayne le averez. E si vus voylez ke jeo la voyse, maundez al rey de
Escoce ke il me trove a tote ma gent a lur custages honurablement: me ben
vus avisez si vus volez ke jo la voyse ou nun, kar jeo crey ke plus vostre pru
freye pur attendre a la curt le rey pur espier et enquere noveles ke pur vus
seent, qar tut ceo ke jeo pus enquere jeo le vus fray a saver. E me maundez
Perot ke fut mon gardeyn en la prison u jeo fu, kar a luy diray chose ke jeo
saveray desore en avaunt, et par luy vus enveray les veies ke jeo ben say.
E pur Deu vus pri ke vous vous remembrez et avisez de les promesses qe
vous moy promistes de par le haut seynur, ceo est a saver c livrees de terre
a moy et a mes heyrs. E pur Deu vous pri de mes enfaunz ke il ne eent
nule defaute taunt come il sunt en vostre garde de manger ne de beyvre
ne de autre sustenaunce. E pur Deu vous pri ke vous avisez coment joe
pus estre pae ensi, kar jeo ne ay ren, ke tut ay perdu ausi bien de ca come
de la et ren ne ay de vous fors vostre grant leaute, en quey jeo moy afy mut.
Hardiement vus afiez en le portur de ceste lettre et curteysie ly facez.
E sachez ke en grant pour suy et en grant dute, kar acone genz unt suspeciun
vers moy, pur ceo ke jeo ay dyt ke jeo suy eschape hors de la prison. Vos
voluntez moy maundez en totes choses. A Deu, ke vous gard.'

That this letter is genuine can hardly be doubted. The mere
fact that it is preserved by Cotton would in itself be strong prima
facie evidence in its favour, since he was demonstrably a well-
informed and careful chronicler who made a point of collecting
contemporary documents and copying them into his chronicle.
But the internal evidence is also strong: the statements made in
the letter about current events in England are in essentials
accurate and consistent, and are borne out by independent
information, as already indicated in the footnotes above.

The letter was written 'on the day after the cardinals were
answered'. The cardinals were two papal legates sent to England
by Boniface VIII to bring about a truce between England and
France with a view to a permanent peace, and their reception
was one of the chief items of business in the parliament summoned for 1 August. As there is no exhaustive official record
of the parliament's proceedings, we have to depend upon the
chroniclers, particularly upon Hemingburgh and the Westminster annalist in the *Flores Historiarum*,[1] and unluckily neither
account is quite free from ambiguity, especially as regards dates.
Hemingburgh is explicit that the cardinals were answered on the
fourth day after that on which they delivered their message from
the pope. This would be 4 August, if Hemingburgh is right in

---

[1] *Flores Historiarum* (ed. Luard, Rolls Series, 1890), iii. 93–4; Hemingburgh, ii.
66–9.

stating that the cardinals delivered their message on 1 August. But as the writs summoning the parliament to meet on 1 August had allowed two days' grace, and as the beginnings of medieval parliaments were apt to be rather dilatory, it is by no means unlikely that proceedings might not actually begin until 3 August, and in that case the answer to the cardinals would be given on 6 August. This supposition seems to be borne out by the Westminster annalist, who was in a position to be accurately informed. He says that on 5 August a statement was made in parliament by Earl Edmund the king's brother and John de Lacy about the beginnings of the war. These two speakers are not, indeed, specifically mentioned by Hemingburgh, but he does say that a long statement was made about the origins of the war, and he assigns this statement to the day before the cardinals were answered. It seems not unlikely, therefore, that the cardinals were answered on 6 August. In that case, Turberville's letter would be written on 7 August. In any case, it must have been written very near that date.[1]

By implication the letter throws some light on Turberville's doings during the obscure four months since his capture in April. Whether the treasonable scheme was first proposed by the French or by Turberville himself is not clear, but the arrangements for it had evidently been made through the mediation of the provost of Paris and of Turberville's jailer Perot. Turberville had given two guarantees of good faith. He had become the 'liege man' of the provost, and had left his children in France as hostages. The chroniclers are agreed that these children were his two sons: presumably they had accompanied him to Gascony, possibly in the capacity of esquires. The reward of his treason was to be a grant of 100 librates of land for himself and his heirs.

About Turberville's movements after he had returned to England, the implications of the letter are less clear. The fixed points are that the king arrived in London on or just before 1 August, and that Turberville had already had at least one audience with Edward when he wrote his report on or about 7 August. In the course of that report he asserts that 'si ceus de Escoce se relevent contre le rey de Engletere, le Gualeys se releverunt autresi: e ceo ay jeo ben fest, et Morgan me ad ceo

---

[1] If Hemingburgh is right in spreading the proceedings over four days, the earliest possible date for the answer to the cardinals would be 4 Aug. The latest possible date would be before 14 Aug., which is the date of the patent empowering the cardinals to arrange a truce with France; *Foedera*, I. ii. 824.

ben encovenaunte'. This Morgan had been the leader of the Welsh of Glamorgan in the rising of 1294–5; he had ultimately submitted to Edward, and had been received into the king's peace about the middle of June 1295.[1] Now Morgan could not have made the promise reported by Turberville unless the two had already been in communication, either personally or by messenger. Such communication would necessarily take a little time. So we must probably infer that Turberville had arrived in England sufficiently long before 7 August to allow time for his negotiations with Morgan: how long before 7 August we cannot guess. But his negotiations with Morgan were dangerous, and therefore not to be entered upon by either party without due circumspection. And circumspection is often a thief of time.

The validity of these inferences depends, of course, on the assumption that Turberville's statement about Morgan's promise can be taken at its face value and accepted as true. That assumption, however, is not free from difficulties. The path of traitors was beset with many pitfalls. If Morgan really had promised, as Turberville alleged, to raise a rebellion in Wales if the Scots rose, that promise would itself have been treasonable. Even if, on receiving Turberville's treasonable suggestion, Morgan had rejected it, he would nevertheless have been guilty of treason unless he had promptly disclosed the fact that the suggestion had been made. On this subject Bracton has some ringing words. Anyone, he says, who becomes aware that treason is afoot must inform the king or one of the king's *familiares* without delay: 'non enim debet morari in uno loco per duas noctes vel dies antequam personam regis vidcat, nec debet ad aliqua negotia quamvis urgentissima se convertere, quia vix permittitur ei quod retro aspiciat'.[2] But there is no indication in the chronicles that it was through Morgan that Turberville's treason was discovered: on the contrary, its disclosure, according to them, was due to someone very different from Morgan. Moreover, when Turberville's letter to the provost did ultimately come to light, we may suppose that Edward would probe very thoroughly into the allegation that Morgan had given the treasonable promise to raise a rebellion in Wales if the Scots should rise. But we get no tidings that Morgan was punished or even tried for treason. He may, of course, have been both tried and executed without our

[1] Ann. Worcester in *Ann. Mon.* iv. 520–1, together with the king's itinerary in P.R.O. Treasury of Receipt Misc. Books 202, give a fairly clear indication of the date.   [2] *De Legibus Angliae*, ed. Woodbine, ii. 335.

knowing it, for the gaps in the evidence are many. But equally he may never have been brought to trial because he was able to satisfy the king that Turberville's allegation was not true. We must also remember in this connexion that although Morgan had indeed led the Welsh of Glamorgan in the rising of 1294–5, his quarrel had not been with the king, but with the earl of Gloucester, who was the lord of Glamorgan, and that when Edward had received Morgan into his peace in June 1295 he had done so, as the Worcester annalist expressly points out, *contra voluntatem dicti Comitis*.[1] Altogether, therefore, it is unsafe to assume without question that Morgan would necessarily have been quite so ready to dabble in treason as Turberville alleged.

The letter to the provost gives one more glimpse of Turberville's relations with Morgan. He begins his report by announcing his safe arrival in England and his audience with the king, and then goes on immediately to say that he had found Wales at peace, 'dunt jo ne osay bayler la chose ke vus bien savez a Morgan'. What was this mysterious but evidently important 'thing' that he had not 'dared' to give to Morgan? A possible answer is suggested by a tantalizing document in the Public Record Office. Among the Miscellanea of the Chancery there is a detached slip of parchment containing a bald list, written in a fourteenth-century hand, of various documents connected with Turberville's treason: it has no heading, and ends as abruptly as it begins. It reads thus:[2]

'Transcriptum littere regis Francie directe domino [*blank*] quod insurgat contra regem Anglie cum Wallensibus.

'Transcriptum littere regis Francie directe domino Galfrido de Geinvill quod non insurgat cum rege Anglie contra aliquos de Hibern[ia].[3]

'Transcriptum littere Thome de Tourbevill directe domino [*blank*] quod insurgat contra regem Anglie cum Wallensibus.

'Transcripta quarundarum [*sic*] cedularum continencium confessiones dicti Thome Tourbevill et aliorum proditorum regis Anglie de terra Scocie.

---

[1] The annalists of Dunstable (*Ann. Mon.* iii. 387), of Worcester (ibid. iv. 526), and of Merton (*Flores Hist.* iii. 27), and also Cotton (p. 253) state explicitly that the men of Glamorgan rose against the earl, and Trevet (*Annales*, ed. Hog, 1845, p. 333) explains that Morgan's grievance was that Earl Gilbert 'progenitores suos exheredaverat de terra sua'. The reference seems to be to Morgan's father, who was apparently dispossessed by the earl in 1273; Bridgeman, *Hist. of Princes of South Wales* (1876), p. 72.

[2] P.R.O. Miscellanea of the Chancery, C47/27/3/31.

[3] Geoffrey de Genville, lord of Trim from 1254 to 1307, was a prominent Anglo-Norman baron in Ireland. For Turberville's interest in Irish affairs see above, p. 298, n. 5.

'Item transcripta quarundam litterarum gentibus Scocie directarum ad ipsos confortandum per Gallicorum promissiones ad continuandum guerram contra regem Anglie.'

The transcripts which are here listed were evidently in official custody, but if they still exist they do not seem to have been yet identified.[1] Two of them, it will be observed, were copies of letters urging some unnamed person to rise in rebellion with the Welsh against the king of England: one of these was from the French king and the other from Turberville himself. Now the only one of the Welsh leaders of 1294–5 who had escaped with liberty as well as life was Morgan, so he might well be regarded as the one hope of those who wished to make further trouble in Wales. It is therefore quite probable that Morgan was the unnamed person for whom the two letters were intended. If so, it is not difficult to suggest a possible explanation of Turberville's reference, in his letter to the provost, to the 'thing' which he had not 'dared' to give to Morgan. This mysterious 'thing' may quite conceivably have been the letter from the French king. Even if Turberville sent his own letter to Morgan, he might well have had reasons for deciding that the time was not yet ripe for disclosing the communication from the king of France. But however this may be, it is at any rate clear that the authorities in England not only came to know of Turberville's allegations about Morgan in the report to the provost, but also actually acquired copies of letters from Philip the Fair and Turberville inciting some unnamed person to raise a rebellion in Wales. It is not credible that the authorities would fail, in such circumstances, to suspect that the Anonymous was Morgan. It is still less credible that Edward I (of all people) would omit to sift the whole matter to the bottom. And if Morgan were then unable to clear himself, 'vix permittitur ei quod retro aspiciat' would

---

[1] These documents may possibly be referred to in P.R.O. Miscellanea of the Chancery, C47/28/4/7, which consists of a number of memoranda made in Edward III's reign about various confoederacies that had been made by the French against England, starting with their alliance with the Scots in 1295. The fourth memorandum is as follows: 'Item, dominus Thomas de Torbeville pro simile confoederacione innuenda inter Gallicos et Wallenses et alios a carcere regis Francie erat liberatus, et ad partes Anglie et Wallie transmissus, et in partibus Kancie in prodicione sua deprehensus, et Londoniis suspensus. Et litere prodicionis predicte inveniri possunt in thesauro domini nostri regis in Turri Londoniis inter literas executorias ordinacionis tendentis ad finem destruccionis et exheredacionis nacionis Anglicane. Vacat.' (This item was printed by Stevenson in *Chron. Lanercost*, p. 482, and by Aungier in *Croniques de London*, p. 95. I am indebted to Mr. H. C. Johnson for identifying the document.)

become precisely applicable, and would doubtless be punctually applied. Here, however, we are brought back to the fact that the chroniclers, though they are much interested in Turberville's treason, give no hint that Morgan shared his fate as an accomplice. Of course, we may not argue from their silence, but at least we must take note of it.

After the compiling of his report to the provost of Paris on or about 7 August, Turberville disappears from view once again, this time for about six weeks. During that interval his report was apparently dispatched to France, and according to some of the chroniclers, he received answering letters from his employers. Then, on Saturday, 24 September, his arrest is laconically recorded by Cotton. Hemingburgh, without mentioning dates, adds the information that Turberville fled secretly from the king's court—which was down in Kent at the time—and was arrested after two days when trying to make his escape to Wales. This would imply that he fled from court on 22 September. The inference is absolutely confirmed by two entries in the Wardrobe Accounts:[1]

'Magistro Nicholao de Luvetot eunti ad querendum dominum Thomam Turbevill cum festinacione pro quibusdam negociis regem specialiter tangencibus, de prestito super expensis suis per manus proprias apud Wengham 22 die Septembris, 13s. 4d.

'Willemo de Aulton eunti similiter ad querendum eundem dominum Thomam, de prestito super expensis suis per manus proprias ibidem eodem die, 20s.'

How Turberville's treason came to be discovered is only an incidental question, but it is not entirely without interest. 'The famous traitors of Edward I's day', as Maitland has called them, that is, David of Wales and William Wallace (and also, we might add, Rhys ap Maredudd), had committed their treasons openly, whereas Turberville's crime was essentially secret, and therefore not easy to discover. It was eventually detected, according to the chroniclers, through an informer, but they disagree about his identity, and give no hint of his name. The point is sufficiently intriguing to be pursued a little further.

In 1317, a writ under the privy seal of Edward II was issued in the following terms:[2]

'Edward par la grace de Dieu roy Dengleterre seignur Dirlaunde et ducs Daquitaine, al honurable pere en Dieu J. par la meme grace euesqe de

---

[1] P.R.O. Treasury of Receipt Misc. Books 202, p. 45.
[2] P.R.O. Warrants for the Great Seal 100/4241; summarized in *Cal. Chancery Warrants*, i. 470.

Wincestre nostre chauncellier, saluz. Come por le bon et greable service qe nostre bien ame . . .[1] ad fait a nostre chiere piere qui Dieux assoille taunt come il vesquit, prenaunt Thomas de Turbeville enemy nostre dit piere, et uncore fait a nous de iour en autre, luy voilloms porveer de sustenaunce a tote sa vie, vous maundoms qe par lettres desous nostre graunte seal facez maunder en covenable fourme a nos chiers en Dieu abbe et covent de Redynges qe en le lieu Johan le Convers, qest a Dieu commaundez, qui avoit sa sustenaunce en lour dite maison, receivent le dit Robert, et lui facent trover en ycele au tiele sustenaunce en totes choses come le dit Johan y avoit taunt come il vesquist, et qe sur ce luy facent aver lettres patentes sealees du commun seal de lour chapitre en due forme feissantes express mencion de quantquil recevera de eux por sa dite sustenance, et que par lour lettres et par le portour des noz nous remaundent ce quil en averont fait. Et por lesploit de ceste busoigne facez faire por le dit Robert tauntz des lettres come mester luy serront. Done souz nostre prive seal a Windesore le 14 jour May lan de nostre regne disme.'

In pursuance of this warrant a writ under the great seal was duly issued, and a copy is entered on the Close Roll.[2] This enrolment supplies the name which is no longer legible in the warrant. That name is 'Robert de Crouland'.

The purport of the two writs, as will be evident, was to grant a corrody in Reading abbey to Robert Crouland, on account of the good service that he had done to the king's father 'in taking Thomas Turberville, the enemy of our said father'. So Crouland had evidently played some important part in the 'taking' of Turberville.[3] Who was this Robert Crouland?

It will have been noticed that the writ of privy seal speaks of Crouland, not only as having served Edward I, but also as still serving Edward II 'from day to day'. Such words naturally suggest some sort of employment in the king's household, the more so as the deceased John Convers, to whose corrody Crouland was succeeding, had also been a household functionary. Within the household, the Wardrobe is obviously the place that should be searched first. Of the detailed Wardrobe Accounts surviving from the reign of Edward II, the nearest in date to 1317 are those of 8–9 Ed. II (1314–16).[4] Here, among other things, are recorded,

---

[1] The parchment has rotted away at this point and the name is therefore missing.

[2] *Cal. Close Rolls, 1313–18*, p. 463.

[3] Grants of corrodies are often entered on the Close Rolls in small batches. On 15 May 1318 there was evidently some further grant to Crouland, but as the enrolment is incomplete, the nature of the grant is unknown; it is accompanied, however, by the grant of a corrody to another person, and may therefore have related to Crouland's corrody; ibid., p. 610.

[4] P.R.O. Exch. Accts. Various, E101/376/7, ff. 74ʳ, 74ᵛ, 76ᵛ, 77ʳ.

under the heading *Nuncii*, the prests made to the messengers of the Wardrobe for their expenses in carrying letters. Five of these prests are made to 'Robert de Crouland' (also spelt 'Crowland' and 'Croyland'), who is described as *cursor regis*. He appears similarly in the *nuncii* sections of the Wardrobe Accounts of 6 Ed. II (1312–13),[1] of 1 Ed. II (1307–8),[2] of 34 Ed. I (1305–6),[3] of 29 Ed. I (1300–1),[4] of 28 Ed. I (1299–1300),[5] and of 25 Ed. I (a fragment covering only February–March 1297):[6] in these accounts he is usually designated *cokinus*, which was, like *cursor*, an established name for the regular messengers of the Wardrobe.

If this Robert Crouland, *cokinus* or *cursor regis*, may be identified with his namesake who was rewarded with a corrody in 1317— and the identification seems quite probable—the Crouland who appears as a royal messenger between 1297 and 1316 had played some unspecified but evidently notable part in 'taking' Turberville in 1295. The gaps in the surviving Wardrobe Accounts of Edward I unluckily prevent our knowing when Crouland first began to serve in the Wardrobe: all we can say is that by March 1297 he was on the establishment of Wardrobe messengers. And March 1297 was only eighteen months after Turberville's arrest. Now Cotton, who provides the most valuable of all the accounts of Turberville's treason, says that it was a messenger who informed against him—the messenger whom he employed to carry his report to France.[7] Now if, in 1295, Robert Crouland was already a *cokinus* in the Wardrobe, it seems hardly likely that Turberville would have ventured to employ him as his own messenger. In that case, the part which Crouland played in 'taking' Turberville would have to remain unspecified. But if, in 1295, Crouland had not yet become a Wardrobe messenger, he might very well have been employed by Turberville. In that case, his long-remembered service in the 'taking' of Turberville would not be beyond conjecture. Would he not be the messenger who turned informer, and thereby brought the traitor to his

[1] P.R.O. Exch. Accts. Various, E101/375/8, ff. 38ᵛ, 39ᵛ.

[2] Ibid., E101/373/15, ff. 23ᵛ, 24ᵛ.

[3] Ibid., E101/369/11, ff. 143ʳ, 143ᵛ, 145ʳ, 145ᵛ, 146ᵛ.

[4] Ibid., E101/359/6, f. 22ʳ.

[5] *Liber Quotidianus Contrarotulatoris Garderobae 28 Ed. I* (1787), pp. 281, 284, 289, 293–4, 297–300.

[6] P.R.O. Miscellanea of the Chancery, 4/6, f. 12ᵛ. The prest to Crouland there recorded is dated 19 Mar. (1297).

[7] Cotton, p. 304. Hemingburgh, ii. 62, states that the informer was the clerk who acted as Turberville's amanuensis.

doom? If so, his appearance soon after 1295 among the couriers of the Wardrobe would be in no way surprising. What more fitting reward for a traitor's messenger who had shown loyalty to the king than to appoint him a king's messenger?

The precise nature of Turberville's treason, is not, of course, in doubt. He himself, in his letter to the provost of Paris, described his activities as being 'pur attendre a la curt le rey *pur espier et enquere noveles ke pour vus seent*'. This was the form of treason later to be defined in the statute of 1352 as 'adherant as enemys nostre seignur le roy en le roialme, donant a eux eid ou confort en son roialme ou par aillours'. That 'adhering to the king's enemies' by spying was already recognized as treasonable before 1295 is clear,[1] but this particular form of treason was to prove very rare in English history,[2] and Turberville's case seems to provide the earliest notable instance of it. One would therefore be glad to have the legal 'record' of his trial. But in a reign otherwise so rich in legal archives as Edward I's, the comparative dearth of information about treason trials is a surprising and disappointing feature. There were, during the reign, at least four or five such trials sufficiently important to be leading cases— those of Prince David, of Rhys ap Maredudd, of Turberville, of Nicholas Segrave, and of William Wallace—but the 'record' survives in only two of these cases, and unluckily Turberville's is not one of the two.[3] Some useful information about Turberville's trial can, however, be gleaned from the chroniclers, especially from the annalist of Merton,[4] and above all from Bartholomew Cotton, who has preserved a vivid description of Turberville's end, which he quotes verbatim from what was evidently a contemporary account, apparently written while the traitor's dead body was still actually hanging on the gallows.[5]

His trial took place on Saturday, 8 October, on the dais of the great hall at Westminster. Either before or during the trial he

[1] See the case of 1285 in *Oxford City Documents* (ed. Rogers, 1891), pp. 204–5, cited by Maitland, *Hist. Eng. Law*, ii. 507, n. 8. Master Nicholas de Wantham, parson of the church of Banbury, was outlawed for non-appearance on a charge that he had, *seditiose ut seductor*, acted as a spy for Guy and Aimery de Montfort and for Llywelyn prince of Wales, *et parti eorum adhaesit*.

[2] Stephen, *Hist. of the Criminal Law of England* (1883), ii. 282.

[3] The two are Segrave (*Rot. Parl.* i. 172–4, where, however, his offence is not specifically called treason) and Wallace (*Chron. of Ed. I and Ed. II* (ed. Stubbs, Rolls Series, 1882–3), i. 139–42). As already remarked (p. 296, n. 2, above) only the sentence of Rhys ap Maredudd is entered on the Close Roll of 20 Ed. I.

[4] *Flores Hist.* iii. 282.

[5] Cotton, p. 306; the account which he quotes ends with the words: 'et la est il pendu de une chene de fer, *et pendra taunt ke ren de ly durer pura.*'

evidently made various confessions.[1] Sentence was pronounced by Roger Brabazon, then newly appointed Chief Justice of the King's Bench, but acting on this particular occasion, we may surmise, as the head of a special commission of jail delivery appointed expressly to try Turberville: such at least was the procedure adopted for the trial of Rhys ap Maredudd in 1292[2] and of William Wallace in 1305.[3] The sentence was evidently one of simple drawing and hanging:[4] there were none of the added severities of disembowelling, burning, beheading, and quartering suffered by Prince David and William Wallace. As Rhys ap Maredudd had also been spared these horrors, we may perhaps infer that the extreme barbarities heaped upon David and Wallace had not yet become established as the standard punishment in cases of high treason.[5]

Turberville's trial and execution were accompanied by some characteristic pageantry. He was led across London from the Tower to Westminster 'mounted on a poor hack', with his feet bound under the horse's belly and his hands tied in front of him. Around him rode six 'tormentors', dressed up like devils; one of them held the hack's rein, while the hangman held its halter. After sentence, Turberville was laid on a fresh ox-hide, and drawn by the six horses all the way from Westminster to the Conduit in Cheapside, and thence 'back to the gallows', a phrase which probably indicates that these were set up at the elms of Smithfield, where Wallace in his turn was executed ten years later. On this journey

> Cillante pierres a graunt fusiun
> Aveit il entur son flanc,
> Ke li raerent le sanc,[6]

and meanwhile the 'tormentors' insulted him and beat him. In the end he was hanged, and in accordance with the sentence of the court, his body was left to hang 'as long as anything of him should remain'.

---

[1] See the document quoted above, p. 302.

[2] Above, p. 296, n. 2.

[3] *Chron. of Ed. I and Ed. II*, i. 139.

[4] 'Et sire Roger Brabazun luy dona soen jugement, ke il fut treyne et pendu, et ke il pendereyt taunt come ren feut enter de ly.'

[5] It is perhaps worth noticing that the annalist of Osney, before summarizing the sentence passed on David, remarks that 'judicialiter adjudicatus est *morti retroactis temporibus inauditae*'; *Ann. Mon.* iv. 294.

[6] From the description of Turberville's execution in the 'song' mentioned above, p. 296, n. 4.

Much of this procedure was, of course, common form on such occasions, but it may well have had a heightened significance at that particular point of time. While Turberville lay in the Tower awaiting his tumultuous end, the king had summoned the assembly that was to become celebrated, in the placid pages of constitutional history, as the 'Model Parliament'.[1] This parliament was convoked 'super remediis contra pericula quae toti regno nostro hiis diebus imminent providendum', and the writs addressed to the prelates dilated, not only upon the high principle 'quod omnes tangit ab omnibus approbetur', but also upon the iniquities of the French king: he, it was alleged, 'linguam Anglicam, si conceptae iniquitatis proposito detestabili potestas correspondeat (quod Deus avertat), omnino de terra delere proponit'. There was always good reason why the punishment of traitors should have the utmost publicity, but there was an added reason why the traitor Turberville should be so memorably exhibited in the streets of London. His treason had been part of the 'detestable design', and when, in due time, the whole realm assembled in parliament at Westminster, his grinning corpse, hanging by its iron chain at the Smithfield elms, could bear eloquent witness to the 'dangers' against which the parliament had been called to 'provide'.

J. G. EDWARDS

[1] Palgrave, *Parl. Writs*, i. 29–31: the writs to the prelates are dated on 30 Sept., those to the lay magnates on 1 Oct., and those to the sheriffs (for the election of knights and burgesses) on 3 Oct. The meeting was originally fixed for 13 Nov., but was subsequently postponed to 27 Nov.; ibid., pp. 32–3.

THE ENGLISH FORCES IN FLANDERS,
AUGUST—NOVEMBER 1297

EDWARD I's Flemish expedition of 1297 is notable in English history mainly because of its intimate connexion with the constitutional crisis of the Confirmation of the Charters. It is important also, however, from the more specialized point of view of military organization as a landmark in the development of the contract system of military service and, though to a less extent, of the use of the commission of array. For though these two methods of raising and organizing troops had been systematically used by Edward I in his Welsh campaigns and were to be still further developed in those in Scotland, the Flemish expedition was the first and remained the only occasion on which he used the two methods in combination for a large-scale overseas expedition under his own command. And since it was on a combination of these two systems that Edward III relied for the overseas campaigns of the Hundred Years' War, it is of some interest to see just what capacity they showed for providing a force adequate for the purposes of continental war on the first occasion of their use for this purpose.

This question has, of course, been considered by Dr. J. E. Morris who, in his *Welsh Wars of Edward I*,[1] estimates the size and analyses the composition of the army, and concludes that it consisted of just over 800 cavalry (127 knights and bannerets with 695 troopers) and some 8,500 infantry. But in arriving at these figures he relied almost entirely on one rather limited source of information, namely, the horse inventories,[2] in which were recorded the names of the various leaders and their followers with the description and valuation of their mounts, for purposes of compensation if they were killed on service. While these lists give, in the main, an accurate and detailed record of the cavalry troops with which they deal, they do not necessarily cover the whole force; and since, on the other hand, they give no systematic indication of how long each leader and his troopers remained on service, it is possible that by adding up the number of all those whose horses were valued during the course of the campaign we

---

[1] pp. 277–80.
[2] Exch. Accts. 6/19, 28, and 37. Morris quotes only the last two but seems to have used all three.

may be including in the total some who were never present at the same time.[1] As a means of estimating the size of the infantry force they are still less reliable since the only indication they give of its numbers is that of the mounted centenars by whom the infantry were led. Morris himself points out, moreover, that not all the centenars who had their horses valued are described as such in the list, so that he was compelled to rely very much on conjecture in assessing the total. It is, however, possible to supply most of these deficiencies from another source of information which Morris did not use—the Wardrobe Book for the regnal year which contains, among other accounts for the expenses of the campaign, a list of the wages paid to both the cavalry and the infantry who took part in its early months.[2] In one respect this record is less complete than the horse inventories, since its purview is limited to the regnal year which ended on 19 November 1297, whereas the inventories cover the whole campaign, including some reinforcements which arrived as late as February 1298. The number of such late arrivals was, however, small and in most other respects the wage book is a more satisfactory source of information since it includes two substantial contingents which do not appear in the inventory; it classifies the troops into household and non-household contingents and, unlike the inventory, it gives the dates of departures and promotions as well as of arrivals, so that we can not only assess the total strength of the army and analyse its composition more precisely but trace its fluctuations and calculate its strength at any given date.[3] This new material necessitates some appreciable modifications of Morris's estimates and reveals more clearly one feature of vital importance. The real total of the infantry, it seems, must be reduced by some 700, the maximum number present at any one time being, apparently, about 7,810, made up of 5,297 archers from Wales (led by 45 mounted constables and the captain of the north Welsh) and 2,285 archers from the English counties and

---

[1] There is, again, a third, though minor, possibility that (as in the case of the earl of Warwick, quoted by Morris) some of those who had their horses valued ready for the campaign did not, in fact, set out.

[2] Wardrobe Book, 25 Edward I: Brit. Mus. Add. MS. 7965, ff. 64–87. T. F. Tout has called attention (*Chapters in the Administrative History of Medieval England*, ii. 119, n. 2) to the heavy totals of some of these accounts.

[3] And since it only records pay for service performed, it excludes those who, having had their horses valued for the campaign, failed to go. The one respect in which the wage book is less satisfactory than the horse inventory is that it normally gives only the *number* of troopers following each leader, whereas the inventory gives their names.

the Welsh March (led by 21 mounted constables) together with 150 Irish footmen, 48 archers, and 22 cross-bowmen of the king's Wardrobe and 10 foot-lancers attending the king's person. The Welsh contingents began to come into pay on 31 July or 1 August and the English on 21 August and the force reached its maximum on 15 October with the arrival of 250 recruits from the English counties and maintained its strength till the end of the period of account.[1] Morris, therefore, in spite of the very conjectural (and apparently mistaken) assumptions on which his estimate was based,[2] came very close to the real total of the archers. He does, however, considerably underestimate the proportion provided by the Welsh who contributed not, as he surmised, approximately equal numbers with the English but more than two-thirds of the whole.[3]

In the figures of the cavalry force also the pay-book necessitates some modification and shows that when Edward set sail from Winchelsea on 22 August he had with him a force of some 670 men-at-arms including 100 knights and bannerets and 570 squires.[4] By 29 September, this had risen to a peak figure of

[1] There was also a small body of carpenters (varying from 10 to 30) and 2 master engineers, to work various engines and supply them with quarrels, and a force of 68 archers in charge of a yeoman of the king's kitchen and the keeper of the larder engaged from 24 to 26 Sept. in guarding the king's supplies from his enemies while crossing the Channel. Add. MS. 7965, ff. 86 and 86d.

[2] All the leaders whom he mentions by name (p. 280) as having probably acted as centenars of infantry appear in the cavalry pay-roll whereas those who really acted as centenars are entered with the infantry.

[3] Morris says (p. 280) that 'The foot were very largely Welsh' but of his conjectural total of 8,500 he assigns only 4,400 to Wales and 4,100 to England. Whether any particular significance attaches to this Welsh preponderance is doubtful: it was, as Morris himself shows (pp. 93–7), not uncommon for the Welsh to supply a large proportion and sometimes a majority of the infantry of an English army.

[4] One other record which Morris did not use also throws some light on the presence of unpaid as well as paid contingents with the army. This is the roll of letters of protection (Supplementary Patent Roll no. 12: 25 and 26 Edward I), issued to those who intended to join the expedition. The roll does not, of course, add anything appreciable to our knowledge of the paid contingents since it makes no reference to the terms of service, but a comparison of the names contained in it with the horse inventories and the pay-book shows that a certain number of men, some of whom led appreciable contingents, apparently served gratuitously. How many such there may have been could only be ascertained by a meticulous collation of the thousands of names included in all three records but a rough comparison reveals the names of a number of men of high position; among ecclesiastics the archbishop elect of Dublin, the bishop of Durham (with thirty followers also having protections), the bishop of Coventry (with two), and among lay magnates the earl of Athol, Hugh le Despenser (with seven followers), Bartholomew Badlesmere, Robert de Monthaut, and John Hastings (with one or two followers each). It seems also that the king's two young nephews, Thomas and Henry of Lancaster,

895 (140 knights and bannerets with 755 squires) dropping slightly again by the beginning of November to about 870. Thus, although for the first month the force was considerably weaker than the figure which Morris derived from the horse inventory, it was for the rest of the period covered by the Wardrobe Book some 50–70 men stronger, quite apart from any unpaid contingents.

More important, however, than this slight change in the total strength of the force is the light which the pay-book throws on its composition. For of the total of 895 men-at-arms it shows that no less than 96 were not English troops serving under normal contract terms, but consisted of an Irish contingent of 3 knights and 56 squires (under John FitzThomas, lord of Offaly) who drew pay at rates substantially above the English standard,[1] and a Scottish contingent of 10 knights and 25 squires (under Sir Edward Comyn) whose service was a condition of their release from prison:[2] while of the 800 English troops remaining a substantial majority were enrolled in the king's household and of these the greater part were drawn from its standing members.[3]

still under the royal tutelage, accompanied him in person with a body of their household knights and squires. The contingent does not appear in the pay-book nor did either of the brothers register his horse, but they appear on the protection roll (mm. 8 and 3) as leading a contingent and their household roll records payments for lodgings and other expenses with the army in Flanders (Chanc. Misc. 3/28. See Tout, op. cit. ii. 184). The horses of their two knights and eighteen squires were registered (Exch. Accts. 6/37, m. 8) though no wages appear to be entered for them in the pay-book. So that, in spite of the uncompromising refusal of the majority of the magnates to acknowledge any obligation to serve in Flanders, it seems that the king was not entirely deprived of gratuitous support. It is interesting to note that Hugh le Despenser and the bishop of Durham are two of the three magnates whom Rishanger (*Gesta Edwardi Primi*, pp. 412–14) mentions by name as having accompanied the king; the other being Aymer de Valence who led the largest of the paid contingents.

[1] The knights took 2s. 9d. and the squires 1s. 4d. a day instead of the standard 2s. and 1s. a day, respectively, and it is interesting to note that on 23 Oct. 1297 the king, having seen the draft agreements with FitzThomas and others, found them 'very exacting' and ordered the justiciar of Ireland, by whom they had been negotiated, to 'withdraw from them as courteously as possible' and to keep the men in Ireland (*Cal. Close Rolls, 1296–1302*, p. 69). By this time, however, (if these are the agreements referred to), FitzThomas and the contingent had been in pay for a month and continued to draw pay till the end of the period covered by the account (Add. MS. 7965, f. 68d).

[2] Ibid., f. 70. The names of a number of those who agreed to serve on these conditions are given in *Foedera* (Hague ed.), i. iii. 182, 185, 188.

[3] One of the horse inventories (6/37), as Morris realized (p. 87), deals almost entirely with household troops, but it was not explicitly labelled as a household list by the clerk who drew it up, though the list 6/28 is headed 'Forinsec'. Morris, however, did not distinguish in his analysis of the force between household and non-household troops; and, in any case, the inventory does not distinguish between permanent and temporary members, whereas the Wardrobe Book with its list

For when the king started for Flanders in August, 475[1] of his 670 horse were troops of the household and only 195 outside it; and though by 29 September the 'forinsec' contingent had risen to 368 (mainly owing to the arrival in late September of the Scots and Irish) while the household only rose to 527, the 'forinsec' contingent had by 1 November sunk again to 320, while the household had risen still further to 550.[2] The household contingent was therefore not only the greater part but the most stable and reliable part of the force, the first to muster in something like its full strength and the only one which continued to grow throughout the period.[3]

If we analyse the 'forinsec' contingent still more closely it becomes apparent that, even in proportion to its size, it rested on a narrow basis. For of the 25 English contingents which it comprised only 6 reach a strength of a bare dozen, and of these only the earl of Pembroke (with 2 bannerets, 6 knights, and 40 squires) and Geoffrey de Geneville (with 4 knights and 22 squires) have contingents which are at all substantial.[4] These two were both men who, being descendants or connexions of Henry III's 'foreign favourites', had special ties with the royal family and of them Geneville, at least, had long devoted himself to the royal service.[5] So that when we subtract the Scots who served to gain their freedom, the Irish who had the special inducement of higher pay, and the contingents brought by the king's two intimates, the maximum cavalry force supplied by the general body of his subjects barely amounted to 200. These figures, therefore, made available by the Wardrobe Book, suggest very strongly the incapacity of the contract system at this early date to provide an adequate force for large-scale continental warfare. The infantry, it is true, seems to have been sufficient for its purpose; since, though smaller than the forces which Edward raised on various occasions for campaigns in Great Britain,[6] it was, in the opinion of Hemingburgh,[7] at any rate, formidable enough to deter the

(ff. 60–1) of those who received the regular fees and liveries of clothing enables us to recognize those who were undoubtedly permanent.

   [1] Of these nearly 400 were certainly permanent members.
   [2] Of these about 420 were certainly permanent.
   [3] Thereby illustrating very strikingly the truth of Tout's description of the king's army at this period as being 'essentially the household in arms' (op. cit. ii. 133).
   [4] And in the whole force only Pembroke himself, his retainer Thomas de Berkeley, and Edmund de Stafford can be described as being of substantial baronial position.
   [5] See F. M. Powicke, *Henry III and the Lord Edward*, ii. 699–700.
   [6] Morris, op. cit., pp. 95, 96.   [7] *Chronicon*, ii. 159.

French from attack. The cavalry, on the other hand, though forming, as Morris says, a 'very fair force', equalling if not exceeding any which Edward had so far raised by contract,[1] was too small to enable him to take the initiative and attack the French. He was reduced to the passive role of entrenching himself in Ghent,[2] and holding the French in check while his unruly followers expended their energy in quarrelling with their Flemish hosts. Nor does it seem that Edward intentionally confined his army to the numerical limits which forced this defensive strategy on him. He had clearly wanted the maximum force possible for the occasion and had called into play almost every royal prerogative and tapped almost every source of manpower—native and foreign—to provide it.[3]

It may be true, as Morris points out, that the need to leave adequate support for the young regent at home against the baronial opposition and against the danger of Scottish revolt deterred Edward from taking with him some loyal and experienced supporters who might have been willing to come,[4] but the repeated appeals he made from Flanders during the campaign for more men from England to join him[5] seem to show both that he was dissatisfied with the strength of his army and that he believed he could with safety draw more men from home if they could be induced to come.

The fact that only 200 men outside the king's household could be so induced seems to be attributable to a great extent to

[1] Morris, op. cit., pp. 14, 133, 159, 248 and *passim.* Forces of contract cavalry often seem to have been no more than 100 strong and rarely rose above 300 at a time.

[2] The static character of the campaign is emphasized by another entry in the Wardrobe Book (ff. 86 and 86d) which shows that Edward raised a large native labour corps of Flemish diggers and sappers to strengthen the defences of Ghent with a ditch. Beginning on 12 Sept. with a master and 29 workmen, the force rose rapidly to a maximum of 400 workmen with 4 masters by the 21st, sinking again in the second half of the month and apparently disbanding on the 30th.

[3] The Scots and Irish as well as the English magnates and middle class were ordered or requested to muster with horses and arms: continental allies were urged to send assistance and, as we have seen (*supra*, p. 313, n. 2), Scottish prisoners were released on condition of giving service. (*Cal. Close Rolls, 1296–1302*, pp. 112, 113; *Cal. Pat. Rolls, 1292–1301*, pp. 247, 249; *Parl. Writs,* i. 281–4; and *Foedera* (Hague ed.), I. iii. 183–4.)

[4] Op. cit., p. 281. Some colour is given to this view by the fact that some men who took out letters of protection preparatory to going to Flanders (e.g. John Tregoz, Guncelin de Badlesmere: Suppl. Pat. Roll 12, mm. 5 and 9) are found acting on the regent's council at home (Morris, loc. cit.).

[5] Requests were sent on 26 Oct. 1297 to fifty-four individuals to come with horses and arms to join the king in Flanders, and similar appeals to diminishing numbers of men were made on 24 Nov. and 14 Dec. (*Cal. Close Rolls, 1296–1302*, pp. 76, 187, 190).

the widespread and intrinsic unpopularity of the form of service required. It is true that the circumstances of the time were not favourable to the raising of military forces. Relations between king and baronage were strained, and the king's recent arbitrary actions and his repeated demands for military service might well have deterred some from volunteering who in more normal times would have been prepared to respond. But if this had been the only or even the main reason for the poor response, it seems hardly likely that a few months after his return, when suspicion and discontent were by no means allayed, Edward would have been able, as he was able, to raise against Wallace, without apparent difficulty, not only an unpaid feudal array which Morris estimates at some 1,000 to 1,100 men, but also a contract force nearly half as large again as that which went to Flanders.[1] It seems clear, therefore, from this comparison that whatever share the special discontents of the moment may have had in keeping down the number of Edward's army in 1297, one of the essential causes for its small size was the deep-rooted suspicion of the military class for contract service in general and an invincible dislike for foreign service in particular. It was this double antagonism which, in Edward I's day, prevented the contract army from being an effective instrument for overseas campaigns, and the success of Edward III in raising, as he did on more than one occasion, forces of 3,000 or 4,000 cavalry by contract[2] is a measure of the revolution which, in the interval between the two reigns, had taken place in the attitude of both aristocracy and middle class to both these forms of service.[3]

[1] Op. cit., pp. 290–2.
[2] A. E. Prince, 'The Strength of English Armies in the Reign of Edward III', *Eng. Hist. Rev.* xlvi. 361, 363, 364, 368.
[3] I should like to express my thanks to the University of Sheffield for a grant from the University Research Fund, which facilitated the collection of the manuscript material used in this article.

APPENDIX

Maximum[1] Forces of Welsh Infantry recorded in Add. MS. 7965, ff. 81–5

Glamorgan		900
West Wales and the Barons' Lands		
Cardigan	636	
Carmarthen	400	
Cantrefmawr	270	
Cantref Bychan	169	
Kidwelly	189	
Carnwyllion, Maelienydd, and Cydevain	200	
Talgarth and Builth	240	
Clouy[2]	100	
Elvael	100	
Gower	200	2,504
North Wales		
Snowdon and Carnarvon	609	
Anglesea and Englefield	654	
Powys	320	
Dyffryn Clwyd and Penllyn	240	
Denbigh and Nanhendwy	140	1,963

Maximum Size of Principal Cavalry Contingents

Household Name	Rank	Contingent Kts.	Esqs.	Total
Beauchamp, Walter, de (Steward of Household)	ban.	2	15	18
Benstead, John de (Controller of Wardrobe)	kt.	2	12	15
Berwick, John de	kt.	4	28	33
Botetourt, John de	ban.	1	7	9
Chavent, John de	kt.	1	8	10
Chavent, Peter de	ban.	2	10	13
Drokensford, John de (Keeper of Wardrobe)	kt.	3	29	33
Engayne, John de	ban.	3	5	9
FitzPain, Robert de	ban.	5	20	26
Leybourne, Wm. de	ban.	4	17	22
Planche, James de	kt.	1	8	10
Teye, Walter de	ban.	2	8	11
Tony, Robert de	ban.	2	12	15
Touchet, Wm.	ban.	4	12	17
Warwick, Guy	ban.	2	11	14
Welles, Adam	ban.	1	12	14

[1] These are the maximum contingents for each district: they were not all present at the same time so that when added together they come to slightly more than the maximum force given in the text (p. 311).

[2] ? Clun (see H. Owen, *Description of Pembrokeshire*, Pt. III, p. 196, n. 2): probably a corruption of the original Welsh form Colunwy. I am indebted to my colleague Dr. G. P. Jones for advice on the spelling of the Welsh place-names.

Non-household

Name	Rank	Kts.	Esqs.	Total
			Contingent	
Beauchamp, Humphrey de.	kt.		12	13
Beauchamp, John (of Somerset)	ban.	1	10	12
Caunville, William (or Gerard) de . . .	kt.	1	9	11
Geneville, Geoffrey de	ban.	4	22	27
Ghent, Gilbert de	ban.	1	10	12
Stafford, Edmund de	ban.	2	7	10
Tateshale, Robert	ban.	2	9	12
Valence, Aymer de	ban.	8[1]	40	49

Promotions during the course of the expedition
  To the rank of banneret:

Household: John Botetourt	23 Aug.
Walter de Teye	5 or 15 Sept.
Robert Scales	6 Oct.
Robert de Tony	1 Nov.
Non-household: Edmund Stafford	27 Sept.
Maurice Berkeley (with Valence) . . .	8 Oct.
John Beauchamp of Somerset . . .	1 Nov.

  To the rank of knight:
    12 squires, the following named:

Household: Henry de Beaumont.	
Peter de Braose.	
John de Chavent	1 Nov.
William Russell.	
Roger St. John.	
Non-household: Herbert FitzJohn[2]	29 Sept.
William Caunville	1 Nov.

N. B. LEWIS

[1] Including two bannerets, Thomas de Berkeley and (after 8 Oct.) his son Maurice who raised his banner on that day.

[2] He had been a squire of the household up to 29 Sept. but apparently left the household on being knighted. (Add. MS. 7965, ff. 69d and 76.)

EDWARD I AND THE STRUGGLE
FOR THE CHARTERS, 1297–1305[1]

IN 1294 Edward I went to war in defence of his rights in
Gascony. For his needs, arising from his campaigns and from
an expensive diplomacy, he made unprecedented demands upon
his subjects. The new taxes on movables became annual during
these years. There was a savage increase in the customs on the
main commodities of the export trade, wool, woolfells, and leather.
The royal right of prise was exercised to such an extent that prises
in these years assumed new, national dimensions.

The taxes were taxes of a new sort with a new incidence. The
maltote had not been granted as the old rate of half a mark had
been, if it had been granted at all. Prises were now for the Great
Wardrobe, demands for supplies for whole armies. These things
made the Charters look out of date. Certainly such developments
made the Great Charter, on a literal interpretation of the existing text, inadequate. We know that the leaders of the nation in
1297, in the emergency after the Scots' victory at Stirling Bridge,
forced on the king an addition to the Charters, the so-called
Confirmatio Cartarum, additional articles bringing them up to
date.[2]

The use the late-thirteenth-century Englishman made of his
moment of power shows his mind. In 1297 the Charters still
embodied his idea of political justice. Even the 'new medicines
for new diseases'[3] were better in the old bottles. This was not so
in 1311, the next revolutionary occasion, or ever again. Somewhere between 1297 and 1311 'The Charters' ceased to be a
sufficient slogan: a chapter in our history ends. It ends, we
believe, between 1297 and 1305 in an ill-known struggle for the
Charters.

This is not the accepted view of the last years of Edward I's
reign. Stubbs wrote: 'The remaining years of Edward I's reign
[i.e. after the Confirmation of the Charters, 1297] owe such constitutional interest as they have to the fact that they witnessed the
supplementary acts by which the Confirmation of the Charters
was affirmed and recognized as the end of the present disputes

---

[1] I am deeply indebted for helpful criticisms to my friend Professor V. H.
Galbraith.

[2] *Eng. Hist. Rev.* lx (1945), 181 and 190–1.

[3] This phrase is Winchelsey's (*Reg.*, p. 157); cf. T. S. R. Boase, *Boniface VIII*
(1933), p. 141.

and especially as the close of the long disputes about the limits
and jurisdictions of the Forests.'[1] But it is here suggested that
the years after 1297 have an interest of their own, that far from
the constitutional crisis of Edward I's reign being a short, sharp
affair, the *Confirmatio Cartarum* of 1297 is not the end but a
cause, and that it was not affirmed but reversed in the larger
conflict that followed it.

After 10 October 1297, with its political difficulties out of the
way, the regency was able to give its attention to the Scots and
it ordered a muster at Newcastle-on-Tyne for 6 December. To
finance the campaign it lost no time in setting the Chancery and
the Exchequer to work on the ninth which it had been agreed
should supersede the eighth. Meanwhile, also in accordance with
the October settlement, the archbishops summoned convocations
for a clerical grant.

The regent and council did their part. They published the
Charters, prepared a perambulation of the forests, released
arrested wools, and (this with the utmost publicity) abandoned the
maltote on wool. They accepted the conditions which the convocations, when they met, attached to the grants they made.
They even allowed the provision made by the convocation of the
Southern Province that, to avoid a violation of *Clericis laicos*,
payments from the proceeds of its tenth should be made directly
to the earls engaged in the Scottish expedition in order to exclude
completely the royal authority.

The king on his return from Flanders in March 1298 continued
this vigorous but conciliatory policy. The news of his return was
sent to the forces already in Scotland to hearten them, and a
council was called to meet at Westminster on 30 March. The
collectors of customs were ordered to account at the Exchequer
after Easter for all the wool which had passed through their ports
since the beginning of the war with France in 1294. On 4 April
a nation-wide inquiry was ordered into another major grievance
of the people, the unprecedentedly heavy and manifold prises
since 1294, though it is noteworthy that the inquiry was into
maladministration of them and the question of the legality of the
prises themselves was not raised. The council which met on
30 March decided to move the Exchequer and Bench to York
and ordered another muster at York for Whitsuntide (25 May).
On 30 April 1298, at the king's instance, Archbishop Winchelsey
summoned another convocation.

[1] Stubbs, *Constitutional History of England*, ii (1906), 153–4.

When it met on 25 June, at the New Temple, London,[1] the king by 'sire Johan del Isle e sire Willame de Sutton' chivalers' his spokesmen, informed the assembled clergy that he had no intention of asking them for an aid this time or at any other time unless compelled to do so by sheer necessity. Instead, in this war of his against the Scots, he told them, he would live of his own as long as he could. But he asked four things of them. Firstly, that in view of the dangers which might ensue, he might be given some expectation that an aid from them would be forthcoming when he called for it to defend the kingdom and Holy Church, if the danger lasted so long that he could not otherwise provide what he needed. Secondly, that the remainder of the tenth lately granted by the clergy to the earls to repel the Scots be put at his disposal if need be, to defend kingdom and Holy Church.[2] Thirdly, he asked for their prayers in his undertaking against the Scots. Fourthly, he asked for solemn excommunication of Scots who were ravaging the Church and the kingdom and disturbing the peace.

Convocation's reply to the first of these requests was that without the pope's consent they could not give the assurance asked for. The pope had bound them tightly by *Clericis laicos*.[3] To the second they replied that they would put the remainder of the recently granted tenth at his disposal if the emergency was once again so great that it was proper for them to do so, otherwise they could not do it without the pope's consent. Convocation found no difficulty in granting the king's third and fourth requests.

But convocation did not stop with the consideration of what the king had put before them. It went on, unasked, to consider the working of the agreement of Michaelmas 1297. In the *Confirmatio Cartarum*, the king had agreed to sealed copies of the Charters being deposited in cathedral churches so that they could be read to the people twice a year, and to greater excommunication being pronounced twice a year by the bishops on all infringing the Charters.[4] But without discipline, as the *Confirmatio*

[1] The following account of this important convocation is based on the documents in *Registrum Roberti Winchelsey*, ed. R. Graham (Canterbury and York Soc., in progress), pp. 260–2, 536–8, and 268–72.

[2] The contemporary Bury chronicler in reporting this request words it less delicately than the official record (*Reg. Winchelsey*, ed. Graham, pp. 261 and 537). My summary owes something to his blunt '. . . ut placeret clero regi concedere residuum pecunie comitibus concesse' ('St. Edmundsbury Chronicle, 1296–1301', ed. V. H. Galbraith, in *Eng. Hist. Rev.* lviii (1943), 71).

[3] '. . . nous sumes liez estreytement par le pape' (*Reg. Winchelsey*, ed. Graham, p. 262).   [4] Art. 3 and 4. Cf. *Eng. Hist. Rev.* lx (1945), 182.

Cartarum had recognized, some bishops might be negligent or faint-hearted over the excommunications. It was now ruled that the readings and excommunications be fixed for Palm Sunday and All Saints' Day each year, and that the form of excommunication be the 'vulgar' (French)[1] form used in 1297 on the occasion of the Confirmation of the Charters. It was further provided that this excommunication should be expounded in English *seriatim in omnibus ac patenter*. Measures were also taken to strengthen the hands of the lower clergy. The *Confirmatio Cartarum* had provided in clause 6 that no one's goods should be taken in the king's name without the common assent of all the realm. But it might be difficult, even harmful, for a minor dignitary or a rector or vicar whose ecclesiastical property was taken in spite of this, always to have recourse to his bishop. It was ruled, therefore, that power be extended to the lower clergy of denouncing evident and notorious offenders in this matter without recourse to their bishop. Finally, the use of the weapon of an interdict was authorized to protect clergy of all grades from intimidation. These instructions went out to the dioceses on 15 July along with the instructions for the prayers and excommunications which the king had asked for against the Scots.

The king, too, claimed to interpret the *Confirmatio Cartarum*. He was as masterful as ever. The worst consequences of *Confirmatio Cartarum* could be postponed by asking for nothing, by doing what in fact he told convocation on 25 June 1298 it was his intention to do: live of his own as long as possible.[2] It would be difficult to do this and wage war at the same time, but Edward seems to have attempted nothing less. His devices at this time are as manifold as his straits are obvious. His treasury was empty on 4 December 1297.[3] His jewels, even to a treasured keepsake of his late wife Eleanor, were pawned.[4] He was pledged to pay off a good many old debts in April 1298,[5] and he could not so easily incur new ones. For supplies for his armies he had now to pay or definitely promise to pay. Some money was raised on the royal forests by sales of 'waste' and timber enough to bring in

---

[1] This must be the form still preserved along with the other documents of the 10 Oct.–5 Nov. crisis in *Reg. Winchelsey*, ed. Graham, p. 204. We now, therefore, know the occasion of this form.

[2] This appears from the reply of convocation to the king on 28 June 1298; see *Reg. Winchelsey*, ed. Graham, p. 260.

[3] *Reg. Winchelsey* as cited in *Eng. Hist. Rev.* xxxiv (1919), 202.

[4] Public Record Office, Exch. L.T.R. Memor. Roll, no. 69, m. 76d.

[5] e.g. *Cal. Pat. Rolls, 1292–1301*, pp. 321–3.

certain specified sums.[1] London bought renewal and confirmation of its liberties by taking over the king's debts to certain merchants amounting to 2,000 marks.[2] Anything to get ready money. And yet such things could only be palliatives. Unable to dispense with prises for war purposes, driven to exploit his prerogative rights, the king himself helped to bring the forests, the escheatries and, above all, prises to the forefront as political issues by 1300–1. Meanwhile, naturally enough, he resisted any diminution of 'his own' such as disafforestment would have involved. On 18 November 1298, eight months after his return from abroad and a full year after the regency's writs[3] for the perambulation of the forests, he conceded an inquiry into maladministration of the forests but said nothing more about perambulation.[4] Men ceased to trust him.

A Statute of 2 April 1299, the so-called *De Finibus Levatis*,[5] confirmed their suspicions, making it quite certain that the king's interpretation of his concessions in 1297 was not that of his subjects, nor that of an honest man. The king publicly for the first time sought to go back on his engagements. The Statute indeed promised a perambulation of the forests when foreign affairs (he was at that time negotiating the Treaty of Montreuil with France) permitted him to release members of his council for the purpose,[6] but with the saving clause that it was to be made only within the limits imposed by his oath, the rights of his crown, his interests and claims, and those of all other men,[7] and no action was to be taken upon the perambulation until its findings had been reported to him. This saving clause was sufficient in itself to provoke a great outcry, but there was worse in the Statute. The king, it

---

[1] e.g. ibid., pp. 344–5.

[2] *Cal. Chart. Rolls*, ii. 477–8 and *Cal. Close Rolls, 1296–1302*, p. 303.

[3] The regency issued two sets of writs on the subject. Those of 16 Oct. 1297 (*Cal. Pat. Rolls, 1292–1301*, p. 312) referred the perambulators to a previous perambulation instead of to the Forest Charter itself. This was corrected in a reissue of 26 Nov. (*Parl. Writs*, i. 396–7, nos. 38–9).

[4] *Parl. Writs*, i. 397 (no. 41). Cf. Petit-Dutaillis, *Studies Supplementary to Stubbs' Constitutional History*, ii. 220.

[5] *Statutes of the Realm* (Rec. Com., 1810), i. 126–30—in reality, of course, a miscellaneous Statute.

[6] Roger le Brabazon, John de Berewyk, Ralph de Hengham, William Inge, and John de Crokesle were appointed on 23 Sept. 1299 (*Cal. Pat. Rolls, 1292–1301*, p. 441).

[7] 'Salvis semper juramento nostro, jure corone nostre, & racionibus nostris atque calumpniis ac omnium uliorum' (*Stat. of the Realm*, i. 128). Edward refers to this oath again as a difficulty in 1301 (*Parl. Writs*, i. 104, no. 44). The oath referred to may be the coronation oath; and this would be important because of the change of the oath at the coronation of Edward II.

tells us, had 'deliberated' upon his grant of 1297, and there emerges the fact that while the king wills still that the Forest Charter be observed, it is not his will that it be observed in all its points.[1] The critical clauses 1–5, which include those on dis-afforestment, are omitted from the recital of the clauses of the Forest Charter which follows.[2] The king went so far as to deny that he had in 1297 granted that the Forest Charter should be kept in all its points—his undertaking, as he now represents it in 1299, had been subject even in 1297 to the reservation of his oath, the rights of his crown and his interests and those of other men.[3] Such a claim is, of course, flatly contradicted by *Confirmatio Cartarum*, which the king had personally accepted at Ghent on 5 November 1297. But in the Statute of 2 April 1299 Edward prefers to rely upon the verbal agreements of July 1297 and his proclamation of 12 August 1297, and to ignore the *Confirmatio Cartarum*.[4]

A chronicler tells us that after this Statute was read at St. Paul's there was an uproar and that even before it the king had found it expedient to seek the country air.[5] Certainly on 2 April 1299 a mandate went out to the city of London 'to arrest, try and punish persons congregating by day and night, and speaking ill of the king and his subjects'.[6] The Bury St. Edmunds chronicler, too, can be believed when he says that men were 'exasperated' with the king's 'morosis ac supervacuis verbosisque . . . intricacioni-bus'.[7] By midsummer they were going about saying that he did not intend to keep the Charters, and Edward tried in vain to contradict them.[8] On 30 October 1299 he felt it necessary to warn the convocation of the Southern Province, which was to meet at the New Temple in November, not to attempt anything 'against the crown, the king's dignity, or the council',[9] and

---

[1] 'Nos diebus istis quatenus nobis vacat . . . habuimus deliberacionem super concessione nostra predicta et . . . Volumus quod predicta magna carta de libertati-bus observetur in omnibus punctis suis; et carta eciam de foresta, secundum sub-scriptos articulos . . .' (*Stat. of the Realm*, i. 127).

[2] Ibid., pp. 127–8. M. Petit-Dutaillis drew attention to this omission in *Studies Supplementary to Stubbs*, ii (1915), 220.

[3] The preamble to *De finibus levatis*: 'salvis tamen juramento nostro, jure corone nostre, et racionibus nostris, ac eciam aliorum' (*Stat. of the Realm*, i. 126–7).

[4] Ibid. The whole preamble deserves careful study.

[5] *Chronicon . . . Walteri de Hemingburgh*, ed. Hamilton, ii. 183.

[6] *Cal. Pat. Rolls, 1292–1301*, p. 403.

[7] 'The St. Edmundsbury Chronicle, 1296–1301', ed. Galbraith, *Eng. Hist. Rev.* lviii (1943), 72.

[8] King to the 'commonalty' of every county, 25 June 1299, Lewes (*Cal. Pat. Rolls, 1292–1301*, p. 424), a very revealing proclamation.   [9] Ibid., p. 451.

Walter Langton, bishop of Coventry and Lichfield and treasurer, was deputed to present the king's point of view to the assembly.[1] As the year drew on his difficulties mounted. The muster due at Newcastle in November had to be put off to mid-December at Berwick.[2] The foot that were being arrayed in the shires were unwilling to march 'either on account of the bad money current in the kingdom or of the inclemency of the season'.[3] Even the promise of a bounty does not seem to have moved them and the muster had to be again put off to midsummer 1300 at Carlisle. Meanwhile there was to be a parliament. The issue between the king and his subjects was joined. The writs went out for a parliament to meet on 6 March 1300 at London.[4]

Both parliament and muster were on an unusual scale, the latter evidently[5] for an all-out military effort after a year of inaction, the former to remove political impediments thereto. To the parliament were summoned, besides an unusually large number of earls and barons and abbots, representatives of the shires and boroughs and of the inferior clergy, and thirty-eight officials, judges, and others of the council[6]—a fuller parliament even than that in the crisis of Michaelmas 1297.[7]

The outcome of the parliament was the document known as *Articuli super Cartas*.[8] The title is modern, but the articles themselves are not in doubt, being enrolled upon the Statute Roll.[9]

[1] Inferred from ibid., p. 450: '31 October, 1299. Langley. Letter of credence for W. bishop of Coventry and Lichfield, directed to clergy of forthcoming convocation at New Temple.'
[2] *Parl. Writs*, i. 325–6 (nos. 3–4): 16–17 Nov. 1299, York.
[3] Ibid. i. 326 (nos. 6–7): 21 Nov. 1299, Wigton, for outcome of which see ibid. i. 339–40 (no. 22) and ibid. i. 329 (no. 12).
[4] Ibid. i. 82–5 (nos. 1–7): 29 Dec. 1299, Berwick, writs for parliament; ibid. i. 327–8 (nos. 8–10), writs of 30 Dec. for muster.
[5] Besides the individual writs of military summons mentioned in note 4 above (on which see Morris, *Welsh Wars of Edward the First*, p. 298), commissions (*Parl. Writs*, i. 330–9, nos. 15–21) to all counties to summon all holding lands or rents, whether knights or not, inside as well as outside franchises, and whether tenants-in-chief or not, worth £40 per annum. Cf. also *Cal. Pat. Rolls, 1292–1301*, pp. 487–8. Ireland also was to be drawn on for men, materials, and money (*Parl. Writs*, i. 329–30, nos. 13–14; *Cal. Pat. Rolls, 1292–1301*, pp. 488 and 490).
[6] See n. 4, *supra*. Cf. Pasquet, *An Essay on the Origins of the House of Commons*, trans. Laffan (Cambridge, 1925), p. 112.
[7] '. . . the most completely constituted parliament . . . since 1296' (Stubbs, *Const. Hist.* ii. 155).
[8] *Stat. of the Realm*, i. 136–41.
[9] They are also referred to on 30 Oct. 1300 in unmistakable terms (cf. the *Articuli*: 'en aleggeance des grevances qe soen poeple ad eu par les guerres qe unt esté') on the Close Roll (*Cal. Close Rolls, 1296–1302*, p. 410) and again in the Lincoln parliament of the following year (*Parl. Writs*, i. 104–5, no. 45).

Something of the preceding debates may be inferred from a version of the *Articuli* in Sir Alexander Acland-Hood's collection of manuscripts described by A. J. Horwood in the *Royal Historical Manuscripts Commission*, Sixth Report (1877), App., pp. 344–52. Horwood's view of this text is that it 'would seem to be the form proposed for, or the statement of grievances on which was based, the Statute of 28 Edw. I, commonly known as "Articuli super Chartas" '. I have adopted Horwood's view because the text can be dated to the year 1300 and within the limits 14 January–11 April 1300;[1] it certainly relates to the business of the *Articuli super Cartas* parliament. A careful reading shows that it must be reckoned prior to the *Articuli* and, if not quite a petition *formam actus in se continens*, then heads of the proposals for a settlement, very much nearer the proposals than the settlement. The following account of the parliament is based upon either the *Articuli* themselves or a comparison of the Acland-Hood text[2] and the *Articuli*.

The first thing was to bring the king back to the Charters, 'every article and every point of them', as fully as he had granted them in 1297. This was secured by a fresh *inspeximus et confirmavimus* of the Charters[3]—the full texts, not omitting the articles which the king had omitted in reciting the Forest Charter in 1299. Nor was it even considered a sufficient guarantee that this time the king himself, and not the regent, as on 12 October 1297, had inspected the Charters. It was insisted that the *inspeximus*es should be in charter form (those of 12 October 1297 had been simple letters patent), which would enable the inspection to be attested by witnesses as well as the king. The long lists of witnesses to the *inspeximus*es of 28 March 1300 are remarkable and are convincing proof of the importance attached to the occasion.[4]

---

[1] The words 'Dautrepart la comm[un]e des chevalers e de autre gentils hommes du realme ke hount la somounse de xl. livres de tere, *etc.*' refer to writs of 14 Jan. 1300 (*Parl. Writs*, i. 330–9, nos. 15–21), which were in fact reissued in a revised form on 11 Apr. 1300 (ibid. i. 341–2, no. 29).

[2] As known from the *Hist. MSS. Com. Report*. I have not seen the manuscript itself.

[3] 28 Mar. 1300.

[4] The lists are headed by Robert, archbishop of Canterbury, and Antony Bek, bishop of Durham. Then follow eight bishops: London, Ely, Exeter, Coventry and Lichfield, Sarum, Rochester, Norwich, Llandaff, and one bishop-elect, Lincoln. The earls are headed by John de Warenne, earl of Surrey, Thomas, earl of Lancaster, Roger Bygod, earl of Norfolk and Marshal, Henry de Lacy, earl of Lincoln, followed by Ralph de Monthermer, earl of Gloucester and Hertford, the young Humphrey de Bohun, earl of Hereford, the young earl of Warwick, and

Edward I was now bound to the whole text of the Charters beyond cavil. As for their execution, he now added the further sanctions at parliament's request of publication of the Charters four times a year in each county at fixed times and 'devant le poeple en plein conté', and the election in each county 'par la commune de meisme le conté' of three *prodes hommes*[1] who would be commissioned royal justices of oyer and terminer to try and to punish infringements of the Charters in their shire. The settlement of Michaelmas 1297 had gone back some way towards the Confirmation of the Charters of 1265 in reviving regular publication of the Charters. Regular royal publication was a still closer approximation to the Confirmation of the Charters of 1265.[2] The device of elected justices to deal with infringers of the Charters seems also to have been inspired by the example of 1265, though on that occasion it had been resorted to for infringements of the *Forma Regiminis* of that year and not for infringements of the Charters themselves. But, in any case, justice elective and summary for offences against the Charters, in fields where there had previously been no redress save by royal grace, was a most notable concession.

Besides these things, which he granted at the request of his barons, the king also granted of his own special grace nineteen other articles which endeavoured to provide remedies for the grievances of the people in 1300.

And yet the parliament of 1300 must be reckoned a victory for the king. All his concessions in the *Articuli super Cartas* were qualified by the saving of the prerogative in the concluding passage: 'In each and all of the aforesaid things it is the king's will and the intention of him and his council and of all those who were present at the making of this ordinance that the right and lordship (*Seignurie*) of his crown be saved.'[3] Further evidence of

Richard, earl of Arundel. Then—Reginald de Grey, John de Hastings, Henr. de Percy, Hugh le Despenser, Hugh de Veer, Robert de Tateshale, Hugh Bardolf, Hugh de Courtenay, John de Segrave, Henry de Grey, William de Ros of Helmsley, Alan la Zousche, Robert de Tony, Robert de Monte Alto, William de Braose, Thomas de Furnivall, John Engaigne, Peter Corbet, William de Leyburn, William le Latimer, Walter de Beauchamp 'Sen. hospicii nri.', Walter de Huntercumbe 'et aliis'. *Stat. of the Realm*, i (Charters), pp. 38–44.

[1] They might be 'chivaliers ou autre loiaux sages et avisés'. The three elected for Hampshire and commissioned on 10 May 1300 seem to have been plain gentry. Certainly they were not chosen for wealth or social standing. One was a knight and a tenant-in-chief, but none had lands and rents worth £40 a year. With *Parl. Writs*, i. 399 (no. 43) compare ibid., pp. 338–9 (no. 21).

[2] Stubbs, *Select Charters*, 9th ed., p. 406. Cf. *Eng. Hist. Rev.* lx (1945), 182.

[3] 'En totes les choses desus dites, e chescunes de eles, voet le Roi et entent, il

the success of Edward's stand for the prerogative is the new commissions of 1 April 1300 for the perambulation of the forests.
These contained the saving clause whose introduction into *De
Finibus Levatis* had provoked a storm just twelve months before.[1] But the best evidence is what the king did not grant in
1300. He had to bind himself more strictly than ever to the
Charters, but he did not repeat the *addicio* of 1297 to the Charters.
The *Confirmatio Cartarum* was neither re-enacted nor formally
revoked. It was ignored as Edward had ignored it in 1299.[2]
Ignored, too, was convocation's attempt in 1298 at definition of
the ecclesiastical sanctions provided by the *Confirmatio Cartarum*,[3]
though it seems to have been parliament's original intention to
incorporate at least some of it into the settlement.[4] Parliament
had wanted more than it got, too, in the way of lay sanctions for
the Charters. Besides the elective county justices for the local
offenders, it had asked also for the punishment of the king's
ministers of the Chancery, the Exchequer, the Wardrobe and
the two Benches, King's Bench and Common Pleas, no less than
other people if they infringed the Charters.[5] They might be tried
by the king himself, or those to whom he might assign the task,
if the offence was committed while they were *en lur place demeyne*,
but by the elected justices of the county concerned like other
people if while they were *hors de lur place*. In either case, if they
were found guilty their punishment should be the same as for
les autres de la commune.[6] The king granted the latter demand, the
treatment of his ministers like other people for infringements of
the Charters in their private capacities,[7] but as to the former,
Articuli super Cartas allows no action against the king's ministers
for offences in the course of their duties (*en lur place*) except in

et soen consail, et touz ceus qui a cest ordenement furent, qe le droit et la seignurie
de sa coroune savez lui soient par tout' (*Stat. of the Realm*, i. 141).

[1] The clause 'salvis semper juramento nostro, jure corone nostre, racionibus
nostris atque calumpniis et omnium aliorum' (cf. p. 323, *supra*). The writs of 1 Apr.
1300 are printed in *Parl. Writs*, i. 397–8 (no. 42).

[2] See *supra*, p. 324.   [3] See *supra*, pp. 321–2.

[4] This much is certain: that the Acland-Hood version of *Articuli super Cartas*,
c. 1 (*Hist. MSS. Com. 6th Report*, 1877, App., pp. 344–52), even in its present only
partially legible state, provides ecclesiastical sanctions which do not appear at all
in the *Articuli super Cartas* themselves and which are more than a repetition of the
ecclesiastical sanctions provided by the *Confirmatio Cartarum*.

[5] Acland-Hood (*Hist. MSS. Com. 6th Report*, App., p. 344): 'ministres le Rey
de la chancelerie ou de la Chekere ou de la Garderobe ou du Baunk le rey ou
dautre Baunk'.

[6] Acland-Hood text corresponding to *Articuli super Cartas*, c. 1.

[7] *Articuli super Cartas*, c. 1: 'ausi bien des ministres le Roi hors de leur places
come des autres'.

the one matter of prise, and offences in that matter it does not treat as infringements of the Charters.

The *Articuli super Cartas* treats prise-offences as maladministration of the prerogative. In 1297 prises were treated as a matter to which the Charters were applicable and clause 6 of the *Confirmatio Cartarum* had extended their application beyond the very few and particular limitations which they originally imposed upon this prerogative, to cover also the new great national prises for war purposes that had arisen since 1225. The inquiry made in 1298-9 had shown a considerable degree of petty misconduct,[1] and if the king himself was willing to put that right, the leaders of the nation were not disposed to insist too strongly upon the particular ground of action. But the way in which the *Articuli super Cartas* separates the prise-question (c. 2) from the question of the Charters (c. 1), dealing with it as a matter of pure prerogative, remedies for the wrongful administration of which are accorded as a special grace,[2] is too deliberate to be mistaken, and must be reckoned the supreme evidence of the success of Edward's stand for the prerogative in 1300.

The advantage gained in 1300 Edward kept in the Lincoln Parliament of 1301. In 1300 he had reconfirmed the Charters, but not the 1297 addition to the Charters. Not yet strong enough to challenge the *Confirmatio Cartarum* directly, he nevertheless succeeded in large measure in withdrawing attention from it to another set of articles. In these he gave greater safeguards for the Charters—in return for safeguards for the prerogative—but his concessions were not added to the Charters as the *Confirmatio Cartarum* of 1297 had been. His victory in 1301 was that the fight in that year was on the 1300 and not the 1297 basis. He even got an aid without renewing the *Confirmatio Cartarum*.

Some concessions, of course, he had to make. He needed parliament's backing[3] in the matter of the pope's claim to Scot-

---

[1] See p. 320 *supra*; *Eng. Hist. Rev.* xlviii (1933), 263-4 and W. S. Thomson, *A Lincolnshire Assize Roll for 1298* (Linc. Rec. Soc., 1944).

[2] Between c. 1 and the rest of *Articuli super Cartas* occurs the following: 'e, estre cestes choses grantées sur les pointz des chartres avantdites, le Roi, de sa grace especiale, en aleggeance des grevances qe soen poeple ad eu par les guerres qe unt esté, et en amendement de leur estat, e pur taunt q'il soient plus prestz a soen service e plus volentiers aidantz quant il en avera afere, a granté ascuns articles, les quieus il entent qui tendront ausi grant lieu a son poeple et ausi grant profist ferront, ou plus, qe les pointz avant grantés' (*Stat. of the Realm*, i. 137).

[3] The Barons' Letter supported by 'seven earls and ninety-seven barons for themselves and for the whole community of the land' (see Stubbs, *Const. Hist.* ii. 159).

land and his need, too, of money by this time was such that he had to accept the fifteenth which parliament was prepared to grant him, whatever the conditions attached to it.[1] In granting that statutes contrary to the Charters should be null and void,[2] he added to all his previous concessions. And he gave way (but, as events were to show, only for the time being) on the question of disafforestments. But the first item of the petition in the famous bill presented by the knight Henry Keighley for the barons and the whole community[3] merely asked him to reaffirm his grant in 1300 of the Charters in every article and every point.[4] The petition that the powers of the justices elected to enforce the Charters[5] should be clarified presupposes the 1300 settlement, though the reply *Placet tacite* may indicate some demur at the idea of doing it by taking counsel with the magnates in the matter.[6] Again, although the magnates returned to the attack on the question of the king's ministers and still wished for means of bringing them to justice like other men for offences against the Charters, they now accepted at the outset the distinction drawn by *Articuli super Cartas* in 1300[7] between offences against the Charters and prise-offences.[8] This, naturally, was acceptable to the king—*Placet expresse*. But to their petition now that ministers' misprisions be dealt with by *auditores* 'qe ne soient pas suspecionus des Prelatz Contes e Barons de la terre' the answer is that 'Dominus Rex vult providere aliud remedium . . . set non per tales auditores'.[9]

---

[1] For the conditions and how severe and unusual they were see Stubbs, *Const. Hist.* ii. 157 and Willard, *Parliamentary Taxes on Personal Property, 1290–1334* (1934), pp. 22–5.

[2] Be it noted that the sole purpose of the letters patent of 14 Feb., the so-called Confirmation of the Charters 1301 (Bémont, *Chartes des libertés anglaises*, 1892, no. xvi), is to give effect to this. They are not in themselves a confirmation of the Charters.

[3] This, with the king's replies, is printed in *Parl. Writs*, i. 104–5 (no. 45).

[4] Ibid.: *en touz lur pointz entirement*.

[5] Ibid.: 'E qe par le conseil de Prelatz Contes e Barons soit mis en certein le poer des justices assignez en les Conteez pur les chartres garder.'

[6] This 'parliamentary' idea is considerably developed by the magnates in the Ordinances of 1311. Nothing concrete came of it in 1301—perhaps because of the king's grudging acceptance.

[7] See *supra*, p. 329.

[8] *Parl. Writs*, i. 104 (no. 45): 'E les mesprisions e trespaz fetz par les ministres le Roy contre la tenur des dites Chartes, e les prises torcenusement fetez saunz gre ou paie fere encountre la forme del estatut nostre Seignur le Rey fet a Wemonster en quareme drein passez desoremes cessent.'

[9] Ibid.: 'E ce ke mespris est par nul ministre soit amende solom ce ke le trespas le demaunde par auditours a ceo assignez qe ne soient pas suspecionus des Prelatz Contes e Barons de la terre solom ceo kil mesmes ainz ces houres ad fet e qe ce seit

After 1301 and the humiliations attached to the grant of the fifteenth, Edward financed himself without recourse to parliament except on one occasion, and then for feudal not gracious aid. He neither used nor infringed the clauses of *Confirmatio Cartarum* which obliged him to obtain 'common assent' to taxes and customs.[1] By 1305 he was in a position to reveal his purpose with impunity, and with papal help repudiate the *Confirmatio Cartarum*.[2]

What Edward I fought against successfully between 1297 and 1305 was enlargement of the scope of the Charters, either by additions to them such as the *Confirmatio Cartarum* of 1297 or by enlargement of the interpretation of what constituted an offence against them, which would have given the Charters a constructive value exceeding their literal content.[3]

This view of the last years of Edward I's reign has a bearing upon the first crisis of Edward II's reign. The usual comparison of the work of the Ordainers with the action of the barons in 1258 has its uses; but the contrast with 1297–1305 is more revealing. The most striking thing about the *Ordinances* is that the begetters of *Confirmatio Cartarum* 1297 ignored it in 1311. The Charters themselves are confirmed (in the texts of 1225), but they have in any case dropped curiously into the background. Baronial policy has changed. The Charters remain in the pharmacopoeia but they are no longer the sovereign remedy. The *Ordinances* are not added to the Charters. In 1311 the leaders of the nation were still, indeed more than ever, concerned with the king's ministers and ways of proceeding against them for wrongdoing—a problem which Edward I's reign had failed to resolve. But their attention was chiefly directed to their unquestioned right of

meintenant mis en œvre. *Dominus Rex vult providere aliud remedium super hoc set non per tales auditores.*'

[1] In 1302 he collected the aid granted in 1290 *pur fille marier*. In 1303 he sailed as near as he could to the *Confirmatio Cartarum* first by negotiating a new custom (in return for the *Carta Mercatoria*) from *foreign* merchants and then by trying less successfully a similar negotiation with the native merchant interest—which, from whatever motives, was loyal to the community and refused, and Edward withdrew. (This manœuvre of 1303 did not pass unnoticed in the Ordinances of 1311.) In 1304 he had resort to a tallage of the demesne lands, cities, and boroughs. In 1306 he resorted to parliament for aid for knighting his eldest son—the feudal aid referred to. The facts and references are collected in Stubbs, *Const. Hist.* ii. 163–4.

[2] Clement V's bull of 29 Dec. 1305, with its proviso that the rights of the English people should remain as they were before 10 Oct. 1297 (for that is what it amounts to), is printed by Bémont, *Chartes des libertés anglaises*, no. xvii. Cf. Petit-Dutaillis, *Studies Supplementary to Stubbs*, ii (Manchester, 1915), 226.

[3] He resisted, for instance, their extension, explicitly or implicitly, in the matter of prise, a prerogative hitherto limited in a few particular cases only by the Charters.

being taken into counsel by the king. They sought to develop the implications of that right and particularly to develop parliament as the instrument of good counsel, and through that, of right government too. That the same generation, with the same problems, with an even greater opportunity and with the same leadership, made no attempt to repeat the policy of 1297, that the organic history of the Charters ends here and English liberties have not in fact been developed by development of the Charters, gives the years 1297–1305 some claim to be considered decisive in our constitutional history.

H. ROTHWELL

THE NEGOTIATIONS PRECEDING THE 'TREATY' OF LEAKE, AUGUST 1318

I

IN an illuminating article on the negotiations which led up to the 'treaty' of Leake in August 1318,[1] Mr. J. G. Edwards was able to establish the fact of a very important preliminary agreement, which he dated shortly before 21 July.[2] Mr. Edwards suggested that the only other important agreement of this period, of which we have knowledge, was that of 12 April, at Leicester. J. H. Ramsay had argued[3] that there were several meetings at Leicester, besides that described by the canon of Bridlington under the date of 12 April; but Mr. Edwards agreed with J. C. Davies[4] that the different versions given in the chronicles were only different descriptions of the same assembly.

In this assembly of 12 April, it was agreed, he suggested, (1) that the ordinances of 1311 were to be faithfully observed, (2) that evil counsellors of the king were to be removed, (3) that all lands given by the king contrary to the ordinances were to be taken into the king's hand, (4) that those who had received lands of the king's gift were to be attached to account for the issues at the Exchequer, and that they were to give security to appear at the next parliament to receive judgement of the peers of the land, (5) that all trespasses committed by Lancaster and his followers were to be pardoned, (6) that Lancaster should promise *debitam fidelitatem et securitatem* to the king and his friends, except Warenne, and (7) that Lancaster should meet the king.

Mr. Edwards—like Stubbs, Ramsay, Tout, and Conway Davies before him—relied upon four chroniclers for his account of the meeting at Leicester.[5] He believed that he could fairly add

---

[1] 'The Negotiating of the Treaty of Leake, 1318', in *Essays in History Presented to R. Lane Poole* (ed. by H. W. C. Davis, Oxford, 1927), pp. 360–78. My obligation to Mr. Edwards will be evident at every stage of this essay. A final obligation was the fact that he generously read the manuscript of this essay and discussed it with me.

[2] From a letter printed by R. L. Poole in *Hist. MSS. Com., Report on MSS. in Various Collections*, i. 267–70. This letter is discussed below.

[3] *Genesis of Lancaster*, i (Oxford, 1913), 90.

[4] *Baronial Opposition to Edward II* (Cambridge, 1918), pp. 444–9.

[5] The 'Gesta Edwardi de Carnarvan', by the canon of Bridlington, in *Chronicles of Edward I and Edward II* (ed. W. Stubbs, Rolls Series, 1883), ii. 54; the 'Vita Edwardi Secundi', by the monk of Malmesbury, ibid. ii. 233; the *Flores Historiarum*, by Robert of Reading (for the reign of Edward II) (ed. H. R. Luard, Rolls

together all that the chroniclers had to say. This method, how-ever, legitimate though it may be, does in fact leave out of account a fifth description of an assembly at Leicester, that of John of Trokelowe.[1] John seems to describe an agreement at Leicester dated about 24 June.[2] It is suggested below that we have, there-fore, to allow for the possibility of two meetings at Leicester, one on 12 April, the other about 24 June. If this is the case, we may have to revalue the chronicles. One of them, the monk of Malmesbury, may possibly describe the same meeting as John of Trokelowe.

The arguments in favour of this are given briefly below. But it must be emphasized that the evidence remains extremely ambiguous. There is room for different interpretations. John of Trokelowe is, as Professor Tout has warned us, 'lacking in chronological precision'. The interpretation of Mr. Edwards and Mr. Davies follows the sound canon of historical interpreta-tion which says that, other things being equal, the simplest hypothesis is the best. The most that it is hoped will be achieved by the following reconstruction is to underline the complicated nature of the problem presented by the political negotiations of 1318, and to put one more very tentative interpretation of this, alongside that which already holds the field.

For the sake of clarity, the essential facts in the four accounts are given side by side (see opposite). It will be seen that the canon of Bridlington described a 'parliament' at which every-body, including Lancaster, swore to see that the ordinances should be observed and other important reforms carried out. There was no mention that Edward was present, or that any-body spoke on his behalf. Apparently the king was not a party to the agreement. The second writer, Robert of Reading, de-scribed a similar meeting. It was not between Thomas and the king, but between Thomas and the cardinals, and the *proceres et episcopi regni*. An oath to keep the ordinances was sworn by *omnes et singuli*. On the whole it does not seem likely, from the report of these two writers, that the king was a party to the

Series, 1890), iii. 184; and the *Chronicon* of Henry Knighton (ed. J. R. Lumby, Rolls Series, 1889), i. 413. The first clause was from Bridlington, Malmesbury, Robert of Reading (in the *Flores*) and Henry Knighton; the second from Bridling-ton; the third from Bridlington and Knighton; the fourth from the same; the fifth from Bridlington; the sixth from Malmesbury, and the seventh from Knighton.

[1] *Annales* (ed. H. T. Riley, Rolls Series, 1866), p. 102.
[2] The feast of St. John Baptist. An alternative date, 24 Aug., for St. John, may be left out of account. John's exact words are quoted *infra*, p. 343.

Gesta Edwardi de Carnarvan, by the canon of Bridlington.	*Flores Historiarum*, by Robert of Reading.	*Vita Edwardi Secundi*, by the monk of Malmesbury.	*Chronicon*, by Henry Knighton.
Meeting at Leicester between the archbishop of Canterbury, the bishops of Norwich, Chichester, Winchester, Llandaff, Hereford, the earls of Lancaster, Pembroke and Hereford, and twenty-eight barons. It was a 'parliament'— *in parliamento ibidem indicto*. All swore an oath that the ordinances should be kept, that evil counsellors should be removed, that lands given against the ordinances should be taken into the king's hand, &c.	The 'regni proceres una cum saepedictis cardinalibus et episcopis apud Leycestriam coram dicto comite quasi vir unus comparuerunt'. They swore to keep ordinances: 'omnes et singuli ad observationem ordinationum praemissarum et pacis de novo per sacramentum praestitum fuissent astricti.' And they went to London to meet the king.	'Convenerunt apud Leicestriam archiepiscopi comites et barones ex parte domini regis, et consiliarii comitis.' After some negotiation: 'Videntes archiepiscopus et ceteri comites animum comitis inmobilem, concesserunt pro domino rege et pro se ordinationes universas fideliter observari. . . . Et comes Lancastriae e contra domino regi et suis debitam fidelitatem et securitatem sub fide promisit.'	The meeting was *inter Thomam comitem et clerum*. At this meeting, 'certi articuli concordati [fuerunt] . . . et postea fuerunt ordinati et confirmati Londoniae per cardinales, archiepiscopos Cantuariae et Dunelmiae[a] et alios praelatos provinciae Cantuariensis'.
			[a] *Sic.* A mistake for *Dubliniae*.
The date is given as 12 Apr.	*No date is given.*	*No date is given.*	*No date is given.*

agreement of 12 April. When the agreement had been made, Robert of Reading said, the *consilium communitatis* went to meet the king. The canon of Bridlington seems to imply that the agreement was intended to coerce Edward.[1] We have other evidence to suggest that pressure was still being applied to Edward in order to reconcile him with Lancaster, as late as 8 June.

On the other hand, the monk of Malmesbury described a meeting between the archbishops, earls, and barons on behalf of the king, and the advisers of the earl. Its conclusion took the form of a pact between Lancaster and the king's party, in which the former swore fealty and security to the king and his supporters, whilst the latter swore that they and the king would faithfully observe the ordinances. This was a true 'reformation of peace'

[1] Op. cit., p. 55. 'Ecce legum mirabiles conditores; nam dominum suum regem, ut praedicitur, per asperitatem debent ad bonum regni regimen coartare; sed pacis corruptores per approbatas leges regni nolunt permittere castigari.'

between the king himself and the earl. The matters in which the monk differs from the first two chroniclers are, therefore, not incidental. It would have been an egregrious blunder for a chronicler, in the midst of the grave events of 1318, which actually turned on an attempt to bring the king and the earl together, to say that a definite agreement between Edward and Thomas had been achieved at a particular meeting, if it had not. It is very hard to think that the monk of Malmesbury would be guilty of such a blunder. This makes it probable that his observation applies to some other meeting than that described by the canon of Bridlington. There is no reason why it should not. The monk did not give any date for his meeting at Leicester.

The case of Henry Knighton is different. He described a meeting only between Thomas and the *clerus*, with 'certain articles' accepted. His description is so brief that it seems impossible to say whether it agrees or disagrees with either the canon of Bridlington or the monk of Malmesbury.[1]

It seems wiser for the moment to exclude both Henry Knighton and the monk of Malmesbury from the sources which tell us what happened at Leicester on 12 April. If we do that, we have to fall back on the canon of Bridlington and Robert of Reading in the *Flores Historiarum*. If we may venture to take these two accounts together, all the information which the two writers give us is that on 12 April the archbishop of Canterbury, five bishops, three earls (Lancaster, Hereford, Pembroke), held a 'parliament' at Leicester,[2] in which they swore a common oath to see that the ordinances should be kept, that evil counsellors should be removed, &c. There was no agreement between Lancaster and the king and no undertaking by Thomas to meet his ruler. If this meeting can be described in general terms, it would seem to represent an agreement between Thomas of Lancaster and the 'middle' party of Pembroke and the bishops, on the basis of the ordinances of 1311. This is at sharp variance with the accepted idea of the policy and actions of the 'middle' party in the negotiations leading up to the indenture at Leake. Perhaps before the next stage in those actions is considered, the aims of the 'middle' party should be very briefly discussed.

[1] Though it does not seem likely that the clergy of the Southern Province would have been called on to confirm articles which had been—according to the monk of Malmesbury—agreed on by both Thomas and the king.

[2] According to the *Flores*, the two cardinals also were present at Leicester, but is doubtful whether they attended the 'parliament'. The canon of Bridlington did not say that they were present *in parliamento*.

II

One root of the 'middle' party was probably the earl of Pembroke. A part of his activity in organizing the 'party'[1] was the very well-known indenture of 24 November 1317, in which Roger D'Amory bound himself to persuade Edward II to be guided by the counsels of Pembroke and Badlesmere. This is regarded as being aimed against Thomas of Lancaster,[2] and 'decisive proof' of this fact is supposed to have been found in a 'political agreement' of June 1318, discovered by Mr. Salisbury in 1918.[3] This agreement will be discussed in a moment. Meanwhile we may venture to suggest that the theory that the indenture of 1317 was 'hostile to Lancaster'[4] can only be accepted with certain reservations, some of which are suggested below.

Perhaps the initial problem has been wrongly stated. The problem at the time of this indenture was not to exclude Lancaster from the royal councils. He had already excluded himself, as may be seen in the correspondence between him and Edward in 1317.[5] The problem was to get him back into effective co-operation with the king. There is complete agreement in all the sources alike that England was paralysed by the withdrawal of Thomas from the business of government. There could be no effective opposition to the Scots until the country was freed from the dangerous division into two armed camps, with its threat of civil war.[6] The indenture of 1317 proves clearly enough that Pembroke wanted to make himself foremost in the royal councils; but perhaps the prime purpose for which he wished to use this position was to heal the schism between Edward and Lancaster on reasonable terms,[7] not to exclude Lancaster from the councils of the king. Some slight confirmation of this is offered by the

---

[1] We must be careful not to read any modern connotation into this word.

[2] At least, as an organized effort to replace Earl Thomas by Earl Aylmer as the king's chief counsellor; Tout, *Place of Edward II* (2nd ed.), p. 104.

[3] 'A Political Agreement of June 1318', *Eng. Hist. Rev.* xxxiii. 78–82; Professor Hilda Johnstone in *Place of Edward II*, p. 104, n. 3; T. F. Tout, *Chapters*, ii. 205, n. 1.

[4] Stubbs, *Chronicles of Edward I and Edward II*, ii, Introduction, p. lxxx.

[5] Ibid. ii. 50–2.

[6] Malmesbury, ibid. ii. 229: 'Satis enim liquet ex Britonum historia quam sit plena periculis civilis discordia.' Archbishop Walter Reynolds wrote as if civil war had been very near, in a letter of 21 July; *Hist. MSS. Com., Various Coll.* i. 268.

[7] It seems probable that Pembroke and his supporters were hostile to any claims of Lancaster to continue the exceptional position in the council which he had been given in 1316. In this sense they were hostile to Thomas. But there is no evidence that Thomas was holding or claiming this position on the council during 1317.

close connexion between Pembroke and the clergy, who seem to have pursued consistently the main objective of ending political strife.

The 'middle' party was, indeed, largely composed of the clergy, led by two cardinals, Gaucelin of Eauze and Luca Fieschi. These cardinals had been sent by John XXII for a twofold political purpose: to bring about peace, firstly between Edward II and Robert Bruce, and secondly between Edward and Thomas of Lancaster.[1] The cardinals were possibly sent to England at the request of Edward himself.[2] The request may have been made by a mission of December 1316, composed of exactly the same magnates, ecclesiastical and lay, who were the core of the 'middle' party.[3] Whether or not the same embassy asked John to agree to Edward's breaking of his oath to keep up the ordinances is uncertain. On the whole it is unlikely.[4] In any case the request, if made, was refused.[5] The main aim of the cardinals and the bishops was, therefore, reconciliation on the basis of the ordinances.[6] About 30 November 1317 the cardinals, with the bishops and clergy of the province of Canterbury, publicly pronounced 'formidable sentences' in St. Paul's, against all violators of the ordinances.[7] The archbishop of Canterbury and five bishops, outnumbering the earls, attended the 'parliament' of 12 April which once more reaffirmed the necessity of maintaining the ordinances of 1311.

The outlook of the 'middle' party, it seems likely, was sub-

[1] Henry Knighton, *Chronicon*, i. 412. Besides, of course, taxing the Church.

[2] John of Trokelowe, *Annales*, p. 99: 'ad petitionem tamen Domini Regis'. Cf. *Flores*, iii. 179.

[3] The earl of Pembroke, Lord Badlesmere, and the bishops Hotham of Ely and Salmon of Norwich. To these should be added, as leaders of the 'middle' party, the archbishops of Canterbury and Dublin. It was very much a clerical party.

[4] J. C. Davies thinks it did; op. cit., p. 429. T. F. Tout thought it unlikely; *Place of Edward II*, p. 101. Mr. Davies relies on the monk of Malmesbury, ii. 227. The monk said that 'misit rex nuntios ad curiam Romanam, qui cum venissent petierunt ex parte regis Angliae quatinus dominus papa dictum regem ab observatione quarundam ordinationum . . . dignaretur absolvere'. Pembroke apparently received his protection on 7 Dec. 1316; *C.P.R. 1313–1317*, p. 573, cited in Tout, *Place of Edward II*, p. 101, n. 2. The 'messengers' described by Malmesbury went *instante jam verno tempore* in 1317. It is not at all unlikely that some mission from Edward made this request. The fact that it was refused may well have had a decisive influence on Edward's policy.

[5] Malmesbury, ii. 227–8.

[6] On 1 Aug. 1317 Pope John XXII wrote to the archbishop of Canterbury hoping that 'verbum Dei in ore tuo . . . specialiter carissimum in Christo filium nostrum Edwardum . . . ad viam veritatis et justicie . . . reducat'; Canterbury Register, i, f. 362, cited *Hist. MSS. Com., App. to Eighth Report*, p. 354.

[7] *Annales Paulini*, i. 281; *Flores*, iii. 182.

stantially the same as that of its clerical members.[1] It stood, or tried to stand, squarely between the king and the earl. It was not simply anti-Lancastrian. On 12 April it was apparently closer to the earl than to the king.[2] It seems to have been prepared to demand Edward's acceptance of the ordinances on which Thomas had always taken his stand. With this conclusion in mind we may approach the next important stage in the negotiations, that represented by the 'political agreement' of 8 June at the Exchequer in Westminster, and the declaration on behalf of Edward II of his adherence to the ordinances, made immediately after, in St. Paul's.

III

The 'political agreement' of 8 June was made between the archbishops of Canterbury and Dublin, the earls of Pembroke and Hereford, Hugh Despenser and (probably) others.[3] The fact that these magnates included Hugh Despenser, and that the agreement was immediately followed by Edward's declaration that he placed himself on the counsel and aid of the barons has made the agreement seem like 'a combination definitely against Lancaster'.[4] This view falls in line with the theory that the 'middle' party was anti-Lancastrian. If we modify our concept of the 'middle' party, as suggested above, we should perhaps also modify our interpretation of the agreement of 8 June.

The bishops and magnates met in the Exchequer to discuss with

---

[1] For information about the bishops during this period see the useful paper by Miss K. Edwards, 'The Importance of English Bishops in the Reign of Edward II', in *Eng. Hist. Rev.* lix (Sept. 1944), 311–47. Miss Edwards may not have brought out fully the role played by the bishops and cardinals as intermediaries between Edward and Thomas of Lancaster. Walter, archbishop of Canterbury, wrote feelingly of the long labour of mediation which had been performed *per nos et mediatores alios.* The occasion was the final reconciliation at Leake, and the date of his letter was 8 Aug. 1318; *Hist. MSS. Com., Various Coll.* i. 269. His letter shows the high hopes built on this short-lived reconciliation of 1318.

[2] Actually, according to Robert of Reading, the cardinals had already, in late 1317, obtained a firm promise that Edward and Thomas would meet and be reconciled at the parliament of Jan. 1318; *Flores,* iii. 180. T. F. Tout gives all the details in *Place of Edward II* (2nd ed.), p. 107. On the whole, it seems likely that it was the king rather than the earl who destroyed this particular attempt to bring about peace. That may just possibly account for the strong position of Lancaster in Apr. 1318.

[3] It was discovered and printed by Mr. E. Salisbury in 1918, *Eng. Hist. Rev.* xxxiii. 78–83, 'A Political Agreement of June 1318.' Unfortunately the document is in part illegible. I have adopted the date 8 June, suggested by Mr. Salisbury, but the date is illegible on the document and it is possible that it was a day or two earlier than 8 June.

[4] T. F. Tout, *Chapters,* ii. 205, n. 1.

the council of the king. This may have been preliminary to a combination against Lancaster; but it also may have been a natural sequel to the meeting of 12 April, with Thomas of Lancaster. On 12 April the 'middle' party had come to an agreement with Lancaster; now, on 8 June, it may be guessed, they sought an agreement with the king. The agreement of 8 June did, in fact, include much more than an undertaking to oppose Lancaster if he continued to act in an unlawful manner. It seems to have stated that the main remedy to be sought for the crisis caused by the Scottish invasions was the return of the earl to political life.[1] It condemned the earl's recourse to violence and *assemblees des gentz darmes*; but almost certainly agreed to maintain the ordinances '[aus]sibien as prelatz e grandz susnometz e par eus furent jurees come le dit Counte de Lancastre'. It invited Thomas to attend parliament as a peer of the realm, 'sanz sovereinete a li accrocher vers les autres'; but it also promised the earl redress of his grievances towards individuals. It asserted that, if Thomas would not come into the government, the magnates taking part in the agreement would take over the business of the king and of the realm,[2] without waiting for the earl.

It seems clear that in entering into such an agreement the leaders of the 'middle' party had moved so far from the pact of 12 April that Lancaster could consider their action a betrayal.[3] In its condemnation of his policies and actions it was hostile to him. The implied charge of taking to himself sovereignty over others was almost as severe as that of assuming royal power for which the Despensers and Mortimer were later condemned. It is clear that those who accepted the agreement of 8 June were prepared, under certain conditions, to exclude Lancaster from the government altogether, and this goes far to justify the interpretation of their attitude by Professor Tout.

---

[1] 'et plus grantdz font a douter si remede ne soit mise de ceo qe le Co[unte] de [Lancastre se] est sustreit e ne se est pas donc a conseiller ne aider a nostre seignur le Roi en ses busoignes'.

[2] '. . . Roiaume e les grandz susnometz vivement empreignent les busoignes nostre seignur [le Roi] e du roiaume al [honur et profit de seinte eg]lise, e du Roi e la sauvaucion du poeple e de lestat le Roi sanz attendre ou regard a[uoir . . . Counte] de Lancastre.'

[3] This may account for the distrust of the secular leaders of the 'middle' party which Thomas showed later at Tutbury. His distrust would include the archbishops of Canterbury and Dublin; but he may have been less hostile to the *clerus* who do not seem to have participated, as a body, in the agreement of 8 June. In his public declaration at St. Paul's the king submitted to the counsel and help only of the earls and barons.

Yet this does not seem to have been the first purpose of the agreement. The first purpose seems to have been to get Lancaster into the government, not to exclude him. Only if he would not come in on what they considered reasonable terms would the magnates assembled on 8 June take over the government alone. This main conclusion is strongly supported by Edward's declaration on 8 June, in St. Paul's, with a full measure of publicity and solemnity, that he would confirm the ordinances, have peace with Lancaster,[1] and place himself on the help and counsel of his barons.[2] There can hardly be a doubt that the declaration of the king was a direct sequel to the negotiations in the Exchequer. It summed up, and bound Edward irrevocably to, the main agreement which had been reached. If this is true, two important conclusions seem to follow. In the first place, it shows that the main purpose of the proceedings on and before 8 June was, indeed, peace between Lancaster and Edward, not a combination against the former. In the second, it suggests that the earlier argument above, to the effect that Edward had not yet (before 8 June) pledged himself to accept peace with Thomas and enforce the ordinances, may be correct. Edward's declaration on 8 June would lose some of its effect if he had already on 12 April bound himself, through his representatives, to enforce the ordinances, and had accepted Thomas's pledge of security and peace. Alternatively, Thomas's unilateral pledge of peace and security, recorded by the monk of Malmesbury, is easier to understand if it was made after 8 June, when Edward had himself publicly proclaimed his peace with Lancaster.

The proceedings of 8 June were, therefore, it seems probable, in line with the objects of the 'middle' party as suggested above, and with the theory that Edward and Thomas had not yet exchanged mutual assurance of peace on the basis of the ordinances of 1311. On the other hand, it must be emphasized that, if this is true, a political revolution had, indeed, taken place since the meeting of 12 April as recorded by the canon of Bridlington. In April the 'middle' party was very close to Thomas, and came to an agreement with him before negotiating finally with the king. In June, on the contrary, the king placed himself completely on the counsel and help of the barons,[3] which seems, in its context, to imply primarily the counsel and support of the 'middle'

---

[1] *Flores*, iii. 184. [2] *Annales Paulini*, i. 282.
[3] He said that he would 'omnino adhaerere et coaptare se consilio et auxilio comitum et baronum suorum'; *Annales Paulini*, i. 282.

party. Edward and the 'middle' party had moved very close together, and the latter had moved very far from the earl. This political revolution had important repercussions for a number of years to come, and was indeed, in some sense, the turning-point in the political struggles of the reign.

IV

Whether or not this is true, the next stage in the negotiations would seem to be clear. Both the king and the earl had now (8 June) separately accepted proposals for a new concord on the basis of the ordinances. So far, however, they had only given their assurances to the 'middle' party. The next logical step was that they should give their pledges directly to each other. This suggests that there would have to be still another conference, this time between the king and the earl or their representatives. Such a conference is exactly what is described by the monk of Malmesbury, as recorded above, and there is therefore a case for thinking that this conference (which is undated) may have fallen after 8 June.

There are two pieces of evidence which might support this theory, both of them unfortunately ambiguous. Archbishop Reynolds wrote on 9 June 'quod dominus Rex vie pacis innite (inite?) annuit amplectende apud Leicestr' prelocute'.[1] There is perhaps no need to discuss this puzzling phrase at length. It can unfortunately be used, in its ambiguity, to support the view either (a) that the king had agreed to the previous agreement of 12 April at Leicester, or (b) that he proposed to take part in a future agreement at Leicester (of 24 June?). The only argument in favour of the second alternative seems to be that it was the one favoured by R. L. Poole;[1] though it might possibly be argued also in its favour that the way of peace which Edward II actually embraced on 8 June was decidedly not the way designated on 12 April at Leicester, even if all the accounts of such an assembly are taken together. The archbishop was misleading his correspondent if he suggested that it was. Prima facie, it seems reasonable to believe that the great news which Reynolds had to

---

[1] Canterbury, Eastry Correspondence, portfolio i, no. 13. *Hist. MSS. Com., Various Coll.*, cited by J. G. Edwards, op. cit., p. 368. For J. G. Edwards's interesting discussion of this phrase, see ibid., p. 368, n. 1. Mr. R. L. Poole said that he gave the date of this letter doubtfully as being in June 1318. He thought that it was questionable whether the place of the king's meeting at Leicester early in Aug. 1318 was likely to be fixed two months earlier. But this difficulty does not arise if there was a meeting about 24 June.

impart on 9 June was that Edward had finally pledged himself to peace with the earl; and this, as pointed out above, suggested a meeting between Edward and Thomas in the future, rather than referred to one in the past.

The other evidence is that of John of Trokelowe, already referred to above. John is sketchy and uncertain in his chronology. Nevertheless, he does make one invaluable observation to the effect that peace was re-formed between Edward and Lancaster, at Leicester about 24 June. This statement cannot be assessed in isolation and the different accounts which may possibly refer to such a meeting—John himself, the monk of Malmesbury, and Henry Knighton—may be put side by side.

John of Trokelowe[1]	*Malmesbury*[2]	*Henry Knighton*[3]
(1318) The Scots consumed the North with fire and sword. Then 'Deus . . . cordibus praelatorum instillavit ut, una cum Cardinalibus, Regem adirent, et inducerent, quatenus Articulos, totiens pro statu Ecclesiae et regni petitos et concessos, bona fide confirmaret, et in usu et opere stabiles esse permitteret, ne sibi et regno gravius periculum immineret. Ad quod faciendum, dies circa festum sancti Johannis Baptistae apud Leicestriam assignatur; ubi pace inter Regem et Comitem quodammodo reformata, Articulisque pristino more concessis, Cardinales licenciati ab Anglia recesserunt.'	Convenerunt apud Leicestriam archiepiscopi comites et barones ex parte domini regis, et consiliarii comitis. The archbishop (*sic*: singular) and the other earls, finding the earl unyielding, pledged the king and themselves to observe the ordinances 'et cartam testimonii sacramento singulorum et sigillorum impressione roborari. Et comes Lancastriae e contra domino regi et suis debitam fidelitatem et securitatem sub fide promisit.'	Certi articuli locuti et concordati apud Leycestriam inter Thomam comitem et clerum, et postea fuerunt ordinati et confirmati Londoniae per cardinales, archiepiscopos Cantuariae et Dunelmiae[a] et alios praelatos provinciae Cantuariensis. [a] *Sic*. A mistake for *Dubliniae*.

[1] *Annales*, p. 102.   [2] *Vita Edwardi Secundi*, ii. 233.   [3] *Chronicon*, i. 413.

Henry Knighton may be dismissed immediately from the company of the other two writers. His reference to an agreement *inter Thomam comitem et clerum* is unlikely to be a reference, however loose, to the agreement described by Malmesbury, for instance, between the advisers of the king and of the earl.

On the other hand, it will be seen that John of Trokelowe and the monk of Malmesbury may well describe the same meeting. It was a meeting where peace was 're-formed' between the earl and the king. There are important discrepancies between the accounts, but they do agree on this one essential point. The difficulty of Trokelowe's narrative lies in its brevity and general lack of precision, so that it is possible that John actually referred to the assembly of 8 June when he spoke of a meeting 'about' the 24th. On the whole this seems to be unlikely. Trokelowe makes the *pax reformata* appear as the end of the negotiations for peace, preparatory to the departure of the cardinals; but there is nothing in the surviving evidence for the meeting of 8 June to suggest that this could be regarded as the climax of these negotiations. It is hard to believe that he was so confused in his narrative that he placed the meeting of 8 June at Leicester instead of London, ascribed to it a reconciliation between Thomas and Edward which almost certainly did not then take place, and said that it occurred about 24 June.

The difficulty of equating the assembly described by the monk of Malmesbury with this assembly of about 24 June lies in the assertion of the monk that after the agreement at Leicester 'they' accepted (*acceperunt*) a date of 19 June for parliament.[1] This would mean that the agreement itself fell before 3 March, the date when the parliament of 19 June was actually agreed upon.[2] Now it is possible to believe that the king's advisers agreed on a policy of conciliation as early as 3 March, but hardly possible that the king and the earl gave mutual pledges as described by Malmesbury as early as this. That would have made almost pointless the proceedings of 12 April as well as those of 8 June. It must be assumed that, as frequently happens in medieval chronicles, the narrative of the monk is, at this point, logical rather than chronological. In any case, we have three, not one, possible dates for the meeting described by the monk of Malmesbury—before 3 March, 12 April, about 24 June. Neither of the last two fits in with the strict chronology of the chronicle, a point not previously emphasized. If either is to be accepted, there seems

---

[1] Malmesbury, ii. 233.

[2] *Parl. Writs*, ii, pt. ii, p. 180.

As Stubbs suggests, the discussion in council recorded by Malmesbury (ii. 233) possibly took place about 4 Jan., in connexion with the postponement of the parliament summoned for 27 Jan. 1318 (*Chronicles of Edward I and Edward II*, ii, Introduction, p. lxxx). Malmesbury then described the logical outcome of this discussion, which was an agreement between Thomas and Edward. He then goes back to tell how parliament was summoned for 19 June, but omits to inform us that this summons was cancelled by Edward on 8 June. *Parl. Writs*, ii, pt. ii, p. 181 (not 4 June, as Stubbs op. cit. lxxxi). There are some good arguments for placing this discussion in the council at some date just before 8 June. The cancellation of 8 June would then be the result of a decision to seek an agreement with Lancaster, as advised by members of the council. This seems, however, to involve the somewhat dangerous assumption that the monk simply did not know of the cancellation of 8 June.

to be a somewhat dubious preference in favour of 24 June. But whatever the date at which we place the meeting described by the monk of Malmesbury, we may tentatively accept Trokelowe's evidence for a meeting at Leicester about 24 June and proceed to discuss the subsequent negotiations for which the agreement between Edward and Lancaster paved the way.

V

The next and final agreement preceding the meeting at Leake in August 1318 was that reflected in the letter reprinted by Mr. Edwards,[1] which he dates with almost absolute certainty as being 21 July. This was not a formal agreement; it was simply a report on negotiations between Thomas on the one hand and certain persons not named on the other. It is dissociated by Mr. Edwards from the negotiations which took place at Tutbury, between Thomas of Lancaster and the bishops of Norwich and Ely. His main reason seems to be that 'for the conversations of 4–16 July and 20–9 July there is independent evidence which shows that Lancaster did not then take up the intransigent attitude which he adopted [at Tutbury] on the occasion recorded by Knighton'.[2] The Tutbury discussions, recorded by Knighton, he concludes, probably occurred on some occasion prior to 4 July.

There are one or two objections to this conclusion, however. In the first place, Knighton himself appears to have looked on the discussion at Tutbury as being the prelude to the final meeting between Thomas and the king, which occurred on 7 August.[3] We should not, therefore, expect the discussions to be very much earlier than this.

In the second place, there are points in common between the discussions at Tutbury and those reported in the letter of 21 July. Both were carried on between Thomas and bishops.[4] Both were

---

[1] It was first printed in *Hist. MSS. Com., Various Coll.* i. 268. It came from the Eastry correspondence, Canterbury—no. 34 of a roll (iv) of miscellaneous letters from Archbishops Pecham, Winchelsea, and Reynolds.

[2] Op. cit., pp. 369–70.

[3] *Chronicon*, p. 421: 'Cumque antedicti episcopi sub tali ordine nuncium suum ordinati fuissent, comesque ad singula, ut praedictum est, responsum dedisset, tandem placuit comiti occurrere regi obviam apud Sotysbrig ad sibi mutuo collo- quendum.'

[4] In the first case we know there were the bishops of Norwich and Ely; in the second there were certain *episcopi missi* (Edwards, op. cit., p. 372). The first mission described by the letter of 21 July, it is suggested below, was that of 4–16 July. The reference to *episcopi missi*, in the letter, does not really make it clear whether or not only bishops had gone on this mission. There may, of course, have been others, including Pembroke himself. One difference between the position of

concerned with the questions of the resumption of lands into the king's hands, the removal of evil counsellors, and the meeting between the earl and the king. The discussions at Tutbury covered some things not mentioned in the letter, and the letter covers one extremely important matter which, as far as our record goes, was not touched on at Tutbury. But the agreement on other points seems to be so close that the two sets of negotiations are unlikely to have been very far apart.

Finally, it may be argued, though Thomas was indeed intransigent on some points at Tutbury, his attitude may not have differed much from that which we can deduce from the report of negotiations given in the letter of 21 July. The proposal of the bishops at Tutbury that gifts contrary to the ordinances should be

the clergy at their first agreement at Leicester, as described by Henry Knighton, and in the negotiations at Tutbury seems to be worth pointing out. At Leicester, on 12 Apr., the *clerus* were part of the 'middle' party. At Tutbury they seem to have spoken on behalf of the king. This may have been a result of the political revolution of 8 June already discussed. It perhaps explains why some of the points already settled on 12 Apr. had to be negotiated all over again at Tutbury. Compare, for example, the clause of the agreement recorded by Bridlington, ii. 54, on 12 Apr.: 'quod omnes terrae contra ordinationes per regem datae in manum regis capiantur festinanter', &c., with the first suggestion by the prelates at Tutbury (Knighton, i. 413): 'Que les terres, rentes et tenemens donez encontre la fourme dez ordinancez seiont renduz et remisez en la mayn le roy', &c. Mr. Edwards regards the proposal of the prelates as an attempt to modify the earlier concession (op. cit., p. 365): 'the two bishops endeavoured to persuade the earl to agree that there should not be an absolute resumption, but that parliament should be left to decide whether or not each grant was "convenable", and then to allow it to stand or not as seemed reasonable'. To this, he suggests, Lancaster refused to agree, demanding that 'les dites choses furent mises en oeure si come fuist accordes a les perlancez a Leycestre'. But it is a little difficult to see enough difference between these two clauses to account for the fact that negotiations were reopened on the question of lands granted contrary to the ordinances, if it had just been settled at Leicester. A much greater difference is between the clauses of Bridlington to the effect that those who had received grants contrary to the ordinances should receive judgement of the peers in parliament, and the suggestion of the prelates that such people should surrender their grants but should not be punished. In this case it is not easy to reconcile such a suggestion with good faith on the part of the bishops, if Thomas and the king had both agreed on these points on 12 Apr. With regard to both points at issue, the situation was entirely different if only Thomas and the 'middle' party had agreed on them. They would clearly, on this hypothesis, have to be negotiated again, between Thomas and the king. The prelates, now representing, or speaking on behalf of, the king, might well wish to water down their previous agreement of 12 Apr. Thomas no less naturally kept reminding them of what they, together with him, had sworn on that occasion on 12 Apr. Whether the differences between the points at issue in the negotiations of 12 Apr. and at Tutbury are great or small, the difficulty, inherent in Mr. Edwards's thesis, would seem to remain. If there was no real difference, it is hard to see why the points had to be negotiated again; or, if there was a sharp difference, it is equally difficult to see how the bishops could bring forward proposals so far removed from those of the 'definitive' agreement of 12 Apr.

surrendered followed closely the lines of the Leicester agreement. Thomas accepted. The procedure should be followed, he said, 'si come fuist accordes a lez perlancez a Leycestre'.[1] It is not altogether impossible to reconcile his answer with the agreement reported in the letter of 21 July: 'quod omnia collata quibuscunque personis per regem contra ordinaciones tam in redditibus quam peccunia ipsi domino regi restituerentur'. It would seem logical to conclude that the latter was derived from the former, though whether or not it was directly derived it seems impossible to say.

The bishops apparently said that they had undertaken, 'sil pleace a nostre seigniour le roy', that those who returned such grants to the king should not be punished.[2] By undertaking this, Thomas told them, they had gone against the ordinances and against their oath and his, and he quoted the relevant passage of the ordinances. No mention of this matter was made in the letter of 21 July. It might perhaps be argued that the strong attitude of Thomas prevented a clear-cut agreement on the point, though this would not affect the promise of immunity which the bishops had, according to Thomas, already made.

---

[1] Knighton, *Chronicon*, pp. 413–14: 'Que les terres, rentes et tenemens donez encontre la fourme dez ordinancez seiont renduz et remisez en la mayn le roy sanz estre redonez a mesmes ceaux eynz demourront en la mayne le roy a son profite, et al parliment soient regardez queux chosez estoient covenablement donez et queux altrement, et adonkes soit la chose discusse solom ceo que lem verra que soit affaire par reson.'
The answer was: 'Sires mout a vous plerroit que les ditez choses furent mises en oeure si come fuist accordes a les perlancez a Leycestre, et sils soyent redonez desore buseygneroit que vou sires ou altres peres de la terre nyent suspecions enpreystez et les ditez chosez, terrez et tenementz etc. soient mises en si covenable garde que les usez veignent pleynement a lescheker le roy al commune profit de luy et de sonn realme, et dispenduz en la deffence de la terre. Issi qils ne fussent desorenavant gastez ne en malveys oeps despenduz sicome avant ont estre.' Mr. Edwards says (op. cit., p. 365), 'to this Lancaster refused to agree, demanding that "les dites choses furent mises en oeure si come fuist accordes a les perlancez a Leycestre", and that all the issues should come to the exchequer for the king's use'. Perhaps the demand that all issues should come to the exchequer was not necessarily in conflict with the proposal of the bishops. Both the proposal of the bishops and the earl's reply permitted a possible re-granting of lands under the proper safeguards, though those proposed by the earl were more specific.

[2] Mr. Edwards (op. cit., p. 365) believes that the earl refused to agree. His reply was: 'Par la sires ou vous avez enpris que ceux que ont pris del roy contra la ordinaunce, queux ne serront punys, sires il nous semble que vous avez méspris contre les ordinaunces e encontre vostre serment et nostre, car les ordinaunces voilent que ceux soient punis en parlement'. (He then quoted the relevant article in the ordinances.) It is true, of course, that Thomas did not agree. He was informed of a step which the bishops were apparently prepared to recommend, whether it was agreeable to Thomas or not. They only seem to stipulate the agreement of the king.

On the question of his enemies, the evil advisers around the king, the earl took a positive and effective stand. He could not trust the king's surety, offered him for a meeting, he said, whilst those who had taken gifts and forsworn themselves were around the king. Even if this surety was reinforced by the prelates and lords who were at Leicester (12 April), he still would not be safe. The further suggestion that those whom the earl suspected should add their letters of surety, fortified by the cardinals' threat of excommunication against those who broke their promise, did not move Lancaster. Finally[1] the bishops suggested that those of whom Thomas felt 'qils sont sez enmys mortelez, e quils ont procure male devers son seigniour lige' should absent themselves *un pecee* whilst the earl and the king met. This again the earl refused. He would have the evil advisers removed *de tut*.[2] Here, and only here, Thomas seems to have been quite uncompromising. Here he seems to have gained his point. In the letter of 21 July, the mission was said to have agreed 'quod illi quos dominum regem male consuluisse pretendit omnino a regis lateribus amoveantur'.

Finally, there was the question of forgiving his enemies, on which point in particular Thomas is thought to have been more accommodating as reported in the letter of 21 July than he was at Tutbury.[3] It is true that at Tutbury he was reluctant. The bishops asked him to receive his enemies into friendship, provided that those who were guilty towards him should make amends in reason. The bishops promised to take action against either side that refused to enter the peace. Thomas replied that he could not receive his enemies into friendship until the things which they had done[4] against king and people be 'arrested' in parliament. He welcomed the promise of the bishops: he had always wanted harmful things to be redressed so that peace could be kept. It is very hard to know what to make of his reply. One thing is

---

[1] Part of the discussion is missing, p. 418, after *al parlement quele houre que*.

[2] Knighton, *Chronicon*, p. 420. The understanding was that, with all this security offered, the earl, at the request of the king, the prelates, and the cardinals, would be reconciled with his enemies on the basis that those who had committed offences against him would make *covenable* amends. With regard to this reconciliation with his enemies, Thomas seems to have given a very guarded and typically ambiguous agreement (pp. 420–1).

[3] J. G. Edwards, op. cit., p. 372, n. 1.

[4] His words were: 'nous ne purroms a eux accordere [i.e. to the request of the prelates] et nostre seourment saver avant que lez chosez qils ont myspris contre le state le roy al damage de luy et de son people soient arestez par agarde des pieres en parlement, si come il est contenue en les ordinauncez.'

certain: it was not an outright refusal. Whether it could have led to the conclusion recorded in the letter of 21 July[1] must remain a matter of doubt. On the whole it seems just possible that it could.

At least on three of the major points discussed at Tutbury— the question of gifts contrary to the ordinances, of the punishment of those who had taken such gifts, and of evil counsellors— the attitude of Thomas seems to have been reflected in the letter of 21 July. It seems not unreasonable to conclude that the negotiations at Tutbury were not far separated in time from those whose outcome was recorded in the letter.

The only evidence as to the exact time of the Tutbury discussions seems to lie in the movements of the bishop of Ely who was present at them.[2] The bishop left London on the king's business on 13 June,[3] and he was again absent from court 4–16 July and 20–9 July. On 1 August he visited the earl 'a third time'.[4] As Mr. Edwards points out, this seems to make the visit of 4–16 July the first occasion.[5] Unless the Tutbury discussions occurred after 1 August, and long after the agreement recorded in the letter of 21 July, which seems highly improbable, their date would have to be either 4–16 or 20–9 July. It seems more likely to have been the former. The purpose of the mission of 20–9 July will be dealt with in the next section: it is not likely that it covered the questions discussed at Tutbury. But the discussions of 4–16 July are, almost beyond question, those described in the letter of 21 July. The conclusion seems to be, therefore, that the discussions at Tutbury and those recorded in the letter are the same.[6] It follows that, after the agreement of about 24 June, there were only two sets of negotiations. The first from 4 to 16 July was recorded by both Henry Knighton and in the letter of 21 July. As a result of these negotiations, there was agreement,

---

[1] The agreement in the letter was: 'dixit se velle remittere omnibus quamquam transgressionem sibi factam et offensionem quam pro transgressionibus conceperat erga eos preter quam duobus . . . .'

[2] These have been traced in the discussion by Mr. J. G. Edwards noted above, which has provided the starting-point of this work. See *Parl. Writs*, ii, pt. i, p. 208; ibid. ii, pt. ii, App., pp. 123–4.

[3] Edwards, op. cit., p. 369; the bishop returned to court on 2 July.

[4] Ibid., p. 369, n. 3; citing *Parl. Writs*, ii. pt. ii, App., pp. 123–4.

[5] It also enables us to guess, though we can do no more than guess, that the first absence, beginning 13 June, was connected with the meeting at Leicester of about 24 June.

[6] The only strong objection seems to be the fact that Knighton's account of the discussions at Tutbury did not include the proposal for a baronial council. But, as Mr. Edwards points out, Knighton's account was incomplete.

though far from complete agreement, between Thomas and the king, on most of the outstanding points at issue; but there was one major issue on which the settlement of 4–16 July was not acceptable to Edward's advisers. It was on this issue that the mission of 20 July went *ad mitigandum comitem*. The problem of this major issue should finally be briefly discussed.

VI

What was this final issue? It is hard to believe that the mission went to persuade Lancaster to forgo the removal of evil coun- sellors from the king's side, or the resumption of lands given by the king contrary to the ordinances. Even though these concessions by the king were not mentioned in the 'treaty' of Leake, both sides had come very close to agreement on them in the negotiations at Tutbury. Action, though admittedly not very drastic action, was, in fact, taken with regard to them in the parliament at York. How far the earl had to be 'mitigated' on these points must apparently remain uncertain.

There remains the question of setting up a baronial council. This, we now know, in spite of the silence of Henry Knighton, was probably raised at Tutbury: at least, it was recorded in the letter of 21 July. Indeed, agreement on the point was actually obtained. Thomas apparently proposed a council of eight bishops, four earls, and four barons, to hold office for a year. Two bishops, one earl, and one baron were to act in each quarter. He persuaded the negotiating bishops[1] to accept this scheme. But it is precisely this feature of the settlement which we know to have been later modified. On the whole it seems likely, although it was not explicitly stated, that it was this feature of the agreement at Tutbury which was rejected by the king's advisers,[2] and that it was primarily to 'mitigate' this feature that the final mission to Thomas set out on 20 July. What this mission achieved, apparently, was the addition to the council of a banneret repre- senting the earl. The main question seems to be, therefore, not which particular feature of the agreement of 4–16 July was sub- sequently modified, but rather what was the purpose of the king's advisers in persuading Thomas, on 20–9 July, to modify the form of baronial council which he had earlier proposed. The problem is of considerable importance because of the light it throws on the attitude of both Thomas and of the 'middle' party.

[1] There may have been others as well, as pointed out above.
[2] Is it permissible to guess that this was why it was omitted by Henry Knighton?

There can be little doubt that the form of the council first proposed at Tutbury came from Thomas. On the whole it seems likely that his intention was not to include himself. This is supported by two considerations. In the first place, although it was possible, under his scheme, for Thomas to be elected as one of the four earls on the council, all that Thomas in fact promised to do, according to the letter of 21 July, was to meet the king and to accompany him to war. Considering how urgent the need was for his presence on the council, it seems likely that his failure to give a definite promise to serve has considerable significance.

In the second place, if the arguments above have any validity, the one over-riding aim of the 'middle' party in 1318 was to secure the co-operation of Lancaster with the government 'sanz sovereinete a li accrocher vers les autres'. It was not, and could not be, to exclude him from the council. Such an exclusion would have brought matters back, after six months of tedious negotiations, to exactly where they had been at the end of 1317. This seems to be the most logical explanation of the consternation of the king's advisers, on the return of the embassy of 4–16 July. They were afraid, not that Thomas had secured the possibility of his election to the council, but that he had virtually denied that possibility, just as he was doing when the negotiations had first begun.

One or two minor points seem to support this conclusion. The first and most obvious is that it was a strange way of 'mitigating' the earl, to exclude him from a council which he proposed to attend. It was certainly not conducive to the reconciliation for which the bishops had worked so hard. The second is that the election of a banneret was a very clumsy method of preventing Thomas's election. All that was necessary, apparently, for this purpose, under the scheme which Thomas himself propounded, was not to elect him amongst the earls. Thomas himself had proposed no safeguard whatever against his own exclusion. The third point is that the method was very ineffective. If Thomas was not a member of the council, as nominated at York, his representative was a permanent member. If the latter had no great constructive, he had great obstructive, power.

On the whole Thomas's attitude, towards the end of these long negotiations, seems to be indicative of a deep dissatisfaction with the pressure that had been put on him by the 'middle' party,[1] and with the concessions he had been forced to make in the interests of peace. Thus, the final agreement obtained by the mission of 20–9 July was, as we should judge by its provisions, a compromise which really satisfied nobody. It was the best which, under the circumstances, could be obtained. It finally enabled the indenture at Leake, on 9 August, to be sealed. But it could not, and in fact it did not, provide the basis for a permanent peace.[2]

VII

To summarize these conclusions the following list of meetings preliminary to the 'treaty' of Leake may be tentatively suggested.

1. The meeting of the clergy in London, November 1317. In this the ordinances of 1311 were accepted as the basis for a determined effort to 're-form' the peace.

2. The first meeting at Leicester, 12 April 1318. This was between the 'middle' party and Lancaster's advisers. The agreement bound the earl and the 'middle' party, not the king.

3. The assembly in the Exchequer at Westminster, about 8 June. This was between the 'middle' party and the king's advisers. It represented the second important stage in the negotiations. The basis of peace had now been accepted by both sides. The agreement incorporated some of Thomas of Lancaster's reforming programme, but it also established safeguards against a continuance of lawlessness by the earl. It brought Edward and the 'middle' party close together. It was followed immediately by the king's public acceptance of the ordinances, at St. Paul's, with a profession of his willingness to be guided by the magnates. Taken together, these developments, it has been suggested, amounted to what was, for that period, an important political revolution, which had very important consequences later on.

4. The second meeting at Leicester, about 24 June. In this the king and the earl for the first time gave a mutual pledge to keep the peace and accept the ordinances.

5. The negotiations at Tutbury and near Northampton, 4–16 July. These were an attempt to settle the remaining points at issue, preliminary to a meeting between the king and the earl. They were partly, though not completely, successful. They left

---

[1] Perhaps it is significant of the gulf between Pembroke and Lancaster by 21 July that the former was prominent in supporting the original agreement, in the discussions in the king's council; that is he, was content to have Thomas excluded from the council.

[2] See note below.

the earl disgruntled and suspicious.[1] But they led to an agreement recorded in the letter of 21 July.

6. The final settlement of 20–9 July. The central issue here was probably raised by an attempt to bring Lancaster in some way into the king's council. This again was partly successful. Lancaster was only to be represented on the council; but this was enough to make possible, finally, the indenture of 9 August at Leake.

7. The indenture at Leake on 9 August. This may not have been entirely a 'virtual surrender' by Thomas,[2] though the facts go far to justify the verdict of Professor Tout. Thomas was called upon to make most of the concessions for peace; but the 'treaty' was really a compromise which satisfied nobody and contained within it the seeds of the crisis of 1321.

B. WILKINSON

[1] Henry Knighton, *Chronicon*, p. 417: 'Quant a la soerte des altres grantz quae furent a Leycestre il nous semble que nous ne poems de tut fyere, puis que ascuns de eux que illocques furent ount dedit lour serement qils fyrent a Leycestre en voz presencez.' Presumably this was because Pembroke and others did not impose on Edward all the terms to which they had sworn on 12 Apr. Thomas never forgave Pembroke for what he considered a betrayal, and this contributed to Thomas's downfall in 1322. See Malmesbury, ii. 263: 'Sed et comes de Penbrok divertebat se ad partem regis eo quod comes Lancastriae imposuerat se proditionis. Expertus erat comes Lancastriae, ut dixit, hominem illum infidum et varium, et baronibus indixerat auxilium ejus repudiandum.' All this helps to explain Lancaster's actions in 1321–2, and to illuminate Adam of Murimuth's remark about the 'treaty' of Leake (*Cont. Chronicarum*, p. 29): 'sed vera pax non fuit, sicut inferius apparebit.'
[2] T. F. Tout, *Chapters*, ii. 205.

IDEALS OF KNIGHTHOOD IN
LATE-FOURTEENTH-CENTURY ENGLAND

THE slowly altering ideals of knighthood and of knightly conduct are crucially significant for the development of social theory in medieval England. It is probable that for a considerable section of the ruling class they formed a standard of values, at times consciously followed, at times consciously sinned against, but always presupposed. They contained conceptions of personal loyalties that were to have direct political consequence and could provide the avowed motives for political action. Two manuscripts can illustrate the form in which they were taught in late-fourteenth-century England. But the value of these manuscripts as sources largely depends on the precision with which it is possible to determine their provenance, the public for which they were intended, and the contemporary sense of the epithets that they employ.

A manuscript in the library of Worcester College, Oxford,[1] contains a verse account of the life and deeds of arms of the very noble prince of Wales and Aquitaine who had by name Edward. Its purpose is explicitly didactic.[2] It aims at teaching the hearer how to know the good and to gain honour[3] and seems an Anglo-French counterpart of the 'Livre des Faicts de Jean Bouciquaut'.[4] The manuscript, in an admirable hand and carefully rubricated, is by a good professional scribe, probably about the end of the fourteenth century. It was possibly commissioned for some lord's household, but nothing in its known history can help to establish the part of England from which it came. Worcester College gained it from Dr. Clarke of All Souls; its first recorded owner was Sir William le Neve.[5] A note *defic' hic* written in the scribe's hand on f. 37ʳ seems to make it clear that it is a copy of another manuscript. It is stated in the text that the author had been herald in the household of Sir John Chandos.[6] It seems possible that either he or his patrons had some connexion with the

---

[1] Worcester College Library, MS. 1; *The Life of the Black Prince by the Herald of Sir John Chandos*, ed. M. K. Pope and E. C. Lodge (Oxford, 1910); cited below as *Chandos Herald*.

[2] Ibid. ll. 1–43.

[3] Ibid. l. 36 seq.

[4] Ed. J. A. C. Buchon, *Froissart* (Paris, 1840), vol. iii.

[5] 1600?–61.

[6] *Chandos Herald*, f. 59ᵛ, ll. 4187–8.

affinity of the Duke of Lancaster.[1] But the original poem has been handled by a redactor who added the descriptive titles, composed the verses on the officers of the prince's household,[2] and on some occasions may have altered the text. This redactor used an already old-fashioned Anglo-Norman, was unfamiliar with Paris French, and was possibly linked with the household of the Devereux of Herefordshire.[3] His work is the more easily traced since the main body of the poem is in a French similar to that of Froissart.[4] It is probable that the conflation had already taken place in the manuscript from which that at Worcester College was copied, for similar scribal errors occur in the French verses and in the Anglo-Norman additions. It is impossible to date the original poem with exactness. It was apparently composed after 1376, since the conquest of Castille by Henry of Trastamar is stated to have occurred about twenty years earlier.[5] It has been suggested that it was written before 1385 since the princess of Wales is referred to in the present tense,[6] but this is inconclusive since the present tense is also used for the queen of Navarre who died in 1373.[7] It seems safest to hold that the poem assumed its present form between 1376 and 1400.

It is possible to place the second manuscript with more exactness. Brit. Mus. MS. Cotton, Nero A. x, ff. 37–126,[8] was bound into its present volume of miscellanea by Sir Robert Cotton. It had come into his possession from that of the Yorkshire antiquarian Henry Savile of Bank (1568–1617).[9] This already suggests a northern provenance and two annotations[10] in fifteenth-century hands seem to imply a secular rather than a monastic ownership before the Dissolution. It contains four poems in Middle English, *Gawayne and the Grene Knight*, *Pearl*, *Patience*, and *Cleannesse*. All are in north-west dialect. The collection seems intended for recitation, perhaps for the instruction and entertainment of some lord's household. Closely as all four poems are interwoven they represent three different literary genres. In spite of echoes from

---

[1] For the apparent bias in favour of the duke of Lancaster, ibid., f. 45ᵛ, l. 3197 seq.

[2] Ibid., ff. 60ʳ–61ʳ, ll. 4189–255.

[3] Cf. ibid., f. 32ᵛ, where the name of Sir John Devereux has been inserted at the expense of a rhyme, l. 2281.

[4] Cf. the discussion of the linguistic problems of the text in the preface of the edition by M. K. Pope and E. C. Lodge.

[5] Ibid., l. 1816. [6] Ibid., l. 2142. [7] Ibid., ll. 2485–6.

[8] Facsimile in E.E.T.S., O.S. 162.

[9] Cf. Brit. Mus. MS. Harl. 1879.

[10] Brit. Mus. MS. Cotton, Nero A. x, ff. 124ᵛ, 125.

Mandeville and the *Romaunt of the Rose*, *Patience* and *Cleannesse* belong to an antique tradition of Bible paraphrase and homiletic verse. *Pearl* is part of the new literary movement in fourteenth-century Europe, a didactic elegy by a learned man, *fictio rhetorica musice composita*. *Gawayne*[1] is a metrical romance portraying the conduct of the perfect knight. Yet close similarities between all four suggest a single author or a single redactor, perhaps a clerk or esquire in some household. Possibly it might be a repertory book composed by the author of *Gawayne*, who included his own poem, *Pearl*, perhaps a favourite piece of recitation that had influenced his own verse strongly, and *Patience* and *Cleannesse* which he had interpolated and polished.

The one surviving manuscript was prepared, written, and illuminated professionally and clumsily. The dialect forms make it possible that it was the work of a professional scribe in some such town as Chester; from the hand the period would seem to be early fifteenth century. Only the illuminations[2] suggest the kind of manuscript of which it is a copy; slovenly executed, with the figure work curiously out of proportion, they are yet obviously related to the new experiments in the representations of natural scenery and of architectural background which marked sophisticated French court art at the turn of the century. They can be best explained as the clumsy copies of larger illuminations in a contemporary manuscript de luxe. On such an hypothesis the lost original behind the *Gawayne* manuscript was a repertory book commissioned by a magnate of wealth not much before 1390. It was composed for the use of a household where the primary language was a rather archaic north-west dialect of Middle English surcharged with a class dialect and grammar—for some such household, for example, as that at the earl of Arundel's Castle of Holt.

Even when it is granted that both the Chandos Herald and the author of *Gawayne* wrote for recitation, the public they envisaged must have been far smaller than that of the minstrels' romances of seventy or eighty years earlier, for it was now a public familiar with courtly usage, courtly grammar, and the nuance of knightly epithet. The ideals of knighthood that they portray seem almost identical and both have a similar religious décor. Two virtues are emphasized throughout by the Chandos Herald and his redactor, 'proesce' and 'loiautee'.[3] They give its purpose to the

---

[1] Ed. J. R. Tolkien and E. V. Gordon (3rd ed., Oxford, 1936).
[2] Cf. ibid., ff. 37, 38, 56, 82[r], 90[v], 125[r], 125[v], 126.
[3] Cf. *Chandos Herald*, f. 58[v], ll. 4103–7, f. 60[r], ll. 4211–12, f. 44[v], l. 3126 seq.

plot of *Gawayne*. They are closely linked with a group of qualities; Edward of Wales is shown as possessing 'franchise' and 'largesce'[1] and 'pite',[2] it is his pleasure to aid the right and him who asks on plea of suffering,[3] he is always 'curtois'; while the pentangle on Sir Gawayne's shield symbolizes his 'franchyse', 'fellowship', 'clannes', 'cortaysie', and 'pitie'.[4]

The contemporary meaning of such epithets can be clarified from a group of late-fourteenth-century romances. *Sir Degrevant*[5] describes in nearly 2,000 courtly verses the motives and manners of the perfect knight. The two manuscripts[6] in which it survives are probably of the middle fifteenth century, the dialect forms show that is from the north, its most probable date of composition is between 1380 and 1420. The *Lyfe of Ipomydon*[7] was written in East Midland perhaps at the same period, but it is only a version of the Anglo-Norman *Ipomadon* of Hugh of Rutland. *Sir Cliges*[8] is an obvious popularization into North Midland by a fifteenth-century minstrel. *Sir Eglamour*,[9] *Sir Isumbras*,[10] and *Sir Firumbras*[11] would also seem to have been intended for a wider public than *Sir Degrevant*. They probably took shape between 1370, the first in the north, the second in the midlands, the third in the south. *Sir Eglamour* has a close relation to *Sir Torrent*,[12] which was being recited in North-East Midland a generation later. Of all this grouping the East Midland *Sowdone of Babylone*[13] and the Northern *Rowlande and Otuel*[14] are the closest to *Sir Degrevant* in their analysis of motive and their assumption of an almost esoteric knightly code; both date from about 1400. Among didactic romances the dating of *Sir Amadas*[15] and of the English version of *Amis and Amiloun*[16] depends upon that ascribed to the Auchinleck manuscript. It is perhaps safest to place them near the middle of the fourteenth century. *William of Palerne*[17] was written for the De Bohun household[18] apparently about 1360.

---

[1] e.g. ibid., ll. 62–7, 75.   [2] e.g. ibid., l. 2927.
[3] Cf. ibid., f. 26, ll. 1877–9.
[4] *Gawayne and the Grene Knight*, ii. 640–65.
[5] Ed. J. O. Halliwell (Camden Soc. xxx).
[6] Thornton MS. and Cambridge Univ. Libr., Ff. 1. 6.
[7] Ed. H. Weber, *Metrical Romances* (Edinburgh, 1810), ii. 281 seq.
[8] Ibid. i. 331 seq.
[9] Ed. J. O. Halliwell (Camden Soc. xxx).   [10] Ibid.
[11] Ed. E.E.T.S., e.s. xxxiv.   [12] Ed. E.E.T.S., e.s. li.
[13] Ed. E.E.T.S., e.s. xxxviii.
[14] Ed. E.E.T.S., e.s. xxxv.
[15] Ed. Weber, *Metrical Romances*, iii. 241 seq.
[16] Ibid. ii. 367, or ed. E. Kölbing, or E.E.T.S., o.s. cciii.
[17] Ed. E.E.T.S., e.s. i.   [18] Ibid., l. 5529 seq.

Taken in conjunction these texts provided a very consistent standard by which to judge knightly or unknightly conduct. It is not possible to argue from romances as to which virtues were practised. It is easy to gather from them which virtues were admired.

Two virtues above all were held to mark the good knight and bring him honour. They were prowess and loyalty. Prowess would seem to imply an acquired habit of skill at arms and two natural qualities, indomitability and rashness, 'Magnanimitas' and 'Audacia'. In *Gawayne* fearlessness is illustrated most often by indomitability.[1] It is 'Audacia' that is emphasized by the Chandos Herald. He writes of Sir Ralph Hastings that he did not value death at two cherries[2] and of Sir William Felton that he threw himself among the enemy like a man without sense and without counsel.[3] 'Outrageus', rash, is used as a term of praise.[4] The same emphasis can be found in most fourteenth-century metrical romances; in *Amys and Amiloun* where Amiloun fights as if 'wode'[5] and in the battle scenes in *Rowlande and Otuel*[6] and in *William of Palerne*[7]; the glory of Sir Degrevant is his 'Audacia'.[8] The skill at arms that was presupposed was commonly illustrated by good swordsmanship and was held to be governed by a code of fair fighting.[9] For the Chandos Herald it is the possession of prowess which merits the term 'bon chivaler'[10] or 'chivalerous'.[11]

The sense given to 'loiautee', loyalty, at this period is more intricate and more significant. It is a quality of the soul; 'Ot coer loiall' is a recurrent phrase in the Chandos Herald and his redactor,[12] just as a contemporary allegorist saw all right living guarded by the keep of 'Loial Coer'. It implied fidelity to the pledged word, or loyalty to an individual owing to a transient relationship such as that of guest and host in the case of Gawayne, or loyalty to an individual because of love or friendship, 'amur or 'amistie', at a time when love was conventionally phrased in terms of friendship and friendship in terms of love. In the first case it was held to last until the pledge had been fulfilled; in the second until the mutual relationship which had given rise to it

[1] Cf. *Gawayne*, l. 563 seq., or l. 2292 seq.
[2] *Chandos Herald*, ll. 2729–30.   [3] Ibid., ll. 2739–40.
[4] Ibid., l. 166.   [5] *Amis and Amiloun*, l. 1307 seq.
[6] *Rowlande and Otuel*, l. 1809 seq.   [7] *William of Palerne*, l. 3852 seq.
[8] *Sir Degrevant*, passim.   [9] Cf. *Amis and Amiloun*, ll. 1330–45.
[10] Cf. *Chandos Herald*, ll. 3213, 4224.
[11] Cf. ibid., ll. 315, 1225 (for a contrary contemporary opinion, cf. John Gower, *Mirour de l'omme*, ll. 24001–2).
[12] e.g. op. cit., ll. 2266, 4200, 4212, 4236.

had ended. In the third it was ideally held to be irrevocable and of its nature incapable of change. The conflict between such loyalties or their testing was to provide both the psychological tension and the plot of most fourteenth-century romances. Through such plots it is easy to trace the steady weakening of the sense of the family unit and of the old emphasis on the bond between man and lord. But it is probable that the idea of loyalty narrowly and personally conceived had retained a strength of emotional appeal which enabled the audience of a romance to sympathize with the dilemmas of its heroes. Sir Gawayne searches the wilderness for the Green Knight that he may offer himself to be beheaded rather than break knighthood by breaking troth. Sir Amadas is persuaded by his wife to cut her and their child in two in order to fulfil a pledge, just as Arviragus would prefer that the wife he loved should commit adultery rather than break her word. Amiloun chooses leprosy and poverty rather than desert Amis in an unjust quarrel. Amis kills his two small sons in order to heal his friend.

In practice, as in the fantastic situations of romances, such a conception of honour could be a supplement to conventional Christian morality, at times strengthening and at times superseding it. Perhaps in the same fashion personal loyalty thus conceived could either strengthen or supersede the ties of a bastard feudalism. For personal friendship in itself was conceived as an alliance:

> To hold to gider at eueri nede
> In word in werk in wille in dede.[1]

Like friendship 'Pitie' could provide the course or the excuse for direct political action. The Chandos Herald notes that the prince undertook the Spanish campaign 'pur pitie' and 'pur amistie'.[2] For 'Pitie' seems essentially a compassion for an individual which finds expression in immediate action. John Gower could write that 'Pites la doulce et debonnaire' has Mercy for her secretary,[3] and the Chandos Herald that the prince found his pleasure in giving aid to him who asked it on plea of suffering.[4] The epithet had survived into the late Middle Ages from the primitive conception of the hero of the *chanson de geste* as a

---

[1] *Amis and Amiloun*, ll. 151–2 (cf. *La Lessoun a leals amantz*, ed. T. Wright, *Specimens of Lyric Poetry*, p. 18).
[2] *Chandos Herald*, f. 26ᵛ, ll. 1871–9; cf. ll. 2927–8.
[3] *Mirour de l'omme*, l. 13897 seq.
[4] *Chandos Herald*, f. 26ᵛ, ll. 1877–9 (cf. *Marchants Tale*, l. 742).

'Justicier', a punisher of wrong-doers; it remained linked with it.
To John Gower the function of the true knight is to give battle
against injustices.[1] To the author of *Piers Plowman* an essential
note of true knighthood is to put down wrong-doers[2]—not a
magistracy but a substitute or supplement for magistracy. The
Chandos Herald emphasizes the prince's determination 'en tenir
justice et droiture' 'et pur droiture sustener'.[3] The exact meaning
of 'justice' and 'droiture' in such contexts is yet to be determined;
it may be suggested that though it includes both written law and
custom it primarily refers to natural equity.

Three other qualities are persistently inculcated, 'largesse',
'franchise', and 'cortaysie'. 'Largesse' is a prodigal generosity.
It is perhaps primarily valued because of the detachment from
possession and the disregard for wealth that it implies. The
Chandos Herald illustrates it by the 'beals dons' given by the
prince, the gold and silver and rich jewels,[4] and by 400 men that
he entertained daily at his table at Bordeaux.[5] Its moral is
suggested by the statement in the *Livre des faicts* that it is a
notorious thing that the good knight must be without the desire
to amass treasure and riches. No epithet is more closely illustrated
in fourteenth-century romances[6] or had passed through so many
evolutions since the *chansons de geste*.

By this period Franchise would seem to have taken the place of
the 'debonneirete' of the early *romans courtois*. In the *Romaunt of
the Rose* it had been the arrow winged by Courtesy and Courage.[7]
It remained the mark of the well bred, 'the frely fode', it implied
a certain freedom and naturalness in manner and form of approach.
For the Chandos Herald it was perhaps an example of the prince's
'fraunchyse' that on meeting his wife and his son Edward during
his triumphal entry into Bordeaux he dismounted and walked into
the city holding their hands.[8] Franchise was the antithesis of
'wrecced Churlishness' as in the *Frankleyn's Tale*. A form of
generosity of spirit, it was close linked with fellowship as in
Gawayne. It was controlled by courtesy.

The sense of *courtoisie* had been slowly narrowing; now it

---

[1] *Mirour de l'omme*, l. 23610 seq.; for context cf. ibid., ll. 23593–4180 (ed.
Macaulay, pp. 260–7).
[2] *Piers Plowman*, B, I, ll. 94–101.
[3] *Chandos Herald*, ll. 71, 1627, 2298; cf. *Livre des faicts de Jean Bouciquaut*,
Pt. iv, c. 8.
[4] *Chandos Herald*, ll. 3810–12, cf. l. 75.   [5] Ibid., ll. 1610–15.
[6] Cf. *Sir Cleges*, ll. 13–72; *Sir Amadas*, ll. 50–61; *Sir Degrevant*, ll. 81–7; *Sir
Isumbras*, ll. 19–24.
[7] Verse 491.   [8] *Chandos Herald*, f. 53, ll. 3769 seq.

primarily meant good manners, whether in action as in the 'cortaysie' books,[1] or in the 'techeles termes of talkyng noble' as in *Gawayne*.[2] It still retained some of its earlier moral implications through its association with the 'coer gentil' and with 'Bel Accueil'. On this reading the Chandos Herald is recording examples of the prince's *courtoisie* when he relates that he attempted to do squire's service to the captive king of France[3] and that he thanked his own knights 'moult humblement'[4] and that he would say to his household 'Fair sweet lords you are more than 100 times welcome';[5] just as it is Gawayne's cortaysie that leads him to thank in turn the servants of his host.

A class attitude towards woman was inextricably involved with such good manners. Its character reflected the thirteenth-century adage 'Gawayn was a perfect knight, he went on foot, the lady rode'. It was expected to find expression in acts of service and its primary object in 'dames et demoiselles de noble lignee'.[6] But often as in the *Lyfe of Ipomydon* and in *Gawayne and the Grene Knight* such 'druerie' is deliberately contrasted with love.[7] It was the fashion throughout the knightly class to portray marriage in terms of love service and of *amour courtois*.[8] In fiction romantic love was very rarely associated with adultery.[9] It was conceived to be the stimulus of achievement.[10] It was held to be irrevocable and unique.

Accomplishments[11] and physical beauty[12] and a power of vivid sense-perception[13] were highly valued. Even the heroes of metrical

[1] Cf. E.E.T.S., E.S. xiii.   [2] *Gawayne*, l. 917.
[3] *Chandos Herald*, f. 20ʳ, ll. 1419–20.
[4] Ibid., f. 54, l. 3799 seq.   [5] Ibid., ll. 2577–8.
[6] *Livre des faicts de Jean Bouciquaut*, Pt. i, c. 37—for the rules of the order of the 'escu verd'.
[7] *Lyfe of Ipomydon*, ll. 696–718; *Gawayne*, passim, e.g. l. 976.
[8] e.g. *Chandos Herald*, f. 22ᵛ, ll. 1585–98, f. 29, ll. 2050–70 (for the relationship between the prince and princess of Wales), or *Book of the Duchesse*, l. 1285 seq. (for the first marriage of the duke of Lancaster); cf. *Livre des Faicts de Jean Bouciquaut*, Pt. ii, c. 10.
[9] For the conventional union between love and marriage apparently expected by the audience of metrical romances, e.g. *Sir Degrevant*, ll. 513–76, *Sir Eglamour*, ll. 145–80, l. 1297 seq., *William of Palerne*, ll. 4832–5516, *Partonope of Bloys*, ll. 1220–60, 5219 seq.
[10] e.g. *Sir Torrent of Portyngale*, l. 37 seq. (E.E.T.S., E.S. li).
[11] e.g. *Sir Degrevant*, ll. 33–40; for the accomplishments valued at this period, cf. those attributed to the squire in Chaucer's *Prologue*, l. 94 seq., and *Livre des Faicts de Jean Bouciquaut*, Pt. i, c. 8; Pt. iv, c. 10.
[12] e.g. *Ipomedon*, ed. E. Kölbing, ll. 377–86 and its derivatives.
[13] e.g. 'The fyve wittes' symbolized by the Pentangle in *Gawayne* or the emphasis on the joys of the five senses in *Alexander and Dindimus*, E.E.T.S., E.S. xxxi, l. 945 seq.

romances are on occasion[1] lettered. The capacity of listening to fine books is admired.[2] 'Sage' or 'Sachant' is a term of praise and even seems included in the collective noun 'Preudhomye'.[3] Yet the ideals of knighthood remained a simple individualist code of ethics in which honour and dishonour had the sharp contrasts of heraldic colours—like the blood upon the snow in *Gawayne*. Some of its quality seems best conveyed by the delight in clear bright colours and fine stuffs which marks the literary sources for it; the gold, azure, silver, gules, and sable, the fine silk and sendal of the Chandos Herald[4] or the violet and azure in the story of Sir Degrevant and the jewels of Melydor.[5] Some of its individualism could be suggested by that other note of this group of metrical romances, the perpetual sense of the forest, the absence of horizon. For it is a system of ethics which seems to presuppose a class society in which personal relationships hold primary importance and in which the emotional content is provided by a romantic, perhaps rather adolescent, conception of personal loyalty, friendship, and adventure.

Yet even if such ideals formed an essential part in the education of most members of the knightly class in late-fourteenth-century England, it is not possible to tell how far they remained accepted by them. In the new court at Eltham or at Sheen such standards may at times have seemed as naïve and as remote as the bourgeois romances parodied in *Sir Topas*. By 1390 the ideals in the Chandos Herald poem or in *Sir Gawayne* or in *Sir Degrevant* were perhaps consciously old-fashioned. They were even becoming a little insular. The French influences with which they were linked were no longer dominant among the Valois patrons with their taste for delicate sensibility, tenderness, and irony and the savour of good letters. It is Chaucer, not the author of *Sir Gawayne*, who could have been appreciated in contemporary Paris. But in England the new court culture was to vanish, perhaps in Henry of Derby it had produced its own grave-digger. The ideals of knighthood were to survive past Malory, fluctuating, modified, at last formalized in a code of honour.

GERVASE MATHEW

---

[1] e.g. *Lyfe of Ipomydon*, ed. H. Weber, l. 53 seq., or *Floris and Blaunchflur*, E.E.T.S., o.s. xiv, ll. 33–4.

[2] *Livre des Faicts de Jean Bouciquaut*, Pt. iv, c. 7.

[3] For the use of 'preudome' and 'preudhomye' by the *Chandos Herald*, cf. ll. 559, 1414, 1858, 2282, 3829, 4105.

[4] e.g. *Chandos Herald*, l. 985 seq., l. 2595 seq.

[5] e.g. *Sir Degrevant*, ll. 625–55.

TWO TREATISES OF UTHRED OF BOLDON ON THE MONASTIC LIFE

UTHRED OF BOLDON is one of the most interesting of the English monk-scholars of the later Middle Ages. His career is a good illustration of the system by which the intellectual *élite* of the monasteries received a university training, while his numerous writings reflect the interests and controversies of his age. The two treatises which will be examined in this paper are particularly important as giving a rationale of the monastic life as seen by an active and intelligent monk of the fourteenth century.

Uthred was probably born between 1315 and 1325;[1] he would thus be a few years senior to Wyclif. He was at Oxford in Lent 1337–8, possibly as one of the secular students maintained there by the monks of Durham. He took the Benedictine habit at Durham in 1341, and must have been professed in 1342, since he celebrated his jubilee in 1392. He was at Durham College, Oxford, from 1347 until probably about 1367. During part of this time he was warden of the College. He was B.D. in 1354 and incepted D.D. in 1357. At various times between 1360 and 1381 he was actively employed in the business of the Benedictine provincial chapter, as proctor for his house, as definitor, and as visitor; he was one of the special visitors appointed to deal with the very difficult case of Whitby in 1366. He divided the last thirty years of his life between Durham and its cell of Finchale. He was appointed prior of Finchale three times, in 1367, in 1375, and in 1386, and sub-prior of Durham in 1368 and again in 1381. He was sufficiently eminent as a theologian to be chosen as one of the delegation sent by the king to Avignon in 1373, to discuss papal provisions and papal subsidies.[2] According to the continuator of the 'Eulogium historiarum', Uthred attended the conference of lords, prelates, and doctors in London in May 1374, where he supported the papal claims with the text *Ecce duo gladii hic*; but unfortunately the chronicler's account seems to be

---

[1] For Uthred's biography, see *Bulletin of the Institute of Hist. Research*, iii (1925), 46; M. E. Marcett, *Uthred de Boldon, Friar William Jordan and Piers Plowman* (New York, 1938), chap. i; *General and Provincial Chapters of the English Black Monks*, iii (Camden Soc., 3rd series, liv), 278, 309, 318; Tanner, *Bibliotheca*, p. 743.

[2] E. Perroy, *L'Angleterre et le grand schisme d'occident*, p. 32.

as unreliable as it is picturesque.[1] In 1383 Uthred again visited Oxford, possibly as part of a campaign against Lollardy. He died on 31 January 1397.

Uthred's writings may be listed and classified as follows:[2]

(i) *Controversy with the Friars, c. 1366–8*

  1. *Contra fratrum mendicitatem,* inc. 'Utrum paupertas mendicitatis que est ultima . . .' (B) = Paris, Bibliothèque Nationale, MS. Lat. 3183, f. 160ᵛ.[3]

  2. *Contra iniustas fratrum querelas,* inc. 'Periculis in falsis fratribus . . .' (B) = Bodleian MS. Wood Rolls 1; Brit. Mus. Royal MS. 6 D. x, f. 283; Balliol MS. 149, f. 63.[4]

(ii) *Controversies on relations of Church and State, and Church endowment, mainly anti-Wycliffite*

  3. *De regalia et sacerdocio,* inc. 'Dato quod progressus innocencie'[5] (or perhaps inc. 'Quod solus Dominus noster Ihesus . . .') = Durham Cathedral Library MS. A. iv. 33, f. 1 (cf. f. 9ᵛ); perhaps cf. *De regia dignitate Christi,* inc. 'Videns esse planum Dominum Iesum Christum ab ipso . . .' (B, L).

  4. *De naturali et necessaria connexione ac ordine sacerdotalis officii et regalis* (cf. L), inc. 'Sicut ex duobus spiritu scilicet et corpore . . .' = Durham MS. A. iv. 33, f. 24.[6]

---

[1] *Eulogium historiarum* (Rolls Series 9), iii, 337; cf. Perroy, op. cit., p. 35.

[2] (B) = J. Bale, *Index Britanniae Scriptorum,* ed. R. L. Poole and M. Bateson (Oxford, 1902), p. 462; (L) = J. Leland, *Commentarii de scriptoribus Britannicis* (Oxford, 1709), p. 392.

[3] I owe this identification to the Rev. Stephen Forte, O.P.

[4] In this treatise, printed by Marcett, op. cit., p. 25 ff., Uthred deals with twenty-eight articles containing his alleged 'errors', drawn up by the Friars. His chief antagonist was William Jordan, O.P. The archbishop of Canterbury imposed silence on both Uthred and Jordan on 18 Feb. 1368, and on 9 Nov. 1368 condemned thirty articles, of which twenty-four correspond to Uthred's 'errors', Lambeth, Reg. Langham, f. 60ᵛ, 70ᵛ; Wilkins, *Concilia,* iii. 75. This controversy dealt, not with mendicancy, but with purely theological questions, such as Grace, Justification, the salvation of infidels. The archbishop's condemnation, though not mentioning him by name, must have constituted a defeat for Uthred, a fact, I think, not hitherto noticed; but this does not seem to have damaged his reputation or career. Theological controversy in England, though violent on paper, was in fact a gentlemanly business before Wycliffism introduced a state of war. For Jordan, see also A. Gwynn, in *Review of English Studies,* xix (1943), 19 ff. Worcester Cathedral MS. F. 65 contains four *conclusiones* by Uthred, connected with this controversy, on f. 19ᵛ, and two arguments against Uthred's doctrine on ff. 7 and 11ᵛ. The Rev. S. Forte has made a special study of this manuscript.

[5] This treatise, as given in Durham MS. A. iv. 33, is in a confused state, with numerous cross references to the rest of the manuscript, and it is not clear what the correct incipit should be.

[6] This and the two next treatises are the subject of a Ph.D. thesis (University of Manchester) by Mr. C. T. Thompson.

5. *De dotacione ecclesie sponse Christi* (cf. B, L), inc. 'Ad veritatis lucidam declaracionem . . .' = Durham MS. A. iv. 33, f. 69; MS. Bodley 859, f. 277.

6. *Contra garrulos dotacionem ecclesie impugnantes* (cf. B), inc. 'Quoniam propter quosdam falsos fratres . . .' = Durham MS. A. iv. 33, f. 99; perhaps identical with *De non auferendis ecclesie possessionibus ministris abutentibus* (L).

(iii) *Other theological treatises, including some anti-Wycliffite*

7. *Tractatus parvus de ecclesia militanti*, inc. 'Ecclesia militans mater nostra . . .' = Durham MS. A. iv. 33, f. 110ᵛ.

8. *De eucharistie sacramento* (cf. B, L), inc. 'Tractaturus de supernaturali et preciosissimo . . .' = Durham MS. A. iv. 33, f. 122.

9. *De divina predestinatione* (L): unidentified.

10. *Contra blasphemos in Christum* (L): unidentified.

(iv) *Monastic treatises*

11. *De esu et abstinentia carnium* (L) = treatise inc. 'Numquid licitum sit mon. S. Bened. . . .' Brit. Mus. MS. Cotton Vitellius E. xii, f. 97 (damaged by fire);[1] perhaps cf. Add. MS. 6162, f. 36.

12. *Pro monachis veris*, inc. 'Abbas, prior seu quiscumque presidens . . .' (B) = *Abbas vel prior*, a treatise on law affecting monks, Durham MS. B. iv. 26, f. 148ᵛ; B. iv. 41, f. 83; B. iv. 45, p. 125; Jesus College, Cambridge, MS. 61, f. 48; cf. Jesus MS. 41, f. 102ᵛ.

13. Visitation articles, formerly in Cotton MS. Vitellius E. xii, art. 11 (now burnt); perhaps = those printed in *Chapters of the English Black Monks* (Camden Soc. 3rd series, xlvii), ii. 83 ff.

14. *Super Bernardum Clarevallensem, de precepto et dispensatione*, inc. 'Abbas supra regulam non est . . .' (B); probably = table on *De precepto*, compiled by Uthred, Jesus College, Cambridge, MS. 41, f. 88.

15. *De institutis monachorum*, cited by Thomas Rudbourne (*Anglia Sacra*, i. 220–2); probably = Cotton MS. Vitellius E. xii, ff. 56 ff.; cf. Dugdale, *Monasticon*, i (ed. 1848), xix.

16. *De substantialibus regule monachalis*, inc. 'Novicio inquirenti . . .' (cf. B) = Durham MS. B. iv. 34, f. 80; Corpus Christi College, Cambridge, MS. 103, p. 291; probably identical with *De variatione professionis monachorum et aliorum* (L).

17. *De perfectione vivendi in religione*, inc. 'Sacratissimo siquidem Dei evangelio . . .' = Durham MS. B. iv. 34, f. 97; Corpus Christi College, Cambridge, MS. 103, p. 310; the *De perfeccione ecclesie graduali*,

---

[1] For a complete description of the manuscript, cf. Thomas Smith's *Catalogus Lib. MSS. Bibl. Cotton.*, Oxford, 1696, pp. 99–100.

Durham MS. A. iv. 33, f. 116ᵛ, is in reality an extract from the *De perfeccione vivendi* (see *infra*, p. 376, section E).

18. Alphabetical list of monastic saints and writers, MS. Cotton Vitellius E. xii, f. 62; this is probably the work of Uthred referred to at the end of the *De perfeccione vivendi* (see *infra*, p. 381).

(v) *Devotional*

19. *Meditatio devota*, inc. 'Domine recogitabo' (B, L); for the numerous manuscripts, see A. Wilmart, *Auteurs spirituels*, p. 424. One group of manuscripts has invocations of Durham saints at the end: Cambridge, Jesus College, MS. 41, Harley MS. 5234; the other group has St. Albans saints: Bodley 797, Brasenose 15, Cambridge Univ. Library Gg. 4. 11, Paris Arsenal 412.

20. *De diligendis inimicis* (B), inc. 'Ad dilectionem inimicorum invitat . . .'; not identified.

21. A *proverbium magistri Uthredi* quoted below.

Uthred was probably best known in the later Middle Ages as the writer of the *Meditatio devota* (no. 19), judging from the number of manuscripts. Himself a typical product of the university, he seems to have felt, like so many men in his age, a certain distrust of the excessive intellectualism of the schools, or at least a desire to subordinate intellectual to spiritual values. This is brought out in a saying of his, which was still being quoted at Durham half a century after his death, when Prior Wessyngton wrote to a monk-scholar:

'proverbium magistri Uthredi, quod tibi et omnibus scolaribus a tempore suscepti regiminis prioratus ad studium destinatis, quasi peculiare mandatum dedi: videlicet quod non est bonum perdere substanciam propter accidens; substanciam dico, missas celebrare et audire, divinum servicium debitis horis dicere, ac alia que monachicam decent conversacionem primo perimplere; secundario vero, prout opportunitas permiserit, libris et doctrine vacare.'[1]

Of Uthred's monastic treatises, some were clearly inspired by the practical interest in monastic discipline which Uthred had as an experienced visitor and legislator; thus we have the visitation articles (no. 13), the treatise on the time-honoured question of the eating of flesh-meat (no. 11), the treatise *Abbas vel Prior* (no. 12), and the table on the *De precepto et dispensatione* (no. 14). Uthred's other monastic treatises are more theoretical or historical, and form part of a widespread literary tradition. Throughout the fourteenth century a series of treatises were compiled in

[1] *Hist. Dunelm. Scriptores Tres* (Surtees Soc.), App., p. cclxiii; I have emended 'secularibus' to 'scolaribus'.

various monastic centres, such as Bury St. Edmunds,[1] St. Albans,[2] Durham,[3] and Glastonbury;[4] though differing in some respects, they have certain common features and a common apologetic purpose. They begin by tracing the origins of monasticism back to Old Testament times, and conclude with lists of monastic saints and writers. They seem to have been intended at first as an apologetic against the Friars and later against the Wycliffites. Uthred's treatise *De institutis monachorum* (no. 15), so far as can be judged from surviving fragments, and the alphabetical list of monastic saints and writers which I believe to be his (no. 18), both belong to this type of literature. Moreover, the two treatises *De substantialibus* and *De perfectione vivendi*, which we are about to consider, may well have grown out of the historical discussion of the origins of monasticism which is common to all the treatises; and the closing words of the second treatise (below, p. 381) show that it was intended as an introduction to an alphabetical list of monastic saints.

Two other English monastic writers, in the earlier part of the fourteenth century, had already commented on the Rule of St. Benedict. Richard of Wallingford, abbot of St. Albans and a celebrated mathematician (d. 1336), wrote a commentary on the Rule, or at least on its prologue, which is only known to us from a chance reference.[5] John of Beverley, D.D., a monk of Durham, prior of Durham College, Oxford, and active in the affairs of the provincial chapter *c.* 1338–43, wrote a commentary on the Rule in the form of a dialogue, which is also only known to us from quotations. In fact it is with a quotation from John of Beverley's dialogue that Uthred begins his treatise *De substantialibus*.[6] The main purpose of this essay is to study Uthred's two treatises on the monastic life. The first of these, starting from the three vows, demonstrates the origin and lawfulness of the monastic life; the second discusses whether perfection is to be found in the monastic or the secular life. Their contents may be summarized as follows:[7]

[1] Vatican MS. Reg. Lat. 127, f. 165; cf. MS. Bodley 240, p. 765.
[2] Brit. Mus. Cotton MS. Claudius E. iv, f. 322ᵛ.
[3] Durham MS. B. iii. 30, f. 1; Cotton MS. Vitellius E. xii, f. 56; Harleian MS. 4843 m, f. 187.
[4] Queen's College, Oxford, MS. 304, f. 58.
[5] Cited in Brit. Mus. Add. MS. 6162, f. 42ᵛ.
[6] Other quotations are in Brit. Mus. Add. MS. 6162, ff. 40ᵛ, 42–4.
[7] This attempt to summarize some seventy pages of manuscript has involved some omissions, and perhaps some unwitting distortions, but I hope it may give some idea of the author's argument.

(I) *De substancialibus regule monachalis*

Durham Cathedral Library, MS. B. iv. 34, f. 80 (alias 76);[1] Corpus Christi College, Cambridge, MS. 103, p. 291;[2] Emmanuel College, Cambridge, MS. 142, f. 83 (alias 82).[3]

'Novicio inquirenti quare hec duo, puta castitas et proprietatis abdicacio, que famosius dicuntur esse de substancia voti monachalis, non inserantur[a] in monachorum professione, sed stabilitas et morum conversio, que minus videntur de voti substancia quam alia[b] supradicta, respondet doctor eximius magister Iohannes de Beverlaco, quondam professus huius ecclesie Dunolmie nostre, in tractatu suo super regulam beati Benedicti, in 3° dubio primi articuli principalis, dicens . . .'

  [a] inserantur D; inseruntur C, E.   [b] quam duo alia E.

The explanation given is that the monastic life is formally distinguished from others, by stability from the Girovagi, by *morum conversio* from the Sarabaites, by obedience according to the Rule of St. Benedict from seculars and other religious and *aliqualiter* from hermits. 'Hec ille. Verumptamen pro responsionis materia de substancialibus voti monachalis . . .'; the main part of the treatise begins:

(A) *Naturalis regula racionis* (D, f. 80; C, p. 291)

The three *substancialia* are binding in some measure, not only on all monks and all Christians, but even on all men having discretion and the use of reason, by a kind of natural vow and obligation:

1. *Primum principale*: Abdication of property (as against the world): no man has unrestricted dominion, but only a permitted use of goods, which belong to God only, man being merely a *dispensator* or *villicus Dei*; therefore abdication of true property is imposed by nature on all men.

---

[1] Cited as D: written in a hand of *c.* 1400; cf. T. Rud, *Codicum MSS. eccl. cath. Dunelm. catalogus*, p. 238; *Eng. Hist. Rev.* (1944), pp. 163-4. I have to thank the Dean and Chapter of Durham for the use of this and other Durham manuscripts.

[2] Cited as C: this is a miscellaneous collection of treatises; Wyclif, Kilwardby, Bonaventure, William of St. Amour, and Fitz-Ralph, some of them bearing on the Mendicant controversy; it is written in several hands of the fourteenth and fifteenth centuries, these two treatises of Uthred's being in two hands of the early fifteenth century. Cf. M. R. James, *Descriptive Catalogue of the Manuscripts in the Library of Corpus Christi College, Cambridge* (Cambridge, 1912), i. 198 ff.

[3] Cited as E: this is the note-book of a monk of Norwich, John Stowe, *c.* 1446-9; cf. M. R. James, *The Western Manuscripts in the Library of Emmanuel College, Cambridge, A Descriptive Catalogue* (Cambridge, 1904), pp. 111 ff. The manuscript breaks off in Section (C), in the middle of objection (10). The book contains among other things a number of scholastic exercises and orations, perhaps connected with Cambridge.

Objections: (i) *Crescite et multiplicamini . . . Ecce dedi vobis omnem herbam . . .* (Gen. i. 28–9); (ii) all laws, human and divine, attribute property to men, hence litigation and wars; answers, as to (i), God gives man the use of things, but must retain to Himself the *proprietas et dominium principale*; (ii) it was Cain who first usurped dominion and property.

2. *Secundum principale.* Continence (as against the flesh): no man may indulge in eating, drinking, sexual acts, &c., according to bestial appetite or his own will, but in due measure and time, as suited to his complexion, age, &c.; Aristotle (*Ethics*, vii) is cited; therefore natural reason imposes some continence on all men.

Objection: according to this argument it would follow, among other things, that lords and prelates should not be allowed more delicate food, clothes, &c., than *populares* with the same bodily disposition; answer: according to Aristotle (*Politics*, i), superiors are occupied with the mental and spiritual work of government, subjects with bodily work; and superiors are more discreet in avoiding excess, and so may be allowed more subtle food, &c., while subjects are less able to restrain themselves. But illicit self-indulgence is even less lawful for superiors than for inferiors, for a number of reasons. Thus incontinence is forbidden to all men, and to superiors more than to subjects.

3. *Tercium principale.* Obedience (as against the Evil Spirit): all men, like the angels and all other creatures, need to be regulated by obedience to God and to each other. There are three kinds of obedience: (i) 'natural' or involuntary, as of insensitive creatures; (ii) 'sensitive', due partly to compulsion, partly to attraction; (iii) 'rational', belonging only to rational creatures; all men are bound to this kind of obedience.

'Et sic prout in principio est assumptum, hec tria que dicuntur omnium religionum substancialia, scilicet[a] proprietatis abdicacio, continencia, et obediencia, sunt omni homini habenti discrecionem et usum racionis ex obligacione nature indita et inscripta, et in hiis tribus religionum substancialibus instituitur a natura contra mundum, contra carnem, contra spiritum,[b] regula naturalis sive regula racionis . . .'

[a] scilicet *om.* C.   [b] contra spiritum *om.* E.

(B) *Regula Paradisi superaddita, and its derivatives* (D, f. 83; C, p. 295; E, f. 85)

Objection: if this *naturalis regula racionis* is binding on all men by nature, then all other *religiones*, instituted by men and approved by the Church, must be superfluous, because the rule of reason is better, more certain, &c. Answer: *religiones voluntarie* aid the observance of the rule of reason, and need to be founded in reason; thus as regards the three *substancialia*, each of these must be exercised reasonably and not indiscreetly or excessively.

The rule of reason was not by itself sufficient for man *in statu fidei*, even when he was in the state of innocence; hence the Creator imposed the *Regula paradisi superaddita*, by His commands as to what fruits in paradise might or might not be eaten; these commands imposed (1) abdication of property, (2) continence, (3) obedience; and this was the first particular *religio* or rule:

'Ista itaque[a] regula paradisi superaddita regule naturali, continens et exprimens et imponens ista tria substancialia tam regule racionis naturalis, quam regule ipsius paradisi, immo cuiuscumque religionis posterioris[b] ab ecclesia approbate, ut est dictum, erat prima religio sive regula particularis vivendi ab ipso Deo patrono excellentissimo et abbate notorie discretissimo ac scientissimo primarie instituta.'

a utique C.

b posterius E.

Monasticism is traced in the Old Testament, as illustrated in Samuel, the sons of the Prophets, Elias, and Eliseus (the *Magister Historiarum* and St. Jerome are quoted);[1] the *substancialia* were practised, but not mendicancy, since this was forbidden by the Law (Deut. xv. 4). Monasticism is also traced in the New Testament: Christ, as the Second Adam, practised the *Regula paradisi superaddita*, by obedience (being obedient unto death), by continence, and by voluntary poverty; He was *pauperrimus*, but not *mendicus*; He made a double use of the necessaries of life, (i) sometimes using them 'iure ac dominio innocencie hominis naturalis', (ii) sometimes by *providencia mundialis*, having *loculos* for buying things, &c.

From the *Regula paradisi*, exemplified by Christ and followed by the Apostles, was derived the *religio* of the Primitive Church, and hence are derived all other reasonable and approved *religiones*, though there are fruitful variations among them. Mendicancy, however, is not founded in the *Regula racionis*, nor in the *Regula paradisi*, nor in the Old Testament, nor in the practice of Christ and the Primitive Church.

---

[1] Compare the accounts of monasticism in the Old and New Testaments here and *infra*, p. 375, with the account probably by Uthred, printed in Dugdale's *Monasticon*, i. xix ff., from MS. Cotton Vitellius E. xii. Cf. also Wyclif, *De civili dominio*, ed. J. Loserth (Wyclif Soc. 1903), iii. 17.

Christ (1) by creating man, laid down the *Regula racionis*, (2) by instructing man, added the *Regula paradisi*, and (3) by re-creating man, exemplified the *Regula paradisi.*

'*Solucio argumenti.* Hiis pro religionum fundacione breviter declaratis, plane solvitur argumentum quod ex quo pro statu innocencie fuerat lex talis sive religio regularis per Deum homini in paradiso superaddenda, ut declararet, facilitaret et adiuvaret[a] regulam racionis homini inditam a natura;[b] a multo forciori iam pro statu lapsus, quando nostra racio multi-pliciter excecatur, sunt necessarie leges, religiones et regule varie ad declarandum, facilitandum et iuvandum nos ad debitam execucionem nostre naturalis regule racionis, dum tamen omnes ille religiones, leges et regule fundentur ut dictum est in ipsa regula racionis; propter quod non sunt superflue, sed multum necessarie huiusmodi religiones et regule ab hominibus habentibus sufficientem et notam auctoritatem et scienciam racionabiliter et sic a Deo principaliter institute; presertim cum ipsemet Dominus noster Ihesus ad reformandum et informandum nos personaliter huc accedens, ad precepta legis superaddiderit nobis illa consilia evangelica, Mat. 5, ad informandum, iuvandum nos et facilitandum ipsa legis precepta melius, securius et integrius observare . . .'

[a] iuvaret C, E.   [b] natura originali E.

(C) *Objections* (D, f. 88; C, p. 301; E, f. 89)

1. The first *religio* and the origin of all *religiones* is the *naturalis regula racionis*, not the *regula paradisi.*

2. The *regula paradisi* was imposed on all men; but a *religio* is a *lex privata*, instituted only for its professors;[1] therefore the *regula paradisi* is not to be called a *religio.*

3. The *regula paradisi* was imposed on man compulsorily under pain of sin; but a *religio* is something not imposed, but proposed to a man, to be freely accepted or rejected; therefore the *regula paradisi* is not a *religio.*

4. Against the distinctive profession formula, *Obedienciam secundum regulam beati Benedicti*: the *regula paradisi*, since it is not a private *religio*, ought to be called *humana religio* (since it is binding on all men), or *religio Christiana* (since it is imposed by Christ on all Christians); but the *religio monachalis*, by the profession formula, is distinguished and different from these, and is therefore illicit and profane.[2]

5. The profession formula, *Obedienciam secundum regulam*, &c., divides existing monks from all pre-Benedictine monks, both of the Old and of the New Testaments, and from those of the

[1] Cf. Wyclif, *De civili dominio*, iii. 31, l. 6.
[2] Cf. Wyclif, loc. cit.

Rules of Pachomius, Basil, &c.; therefore existing monks cannot claim early monks like St. Martin, Jerome, &c., as their fathers and patrons.

6. The obedience, stability, and *morum conversio* of the profession formula are imposed on all men by natural reason; hence the *religio monachalis* does not differ substantially from that of seculars or other religious orders, but only by certain observances and rites humanly invented, and these are details which might for instance distinguish members of the same order or even of the same community.[1]

7. Since external observances and ceremonies are liable to be changed from time to time, a *religio* cannot be established or distinguished from others or from seculars by such things, but only by the perfect or imperfect observance of the law of Christ can any distinction between *religiones* be made.

8. Any true *religio* exists for the true and due worship of God; but a monk, a secular, and a regular canon may all three worship God equally well; therefore they must all be of the same *religio*;[2] therefore either one of them must be an apostate from his own *religio*, or else all *religiones* must be the same, with no distinction between them. Again, a *religio* must be founded on something that cannot be taken away; but external observances can be taken away; therefore the only distinction in *religiones* must be in interior virtues. There must be parity or identity of *religio* where there is parity of virtue.[3]

9. Whatever the Rule of St. Benedict adds to the law of Christ cannot add greater perfection or goodness; therefore it is a useless distinction and frivolous, and should be abolished.[4]

10. Diversity of *religiones* provokes strife and envy, and was not introduced by Christ, but by carnal men; therefore it should be extirpated, to promote unity.[5]

(D) *Answers to objections* (D, f. 90ᵛ; C, p. 304)

1. The word *religio* is derived from *religere*, i.e. *eligere*, or from *religare*;[6] in either case, *religio* presupposes a pre-existing law, for the better understanding and observance of which it is imposed; further, *religio* implies deliberation and assent, which could have no place in the natural law.

---

[1] Cf. Wyclif, op. cit. iii. 20, l. 15. [2] Cf. ibid. iii. 19, l. 9.
[3] Cf. ibid. iii. 22, l. 5.
[4] Cf. ibid. iii. 13, l. 15; 20, l. 3.
[5] Cf. ibid. iii. 14, l. 4.
[6] Cf. S. Thomas, *Summa Theol.*, 2a 2ae, q. 81, a. 1.

2. Even if the state of innocence had continued, there would have been different ways of living among men, yet all would have observed both the *prima regula naturalis* and the *superaddita regula paradisi*; just as now all men ought to observe both the natural law and Christian religion, and yet the Christian religion is not the less properly so called, because it is common to all men.

3. The *religio* of the Primitive Church and the Rule of St. Benedict are not imposed on any man to be accepted under pain of sin, but are imposed on all men disposed to this way of life, in order to make the observance of the Christian religion easier.

4. The terms *religio, religio Christiana, religio vera*, and *religio paradisi* are in reality the same thing, and stand as *genus* in relation to the *religio monachalis*; the particle, *Obediencia secundum*, &c., is the *differentia*, which does not divide *religio monachalis* from its *genus* (as 'man' is not divided from 'animal'), but only from other species of religion.

5. Just as the Christian religion existed from the beginning of mankind, though it only later received its name from Christ (cf. St. Augustine, *Retractationum* lib. i, c. 13, § 3);[1] so the *regula* and *religio* of St. Benedict existed *realiter* from the beginning of monasticism, though it only later received its name from St. Benedict.

6. Granted that obedience *secundum regulam beati Benedicti* does not distinguish monastic *religio* from others as regards *religionis materia* or as regards *genus*, yet it does so as regards *forma religionis*; the formula does distinguish monastic *religio* from other ways of life, not only *accidentaliter* but *specifice*; such a distinction does not arise between professors of the same rule.

7. The *religio* of monks is not based on ceremonies, but upon obedience according to the Rule of St. Benedict; the observance of Christ's law, like charity, is the end towards which *religiones* are ordered; 'sed finis nec constituit nec distinguit inter operaciones in ipsum finem dirigentes', since different operations may be ordered towards the same end.

8. The worship of God is the end, *religiones* are the means, but different means often lead to the same end; again, any corporal observances might be changed or taken away, if charity demanded it, and yet the Rule of St. Benedict would remain;[2] true religion must be founded both in interior virtues and in some

---

[1] *Pat. Lat.* 32, col. 603.
[2] Cf. St. Bernard, *De praecepto et dispens.*, c. ii. iv; *Pat. Lat.* 182, cols. 863, 865.

corporal observances, according to what charity demands, since man consists of soul and body.

9. Just as the epistles of the Apostles, &c., did not perfect the law of the Gospel, but declared and explained how that law might be more easily and perfectly observed; so *religiones* arose as new remedies for the growing wickedness of the world (Mat. xxiv. 12); and the *religio monachalis* adds no perfection to the law of Christ, but only helps its observance.

10. *Diversitas vivendi* is very profitable and necessary; examples are cited from the New Testament, the disciples of Christ and of St. John the Baptist, St. Paul (1 Cor. vii. 7; Rom. xii. 4; 1 Cor. xii. 4). It is not diversity that produces strife and envy, but indiscreet persons contending about the dignity or perfection of their state; there were contentions even among Christ's disciples (Luc. xxii. 24). There are many branches from one root; the supreme Shepherd has many sheep of different pastures, different fleeces, different colours; so with the different *religiones*.

'Nec sunt igitur religiones iste seu varii modi vivendi tam utiles et fructiferi ab ecclesia exstirpandi[a] . . . sed illi pocius, si qui forent, qui huiusmodi religiones et vivendi modos varios approbatos conati fuerint adnullare, tanquam ecclesie previgni et contra stimulum calcitrantes, immo malediccionis filii . . .'

[a] ab—extirpandi *om.* C.

(II) *De perfectione vivendi*

Durham Cathedral Library, MS. B. IV. 34, f. 96ᵛ (alias 92ᵛ); Corpus Christi College, Cambridge, MS. 103, p. 310.

Pretractato[a] superius de substancialibus regule monachalis et de fructifera et necessaria fundacione religionum et aliorum vivendi modorum et statuum in ecclesia variorum ac quomodo[b] ab invicem distinguantur, subsequitur[c] tractatus 2ᵘˢ de perfeccione vivendi in eisdem, quatinus inter hec membra necessaria ordo debitus agnoscatur.[d]

[a] Pretracto D.   [b] ac quomodo *om* C.   [c] sequitur C.   [d] agnoscitur C.

[D, f. 97.] Incipit tractatus secundus de perfeccione vivendi.

Sacratissimo siquidem Dei evangelio, Mat. 19, asserente observacionem legalium mandatorum homini non sufficere, sed adhuc unum sibi deesse ad vite perfeccionem, ideo querunt plures, an talis perfeccio in vita seculari an in conversacione regulari verius sit ponenda.

(A) *Arguments for seculars* (D, f. 97; C, p. 310)

1. The example of Christ, who lived in secular habit in common with other men. There existed among the Jews three famous

religiones, the Pharisees, Sadducees, and Essenes,[1] which were not followed by Christ, but condemned by Him.

2. In giving the evangelical counsels and precepts, Christ did not tell anyone to vow continence, &c. The traditions of men cannot add anything to the evangelical counsels and precepts; those who try to do so, follow Mahomet, who said that Christ was a good and wise prophet, but that His law was not complete because He was killed in His youth.

3. Man is free by nature, therefore the more free he is, the more perfect; but the life of seculars is more free than that of regulars.

(B) *Arguments for regulars* (D, f. 97ᵛ; C, p. 313)

1. To the young man in the Gospel (Mat. xix. 16), Christ said, *Si vis perfectus esse . . .*, laying down the three *substancialia*. This is confirmed by the life of the apostles with Christ; *Ecce nos reliquimus omnia* (Mat. xix. 27).

2. The Apostles in the Primitive Church after Pentecost led the cenobitical life as regards poverty, continence, contemplation, &c. St. Mark at Alexandria led a similar life (St. Jerome, Philo, and Eusebius are cited).

3. The *regula racionis*, which St. Bernard calls the *regula caritatis* (*De precepto et dispens.*),[2] binds all men having the use of reason, and this rule is facilitated by the particular rules derived from it, as explained in the previous treatise.

(C) *Definition of perfection* (D, f. 99; C, p. 315)

According to the *Sentences* (lib. ii, dist. iv), perfection is threefold: (1) perfection *secundum tempus*, proper to *natura condita*; (2) perfection by nature, proper to glorified man; (3) universal perfection, proper only to God. The present discussion concerns the first form of perfection.

(D) *Personal perfection* (D, f. 99; C, p. 315)

Man's *via* is twofold: (1) of first innocence, (2) of *reparacio graciosa* through Christ. By sin man was wounded in his natural and intellectual powers, and despoiled of gratuitous and moral virtues (cf. *Sent.*, dist. ii, c. xxv); by penitence the theological virtues are regained. Perfection consists of the practice of the three theological virtues. According to Aristotle (*Ethics*, i. 10, 11; ii. 1), moral virtue requires to be exercised (1) *scienter*, (2) *libere*, and (3) *habitu*.

---

[1] Cf. Wyclif, op. cit. iii. 17, 1. 22.
[2] St. Bernard, op. cit., c. iv; *Pat. Lat.* 182, col. 866.

'Ex quo concludi poterit quod ipse tres theologice virtutes continent quicquid tempus huius vie requirit et convenit secundum tempus hoc haberi, quod, ut predicitur, est perfeccionis primum membrum. Nec gradus aliquis nec status in Christianismo secularis, religiosus aut ecclesiasticus qualiscumque reddit aut efficit hominem sic perfectum esse, sed eius conversacio virtuosa, quamvis gradus et status huiusmodi multum iuvent . . . et quanto gradus superior, tanto perfeccior, quia Deo propinquior, occupans debet esse . . .'

The world is divided according to St. Anselm (*De similitudinibus*, c. 131)[1] into *oratores, defensores, agricultores*; or into secular and regular; or into clerical and lay; a man may be perfect in any walk of life; 'alicui homini utilis et perfecta est conversacio secularis, cui foret vita regularis inutilis et penitus inperfecta', and conversely.

(E) *Gradual perfection (i.e. perfection of grade or state)* (D, f. 101; C, p. 318)

'Oportet investigare unde consurgat perfeccio gradualis, id est perfeccio gradus sive status ecclesie militantis, quatinus perfeccionem hominis personalem et perfeccionem militantis ecclesie gradualem insimul combinando, tam ad quesitum, quam ad utriusque partis motiva responsio patefiat.'

The life of the Church Militant is divided thus:

1. Contemplative life, (*a*) superior, concerned with divine things (superior reason), (*b*) inferior, concerned with *sciencia* (inferior reason); cf. the speculative life, according to the philosophers, concerned (*a*) with immaterial, (*b*) with material things;

2. Active life, (*a*) concerned with the utility of the soul, (*b*) concerned with the necessities of the body; cf. the practical life, concerned (*a*) with moral virtues, (*b*) with bodily governance.

The quadruple life, exercised now in one way, now in another, is the perfect life, as exemplified in Christ, St. John the Baptist, and the Apostles. A digression concerning ecclesiastical endowment follows. It was the Devil who cried in the air, at the endowment of the Church, *Hodie effusum est venenum in ecclesia*,[2] and he still inspires those who say the Church is too well endowed and that kings and princes should disendow it.

(F) *Conclusion* (D, f. 103ᵛ; C, p. 323)

'Primo constare poterit ex premissis in quo modo vivendi sit ponenda pro hac vita hominis perfeccio personalis, quia videlicet in vita virtuosa secundum

---

[1] *Sic*, for c. 127; *Pat. Lat.* 159, col. 679.
[2] Cf. Langland's use of this story in *Piers Plowman*, B, passus xv. 519 ff., and Skeat's note.

istas tres virtutes theologicas, et pro quanto in illis est virtuosior, de tanto perfeccior est persona, ut superius est ostensum; 2° quod perfeccio status sive perfeccio gradualis ecclesie militantis consistit in illa vita quadruplici varie prout oportunitas exegerit executa, quam Dominus noster Ihesus in persona propria exemplavit, Iohannes Baptista, apostoli et eorum successores inferioresque prelati diligencius exequebantur et adhuc singuli secundum quod eis competit exequuntur exequive deberent.

'Et quanto gradus vel status talis fuerit superior in ecclesia militante, de tanto est perfeccior iudicandus, et consequenter conveniret quod proficiendus in gradum vel statum talem foret excellencior in perfeccione hominis personali, et in gradibus seu statibus inferioribus ecclesie sive magis particularibus sufficit correspondenter minor perfeccio personalis, ut cum simul coincidunt perfeccio status sive perfeccio gradualis ecclesie ac correspondens perfeccio hominis personalis, in tali vivendi modo videtur cuiuscumque hominis habentis perfeccionem ponenda perfeccio suprema sibi competens hic pro via.'

(G) *Objections to the quadruple life as perfect* (D, f. 104; C, p. 323)

1. The contemplative life, being *quasi vita patrie*, must be more perfect; and the speculative is higher than the practical.

2. Christ did not tell Mary to stop contemplating and help Martha; Peter represents the active life, John the contemplative. Answers are given to these objections.

(H) *The claims of (A) seculars and (B) regulars reconsidered* (D, f. 105; C, p. 325)

Definition of *regularis vita*: not only Christ and the Apostles but all the saints and all *bene viventes*, although in secular habit, may in a sense be called *regulares*, because they observe the three *substancialia* (cf. the previous treatise); and again, *loquendo de ordine facticio*, in all grades of the Church, and in the sacraments, &c., there are bodily observances, and so all ecclesiastics and even laymen may be called *regulares*;[1] but to follow the commonly used way of speaking, *regulares* are those who by profession live under one of the rules approved by the Church; and all others are seculars.

'Dicitur ad quesitum quod utrumque membrum illius quod queritur est negandum, quia nec in vita seculari nec in conversacione regulari est generaliter ponenda hominis perfeccio pro hac vita, quia nec generaliter hominis perfeccio personalis, nec generaliter hominis perfeccio gradualis, immo in omni gradu seu statu ecclesie militantis poterit quis perfectus esse, cuius vocacioni competit status talis, et perfeccior quis in inferiori

---

[1] Cf. Wyclif, op. cit. iii. 4, l. 29.

quam foret idem in superiori, et de aliis secundum vocaciones alias e converso, sicut est superius aliqualiter declaratum . . .'

(I) *Answers to (A) arguments for seculars* (D, f. 106; C, p. 325)

1. Likeness to Christ consists not 'in habitu exteriori seculari vel regulari aut observanciis corporalibus quibuscumque', but *in virtuoso habitu interiori*,[1] according to the three theological virtues. The three Jewish sects were heresies, not *religiones*. Three reasons are given why Christ did not follow the legitimate *religiones* of the Old Testament, like the Sons of the Prophets.

2. As it was necessary for Christ to add counsels to precepts, to help men to observe the precepts, so with the growing wickedness of the world, it was necessary to add approved *religiones* to counsels.

3. No creature is entirely free, but all have obligations to God. 'Inest tamen naturaliter libertas creature racionali, ut libere eligat et libere exequatur quod racio sibi suadet'; but such liberty has to be limited, because reason is obfuscated. This discussion continues for three pages.

(J) *Answers to (B) arguments for regulars* (D, f. 109; C, p. 329)

1. All men, regular and secular, are bound to observe the three *substancialia*, as shown in the previous treatise. Moreover:

'. . . Perfeccio vivendi consistit in sequi Christum, et de quanto quis propinquius vel similius sequitur in vivendo, de tanto perfeccior erit talis, et de solo habitu exteriori, sive seculari sive regulari, penitus non est cura, immo nec relinquere huiusmodi, nec illa tria que dicuntur religionis substancialia profiteri arguit vel probat relinquentem vel sic profitentem ex hoc perfectum esse, sed talia multum adiuvant et facilitant quoad quasdam personas ad perfeccionem non habitam adquirendam sive ad perfeccionem habitam nutriendam ut amplius augmentetur.'[2]

2. In the Primitive Church, the cenobitic and contemplative

---

[1] D has a note in right margin, partly cut away: *Nota bene contra* . . . with the first stroke of what may be a W for Wodford; cf. *infra*, n. 2.

[2] Against this passage, D has the following marginal notes added: (i) in the left margin: 'Nota bene contra errorem M. Willelmi Wodforth contrarium sentencie infrascripte'; (ii) in the right margin, in a later hand, partly cut away by the binder: 'Nota bene [contra?] errorem M[. . .] Wodfor[th . . .] ipse tenet contra [. . .] infrascript[. . .]' This clearly refers to the Franciscan anti-Wycliffite writer, William Woodford (d. 1397). The implication seems to be that he attached too much importance to external observances, in contrast to Uthred. The reference may perhaps be to Woodford's four Determinations, which deal largely with the question of 'private religions', or to his sixty-five *Responsiones*, which deal with the observances of the Friars in some detail (MS. Bodley 703, ff. 69 ff., 41 ff.); but I have not traced the particular passage.

life was necessary and holy, as now; but the apostolic life, as lived by Christ, combining now contemplation, now action, according to need, was most perfect (cf. (E) above).[1]

3. The *regula paradisi* and other particular rules help men to perfection, but it does not therefore follow that the life of regulars is generally to be called more perfect than that of seculars, who may perhaps be more discerning and stronger in resisting temptations, &c.

(K) *Practical argument, from the examples of the saints* (D, f. 111)

'Verumptamen quia non sermone est regnum Dei, sed in virtute . . . ideo in istis de perfeccione vivendi tam secularium, quam regularium per argumenta vocalia seu verbalia generaliter declaratis non videtur simpliciter quiescendum; sed ulterius est ad argumenta realia et practica transeundum. Quot enim sanctos et viros perfectos seculares generavit, educavit et ad finalem perfeccionem felicissime perduxit sancta ecclesia mater nostra, dinumerare seu transcribere nequc calamus michi sufficit neque lingua; nec eciam quot regulares vita et sanctitate preclaros, doctrina evangelica precipuos, ac ecclesie validissimos defensores produxit sancta religio ad perfectum. De quibus tamen inter ceteros michi innumerabiles narraturus, de aliquibus religiosis, quamvis respective ad[a] eorum omnium numerum valde paucis, incipiam a prima et inter omnes religiones sacras sacratissima, accipiendo religionem sicut superius limitatur, ordine scilicet altissimo monachorum, quoniam secundum beatum Dionisium *de ecclesiastica ierarchia* capitulo 6°,[2] quod capitulum intitulatur secundum unam translacionem *De hiis ordinibus qui perficiuntur*, et incipit capitulum istud 6m *Isti quidem sunt ierarchici ordines*; secundum aliam translacionem quam exponit Lincolniensis intitulatur capitulum istud 6m *De eorum qui perficiuntur ordinibus*, et incipit capitulum illud *Hii quidem sacerdotales et ordines*; secundum vero 3am translacionem quam sequitur et exponit Thomas abbas sancti Andree Vercellensis incipit capitulum istud 6m *Explicitis tribus ordinibus proficiencium*; secundum translacionem autem 4am quam exponit frater Albertus intitulatur capitulum istud 6m *De perficiendorum*[b] *ordinibus*, et incipit capitulum istud 6m *Hii quidem sacerdotales et particiones*; sed secundum 5am translacionem isti translacioni 4te similimam, quamvis in vocabulis aliquociens discrepantem, incipit capitulum istud 6m *Hii sunt igitur sacerdotales ordines*.[3] Verumptamen in sentencia, quamvis diversa

---

[a] de D. [b] proficiendorum D.

[1] The rest of the treatise, from this point, is missing in C.

[2] Pat. Lat. 122, col. 1101.

[3] There were five translations of the principal works of Pseudo-Denis, made before the fifteenth century: (1) by Hilduin of Tours, 832–5; (2) by John Scotus Eriugena, 860–2; (3) by John the Saracen, c. 1160; (4) by Robert Grosseteste, c. 1239–13; (5) the *Extractio* by Thomas Abbot of Vercelli, c. 1238–44; cf. S. H. Thomson, 'An Unnoticed Translation of the Ps.-Dionysius' De ecclesiastica Hierarchia', *Révue Bénédictine*, 1 (1938), 246 ff.; M. Grabmann, *Mittelalterliches Geistesleben*, i (Munich, 1926), 449 ff. For the date of Grosseteste's translation of

habeant vocabula, sic conveniunt omnes isti quod secundum beatum Dionisium capitulo illo 6 de ecclesiastica ierarchia, *Omnium proficiendorum alcior est ordo monachorum*,[1] imo litera Dionisii quam Lincolniensis exponit sic habet *Perfeccior autem omnium excellencior ordo monachorum sacra ordinacio repurgata secundum omnem purgacionem* ... Oportet enim secundum Lincolniensem monachos purgari cum purgatis, et deinde illuminari cum illuminatis, et insuper habere vite sue agende regulas speciales ...'

Monks are sometimes called *therapeute*, sometimes *monachi*; the interpretations of these names are given.[2] The *misterium monastice perfeccionis* or consecration ceremony of a monk, according to Denis, contains seven *theorie* or rites; (1) the monk to be consecrated stands behind the priest, *nullum genu flectens*; (2) renunciation; (3) *cruciformis signacio*; (4) tonsure; (5) *mutacio vestium*; (6) the kiss; (7) the Communion.[3]

The ecclesiastical hierarchy contains nine orders:[4]

(i) three *Ordines infimi*, called *Perfecti*:

    (1) *Ordo purgativus* = converts,
    (2) *Ordo illuminativus* = *sacer populus*,
    (3) *Ordo perfectus* = monks.

(ii) three *Ordines medii*, called *Perfectivi*:

    (4) Ordo *purgativus* = *ministerialis seu leviticus*,
    (5) Ordo *illuminativus* = priests,
    (6) Ordo *perfectivus* = bishops.

(iii) three *Ordines supremi*, called *Perfecciones*:

    (7) *Ordo purgans* = Christ redeeming,
    (8) *Ordo illuminans* = Christ preaching,
    (9) *Ordo perficiens* = Christ judging.

The six lower orders belong to the body of the Church Militant, the three highest, to its Head.

Pseudo-Denis see D. A. Callus, 'The Date of Grosseteste's Translations and Commentaries on Pseudo-Dionysius and the Nicomachean Ethics', *Recherches de Théol. ancienne et médiévale*, xiv (1947), 66–90 (the *De Angelica Hierarchia*, c. 1239–40; the other three, c. 1240–3). The *Extractio* of Thomas Gallus was completed in 1238, cf. G. Théry, 'Chronologie des œuvres de Thomas Gallus, abbé de Verceil', *Divus Thomas* (Plac.), xxxvii (1934), 268–75, 493–4. For Hilduin's translation (832–5), see G. Théry, *Hilduin, Traducteur de Denys* (Études de Phil. méd. xvi, xix), Paris, 1932–7. For Eriugena's translation (860–2) see G. Théry, 'Scot Érigène, Introducteur de Denys', *The New Scholasticism*, vii (1933), 91–108; M. Cappuyns, *Jean Scot Érigène, sa vie, son œuvre, sa pensée* (Paris, 1933), pp. 150–61. I have to thank the Rev. D. A. Callus for help on this subject.

  [1] *Pat. Lat.* 122, col. 1102.
  [2] Cf. also R. Grosseteste, *Epistolae*, ed. Luard (Rolls Series, 1861), pp. 173–8.
  [3] *Pat. Lat.* 122, cols. 1102–3.
  [4] For orders (1)–(6), cf. ibid., cols. 1103–4; I cannot trace the source of the last three orders.

'Igitur hec predicta quamvis prolixius iam adduxi, quatinus ex testimoniis sanctissimi et antiquissimi doctoris Dionisii secundum sentenciam 5 variarum translacionum et 3 exposicionum superius iam tactarum sicut primo supposui declararem, scilicet ordinem monachorum inter omnes sacras religiones esse primum, sacratissimum et altissimum in ecclesia Dei merito nominandum' (D, fo. 114ᵛ).

The reasons for this are: (1) the useful and necessary institution of the monastic order, required to complete the ecclesiastical hierarchy; (2) its antiquity; (3) its cleanness and purity of conscience; (4) its excellence and dignity; (5) its concord and indivisible unity; (6) its purgation and contemplation of divine things; (7) its renunciation of secular things.

Thus the monastic order can never be destroyed 'emulorum latratibus, nec adversariorum insultibus, nec ullis tempestatibus vel procellis'; nor is it defiled or lessened in sanctity by its unworthy members, any more than the angelic order was defiled by the fallen angels, or the apostolic order by Judas, or the ecclesiastical order 'propter multitudinem dampnabiliter viventium, qui tamen ecclesie sancte filii nominantur'.

Finally, 'vocabuntur monachi aliqui sancti qui fuerant de ordine perfecto'. According to Denis, there are (1) the *ordo perfectivus* (episcopal); the *ordo illuminativus* (sacerdotal) exercising three offices, viz. (2) *perficit monachum* (abbatial), (3) *conficit sacramentum* (sacerdotal), (4) *informat populum* (doctoral), and (5) the *ordo perfectus* (*ordo singularium monachorum*).

'De hiis 5 ordinibus sacris aliqui, quamvis pauci in comparacione ad numerum omnium sanctorum precedencium monachorum, seriatim interius subscribentur, ut realiter et practice arguatur religionem hanc sacratissimam monachorum plurimos conversacione ac sanctitate precipuos, pastores ecclesie nobilissimos, doctrinis sanis strenuissimos, ad omne opus perfectum paratissimos, et ad contemplandum devotissimos genuisse, aluisse ac ad perfeccionem tam personalem, quam gradualem, quatenus hominibus competeret, produxisse, sicud in recitando nomina et facta preclarissima monachorum de iam prefatis ordinibus quinque sacris, veluti in antiquis fidedignis historiis sunt inscripta, ponenda tamen singula secundum litterarum ordinem alphabeti, ut cuicumque occurrat facilius id quod querit.¹ Explicit.'

With regard to the date and occasion of the writing of these treatises, it may be noted, first, that the second treatise refers to and depends upon the first, and the two were probably written

---

¹ This last sentence is evidently intended to introduce an alphabetical list of monastic saints and writers, such as that in Cotton MS. Vitellius E. xii, f. 62.

together. It is unlikely that they represent a verbatim report of a scholastic act, though they may have grown out of something of the sort. While there are occasional thrusts against the Mendicants, Uthred is mainly concerned to meet the kind of objections that Wyclif raised against 'private religions'. The ten objections at the end of the first treatise (p. 371, *supra*) do not seem to correspond to the later and more violent tracts against the religious orders, written by Wyclif *c.* 1383, published in his *Polemical Works*;[1] they bear more resemblance to some of the arguments used by Wyclif in the third book of his *De civili dominio*.[2] At this time Wyclif, in spite of his criticisms, still makes occasional tributes to monasticism;[3] while Uthred seems to show a polite uncertainty as to whether his antagonists really mean business— *si qui forent* (p. 374, *supra*). We may conjecturally assign Uthred's two treatises to the period *c.* 1374–6, when Wyclif seems to have been preparing for and writing the *De civili dominio*, and when he actually crossed swords with Uthred in his *Determinacio*.[4] In fact the treatises may have been a by-product of Uthred's controversy with Wyclif over dominion, endowment, and the relations of Church and State; while from another point of view, as has been pointed out, they form part of a literature dealing with the origins of monastic history, monasticism, and monastic hagiology.

Uthred's two treatises are remarkable and, indeed, unexpectedly impressive. In view of the date, one might have expected something excessively formal, arid, and hair-splitting; but although the plan is highly articulated, with *principalia*, numbered arguments and counter-arguments, and syllogisms, the argument is fairly easy to follow, even for a layman, far more so, for instance, than the scholastic exercises reproduced in Little and Pelster's *Oxford Theology and Theologians*. Again, while Uthred undoubtedly has current controversies in mind, and is at pains to confute the claims of the Mendicants[5] and the Wycliffite objections to 'private religions', yet the controversial element is subordinated to the general plan, in an attempt to work out a constructive theory of the religious life. Perhaps it would hardly be an

[1] Ed. R. Buddensieg (Wyclif Soc.), 2 vols., 1883.
[2] *De civili dominio*, iii. 1–32.   [3] *Op. cit.* iii. 17.
[4] Printed in *Opera Minora*, ed. J. Loserth (Wyclif Soc.), 1913, pp. 405 ff. For this period of Wyclif's work, see Workman, *John Wyclif*, i. 231 ff., 257 ff.; A. Gwynn, *The English Austin Friars in the Time of Wyclif*, pp. 230 ff.
[5] As put forward for instance in Geoffrey Hardeby's *De vita evangelica* (*c.* 1357–8); cf. Gwynn, op. cit., p. 93.

exaggeration to say that Uthred seems, like Mabillon, to be one of those people who are stimulated by a controversy into producing a constructive piece of work. What perhaps impresses one most, one may say surprises one most, is the moderate tone, a certain serenity and rationality, which contrast favourably with the style of contemporary controversialists, both orthodox and unorthodox, with the violent and bitter language of Wyclif, for instance, and with Uthred's own earlier invectives against the Friars. Perhaps Uthred now felt more sure of himself. Although he is, metaphorically speaking, fighting for his life, defending the very existence of 'private religions', he does not lose his temper or make exaggerated claims. He brilliantly outflanks the Wycliffite objections to 'private religions' by arguing that monasticism is not merely lawful, but is something deeply rooted in man's nature as a rational being. All men are in a sense monks; man is, to adapt Aristotle's phrase, 'by nature a monastic animal'. The analogy between the baptismal vows and the vows of the monastic profession is a familiar one,[1] of which Wyclif himself makes use on occasion;[2] but here the analogy is pushed farther back still, to the creation itself. Uthred's efforts to show the rational and natural character of monasticism almost remind one of the eighteenth-century Deists' attempts to prove the entire rationality of Christianity—'Christianity as old as the creation', though needless to say Uthred's principles are entirely different. Uthred shows the same desire to trace things back to the Garden of Eden that we see in the writings of Fitz-Ralph and Adam Easton and in the popular slogan 'When Adam dalf and Eva span'; quaint as it sounds, this represents a serious attempt to examine first principles, and is analogous to the later preoccupation with the 'state of nature'. It may be noted that Uthred, here, and still more explicitly in his other writings, accepts a theory of Dominion resembling that of the school of Giles of Rome.

In his discussion of the claims of regulars and seculars to perfection, Uthred shows his balance and restraint. One might have expected him, under the circumstances, to make an out-and-out case for the religious; but on the contrary, he is at pains to insist that perfection does not consist in external observances or in any particular state of life, but in interior dispositions, attainable in any walk of life; and that the 'mixed life', partly con-

[1] See references collected in H. Denifle, *Luther et le Luthéranisme*, trans. J. Paquier, ii. 20 ff.
[2] *De civili dominio*, iii. 4 ff.

templative, partly active, is the highest of all.[1] Here is something very different from the picture, drawn by later humanist and Reformer critics, and until recently still sometimes accepted as historically true, of a monasticism eaten up with formalism, ceremonialism, and superstition, and claiming a magical efficacy. Uthred was in the main simply following the normal, classical tradition among patristic and medieval writers, who taught that perfection consists in interior virtues and above all in charity, and that it is enjoined upon all men, and is not something extra, with which religious alone are concerned.[2] At the same time, one cannot help feeling that a writer like St. Peter Damian would have treated the question with at least a different emphasis. Perhaps Uthred reflects the growing desire to open up the spiritual life to the devout laity, which is such a marked feature of the later Middle Ages, as shown for instance in Hilton's epistle on the mixed life, and indeed in the whole of the vernacular mystical literature in England, Germany, and the Netherlands.

Another feature of Uthred's teaching, in these treatises and elsewhere, is his Aristotelianism. He is always introducing nature and reason,[3] and the natural superiority of the rational and spiritual over the material; government is the natural function of a spiritual *élite*. So far from it being improper for ecclesiastics to be concerned with government and property, they, as being more spiritual and more discreet, are precisely the persons most fitted to exercise dominion;[4] in fact they seem to correspond to the Aristotelian citizen or natural master. This may be regarded as Uthred's answer to objections against 'Caesarian prelates'. The weakness of the argument is that so many leading ecclesiastics were not spiritual men saddled with secular duties (like

---

[1] Cf. the life of Dowel, Dobet, and Dobest in *Piers Plowman*, corresponding to the active, contemplative, and mixed life. Langland, like his contemporary Uthred, was very much concerned with the problem of perfection.

[2] See the authorities collected in Denifle, op. cit. i. 238–315 *passim*. Cf. especially St. Thomas, *Summa Theol.*, 2a 2ae, q. 81, 184, 186, 188. Uthred does not seem quite decided on the claim of the religious state to be the state of perfection; at one point he seems to doubt it (section E), while elsewhere he admits it (sections F and K), in fact his quotations from Denis seem intended to show the 'perfect' character of the monastic order. He seems to ignore the important point made by St. Thomas, that the religious life is called the state of perfection, not because its members are perfect, but because they solemnly bind themselves to strive for perfection (*Summa Theol.*, 2a 2ae, q. 184, a. 4 and a. 5).

[3] Uthred's appeals to natural reason, while balanced by appeals to authority, may perhaps be compared with the rationalist apologetic against the Lollards which was carried to such extremes later by Pecock.

[4] This argument is specially used in the *De dotatione ecclesie*.

Langton), but secular administrators disguised as spiritual men (like Wykeham). Neither the critics nor the apologists seem to have realized that the Church was not the exploiter but the exploited. But curious as Uthred's argument may seem, one can see how it would seem confirmed by the existing arrangement of things, by the traditional preponderance of clerics in government and administration from the days of the Witan to the days of William of Wykeham, a tradition only just being consciously challenged; by the wide lordships, privileges, and jurisdictions of ecclesiastical persons and bodies from the Palatinate of Durham, for instance, down to the halimotes; or again by the more elaborate and long-standing administrative machinery prevailing on the ecclesiastical lordships. In one sense, Aristotle's picture of a small *élite* of citizens devoted to the good life, to intellectual and moral virtue, and supported by the labours of slaves and artisans, might well have seemed to a man like Uthred to find a realization, Christianized, spiritualized, and safeguarded, in a monastic community like Durham or St. Albans. Aristotle, too, would reinforce a certain aristocratic point of view, as in the curious argument for a more delicate standard of living for superiors, because they are more able to restrain themselves. However much belied in practice, the ideal of self-restraint must always have been an essential element in *courtoisie*. In general, Uthred's Aristotelianism, not only in dialectic and metaphysic, but in outlook on the world and on society, is interesting as showing how the intellectual revolution of the thirteenth century continued to take effect; thus among other things we can see it reinforcing the old claims for the superiority of the spiritual over the temporal, just at a time when Marsilius, for instance, was using Aristotle in an opposite direction. Uthred's Aristotelianism naturally shows itself more clearly when discussing semi-political issues like church endowment, but there are clear traces of it even in these two more or less ascetical treatises on monastic life.

Finally, an interesting light is thrown on late medieval scholarship and criticism, when Uthred brings together five translations of and three commentaries on the Pseudo-Denis. This is the more remarkable, since the Durham library does not seem to have been very rich in Denis's works, to judge from the surviving catalogues;[1] perhaps Uthred relied on the libraries of Oxford.

W. A. PANTIN

---

[1] *Catalogi veteres librorum eccles. cath. Dunelm.* (Surtees Soc. 1838), p. 72.

CHICHELE AND CANTERBURY[1]

'PAUCIS diebus vel nullis mansit in Eboraco', wrote Gascoigne of Archbishop Kemp, when castigating him for staying in his diocese only two or three weeks at a time at intervals of ten or twelve years.[2] If we substitute Canterbury for York, to no medieval archbishop could such a stricture be less appropriately applied than to Henry Chichele. While his main administrative headquarters were at Lambeth, whence he could quickly be ferried over the river to the council at Westminster or, farther down stream, to his chambers in the City, his itinerary[3] during the twenty-nine years of his primacy shows him steadily moving round his Kentish and Surrey manors, and, save for 1439 and 1440 (when he was having bouts of illness), regularly spending part of his time in the palace of Canterbury.

At Canterbury he kept his first Christmas before his primary visitation of his diocese at the new year. His subjects could have seen him there in March, April, June, and September 1415. In 1416 he was there for four periods, during April, July, August, and October, residence only paralleled in 1422, 1425, and 1436; most years he kept Easter there as well as one other period, which might be the Purification, or August, or late October–November. The visits were not for a few hurried days: they generally lasted from two to three weeks, sometimes longer.[4] The considerations which kept most diocesan bishops from their cathedral cities scarcely affected the tactful and pacific Chichele, with whom the priory of Christ Church was on friendliest terms. At the creation of William Molassh as prior, the archbishop in his sermon firmly upheld the tradition of peace. Commenting on the text *Vidi spiritum descendentem sicut columbam*, he pointed to the need, in prelates, for kindliness and readiness to forgive wrong, and went on punningly to derive William Molassh's name from the phrase *vir almus molliens sive mulcens*.[5] Chichele's gifts to Christ Church

---

[1] I am greatly indebted to the Hon. Chapter Librarian, Mr. W. P. Blore, for sending me transcripts from the muniments of the dean and chapter, and particularly for the extract printed at the end of this paper.

[2] *Loci e libro veritatum*, ed. Thorold Rogers, p. 37. Professor Hamilton Thompson observes (*The English Clergy and their Organization in the Later Middle Ages*, p. 43) that Gascoigne did not exaggerate greatly on this point.

[3] *The Register of Henry Chichele, Archbishop of Canterbury, 1414–1443, passim.*

[4] e.g. 10 Mar.–4 Apr. 1425; 5 Mar.–4 Apr. 1438.

[5] Dean and Chapter of Canterbury, Register S, f. 98ʳ: 'Est inquam columba

were numerous and important, and he used his influence freely on its behalf.

His donations to the fabric, put on record by the convent, amounted to 1,000 marks,[1] exclusive of the New Library, built by him above the Prior's chapel, which he 'abundantly stocked with valuable books of the various faculties'.[2] The south-western tower, called the Dunstan-Steeple, was begun in 1424, and in the next ten years Chichele contributed to it £474. 8s. 2d. through his treasurers.[3] It was probably he who brought on visits to Canterbury the king's master-mason, Thomas Mapilton, to act as supervisor of the work.[4] Mapilton was in 1429 to be employed by the archbishop's grocer brother, Sir Robert Chichele, in the rebuilding of St. Stephen's, Walbrook.

There were other munificent gifts to his 'sons and chaplains in Christ': there was the festival set of vestments in white velvet 'splendidly starred with Saracen-flowers';[5] and the fine plate listed in an inventory of 1465:[6] in the prior's house, a gilt and enamelled drinking-cup, two heavy gilt jars with the archbishop's arms on the covers, and a gilt ewer; in the refectory, two silver gallon pots, a silver-gilt drinking-cup 'with chaplets on the lid and daisies round the base', a great silver bowl for rose-water, and 'a great silver ship' for collecting alms (ad opus elemosine) on the prior's table. There were others besides.[7] More important than the gifts was his friendship with a succession of priors, John Woodnesburgh to whom he was evidently devoted,[8] William Molassh, and John Salisbury. To the obedientaries, whom it was his duty to change from time to time,[9] and to the monks and novices, he probably appeared as more than the visitor of a great

animal mansuetum, felle carens, iniuriarum vix reminiscens, quam conditionem eo magis quilibet prelatus habere tenetur quo magister noster Christus iniurias sibi factas remisit.'

[1] *Literae Cantuarienses*, ed. J. B. Sheppard (Rolls Ser.), iii. 171–2.

[2] *Reg. Chichele*, i. 123–4; cf. Woodruff and Danks, *Memorials of Canterbury Cathedral* (1912), p. 385.

[3] C. E. Woodruff, 'The Rebuilding of the South-Western Tower of Canterbury Cathedral', *Archaeologia Cantiana*, xlv. 41.

[4] Mr. John Harvey, *Gothic England*, p. 97, calls the south-west tower 'Mapilton's principal extant work'; but Prior Goldstone finished the decoration: *Somner's Antiquities of Canterbury*, ed. N. Battely (1703), 'The History of Christ Church Canterbury', p. 24; and Woodruff, op. cit.

[5] *Litt. Cant.* iii. 171. *Flores saracenorum* are oriental daisies worked in gold.

[6] Dean and Chapter of Canterbury, Register N, ff. 223–350.

[7] *Litt. Cant.*, loc. cit. We are told that he gave the ship, evidently a collecting-box, *conditionaliter*.

[8] Cf. *Reg. Chichele*, i. lxxxv, for Chichele's grief at his death.

[9] Ibid. lxxxiii–lxxxiv and the references there cited.

college. Accounting for the jubilee year of 1420, the clerk to the prior-treasurer headed his return of rents from the City of Canterbury with a solemn precision that may bear more than formal testimony to the archbishop:

'Redditus ecclesie Christi Cantuariensis de domibus et shoppis et aliis diversis placeis locatis anno domini Millesimo CCCC^mo XX^mo anno videlicet jubileo sancti Thome martiris gloriosi et anno regni regis Henrici quinti VIII°, patriarchatus autem reverendissimi in Christo patris et domini domini Henrici Chichele Cantuariensis archiepiscopi anno VII°, prioratus vero venerabilis in Christo patris et domini domini Johannis Wodenesberghe prioris ecclesie Christi supradicte anno IX°.'[1]

Patriarchatus would have confirmed Martin V's worst suspicions.

By 1424, ten years after he had become archbishop, Chichele had erected on the north side of the presbytery his tomb, on which lay his effigy with the cadaver underneath, the whole surmounted by the magnificent tester adorned with angels bearing heraldic shields.[2] To this mausoleum his body was eventually borne, in accordance with the undertaking made to him by the convent, on 15 April 1443. The procession, escorted from Lambeth by 200 gentlemen on horseback with their retinues and by a hundred torches, carried the coffin, and upon it Chichele's effigy dressed in full pontificals, to the west door of the priory, where it was met by the prior, John Salisbury, and John Eltham the subprior, with the taperers and thurifers, and by the whole convent in order of seniority, and carried into the cathedral church to the singing of the responsory *Subvenite et libera me, Domine.* After the exequies next day, the interment took place in the presence of Chichele's suffragan, Robert, bishop of Ross, and the abbots of St. Augustine's and Faversham.[3] As they stood about the iron grille surrounding the tomb, some of those present may have remembered a scene, eighteen years before,[4] when the eucharist was interrupted by the noise of blows and the shouts of the citizens of Canterbury.

[1] D. and C., Reg. H, f. 102^r. It is worth remembering that Lyndwood, in dedicating his *Liber provincialis* to Chichele, called him *dei gratia archiepiscopus*.
[2] In the seventeenth century, as an early illustration shows (*Somner's Antiq. of Cant.*, ed. Battely, 'Christ Church', opp. p. 34), the original figurines on the supporting columns, which had probably been destroyed, were replaced by characteristic symbolical statuettes, some of which were placed in the choir screen when All Souls College redecorated the tomb at the end of the last century and put in new figures of painted wood.
[3] D. and C., Thomas Causton's obituary, MS. D. 12, f. 24^v.
[4] 'die sancte Agathe virginis (5 Feb.) quo die omnia premissa perpetrata erant, A.D. 1425': D. and C., Reg. S, f. 93; *Litt. Cant.* iii. 146–8.

To the grille was clinging then a young goldsmith, as he tried to protect himself from the bailiffs and 'an undisciplined multitude of the city'. Bernard Oswyk, described as *juvenis de partibus transmarinis*,[1] had been arrested by the bailiffs and jailed on a plea of trespass: he escaped and fled to Christ Church. Though threatened with angry and abusive language and charges to the effect that the priory was wont to harbour such thieves, murderers, and robbers as Bernard, the prior, John Woodnesburgh, refused to surrender the man; whereupon with great noise and shouting (disturbing Thomas Moonie, the commissary-general, who was holding his court in the building) the citizens dragged the wretched Bernard away from the tomb, and were carrying him down the nave when the commissary-general stopped them and prevailed upon them to let him go. A later account says that the prior would not allow the prisoner to make confession, 'but so kept hym, housyd hym and herberghede hym for XL days and let hym escape in contempt of the kynge and gret grevaunces to the same Baylyffs and citesines'.[2] Chichele was at once informed of the outrage upon sanctuary, and, through Thomas Moonie, issued a citation to the citizens which named three persons, William Byllyngton, bailiff, William Chylton, citizen, and Thomas Topclyff, chaplain, along with their accomplices. The entry in Register S breaks off incomplete, so the ensuing action is unknown. In striking contrast to this had been the proceedings of 1304, when a leathermaker called Adam had killed a carter named Alexius of Westwell, and fled from sanctuary 'into the Chamber of the great Hall by the outer gate of the prior's court in which were many goods of the wardrobe of the Lord Edward, son of King Edward'. Adam had been appointed custodian of these by the prince's treasurer, who had just left the city,[3] and when called upon by the steward of the liberty of Christ Church 'to come to the king's peace', declined and locked himself in. The steward at once informed the king's council, which, after deliberating, sent from London an official to replace Adam, and ordered the steward to arrest Adam and keep him in jail. In the meantime an inquest was held by the coroners of the three lathes of the neighbourhood, St. Augustine's, Shepway, and Scray, with the hundred of Westgate and the four neighbouring vills as jurors. The verdict was one of wilful homicide, and Adam was accordingly brought before the royal justices, at Canterbury, on

---

[1] D. and C., Cart. Antiq. C. 1282.   [2] *Infra*, p. 401.
[3] William of Blyborough: Hilda Johnstone, *Edward of Carnarvon*, p. 11.

9 September 1304, and, on claiming his clergy, was handed over to the ordinary as one found guilty of slaying. 'Et missus fuit apud gayolam de Meydestone', says the record, and we know no more. The Church may have protected his life, but did not oppose incarceration.[1] In this case the civil authorities behaved with complete propriety, and the immunity of Christ Church was respected.

The angry words addressed in 1425 to the prior need cause no surprise to any student of the relations of the city and priory in the past.[2] As early as 1227, when the city was called upon to furnish a number of men-at-arms for war in Scotland, the convent claimed that it was free from all secular service, whereupon the mayor and commonalty assembled to consider a plan for coercing the monks, and were only deterred by the spokesmanship of William de Ely.[3] A religious house so discharged was always likely to be in a difficult position when asked to subvent or contribute to local defence works or to assist with men in guarding the city. As in the time of Hubert de Burgh,[4] so in 1415 the priory had helped the city authorities, while protesting that its action should not be made a precedent. In July of that year Prior Woodnesburgh sent, on these express conditions, a contingent to help defend the city against any possible pillaging by the French embassy returning (as it was supposed that they would do) from London to the coast, after Henry V had embarked and the army had left Southampton for Normandy.[5] It was perhaps a little hard, therefore, that the convent should have been made the object of attack ten years later; but the commanding position of the great house invited criticism. The wealth and splendour of a highly privileged community;[6] the extensive ownership of

---

[1] D. and C., Reg. K, f. 143, which takes the case farther than the Christ Church Register in Trin. Coll., Cambridge, MS. O. 9/26, f. 120, from which Mr. R. A. L. Smith summarized the proceedings in *Canterbury Cathedral Priory*, p. 87.

[2] *V.C.H., Kent*, ii. 118, gives examples.

[3] *Hist. MSS. Comm., App. to Fifth Rep.*, p. 433. The freedom from secular service was claimed in virtue of the charters of Cnut (1020) and William I (1071).

[4] *Hist. MSS. Comm.*, op. et loc. cit.

[5] *Somner's Antiq. of Cant.*, ed. Battely, App. lvi, p. 64. The priory sent 9 lances and 24 bowmen.

[6] The citizens would have been interested to hear Chichele's auditor, Richard Andrew, thus describe the monks of Christ Church in his sermon at John Salisbury's creation as prior (6 Mar. 1438): 'O gloria beatorum, felix congregacio monachorum, qui omnem preeminenciam libertatis adquirunt ministerio servitutis, qui delicatarum vestium despectis ornatibus abiectarum ignominias amplectuntur, qui asperitatis onera supportantes delicias aspernuntur, postpositis diviciarum illecebris degunt voluntarie sub pallio paupertatis.' D. and C., Reg. N, f. 176.

urban property and shops; the employment of a large staff of servants and retainers living round and about the priory; the abutment of the monastery upon the city wall and the ditch on its north and eastern frontages; the possession of valuable riparian rights on the Stour, and the ownership of some of the best meadowland on the west and south-west of the city: all these things brought Christ Church into constant and not too cordial relations with the townsfolk, who watched with jaundiced eyes what they regarded as the 'accroachments' of the monastery. Especially was this so under the régime of Thomas Chillendon, a great building prior, who started (1412–13) rebuilding the existing wall from Northgate southwards, and by becoming the tenant of a tower, a postern, and a piece of waste land under the wall at Queningate began, as Canon Livett has shown,[1] the work which led in later years to his successors becoming owners of a large part of the city wall.[2]

Between 1425 and 1427 grievances between the city and the convent reached proportions that made a general settlement necessary. Three documents, two of them preserved among the *Cartae Antiquae* of the Cathedral Library, give the story. The first, printed by Dr. Sheppard, from Register S, is a bond (10 April 1428) by which the prior and chapter oblige themselves under penalty to abide by the decision of John Martyn, one of the judges of the Bench, and Geoffrey Lowther esquire, in their dispute with the citizens. If the arbitrators cannot agree, both parties will submit to the ruling and judgement of Archbishop Chichele, the neutral (*imparis*) elected by both sides, to be given before the following August.[3] The city records show that John Martyn had been cultivated at an earlier date: in one of the cofferer's registers for 1421–2 a sum is entered: 'Pro una pipa vini empta et data Johanni Martin pro amicicia habenda pro negociis civitatis.'[4] Lowther, an official of high standing in Kent,[5] would probably favour the convent, while Martyn must be presumed to have been on the side of the citizens. The particular points at issue are mentioned as 'the seizure and abduction of a

[1] 'Queningate and the Walls of Durovernum', *Arch. Cant.* xlv. 92 f. The area about Queningate *within* the wall is described by E. Hasted, *Hist. of Kent*, iv. 572. For Chillendon as a builder, cf. William Gostling, *A Walk in and about the City of Canterbury* (4th ed., 1796), pp. 171–3.

[2] *Hist. MSS. Comm., App. to Ninth Rep.*, pp. 138, 168.

[3] *Litt. Cant.* iii. 150–1.

[4] *Hist. MSS. Comm., App. to Ninth Rep.*, p. 138. Such gifts were quite normal.

[5] Keeper of Dover Castle, 1424: *Foedera*, x. 337.

fish in the time of John Woodnesburgh, lately prior of the Church written below, and the buying of victuals within the liberty of the said city, and of all manner of trespasses, complaints, demands, debates, touching the prior and chapter and the said city and community'. The grievances of the priory along with the answers of the city, the second of the documents, are preserved in a roll in the *Cartae Antiquae*,[1] and these are followed in the roll by the more comprehensive complaints of the bailiffs and citizens, with the archbishop's rulings in the majority of cases where the plea was not withdrawn. The arbitrators therefore failed to agree, and the third document of this little series, printed below, reveals Chichele as the impartial arbitrator between *civitas* and *coenobium*.

The territorial complaints[2] mainly concern disputed rights in the meadows outside the city, from Riding Gate on the south-east to the Barton of the priory in the extreme north. The prior's grievances alleged that the citizens had made a carriage-way through the south side of the city at Riding Gate: to prepare the 'open way for alman[ey] cariage', it seems that they had either enlarged the gate itself[3] or (perhaps *and*) pulled down the adjacent wall, which, as the prior complained, imperilled the defences of the city and the priory 'havyng consideracion both to the werres and the hygh maleys of thys mischevous heresyys and lollardrie'. No answer was made to this charge: but a firm denial of any illegality met the prior when he complained that the city had pulled down the fences round his mill at St. Mildred's,[4] erected as the result of a judicial award. The citizens protested that they had never assented to any award, and that they were within their rights in demolishing the barriers placed by the prior in the Stour since they had the right of fishing and fowling there. The prior then complained that the citizens had ignored his rights and carted away hay from his meadow near the Wyncheap Gate, from the island of Binnewith (near where the Franciscans made their early settlement) and the Rosery's Mead, or the Rosier, the meadow close to, and on the west side of, the church of Holy Cross.[5] The citizens replied that the Rosier was theirs, not the

---

[1] Ch. Ant. C. 1232.

[2] My thanks are due to the Clarendon Press for the map.

[3] An interesting drawing (1722), showing the remains of the Roman masonry, is in William Stukeley, *Itinerarium Curiosum* (1724), opp. p. 115.

[4] For the topography of this area, cf. the plan in Gordon Ward, 'The Age of St. Mildred's Church, Canterbury', *Arch. Cant.*, liv. 66.

[5] In 1500 it was said to consist of five gardens near Holy Cross, Westgate: *Hist. MSS. Comm., App. to Ninth Rep.*, p. 146.

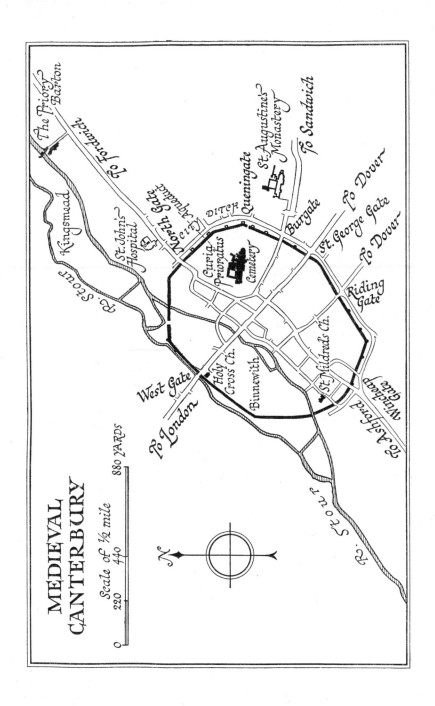

MEDIEVAL CANTERBURY

Scale of ½ mile

0   220   440   880 YARDS

The Priory Barton
To Fordwich
Kingsmead
R. Stour
St. John's Hospital
North Gate
St. Augustines' Monastery
To Sandwich
Queningate
Quenin[gate]
Northgate
DITCH
CITY
Curia Prioratus
Cemetery
Burgate
St. George Gate
To Dover
To Dover
Riding Gate
West Gate
Holy Cross Ch.
Binnewith
St. Mildred's Ch.
To London
Worthgate
To Ashford
R. Stour

prior's—a claim which in spite of the archbishop's award was to last on beyond the settlement of 1492.[1] Apart from the dispute over the Rosier, the citizens were claiming that, in modern terms, they had sporting rights which the riparian owner could not interfere with; but their manner of proceeding suggests that they were suffering under more serious grievances.

The fifth of the citizens' complaints, as they were laid before the archbishop, was that the prior, as the then farmer of Kingsmead, had diverted the Stour to bring the current through his own mill, thereby reducing the acreage of that meadow, and, when he was no longer farmer, had dammed the stream so that flooding took place, presumably at high water. Kingsmead was the meadow to the west of the Barton mill (the priory mill),[2] and the archbishop's directions show that the prior had diverted the channel from east to west. Chichele now ordered that the river should 'be turned and have its right course by St. John's Hospital directly to his (the prior's) mill of Barton Manor', and the obstructions in the stream were to be removed. Kingsmead was to be measured by John Darell (the archbishop's *scutifer*) and Geoffrey Lowther, and the ground lost through the diversion was to be made up out of a carrier called the Malt Ditch. As concerns the Rosier, Chichele adjudged it to the prior and convent, though if conclusive evidence of the citizens' right to it could be produced, there was to be a fresh award. The archbishop also dealt with the claim of the citizens to fishing rights on the Stour both within and without the city wall. Within the wall, he upheld the priory's right on the ground that the monks were entitled to fish from the banks of the land they owned: without, they were to be treated as ordinary citizens participating with the others in whatever rights were enjoyed. A further group of articles complained of various encroachments by the prior within the city: erection of gutters, poyes (pent-houses or pigsties), stalls, stairs, and so forth—without the sanction of the city authorities. Here Chichele decided that when such buildings constituted a nuisance, they were to be 'reformed', i.e. pulled down or altered, by view of certain jurats of the city.

An important, if extremely tiresome, source of complaint on either side was the city ditch which the citizens claimed as their property. The ditch lay immediately outside the wall. From

---

[1] *App. to Ninth Rep.*, p. 148. There was to be a neutral custodian put in (1501).
[2] For the Prior's Barton, cf. R. A. Lendon Smith, 'The Barton and Bartoner of Christ Church, Canterbury', *Arch. Cant.*, lv. 16 f.

Northgate to Burgate on the east the wall bounded the Liberty, and was steadily being rebuilt by the priors at a thickness of some 6½ feet in place of the ancient rampart and its containing wall.[1] The citizens complained that the effluents of the 'Petydortur' and other latrines in the prior's court were draining out through loopholes in the wall and the ditch, to the annoyance and peril of the inhabitants. From the monks' grievances we know that the citizens had filled up the ditch where the nuisance was greatest and had actually built right up to the wall, so that the prior's house and court could now be overlooked.[2] To remedy these insanitary conditions the archbishop gave a drastic and impartial order; the city was to 'scour' the ditch under the wall of the priory from the 'Petydortur' to Queningate, and was to pull down all buildings in the ditch between the former and Northgate; the priory, on its side, was, so soon as the buildings had been removed, to scour the ditch from the 'Petydortur' to the Stour. Eventually, by the agreement of 1492, the monastery got undisputed possession of the wall surrounding the priory on the north and east, as well as the bastion towers.[3]

Lastly came the problem of supplies. The citizens charged the prior's servants with forestalling, i.e. with going to meet the tradesmen bringing food to market, especially fish from Reculver, and buying from them before they reached their stalls. This and another accusation, directed against the prior's catour, of buying food above market price so as to make sure of selling it, were withdrawn in the end, but the main grievance was pressed: it was that the priory bought victuals in gross when there was a local custom that if any fish or article of food arriving in the market exceeded 12*d.* in value it should be divided and sold to any persons wishing to buy. Contrary to this custom, so the citizens asserted, the priory bought before 7 a.m. one morning a large halibut which, when impounded by the bailiffs, was forcibly carried off in a scuffle by the priory servants. The battle of the

[1] Livett, op. cit., p. 106.

[2] 'Also ther as the sayd Priour and Covent shold' have of ry3th and thei and alle her' predecessoures have had be the graunt of Seynt Ethylberd' foundour of the sayd Chyrche in hys fyrst fundacion the use and the possessioun' of the issue goynge owt of the petydortur of the said Chyrche in to the frehold' and the possessioun' of the same dych . . . the Baylyffz and the Cominalte of the sayd Citee in late tyme have streyled' mystornyd' and almost fulli stopped the sayd issue wyth stakes timber houses erthe and dong' and have bilteth houses and layd dong' in the sayd dych so that the peopple my3the clymbe and come on the walle of the sayd Chyrche. . . .' D. and C., Ch. Ant. C. 1232.

[3] *Hist. MSS. Comm., App. to Fifth Rep.*, p. 433.

halibut recalls the dependence of the monks upon regular supplies of fish from the coast. The 'mullets, bass, whelks' for which the catour and his men were waiting (perhaps first in the queue) would not often be seen on the citizens' tables, and at certain seasons were wholly unprocurable. The pathetic lament of John Ryman, the Franciscan poet, recently unearthed by the late Dr. A. G. Little,[1] shows what austerity followed in the train of Advent towards the close of the fifteenth century:

> There was no fresshe fisshe ferre ne nere,
> Salt fisshe and samon was too dere,
> And thus we have had hevy chere.
> > Fare wele, advent, cristemas is cum.
> > Fare wele from us both alle and sume.
>
> Thou hast us fed with plaices thynne,
> Nothing on them but bone and skynne,
> Therfore our love thou shalt not wynne.
> > Fare wele, *etc.*
>
> With muskilles gaping afture the mone
> Thou hast us fedde at nyght and none
> But once a wyke and that to sone.
> > Fare wele, *etc.*

The archbishop's ruling was quite clear. The prior and convent had the right to buy 'all maner of victual at all times' for their use, without restriction. He had been concerned with such domestic considerations before. When in 1419 he was with Henry V in Normandy, Thomas Felde and John Langdon, proctors of the priory, had brought him the necessary evidence substantiating its claim to the annual allowance of wine given by Louis VII in 1179 as a propitiatory offering to St. Thomas.[2] By the terms of the original deeds the convent was allowed to claim 100 *modii* of wine, at vintage-time, at the castle of Poissy, and free passage was to be accorded it, as far as this lay within the 'French king's power'.[3] Although the convent was effusive in its thanks to Chichele for his services 'circa negotia nostra in partibus Francie et Normannie'—and the supply of wine was by no means the only interest here—it seems doubtful whether it —or an equivalent—ever reached Christ Church; since, after Chichele's death, a petition of Prior Goldstone to the king of

[1] 'John Ryman, a Forgotten Kentish Poet', *Arch. Cant.*, liv. 2.
[2] *Litt. Cant.*, iii. 138.
[3] *Hist. MSS. Comm., App. to Fifth Rep.*, p. 460.

France stated that the delivery of the wine had been discontinued for many years owing to the wars. It appears to have been resumed under Prior Sellyng.[1] It has been shown that the wine, being of an inferior quality, usually got no farther than the agent of the convent in Paris, who sold it for cash and bought something of better character to be shipped to Sandwich.[2]

No comment appears to have been given by Chichele upon the final complaint that the priory was 'accroaching' part of the market and the periodical fairs of the city by inducing retailers to set up their stalls within the cemetery for the sale of cloths, woollens, laths, tin, &c., and by allowing persons living within the cemetery gates to open shops. The charge may have been 'left' or dropped, like the complaints against the priory for protecting Bernard the Goldsmith; for refusing to allow the coroner to hold an inquest into the death of John Grove, the monk who fell from the south-west tower in 1425;[3] or for erecting without licence a stone arch over the city ditch to carry the aqueduct in on the north side of the priory. There is only one grumble about jurisdiction, evidently well founded. The prior, it was claimed, was making dwellers in Burgate ward attend his lawdays at Prior's Barton. Here Chichele awarded a compensation payment of 12d. a year to the alderman of Burgate for the loss of suit. The same thing had been done earlier in the case of St. Martin's Ward.

A number of these complaints may seem very small beer: hardly worth bringing in the archbishop to settle. None the less the grievances persisted long after Chichele's day. There was another settlement, when relations were better, in 1492, and a long-term agreement was made. Yet the strife broke out in an aggravated form in 1500, when the 'Mayor's ryot' took place and violence under official leadership was done both to the priory servants and to the monks themselves. The grievances of the priory on this occasion[4] reveal a more sinister and determined hostility to the monks than in 1428. Apart from the charges of battery, robbery, and unlawful imprisonment, two of the monastic articles are specially significant. The mayor (William Atwood) and citizens, 'for such malice and grugge as they owed to the seid priour', had discontinued the old custom of assembling at

[1] *Hist. MSS. Comm., App. to Fifth Rep.*, p. 461.

[2] R. A. L. Smith, op. cit., p. 43, and the references there cited.

[3] *The Chronicle of John Stone, Monk of Christ Church, Canterbury, 1415–1471*, ed. W. G. Searle, p. 12.

[4] D. and C., Ch. Ant. C. 1235.

Christmas at the tomb of Archbishop Sudbury to pray for his soul, and held their orisons instead beneath the Westgate prison; again on St. Thomas's day (29 December) they had deliberately declined to accompany, as they did heretofore, the nobleman who bore the king's offering to the martyr's shrine. To what a pass were things coming when in the fields outside the city the sight of a priest of the almonry 'with a sparrow-hawk upon his fist' so enraged the mayor and his riotous friends that the offender was hailed off to the Westgate! And thus, continues the querimony:

'the seid Maior and his brothern dayly shewe unkyndenesse to the seid monastery sekyng quarelles a yenst theyme and induce the inhabitauntes of the same cite to the same. Whiche unkende demeanour more grevyth the seid priour and his bretherne then the losse of wordely goods. For the said priour seyth he never dyd nor mynded to trouble nor myscontent the seid cite butt to have ther favour and goode wyll and wolde take losse for to wyn ther favour, the inheritaunce of his seide monasterie savyd, which inheritaunce the seide priour ys bounde to maynten and kepe.'

The inheritance had only forty years to run.

APPENDIX

The Complaints of the Mayor and Commonalty followed by the Awards of the Arbitrator, Archbishop Chichele

D. and C. of Cant., Ch. Ant. C. 1232.

[*The first two items are missing.*]

(iii) Also wheras Tenauntes of the Burgh' of Seynt Martynes owten and of ry3th' sholden' come to the lawday to be halden fowr tymes in the yer to fore the alderman of the Warde of Burgate of the Citee of Cantyrbyry and ther to presente allthyng' that langyth to the day of lete and also to come to the Burghmoot of the sayd Citee, als ofte tymes as the comyn horn of the same Citee is blawyn by the somaunce of the Baylyffes of the same Citee for the tyme beynge, of whyche sewtys the same Baylyffys and Citesines hav be alowyd of in Eyr to for Justic' etc. and pesubly possessyd, in to now late tyme that the same Priour hath encrochyd the receauntes[1] dwellyng wytinne the sayd Burgh to come to his lawday holdyn at the Priowrys Berton' and wyth drawe her'sutes that they shulde do to the Citee aforseyd in deseriteson of owr' lorde the Kyng' forsayd and amenusyng[2] of the ferme of hys sayd Citee.

As to thys article my lord of Cantyrbyry awardyth and ordeynyth be assent' of the syd parties that xiid be payd yerly to the aldyrman of Burgate

---

[1] Perhaps for 'residents'?   [2] 'diminishing'.

for all' sutys to lawdayes and burghmotes as hyt hath' be payd of old tyme
be the tenauntes of the sayd burgh of Seynt Martynes.

(iiii) And also wher as the forsayd Citesines hav be sesyd of certeyn
parcell' of ground that lyyth jionyng under the town walle at the Roser,
the whyche grownde is parcell of the syd citie wall and dyche of the same
Citee, and is swared[?] fore and be a dyche severed fro the medys of the
sayd Priour and evere hath bee severed, in to now late that the same Priour
hat maad claym of the same parcelle of ground and lettyth the same
Citesynes that thay ne mowe have the profyt in the same ground as they
hav had to gret grevance and to deseriteson' of owre lyge lorde the kynge
and amenusyng of the ferme of hys sayde Citee.

As to thys article my sayd lord be the assent aforsayd awardyth and
ordeynyth that the sayd Priour and Covent enioye and have pesybly to hem
and to her' successours the forsayd ground atte the forsayd roserys and
encas the sayd Bayliffs and cominalte of the sayd Citee in tyme comynge
shewe sufficient and notable evidence to my sayd lord of Cauntyrbury or
to hys successor of the sayd ground that hyt be aiugged and demyd after
the same title and evidence be my said lord or his successors.

[The above award has been scratched through.]

(v) Also wher[as] a meed clepyd Kingesmeed langynge to the Cite
aforsayd forth wyt a ryver clepyd the Kynges stowr the forsayd Priour hat
holdyn to ferme the same meed of the same citesines for a certeyn summe
yerly be twene hem acordyt thys xii yer and more wythinne whyche time
the forsayd Priour hat turned the forsayd River owt of hys rygth cowrs fro
the on syde of the sayd meed in too the other syde and wyt the cowrs of the
same Ryver the forsayd Priour hat susteynyt a melle of hys owene and so be
that turnynge of the Ryver that same meed hat lost a gret part of hys
ground in the [di]seriteson' of owre lyge lorde the Kynge a[nd] gret
damage to the same Citesines.

Also the forsayd Priour now late dys yer for als so myche as he was no
longyr fermour of the same meed hat maad and reysed a baye[1] of ston and
tymber overtwart in the Kynges heygh ryver of swyche hygthe that the
cowrs of the Kyngestrem is so stoppyd that the sayd meed and other medys
lyynge ther too be ofte tymes over flowen so that the forsayd Kyngesmeed
is lykly in schort tyme to be surunded and of lasse valew fro yer to yer in
deseriteson' of owr lyge lord and amenusynge of hys ferme aforesayd.

As to thys two articles above conteynyd my said lord be the assent
aforsayd awardyth and ordeynyd that the River there be turnyd and have
hys rygth cours be the hospitall of Seynt John directly to the mylle of the
sayd Priour of hys manoure of the Berton wythowte interuption of the
Baylyffes and Cominalte of the sayd Citee or of her' successors and that
the floodyatys of the sayd Baye newe maad be take away.

(vi) Also wher as the sayd Citesynes hav sufferyd the sayd Priour and his

---

[1] 'dam.'

predecessors to have ows and ese of a dyche callyd the malt-dyche whych is parcelle of the forsayd Kyngesmeed by the whyche dych the water of the Kynges hy3gh Ryver is caryed un to the sayd Priowr' melle callyd the maltmylle, for whyche dyche and esement the same Priour and hys predecessowrys hav payd yerlych to the Chambyr of the forsayd Cite xviii d., un to now late thys Priour and hys predecessowres the same ferme hav wytdrawen in disheriteson of the sayd citesines.

As to thys article my sayd lord be the assent aforsayd awardyth and ordeynyth that the Kyngesmeed aforsayd be mete by discrecioun of Jon Darel and Geffrey Lowther, and encas hyt lakke of the number of acres due thertoo takynge concideracion of the weryng of the sayd meed wyth the River, that hyt be denudnyd[1] after the sayd metyng, and as moche as lackyth of the sayd meed be take of the dych icallyd the maltdych.

(vii) Also wher as the ryver wytinne the Franchyse of the forsayd Cite was annexit as parcelle of the Cite at tyme that the forsayd Citesynes haddyn the same Cite to ferme fro whych tyme thay and non other hav had several fysshynge wytinne the sayd Ryver and hav had the profytes ther of letynge the fyssynge in the same ryver to ferme fro yer to yer for xxxiiis. iiiid. and sum yer for xxvi s. viii d., un to xvi yer now late apassed that the sayd Priour by on Laurens Tent[2] hys monk by makynge of barrerys in the sayd Ryver and by grevous manases maad un to the fermours of the fyssynge forsayd so that the sayd Baylyffes and citesynes hav lost the profytes of the forsayd fysshynge by the forsayd tyme in dysheriteson of our sayd lyge lord and amenusynge of the ferme aforsayd.

As to thys article my sayd lord be the assent aforsayd awardyth and ordeynyth that there as the sayd Priour and Covent have lond innynge to bothe sydys of the River above Seynt Mildreedys and in all other placys wyth oute the wallys of the sayd Cyte they have several fysshynge, and ther they have lond innynge on the Ryver on that on sythe wyth oute the wallys of the sayd Cyte they have fysshynge incomyne wyth such persones as owthe of ry3th to have fysshynge there, and as to fysshynge wythynne the walles of the sayd Citee that the sayd Priour and Covent and her' tenauntys be demenyd as other of the sayd Cytee beth after the use and custom of the same Citee.

(viii) Also wher the forsayd Cite is walled and dykyd abowte for strengthe and savacioun of the forsayd Cite by comaundement and ordinaunce of the progenitowres of owre lyge lord the Kynge that now is, the forsayd Priour wyt owtyn warant or lycense of the Kynge or of the Citesynes the dyche of the same Cite hath dystroyed wyt the ordure and felthe of the petydorture and other foreynes of hys place whych been letyn ownt be lowpes[3] in to the same dych atte divers tymes in the monthe, and the pople dwellynge up on the same dyche and others that passe by the wey

---

[1] Probably, as Mr. Blore suggests, for 'demenyd' or 'demanyd', i.e. treated or dealt with.

[2] Laurence of Thanet, d. 1405.   [3] 'loop-holes'.

toward and froward the cite by the evyl sans' and the eyr enfectyt gretly and grevously beth dyssesyd in contempt of owre lyge lord Kynge and gret damage to the Citesines aforsayd.

As to thys article my sayd lord be the assent aforsayd awardyth and ordeynyth that the sayd Baylyffes and Cominalte shall do scoure the dyche of the sayd priorie undyr the walle of the same priorie fro the sayd issue of the petidorture un to Quenyngate and do voyd and put away all the foreynys and byldynge innynge up on the walle of the close of the sayd Priorye and stondynge in the dyche be twene the sayd issue and Northgate and the sayd Priour shall do scure the sayd dyche after the sayd byldynge i[s] putaway in the manere aforsayd fro the issue aforsayd unto the Ryver.

[1]Also how the forsayd Priour hat Arche of stone to bere hys condyt over the dyche of the same Cite in to the forsayd Priorye wyt owte lycence or agrement maad wyt the Kynge other[2] hys citesines of the sayd Cite, the wyche arche in tyme of werre my3the be cause of gret dyssese of the sayd Cite.

As to thys article the sayd Baylyffes and Cominalte leve[3] here complaynt.

(ix) Also wher as the Priorye of Crystyschyrche and alle the Cyte of the same is wyt inne the presaynte of the forsayd Cite and is parcelle of the same Cite and that the coroner of the same Cite shal have the sy3the of that that belanged to the offys of the coroner when hyt fallyt and alle that belanget to hys offys as well in the same Priorie as in any place of the Cite aforsayd and of doynge the sayd offys of coroner wyt inne the same Priorie, the Coronerys of the same Cite have don hyt and noon other as hit is aperyd of record to fore justises en eyr, in to now late what is to say the sonynday next after Crystmasseday the yer of owre lyge lord that now is the vi the fawrthe yer wytinne the same Priorye a monk of that same place be ny3the was slayn as he fyl down of a scaffold so that anon forth wythe he dyde and was byryed wyt owtyn sy3the of coroner and the sayd Priour wolde nowthe suffre the coroner aforsayd to do hys offys in contempt of the Kynge and disheriteson of the said Citesynes.

As to thys article the said Baylyffes of Cantyrbyri leve here complaynt.

[4]Also wheras on Barnard Oswyk goldsmyth fern[5] agoo was arestyd in the forsayd Citee of Cauntyrbyry at sewte of John Yve upon a playnt of trespas up on whyche arest the same Barnard made rescus and ran in to the Chyrche of the same Priorie and there William Billyngstone and Richard Curteler thanne Baylyfys of the same Cite folwynge here sayd prisoner axydyn[6] restitucion of hym as thay hav had aforn thys tyme and of ry3th sholdyn have, and ther the sayd Barnard was kept and the forsayd Priour wolde no3th suffre the sayd Prisoner to make non confession but so kept hym housyd hym and herbeghede hym xl dayes and let hym ascape in

---

[1] A cross stands in the margin against this next item, and no number is assigned to it.

[2] 'or'.

[3] i.e. 'drop'.

[4] This item has crosses in the margin and no number to it.

[5] 'long'.

[6] 'asked'.

contempt of the Kynge and gret grevaunce un to the same Baylyffs and Citesines.

As to this article the sayd Baylyffes and cominalte leve here complaynt.

(x) Also how that the forsayd Priour hat do maad a goter to brynge owt watyr felthe and offall out of a tenement called Sheremannystenement to the dyche of the Kynges Cite of Cantyrbyri forsayd whereby the same dyche is swared and hyndered wyt owten leve of the Kynge or of hys Citesines in hynderynge of the same Citee.

(xi) Also how the forsayd Prior hat don maad upon the Kynges heghe strete a poye to pote swyn therein besyde the tenement of Sherman forsayd in the parysshe of Seynt Paule and anexed to the same tenement wyt owte lycence of the Kynge or the forsayd Citesynes in usurpacion and acroche-ment in contempt of owre lygelord the Kynge and great damage to the forsayd Citesines.

(xii) Also how the forsayd Prior occupieth and menuryt[1] every day and every yer be hys tenauntys at the Bolstake in the Cite the Kyngestallage that is to sayn certeyn poyes wyt owte hys tenauntes up on the Kyngessoyl of whych stallage the bedemen at Herbaldowne have every yer xx mark of the Kyngesalmasse By the handys of the Baylyffes for the tyme and so dys almasse wylnogth be reysyd of the sayd stallage be cause of the said Priores acrochement in disheriteson' of owre lyge lord the Kynge and gret damage of the sayd Citesines.

(xiii) Also how the forsayd Prior hat don maad certeyn steyres an[d] celeres dores at the olde spechous and in the mercerye in Burgate and in mani other place wyth inne the sayd Citee up on the Kynges soyl to nois-aunce etc. in acrochement wyt owt lycence or agrement wyt the Citesines of the sayd Citee in disheriteson of the sayd Citesines.

(xiiii) Also how the forsayd Prior hat don maad up on the kyngessoyl a bothe of tymbyrwerk in manere of alesceller and a porche at hys taverne called the sonne besyde Cristyschyrche-gate[2] whych Byldynge he hat acrochyd and usurped upon the Kynge wytowte licence of the Kynge or agrement wyt the Citesines of the sayd Citee in disheriteson of owre lyge lord the kynge to gret damage of the Citee.

As to these vyve articles next above conteynyd my sayd lord be the assent aforsayd awardyth and ordeynyth that such gotteres poyes stalles peyntiz and steyres in the sayd Citee that standyth to nusaunce be reformyd and seyn be Thomas Stanle, Jon Ley, William Avery, Thomas Usbran sworn to the sayd Citee after the universelle demenynge and custom of the same Citee and such maner thyng as ys be the vewe of surveyowres indyfferently and trwly knowyn for comyn nusaunce to be reformythe or agreyd as the partyes may acorde [and all other such maid thyng' to stande and be demenyth after the generalte of the use and usage of the same Citee whyche of ry3th and old custome hath be had and usyd evere afore thys tyme.][3]

---

[1] 'holds in occupation'. [2] The Sun Inn, in Sun Street.
[3] The words in brackets above are scratched through.

+Also how the servantys of the forsayd Prior on dayes of market awayted vytelerys that bryngen fysshe fro Recolvre and other places and beyn[1] of them the same vytayle that is to sayyn molettys, baas, welkys and other vytayle er hyt come to the comyn market of the Citee and maketh lede hyt in to the place and so forstallyn the Kynges market in contempte and damage of the Citee and of the Comyn pepple.

As to thys article the sayd Baylyffes and cominalte leve here complaynt.

+Also how on William Goodwyne cator of the same Priorie many tymes and ofte wytinne the same Citee on marketdayes usyt in the begyn-nynge of the market to come to the vitelerys that brengyt vytayle and conceyl' yt hym to sylle derrer then dey wolde under dese termes but ye may have so moche therefore that they sholde kepe hyt for hym and so he hegyt[2] de kynges market in contempt of the kynge and gret damage to the kynges pepple and namly to the Kynges Citee.

As to thys article the sayd Baylyffes and cominalte leve her complaynt.

(xv) Also wher hyt hat be usyt fro tyme of no mynde in the same Citee for comyn profyt of the same Cite and of the contre that whenne ony fysshe or othyr vytayle be browt into the market for to sylle yf hyt passe the valew of xii d that hyt shal no3th be soold in groos yf fremen of the same Citee wille have apart ther of and also that hyt shalle no3th be put to the sale to fore the owre of vii atte Clokke up [on] peyne of forfeture of the same vytayle and fyyn of the sellere and now late thys same yer anno V^{to} wher ther came an halybut to market at the exitation of on of the Baylyffes to be solde ther, thys same halibut was sold to the forsayd Prior in gros to fore the owr assygnyt and no3thwytstandynge that fremen of the same Citee wolde have part and therupon the forseyd halybut was arest be officerys of the same Citee for the same cause and ther the servauntys of the same Priorie that is to say Robard Newlond, Thomas Cadbery, John Lardyner, William Goodwyne, Bette Wylmynbone and many other' wyt fors of armys ayens the pees etc. brokyn the Kynges areest forsayd of the same Fysshe and bar hyt to another mannys hous in contempt of the Kynge and gret damage to the sayd Citesines etc.

As to thys article my sayd lord be the assent aforsayd awardyth and ordeynyth that the sayd Prior and Covent and here successors and alle here servauntys have free and playn liberte to bye alle maner of vytaylle in the sayd Citee at alle tymys to the use of the sayd Prior and Covent wyth owte interrupcion or impediment of the sayd Baylyffes and cominalte or of here successors.

(xvi) On ys wheras the forsayd Baylyffys and citesines of Cauntyrbyry holdyn to Feferme the forsayd Cite of owre lyge lord the Kynge wyt alle hys aportenaunces payinge therfor yerly lx li. to the whyche Cite at tyme of the lees amonge alle other commoditees ther were annexyd to the same Cite market be certayn dayes in the wyke and two fayres erlyche at the festes of Whytsontyyd and Michelmasshe wyt alle the profytes and

---

¹ 'buy'.   ² 'limited'.

commoditeis to the same markette and fayres belangynge of whych market and Fayres the sayd baylyffys and Citesines hav be pesably possesit in to the tyme now late goon that thys Prior and hys predecessowrys hav acrochyd un to hem parcelle of the sayd market and fayres wyt inne the Cimiterie of the sayd Priorie and the profyt of the same market and fayres wyt in com-ynge thedyr to be sold, that is to wyte clothe, lynnen and wollen, boord, latthes, yrone and othyr diverse marchandyses takyn and reysen and suf-feren men dwellynge wytinne the yates of the sayd Cimiterye to holde opyn shoppes and diverse marchandyses in desheriteson of oure lyge lord aforsayd and amenusynge of the ferme of the sayd Cite.

E. F. JACOB

AT THE DEATHBED OF CARDINAL BEAUFORT[1]

THE two very different accounts of the last hours of Cardinal Beaufort which have come down to us have one feature at least in common: each claims an eye-witness's authority. Thanks to the melodramatic crudities with which it was embellished by the youthful Shakespeare, the version preserved for us by Edward Hall for long enjoyed the wider vogue. Recent historians, however, following Stubbs, have preferred the more sober account given by the last of the anonymous continuators of the *Croyland Chronicle*, in which Beaufort is described as dying 'with the same business-like dignity in which for so long he had lived and ruled'.[2]

Though it must be admitted that Hall himself was a deeply prejudiced witness and one besides who was not over-critical of the materials at his command, it would, nevertheless, be unwise to dismiss his story as a deliberate fabrication. The temptation to do so would be less were it not for the nonsense in which he has embedded it. For throughout his treatment of Beaufort's policy and character Hall's judgement was disturbed by two powerful influences, his faith in the goodness of Humphrey, duke of Gloucester, and his hatred of Wolsey and the Roman Church. The first led him to accept as truth the whole mass of misrepresentation and abuse with which Gloucester hoped to overwhelm the most successful of his political opponents. The second so violently distorted his vision that he was incapable of keeping the images of the two cardinals for long distinct. As if they had not already enough points of resemblance, Hall frequently transfers to Beaufort the less attractive qualities with which as a strong partisan of the English Reformation he had already endowed Wolsey. As a result the passage in which he sums up Beaufort's life is an indiscriminate medley of phrases drawn some from Gloucester's 'Complaint' and others from his own far from objective 'discripcion' of Henry VIII's minister.[3] But the speech which he puts into the mouth of the dying

---

[1] Thanks are due to Dr. C. T. Onions, Prof. M. D. Knowles, and Mr. L. H. Butler for help on various points in this paper.

[2] W. Stubbs, *Constitutional History of England*, iii (5th ed., 1903), 143.

[3] Compare, for example, the passages on pp. 210–11 and 773–4 of the 1809 edition (by Sir Henry Ellis) of *Hall's Chronicle*.

Beaufort is derived from neither of these sources. Nor is it one of those set orations which he was fond of composing for his principal actors. It is given on the specific authority of 'doctor Ihon Baker his [i.e. Beaufort's] pryuie counsailer, and his chappelleyn'. It would be rash to assume that Hall was content to quote Baker's text verbatim; and, indeed, part at least of the speech is obviously apocryphal. But it would be rasher still to argue that Baker was a mere figment and that Hall had no better evidence than his own imagination. When Hall invents he does not trouble to shed his responsibility on to another.

Who then was John Baker? As an author he was, it seems, unknown to Bale since he does not feature in the *Index Britanniae Scriptorum*.[1] As a chaplain and councillor he is not mentioned in the scattered and incomplete references to Beaufort's presumably large *familia*;[2] he will not be found, for example, among the executors of the cardinal's will;[3] nor by name at least as one of its beneficiaries, though he may have received his share of the 100 marks which were to be divided between the clerks of the testator's chapel.[4] Finally, while it is known that Beaufort, like most of his class, possessed a council, no list of its members has so far come to light.[5] It is impossible therefore at present to connect Hall's informant with the cardinal's service.

To identify anyone with both a surname and Christian name as common as those of John Baker is at first sight to attempt an almost hopeless task. A dozen John Bakers flourished in England about the middle of the fifteenth century, most of them obscurely. Only the fact that our man was a doctor as well as a clerk makes the problem manageable, for it would seem to reduce the possible field of choice to one. This John Baker, who supplicated for the degree of Doctor of Divinity at Oxford on 3 July 1454, was a native of Aldermaston, Berkshire.[6] Since he was admitted a

[1] Ed. R. L. Poole and M. Bateson in *Anecdota Oxoniensia*, Medieval and Modern Series, part ix.

[2] The disappearance of all but the first quarter of Beaufort's register as bishop of Winchester is only one of the obstacles to a complete list of his servants. The Winchester Pipe Rolls, deposited by the Ecclesiastical Commissioners in the Public Record Office, are of little use except for his estate-officials.

[3] *A Collection of Royal Wills*, ed. J. Nichols, p. 331. These include the master of his household, the steward of his temporalities, and his treasurer of Wolvesey.

[4] Ibid., p. 329.

[5] 'The Book of Declaration' of Sir Robert Whittingham as an executor of John, duke of Bedford (Exchequer K.R. Accounts, Wardrobe and Household, E 101/411/7).

[6] T. F. Kirby, *Annals of Winchester College*, p. 210 seq.; *Register of the University of Oxford*, ed. C. W. Boase (Oxford Historical Society), i. 20; M. E. C. Walcott,

scholar of Winchester in 1431 he was probably born about 1420. Proceeding to New College, of which he was elected a fellow on 23 October 1438, he was senior proctor for the year 1448–9.[1] On 2 July 1454 he succeeded his friend and slightly older school-fellow, Thomas Chaundler, as warden of Winchester College. There he remained until his death in February 1487, having added considerably to the lands and buildings of his house. His other preferments seem to have been few, but on 24 March 1481 he was installed as prebendary of All Saints in Lincoln Cathedral.[2] The most interesting thing about him is his membership of that distinguished band of Wykehamist friends commemorated by Chaundler, who as warden of New College was the first serious Oxford humanist, in the *Collocutiones* which between 1463 and 1465 he presented to his patron, Bishop Beckington of Bath and Wells.[3]

It should now be clear that if Hall owed his information to some lost writing of Warden Baker's he was fully justified in making use of it. There is, moreover, nothing improbable in his statement that Baker was the cardinal's privy councillor and chaplain, though the second term is perhaps more credible than the first. Beaufort was after all intimately connected with the two foundations in which almost the whole of Baker's life was spent. In January 1434, not for the first time, he formally visited Winchester College while Baker and his friend Chaundler were among its scholars.[4] Thanks to his many benefactions and watchful interest his anniversary was kept by the grateful society after his death.[5] When that event occurred Baker was a fellow of New College to which the cardinal was perhaps, though not certainly, less attached.[6] But even if he was not one of those present in Wolvesey, he was bound to be informed of the circumstances

---

William of Wykeham and his Colleges, p. 352; A. F. Leach, *A History of Winchester College*, p. 218.

[1] C. W. Boase, op. cit., p. 287.

[2] Le Neve's *Fasti Ecclesiae Anglicanae*, ed. T. D. Hardy, ii. 100. To this should be added the prebend of Wedmore IV in Wells Cathedral which he may have owed to Bishop Beckington (*Cal. MSS. of Dean and Chapter of Wells*, Hist. MSS. Com. ii. 110).

[3] *The Chaundler MSS.*, ed. M. R. James (Roxburghe Club, 1916), p. 55. For Chaundler see *Official Correspondence of Thomas Bekynton*, ed. G. Williams (Rolls Series), i, pp. xlviii–liv, &c.; the article in the first Supplement to the *Dict. of Nat. Biog.*, by A. F. Pollard; and R. Weiss, *Humanism in England*, pp. 133–6.

[4] Walcott, op. cit., pp. 343–4.

[5] Ibid., pp. 206 and 251; Kirby, op. cit., pp. 171 82.

[6] The archives of the college have been even less carefully searched than those of Winchester.

of the Visitor's last illness; all the more so if they were in any way unusual. Could we be sure that it was his report that Hall garbled, we should have the strongest possible ground for believing that the Rich Cardinal spoilt a good death by cries of thwarted ambition and despair.

This might hardly seem to be borne out, though it is not specifically excluded, by the terms in which the scene is described for us by the writer whom it will be convenient to label *Anonymus Croylandensis*.[1] His Chronicle, of which only the first few paragraphs have survived, begins with some refreshingly unorthodox remarks about the *de facto* title of Henry VII. These and the evidence it provides of discontent with the usurper's policy in his first parliament are all the more memorable for not having received the attention they merit from recent writers. It next records the death of Thomas Bourchier and after recalling that of Henry Beaufort takes a perfunctory glance at national affairs before launching out on a detailed description of a local event to which the greater part of what we have is devoted. This was the visit of the diocesan, John Russell, to the monastery in April 1486 to arrange for the appropriation of the church of Bringhurst, co. Leicester, to the abbey of Peterborough. In the middle of this well-documented but somewhat tedious business the narrative breaks off. Apart therefore from the passage which is our present concern its subject-matter is confined to the first year of Henry VII's reign. It is impossible to decide precisely how long after 1486 the chronicler began to write, though his opening sentences imply that the interval was a short one. And unless he incorporated his account of Beaufort's death from an earlier source he can scarcely have been born much later than 1430; for that account ends with the definite statement that 'he who wrote this was present, and both saw and heard these things, "and we know that his testimony is true"'.[2]

His recollections are sufficiently extraordinary to deserve full quotation:[3]

'There occurs to my memory as I write this a notable action, and one worthy of imitation by others, of that glorious and catholic man, the said

---

[1] Printed by W. Fulman in his also anonymous *Rerum Anglicarum Scriptorum Veterum*, tomus i, Oxford, 1684. This is often said to be the work of John Gale, but although Fulman acknowledges Gale's help there is no reason for believing that this was considerable enough to justify our calling him an editor. Most of the copy from which Fulman's edition was printed survives as Corpus Christi College, Oxford, MS. 208.

[2] John xxi. 24.   [3] Fulman, p. 582.

Cardinal of Winchester. When he was languishing at the point of death in his palace of Wolvesey beside his cathedral church of St. Swithun in the said year 1447, on the Saturday before the Sunday of the passion of our Lord, on which day the office *Sitientes* is sung,[1] he caused all the ecclesiastics of the parts adjacent, both regular and secular, to be collected in the great chamber of the same palace. Here he had his solemn exequies with the mass of *Requiem* chanted in his presence as he lay in bed. On the fifth day thereafter[2] the prior of his cathedral church as executor of the whole office celebrated mass in full pontificals.[3] In the evening after the exequies had been performed the testament of his last will was read aloud before all; and early on the morrow of the mass, when he had added certain corrections and codicils, all these testamentary matters were once more recited, and publicly and in an audible voice he confirmed them.[4] And thus he bade farewell to all and died at the time above-mentioned.'[5]

It would be foolhardy for anyone but a liturgiologist to venture to comment on the significance of these unusual ceremonies.[6] That they were remembered and set down in such detail at a distant fenland monastery some forty years later is itself remarkable. It is the greater misfortune that the chronicler has done so little to reveal his identity. The deduction that he was a monk of Croyland, though reasonable, is by no means certain. The space which he devotes to Russell's visit to the abbey on business of purely local interest would suggest it. But if he was, it is curious that he should not know who was the author of the previous Continuation of the Chronicle, especially when it is noted that that extremely valuable section was composed at Croyland during April 1486.[7] It is perhaps easier to account for his presence at Winchester in 1447. For the family of Beaufort had connexions with Croyland Abbey. On the death of Edmund Holland, earl of Kent, in 1408 the neighbouring Wake manor of West Deeping

---

[1] Saturday, 25 Mar. The Introit for that day was 'Sitientes venite ad aquas, dixit Dominus'.

[2] Wednesday, 29 Mar.; and presumably the evening before.

[3] For *executor officii* see W. H. Frere, *The Use of Sarum*, i. 60–1, &c.

[4] I take this to mean that the first reading occurred on Saturday, 25 Mar., and the second on Thursday, 30 Mar.

[5] 11 Apr. (Fulman, p. 581).

[6] For an earlier parallel see the case of Thurston of York (D. Knowles, *Monastic Order in England*, p. 478). Philip Repingdon, bishop of Lincoln (*ob.* 1424), in his will gave orders that his funeral mass should be celebrated in the parish church of St. Margaret in the close at Lincoln if possible while he was dying. See *Register of Henry Chichele*, ed. E. F. Jacob, ii. 285.

[7] Fulman, p. 578. C. L. Kingsford (*English Historical Literature in the Fifteenth Century*, p 181, n. 7) suggests that Peter Curteys may have been the author of the second Continuation, but there are serious objections to this proposal. Kingsford was himself aware of them. The plan of his book precluded him from dealing with the third Continuation.

had been brought by his sister and co-heir Margaret to her
husband John Beaufort, the cardinal's elder brother.[1] The
relations of the abbey with the lords of Deeping were rarely
cordial and never worse than in the 1430s.[2] But with the death
of John, the first duke of Somerset, in 1444 they entered on a
peaceful and happy period. The duke's widow Margaret, as the
prior gratefully records, 'had always shown herself gracious and
well-disposed towards our monastery' and in 1465 she and her
daughter, a more famous Lady Margaret, were together admitted
to the confraternity.[3] Apart from this, Cardinal Beaufort was the
son of Croyland's most powerful protector in Richard II's reign[4]
and had himself in his youth been bishop of Lincoln.[5] His death
is recorded in the 'First Continuation' with many laudatory
epithets and it would not therefore be altogether surprising if the
abbey had sent one of its monks to visit him in his last illness.[6]
It may even have been the conversation of John Russell, in 1447
a scholar of Winchester, which during April 1486 recalled to the
ageing chronicler this impressive memory of his youth.[7]

Time had certainly dimmed the accuracy of his recollections
in spite of their apparent precision. This is shown by the dating
of Beaufort's extant will and its codicils.[8] According to the
chronicler the will was read first on 25 March 1447 and then
again, after the codicils had been added, on 30 March. Since the
body of the will is dated Wolvesey, 20 January 1447, there is
nothing improbable about the earlier of these ceremonies. But
the codicils (there are two of them) are dated 7 and 9 April
respectively. As will be seen presently the second modifies the
first in an important respect and therefore it is unlikely that
drafts of both were read on 30 March. We are forced to conclude
that at least as far as the chronology goes our eye-witness is in
error, though this need not detract from the general truth of his
account. It would after all have been much more extraordinary

---

[1] G. E. C., *Complete Peerage*, vii. 159–63; Fulman, p. 499.

[2] Ibid., pp. 518–19.   [3] Ibid., pp. 539–40.   [4] Ibid.

[5] The abbey had also suffered from the ascendancy of Beaufort's opponent
Gloucester in 1432–3 (ibid., p. 517). It received no bequest under the cardinal's
will.

[6] The fact that the steward of Beaufort's temporalities, William Whaplode, bore
the name of a village near Croyland, strengthens the possibility of the connexion.
Whaplode seems to have settled at Chalfont St. Peter, Bucks. (*V.C.H. Bucks.* iii.
187 and 196–7).

[7] For Russell see Kirby, op. cit., p. 195 and *Dict. Nat. Biog., s. n.*

[8] Printed from the Canterbury Registers in Nichols, op. cit., p. 321 seq. There
is a summary in N. H. Nicolas, *Testamenta Vetusta*, i. 249–55.

if he had remembered exactly what happened without mistake after so long an interval. But the result of his proved inaccuracy is to leave us at liberty to believe as much or as little as we please. Perhaps it was an intuitive realization of this which caused Stubbs to telescope events that are said to have occupied eighteen days into the final two.[1] All that we can conclude is that to one observer, though not necessarily a very close one, Beaufort's last weeks were nicely divided between concern for the repose of his soul and the disposition of his worldly goods. The business-like element in his last public appearance has at least that much support; the dignity can only be inferred.

The truth is that we can never hope to see into the mind of the dying cardinal through the eyes of such doubtful and conflict-ing witnesses as Dr. John Baker and *Anonymus Croylandensis*. Whether we prefer one to the other will depend upon our pre-vious reading of that dark problem, Henry Beaufort's character. Upon the solution of that problem much hangs and it is only just that every clue should be considered, even the denunciations of his most implacable critic, Gloucester.[2] 'For fifty years', wrote Stubbs with but slight exaggeration, 'he had held the strings of English policy.'[3] An understanding of his aims and motives is quite essential to our reading of the political history of at least half that period, the quarter-century since Henry VI's accession. In any state in which kingship implies personal rule, a long minority must always put a heavy strain both on the institutions themselves and still more on those who have a duty to make them work. Henry VI's ministers had the added burden of conducting a great half-finished war of conquest in France. Prolonged almost indefinitely by the king's lack of will, his nonage was a challenge to the statesmanship and self-restraint of the governing classes as testing as it was abnormal. Even had Beau-fort wished it, his birth, prestige, wealth, and experience would have made it impossible for him to avoid a large share of responsi-bility. And yet his contribution to the outcome, which was defeat in France and ruinous civil war at home, is hidden from us in the dust of controversies not yet entirely dead. How far did he subordinate the good of the realm, as his enemies alleged, to the satisfaction of his own greed and ambition? The answer is

---

[1] Op. cit. iii. 143. He is faithfully followed by L. B. Radford, *Henry Beaufort*, pp. 289–90. W. Hunt (*Dict. Nat. Biog., s. n.*) tells much the same story.
[2] The duke has received even less attention than Beaufort.
[3] Op. cit. iii. 143.

still doubtful. In spite of the evidence, plentifully scattered throughout the records, of his all-pervasive influence in these years, it is, nevertheless, far from clear what manner of man he was. His few surviving letters offer the barest of hints and are usually on purpose non-committal. He so rarely speaks to us with his own voice that when he does his words deserve the closest scrutiny. It is, therefore, strange that one such utterance has not received more minute attention: that will which he was so anxiously ruminating as he lay *in extremis* and to which he added several fresh paragraphs on the two days, Good Friday and Easter Sunday, when he might pardonably have been thinking of other things. In view of the charges with which he stands accused it is pertinent to ask whether the two codicils and the will itself contain any evidence of uneasiness or remorse.

Among the provisions for masses, the numerous charitable bequests and the legacies to kin and servants with which all three documents abound, one theme recurs, namely, the disposal of certain jewels formerly the property of the king.[1] These, the testator twice affirms, had been pledged to him 'by my lord the king and his officials acting in this matter by his authority and that of his parliament' in the year 2 Henry VI in return for a loan and had been lawfully retained by him when the treasurer had failed to content him on the dates agreed. It may be worth seeing whither this scent leads us. The loan can easily be identified as that of 1 March 1424, the first of the new reign. But before its details are investigated something needs to be said about Beaufort's previous financial dealings with the government during the early years of Gloucester's nominal Protectorate.

When Henry V died he owed his uncle the balance of the two great loans of 12 June 1417 and 13 May 1421.[2] This amounted on 31 August 1422 to £20,149. 0s. 5d.[3] By the settlement of 19 May 1421, which merely expanded the provisions of that of 18 July 1417 to cover the recent new loan, the bishop held what was usually described as a 'long commission' of the port of Southampton and its subsidiary havens.[4] The terms of this grant were the

---

[1] Nichols, op. cit., pp. 329, 334–5, and 338.

[2] For these see *Eng. Hist. Rev.* lx (1945), 345–8.

[3] Of the £25,973. 11s. 8d. owed on 13 May 1421, £1,058. 19s. 4½d. had been cancelled against the arrears of the bishop's clerical tenths, £1,666. 13s. 4d. had been repaid from the customs of London, and £3,098. 18s. 10½d. from the receipts of Southampton (Exchr. of Receipt, Receipt Rolls, E 401/696, 699, and 702; Issue Rolls, E 403/652 and 655).

[4] *Calendar of Patent Rolls, 1416–1422*, 122 and 372; *Rotuli Parliamentorum*, iv. 111–13 and 132–5; Exchr. K. R. Memoranda Roll 1 Henry VI, E 159/199,

model for many of his later concessions and are therefore important. They empowered him to appoint one of the two customers and to enjoy all the profits of the port from customs, subsidies, and tonnage and poundage, exclusive of any assignments made, and annuities granted, from them before 18 July 1417, until such time as he should be fully repaid. Meanwhile, the great crown of England was to remain in his hands as security. Neither the king's death nor the bishop's was to impair the validity of this grant. Finally, as an additional safeguard, it was provided that

'if it should happen that by reason of war, or ordinance or any other contingent cause whatsoever, the course or exercise of merchandise in the aforesaid port should have ceased, or that merchants seeking access to the aforesaid port should have been hindered or disturbed to the detriment of the customs and subsidies in the same port',

then the bishop should have the right to make good his losses by taking over, on the same terms as he had been granted Southampton, the port of London 'or any other port or ports whatsoever'. Although apparently he or his nominees were to be sole judges of the necessity for putting the dormant provisions of this clause into effect, there can be little doubt that it was never intended to receive the wide interpretation which he was to place on it soon after Henry V's death.

The occasion arose in the first parliament of the new reign. On 9 November 1422 the Commons, while subjecting alien merchants to taxation at the old rates, considerably lightened the burden for natives; these were to pay customs and subsidy on wool at the reduced rate of 40s. the sack (instead of 50s.) and were exempted from tonnage and poundage altogether. These grants were made on condition that no part of their yield should be spent on any 'other use but only in and for the defence of the ... realm'.[1] It therefore became necessary for the law officers of the Crown to declare in council that, since Beaufort's loans had been made to help finance the war, this act of parliament did not invalidate his patent.[2] It had, however, unquestionably retarded the speed at which he could hope to obtain repayment. Taking advantage of this, he immediately invoked his right to assume control of other ports and on 17 November began to nominate his own customers.[3]

Commissiones, Mich., Ebor, m. 1. His customer was John Foxholes (Exchr. K. R., Customs Accounts, E 122/140/15).

[1] *Rot. Parl.* iv. 173–4. The new rates dated from 1 Sept. 1422.
[2] *Proceedings and Ordinances of the Privy Council*, ed. N. H. Nicolas, iii. 34–5.
[3] *Calendar of Fine Rolls*, xv. 18–19 and 22–3. He seems to have indented with his nominees for their services. Richard Ulverston, his collector at Hull, appointed

Although the Exchequer acquiesced, the legality of his action may have been challenged; for on 15 February 1423, a week after a further list of nominations, his claim to appoint one customer in every English port was formally recognized by the king's council, of which he was the second most important member.[1] Thenceforward the whole of the government's steadiest source of revenue was diverted to his use. Before the end of the year he had received more than £11,000,[2] though it was not until 21 May 1425 that the whole of Henry V's debt was paid off.[3]

The inevitable result was to force the council to resort to fresh borrowing. Parliament had granted no direct taxation since December 1421; the clergy refused to be more generous until in the summer of 1425 they reluctantly consented to vote half a tenth;[4] the hereditary revenues of the Crown produced a negligible fraction of its expenditure;[5] and the one really valuable group of indirect taxes upon the yield of which the government was normally dependent was pledged indefinitely to a single creditor. He, it is true, was willing to make new loans as the old were repaid, but only on terms that would extend still further the period during which he was virtually farming the customs. The patent of May 1421, as it was interpreted after Henry V's death, had in short given Beaufort the beginnings of a stranglehold over the royal finances which might easily have become permanent. It was only broken by the settlement which followed his armed conflict with Gloucester in October 1425 and which involved his withdrawal from England for service at the Roman Curia. Between 1 March 1424 and 21 May in the next year he lent the Exchequer rather more than £18,000.[6] By this means he retained

on 17 Nov., on 18 Dec. exhibited his indenture, dated 8 Dec., to the barons of the Exchequer (Exchr. K.R. Mem. Roll 1 Henry VI, E 159/199 Commissiones, Mich., Ebor., m. 1). He had already on 8 Dec. paid over £200 to Beaufort's representative (E 401/703; E 403/658 under 21 Dec.).

[1] *Proceedings*, iii. 35. On the following day, Beaufort being present, the council reduced the subsidy and customs on wool for aliens from 63s. 4d. to 53s. 4d. notwithstanding the decision of parliament. A year later on 28 Feb. 1424 the Commons, when renewing their earlier grant, accepted the council's amendment (*Rot. Parl.* iv. 200–1).

[2] By 15 Dec. 1423 he had received £11,302. 9s. 2d. (E 401/696; E 403/658, 660, and 663).

[3] Ibid. and also E 401/677 and 711; E 403/666, 669, and 671. The delay shows the extent to which this form of revenue had been previously assigned in advance to other creditors and annuitants.

[4] *Reg. Chichele*, iii. 91–8 and 103–17.

[5] How little can be seen from Treasurer Cromwell's 'budget' of 1433 (*Rot. Parl.* iv. 433–5).

[6] £9,333. 6s. 8d. on 1 Mar. 1424; £1,000 in obligations on 13 Dec.; £4,000 on

his 'long commission' of all the ports until, having ceased to lend, he allowed it to expire when repayment was completed on 18 April 1426.[1] If, as seems more than likely, he enjoyed a concealed reward from all these loans, there is no need to look for reasons other than financial for his willingness to lend.[2] Starting with little beyond the temporalities of his see, he had by 1424 made his name a byword for great wealth.[3] In the 'long commission' which enabled him to lend the king the proceeds of the one regular national tax as it was collected, he had found a method of multiplying his capital at compound interest as safe for him as it was ruinous for his debtor. On the other hand, he cannot have been blind to the advantage his financial hold gave him in the councils of the minority. His loans reinforced his political influence and this in its turn improved his position as a creditor. Only an appeal to force could shake his ascendancy.

The one loan in these years which was not repaid, though all the others were to the last penny, was that of £4,000 advanced on 1 March 1424.[4] It is the one to which his will refers. Preparations were being pushed forward that spring for an early offensive in France, and in June Lords Willoughby and Poynings were sent across the Channel with a small force in time to take part in the campaign of Verneuil.[5] During February, in anticipation of this, the council was empowered by parliament to negotiate a loan of 20,000 marks on the security of 'the customs and subsidies and all other profits, commodities and revenues of the king . . . and of the goods, jewels, and chattels of the crown', between then and the following Michaelmas. Beaufort had probably already consented to subscribe, for his name alone was mentioned among those with whom the council were to treat.[6] By 26 February,

22 Mar.; £3,933. 6s. 8d. on 21 May; total: £18, 266. 13s. 4d. (E 401/707, 710, 711, 712, and 713).

[1] *Cal. Pat. Rolls, 1422–1429*, pp. 293–4, where the total was wrongly given as £11,032. 16s. 1d. instead of £9,933. 6s. 8d.; the mistake was afterwards corrected in the Exchequer; *Rot. Parl.* iv. 278–80; Exch. Issue Rolls, E 403–671, 673, and 675. Beaufort did not return the great crown until 26 Feb. 1427 (*Proceedings*, iii. 250). For details of the security offered see ibid., pp. 199–200 and *Rot. Parl.* iv. 275.

[2] For a discussion of this problem see *Cambridge Historical Journal*, ix (1947), 51–68.

[3] In this year Sir John Mortimer was hanged as a traitor after being accused, among other things, of wishing to strike off Beaufort's head for he 'would play with his money' (*Chronicles of London*, ed. C. L. Kingsford, p. 283).

[4] On the same day he also lent 8,000 marks, making a total of £9,333. 6s. 8d. or 14,000 marks.

[5] *Proceedings*, iii. 135; J. de Waurin, *Recueil des croniques et anchiennes istories de la Grant Bretaigne, 1422–1431*, ed. W. Hardy (Rolls Series), p. 94; E 403/666; *Issues of the Exchequer*, ed. F. Devon, 387, &c.   [6] *Rot. Parl.* iv. 210–11.

at any rate, his contribution had been fixed at 14,000 marks, and in return the council had agreed to repay 8,000 by immediate assignment on the customs and to hand over crown jewels as security for the remainder. If the latter were not forthcoming, half at Christmas 1424, half at Easter 1425, the pledges were to be forfeit. At the same time the treasurer was commanded to indent with the bishop about the jewels, allowing him a right of sale if the terms of repayment fell through in any particular, and the chancery was instructed to prepare the necessary letters patent.[1] On 28 February a privy-seal warrant read to the council substituted midsummer 1425 for Easter as the final date of settlement.[2] On 1 March the loan was entered on the Receipt Roll,[3] and it appears that parliament that day ratified the whole agreement.[4]

The most unusual feature of this transaction was the council's order to the treasurer to agree with Beaufort on the value of the jewels to be pledged, 'notwithstanding that the said jewels have formerly been priced at a greater price than that at which our said cousin shall perhaps wish to receive them'.[5] If this was not intended as a direct encouragement to Beaufort to place the lowest possible valuation on them that the treasurer would accept, the wording was unfortunate. But that does not prove that he took full advantage of the permission given him. One observer with a long memory and an accumulated sense of grievance was perhaps going beyond the evidence when sixteen years later he raked up everything he could remember about the cardinal's past in order to discredit him. According to Gloucester's Complaint, presented to Henry VI in 1440:

'in the tender age of you, my right doubted lord, for the necessity of an army the said Cardinal lent you four thousand pounds upon certain jewels priced till two and twenty thousand marks, with a letter of sale an they were not quit at a certain day ye should lose them. The said Cardinal, seeing your said money ready to have quit with the said jewels, caused the Treasurer of England that time being to pay the same money for part of another army, in defrauding you, my right doubted lord, of your said jewels, keeping them yet still to his own use, to your great loss and his singular profit and avail.'[6]

---

[1] *Proceedings*, iii. 144.　　　　　　　　　　　　　[2] Ibid., iii. 146.
[3] E 401/707.
[4] The patent (*Cal. Patent Rolls, 1422–1429*, p. 214) is warranted 'by King and Council in Parliament' but it does not appear on the Parliament Roll. See also *infra*, p. 417.
[5] *Proceedings*, iii. 146.
[6] *Wars of the English in France*, ed. J. Stevenson (Rolls Series), ii. ii. 443.

It is not usual to attach much importance to the duke's rancorous diatribe, but to dismiss it as 'sufficient by itself to establish the writer's incapacity for government'.[1] Yet here for once is a specific point on which its accuracy can be tested.

To do this it is first necessary to examine Beaufort's detailed agreement with Treasurer Stafford. That half of the indenture which formerly bore his seal is still preserved among the archives of the Exchequer, presumably because it was never cancelled.[2] This document, which is partly in English and partly in French, is by ill fortune badly perished, but although a satisfactory transcript is impossible, its more important contents can even now be deciphered. It is dated 6 March 1424 and states that the treasurer and chamberlains,

'by authority of parliament as well as by special warrant sent unto them by the advice and assent of the council of our said sovereign lord, have engaged the jewels and goods underwritten parcelly to the value and price as it sueth after in money'.

The list is headed by a gold collar of which 'the half is engaged to the said bishop . . . in parcel of the said bishop's agreement to the value of £1,000 and that other half left with him of trust', and contains a number of other easily identifiable jewels, described in attractive detail.[3] It can be supplemented by a memorandum kept in the Exchequer of a portion of the total which was actually handed over to the bishop three days earlier.[4]

That Beaufort should have been allowed to hold a jewel which even he admitted was worth at least £2,000 as cover for only half that sum is perhaps the first obviously suspicious feature of this transaction. If the whole collar had been pledged to him it would have been only necessary to give him jewels worth another £2,000 to have made up the full security for his loan. As it was the estimated total value of his pledges was by this arrangement raised to £5,000. But there is good reason for believing that the collar was worth much more than he was prepared to admit. For in the very parliament in which the terms of his loan were ratified

---

[1] Stubbs, op. cit. iii. 129.

[2] Exchr. K.R. Treasury of the Exchr., E 101/335/15/1.

[3] The following are the most valuable: the Tablet of Lancaster (1,000 marks), the Tablet of Bourbon (£280), the Tablet of the Salutation (£210), the Sword of Spain (£200), a gold ouch of the Garter (£160), a Tablet of St. George and the Dragon and an Image of St. Michael (together £120). The amounts in brackets are those for which they were pledged

[4] *The Antient Kalendars and Inventories of the Treasury of His Majesty's Exchequer*, ed. F. Palgrave, ii. 117–20.

it was officially priced by the treasurer at £5,162. 13s. 4d.[1] What
is more, half of it had recently been pawned to a group of London
merchants, headed by the alderman and skinner Henry Barton,
for £2,581. 6s. 8d. and redeemed at that price in order that
Beaufort might have it.[2] Finally it and a number of the other
jewels were accepted by Beaufort himself on other occasions at
a considerably higher valuation than he consented to in 1424.[3]
Gloucester may have exaggerated the size of his enemy's profit,
but even that is questionable on the surviving evidence. There
can be scarcely any doubt that Beaufort stood to gain very
considerably indeed by the failure of the government to honour
its bond within the time allowed. And it is difficult to acquit
him of intentionally under-estimating his pledges with this in
mind.

The question how far he contrived to arrange that the Exchequer should default is not answerable with the same degree of
certainty. But the circumstantial evidence against him is black.
This is the one loan in all his long career as the crown's financier
that was not repaid. Most of the others were accepted as a first
charge on the revenues and as promptly dealt with as the stringency of his conditions required. When there was any danger of
his foreclosing or of taking advantage of a letter of sale, he was
persuaded to agree to a postponement.[4] He did not make any
such concession in 1424-5. Yet he was in a position to know
how difficult it was for the government to pay, for he was at that
time its head. He had returned to the Chancery on 16 July 1424[5]
and during Gloucester's absence from England (16 October 1424
to 12 April 1425[6]) he was granted a substantial increase of salary
as chief councillor.[7] When, therefore, the first half of his loan fell
due for repayment at Christmas 1424, he was by virtue of his
offices in the strongest possible position to make his wishes felt
at the Exchequer. On the other hand there is no explicit statement anywhere in the surviving minutes of the council to bear out

---

[1] *Rot. Parl.* iv. 214.   [2] E 403/666, 8 June 1424.
[3] The collar for £2,800, the ouch of the Garter for £200, and the Sword of
Spain for 500 marks (*Ancient Kalendars*, ii. 142-3 and 182-3, and an indenture of
7 June 1434 in B.M. Cotton, Cleop. F. vi, ff. 336-7).
[4] *Proceedings*, v. 16 and 115. It is fair to add that these concessions were almost
certainly at a price.
[5] *Cal. Close Rolls, Henry VI*, i. 154.
[6] *Wars of the English in France*, II. ii. 397. He was officially absent from Michaelmas 1424 to 12 Apr. 1425, during which period he received no salary as Protector
(E 403/707, 17 Feb. 1433).
[7] At the rate of 2,000 marks per annum (*Proceedings*, iii. 165).

Gloucester's assertion that he persuaded the treasurer to spend the money intended for his satisfaction on another army.[1] In any case it is hardly likely that there would be. A decision, however, was taken at a meeting at which Beaufort was present on 28 November for the payment of the troops in the East March against the Scots that could be made to answer Gloucester's vague description.[2] It involved Beaufort's surrender to the treasurer on 13 December of an obligation for £1,000 which he held against the earl of Northumberland and an assignment of just over £3,000 to the latter on 17 February 1425.[3] Since this assignment was on the customs it was contrary to the terms of Beaufort's long commission and could only have been made with his consent and to his disadvantage. Such a decision, taken under his presidency though with the connivance of the rest of the councillors, may well have prevented the redemption of the crown jewels at Christmas.

If the king's chief minister and uncle took advantage of the minority to rob him, it is understandable that the integrity of others was not proof against temptation. But few had Beaufort's opportunities and none his tight grip upon the royal finances. Even so the most effective checks upon such conscienceless self-seeking were the mutual jealousies of those in power. Beaufort's own immunity from criticism did not survive the return of Gloucester. He was driven from office on 14 March 1426,[4] and with him went his colleague, John Stafford, the treasurer,[5] as part of the compromise negotiated by Bedford and the other lords in the Parliament of Bats. His past conduct was to escape scrutiny and his Roman ambitions were to be encouraged in return for his disappearance from English politics, presumably for ever.

But for one small piece of evidence it would be reasonable to suppose that the matter of the crown jewels was overlooked by Gloucester in this crisis. Unlike the complaint of 1440, the duke's charges against Beaufort in 1426 do not refer to finance.[6] According, however, to an entry on the Issue Roll, dated 10 May

---

[1] Ibid. iii. 160–5. Exchr., Treasury of Receipt, Council and Privy Seal, E 28/46.
[2] *Proceedings*, iii. 162–3.
[3] E 401/710; E 403/669.
[4] *Cal. Close Rolls, Henry VI*, i. 269. 14 May in *Cambridge Medieval History*, viii. 391, is a misprint.
[5] Walter Hungerford was already treasurer on 16 Mar. 1426 (ibid.); the date given by the *Handbook of British Chronology*, ed. F. M. Powicke, p. 84, is wrong.
[6] The best text of these charges and of Beaufort's replies is printed by C. L. Kingsford in his *Chronicles of London*, pp. 76–94.

1430, a *breve generale de magno sigillo* ordering the tardy return of the loan of £4,000 was then found filed among the warrants of Easter term 1426.[1] This suggests that at the time of the Parliament of Bats an attempt was made to undo the damage of the period of Gloucester's absence. If so it was at least for the moment ineffective. The position had greatly changed in the spring of 1430. Beaufort was now on the defensive. His Roman plans had gone awry and though he had succeeded in repulsing several attacks by Gloucester he was still exposed to a charge under the Statute of Praemunire. When, therefore, the boy king was being fitted out for his journey to be crowned in Paris, the cardinal was persuaded to disgorge the finest of his spoils, the Rich Collar itself, for less even than he had given for it. On 10 May 1430 his treasurer, John Burton, clerk, received £908. 2s. 1½d. for its return.[2] It was probably at about this time that the Sword of Spain and the ouch of the Garter were also surrendered. The former seems to have been in the king's possession at the date of his French coronation,[3] and both, together with the Rich Collar, were pledged to Beaufort as security for a new loan on 20 June 1434.[4] On the other hand there is no evidence of any payment for their return.[5] It is likely that they, and perhaps some of the much less valuable pieces, were exchanged for a Tablet of St. George, bought by Henry VI for 2,000 marks from Sir William Estfield, which was later counted as part of the 1424 deposit.[6] It is otherwise difficult to explain how this tablet found its way into the cardinal's hands. It was to stay there, along with the remainder of the crown jewels, until his death.

Meanwhile Henry VI was growing up and beginning to take a personal share in the government of the kingdom. He had a right, if he was so inclined, to call upon those responsible for the administration during his minority to render an account of their stewardship. It was probably the thought of this which inspired Beaufort in 1437 to obtain a general pardon from the consequences

---

[1] E 403/694.   [2] Ibid.
[3] Exchr. K.R. Treasury of the Exchr., E 101/335/15/2. It and other jewels were Beaufort's security for a loan of £593. 6s. 8d. made to Sir John Tyrell, the king's treasurer of war, in France between 21 May 1431 and 1 Mar. 1432 (E 403/703, 19 July 1432; *Foedera*, x. 502).   [4] *Antient Kalendars*, ii. 142–6.
[5] If this took place in France it might not be recorded on the Issue Rolls of the English Exchequer. A marginal note in *Antient Kalendars*, ii. 117, suggests that only the Rich Collar was paid for.
[6] See *infra*, p. 428. For Sir William Estfield (*ob.* 1446) see J. C. Wedgwood, *History of Parliament, Biographies of the Members of the Commons House, 1439–1509*, p. 304.

of all his past transgressions and offences. Nothing was more likely than that Gloucester would become a tale-bearer. Now there was no necessary common form for general pardons, and that granted to the cardinal on 26 June 1437,[1] though following the customary lines, had one unusual clause tacked on at the end. The king was made to pardon and quitclaim to his uncle

'also all our jewels and those of our said father which have been delivered to the same bishop as security for wages of war or otherwise in our name or in that of our same father, and also all our right which we have in the same or in any parcel of them'.[2]

Beaufort's legal position, already strong, was thereby rendered impregnable. There remained his conscience.

This showed no signs of premature activity. When he made his will on 20 January 1447 he contented himself with bequeathing to Henry VI the Tablet of Bourbon and a goblet with a ewer 'from which goblet, made from the gold offered by him on Good Friday, the illustrious prince of worshipful memory his [Henry VI's] father was commonly wont to drink'. This legacy was accompanied by a humble request that the king would assist the testator's executors in everything tending to his salvation, 'as I was, God knows, ever faithful to him, desirous for the prosperity of his estate and wishfully eager for whatever could concern his safety in soul and body'.[3] The Tablet of Bourbon, it will be remembered, was in the 1424 indenture priced at £280; Henry V's goblet and ewer seem to have been there too but cannot now be identified.[4] Nothing was said at this time about the rest of the crown jewels.

Eleven weeks of further thought went to produce the first codicil sealed with Beaufort's signet on Good Friday. In this Henry VI received a fresh bequest: 'I leave to my lord the king my gold dish or plate for spices and my gold goblet enamelled all over with figures (*cum ymaginibus*) together with a ewer of the same work belonging to the said goblet.' This is immediately

---

[1] *Foedera*, &c., ed. T. Rymer, x. 670–1. Compare that of 2 Mar. 1443 (ibid. xi. 20–1).

[2] Ibid. x. 671. This clause was discussed in the council ten days before (*Proceedings*, v. 33–4). The proviso then introduced I take to refer to the jewels pledged for a loan of 4,000 marks made on 15 Feb. 1436 (E 401/744; Exchr. Treasury of Receipt, Council and Privy Seal, E 28/56, 20 Feb. 1436), the settlement of which Beaufort had consented to postpone on 18 Apr. 1437 (*Proceedings*, v. 16). There was an obvious danger that otherwise the pardon might release him from the obligation to return these jewels too.

[3] *Royal Wills*, p. 329.

[4] This appears from a statement in the codicil of 7 Apr. (ibid., p. 335).

followed by an order to his executors to offer to the king at the price he had given for them all the jewels and plate pledged in 1424, 'notwithstanding that by the non-observance of the said condition on the part of the lord king and by the non-payment of the said sums they are mine by the best right'. A year was to be allowed for this offer to be taken up; if it was declined the jewels were then to be sold along with the cardinal's other chattels and the proceeds spent for the good of his soul.[1]

Even this did not satisfy him, for two days later in the second codicil he returned once more to the subject. Not only was the time-limit now omitted, but the executors were to apply the greater part of the money repaid by the king to pious uses likely to be particularly pleasing to Henry VI. Eton and King's Colleges were to receive £1,000 each. And once more the dying Beaufort insisted that the jewels were his to do with what he willed.[2]

Henry was slow to exercise his option. It was not until 22 August 1449 that the more interesting and costly of the jewels were deposited with the treasurer in return for a payment of £2,043. 8s. 9d.[3] Nothing was done about the unimportant residue, mostly silver-gilt; if it had not already been dispersed, the task of disentangling it from the cardinal's own immense collection of plate[4] may well have been found too troublesome. One contemporary, the unreliable hagiographer John Blackman, has preserved for us what must be a badly distorted account of Henry VI's dealings with the executors.[5] In this the king is made to refuse their offer of £2,000 for the relief of the kingdom's burdens with the words: 'He was a very dear uncle to me and most liberal in his lifetime; the Lord reward him. Do ye with his goods as ye are bound: we will have none of them.' He then at the entreaty of the executors consented to accept the money on behalf of his two colleges. The will itself disproves this story. Few would in any case attach much value to Henry's judgement of character;[6] but in this instance there is no reason for believing that it was ever uttered.[7]

---

[1] Ibid., pp. 334-5.
[2] Ibid., pp. 338-9.
[3] For the indenture of receipt see *infra*, pp. 427-8. See also *Antient Kalendars*, ii. 201-2 and *Proceedings*, vi. 86-7.
[4] Some notion of what this amounted to in Feb. 1432 can be derived from Exchr. K.R. Memoranda Roll, E 159/208 (10 Henry VI), Communia Recorda, Easter Term, m. 2 seq.
[5] *John Blacman's Henry the Sixth*, ed. M. R. James, pp. 10 and 32.
[6] But see Stubbs, op. cit. iii. 143.
[7] Henry did not refuse a *loan* of £2,000 in 1452 from the executors (*Cal. Patent Rolls, 1446-1452*, p. 561).

This minute examination of the history of but one of the many matters which are known to have been occupying the thoughts of Cardinal Beaufort on his deathbed will, it is hoped, have shown that he had grounds for uneasiness. The will itself bears witness to the extent to which it preyed on his mind with increasing force as his end approached. Even the repeated emphasis with which he alludes to his lawful title to the jewels betrays his consciousness of the need for self-justification. He maintained this firm attitude as far as we know to the last. If, after a struggle, he brought himself to make amends it was done in the clearest possible terms as an act of grace; it had not been in the bond.

It is not so very surprising that this exigent moneylender was believed to have tried to drive a hard bargain with death. When, however, he came to part with his money for the last time, the investment was made on poor security. It is unfortunately impossible to make an accurate estimate of his total wealth, but a rough idea of its magnitude may be guessed at from various hints. Thus in February 1433 when he obtained a licence to export £20,000 in money, jewels, and plate to the Council of Basle,[1] he departed leaving rather more than that sum in the king's hands.[2] The total certainly did not decrease with time.

For some years before his death he had become a landowner apart from his temporalities. His most important land purchase was made on 25 May 1439, when a bargain was struck with the king in the presence of the latter's councillors at Cold Kennington in Middlesex.[3] In return for the sum of £8,900 Henry VI 'of his own motion' and without the council's advice being formally tendered granted to his uncle, his heirs and assigns the castle, lordship, and manors of Chirk and Chirklands in North Wales, together with a number of other manors (mostly in reversion) in Somerset, Dorset, and Wiltshire.[4] For this 'delapidation of his crown' Henry was much blamed by Sir John Fortescue, 'whereof

---

[1] *Foedera*, x. 538–9. From this he lent the king's French government 10,000 marks at Calais in May 1433 (*Proceedings*, iv. 162–3, 202–3, and 242–3).

[2] £6,000 deposited for the return of his jewels seized at Sandwich in Feb. 1432 (*Rot. Parl.* iv. 391–2), not repaid until May 1434 (*Proceedings*, iv. 238–9); £14,473. 6s. 8d. in loans made on or before 19 July 1432, on which date assignments were granted to him on the lay subsidy payable at Martinmas 1433 (*Rot. Parl.* iv. 389 and 391–2; E 401/731 and E 403/703).

[3] Exchr. T.R. Council and Privy Seal, E 28/60; *Cal. Patent Rolls, 1436–1441*, pp. 276 and 311. The place is now Kempton.

[4] These were: the manors of Henstridge and Charlton Camville, Somerset, of Canford with Poole, Dorset (already granted him for life, 28 July 1436: *ibid., 1429–1436*, p. 601), and of Amesbury, Winterborne Earls, and Wilton, Wiltshire.

never man see a precedent, and God defend that any man see
more such hereafter';[1] a view shared, one need hardly add, by
Duke Humphrey.[2] If we may judge from the fact that on the very
same day, this time with the council's approval, Beaufort was
allowed to buy the reversion of an estate worth at least £40 a
year for 350 marks,[3] these lands were cheap at the price. They
were, moreover, conveniently situated, being near to the centres
of his nephew Somerset's territorial power at Corfe, Glyn
Dyfrdwy, and Cynllaith Owain.[4] By February 1442 he had
further bought out, possibly with financial aid from the king,[5]
the occupants of those manors in which he had been sold the
reversionary interest;[6] while a year later, if not before, he had
acquired a Dorset manor formerly the property of the abbey of
Holy Trinity, Caen.[7] Yet in spite of all this expenditure, which
can hardly have amounted to less than £10,000, he was still able
to lend money on his old lavish scale to the government. For
when on 25 May 1443 he agreed to advance £11,000,[8] he was
already owed at least another £14,000 by the Crown.[9] To a
minimum of £35,000 in lands and money must be added his

[1] *Governance of England*, ed. C. Plummer, p. 134. This was no doubt why the
council refused to endorse it. Compare *Proceedings*, v. 253, where councillors
'abstained them in all wise to speak nor durst not advise the king to depart from such
livelode nor to open their mouths in such matters' when the earldom of Kendal
was granted to Beaufort's nephew, Somerset.

[2] *Wars of the English in France*, II. ii. 448-9.

[3] E 28/60 (25 May 1439); *Cal. Patent Rolls, 1436-1441*, p. 260; E 401/762
(24 July 1439).

[4] Corfe was granted by Henry IV to his half-brother John Beaufort and his heirs
male (it went to Edmund his youngest son when John, duke of Somerset, died
leaving a daughter Margaret, in 1444) but I cannot find the grant (*Inquisitiones
post mortem*, Rec. Com. iii. 330 and iv. 83 and 268). The inheritance of Owen
Glendower was granted to Somerset and his heirs male on 8 Nov. 1400 (*Foedera*,
viii. 163-4; J. E. Lloyd, *Owen Glendower*, pp. 14-15 and 141).

[5] It was part of the original agreement that the king should grant to Beaufort
and his feoffees to his use lands elsewhere of equivalent value until the reversions
fell in (*Cal. Patent Rolls, 1436-1441*, p. 311). Gloucester says that the cardinal
was given the promise of lands of the Duchy of Lancaster in Norfolk worth 700-
800 marks a year if the king had not made him 'as sure of all the lands toforsaid
by Easter now next coming (1441) as can be devised by any learned counsel' (*Wars
of the English in France*, II. ii. 448).

[6] *Cal. Patent Rolls, 1441-1446*, pp. 46-7, 129, and 133.

[7] Ibid., p. 174 (2 Mar. 1443): the manor of Tarrant Launceston.

[8] Ibid., p. 182; E 401/781 (6 June and 6 July 1443); Exchr. T.R. Council and
Privy Seal, E 28/71 (25 May 1443); *Proceedings*, v. 279-80.

[9] £10,000 lent on 6 Apr. 1443 [E 401/780; *Cal. Patent Rolls, 1441-1446*, 160;
Exchr. T.R. Council and Privy Seal, E 28/71 (16 Mar. 1443)]; £4,066. 13s. 4d.,
part of loans made on 19 Mar. and 7 May 1442, had to be reassigned on Southampton on 29 Nov. 1442 and does not seem to have been repaid until later (*Cal.
Patent Rolls, 1441-1446*, p. 76; E 401/780).

jewels, plate, furniture, and other gear. If we assume that he had the disposal of a fortune in all of more than £50,000 when, having made his last small loan to the king in August 1445,[1] he began to set his affairs in order and to prepare for death, we shall not be guilty of exaggeration. The Rich Cardinal indeed deserved his epithet.

The distribution of this huge property as he finally decided it followed conventional lines. To his only surviving Beaufort nephew, Edmund, marquis of Dorset, he left the castle and lordship of Chirk and the manor of Canford with Poole in Dorset.[2] His other kinsfolk, William the younger son of his half-brother Sir Thomas Swinford,[3] an unidentified John 'bastard of Somerset',[4] his own natural daughter Joan and her husband, Sir Edward Stradling,[5] all received small legacies. More interesting perhaps are the omissions. Nowhere in his will does the cardinal mention his former political associate, William de la Pole, marquess of Suffolk, who until recently had been one of his principal feoffees;[6] it looks as if a coolness had arisen between

---

[1] E 401/790; E 403/757 (18 and 19 Aug. 1445).

[2] His directions to his feoffees for the disposal of his lands have not survived, but in 1450 Edmund Beaufort, then duke of Somerset, was in possession (*Rot. Parl.* v. 187).

[3] For the Swinford family see *Excerpta Historica* (by S. Bentley), pp. 152–9.

[4] His name suggests that he was the illegitimate son either of John, earl of Somerset, the cardinal's brother, or of John, duke of Somerset, the cardinal's nephew. It is tempting to identify him with Dr. John Somerset, Henry VI's physician (*ob. c.* 1455), who had certainly some connexion with the Beaufort family (*Dict. Nat. Biog., s.n.*).

[5] Joan Stradling is said to have been Beaufort's child by Alice, daughter of Richard, earl of Arundel. The Earl Richard who died in 1375 had a daughter Alice, from 1364 to 1397 the wife of Thomas Holland, earl of Kent; she died in 1416 (G.E.C., *Complete Peerage*, new ed. vii. 156; M. R. James, *Catalogue of MSS. of St. John's College, Cambridge*, pp. 269–70). She is a less likely candidate than her niece, Alice, daughter of the Earl Richard who died in 1397. This Alice is generally described but without evidence as the earl's youngest daughter (*Royal Wills*, pp. 128 and 144; M. A. Tierney, *History of Arundel*, pp. 192–3; *Dict. Nat. Biog., s.n.* Richard Fitzalan III); if so she must have been born between 1383 and 1385 (G.E.C. i. 253, where another daughter's age is given as 33 in 1415; their mother died in 1385). Before Mar. 1393 she had married John Charleton of Powys who died in 1401 (ibid. iii. 161). Her liaison with Beaufort therefore probably took place in her widowhood, i.e. when he was already a bishop. This is borne out by the date of their daughter's marriage with Sir Edward Stradling (*c.* 1389–1453) of St. Donat's, Glamorgan and Halsway, Somerset, in or before 1423 (*Cal. Papal Registers, Letters*, vii. 300; *Cartae et Munimenta de Glamorgan*, ed. G. T. Clark, 1910 ed., iv. 1580–5). Sir Henry Stradling, the eldest son of this marriage, was thirty years old when he succeeded his father in 1453 (*Stradling Correspondence*, ed. J. M. Traherne, pp. xviii–xx).

[6] *Cal. Patent Rolls, 1436–1441*, pp. 276 and 311; ibid., *1452–1461*, pp. 233–4; *Monasticon Anglicanum*, ed. W. Dugdale, vi, pt. ii (1830 ed.), pp. 722–4.

them. Nor is Suffolk's wife Alice, the daughter of Thomas Chaucer, Beaufort's cousin and close ally many years before, to be found beside Margaret of Anjou among his beneficiaries. It is more difficult to explain the absence of Richard II from those whose souls are to be prayed for in the Beaufort chantry at Winchester; for to that king he owed his early advancement, his first bishopric, and his legitimation. Though he had been one of the last to desert Richard in 1399, neither gratitude nor remorse caused him to share Henry V's devotion to his memory. It is somewhat curious to find that after almost half a century he still preferred to remember the usurper Bolingbroke.

His will also made suitable, even handsome, provision for his tenants, his household, his officials, his executors, the monks of his cathedral church, and those of St. Augustine's, Canterbury.[1] And a few noble debtors were forgiven their borrowings.[2] But the bulk of his wealth was dedicated to masses and works of charity for the repose of his soul. Prayers were to rise for ever not only in his two cathedrals of Lincoln and Winchester and in the two great monasteries at Canterbury but in the houses of the mendicants in London and in his diocese, in Hyde Abbey, in Eton and King's, Cambridge, in the house of the Bonhommes at Ashridge,[3] and wherever else his executors might decide. Even before his death he had transferred to the Hospital of St. Cross by Winchester six manors and a like number of advowsons, extended at £144. 14s. 6d. per annum, to provide a new foundation there of 'noble poverty'; or, as we should say, for indigent gentlefolk.[4] Compared with the colleges endowed by both his predecessor and successor in his see, this was a very modest establishment; and thanks to his failure to see it firmly started in good time before he died, it was ill equipped to withstand the hazards of the civil war that followed. But with the Lancastrian restoration of 1485 his wishes were at length carried out by William of Waynflete.[5] Finally, in addition to all this, the cardinal left the whole residue of his property to be laid out at

---

[1] St. Augustine's was forgiven a debt of £366. 13s. 4d. in return for masses. He also left £1,000 to Christ Church, Canterbury, which house had admitted him to its confraternity (*Hist. MSS. Com. Report*, ix. 113–14).

[2] £333. 6s. 8d. owed by John lord Tiptoft; £200 by William Stafford.

[3] For this see *Visitations in the Diocese of Lincoln, 1517–1531*, ed. A. Hamilton Thompson (Lincoln Record Soc.), i. p. lxxii, n. 2.

[4] *Cal. Patent Rolls, 1441–1446*, p. 174; *1452–1461*, pp. 233–4; *Rot. Parl.* v. 184–5; *Monasticon*, vi, pt. ii, pp. 722–4.

[5] R. Chandler, *Life of William Waynflete*, pp. 223–6.

the discretion of his executors on pious uses 'as they should believe to be of the greatest possible advantage to the safety of my soul'. There is evidence that they carried out their trust.[1] By whatever methods his wealth was accumulated there can be no doubt that its dispersal was exemplary.

About Beaufort the statesman—and few would be rash enough to deny him that title—it has not been the concern of this paper to speak. His aims as a financier were often hard to reconcile with his duties as his great-nephew's most influential and experienced adviser. It is this conflict between self-interest and loyalty which makes his career so difficult to assess fairly. But it is no use trying, as some have done, to dispose of his activities as a moneylender by emphasizing his statecraft. The measure of his influence on events can only be taken when each is understood. As he lay dying it was natural that the faults into which he had been tempted by avarice should have been uppermost in his mind. It is therefore not easy to accept Stubbs's far-fetched interpretation of the words which he caused to be inscribed on his tomb: 'I should tremble did I not know Thy mercies.' The obvious meaning is the likelier one.

APPENDIX

The indenture for the return of the crown jewels, 22 August 1449
(Exchr. K.R. Accounts, E101/335/15/3)

Thys edenture,[2] maad the xxij[ti] day of August the yer of the regne of oure souuerayn lord kynge Henry the vj[te] xxvij[ti], wytnesseth that the worshipful fader in God Marmaduk Lomley, bisshop of Karlille, tresourer of England, and þe chamberleins of the Eschequier haue receiued of William Port, oon of þe executours of the testament of Henry late Cardinal of England, bisshop of Winchestre, in the name of alle the executours of the sam testament thees jewells vnderwriten layde to þe sayd late Cardinal in hys lyf for seurte of repaiement of m^{l}m^{l}xliij li. viij s. ixd. lent vn to oure seide souuerayn lord in hys greet necessite,[3] the same tresorer & chamberleyns yeuing suffisant assignementes to the seyd executours atte receyuyng of þe same jewells for the seyd somme of m^{l}m^l xliij li. viijs. ixd.

Furst, j tablet of golde called the Tablet of Lancastre, garnisshed wyth xvj balaiz, iij rubiz, liiij perles & ij saphires, weying al togeders lxij marc' iiij vnces of troys.

Item, ij basins of gold, weying xliij marc.

---

[1] L. B. Radford, *Henry Beaufort*, pp. 294–5.   [2] *sic.*
[3] Several words have here been erased.

Item, j cuppe of gold couuered of kerimery werk,[1] wyth iij scuchons of the kynges armes in top, weying iiij marc ij vnces di.

Item, j tablet of gold called the Tablet of Bourgoygne, garnisshed with xxvj[ti] balaiz, xxij saphires, cxlij perles, weying alltogeders lxx marc.

Item, j ymage of Saint George, garnisshed w[t] viij balaiz, clxxviij perles, weying altogeders viij lb. x vnces.

Item, j tablet of Saynt George bought by þe kyng of Estfeld for m[l]m[l] marc, garnisshed wyth xxx diamantes, cxxxij balaiz, xxxij saphires, xxxvj rubiz, v[c]lxij perles & iij emeraudes, weying al togeders lij marc iij vnces.

Item, j ymage of Seint Michel, garnisshed wyth clij perles, iiij saphires, xxiij baleiz, weying altogeders xj lb. v vnces.

In witnesse of which to þat oo partie of this endenture remaining w[t] the seyd tresourer & chamberleyns William Port abouesaid in þe name of þe seyd executours hath put to his seel.[2] And to the tother party of this endenture remaynyng w[t] the same executours the seel of the office of the receyte is put to. Writon the day and yeer abouesaide.

[Endorsed:] Indentura Willelmi Port vnius executorum testamenti Henrici nuper Cardinalis Anglie.

K. B. McFARLANE

---

[1] The meaning of this word is doubtful. The *Oxford English Dictionary* (*s.v.*) suggests '? Filigree work'. See *Ancient Kalendars*, ii. 117, 166, and 202.

[2] The seal has disappeared.

SOME EXAMPLES OF THE DISTRIBUTION AND SPEED OF NEWS IN ENGLAND AT THE TIME OF THE WARS OF THE ROSES

THE precarious equilibrium of English society from the middle of Henry VI's reign until the last years of Henry VII placed an abnormal value upon the dispatch of news. 'Nowe (1461) gon messyngers by twyne contraye and contraye',[1] wrote a London chronicler. Rival messages from conflicting factions added to the confusion. From Lancashire Edward Plumpton wrote on the outbreak of Buckingham's rebellion in October 1483, 'messengers commyth dayly both from the king's grace and the duke into this country'.[2] The necessity for speed in conveying news was well understood. If St. Antoninus, archbishop of Florence (1446–59), appreciated intellectually the value of time,[3] his English contemporaries perceived the material dangers of delay *quia mora trahit periculum*. This was apparently a popular Latin tag in the early years of Edward IV.[4] Within official circles—and owing to 'bastard feudalism' they radiated widely—no one could afford to be a moment behindhand. With cynical amusement de Commynes heard that in a quarter of an hour of the arrival at Calais of the boat from England bringing news of the Lancastrian restoration everyone had discarded his Yorkist badge and put on the 'ragged staff' of Warwick.[5] Experience of civil war had heightened public nervousness, so that in 1483 even university authorities had to hire a man to contradict

---

[1] *Historical Collections of a Citizen of London* (ed. J. Gairdner, Camden Soc., 1876), p. 216.

[2] *Plumpton Correspondence* (ed. T. Stapleton, Camden Soc., 1839), p. 45.

[3] 'Cum autem tempus sit preciocissima res et irrecuperabilis', *Summa*, pars II, tit. 9, c. ii, ed. Nuremberg, 1477 (without signatures).

[4] 1461, *Paston Letters*, ed. J. Gairdner, iv (1904), 9; 1463, *Plumpton Correspondence*, p. 8; prior to 1470, *Historiae Croylandensis Continuatio* (i), ed. W. Fulman, *Rerum Anglicarum Scriptorum veterum tomus*, i. 532. The derivation eludes me; but the danger of delay is common to legal and moral precepts, e.g. *Mora sua cuilibet est nociva* (Lib. Sext. Reg. xxv, *Corp. Jur. Can.*, ed. Friedberg, ii. 1122) and 'Principiis obsta: sero medicina paratur, Cum mala per longas invaluere moras' (Ovid, *Rem. Am.*, l. 91, paraphrased in *De imitatione Christi*, i. xiii). In character it is not unlike a Brocard such as *dolum semper obesse*, but I have not found it in the Brocardic literature accessible to me. *Mora trahit periculum* is quoted but without source by J. Dielitz, *Die Wahl- und Denksprüche* (Frankfurt, 1884), p. 196, and E. Margalits, *Florilegium Proverbiorum universae Latinitatis* (Budapest, 1895), p. 329. Literary use of the idea frequently occurs, e.g. *1 Henry VI*, iii. ii. 33.

[5] *Mémoires*, ed. J. Calmette, i (1924–5), 209.

the rumour—incidentally true—that the northerners were march-
ing south again.[1] The morbid anxiety spread to foreigners whose
contacts with England were purely official. A hard-bitten Milanese agent complained to his government in 1471: 'I wish the
country and people were sunk in the sea. . . . I feel like one going
to the torture, when I write about them, and no one ever hears
twice alike about English affairs.'[2]

Considering the importance of news to those who valued power,
wealth, or even safety, it might be supposed that contemporary
sources would disclose numerous precise entries relating to the
passage of news, specifying the date on which intelligence was
known, and indicating thereby the speed at which news travelled.
But the contrary is true; and the lack of precision pertaining to
the distribution of news must itself be reckoned as an historical
fact of some significance. Because news habitually arrived in
fragments so that an event became known only gradually as
discrepancies were weeded out and piecemeal information brought
together, it was hard and a trifle unreal for a chronicler, letter-
writer, or official to state with any exactness when an event was
first known. Anticipation, as always, was an important, and for
the historian a disquieting, factor, since it was seldom found
necessary to amend records in the light of subsequent verifica-
tion. On what appeared to be excellent authority the mayor of
York learnt on 6 April 1483 that Edward IV was dead. A requiem
was sung on the 7th;[3] and although we know that the king lived
until 9 April, York felt no compulsion to revise the former entry
in the civic minutes. Happily there are exceptions, in which we
can determine within a few hours the time when a faithful report
arrived at a given place. A decisive victory such as Agincourt[4]
must ever be the ideal subject for a sudden and well-remembered
public announcement. When dealing with complex happenings
and those of some duration the modern investigator must imitate
the caution of the more critical contemporaries. 'De telz matières
ne vient point voulentiers ung messaige seul', said de Commynes
reflecting on the crisis, so nearly fatal to Lewis XI, when news

---

[1] 'Solvi uni viro conducto per vice-cancellarium ad cogendum certos rumores de
adventu virorum borialium . . . V s.', *Cambridge Grace Book A* (ed. S. M. Leathes,
Cambridge Antiquarian Soc., extra vol. i, 1897), p. 170.

[2] *Calendar of State Papers, Milan*, i. 154. The original in J. Calmette and G.
Périnelle, *Louis XI et l'Angleterre* (1930), p. 140, note.

[3] *York Civic Records* (ed. A. Raine, Yorkshire Archaeological Soc., Record
Series xcviii, 1938), i. 71. The report came from the dean.

[4] Details in *Chronicle of London*, ed. N. H. Nicolas and E. Tyrell (1827), pp. 101–2.

that the bishop of Liége had been seized by the populace at Tongeren during the night of 9–10 October reached Péronne on 11 October 1468.[1]

Despite their host of spies, the rulers of Europe (outside Italy and Turkey) continued to receive vital information in curiously haphazard fashion. First details of the battle of Barnet came to Ghent by accident. On 15 April 1471, the morrow of the battle, a Norfolk man at 10 a.m. viewed the bodies of Warwick and Montague in St. Paul's, and then, wanting to be the first to bring the news home, left London by boat directly after dinner, probably therefore about midday. Taken at sea by Hansards, he was landed in Zealand, and his story was quickly reported to the sister of Edward IV, Margaret, duchess of Burgundy, then residing at Ghent. A copy has survived of Margaret's letter relating the events to her mother-in-law the dowager of Burgundy.[2] She doubtless wrote also to her husband Charles, who at Corbie, near Amiens, was in possession of the facts not later than 18 April 1471.[3] This time Charles was reliably informed; but the previous autumn the first reports which he received of the Lancastrian readeption were inaccurate and to the effect that Edward IV had perished.[4] If the essential facts were frequently known and acted upon swiftly, the attendant circumstances as often followed with delay. Sandwich was sacked by the French on 28 August 1457, and the next day a commission to repulse the invaders was issued; but only on 3 September did London write an account of the raid to the king, enclosing letters furnishing particulars, which were not received by Henry VI at Northampton until 5 September.[5] When one considers the causes which impelled princes to set up costly relay systems, one is tempted to think that the fragmentary nature of reports from the scene of events was as strong an inducement as the desire for initial speed.

The governments of major powers had nevertheless well-developed methods for procuring information with reasonable celerity; and those who had the management of affairs, and were interested in the complexion put upon events, were accustomed

[1] *Mémoires*, ed. J. Calmette, i. 133. For the events see *Mémoires*, ed. Mlle Dupont, iii (1847), 228 seq. and ed. B. de Mandrot, i (1901), 137, note; G. Kurth, *La Cité de Liége au moyen âge*, iii (1910), 304–5.

[2] *Compte Rendu. Commission Royale d'Histoire* (Brussels) 2, vii (1855), 47–51.

[3] Olivier de la Marche, *Mémoires*, ed. H. Beaune and J. d'Arbaumont, iii (1885), 73; H. Vander Linden, *Itinéraires de Charles duc de Bourgogne* (Com. Roy. d'Hist., 1936), p. 30.

[4] Commynes, *Mémoires*, ed. J. Calmette, i. 206.

[5] R. R. Sharpe, *London and the Kingdom*, iii (1894), 380–2; see *infra*, p. 446, n. 6.

to release full if tendentious accounts for domestic and foreign consumption. After the battle of St. Albans in 1455 and again in 1461 and 1471 after the battles of Towton and Tewkesbury, the victorious party sent out news-letters, of which the latest in date was issued in English and French versions.[1] In November 1468 a Hanseatic agent forwarded to Lübeck for official use a *collectanea* volume of such ephemeral literature containing pieces drawn from England, France, and Burgundy over the preceding seven years.[2] Apart from their utility to governments, official and semi-official narratives supplied individuals with a knowledge of contemporary history. Relations of notable incidents on the Continent probably circulated in England within a few months of their occurrence. In July 1474 John Paston asked his brother in London to send to Norwich 'my book of the Metyng of the Duke and of the Emperour', which indubitably is one of the widely disseminated accounts of the interview at Trier of Charles 'the Bold' and Frederick III in October–November 1473.[3] The daughters of Edward IV also possessed a finely bound and illuminated copy in French of a news-letter from Constantinople describing events following the death of Mohammed II in 1481.[4]

In England, while public interest was solicited and public opinion was canvassed through hand-bills, domestic news, in particular casualties on the battlefield, or the conduct of sieges and campaigns, was distributed in bills and schedules.[5] These papers, especially the shortest, consisting of brief factual statements, were probably the first reliable notification of events. When men claimed 'certain knowledge' of such and such, as distinct from 'flying rumours', it was generally the news-bill that they had in mind as the warrant of veracity.[6] William Worcester,

---

[1] 1455. This paper belongs properly to the Stonor collection, see *Stonor Letters* (ed. C. L. Kingsford, Camden Soc., 1919), i. 52, but was printed most recently in *Paston Letters*, iii. 25–9.
1461. *Calendar of State Papers, Milan*, i. 60–5.
1471. English: *Arrivall of Edward IV* (ed. J. Brie, Camden Soc., 1838); French: C. L. Kingsford, *English Historical Literature in the Fifteenth Century* (1913), pp. 175–6, which mentions most important, but not all, manuscripts.
[2] *Hanserecesse*, 2, vi (1890), 87–8.
[3] *Paston Letters*, v. 207. The principal reports of the meeting in K. Rausch, *Die Burgundische Heirat Maximilians I* (Vienna, 1880), App. III.
[4] See my article in *The Times*, 23 May 1936.
[5] The 'Brief Notes' in *Three Fifteenth Century Chronicles* (ed. J. Gairdner, Camden Soc., 1880) are largely composed of these; see ibid., p. 156 seq.
[6] 'Hec qualiacunque sint, volui his litteris sanctitati vestre nota facere, in quibus scribendis non vulgi opinionem aut varios hominum rumores secutus sum, sed ea tantum que ab hisce principibus vera esse accepi, maximeque a reverendissimo

diligently collecting historical material, received a bill of the proceedings of the Coventry Parliament in 1459 from a correspondent there who procured an official or composed a private report. When in his annals he came to list the persons attainted at Coventry, Worcester cited a copy of this bill transcribed into a note-book, and another copy or extract was also sent in 1459 to Justice Paston.[1] Memoranda such as the report on the Lincolnshire rising of 1470, or on the parliament of 1485 drawn up by the Colchester burgesses for the instruction of their fellow citizens, might fairly be described as official;[2] but the information circulating at any time in the kingdom was largely the product of private correspondence. From capital or camp letters radiated across the country;[3] and at times of crisis such as early May 1471 correspondence between persons of rank was a useful subsidiary source of information for the city of London itself.[4] Although many news-letters, especially those nicely framed to justify a particular government, must have reached their destination long after the events related were tolerably well known, they, together with the surviving copies of bills, are the most reliable evidence we possess for judging the type of document upon which contemporaries formed the conclusions designated as 'certain tidings'.

None the less, events authenticated by schedule or news-letter were the exception rather than the rule. Most people were largely dependent on picking up hearsay. 'My cosyn John Loveday can tell yow, and there be eny flyeng talys for he hathe walkyd in London and so do not I', said John Paston in July 1471.[5] The alarm of successive governments, reflected in the severe penalties uttered against rumour-mongers, leaves no doubt that in a society relying on oral information whispering could be a dangerous weapon in the hands of subversive elements. On the government side there is consistency extending over centuries, alike in the charges brought against purveyors of false news and in the measures to bring them to account, while the same tone of

domino cardinali Anglie, cuius neptis . . ., omnia eidem quo gesta sunt ordine innotescere fecit.' Piero del Monte on the death of James I. R. Weiss, 'Earliest Account of the Murder of James I', *Eng. Hist. Rev.* lii (1937), 491.

[1] *Paston Letters*, iii. 198–9; Worcester's *Annals* in *Letters and Papers . . . of the Wars of the English in France* (ed. J. Stevenson, Rolls Series), ii, pt. 2, p. 771.

[2] (i) published by J. G. Nichols in *Camden Miscellany I* (Camden Soc., 1847); (ii) in *Red Paper Book of Colchester*, ed. W. Gurney Benham (1907), pp. 60–4.

[3] e.g. 1462, *Paston Letters*, iv. 59–61; 1475, *Stonor Letters*, i. 157; 1485–6, *Plumpton Correspondence*, pp. 48–50.

[4] R. R. Sharpe, op. cit. iii. 390.　　　　　[5] *Paston Letters*, v. 107.

alarm rings through the pronouncements at times of recurrent civil tension. Under the Statute of Westminster, prim. c. xxxiv, anyone spreading falsehoods might be put in prison until he could produce his informant, and in the Gloucester Parliament of 1378 that penalty was enacted against the contrivers of false news bent on stirring up discord between the lords or between them and the commons. In 1484 and 1485 Richard III was admonishing towns such as Windsor, Southampton, London, York, for seditious rumours and the 'telling of tales and tidings wherby the people might be stird to commocions . . . , or any strife and debate arise betwene lord and lord, or us and any of the lords and estats of this our land', and he proceeded to enjoin the traditional sanction of the Statute of Westminster, which afterwards served the Tudors.[1]

It was probably to prevent rumours springing up that the unfortunate woman of Kent, who in 1443 at Blackheath made a demonstration before the king in favour of the disgraced duchess of Gloucester, was taken through London with a paper on her head displaying the infamous words she had used to the king.[2] The products of flying rumours, seditious bills, ballads, and prophesyings have naturally left few traces; but there is no doubt that in the official mind they were intimately related,[3] and perhaps deliberately associated with the black arts. The fate of Clarence in 1478 was precipitated by the conduct of Thomas Burdett, one of his gentlemen, who in the preceding year had more than once scattered seditious bills, rhymes, and ballads at Holborn.[4] What seems to have been the most systematic attempt to organize false news for political ends was undertaken by the Yorkist conspirators in 1487. The Crown had wind of what was intended, for during the spring a proclamation was cried in London against 'forged tydynges'.[5] Still, the plans of the rebels gained a partial

[1] *Statutes of the Realm, 2 Ric. II*, Stat. 1, c. v; Richard III to Windsor, 6 Dec. 1484, and Henry VII to an unknown in ? 1487. *Report on Rymer's Foedera*, App. E (1869), pp. 79–80. Richard III to Southampton and York, 5 Apr., 1485, *11th Report Hist. MSS. Com.*, App. III (1887), p. 106, and *York Civic Records*, i. 115–16.

[2] *The Brut*, ed. F. W. D. Brie, pt. ii (Early English Text Soc., O.S. 136, 1908), p. 484.

[3] Proposed legislation in first parliament of Henry VII: 'Also it is in actt [? enacted] that all maner of profycyes is mayd felony.' *Plumpton Correspondence*, p. 50.

[4] *3rd Report of Dep. Keeper of the Public Records*, 1842, App. II, p. 213. Clarence's fall had a background of necromancy, the real importance of which is obscure.

[5] *London Letter Book L*, ed. R. R. Sharpe (1912), p. 243, undated, but between entries of 2 Apr. and 29 May 1487.

success in hampering the king, for as the rival forces closed in to meet at Stoke on 16 June 1487, Yorkist agents set around the theatre of operations spread the news that King Henry was defeated, with the result that reinforcements coming to his side turned back, while some persons of name hastened into sanctuary.[1]

A minor by-product of the chronic crisis of confidence which beset the later Middle Ages was the use of the credence and token. The purpose of each is to confirm trust, the former in the spoken word of the messenger bearing a letter of credence, the latter in the message itself, whether verbal or written. Perhaps the majority of fifteenth-century letters touching vital issues recommend the recipient to trust the bearer, who will supplement and explain the contents. This cautious habit has in general deprived historians of inestimable material, but nowhere more than in relation to the exchange of news. How often do we not suspect that grave news was entrusted to a bearer, whose impressive but wholly uninformative letter of credence alone survives?[2] The arrival in London of the news from Towton invites speculation. 'Please you to know', writes William Paston, 'suche tydyngs as my Lady of York hath by a letter of credens under the signe manuel of our soverayn lord king Edward, whiche lettre cam un to oure sayd lady this same day . . . at xi clok and was sene and red by me. . . .'[3] Now, did Paston mean by 'lettre of credens' an authentic or trustworthy letter, or did he, as I incline to believe, intend a letter under the sign manual, in other words under the king's official token, referring in barest terms to the victory, but with a credence that entire confidence should be given to the bearer's story? Occasionally there is proof that the credence clause was the key which opened for the receiver the specific purposes of a letter, witness the notorious letter of the Protector Richard, duke of Gloucester, dated from London 10 June 1483, addressed to York and received there on 15 June. This letter, which was delivered to the mayor by Sir Richard Radcliff,[4] an adherent of the protector, besought the city to dispatch at once an armed force to London 'as our trusty servaunt this berer shall mor at large shew

[1] *Great Chronicle of London*, ed. A. H. Thomas and I. D. Thornley (1938), p. 241. *Letters and Papers Richard III and Henry VII* (ed. J. Gairdner, Rolls Series), i. 94.

[2] e.g. Richard III's credence for Garter King of Arms to Southampton dated 17 July [? 1485], *11th Report Hist. MSS. Com.*, App. III (1887), p. 104.

[3] *Paston Letters*, iii. 266–7.

[4] Cf. also London 11 June 1483, Gloucester to Lord Nevill, 'and that ye wyll yef credence to Richarde Ratclyff, thys berer, whom I nowe do sende to you enstructed with all my mynde and entent', ibid. vi. 71–2.

you to whom we pray you geve credence'.[1] Since York had to take positive action on the letter, an entry was made in the House Book: 'the credence of the which lettre is that such felichip as the citie may make defensably arraid, as wele of hors as of fute be on Wendynsday at eyn next cummyng [18 June] at Powmfret, their attendyng upon my lord of Northumbreland and so with hym to go up to London'.[2] The use and formula of the credence make too specialized a question for the present study, but in considering the transmission of news it cannot be disregarded.

The parallel custom of tokens had become quasi-universal, so that little confidential business was transacted without an exchange of tokens to vouch for faith and urgency.[3] Though documentary evidence is lacking, it is almost safe to assume that news by word of mouth was commonly, and hasty scribbles frequently, accompanied by a token. The battle of Barnet affords an instance of an impromptu communication authenticated by a token, readily accepted by all and sundry. Owing to the engagement starting at dawn twelve miles from London, wild rumours were early abroad in the city.[4] By 10 a.m. came word that King Edward had the field; but the report was disbelieved, until a rider dashed through the streets on his way to Westminster displaying one of Edward's gauntlets sent to the queen as an assurance of victory.[5] The tragic deaths of the Stuart kings furnish a curious contribution to the history of tokens. In 1437 the papal legate, to confirm his account of the assassination of James I, conveyed to Rome the shirt in which the king of Scotland perished;[6] and a supporter of James III, slain at Sauchieburn 11 June 1488, later paraded his blood-stained shirt to incite the people.[7] After the battle of Flodden, 9 September 1513, when Surrey sent south the first intelligence of victory, the body of James IV had not been recovered,[8] but as soon as it was found, the king's gauntlet and a

---

[1] *York Civic Records*, i. 73–4.

[2] Ibid. i. 74. The York House Books contain other passages distinguishing between letter and credence; cf. i. 34 (13 Aug. 1480), also *infra*, p. 451, n. 7.

[3] In the Paston letters I have counted at least twelve certain references to tokens and there are about six each in the Plumpton and Stonor collections.

[4] The Yorkist official report says that the battle began between 4 and 5 a.m., lasting three hours 'or it was fully achivyd' (*Arrivall of Edward IV*, pp. 19–20). A source favourable to Henry VI says 4 to 10 a.m. (*Chronicle*, by John Warkworth, ed. J. O. Halliwell, Camden Soc., 1839, p. 16).

[5] *Great Chronicle of London*, pp. 216–17.

[6] *The Latin Brut*, in C. L. Kingsford, op. cit., p. 323; cf. R. Weiss, op. cit., pp. 481, 490 note.

[7] A. Conway, *Henry VII's Relations with Scotland and Ireland* (1932), pp. 26–7.

[8] *Calendar of State Papers, Venice*, ii. 144.

piece of his plaid were hurried to the queen of England. On 16 September 1513 Catherine of Aragon, from Woburn, passed on the tokens to Henry VIII, then encamped before Tournay, with the fierce words: 'In this your grace shal see how I can kepe my promys sending you for your baners a king's cote. I thought to sende hymselfe, but our Englishmens' herts would not suffre it.'[1]

When the English carried home with them the body of James IV,[2] they were doubtless prompted less by the desire to retain a trophy than to possess authentication of his death. The end of the Middle Ages teemed with impostors who impersonated the dead. England exhibited the case of Richard II and of the Princes in the Tower, while Europe among others had the false Joan of Arc[3] and Charles the Bold, who, although buried at Nancy expressly as a trophy[4] by his conquerors, kept recurring for years.[5] These spurious survivals are important witnesses to the inadequacy of ordinary means for the distribution of news once popular credulity was aroused by an unusual personality. Only a token which excited the visual imagination could dispel a legend, and Edward IV was a good psychologist when he ordered the bare remains of Warwick and Montagu to be laid in the public gaze at St. Paul's the day after Barnet. Lancastrian partisans did spread rumours that Warwick survived, but in vain, for the report of the scene in St. Paul's everywhere pursued them.[6]

The problem of procuring accurate news is in the first place one of collecting reliable information at source. Within the realm the Crown presumably relied upon its officers on the spot to provide the data. The murder of Suffolk was notified to the king by the sheriff of Kent, who inquired where the body should be buried, an administrative point of some delicacy.[7] The relief of Berwick in 1455 was intimated to the chancellor by the northern magnates in charge of the war against the Scots.[8] Yet

[1] *Letters and Papers Henry VIII*, i (2nd ed.), no. 2268, no. 2391, pp. 1060–1). H. Ellis, *Original Letters*, 1 (1824), i. 88–9.
[2] Hall's *Chronicle* (ed. 1809), p. 564.
[3] A. Molinier, *Les Sources de l'histoire de France*, iv (1904), nos. 4500, 4659–62.
[4] Cf. epitaph on Charles's tomb at Nancy in *Chroniques relat. à l'hist. de la Belgique sous la domination des ducs de Bourgogne*, ed. Kervyn de Lettenhoven (Coll. des Chron. belges), iii. 515–16.
[5] *Calendar of State Papers, Milan*, i. 276.
[6] Ibid., p. 155; *Arrivall of Edward IV*, p. 21. H. Wylie, *Henry IV*, i (1884), 364, for the earlier case of 'Hotspur'.
[7] *Paston Letters*, ii. 147; *Chronicon Angliae*, ed. J. A. Giles (1848), ii. 39.
[8] See *infra*, p. 446, n. 1.

momentous news was collected and carried to court by private individuals, such as the monk who in 1465 told Edward IV of poor King Harry's capture,[1] or the Milanese subject Fra Zuan who was in Exeter—perhaps as a spy—when Warbeck landed in 1497, and brought word to Henry VII.[2] The routine of English government had for centuries depended upon local information supplied by officials to the king's council and courts; but the notification of exceptional occurrences is a subject deserving investigation. Some interest attaches therefore to the arrangements of towns such as London and York for securing information from their own accredited observers. The mayor of London had word of the battle of Towton on Good Friday (3 April) 1461 one day before the king's letter was brought to his mother Cicely dwelling within the city.[3] Since Edward was then reputed to be dominated by his mother,[4] he might have been expected to send the fastest dispatch to her, so that, although there is no evidence to show that the report was brought to the mayor by a messenger of the city, it looks rather as if London had independent means of forwarding information, which in this case brought in news ahead of the royal messenger. Ten years later, when the Bastard of Fauconberge delivered in the Lancastrian interest an ultimatum from Sittingbourne dated 8 May 1471, the mayor of London on the 9th replied that the city knew about the battle of Tewkesbury (4 May), not only from letters signed by Edward IV, but also from the memoranda of its own servants, who, acting as war correspondents with both sides throughout the campaign, had fully reported the battle and its sequel.[5] Similarly in 1485 at York the Council of Twenty Four heard of King Richard's death from their serjeant to the mace, who had been present at the battle of Bosworth for the purpose of reporting to the city.[6]

As usual in European history, war, with its handmaid diplomacy, proved once more the decisive factor for innovating central institutions, and produced in the relay system a new instrument

---

[1] See *infra*, p. 447, n. 10.　　　　　　[2] See *infra*, p. 453, n. 3.
[3] *Great Chronicle of London*, p. 197.
[4] *Calendar of State Papers, Milan*, i. 67.
[5] Exchange of correspondence published by J. R. Scott, *Archaeologia Cantiana*, xi (1877), 359–64, and R. R. Sharpe, *London and the Kingdom*, iii (1894), 387–92. According to the city 'Edward late called prince and other were taken and slain'; this evidence for the death of the son of Henry VI has been generally overlooked, but deserves to be set against Clarence's testimony, writing 6 May 1471 to Henry Vernon, that Edward was among those 'slain in plain battle'. *12th Report Hist. MSS. Com.*, App. IV (1888), p. 4.
[6] See *infra*, p. 451, n. 7.

of absolutism. Outside Italy, the postal innovations of Lewis XI[1] were perhaps epoch-making; but if the French service was certainly working in 1479, the king of the Romans, Frederick III, instituted relays between Feldkirch and Vienna in 1443,[2] while as early as 1425 during their expedition to Domodossola the Bernese set up a temporary system.[3] The first English experiment in posting was probably imitated from France, a state for which after 1475 Edward IV felt alternating attraction and repulsion. During the last years of his reign Lewis XI formed a network of postal routes corresponding with the main lines of his aggressive diplomacy leading towards the Netherlands, Spain, and Provence.[4] In England also the innovation was adopted to serve aggression, but for the purposes of a single campaign. According to the second continuation of the *Croyland Chronicle*, Edward IV in his last campaign against the Scots (summer 1482) invented the new practice of stationing riders at intervals of twenty miles so that a letter passed at the rate of 200 miles in two days, through a chain of messengers, none of whom was allowed to ride beyond his allotted sector.[5] Assuming that he reckoned in computed miles—for he could not have thought in statutory miles—the chronicler intended by 200 miles the distance roughly between London and Newcastle.[6] To prepare for the

[1] G. Zeller, 'Un Faux du XVIIe siècle: l'édit de Louis XI sur la poste', *Rev. Historique*, 180 (1937), 286–92; R. Gandilhon, 'Louis XI fondateur du service des postes en France', ibid. 183 (1938), 37–41.
[2] E. Kiesskalt, *Die Entstehung der deutschen Post* (Erlangen, 1938), p. 165. I am unable to consult this author's *Die Post ein Werk Friederichs III, nicht der Taxis* (Bamberg, 1926).   [3] E. Kiesskalt, *Die Entstehung*, &c., p. 164.
[4] R. Gandilhon, op. cit., pp. 40–1.
[5] *Historiae Croylandensis Continuatio*, ed. W. Fulman, *Rerum Anglic. Scriptores*, i (1684), 571.
[6] In the itineraries printed with the 1541–61 editions of *A Cronycle of Yeres from the Begynynge of the Worlde . . .*, Durham is 200, Newcastle 212, Berwick 248 computed miles from London; see H. G. Fordham, 'Earliest Tables of Highways of England and Wales 1541–61', *The Library*, 4th ser., viii (1927–8), 349–54. These mileages were doubtless already traditional by the fifteenth century, since on the 'Gough Map', prior to 1350 (reproduced Ordnance Survey, 1936), the distanced stages between London and York aggregate 146 miles, and 148 in *A Cronycle of Yeres*. The Gough Map shows no route from York to Berwick. From July to October 1482 Edward IV engaged ten men to maintain communication with Richard of Gloucester who commanded against the Scots. A payment to five of them indicates that they were stationed along the road to Berwick; see C. Scofield, *Edward IV*, ii (1923), 339–40. If Newcastle served as a base (cf. *infra*, p. 446, n. 1) each would have about twenty computed miles to ride, as stated by the chronicler. For computed miles, see H. G. Fordham, *Road Books and Itineraries of Great Britain* (Cambridge, 1924); F. M. Stenton, 'Road System of Mediaeval England', *Econ. Hist. Rev.* vii (1936–7), 1–21; Sir Charles Arden Close, *Geographical Byways* (1947), pp. 12–23.

impending English attack the Scottish parliament early in 1482 took measures to accelerate slothful messengers; but in the first years of his reign, when the Scots and Queen Margaret held the initiative, Edward IV may already have kept a messenger at Grantham.[1] During the readeption of Henry VI the espionage service of Clarence anticipated in one respect the later development of relaying news. The essential was that a minimum of two agents should be continually in the households of Lords Northumberland, Shrewsbury, and Stanley, so that when one was bringing news to Clarence another should always remain to learn what was going on. In March 1471, as soon as he learnt that Edward IV was sailing toward the Humber, Clarence ordered spies to be sent thither with similar instructions.[2]

In common with other dynasties the English kings had kept, certainly since the thirteenth century, a staff of household messengers[3]; but like most aspects of the intensified political activity of the later Middle Ages postal relays imposed a serious burden on public finances. Significantly enough Clarence, instructing Henry Vernon at a moment of crisis, enjoined that no cost should be spared on the messengers;[4] and in France the expenses of Lewis XI's postal network contributed to its reduction in the following reign.[5] In 1484, when Richard III was carrying on the practice of relays, he still possessed a large part of Edward IV's treasure. The second Croyland Continuation states that thanks to the remainder of this treasure, Richard's preparedness for countering an invasion reached a peak in 1484; and the same source implies that in 1485 he may have been compelled by penury to modify or abandon the use of relays.[6]

The collection of intelligences abroad was a function of diplomacy, and an English king, like any other, had his agents at

---

[1] *Acts of the Parliament of Scotland*, Record Commission, ii (1814), 138: 'Payd to a messenger off the kyngg's att Grantham callyd Curteys XX^d', 16 Nov. 1462; 'Expenses of Sir John Howard 1462–9', in *Manners and Household Expenses in England*, Roxburghe Club, 1841, p. 150. On 19 Aug. 1464 the Crown granted custody of an idiot to a Henry Curteys of Grantham. *Cal. Pat. Rolls, 1461–1467*, p. 342.

[2] *12th Report Hist. MSS. Com.*, App. IV (1888), pp. 2–3.

[3] For earlier messengers of the English Crown, see M. C. Hill, 'Jack Faukes, Kings Messenger', *Eng. Hist. Rev.* lvii (1942), 19–30. The ten men retained July–October 1482 (cf. *supra*, p. 439, n. 6) received 12d. by the day (C. Scofield, op. cit. ii. 340). The household messengers of Edward IV got 5d. a day on journeys, but in addition to their regular wages, see 'Liber Niger' in *Coll. of Ordinances*, Soc. of Antiquaries (1790), pp. 48–9.

[4] See *supra*, n. 2.

[5] R. Gandilhon, op. cit., p. 41.

[6] *Hist. Croyl. Cont.*, loc. cit.

large. Henry VII achieved an almost legendary reputation for his subtle use of spies; and his courtiers were so well informed on Italian affairs that the Milanese resident declared he could fancy himself at Rome.[1] But already the female agents of Edward IV had compelled professional admiration from de Commynes.[2] The possession of Calais was invaluable, for well before the sixteenth century the officer commanding there had the recognized duty of reporting on current affairs in Europe. Thus Lord Dynham sent a dispatch to Richard III by a pursuivant who left Calais within two hours of receipt of news that Lewis XI was dead. Dynham was also in regular correspondence with the chancellor on the more routine aspects of foreign politics. Minor items of political value came across quickly; and Sir John Paston at Canterbury on 13 April 1473 knew that the earl of Oxford had been at Dieppe on the 10th preparing to sail for Scotland.[3]

In the field of international news dependence on the mercantile community was still very marked. In 1497 the Milanese ambassador to Henry VII recommended the letter-bag of Florentine or Genoese merchants when speed and secrecy were essential.[4] The Cely letters disclose the usefulness of English merchants in procuring remote news for men of affairs. Their position as staplers at Calais, and their connexion with the international marts in the Netherlands, enabled the Celys to hear from the Mediterranean well in advance of the main news-stream. In the closing years of Edward IV they gathered news for Sir John Weston, prior of the Hospitallers, who was their 'good lord' in the current sense. It was a service which they rendered in return for his patronage; and judging from the urgency with which Sir John pressed them for news, he had few finer sources of information, notwithstanding the place which he held in the council.[5] For over three centuries cosmopolitan commerce had been far ahead in appreciating the value of news, and had transmitted it more systematically than secular governments, whose organizations varied with the wealth and temper of rulers. In the twelfth

---

[1] *Calendar of State Papers, Milan*, i. 323.

[2] *Mémoires*, ed. J. Calmette, i. 199.

[3] *Letters and Papers Henry VIII*, especially vols. i and iv–vii, contain many reports from the deputy; H. Ellis, *Original Letters*, 2 (1827), i. 156 seq.; *Paston Letters*, v. 184.

[4] *Calendar of State Papers, Milan*, i. 323.

[5] *Cely Papers* (ed. H. E. Malden, Camden Soc., 1900), 32, 55, 104; C. Scofield, op. cit. ii. 291, 298; J. Calmette and G. Périnelle, *Louis XI et l'Angleterre*, p. 247.

century Flemish merchants had told Galbert of Bruges how the murder of Count Charles the Good, slain at Bruges very early on 2 March 1127, was heard in London by the morning of 4 March.[1] Exploited by the rising power of centralized states, mercantile society held its pre-eminence, since the remarkable time-tables of 1500 and 1516 for posting between Brussels and the principal centres of Europe show that the Antwerp merchants could achieve progressively higher speeds for their communications.[2]

At any time the measures taken to control news are an index of the worth attached to it. The administrative use of the proclamation was as technically developed in England as in any country, and seeing that the effectiveness of the proclamation depends on publication,[3] it must be allowed that the principle underlying the publishing of news was understood. Excluding news from abroad, which eliminates the war dispatches of Henry V and Thomas, earl of Salisbury,[4] there is yet plenty of evidence for the solemn publishing of capital events. The victory at Towton was declared at Paul's on the day it was confirmed in London;[5] and in 1470 the flight abroad of Edward IV was published by the civic authority.[6] No sooner was the capture of Henry VI notified to Edward IV at Canterbury in 1465 than it was given to the people in the cathedral.[7] News of the royal family was probably sent to provincial centres for diffusion. The royal letter in 1453 announcing the birth of a son to Queen Margaret was published at Canterbury in the cathedral nave, and the public stood by while a *Te Deum* was sung.[8] On 20 September 1486 a yeoman of the queen's chamber brought tidings to Southampton of the birth of Prince Arthur, born at Winchester

[1] Galbert de Bruges, *Histoire du Meurtre de Charles le Bon*, ed. H. Pirenne (Coll. de Textes pour servir à l'étude de l'Histoire), 1891, pp. 20, 22.

[2] J. A. Goris, *Étude sur les colonies marchandes méridionales à Anvers 1488–1567* (Louvain, 1925), p. 136.

[3] 'Not failling in publisshyng thys our commaundement', proclamation of Richard III, Oct. 1483, *York Civic Records*, i. 85.

[4] R. R. Sharpe, *London and the Kingdom*, iii. 359–67, 370.

[5] *Calendar of State Papers, Milan*, i. 66.

[6] 'Memorandum quod primo die Octobris publicatum fuit per civitatem quod Edwardus IV rex Anglie fugerat.' Guildhall, Journal 7, f. 223ᵛ. The translation by R. R. Sharpe, op. cit. iii. 385: '*it was noised abroad* throughout the city', fails to express 'publicatum fuit'.

[7] 'Pronunciatum erat solemniter in ecclesia Christi Cantuariensis coram populo', *Chronicle of John Stone* (ed. W. G. Searle, Cambridge Antiquarian Soc., 8° series xxxiv, 1902), p. 94.

[8] 'Supprior . . . publicavit literam in navi ecclesie . . . et cantor incepit ympnum Te Deum Laudamus, stantibus omnibus ibidem.' Stone, op. cit., p. 87.

before daybreak.[1] Most evidence seems to indicate publication by word of mouth, but copies of official letters may have been posted, for seditious bills certainly were.[2] At London Paul's Cross, the rostrum for political pronouncements, served also for the publication of private affairs. The death of notable ecclesiastics was apparently made known there by a reference in the prayers for the departed after the Sunday sermon. So Richard and Robert Cely on 16 November 1477 first heard of the death of their uncle the dean of York, who had died before 5 November;[3] and the official character of John Lax, a priest attainted in 1461, as an adherent of Henry VI, was rehabilitated in 1462 by papal letters read from Paul's by the chancellor.[4]

The distinction between published and secret information was well recognized; but there were those who felt confident of penetrating official secrets. 'Other tydings', wrote John Russe in 1462, 'the were come to London, but they were not publyshyd; but John Wellys shal abyde a day the lenger to know what they are.'[5] The relationship between propaganda and official publication is always indissoluble; and a good example is the letter of Edward IV (13 March 1462) to Alderman Thomas Cook bidding him assemble the London householders within his ward and declare to them the recently detected Lancastrian conspiracy.[6] Celebrations on receipt of officially welcome news might permissibly be classed with propaganda. The thanksgivings seem to have been mostly of a religious character.[7] There is little evidence of bonfires, common in the Netherlands,[8] to celebrate successes; although after Towton bonfires were lit at Dover and Sandwich with an answering one at Calais.[9] The precocious growth of state intervention produced at Milan in 1386 the Ufficio delle Bollete for inspecting mail;[10] and repeated denunciations

[1] *Book of Remembrance of Southampton* (ed. H. W. Gidden, Southampton Record Soc., 1930), iii. 53.

[2] e.g. Feb. 1470 in London, see *Six Town Chronicles*, ed. R. Flenley (1911), p. 164.

[3] *Cely Papers*, p. 205.

[4] *Rot. Parl.* v. 478a; *Calendar of State Papers, Milan*, i. 22, 107.

[5] *Paston Letters*, iv. 58.

[6] H. Ellis, *Original Letters*, 2 (1827), i. 126–31.

[7] e.g. at London after Agincourt, see *supra*, p. 430, n. 4; after Towton, p. 442, n. 5; after Stoke, *Great Chronicle of London*, p. 241.

[8] e.g. at Bruges 16 June 1471 for the restoration of Edward IV, *Inventaire des archives de la ville de Bruges*, ed. L. Gihliodts van Severen, 1ère Section, vi (1876), 34, where the events are mistakenly ascribed to 1470.

[9] *Calendar of State Papers, Milan*, i. 77.

[10] B. de Mesquita, *Giangaleazzo* (1941), p. 52.

of the censoring of sermons to be preached before Henry VI show that the English government was not blind to the utility of a censorship.[1] In 1445, at a critical juncture for English foreign policy, Agnes, from Norwich, writes to Edmund Paston in London: 'I praye you to sende me tydynggs from be yond see for here thei arn a ferde to telle soche as be reported.'[2] In a crisis the authorities strove to prevent news of the disturbances reaching the Continent. After the first battle at St. Albans the roads out of Calais were guarded, and the earliest reports to reach Bruges came by a vessel which sailed into Dunkirk.[3] To avoid the English censorship, the secretary of the Steelyard, who had to report on the troubled situation at the end of 1468, waited until his arrival on the Continent before committing himself to writing.[4]

Recorded instances of the passage of news within England are sufficiently rare up to the close of Henry VII's reign to justify individual consideration.[5]

1. Murder of James I of Scotland.
   Perth–London, approx. 440 miles.[6]
   21 February–by 28 February 1437, full moon 24 February.

The king was murdered at Blackfriars, Perth, late in the night

---

[1] Thomas Gascoigne, *Loci e libro Veritatum*, ed. J. E. Thorold Rogers (1881), p. 191; *Historical Collections of a Citizen of London* (ed. J. Gairdner, Camden Soc., 1876), p. 203.

[2] *Paston Letters*, ii. 73.

[3] *Calendar of State Papers, Milan*, i. 16–17.

[4] *Hanserecesse*, 2, vi (1890), 94.

[5] Distances are in statutory miles from Ogilby's itineraries which approximate to, but are not identical with medieval roads. The moons from de Mas Latrie, *Trésor de Chronologie* (1889), give some idea whether night travel had the advantage of a full moon. H. S. Bennett (*The Pastons and their England*, 2nd ed. 1932, pp. 262–3) has computed for a number of journeys the average distance covered daily. But I think averages are unreliable, because we seldom possess precise data, e.g. hour of departure and arrival; moreover, what we know of medieval travel points to much variation in the daily mileage of journeys occupying several days.

[6] Perth–Edinburgh (via Queensferry), 42 miles; Edinburgh–Berwick (via Haddington, Dunbar), 57 miles (the above are statutory miles over modern roads); Berwick–London, 339 miles (John Ogilby, *Itinerarium Anglie*, London, 1675, pl. 9). For the fifteenth century we have Hardyng's *Distaunce and Miles of the Tounes in Scotland* (*The Chronicle of John Hardyng*, ed. H. Ellis, 1812, p. 423):
   Edinburgh–Haddington, 12 miles.
   Haddington–Dunbar, 12 miles.
   Dunbar–Berwick, 20 miles.
   Mr. Denys Hay kindly consulted for me James Paterson, *A Geographical Description of Scotland* (3rd ed.), Holy-Rood House, 1687. Paterson (whose book first published in 1681 is very rare) uses 'the length of Endinburgh' which is '1184 paces at 5 foot the pace', and reckons accordingly, Perth–Edinburgh (via Queensferry), 28 miles; Edinburgh–Berwick, 40 miles; Edinburgh–London, 293 miles, 310 miles (via York).

of 20–1 February 1437.[1] On 28 February Piero del Monte, informed by Cardinal Beaufort, wrote from London recounting the murder to the pope. The length and careful Latinity of the letter suggest that its composition occupied not less than a day,[2] and since the messenger can scarcely have left Perth before dawn on 21 February, the news probably travelled to London in $6\frac{1}{2}$ days. In the spring of 1513, when posts from London to Berwick were in operation, royal letters from Greenwich to Edinburgh arrived in five and six days.[3]

> 2. Murder of William, duke of Suffolk.
>> (i) Dover–London, $71\frac{1}{2}$ miles.[4]
>> 2 May–4 May 1450, full moon 30 April.
>> (ii) Dover–Leicester, 170 miles via London.[5]
>> 2 May–6 May 1450.

Taken at sea 30 April 1450, Suffolk was beheaded and his body cast on shore near Dover 2 May. News of his death came to London 4 May, and was known 'for verray trouthe' on 6 May at Leicester where parliament was assembled.[6]

> 3. Birth of Prince Edward, son of Henry VI.
>> Westminster–Canterbury, 56 miles.[7]
>> 13 October–14 October 1453, new moon 6 October.

The prince was born at Westminster about 10 a.m. 13 October 1453, the royal letter announcing his birth was brought to Christ Church Canterbury on 14 October.[8]

> 4. Repulse of the Scots before Berwick.
>> Newcastle–London, 276 miles.[9]
>> 3 July–9 July 1455, full moon 3 July.

The bishop of Durham and others wrote from Newcastle 3 July 1455 reporting the relief of Berwick to the chancellor. Their letter was acknowledged from Westminster 9 July, the

---

[1] R. Weiss, 'Earliest Account of the Murder of James I', *Eng. Hist. Rev.* lii (1937), 481, n. 4, 489, note.

[2] Ibid., p. 481, n. 6, and see *supra*, p. 432, n. 6.

[3] *Letters and Papers, Henry VIII*, i (2nd ed.), no. 1463 (ii), no. 1735, pp. 791, 793.

[4] Ogilby, pl. 18.

[5] Ibid., pl. 40.

[6] *Paston Letters*, ii. 146–8.

[7] Ogilby, pl. 18.

[8] Stone, op. cit., p. 87.

[9] Ogilby, pl. 8. In mileages on the North Road I make no allowance for its medieval deviations, e.g. between Tuxford and Doncaster; see F. M. Stenton, op. cit., *Econ. Hist. Rev.* vii (1936–7), 10.

date given by 'Bale's Chronicle' for the receipt of the news in London.[1]

    5. Murder of Nicholas Radford.
        Poughill (Devon)–London, approx. 185 miles via Exeter.[2]
        23 October–28 October 1455, full moon 29 October.

Radford, councillor of Lord Bonville, was murdered after dark 23 October 1455 at Poughill by the son of the earl of Devon. Special messengers brought the news to the chancellor in London in the 'forenoon' 28 October.[3] Assuming the messenger left Exeter 24 October, the speed is that of Shillingford, mayor of Exeter, who rode out of the city 24 October 1447 and came to the chancellor at Westminster 9 a.m. 28 October. His companion, Dowlish, left Exeter 12 April 1448 and got to London 3 p.m., 16 April.[4]

    6. Sack of Sandwich by the French.
        Sandwich–Waltham, 81 miles via London.[5]
        28 August–29 August 1457, new moon 24 August.

The French landed near by at 6 a.m. 28 August and quickly entered Sandwich. On 29 August a commission was issued from Waltham to repel the enemy from Kent.[6]

    7. Battle of Wakefield.
        Wakefield–London, 182 miles via Ferrybridge.[7]
        30 December 1460–2 January 1461, full moon 1 January.

Fought 30 December 1460, the battle was told to Warwick in London on the morning of 2 January, according to 'Bale's Chronicle'.[8]

    8. Battle of Towton (fought 29 March 1461).
        York–London, 192 miles.[9]
        30 March–4 April 1461, full moon 31 March.

On 30 March 1461 from York Edward IV sent news of the

[1] *Proceedings . . . of the Privy Council*, vi (1837), 248; R. Flenley, *Six Town Chronicles*, p. 142.
[2] Ogilby, pl. 27.   [3] *Paston Letters*, iii. 49.
[4] *Letters of John Shillingford* (ed. Stuart A. Moore, Camden Soc., 1871), pp. 5, 6, 61. For another example of the journey on this route, see Addendum, p. 454.
[5] Ogilby, pl. 93.
[6] Stone, op. cit., p. 69; Wavrin, *Recueil des croniques . . . de la Grant Bretaigne* (ed. W. and E. L. C. P. Hardy, Rolls Series), v. 385; *Cal. Pat. Rolls (1452–61)*, p. 371.
[7] Ogilby, pl. 95.
[8] *Rot. Parl.* v. 466b; R. Flenley, *Six Town Chronicles*, p. 152.
[9] Ogilby, pl. 7.

battle to his mother, who received it in London 11 a.m. 4 April. Tidings sent, perhaps direct from the battlefield, were brought to the mayor of London on 3 April, on which day rumours of a Yorkist victory (one supposes brought by sea) reached Calais, but remained several days unconfirmed.[1] Communications may have been delayed by flooding in the Great Ouse basin.[2] A York burgess returning from parliament left London 26 March 1484 and reached York 31 March.[3]

9. Landing of Queen Margaret at Bamborough.
   Bamborough–London, approx. 325 miles.[4]
   25 October–by 30 October 1462, new moon 26 October.

Margaret landed at Bamborough 25 October 1462,[5] and on 30 October the Common Council of London granted Edward IV a loan for an expedition against her.[6] At this time the king may have had a messenger stationed at Grantham.[7]

10. Capture of Henry VI.
    'Bungerly' Hippingstones–Canterbury, approx. 282 miles.[8]
    13 July–18 July 1465, full moon 12 July.

King Henry was caught at 4 p.m. 13 July 1465 at 'Bungerly' Hippingstones, a ford on the Ribble.[9] A Lancashire monk brought the news to Edward IV at Canterbury about noon 18 July.[10]

11. Flight of Edward IV.
    Lynn–London, 98½ miles.[11]
    ?29 September–1 October 1470, new moon 29 September.

---

[1] See *supra*, p. 435, n. 3; p. 438, n. 3; Fabyan's *Chronicle* (ed. 1811), pp. 639–40; and *Calendar of State Papers, Milan*, i. 67.

[2] 'Brief Notes' in *Three Fifteenth Century Chronicles* (ed. J. Gairdner, Camden Soc., 1880), pp. 154, 155.

[3] *York Civic Records*, i. 88.   [4] Ogilby, pl. 9.

[5] *Collections of a London Citizen* (ed. J. Gairdner, Camden Soc., 1876), p. 218; W. Worcester's *Annals* in *Letters and Papers . . . of the Wars of the English in France* (ed. J. Stevenson, Rolls Series), ii, pt. 2, p. 780.

[6] C. Scofield, op. cit. i. 262 note.   [7] See *supra*, p. 440, n. 1.

[8] Clitheroe–Preston about 15 miles, Preston–London, 212 miles (Ogilby, pl. 38), London–Canterbury, 55 miles (ibid., pl. 28). Ogilby's routes coincide with the itineraries in *A Cronycle of Yeres . . .*, 1541, according to which, Preston–London is 160, London–Canterbury 42, computed miles.

[9] 'In a wode called Cletherwode, besyde Bungerly Hyppyngstones', Warkworth (ed. J. O. Halliwell, Camden Soc., 1839), p. 5. Brungerley bridge now carries the Waddington (Yorks.) to Clitheroe (Lancs.) road across the Ribble (Ordnance Survey 6 in. Yorks. sheet xlvii S.W.).

[10] Stone, op. cit., p. 93.   [11] Ogilby, pl. 43.

King Edward embarked at Lynn Michaelmas 1470, and his flight was published in London on 1 October 1470.[1] However, the announcement in London may have anticipated events, since H. J. Hillen,[2] quoting Lynn Hall Book, no. ii, f. 284, says that Edward entered Lynn at 10 p.m. on Sunday 30 September, and (but without specific reference) that he sailed at 8 a.m. on 2 October.

12. Return of Edward IV.
    Cromer–Wells, 250 miles via London.[3]
    12 March–by 16 March 1471, full moon 10 March.

Edward's fleet appeared off Cromer in the evening of 12 March 1471, but sailed northwards the same night. On 16 March the duke of Clarence wrote from Wells to Henry Vernon: 'We bee adcerteigned that it is said about London that king Edward is saylled by the coste of Northfolk toward Humbre.'[4]

13. Landing of Edward IV at Ravenspur.
    Ravenspur (Holderness)–Bury St. Edmund (? via London 245 miles).[5]
    14 March–by 19 March 1471, full moon 10 March.

Edward IV landed 14 March 1471 near Ravenspur, and on 19 March the earl of Oxford from Bury issued an urgent summons to arms because he had 'credible tydyngs' of the landing.[6] Oxford was the principal Lancastrian magnate in East Anglia and was probably advised from London.

14. Landing of Queen Margaret at Weymouth.
    Weymouth–London, 135 miles.[7]
    14 April–16 April 1471, full moon 9 April.

Queen Margaret landed at Weymouth in the evening 14 April 1471;[8] and it was reported to Edward IV in London on 16 April, when it was also known in the Steelyard.[9]

15. Battle of Barnet.
    Barnet–Cerne Abbas (Dorset), approx. 130 miles.[10]
    14 April–15 April 1471, full moon 9 April.

---

[1] Warkworth, op. cit., p. 11, and see *supra*, p. 442, n. 6.
[2] *History of King's Lynn*, East of England Newspaper Co., Norwich, 1907, i. 195–6.   [3] Ogilby, pls. 35, 46, 74.
[4] *Arrivall of Edward IV*, p. 2; see *supra*, p. 440, n. 2.
[5] Ogilby, pls. 42, 52.
[6] *Arrivall of Edward IV*, p. 2; *Paston Letters*, v. 96–7.
[7] Ogilby, pl. 53.   [8] Warkworth, op. cit., p. 17.
[9] *Arrivall of Edward IV*, p. 22; *Hanserecesse*, 2, vi (1890), 418.
[10] Ogilby, pl. 53.

Doubtless the battle was virtually decided by 8 a.m. 14 April 1471. Margaret learnt the result next day at Cerne.[1]

16. Surrender of St. Michael's Mount.
St. Michael's Mount–London, 288 miles.[2]
15 February–? 20 February 1474, full moon 6 February.

Oxford, having entered into negotiations, obtained a pardon 1 February, and yielded the Mount 15 February 1474.[3] On 20 February Sir John Paston from London wrote 'men seye that the erle of Oxenfford hathe ben constreynyd to sewe ffor his pardon only off hys lyffe, . . . and soo sholde in all haste nowe come in to the kyng, and some men seye that he is goon owt off the Mounte, and yit lefte a greet garnyson theer, weel ffornysshyd in vytayll . . .'. As in the closely analogous case of Pembroke Castle in 1461,[4] the capitulation of St. Michael's illustrates the difficulties experienced by contemporaries in determining an exact date for the receipt of news coming to hand bit by bit. Sir John obviously knew of the pardon to Oxford of 1 February. The reference to Oxford's departure suggests that the capitulation of 15 February was known in London by the 20th, but not yet confirmed, so that it was accompanied by the rumour of a large force left behind.

17. Surrender of Berwick.
Berwick–London, 339 miles.[5]
? 24 August–by 25 August 1482, new moon 17 August.

The terms of surrender for Berwick Castle, as preserved by Hall, are dated 24 August 1482. On 25 August from London Edward IV dated a letter to the pope announcing the submission of Berwick.[6] Even under favourable conditions King Edward's relay system, devised for this campaign, can scarcely have brought the news to London in 36 hours. Presumably the report was dispatched from Berwick or London in anticipation. During the campaign news was being sent home and officially published, for between 13 and 15 August the lieutenant at Calais ordered bonfires in the streets and discharge of ordnance from the walls to celebrate successes against the Scots.[7]

[1] See *supra*, p. 436, n. 4; *Arrivall of Edward IV*, p. 23.
[2] Ogilby, pl. 28.
[3] C. Scofield, op. cit. ii. 88; *Paston Letters*, v. 203.
[4] C. Scofield, op. cit. i. 202; Howell T. Evans, *Wales and the Wars of the Roses* (1915), p. 141; *Paston Letters*, iii. 312.
[5] Ogilby, pl. 9.
[6] Hall's *Chronicle* (ed. 1809), p. 335; *Calendar State Papers, Venice*, i. 146.
[7] *Cely Papers*, p. 113.

18. Death of Edward IV.
    (i) Westminster–Calais, 92 miles.[1]
       9 April–10 April 1483, new moon 10 April.
    (ii) Westminster–Ludlow, 136 miles.[2]
       9 April–14 April 1483.

(i) Edward died at Westminster 9 April, at an unrecorded hour, but probably in the morning, for the relation of his obsequies states that the king was immediately laid out for recognition by the lords and remained exposed for ten or twelve hours.[3] On 10 April a servant of Lord Hastings, lieutenant of Calais, crossed from Dover in a requisitioned vessel and informed Lord Dynham the resident deputy.[4] Provided the Channel was not impassable communications with Calais were rapid. In the Cely correspondence a letter from London dated 9 November (? 1482) was answered normally from Calais on 12 November.[5]

(ii) On 16 April Edward V wrote to Lynn 'the sorowfulle tydynges . . . was shewed unto us the 14th daye of this present moneth'.[6] Unless for personal reasons the news was withheld from him for some days after its arrival, there was no haste on the part of the council in London to inform the young king.

19. Buckingham's Rebellion.
    Lincoln–York 65 miles.[7]
    (i) 11 October–13 October 1484, full moon 9 October.
    (ii) 15 October–16 October.

(i) A signet letter of Richard III dated Lincoln, 11 October 1483, announcing the outbreak of Buckingham's rebellion was brought by a yeoman of the Crown to York on the 13th.[8] The rising started prematurely in Kent by 10 October, on which date Norfolk, the king's principal supporter, wrote from London to summon immediate aid from John Paston. This gives good

[1] Ogilby, pl. 18.
[2] Ibid., pl. 44.
[3] *Letters and Papers . . . Richard III and Henry VII* (ed. J. Gairdner, Rolls Series), p. 4.
[4] F. Devon, *Issues of the Exchequer* (1837), p. 505, from Tellers' Roll, Mich. 22 Edw. IV, 'relacio et prima noticia mortis Edwardi IVti'.
[5] *Cely Papers*, p. 131.
[6] *11th Report Hist. MSS. Com.*, App. III (1887), p. 170.
[7] Lincoln–Burton on Stather, 32 miles; Burton on Stather–Howden (by water), about 15 miles; Howden–York 18 miles, 'the shortest mediaeval route from Lincoln to York', F. M. Stenton, op. cit., p. 20.
[8] *York Civic Records*, i. 83–4.

grounds for supposing that the news covered the 128 miles from London to Lincoln in under 36 hours.[1]

(ii) A proclamation to be published at York was dispatched under privy seal from Lincoln on 15 October and reached its destination next day.[2]

20. Landing of Henry Tudor.
    Milford Haven–Bestwood (Notts.), approx. 242 miles via Carmarthen, Brecon, Monmouth, Gloucester, Coventry.[3]
    7 August–by 11 August 1485, new moon 14 August.

Henry landed 7 August 1485 at Milford Haven, and on 11 August Richard III from Bestwood (four miles north of Nottingham) wrote urgently to Henry Vernon announcing the landing.[4]

21. Battle of Bosworth.
    Bosworth–York, approx. 120 miles via Leicester, Loughborough, Nottingham, Newark.[5]
    22 August 23 August 1485, full moon 29 August.

The sources imply that the engagement, which lasted upward of two hours,[6] began early on 22 August. On the 23rd the Council of York heard the news from 'diverse personnes especially John Sponer [sergeant to the mace] sent unto the feld of Redemore to bring tydings . . . to the citie'. That day York forwarded the news to the earl of Northumberland at Wressel in a letter, which avoided comment but begged him 'to geve . . . credence unto our servant . . . the berer'.[7]

22. Battle of Stoke-on-Trent.
    Stoke–York 76 miles.[8]
    16 June–17 June 1487, full moon 10 June.

Victory did not fall to Henry VII till about noon 16 June, for although his army reached Stoke before 9 a.m., the battle was

[1] *Paston Letters*, vi. 73; A. Conway, 'Maidstone Sector of Buckingham's Rebellion', *Archaeologia Cantiana*, xxxvii (1925), 103; *Stonor Letters*, ii. 163; Ogilby, pl. 41.
[2] *York Civic Records*, i. 84–5.
[3] Ogilby, pls. 15, 17, 40, 70, 72, 77, 84. The itinerary in *A Cronycle of Yeres . . .* 1541, from Brecon to Gloucester ran via Hay, Hereford, Ross, which adds somewhat to the distance.
[4] *12th Report Hist. MSS. Com.*, App. IV (1887), p. 7.
[5] Ogilby, pls. 7, 78.
[6] 'Duravitque dimicatio amplius duas horas', Polydor Vergil, *Hist. Angl.* (ed. A. Thysius, Leiden, 1651), p. 715.
[7] *York Civic Records*, i. 119.   [8] Ogilby, pls. 6–7.

undecided after more than three hours' fighting.[1] At 3 a.m.
17 June the mayor of York received 'certaine knowlege' by a
servant of 'Master Recordour comyng streught from the feld'.
The mayor and council then proceeded to the minster for a
Te Deum. This is exceptional evidence for a message travelling
at night in England. The speed with which York learnt of battles
is so remarkable as to presuppose arrangements for changing
horses on the road. On 16 June from Newark Henry wrote
ordering thanksgivings; when this letter arrived is unknown.[2]

23. Landing of Perkin Warbeck.
   St. Buryan (Cornwall)–Woodstock (Oxon.).
   266 miles via Tavistock, Exeter, Wells, Bristol, Oxford.[3]
   7 September–10 September 1497, new moon 1 September.

Warbeck landed 7 September 1497 in Whitsand Bay, and
according to the Milanese ambassador Henry VII was apprised at
Woodstock on the 10th. The ambassador supposed wrongly that
Warbeck landed 6 September, and implied that the news had
come slowly because the distance from St. Michael's Mount to
Woodstock was only 200 (? computed) miles.[4]

24. Perkin Warbeck's assaults on Exeter.
   (i) Exeter–London, 172 miles.[5]
       17 September–21 September 1497, full moon 16
       September.
   (ii) Exeter–Woodstock, 154 miles.[6]
       18 September–by 20 September 1497.

(i) The unsuccessful attack on the city lasted from 1 p.m. to
about 3 p.m. 17 September 1497,[7] and 'certeyn tydynges' of the
rebels' repulse reached the mayor of London on the 21st.[8]
Between London and Exeter the timing in 1447, 1448, 1455, 1478,
1497 is remarkably even, suggesting that conditions on this route
(served by a carrier in 1480) remained constant for many years.[9]

---

[1] Leland, *Collectanea*, iv (1770), 214; Polydor Vergil, op. cit., p. 729: 'Dimica-
tum est plus tres horas aequo praelio.'
[2] *York Civic Records* (ed. A. Raine, Yorkshire Arch. Soc., Record Series, ciii,
1940), ii. 23–4.
[3] Ogilby, pls. 28, 58, 69, 79. In *A Cronycle of Yeres . . . 1541*, the itinerary ran
via Truro, Bodmin, Launceston, Oakhampton, Crockernwell, to Exeter, which is
longer than Ogilby's route.
[4] *Rot. Parl.* vi. 545a; *Calendar of State Papers, Milan*, i. 327.
[5] Ogilby, pl. 27.   [6] Ibid., pls. 58, 79.
[7] H. Ellis, *Original Letters*, 1 (1824), i. 34.
[8] *Chronicles of London*, ed. C. L. Kingsford (1905), p. 217.
[9] See *supra*, p. 446, nn. 3, 4, and *Stonor Letters*, ii. 105.

(ii) On 18 September the assault was renewed and again beaten off. This second failure was known to Henry VII at Woodstock by the 20th thanks to an *ad hoc* postal service.[1]

25. Perkin Warbeck's flight from Taunton.
    Taunton–London, 152 miles.[2]
    20–1 September–by 25 September 1497, new moon 1 October.

Warbeck deserted his army at Taunton about midnight 20–1 September 1497; on the 25th the Milanese ambassador, who probably resided in London throughout the rising, dispatched the news home via the Genoese merchants at Bruges. Fra Zuan Antonio de Carbonariis 'brought word of everything to Henry VII' at Woodstock, and he may be 'the man that come from Perkyn', to whom the king's chamber paid £1 on 25 September.[3]

26. Landing of Catherine of Aragon.
    Plymouth–London, 216 miles.[4]
    2 October–4 October 1501, full moon 1 October.

Catherine's ship entered Plymouth harbour at 3 p.m., 2 October 1501,[5] and on 4 October 'cam the ffyrst tydyngis of certaynte of þe landyng of dame Katheryn to the mayer [of London] albeit that many tymys ffleyng rumours ran that she was landid sundry tymys beffore. But now certaynte was brought from the kyng . . .'.[6] Such rapidity could not have been achieved without relays. The princess, whose arrival had been delayed by storms, was impatiently awaited by Henry VII, and the speed may be taken as the fastest possible. In 1442 royal letters of importance dated Windsor 23 June were delivered to Bekynton on 29 June at Plymouth.[7]

27. Death of Arthur, prince of Wales.
    Ludlow–Greenwich, 141 miles.[8]
    2 April–4–5 April 1502, full moon 27 March.

Arthur died at Ludlow 2 April 1502. His chamberlain, Sir

---

[1] Letter to the bishop of Bath and Wells, H. Ellis, op. cit., loc. cit.; *Excerpta Historica*, ed. S. Bentley (1831), p. 113.
[2] Ogilby, pls. 32, 58.
[3] *Chronicles of London*, op. cit., p. 217; *Calendar of State Papers, Milan*, i. 327–8; *Excerpta Historica*, loc. cit.
[4] Ogilby, pl. 27.
[5] *Calendar of State Papers, Spain*, i. 262.
[6] *Great Chronicle of London*, p. 296.
[7] *Official Correspondence of Thomas Bekynton* (ed. G. Williams, Rolls Series), ii. 179–81.   [8] Ogilby, pl. 44.

Richard Pole, wrote immediately to the king and council at Greenwich, where the messenger arrived so late in the night 4–5 April that the council preferred not to inform the king, but forthwith summoned his confessor, who broke the news to Henry VII at an early hour on the 5th.[1]

C. A. J. ARMSTRONG

[1] Leland, *Collectanea* (1770), v. 373.

ADDENDUM

p. 446. Bishop Redman of St. Asaph, who left Torre Abbey 3 August 1478, reached London, a distance of 195 miles, on 8 August. (Bodleian, MS. Ashmole 1519, f. 10ʳ). I find no evidence that he did the journey in four days as stated in *Collectanea Anglo-Premonstratensia* (ed. F. A. Gasquet, Camden 3rd Ser., 1906), iii, p. vii.

FIFTEENTH-CENTURY PRESENTATION DEEDS IN THE LINCOLN DIOCESAN RECORD OFFICE[1]

AFTER the final stage in the bishop's part in placing a clerk in possession of a benefice an entry recording institution is made in the bishop's register. Even when the process is perfectly straightforward, with no doubt as to the good title of the patron or the suitability of the clerk, it has for centuries involved the drawing up of at least three documents—the Presentation Deed sent by the patron to the bishop, which sets the wheels of administration in motion (unless the previous incumbent has executed a deed of resignation when the registrar would be bound to notify the patron): the Letters of Institution addressed by the bishop to the clerk: and the Mandate for Induction addressed by the bishop to the archdeacon or other appropriate person and handed to the clerk after institution to be given by him to the addressee.[2] It is with the first document, the Presentation Deed, that this article is concerned.

This deed is found in a rudimentary form in the twelfth century,[3] and from at least the early thirteenth century the responsible official in the bishop's chancery attached importance to the receipt of such letters for his master's protection against possible litigation with patrons.[4] By the third quarter of the thirteenth century these deeds had assumed their modern form,[5]

[1] I am indebted to Mrs. Joan Varley for reading this article and making some valuable suggestions.

[2] I am indebted to the senior clerk of the Lincoln Diocesan Registry for information about modern practice. This, however, seems to vary in some details from diocese to diocese, according to whether the offices of registrar and legal secretary are held by the same person as at Lincoln or by different persons as at Rochester.

[3] For an example see *Facsimiles of Twelfth Century Charters in Oxford Muniment Rooms*, edited by H. E. Salter, Oxford (privately printed), no. 26.

[4] Phillimore in the *History of Ecclesiastical Law*, i. 314, says presentation could at one time be by word of mouth and if so it must be declared in the presence of the bishop; but that since the Statute of Frauds (29. C. II, c. 3) at least it must be in writing. However, the insistence of the clerks on the written document in the early thirteenth century is illustrated in the Rolls of Hugh of Wells: institution to Flixborough (1220–1): *Non habemus litteras presentationis*; institution to Folksworth on the presentation of Crowland Abbey (1219–20): *Exigantur littere presentationis*; institution to Rushden on the presentation of William Basset (1220–1): *Idem Andreas faciet nobis habere litteras presentationis*. (*Rotuli Hugonis de Welles*, ed. W. P. W. Phillimore, Lincoln Record Soc. and Canterbury and York Soc., i. 217, iii. 34 (2).)

[5] For a good example see the presentation by Selby Abbey to the church of

and there is every reason to suppose that after the business of institution had been dispatched, they were filed in the Registry as warrants for the bishop's action as they are to-day. The first surviving deed, however, in the series at Lincoln known as *Presentation Deeds and Grants of Advowson*[1] is a solitary one for 1482, a Grant of Next Presentation which should properly be attached to the presentation to Orby, which it authorized, in 1493.[2] The earliest Presentation Deed proper is for 1484. In spite of various gaps due either to the Civil War, Commonwealth, and Protectorate (1646–60) or to the loss of whole bundles or parts of them, the series may be regarded as continuous to the present day, though for some years in the eighteenth century few but crown presentations have survived.

Since collections of this kind are little known owing to their comparative inaccessibility until recently, it seems worth while to illustrate some of their importance for historians. Presentation Deeds are essential documents for the registrar (or legal secretary) at various stages of his business: from them the Letters of Institution are drawn up:[3] and at the present time it is principally

---

St. Bartholomew, Lincoln, in 1275. *Registrum Antiquissimum of the Cathedral Church of Lincoln*, ed. Canon C. W. Foster, Lincoln Record Soc., xxviii. 169.

[1] Strictly speaking Presentations are not *Deeds* but Letters, but they were given this designation of Deeds in the Registry many years ago and have frequently been referred to as such.

[2] When the right of next presentation had been granted, the grantee had to send with his deed the grant made by the permanent patron. This was usually attached by putting the seal-tag of the temporary patron's seal through both documents, but some were tied with parchment strips at the corners. Where there had been a re-sale the deeds both of the original grant and the re-sale had to be sent in. Some still remain as originally received, but in many cases they have become detached and when they were arranged by Canon R. E. G. Cole in the early years of this century, he placed them under the year of grant, not under the year in which the right was exercised and in which they came to the Registry. In some cases the year is the same, but in others as much as twenty years might have elapsed before the living fell vacant: for grant of next presentation had to be made during the life-time of the incumbent as purchase during a vacancy was simoniacal. In cases where there had been two re-sales, four documents which were originally together may be in four different bundles. The deed of grant in some cases was recited in full in the register when institution was recorded: e.g. Stainby in 1491 (Register 22, f. 147ᵛ), Newport Pagnell Hospital in 1496 (Register 23, f. 311ᵛ), Ashwell, Rutland, 1494 (Register 22, f. 199). In this last case the deed still survives (P.D./1494/23). In other cases, e.g. Orby in 1493, the deed was not recited (Register 22, f. 159ᵛ).

[3] For this reason apart from any other it is easy to understand why the bishop's clerks preferred written to verbal presentations and why the entries occur in the Rolls of Hugh of Wells which show they were anxious to have them regarded as indispensable. It does not seem certain whether at that date Letters of Institution were drawn up for use at the ceremony, as has now been the custom for centuries past, or whether they were issued as Letters Testimonial after the ceremony. In any case the sending in of a letter of presentation would not only be important as

from them that the entry in the register or Act Book is made, the evidence of institution for the writer of the register being supplied either by the registrar in person if he has attended the ceremony; by the return of the declaration of assent if the institution has been performed by the bishop in the parish church concerned; or by the certificate of institution returned to the Registry if the institution has been performed by a commissary.[1]

In the fifteenth century it seems to have been the practice for the registrar, apparently at the time of the ceremony, to endorse on the deed the name of the archdeaconry in which the benefice lay, the date and place of institution, whether the clerk was instituted in person and if not, the name of the proctor: to this was added any other information such as the terms of a pension assigned to the retiring incumbent, which would need to be included in the record of institution. A normal endorsement runs as follows:

'Lincoln'.

ii[do] die Februarii anno domini retroscripto apud Vetus Templum London' personaliter fuit admissus.'[2]

Sometimes the last two words were omitted. Where the clerk was instituted by proxy the entry ran:

'xx° die mensis Januarii anno domini retroscripto apud Sonday in persona magistri Nicholai Trygge notarii publici fuit admissus etcetera [sic].'[3]

Such endorsements are almost invariably made in the hand of a man writing rapidly: for example in *admissus* the four minims of the *m* and the *i* are often reduced to a single horizontal line. Sometimes too the wrong archdeaconry is written, though this happens comparatively rarely and the mistake is corrected in practically every case in the same hand. But this also suggests a note made on the spot from memory and rapidly.

The entry in the register, as some examples to be quoted will show, is a combination of the information in the deed with that on the dorse, to which in some cases was added the content of an

providing a warrant but would also save the clerk the trouble of making a draft of the required information as he had to do in the case of collations. See *infra*, p. 458.

[1] I owe this information to the Registry clerk. Until the episcopate of Bishop Nugent Hicks (1933–42) institutions were performed in the bishop's chapel, but he began the practice of instituting in the parish church concerned. In such cases the registrar is dispensed from attendance, hence the second form of evidence for the writer of the register.

[2] P.D./1493/9. Institution of Robert Nelson to the sub-wardenship of the chantry of the Blessed Virgin in Brocklesby Church on the presentation of the abbot and convent of Newhouse.

[3] P.D./1493/10. Institution of Richard Toppyng to Great Hale.

additional document, such as the grant of next presentation in full or the summary of the findings of a commission *de jure patronatus*. When the entry had been made in the register, a large R.ᵃ was endorsed on the deed indicating that it had been duly registered, and it was then stored away.[1]

When the living or dignity was in the gift of the bishop the registrar made a summary of the information required on a slip of parchment and placed this with the Presentation Deeds.

'xiᵐᵒ die Septembris anno domini mᵒ cccclxxxxiiiᶜⁱᵒ apud Bukden' reuerendus in Christo pater et dominus dominus Johannes dei gratia Lincolniensis episcopus precentoriam ecclesie cathedralis Lincoln' ac prebendam de Kildesby eidem precentorie annexam et unitam vacantes et ad suam collacionem spectantes magistro Henrico Apiohn contulit ac ipsum precentorem et prebendarium inuestiuit et instituit in eisdem etcetera [*sic*].'[2]

When there was doubt as to a patron's right to present, a commission was issued to some qualified person to investigate this, and the fact of issue was usually endorsed: later if his right proved good the endorsement of institution would be added, but the results or even the fact of inquiry were not always mentioned in the register or, as in one case to be quoted below, the precise circumstances might not be stated. Even if the claim was not good the deed was filed and may be evidence for a dispute which never reached the king's court as a plea of advowson.

The deeds are also valuable as showing the time taken over such business, which may be as short as two days or as long as several months. Thomas Herby, presented to Sedgebrooke Deaconry by Eye Priory on 28 August 1492, was instituted on 30 August.[3]

Arthur Wode, presented by St. Michael's Priory, Stamford, to Thurlby by Bourne on 27 April 1492, was instituted at Buckden the next day.[4]

On the other hand when William Horme was presented to Congerstone on 5 October 1492 and exhibited the deed to the

---

[1] Professor Jenkins in 'Documents Subsidiary to Episcopal Registers' in the *Church Quarterly Review*, Apr.–June 1936, p. 50, says they are likely to have been destroyed at some time after the writing up in the register and the issue of the Induction Mandate, when they ceased to be useful for business purposes; but the importance attached to them nowadays as warrants and the careful indexing by seventeenth-century registrars at Lincoln of the fifteenth-century deeds suggests that they were normally preserved. Moreover there is the evidence from Hugh of Wells' Rolls that they were wanted even after registration. See p. 455, n. 4.

[2] P.D./1493/62.   [3] P.D./1492/53.   [4] P.D./1492/55.

bishop at Buckden on 26 October, a commission of inquiry was issued and he was not instituted until 23 March 1493.[1]

The following example concerning the church of Evedon in Lincolnshire shows how the Presentation Deed and its endorsement were combined to form the entry in the register.

'Reuerendo in Christo patri ac domino domino Johanni permissione diuina Lincolniensi episcopo vester humilis et deuotus filius Willelmus Hayrby de Euyden' generosus omnimodas reuerentias tanto egregio patri debitas cum honore. Ad ecclesiam beate Marie de Euyden' dicte vestre diocesis per resignacionem domini Thome Hayrby ultimi rectoris ibidem vacantem et ad meam presentacionem pleno iure spectantem dilectum michi in Christo dominum Hugonem Haryson capellanum vestreque diocesis vestre paternitati reuerendo caritatis intuitu presentium tenore presento humiliter supplicans et deuote quatinus eundem prefatum dominum Hugonem Haryson ad dictam ecclesiam admittere et ipsum rectorem in eadem instituere ceteraque omnia et singula que vestro in hac parte incumbunt officio pastorali peragere dignetur vestra paternitas reuerendus cum fauore. Dat' apud Euyden' sub sigillo quo utor xx° die Maii anno domini m^{llo} cccc° nonagesimo secundo.'

Endorsed.

'Lincoln'.

xxvi^{to} die Maii anno domini retroscripto apud Bukden' personaliter. Juratus que de solvendo pensione xxvi s. viii d. resignanti. Juravit insuper quod se submittet assignacioni alterius pensionis annue per dominum fiende dicto resignanti in casu quo ipse resignans non sit contentus cum dicta pensione xxvi s. viii d. quando ad hoc fuerit legitime vocatus.'

R.^{a}

The entry in the register[2] runs:

'Dominus Hugo Haryson presbiter presentatus per honestum virum Willelmum Harby de Evydon' generosum ad ecclesiam parochialem de Euydon' Lincolniensis diocesis per liberam resignacionem domini Thome Hareby ultimi rectoris eiusdem in manus domini factam et per ipsum admissam vacantem ad eandem xxvi^{to} die Maii anno domini millesimo cccc° lxxxxii^{do} apud Bukden' personaliter fuit admissus rector: que de bene et fideliter annuatim persolvendo supradicto domino Thome Hareby resignanti durante ipsius domini Thome vita naturali annuam pensionem viginti sex solidorum et octo denariorum sibi ad sustentacionem vite sue de fructibus et prouentibus dicte ecclesie per reuerendum in Christo patrem et dominum dominum Johannem permissione diuina Lincolniensem episcopum auctoritate sua ordinaria de consensu etiam quorum in hac parte interest assignatam et limitatam iuratus institutus canonice in eadem.

---

[1] See below, p. 460.   [2] Register 22, f. 150.

Juravit insuper quod se submittet assignacioni alterius pensionis annue per dominum fiende dicto resignanti in casu quo ipse resignans non sit contentus cum dicta xxvi s. et viii d. quando ad hoc fuerit legitime vocatus. Jurata canonica obedientia in forma.[1] Scriptum fuit etc.'[2]

The following is an illustration of information which has not been entered in the register. On 5 October 1492 Thomas Kebeell, sergeant at law, presented William Horme, deacon, to Congerstone, Leicester archdeaconry.[3] The endorsement runs as follows:

'Leicester'.

xxvi⁰ die Octobris anno domini retroscripto apud Bukden' exhibita fuit ista presentacio domino. Eisdem die et loco emanauit commissio ad inquirendum super iure patronatus eiusdem ecclesie directa magistro Johanni Sherman, vocatis vocandis in genere et in specie presentante et presentato retroscriptis necnon Johanne Beaumont armigero et domino Thoma Helen presbytero per ipsum Johannem Beaumont ad eandem ecclesiam primo presentato cum clausula de certificando expedito negotio etcetera [sic].

xxiii^tio die Marcii anno domini retroscripto apud Lydington' personaliter fuit admissus.'

R.ª

The entry in the register[4] contains no reference to the inquiry.

'Dominus Willelmus Horme, presbiter, presentatus per Thomam Kebell, seruientem ad legem domini regis hac vice patronum ad ecclesiam parochialem de Cunston Lincolniensis diocesis, per mortem domini Georgii Holden ultimi rectoris eiusdem vacantem, ad eandem xxiii⁰ die Marcii anno domini millesimo cccclxxxxii^do apud Lydington' personaliter fuit admissus et rector institutus canonice in eadem. Jurata canonica obedientia in forma. Scriptum fuit archidiacono Leicestr' seu eius officiali et cetera [sic].'

The reason for the inquiry was probably that Kebeell had not stated in the Deed that he was patron for one turn and had not sent his evidence of title in the form of the grant of next presentation.

A case, also from 1492, shows the attempt of a minor to exercise the right of presentation which lawfully belonged to his guardians and is an example of additional information from a commissary's report in the entry in the register. William Cuppuldyke of

---

[1] Sic: the registrar at this date always omits consueta.   [2] Sic.

[3] P.D./1492/45. Horme is described as deacon in the Presentation Deed. There would have been time for him to be ordained priest between October and March but his name is not in the Lincoln ordination lists.

[4] Register 22, f. 215ᵛ.

Harrington, who must have been almost of age, as he was born about 1471 or 1472, sent a Presentation dated 25 April 1492 in favour of William Garner for the rectory of Harrington on the death of John Turnley.[1] This he signed:

'Ego Willelmus Cuppuldyke subscribo nomen meum manu mea propria.'

This was not accepted by the bishop and it was endorsed

'Lincoln',

'Non exped'. Nota causam in libro papireo.'[2]

The following month he tried again and a similar deed dated 24 May[3] is endorsed

'Lincoln'.

'xxviii° die Junii apud London' personaliter.[4] Comparuit apud London' retroscriptus patronus et quia recusauit obedire certis iniunctionibus sibi per dominum conceptis non expeditus recessit. Et magis de causa notatur in libro papireo.'

It was not until August that his guardians, a group of local persons, enfeoffed of the manor to his use, presented John Longe, priest. This deed is unfortunately torn in half and part is lost, but the greater part of the endorsement is visible.[5]

'Lincoln'.

xxvii⁰ die Augusti anno retroscripto apud Bukden' emanauit commissio directa magistro Henrico Apiohn etc[6] ad inquirendum de iure patronatus et si ipsa inquisicio faciat pro presentantibus et presentato retroscriptis, ad expediendum cum clausula de certificando citra festum sancti Michaelis proximo futuro vocatis primitus Willelmo Cuppuldyke generoso et domino Willelmo Garner capellano qui dominus Willelmus prius fuit domino presentatus ad dictam ecclesiam per prefatum W. Cuppuldyke.'

The endorsement of the institution of Longe is defective.

'Octavo die mensis Octobris anno d........ apud Bukden' ...... de....'

In the register[7] the institution of Longe is followed by this entry.

'Capta prius inquisicione per magistrum Henricum Apiohn in Decretis Baccallarium commissarium domini generalem in archidiaconatibus Lincoln' et Stowe et in hoc negocio specialiter deputatum per quam

---

[1] P.D./1492/35. Signatures on deeds were unusual at this date. See p. 462, *infra*.
[2] There is no trace of this book among the existing records.
[3] P.D./1492/34.
[4] This is in a different hand from the rest of the endorsement: the second hand is the most usual one of the time.
[5] P.D./1492/76.
[6] *Sic.*   [7] Register 22, f. 152.

compertum est quod dicti feoffati sunt dicte ecclesie de Harington' patroni hac vice pro eo quod Willelmus Cuppuldyke minoris etatis defectum patitur. Et quod Thomas Sowych' ultimo presentauit ad eandem ea racione quod duxit in vxorem quandam Margaretam Cuppuldyke que habuit manerium de Harington racione dotis sue. Et quod dominus Willelmus Garner per prefatum Willelmum Cuppuldyke presentatus nullum ius habet ad ecclesiam predictam pro eo quod dictus Willelmus Cuppuldyke nunc presentans est hac vice in minore etate constitutus.'

The Presentation Deed of the fifteenth century was on parchment and was validated by a seal usually applied on a tongue rather than a tag.[1] Many of the seals have been lost, but several good specimens of those both of corporations and private persons survive.[2] It is interesting to see on some of these deeds the early use of the signature as a validation, though merely as supplement to the seal and at this time by no means an essential part of the document. The earliest one found is that of George Stanley, Lord Strange in 1487:[3] others are those of Jasper Tudor, duke of Bedford and earl of Pembroke, who grandiloquently styles himself *Regum frater et patruus*,[4] Edmund and John de la Pole, earls of Suffolk,[5] John Devereux, Lord Ferrers of Chartley,[6] Alexander Culpeper,[7] Sir John Longvile,[8] Sir Nicholas Vaux,[9] and Henry Veer[10] as well as William Cuppuldyke already mentioned, who seemed to think his signature would strengthen his bad claim.

The signature gradually spread downwards through the various ranks of society during the sixteenth century and by Elizabeth's reign it was so far regarded as essential to these deeds that those who could not write made their mark, whereas in the fifteenth century only a very small minority of the deeds were signed. There were few male patrons in the late sixteenth century who could not sign their own names, but even in the seventeenth there were several women of good family who were wholly illiterate. This collection provides an interesting means of studying the use of the signature.

The deeds were evidently grouped by the year, beginning on

[1] In 1493 out of 116 only eleven have seals on a tag.
[2] Croxton Abbey (P.D./1487/19), Lincoln College, Oxford, seal *ad causas* (P.D./1493/24), Sixhill Priory (P.D./1495/13), Thomas West, knight (P.D./1495/7), Richard Thimbleby (P.D./1495/19), Humphrey Belcher (P.D./1493/73). A card catalogue of the seals is being compiled by Mr. George Dixon, F.S.A.
[3] P.D./1487/8.   [4] P.D./1493/83.
[5] P.D./1490/39; P.D./1491/15.   [6] P.D./1492/2.
[7] P.D./1489/5.   [8] P.D./1490/42.
[9] P.D./1492/5.   [10] P.D./1487/16.

25 March, and were possibly originally filed on a spike, as they have a hole in one corner which suggests this method: they may later have been filed on tapes put through a carefully cut lozenge-shaped hole in the middle of the left side.[1] If so, a stop was probably provided by a knot and the loose end of the tape was then wound round the rest of the bundle. This is conjectural as the bundles in all cases to 1660 had already been broken up into arrangement by the modern calendar year when they were seen by the writer: after that date, although they were by the year beginning on 25 March, they had been placed in brown-paper folders, and no one now can say precisely what state they were in when Canon R. E. G. Cole made the rearrangement. But bundles of Churchwardens' Presentments from the post-Restoration period were found fastened in the manner described, in 1936, having apparently been untouched since they had been put away after the business of the visitation had been completed. It is clear from the surviving indexes, which seem to have been made in the late seventeenth century, that the deeds were carefully examined at that time, and it is possible that they were transferred from spikes to tapes then. But this can be no more than a mere suggestion. The indexes were alphabetical by the first letter of the name only: each parish was numbered in the index, and there was a corresponding number on the deed. Unfortunately with the breaking up of the original arrangement these indexes do not correspond with the present bundles. Nor are all the indexes complete, as they were made on scraps of parchment usually only four inches long by two inches wide, and since several were needed for each year one or more may be lost. The number of deeds surviving for each year varies very much, from two in 1484 to 116 for 1493. The bundles for 1497 to 1502 seem to be entirely lost, as the only documents for any of those years are grants of next presentation which must originally have been attached to deeds of other years.

Collections of this kind have an obvious value when the registers are lost, as they are at Lincoln for many years between 1560 and 1660, but they would also repay study in connexion with pure diplomatic: with the extremely interesting subject of the market for sales of next presentation, for which they are probably the only extensive source before the insertion of advertisements in newspapers; and with the internal workings of the Registry. Over a period of centuries the endorsements vary and form a

[1] It is difficult to see for what other purpose it could be intended.

useful guide to administrative practice. For example, in the time of Bishop Chaderton (1595–1608) but unfortunately not thereafter, the examining chaplain entered a biography of the presentee on the dorse;[1] the bishop signified assent by writing on the fold (for by this time seals on tags were the general rule), 'Ad. W. L.' (Admissus. William Lincoln:). This record of admission written by the bishop himself perhaps indicates that the registrar was in less close attendance on the bishop and now needed this form of authorization for drawing up Letters of Institution because he was not present and could not be authorized verbally. A full study of this series, together with the other collections of documents, might well throw light on the relationship between the registrar and the increasingly important legal secretary. With the greater accessibility of episcopal archives to which we may look forward, it is probable that attention will be paid to records of this kind; it will be of advantage to students if they are kept in the classes in which they were placed by the earlier registrars, since much information is to be gained from a study of office practice, and where, as in one instance, a series of Presentation Deeds has been split up in a parish classification, the resulting disadvantage to the student of administration and diplomatic has not been compensated for by gain to the student of purely parochial history.

K. MAJOR

---

[1] For an example of such a biography see 'Lincoln Diocesan Records as Sources for the Genealogist', *Genealogists' Magazine*, Sept. 1941, p. 170.

SOME BOOK-MARKERS AT PETERHOUSE

THE rarity of English medieval book-markers is surprising. I am not thinking of the marker ingeniously designed for permanent use, such as survive for example in two manuscripts at Cambridge (Corpus Christi 49 and St. John's 90) and in one at Hereford (P. vi. 11); still less of the ornamental *registrum* recorded in inventories;[1] for it would be surprising if they were common. Rather of the odd scrap—the envelope, the stray half-sheet—with which one marks one's place on closing a volume for the day, only to find it embedded years later in the same place, recalling some trivial incident of life long before. Is it because the medieval reader had no such ready source of scrap for markers, that one so rarely finds anything of interest still thrust between the leaves of a medieval book? For, in my very limited experience, if one finds as a place-marker in a manuscript a bit of vellum or paper with anything written on it, it is hardly ever earlier than the sixteenth century. What one supposes to be medieval, and finds not uncommonly, is the piece of grass or straw that so aroused the disapproval of the author of the *Philobiblon*—'uidebis fortassis iuuenem ceruicosum . . . paleas dispertitur innumeras, quas diuersis in locis collocat euidenter, ut festuca reducat quod memoria non retentat. Hae paleae, quia nec uenter libri digerit nec quisquam eas extrahit, primo quidem librum a solita iunctura distendunt, et tandem negligenter obliuioni commissae putrescunt.'[2]

If this is so, it may perhaps be worth while to ask a few moments' attention for some fifteenth-century markers which have come to light in the course of browsing among the manuscripts of Peterhouse in Cambridge.[3] MS. 166, a *Flores Bernardi* in a good hand of the later thirteenth century, has fastened in between ff. 43 and 44 a little slip of paper covered with neat writing of the fifteenth, but one cannot make much of this; it is only a fragment, and appears to come from some recipe or medical prescription. Nor is one much more edified by the long slip of vellum that still stands as a marker at f. 97 of MS. 243, a

---

[1] Chr. Wordsworth and H. Littlehales, *Old Service-books of the English Church* (1904), p. 278.

[2] *The Philobiblon of Richard de Bury*, ed. E. C. Thomas (1888), p. 130.

[3] My most sincere thanks are due to Professor H. Butterfield and the Rev. J. N. Sanders, librarians of the College, for giving me freedom to work in the Perne Library and much kindness and encouragement.

fifteenth-century *Campus Florum* in a neat and rather pretty English hand, which merely bears part of the familiar couplet

Anno mi]lleno centeno septuageno
Anglorum primas corruit ense Thomas.

But MS. 132 is slightly more forthcoming. This is a *Legenda Aurea*, a very ordinary sort of book, written in several hands of the late thirteenth century or early fourteenth, and inserted in it as markers are three long strips of vellum, as much as 14 in. long and from $\frac{1}{2}$ to $\frac{3}{4}$ in. in width, covered with writing in neat fifteenth-century hands, as follows:

(*a*) at f. 61 (the top of the strip has been torn down, as nurses tear bandages, and the two tags thus made tied together in a knot, destroying the beginning of the message):

. . . Willelmus Clerk pridie idus Augusti Johannes xviij° kal. Maii Johannes x° kal. Mart. Johannes vij° id. Oct. Thomas idus Aprilis Johannes Jacobus xvi° kal. Sept. Johannes diaconus canonici et professi Ecclesie sancte Trinitatis London' dominus Robertus episcopus London' Jacobus comes Johannes Walterus (here dirt and damp supervene, and after a short gap we begin the second line) . . . Margar' Willelmus Agnes Johanna Willelmus Johannes Thomas Willelmus Johannes Johanna Johannes Johannes Johannes Franciscus Isabella Thomas Elizabetha Edmundus Robertus Willelmus Thomas Agnes Johannes Emot' Johannes Agnes Thomas Lodwicus Johannes Johannes Alicia (and the last two names are lost).

(*b*) at f. 66, three scrumpled scraps, which flattened and mended make another slip (the beginning lost):

. . . frater Thomas v^to kal. Mart. frater Johannes kal. Julii frater Robertus kal. Oct. frater Willelmus iiij^to Non. Oct. frater Johannes ij Non. eiusdem mensis frater Willelmus et frater Johannes monachi sacerdotes et professi monasterii beate Marie et sancti Nicholai Spald' ordinis sancti . . . (here we break off, and continue on the dorse) . . . Alicia Margeria Margareta Agnes Johanna sorores nostre Alexander Alexander Robertus Katerina. x° kal. Febr. ·o· frater Thomas Alicia Leke ff.

(*c*) at f. 102, another long slip, caught in by the binder so that it cannot be taken out and flattened, but the first words legible are

. . . dominus Willelmus le Poole dux Suff. Johannes Johannes Matilda Johannes Rosa Johannes Mar' (or is it magister?) Johannes Grey Willelmus Johannes (and then follow a round dozen more of these personal names).

Who were all these people? And why are their bare Christian names set out, often with dates, if not that they are members of the great host of the departed, who crave the suffrages of the

living upon the anniversary of their day of death? I do not pretend to understand this, and the donor of the manuscript to
Peterhouse—it came in 1481 with the great gift of books made by
John Warkworth, then master—seemed little help. On the lining
of the lower cover was a greenish smudge, such as is left sometimes by erased inscriptions, and the ultra-violet lamp was called
upon. It was an inscription, but on the underside of the paste-
down, only to be read in a mirror (and it is surprising how few
libraries are so equipped): 'Legenda Sanctorum ecclesie Rameseye si quis . . . erit anatema sit.' Perhaps this gives us the
answer, and all these people were *confratres* of the abbey of
Ramsey, or associated with one of the altars in the Abbey church,
or—if of another foundation—bound to it in some way, by obit
roll or *amicabilis concordia* so as to deserve its prayers upon their
anniversary. If this is so, we are given a vivid glimpse of the
host of individuals for whom prayer was offered every day,
wherein the countless Johns and the Williams and Agneses and
Margarets are on one footing with the monks of Spalding, with
Robert, bishop of London—Robert Braybrooke, who died in
August 1405—and William de la Pole, duke of Suffolk, the great
noble whose beheading in May 1450, with a rusty sword upon
the *Nicholas of the Tower* by one of the lewdest of the ship, is
perhaps the most memorable of all the pictures in the *Paston
Letters*.

My other book-marker recalls a different aspect of fifteenth-
century society, the household of a noble and learned bishop. Anyone who has had much to do with the library of Balliol College,
Oxford, will have a lively interest for anything that touches
William Gray the humanist, who was its greatest benefactor;
who, having lived as a sojourner within its walls, spent nine years
as the king's proctor at the papal curia, and from 1454 till 1478
was bishop of Ely. One watches the newly promoted bishop
presenting to a good living the master of his old Oxford college,
Robert Thwaites; making his nephews useful; choosing as his
chaplains two or three fellows of Balliol, and a fellow of Merton,
John Warkworth aforesaid, who afterwards became master of
Peterhouse and did so much for the College of his adoption. For
the conduct of his secular affairs, this humanist prelate relied on
two trusty servants, both probably north-countrymen. One was
a certain Elias Cliderow, who had remained in London as his
agent while he himself was at the curia,[1] and on his appointment

[1] The evidence for this is a draft among the *Paston Letters* (ed. James Gairdner,

to Ely became his *receptor generalis* and I know not what besides. The other, Richard Thwaites, brother of the master of Balliol and in 1459 executor of his will, had been with Gray at the curia and had served as *camerarius* of the English Hospice in Rome;[1] when Gray returned to England to be a bishop, he brought this Thwaites back with him and made him his *marescallus hospicii* and later keeper of his park at Hatfield, who so continued till his death in 1467. To one possessed of some acquaintance, however slight, with this episcopal household, it was a curious experience, while turning over the books given to Peterhouse by John Warkworth, to find in MS. 165—a fifteenth-century *Distinctiones Januensis*—used as a marker at f. 27, a scrap of paper bearing the words

Hic iacet Ricardus Thwaites [armiger *deleted*] quondam/armiger et marescallus hospicii domini episcopi Eliensis.

Rightly or wrongly, it gave a sudden vivid sense of looking over the shoulder of the bishop's chaplain, as he drafted an inscription for the tombstone of his man of affairs, perhaps at the request of the patron whom for many years they had served together.

These are mere trifles, worthless scraps from a bibliographer who is no historian, and deserve no place in a volume like the present. But he to whom they are offered knows the value in these studies even of trifles; so let them stand as a bibliographer's small tribute of affection and respect for the author of *The Medieval Books of Merton College*.

R. A. B. Mynors

1904, vol. vi, p. 34) which must be dated some thirty years earlier than its editor suggests.

[1] See V. J. Flynn in *Modern Philology*, xxxvi (1938–9), 126.

A BIBLIOGRAPHY OF THE PUBLISHED WRITINGS OF F. M. POWICKE

1902–47

ABBREVIATIONS

C.P. Clarendon Press.
E.H.R. English Historical Review.
J.T.S. Journal of Theological Studies.
M.G. Manchester Guardian.
M.U.P. Manchester University Press.
T.L.S. Times Literary Supplement.
T.R.H.S. Transactions of the Royal Historical Society.

1902

Pierre Dubois: a Mediaeval Radical. *Historical Essays by Members of Owens College, Manchester*, ed. T. F. Tout and J. Tait. London: Longmans Green & Co., pp. 169–91. Reissued 1907.

1906

Impression of F. York Powell in *F. York Powell: a Life*, by Oliver Elton, i. 207–9. C.P.

Roger of Wendover and the Coggeshall Chronicle. *E.H.R.* xxi. 286–96.

The Angevin Administration of Normandy. Part i. Ibid. 625–49.

1907

The Angevin Administration of Normandy. Part ii. *E.H.R.* xxii. 15–42.

REVIEWS: *Histoire critique de Godefroid le Barbu*, by E. Dupréel; *Le Duc de Lorraine Mathieu Ier (1139–76)*, by E. Duvernoy. *E.H.R.* xxii. 773–8.

The Political History of England, ed. William Hunt and Reginald Lane Poole, i–iv. *The Journal of Education*, xxix. 427–9.

1908

The Abbey of Furness. *Victoria County History of Lancaster*, ii. 114–31.

The Chancery during the Minority of Henry III. *E.H.R.* xxiii. 220–35.

REVIEW: *Essai sur les rapports de Pascal II avec Philippe Ier (1099–1108)*, by B. Monod. *E.H.R.* xxiii. 765–6.

1909

Science in the Teaching of History. *Broad Lines in Science Teaching*, ed. F. Hodson, pp. 135–45. (Christophers, London.)

King John and Arthur of Brittany. *E.H.R.* xxiv. 659–74.

REVIEWS: *Papst Leo IX und die Simonie*, by J. Drehmann. *E.H.R.* xxiv. 397.

Henri I, duc de Brabant (1190–1235), by G. Smets. Ibid. 610.

Chronicon universale Anonymi Laudunensis, ed. A. Cartellieri. Ibid. 824–5.

1910

The Pleas of the Crown in the Avranchin. *E.H.R.* xxv. 710–11.

The Saracen Mercenaries of Richard I. *Scottish Historical Review*, viii. 104–5.

REVIEWS: *Recueil des actes de Philippe Ier, roi de France*, ed. M. Prou. *E.H.R.* xxv. 151–4.

La Chronique de Morigny, 1095–1152, ed. L. Mirot. Ibid. 195–6.

The Interdict, by E. B. Krehbiel. Ibid. 398–9.

La Société française au temps de Philippe-Auguste, by A. Luchaire. Ibid. 564–7.

Französische Verfassungsgeschichte, by R. Holtzmann. Ibid. 761–2.

Ex Guidonis de Bazochiis chronographie libro septimo, ed. A. Cartellieri. Ibid. 812.

1911

The Honour of Mortain in the Norman Infeudationes Militum of 1172. *E.H.R.* xxvi. 89–93.

A great French scholar: Léopold Delisle. *Quarterly Review*, 214. 486–9.

REVIEWS: *Das Anwachsen der deutschen Städte in der Zeit der mittelalterlichen Kolonialbewegung*, by A. Püschel. *E.H.R.* xxvi. 413–14.

Quellenkunde zur Weltgeschichte, ed. P. Herre. Ibid. 543–5.

Der Bürgerstand in Strassburg bis zur Mitte des XIII. Jahrhunderts, by K. Achtnich. Ibid. 571–2.

Philipp von Elsass, Graf von Flandern (1157–91), by J. Johnen. Ibid. 619–20.

Zur Datierung und Charakteristik altfranzösischer Krönungsordnungen, by M. Buchner. Ibid. 620–1.

The King's Serjeants and Officers of State, by J. H. Round. Ibid. 774–7.

The House of Lords during the Civil War, by C. H. Firth. *Scottish Historical Review*, viii. 410–12.

1912

King Philip Augustus and the Archbishop of Rouen (1196). *E.H.R.* xxvii. 106–17.

REVIEWS: *La Clameur de haro dans le droit normand*, by H. Pissard. *E.H.R.* xxvii. 596.

Le Parage normand, by R. Génestal. Ibid. 596–7.

Les Communes françaises, by A. Luchaire, ed. L. Halphen. Ibid. 597.

The Cambridge Medieval History, vol. i. *Scottish Historical Review*, ix. 301–3.

1913

THE LOSS OF NORMANDY (1189–1204): STUDIES IN THE HISTORY OF THE ANGEVIN EMPIRE (Manchester University Publications, Hist. Series, no. 16). M.U.P.

The Poetic in history. *History*, ii (4), 175–87.

REVIEWS: *Henry the Lion*, by A. L. Poole. *E.H.R.* xxviii. 395–6.

Die rechtlichen Grundgedanken der französischen Königskrönung, by H. Schreuer. Ibid. 601–2.

Die Entwicklung der Landeshoheit der Vorfahren des Fürstenhauses Reuss, 1122–1329, by W. Finkenwirth. Ibid. 603.

Zur Frage des Ursprungs der mittelalterlichen Zünfte, by W. Müller. Ibid. 604–5.

Le Bourgage de Caen; tenure à cens et tenure à rente (xie–xve siècles), by H. Legras. Ibid. 765–8.

Die mittelalterlichen Erbschaftssteuern in England, by P. Haensel. Ibid. 804–5.

Die Anfänge der französischen Ausdehnungspolitik bis zum Jahr 1308, by F. Kern. Ibid. 806.

Instrucions et ensaignemens, ed. G. Besnier and R. Génestal. Ibid. 807–8.

The Minority of Henry the Third, by Kate Norgate. *Scottish Historical Review*, x. 403–5.

William Pitt and National Revival and *William Pitt and the Great War*, by J. Holland Rose. Ibid. 415–17.

British Borough Charters 1042–1216, ed. A. Ballard. Ibid. xi. 95–8.

1914

BISMARCK AND THE ORIGIN OF THE GERMAN EMPIRE. (People's Books.) London: Jack.

REVIEWS: *Year Books of Edward II; The Eyre of Kent, 6 & 7 Edward II*, ed. W. C. Bolland, F. W. Maitland, L. W. Vernon Harcourt. *E.H.R.* xxix. 358–61.

Chroniques des comtes d'Anjou et des seigneurs d'Amboise, by L. Halphen and R. Poupardin. Ibid. 397.

Calendar of Patent Rolls 1266–72. E.H.R. xxix. 399–400.

The Norman Administration of Apulia and Capua, by E. Jamison. Ibid. 547–50.

Untersuchungen über Heiligenleben der Westlichen Normandie, by B. Baedorf. Ibid. 598–9.

Ordonnances de J. d'Ableiges pour les métiers d'Évreux 1385–7, ed. A. Giffard. Ibid. 788.

The Cambridge Medieval History, vol. ii. *Scottish Historical Review*, xi. 209–10.

The Life of William Pitt, Earl of Chatham, by B. Williams. Ibid. 318–19.

The King's Council in England during the Middle Ages, by J. F. Baldwin. Ibid. 415–17.

A History of England from the Defeat of the Armada to the Death of Elizabeth, by E. P. Cheyney. Vol. i. Ibid. 429–32.

1915

REVIEWS: *Essai sur l'armée royale au temps de Philippe Auguste*, by É. Audouin. *E.H.R.* xxx. 113–14.

Contribution à l'histoire de l'ordre de Saint-Lazare de Jérusalem en France, by R. Pétiet. Ibid. 328–9.

Select Bills in Eyre, A.D. *1292–1333*, ed. W. C. Bolland. Ibid. 330–6.

Studies in Taxation under John and Henry III, by S. K. Mitchell. Ibid. 530–5.

1917

Per iudicium parium vel per legem terrae. *Magna Carta Commemoration Essays* (Royal Historical Society), pp. 96–121.

1918

The Origins of France, I. *History*, iii. 129–36.

REVIEWS: *Recueil des actes de Philippe-Auguste*, vol. i, ed. H. F. Delaborde. *E.H.R.* xxxiii. 392–5.

Norman Institutions, by C. H. Haskins. *T.L.S.* 136.

1919

The Origins of France, II. *History*, iii. 193–204.

St. Bartholomew's Hospital. *Quarterly Review*, 232, pp. 110–21.

REVIEWS: *Modern France, 1815–1913*, by É. Bourgeois. *E.H.R.* xxxiv. 618.

Benedict IX and Gregory VI, by R. L. Poole. *History*, iii. 245–6.

Imperial Influences on the Forms of Papal Documents, by R. L. Poole. *History*, iii. 246–7.

Henry II, by L. F. Salzmann. *T.L.S.* 29.

The Baronial Opposition to Edward II, by J. Conway Davies. Ibid. 220.

The Collected Historical Works of Sir Francis Palgrave, vols. i–ii, *The History of Normandy and of England*. Ibid. 272.

1920

Article 13 of the Articles of the Barons (1215). *E.H.R.* xxxv. 401–2.

REVIEWS: *The Entries relating to Jersey in the Great Rolls of the Exchequer of Normandy*, A.D. *1180*, by G. F. B. de Gruchy. *E.H.R.* xxxv. 152.

Die Mainzer Dompropstei im 14. Jahrhundert, by F. Vigener. Ibid. 152–3.

Le Bailliage de Vermandois aux xiiie et xive siècles, by H. Waquet. Ibid. 265–7.

Staatstheorien Papst Innocenz's III, by E. W. Meyer. Ibid. 469–70.

Les Lorrains et la France au Moyen-Âge, by M. de Pange. Ibid. 618.

Medieval Reckonings of Time, by R. L. Poole; *The Public Record Office*, by C. Johnson; *The Public Record Office, Dublin*, by R. H. Murray. *History*, iii. 219–21.

Histoire de Lorraine, tome i: *Des Origines à 1552*, by Robert Parisot. *T.L.S.* 160.

À travers trois siècles: L'Œuvre des Bollandistes, 1615–1915, by Hippolyte Delehaye. Ibid. 728.

Chapters in the Administrative History of Mediaeval England, by T. F. Tout, vols. i and ii. *The Athenaeum*, July–December, 174–5.

1921

Ailred of Rievaulx and his biographer Walter Daniel. *The Bulletin of the John Rylands Library*, vi. 310–51.

Maurice of Rievaulx. *E.H.R.* xxxvi. 17–29.

History Lessons and the League. *M.G.* 12 March.

REVIEWS: *Das Mittelalter bis zum Ausgange der Kreuzzüge*, by S. Hellmann. *E.H.R.* xxxvi. 143–4.

Geschichte des deutschen Volkes vom dreizehnten Jahrhundert bis zum Ausgang des Mittelalters, vol. vi, by E. Michael. Ibid. 304–5.

Ireland under the Normans, vols. iii, iv, by G. H. Orpen; *Materials for the History of the Franciscan Province of Ireland*, ed. E. B. Fitzmaurice and A. G. Little. Ibid. 451–5.

Studies in Statecraft, by Sir Geoffrey Butler. *Scottish Historical Review*, xviii. 210–11.

Collected Papers, by Sir Adolphus Ward; vols. i and ii: *Historical. M.G.* 1 March.

Histoire de la formation de la population française: les étrangers en France sous l'Ancien Régime, by J. Mathorez, tome i. *T.L.S.* 186.

The Collected Historical Works of Sir Francis Palgrave, vols. iii–vii. Ibid. 797.

Documents illustrative of the Social and Economic History of the Danelaw, ed. F. M. Stenton. Ibid.

Robert Curthose, Duke of Normandy, by C. W. David. Ibid.

1922

AILRED OF RIEVAULX AND HIS BIOGRAPHER WALTER DANIEL. Reprinted from the *Bulletin of the John Rylands Library*, vi, with corrections. M.U.P.

Ailred of Rievaulx and his biographer Walter Daniel. *The Bulletin of the John Rylands Library*, vi. 452–521.

Northern Universities.—I. Manchester. *The Serpent*, vii. 47–50.

REVIEWS: *The Early History of the Monastery of Cluny*, by L. M. Smith. *E.H.R.* xxxvii. 138–9.

Dispensing Power and the Defence of the Realm, by E. F. Churchill. Ibid. 319.

Mediaeval Contributions to Modern Civilisation, ed. F. J. C. Hearnshaw. Ibid. 461–2.

La Première Étape de la formation corporative. L'entr'aide, by G. des Marez. Ibid. 463.

Year Books of Edward II, vol. xiv, part i. Ibid. 464–5.

The Book of Fees, commonly called Testa de Nevill, ed. H. C. Maxwell-Lyte, part i. Ibid. 570–3. Cf. *infra*, 1932.

The History of Remedies against the Crown, by W. S. Holdsworth. Ibid. 626.

Robert Curthose, Duke of Normandy, by C. W. David. *History*, vi. 264–5.

The Cambridge Medieval History, vol. iii. *History*, vii. 208–11; also in *T.L.S.* 331.

The Norse discoveries of America: The Wineland Sagas, translated and discussed by G. M. Gathorne-Hardy. *Scottish Historical Review*, xix. 135.

Somerset historical essays, by J. Armitage Robinson. *Scottish Historical Review*, xx. 58–61.

Histoire de la formation de la population française, by J. Mathorez; tome ii: *Les Allemands, les Hollandais, les Scandinaves.* T.L.S. 372.

La Formation de l'unité française, by Auguste Longnon. Ibid. 694.

1923

REVIEWS: *Newington Longeville Charters*, ed. H. E. Salter. *E.H.R.* xxxviii. 100–1.

Transcripts of Charters relating to Gilbertine Houses, ed. F. M. Stenton. Ibid. 269–70.

Close Rolls of the Reign of Henry III, 1247–51. Ibid. 433–5.

La Vie de S. Thomas le martyr de Garnier de Pont-Sainte-Maxence, ed. M. E. Walberg. Ibid. 462–3.

Year Books of Edward II, vol. xvi. Ibid. 464–5.

1924

The Historical Method of Mr. Coulton. *History*, viii. 256–68, *followed by* Some Observations in Conclusion. Ibid. ix. 13–17.

REVIEWS: *The Inquisition*, by H. Nickerson. *E.H.R.* xxxix. 146.

Curia Regis Rolls of the Reigns of Richard I and John, vol. i, *Richard I– 2 John.* Ibid. 264–72.

Eginhard: Vie de Charlemagne, ed. L. Halphen. Ibid. 307–8.

Histoire de la coutume de la prévôté et vicomté de Paris, vol. i, by Olivier Martin. Ibid. 595–7. Cf. *infra*, 1927 and 1931.

Vita beati ac gloriosi regis Eadwardi, ed. Marc Bloch. Ibid. 628–9.

Plaids de la sergenterie de Mortemer, 1320–1, ed. R. Génestal. Ibid. 631.

The Times of Saint Dunstan, by J. A. Robinson. *History*, ix. 57–8.

The Cambridge Medieval History, vol. iv. *Scottish Historical Review*, xxi. 233–5.

1925

ESSAYS IN MEDIEVAL HISTORY PRESENTED TO THOMAS FREDERICK TOUT. Ed. A. G. Little and F. M. Powicke. M.U.P.

Some Observations on the Baronial Council (1258–60) and the Provisions of Westminster. Ibid. 119–34.

Professor Tout and the Study of Medieval History. *M.G.* 3 October.

Master Simon of Faversham. *Mélanges d'histoire du moyen âge offerts à M. Ferdinand Lot.* Paris, pp. 649–58.

The *Dispensator* of King David I. *Scottish Historical Review*, xxiii. 34–41.

The Rôle of Youth in the Middle Ages. *Vox Studentium* [i.e. I.S.S. Annals], ii. 3–4.

REVIEWS: *A History of Magic and Experimental Science during the first Thirteen Centuries of our Era*, by Lynn Thorndike. *E.H.R.* xl. 111–13.

The Grey Friars of Canterbury, by Charles Cotton. Ibid. 157.

Note sur la ministérialité en Belgique, by G. des Marez. Ibid. 302–3.

Studies in the History of Medieval Science, by C. H. Haskins. Ibid. 421–3.

A History of Medieval Ireland, 1110–1513, by E. Curtis. *History*, ix. 331–4.

Medieval People, by Eileen Power. *History*, x. 183–4.

1926

The Christian Life. *The Legacy of the Middle Ages*, ed. G. C. Crump and E. F. Jacob. Oxford, pp. 23–57. C.P.

Sir Paul Vinogradoff. *E.H.R.* xli. 236–43, cf. p. 496.

REVIEWS: *Year Books of Edward II*, vol. xvii, *8 Edward II, 1314–15*, ed. W. C. Bolland. *E.H.R.* xli. 122–3.

La Provence au moyen âge (1121–1481), by V. L. Bourilly and R. Busquet. Ibid. 156–7.

Le Déshéritement de Jean sans terre et le meurtre d'Arthur de Bretagne, by Ch. Petit-Dutaillis. Ibid. 304–5.

Medieval Cities, by H. Pirenne. *History*, x. 330–2.

History of the Irish State to 1014, by A. S. Green; *Gleanings from Irish History*, by W. F. T. Butler; *The Student's History of Ireland*, by S. Gwynn. *History*, xi. 56–9.

The Cathedral Church of England, by A. H. Thompson. Ibid. 153–4.

The Cambridge Medieval History, vol. v. *Scottish Historical Review*, xxiv. 65–7.

1927

Alexander of St. Albans: a literary muddle. *Essays in History presented to Reginald Lane Poole*. Oxford, pp. 246–60.

The Place Names of Manchester. *The Manchester and Salford Woman Citizen*, 15 October.

REVIEWS: *Anglo-Norman Custumal of Exeter*, ed. J. W. Schopp and R. C. Easterling. *Econ. Hist. Rev.* i. i. 174.

Étude sur les ministeriales en Flandre et en Lotharingie, by F. L. Ganshof. *E.H.R.* xlii. 116–17.

Die Entstehung des deutschen Grundeigentums, by V. Ernst. Ibid. 141–2.

Histoire de la coutume de la prévôté et vicomté de Paris, vol. ii, part i, by Olivier Martin. *E.H.R.* xlii. 143. Cf. *supra*, 1924.

Honors and Knights' Fees, vol. iii, by W. Farrer. Ibid. 302–3.

The Young King Henry Plantagenet (1155–83) in History, Literature and Tradition, by O. H. Moore. Ibid. 459.

Curia Regis Rolls of the Reigns of Richard I and John, vol. iii, 5–7 *John*. Ibid. 604–6.

La Crisi delle compagnie mercantili dei Bardi e dei Peruzzi, by Armando Sapori. *History*, xii. 60–1.

Francesco Petrarch, by E. H. R. Tatham. Ibid. 86–7.

The Great Rolls of the Pipe for 2–4 Richard I, ed. D. M. Stenton. Ibid. 157–8.

History of Mediaeval Philosophy, by M. de Wulf, transl. E. Messenger. Ibid. 180.

The Wandering Scholars, by Helen Waddell. *Scottish Historical Review*, xxiv. 298–300.

The Life of Bishop Wilfrid, by Eddius Stephanus, transl. and ed. B. Colgrave. Ibid. 307–8.

1928

STEPHEN LANGTON, being the Ford Lectures delivered in the University of Oxford in Hilary Term 1927. C.P.

Stephen Langton: an oration delivered at Canterbury. *Theology*, xvii. 83–96.

Gerald of Wales. *The Bulletin of the John Rylands Library*, xii. 389–410, and separately.

H. W. C. Davis. *E.H.R.* xliii. 578–84; also an appreciation in *M.G.* 29 June.

REVIEWS: *The Mediaeval Castle in Scotland*, by W. M. Mackenzie. *History*, xiii. 56–8.

Les Barbares, by L. Halphen. Ibid. 85.

Church and State: political aspects of sixteenth century Puritanism, by A. F. Scott Pearson. *Scottish Historical Review*, xxv. 350.

The Pipe Roll for 1295: Surrey membrane, ed. Mabel H. Mills. *Econ. Hist. Rev.* i. ii. 350–2.

Calendar of Chancery Warrants, 1244–1326. E.H.R. xliii. 101–3.

Mélanges d'histoire offerts à Henri Pirenne. Ibid. 283–4.

Life and Work in Medieval Europe, by P. Boissonnade, transl. E. Power. Ibid. 287.

The Renaissance of the Twelfth Century, by C. H. Haskins. Ibid. 288.

St. Francis of Assisi, 1226–1926: Essays in commemoration. E.H.R. xliii. 288–9.

St. Hugh of Lincoln, by R. M. Woolley. Ibid. 454–5.

L'Anglais Jean dit Bellesmains (1122–1204?), by P. Pouzet. Ibid. 642.

Chapters in the Administrative History of Mediaeval England, by T. F. Tout, vols. iii–iv. M.G. 8 May.

1929

HISTORICAL STUDY IN OXFORD. An inaugural lecture. Delivered . . . on 8 February 1929. C.P.

England: Richard I and John. The reigns of Philip Augustus and Louis VIII of France. *Cambridge Medieval History,* vi. 205–51, 284–330, 881–7, 899–903.

The Middle Ages. *Encyclopaedia Britannica,* 14th edition, xv. 448–50.

The bull 'Miramur plurimum' and a letter to Archbishop Stephen Langton, 5 September 1215. *E.H.R.* xliv. 87–93.

Note on Ch. V. Langlois. *History,* xiv. 229–30.

Thomas Frederick Tout, 1855–1929. *Proceedings of the British Academy,* xv. 491–518.

Preface to *Studies and Notes supplementary to Stubbs' Constitutional History,* iii, by Ch. Petit-Dutaillis and G. Lefebvre, transl. M. E. I. Robertson and R. F. Treharne. M.U.P.

REVIEWS: *Calendar of Plea and Memoranda Rolls of the City of London, 1323–64,* by A. H. Thomas. *Econ. Hist. Rev.* II. i. 149–51.

A History of Medieval Political Theory in the West, by R. W. and A. J. Carlyle, vol. v. *E.H.R.* xliv. 298–300.

Close Rolls of the Reign of Henry III, 1251–3. Ibid. 488–9.

Recueil des actes de Pépin Iᵉʳ et de Pépin II, rois d'Aquitaine, 814–48, ed. L. Levillain. Ibid. 643–4.

L'Anjou de 1109 à 1151, by Josèphe Chartrou. Ibid. 646–7.

Le Speculum perfectionis ou mémoires de Frère Léon, vol. i, by Paul Sabatier. Ibid. 678. Cf. *infra,* 1932.

The Life of Hastings Rashdall, D.D., by P. E. Matheson. Ibid. 691.

Deutsche Rechtsgeschichte, vol. ii, *Die Fränkische Zeit,* by H. Brunner, ed. C. von Schwerin. *History,* xiii. 370.

From Magic to Science, by C. Singer. Ibid. xiv. 65–6.

The Great Roll of the Pipe for 5 Richard I, ed. D. M. Stenton; *The Great Roll of the Pipe for 14 Henry III,* ed. C. Robinson; *The Great Roll of the Pipe for 6 Richard I,* ed. D. M. Stenton. Ibid. 138–40.

1930

History and Place Names. *History*, xv. 193–8.

Robert Grosseteste and the Nicomachean Ethics. *Proceedings of the British Academy*, xvi. 85–104, and separately.

Note on W. S. McKechnie. *History*, xv. 240–1.

The School of Modern History. *Oxford Magazine*, xlviii. 528–30.

REVIEWS: *The Calendar of the Charter Rolls*, vol. vi, *1427–1516, etc.* Econ. Hist. Rev. II. ii. 327–8.

The Calendar of the Close Rolls, Henry IV, 1399–1402. Ibid. 357.

English Ecclesiastical Studies, by Rose Graham. E.H.R. xlv. 148.

Les Influences anglaise et française dans le comté de Flandre au début du xiiie siècle. Ibid. 150–1.

Chivalry, ed. E. Prestage. Ibid. 151–2.

Curia Regis Rolls of the Reigns of Richard I and John, vol. iv, *7–8 John.* Ibid. 298–300.

Studies in Medieval Culture, by C. H. Haskins. Ibid. 478–9.

The Letters of Osbert of Clare, Prior of Westminster, ed. E. W. Williamson. Ibid. 479–81.

L'Interdiction de la guerre privée dans le très ancien droit normand, by J. Yver. Ibid. 497.

Anniversary Essays in Mediaeval History, by students of Charles Homer Haskins. Ibid. 642–4.

Vie de Louis VI le Gros par Suger, ed. H. Waquet. Ibid. 675.

The Collected Papers of Paul Vinogradoff, ed. H. A. L. Fisher. *History*, xv. 56–8.

Otto of Freising's The Two Cities, transl. C. C. Mierow. Ibid. 144–6.

1931

THE MEDIEVAL BOOKS OF MERTON COLLEGE. C.P.

MEDIEVAL ENGLAND 1066–1485. Home University Library. London: Thornton Butterworth, Ltd.

Sir Henry Spelman and the 'Concilia' (The Raleigh Lecture on History). *Proceedings of the British Academy*, xvi (1930), 345–79, and separately.

On the Writing of History. *The Highway*, xxiv. 22–4.

REVIEWS: *Calendar of Plea and Memoranda Rolls of the City of London 1364–81*, by A. H. Thomas. Econ. Hist. Rev. III. i. 147–8.

The Calendar of Close Rolls, Henry IV, vol ii, *Henry V*, vol. i. Ibid. 167.

Simon de Montfort, Earl of Leicester, 1208–65, by Charles Bémont, transl. by E. F. Jacob. *E.H.R.* xlvi. 122–3.

La Tradition hagiographique de S. Thomas Becket avant la fin du xiie siècle, by E. Walberg. Ibid. 155–6.

The Earliest Northamptonshire Assize Rolls, A.D. *1202 and 1203*, ed. D. M. Stenton. Ibid. 287–8.

Études sur quelques points de l'histoire de Guillaume le Conquérant, by H. Prentout. Ibid. 320.

Les Baillis comtaux de Flandre, by H. Nowë. Ibid. 468–9.

Close Rolls of the Reign of Henry III, 1253–4. Ibid. 469–70.

Histoire de la coutume de la prévôté et vicomté de Paris, vol. ii, part ii, by Olivier Martin. Ibid. 677. Cf. *supra*, 1924.

The Saxon Cathedral at Canterbury and the Saxon Saints buried therein, by Charles Cotton. *History*, xv. 378–9.

The Bishop's Register, by C. J. Offer. Ibid. 381–2.

Pipe Roll of 31 Henry I, ed. J. Hunter; *The Great Roll of the Pipe for 7 Richard I*, ed. D. M. Stenton. *History*, xvi. 86–7.

Grundzüge der deutschen Rechtsgeschichte, by H. Brunner, 8th edition, by C. von Schwerin. Ibid. 189.

Introduction au catalogue des actes de Ferri III, duc de Lorraine, by J. de Pange; *Catalogue des actes de Ferri III, duc de Lorraine*, by J. de Pange. Ibid. 248–50.

Church and State in Visigothic Spain, by A. Ziegler. Ibid. 276–7.

The Chancellor's Roll for 8 Richard I, ed. D. M. Stenton. Ibid. 280–1.

Innocent III, by L. E. Binns. Ibid. 282.

1932

THE COLLECTED PAPERS OF T. F. TOUT, vol. i, ed. F. M. Powicke. M.U.P.

Note on William Hunt. *History*, xvi. 328–9.

The Collection and Criticism of Original Texts. Ibid. xvii. 1–8.

Research in the Humane Studies. *Handbook to the University of Oxford*, pp. 167–81. C.P.

English Local Historical Societies. *Canadian Historical Review*, xiii. 257–63.

REVIEWS: *Register of Edward the Black Prince. Econ. Hist. Rev.* III. iii. 428–9.

Close Rolls of the Reign of Henry III, 1253–4. Ibid. IV. i. 115.

The Kings, the Court, and the Royal Power in France in the Eleventh Century, by W. M. Newman. *E.H.R.* xlvii. 149.

The Book of Fees, commonly called Testa de Nevill, ed. H. C. Maxwell-Lyte, &c., part ii and Index. Ibid. 494–8. Cf. *supra*, 1922.

Curia Regis Rolls of the Reigns of Richard I and John, vol. v, *8–10 John*. Ibid. 661–5.

Le Speculum perfectionis ou mémoires de Frère Léon, vol. ii, *Étude critique*, by Paul Sabatier, ed. A. G. Little. Ibid. 665–7. Cf. *supra*, 1929.

Close Rolls of the Reign of Henry III, 1254–6. Ibid. 702.

Medieval Internationalism, by R. F. Wright. *History*, xvi. 371–2.

Notes on the Catholic Liturgies, by A. A. King. Ibid. 372.

A Guide to the Study of Medieval History, by L. J. Paetow, revised edition. *History*, xvii. 52–4.

Les Caractères originaux de l'histoire rurale française, by M. Bloch. Ibid. 157–9.

The Great Roll of the Pipe for 9 Richard I, ed. D. M. Stenton. Ibid. 283.

1933

Loretta, Countess of Leicester. *Historical Essays in Honour of James Tait*, M.U.P., pp. 247–72.

The Limits of Effective Co-operation in the Synthesis of History. *Bulletin of the Institute of Hist. Research*, xi. 75–9.

Bibliographical Note on recent work upon Stephen Langton. *E.H.R.* xlviii. 554–7.

The Early History of Canon Law. *History*, xviii. 11–19.

A Discussion on 'The Modern Methods for the Study of Medieval History and their Requirements', opened by F. M. P. *T.R.H.S.* 4th ser. xvi. 45–54.

REVIEWS: *L'Office héréditaire du focarius regis Angliae*, by J. le Foyer. *E.H.R.* xlviii. 151–2.

La Tutelle, by R. Génestal. Ibid. 152.

The Cambridge Medieval History, vol. vii. Ibid. 465–8.

Feudal Monarchy in the Latin Kingdom of Jerusalem, by J. L. La Monte; *The Administration of Normandy under St. Louis*, by J. R. Strayer. Ibid. 492–3.

La Chanson de la croisade albigeoise, ed. E. Martin-Chabot. Ibid. 493.

Close Rolls of the Reign of Henry III, 1256–9. Ibid. 650–2.

Les Origines de la commune de Tournai, by P. Rolland. Ibid. 688.

The Damascus Chronicle of the Crusades, ed. H. A. R. Gibb. *History*, xviii. 186.

The Great Roll of the Pipe for 10 Richard I, ed. D. M. Stenton. Ibid. 186–7.

A History of the Church in Blackburnshire, by J. E. W. Wallis. Ibid. 277.

Henry Charles Lea, by E. S. Bradley. Ibid. 286.

Henry William Carless Davis, 1874–1928. A Memoir, by J. R. H. Weaver, and a selection of his historical papers, edited by J. R. H. Weaver and Austin Lane Poole. *M.G.* 29 November.

1934

Pope Boniface VIII (Creighton Lecture 1932). *History*, xviii. 307–29.

Some Problems in the History of the Medieval University. Presidential address. *T.R.H.S.* 4th ser. xvii. 1–18.

Introductory note to *Oxford Essays in Medieval History presented to Herbert Edward Salter*, p. vii. C.P.

Paper on the use of Local Archives. *Proceedings on the Occasion of the First Conference of the British Records Association.* B.R.A. Leaflets, no. 1, pp. 8–13.

REVIEWS: *Curia Regis Rolls of the Reigns of Richard I and John*, vol. vi, *11–14 John. E.H.R.* xlix. 111–13.

Recherches sur les tribunaux de châtellenie en Flandre, by F. Ganshof. Ibid. 156.

La Commune de Toulouse et les sources de son histoire (1120–1249), by B. Limouzin-Lamothe. Ibid. 509–11.

Historical Map of South Wales and the Border in the Fourteenth Century, by W. Rees. Ibid. 537–8.

Analecta reginensia, ed. A. Wilmart. Ibid. 727–30.

A History of Aragon and Catalonia, by H. J. Chaytor. Ibid. 736–7.

La Monarchie féodale en France et en Angleterre, by Ch. Petit-Dutaillis. Ibid. 738.

Boniface VIII, by T. S. R. Boase. *History*, xviii. 363–5.

The Place-names of Northamptonshire, by J. E. B. Gover, A. Mawer, and F. M. Stenton. Ibid. xix. 54–5.

The Great Roll of the Pipe for the First Year of King John, ed. D. M. Stenton. Ibid. 86.

Canterbury Administration, by Irene J. Churchill. Ibid. 151–2.

Gibbon's Antagonism to Christianity, by Shelly T. McCloy. Ibid. 185.

Self-government at the King's command, by A. B. White. *History*, xix. 261–3.

Memoranda Roll of the King's Remembrancer, 1230–1, ed. Chalfont Robinson. Ibid. 277–8.

The Growth of Political Thought in the West, by C. H. McIlwain. *Law Quarterly Review*, l. 277–81.

1935

THE CHRISTIAN LIFE IN THE MIDDLE AGES AND OTHER ESSAYS. C.P.

Reprints (with changes) of earlier papers except *Dante and the Crusade* and *Medieval education*.

Nationalism and Scholarship. Letter to editor. *T.L.S.* 463, 477.

Chronological lists. Great Britain and Ireland. *Bulletin of the International Committee of Historical Sciences*, vii. 33–9.

The Study of History in the Universities of Great Britain: a recent enquiry. *History*, xx. 116–23.

Guy de Montfort (1265–1271). Presidential address. *T.R.H.S.* 4th ser. xviii. 1–23.

Miss Kate Norgate. *The Times*, 5 May.

REVIEWS: *Papal Revenues in the Middle Ages*, by W. E. Lunt. *Econ. Hist. Rev.* v. ii. 138–9.

Rolls of the Justices in Eyre, being the Rolls of Pleas and Assizes for Lincolnshire 1218–9 and Worcestershire 1221, ed. D. M. Stenton. *E.H.R.* l. 519–21.

Histoire des croisades et du royaume franc de Jérusalem, vol. i, by R. Grousset. Ibid. 705–7.

Close Rolls of the Reign of Henry III, 1259–61. Ibid. 710–12.

Medieval Religion, by Christopher Dawson. *History*, xx. 61–2.

The Great Roll of the Pipe for 2 John, ed. D. M. Stenton. Ibid. 85–6.

Codex quartus S. Jacobi de expedimento et conversione Yspanie et Gallecie editus a B. Turpino archiepiscopo. Medium Aevum, iv. 122–3.

Studies in Church Life in England under Edward III, by K. L. Wood-Legh. Ibid. 123–5.

La Pecia dans les manuscrits universitaires du xiiie et du xive siècle, by J. Destrez. *T.L.S.* 858.

1936

THE UNIVERSITIES OF EUROPE IN THE MIDDLE AGES, by the late Hastings Rashdall. A new edition in three volumes edited by F. M. Powicke and A. B. Emden. C.P.

The Reformation in England. *European Civilization, its Origin and Development*, edited under the direction of Edward Eyre. O.U.P., vol. iv, pp. 319–488.

Henri Pirenne. *E.H.R.* li. 79–89.

The Archbishop of Rouen, John de Harcourt, and Simon de Montfort in 1260. Ibid. 108–13.

Reflections on the Medieval State. Presidential address. *T.R.H.S.* 4th ser. xix. 1–18.

Sir Charles Firth. *Oxford Magazine*, liv. 492–3.

REVIEWS: *Lehnrecht und Staatsgewalt*, by H. Mitteis. *E.H.R.* li. 127–9.

L'Élaboration du monde moderne, by J. Calmette. Ibid. 164–5.

The Edwardian Settlement of North Wales, by W. H. Waters. Ibid. 165–6.

Bouvines, by A. Hadengue. Ibid. 543.

The Medieval English Borough, by James Tait. *M.G.* 31 July.

1937

The Search for Freedom in the West. *The Individual in East and West*, ed. E. R. Hughes. O.U.P., pp. 171–91.

England and Europe in the Thirteenth Century. A paper delivered at the Harvard Tercentenary Conference of arts and sciences. *Independence, Convergence and Borrowing in Institutions, Thought and Art*. Harvard Univ. Press, pp. 135–50.

The Bodleian Library, its History and Contents. *Oxford*, Special Number, February 1937, pp. 16–20.

Charles Homer Haskins. *E.H.R.* lii. 649–56.

Presidential address. *T.R.H.S.* 4th ser. xx. 1–12.

REVIEWS: *The Itinerary of King Richard I*, by L. Landon. *E.H.R.* lii. 314–17.

Surrey Manorial Accounts, ed. H. Jenkinson and H. M. Briggs. Ibid. 352–3.

The Cambridge Medieval History, vol. viii; *Histoire de l'Europe des invasions au xvie siècle*, by H. Pirenne. Ibid. 690–2.

Curia Regis Rolls of the Reigns of Richard I and John, vol. vii, *15–16 John*; Appendix, *7 Richard I–1 John*. Ibid. 698–701.

Close Rolls of the Reign of Henry III, 1261–4. Ibid. 701–2.

Étude sur les civitates de la Belgique Seconde, by F. Vercauteren. *History*, xxi. 361–3.

Recherches sur la seigneurie rurale en Lorraine d'après les plus anciens censiers, by C. E. Perrin. Ibid. 363–4.

The Royal Domain in the Baillage of Rouen, by J. R. Strayer. Ibid. 378–9.

Les Villes de foires de Champagne, by E. Chapin. *History*, xxii. 258–60.

St. Bernard of Clairvaux, by Watkin Williams. *J.T.S.* xxxviii. 81.

The Early Dominicans, by R. J. Bennett. Ibid. 428.

The Works of Peter of Poitiers, by P. S. Moore. Ibid.

Beiträge zur Geschichte Cölestins V, by Heinrich Baethgen. *Medium Aevum*, vi. 65–6.

The Place of the Reign of Edward II in English History, by T. F. Tout; second edition, revised by Hilda Johnstone. *M.G.* 21 May.

Studies in the Constitutional History of the Thirteenth and Fourteenth Centuries, by B. Wilkinson. Ibid. 21 May.

The Incorporation of Boroughs, by Martin Weinbaum. Ibid. 21 May.

Fourteenth Century Studies, by M. V. Clarke, ed. L. S. Sutherland and M. McKisack. Ibid. 10 August. (An appreciation of Maude Clarke.)

History of Florence from the Founding of the City through the Renaissance, by Ferdinand Schevill. Ibid. 5 November.

1938

HISTORY, FREEDOM, AND RELIGION. (University of Durham. Riddell Memorial Lectures. Tenth series. Delivered . . . in November 1937.) O.U.P.

Observations on the English Freeholder in the Thirteenth Century. *Wirtschaft und Kultur*. Festschrift zum 70. Geburtstag von Alfons Dopsch (Rudolf M. Rohrer Verlag, Baden bei Wien), pp. 382–93.

Observations concernant le franc tenant anglais au xiiie siècle. *Recueils de la Société Jean Bodin*, t. iii, pp. 211–29. Bruxelles: Nouvelle Société d'Éditions. A translation by F. Joüon des Longrais of the previous entry.

Walter de Merton, Bishop of Rochester, 1274–7. *Annales amicorum Cathedralis Roffensis*, being the third annual report of the Friends of Rochester Cathedral (February 1938), pp. 25–30.

Notes on Hastings Manuscripts. *The Huntington Library Quarterly*, i. 247–76.

The Final Honour School of Modern History in the University of Oxford. *Year Book of Education*, pp. 312–15, and reprinted in *The Purposes of Examinations, A Symposium*, pp. 41–4.

The History of Parliament. A letter to the Editor of *The Times*, 2 November.

REVIEWS: *Latin Monasticism in Norman Sicily*, by L. T. Warner, jr. *Econ. Hist. Rev.* ix. 86–7.

Histoire des croisades et du royaume franc de Jérusalem, vols. ii, iii, by R. Grousset. *E.H.R.* liii. 125–6.

A History of Medieval Political Theory in the West, vol. vi, by R. W. Carlyle and A. J. Carlyle. *E.H.R.* liii. 126–8.

Geschichte des Englischen Königtums im Lichte der Krönung, by P. E. Schramm, and translation by L. G. Wickham Legg. Ibid. 287–9.

Rolls of the Justices in Eyre, being the Rolls of Pleas and Assizes for Yorkshire in 3 Henry III, ed. D. M. Stenton. Ibid. 296–7.

An Ecclesiastical Barony of the Middle Ages: the bishopric of Bayeux, 1066–1204, by S. E. Gleason. Ibid. 327–8.

Über die säkularisierende Wirkung der Kreuzzüge, by H. Benary. Ibid. 328.

The Autobiography of Giraldus Cambrensis, ed. H. E. Butler. Ibid.

History of Europe from 1198 to 1378, by C. W. Previté-Orton. Ibid. 330–1.

Le Mariage en droit canonique, vol. ii, by R. G. Esmein, revised by R. Génestal. Ibid. 755.

The Place-names of Surrey, by J. E. B. Gover, A. Mawer, F. M. Stenton; *The Place-names of Warwickshire*, by the same; *The Place-names of Essex*, by P. H. Reaney. *History*, xxii. 348–50.

Bartholomew of Exeter, by A. Morey. Ibid. 353–4.

The Great Roll of the Pipe for 3 John, ed. D. M. Stenton. Ibid. 378.

Guido de Columnis: historia destructionis Troiae, ed. N. E. Griffin. Ibid. xxiii. 70.

Markward of Anweiler and the Sicilian Regency, by T. C. Van Cleve. Ibid. 286–7.

Saint Benedict, by J. McCann. Ibid. 158. Cf. ibid. 345.

The Great Roll of the Pipe for 4 John, ed. by D. M. Stenton. Ibid. 369.

The Pseudo-Turpin, ed. H. M. Smyser. *Speculum*, xiii. 364–6.

Life on the English Manor, by H. S. Bennett. *Medium Aevum*, vi. 242–4.

Inquisition and Liberty, by G. G. Coulton. *M.G.* 25 March.

Le Procès contre Thomas Waleys, O.P., by Th. Käppeli. *Oxford Magazine*, lvii. 32.

Studies in the Life of Robert Kilwardby, O.P., by Ellen M. F. Sommer-Seckendorff. Ibid.

1939

HANDBOOK OF BRITISH CHRONOLOGY. Ed. F. M. Powicke, with the assistance of Charles Johnson and W. J. Harte. *Royal Historical Society Guides and Handbooks*, No. 2.

THE MUNIMENTS OF THE DEAN AND CHAPTER OF DURHAM: a Report to the Pilgrim Trustees (with W. A. Pantin). Printed for private circulation.

Introductory note to *The Medieval Contribution to Political Thought*, by A. Passerin d'Entrèves. O.U.P.

Points of view, *The Huntington Library Quarterly*, ii. i. 8–10.

Tribute to Dr. R. L. Poole, *The Times*, 3 November.

Reginald Lane Poole, *Bodleian Library Record*, i. 114.

REVIEWS: *Piers Plowman and Contemporary Religious Thought*, by Greta Hort. *J.T.S.* xl. 65–6.

Das mittelalterliche Gemeinschaftsdenken unter dem Gesichtspunkt der Totalität. Eine rechtsphilosophische Untersuchung, by W. Dyckmans. Ibid. 66.

The Marian Exiles, by C. H. Garrett. Ibid. 66–8.

Saint Dominique: l'idée, l'homme et l'œuvre, by P. Mandonnet. Re-edited by M. H. Vicaire and R. Ladner. Ibid. 68–70.

The Great Roll of the Pipe for 5 John, ed. D. M. Stenton. *History*, xxiv. 82–3.

Monastic Studies, by Dr. Watkin Williams. Ibid. 83.

L'Organisation corporative du moyen âge à la fin de l'ancien régime. E.H.R. liv. 357–8.

Histoire littéraire de la France, vol. xxxvii. Ibid. 497–500.

Ausgewählte Aufsätze, by K. Brandi. Ibid. 500–1.

A History of Europe from 911–1198, by Z. N. Brooke. Ibid. 526–7.

Vincent of Beauvais. De eruditione filiorum nobilium, ed. A. Steiner. Ibid. 528–9.

Curia Regis Rolls of the Reign of Henry III, 3–4 Henry III. Ibid. 704–12.

A Study of History, by Arnold J. Toynbee, vols. iv–vi. *M.G.* 29 September.

1940

Introductory note to *The Administration of the Honor of Leicester in the Fourteenth Century*, by L. Fox. Leicester: Edgar Backus.

REVIEWS: *Environmental Factors in Christian History*, ed. J. T. McNeill, M. Spinka, and H. R. Willoughby. *J.T.S.* xli. 338–40.

The Cartae Antiquae, Rolls 1–10, ed. L. Landon. *History*, xxv. 56–7.

Studies in Anglo-Papal relations during the Middle Ages. I. Financial Relations of the Papacy with England to 1327, by W. E. Lunt. Ibid. 58–9.

Travaux de la semaine d'histoire du droit normand tenue à Guernsey du 8 au 13 juin, 1938. E.H.R. lv. 153.

The Sicilian Norman Kingdom in the Mind of Anglo-Norman Contemporaries, by E. Jamison. Ibid. 153–4.

La Société féodale, by M. Bloch. *E.H.R.* lv. 449–51.

Close Rolls of the Reign of Henry III, 1264–1272. Ibid. 654–6.

Papal enforcement of some Medieval Marriage Laws, by C. E. Smith. Ibid. 677–8.

Vom geschichtlichen Sinn und vom Sinn der Geschichte, by F. Meinecke. Ibid. 691–2.

1941

THE REFORMATION IN ENGLAND. A reprint from *European Civilization: its Origin and Development*, ed. E. Eyre, vol. iv. O.U.P. Cf. *supra*, 1936.

The Compilation of the *Chronica majora* of Matthew Paris. *Modern Philology*, xxxviii. 305–17 (a number dedicated to W. A. Nitze). Cf. *infra*, 1944.

The Oath of Bromholm. *E.H.R.* lvi. 529–48.

The Murder of Henry Clement and the Pirates of Lundy Island. *History*, xxv. 285–310.

A letter from F. M. P. on 'The Family of Marisco'. *History*, xxvi. 127.

More notes on Adam de Brome. *The Oriel Record*, viii. 135–9.

REVIEWS: *The Cambridge Economic History of Europe. I. The Agrarian Life of the Middle Ages*, ed. J. H. Clapham and E. Power. *Econ. Hist. Rev.* xi. 83–6.

Initiation aux études du moyen âge, by L. Halphen. *E.H.R.* lvi. 154–5.

Littere Wallie, edited with introduction by J. G. Edwards; *The Welsh Assize Roll, 1277–1284*, ed. J. C. Davies. Ibid. 491–4.

The Education of Women at Manchester University, 1883–1933, by M. Tylecote. Ibid. 678.

The Writings of Robert Grosseteste, Bishop of Lincoln, 1235–1253, by S. Harrison Thomson. *Bull. of Inst. of Hist. Research*, xviii. 120–1.

The Monastic Order in England: a history of its development from the times of St. Dunstan to the fourth Lateran Council, 943–1216, by Dom David Knowles; *The Religious Houses of Medieval England*, by Dom David Knowles. *History*, xxv. 358–62.

The Great Roll of the Pipe for 6 John, ed. D. M. Stenton. Ibid. xxvi. 86–7.

Walter Howard Frere. A collection of his papers on liturgical and historical subjects (Alcuin Club, xxxv). *Spectator*, 24 January.

Witchcraft, by Charles Williams. Ibid. 18 April.

Richard II, by Anthony Steele. Ibid. 12 December.

A History of Medieval Austria, by A. W. A. Leeper, ed. R. W. Seton-Watson and C. A. Macartney. *M.G.* 4 February.

Rival Ambassadors at the Court of Queen Mary, by E. Harris Harbison. *M.G.* 21 November.

1942

The Writ for Enforcing Watch and Ward, 1242. *E.H.R.* lvii. 469–73. Also see addendum. *E.H.R.* lviii. 128.

Contribution to *Herbert Arthur Doubleday, 1867–1941* (London: William Clowes & Sons), pp. 1–4.

REVIEWS: *The Sources for the Life of S. Francis of Assisi*, by J. R. H. Moorman. *J.T.S.* xliii. 110–13.

Medieval and Renaissance Studies, ed. R. Hunt and R. Klibansky, vol. i. *Medium Aevum*, xi. 91–5.

English Villagers of the Thirteenth Century, by G. C. Homans. *E.H.R.* lvii. 496–502.

Medieval Libraries of Great Britain: a list of surviving books, ed. N. R. Ker. *History*, xxvi. 297–8.

The English Government at Work, 1327–1336, volume i; *Central and Prerogative Administration*, ed. J. F. Willard and W. A. Morris. Ibid. 298–302.

The Great Roll of the Pipe for 7 John, ed. S. Smith. Ibid. xxvii. 85–6.

The Wool Trade in English Medieval History, by Eileen Power. *Economica*, N.S. ix. 95–7.

1943

Master Simon the Norman. *E.H.R.* lviii. 330–43.

President Beneš as Patriot and Statesman. *The Spirit of Czechoslovakia*, iv. 62, 64.

REVIEWS: *The Jews in Spain: their Social, Political, and Cultural Life during the Middle Ages*, by A. A. Neuman. 2 volumes. *J.T.S.* xliv. 227–8.

The Great Roll of the Pipe for 8 John, ed. D. M. Stenton. *History*, xxviii. 224.

Medieval Feudalism, by C. Stephenson. *E.H.R.* lviii. 495.

Education for a World adrift, by Sir Richard Livingstone. *Oxford Magazine*, lxi. 312–13.

1944

After Forty Years. (An address given at the thirty-eighth Annual General meeting of the Historical Association at Birkbeck College on New Year's Day 1944.) *History*, xxix. 3–16.

The Compilation of the *Chronica majora* of Matthew Paris. *Proceedings of the British Academy*, xxix, and separately. Cf. *supra*, 1941.

James Tait. Obituary notices in *The Times* and the *M.G.* 5 July.

Oxford, *Polish Science and Learning*, no. 5, pp. 23–30. (A lecture, delivered 16 July 1943, to the Association of University Professors and Lecturers of Allied Countries in Great Britain.)

REVIEWS: *Franciscan Papers, Lists, and Documents*, by A. G. Little. *J.T.S.* xlv. 96–7.

Marco Polo's Precursors, by L. Olschki. *E.H.R.* lix. 404–5.

Canterbury Cathedral Priory: a study in monastic administration, by R. A. L. Smith. Ibid. 405–7.

Trinity College: an Historical Sketch, by G. M. Trevelyan. Ibid. 434.

Liberties and Communities in Medieval England, by Helen M. Cam. *Spectator*, 6 October.

Ramsay Muir, an Autobiography and Some Essays, ed. Stuart Hodgson. *Oxford Magazine*, lxii. 186–7.

Essays in the Conciliar Epoch, by E. F. Jacob. *M.G.* 5 January.

1945

The Alleged Migration of the University of Oxford to Northampton in 1264. *Oxoniensia*, viii–ix. 107–11.

Alexander James Carlyle, 1861–1943. *Proceedings of the British Academy*, xxix. 313–27, and separately.

REVIEWS: *English Literary Criticism: the Medieval Phase*, by J. W. H. Atkins. *E.H.R.* lx. 111.

The English Mediaeval Recluse, by F. D. S. Darwin. Ibid. 269.

George Lincoln Barr, his Life, by Roland H. Bainton; *Selections from his Writings*, ed. Lois Oliphant Gibbons. *Medium Aevum*, xiii. 22–6.

Medieval and Renaissance Studies, Richard Hunt and Raymond Klibansky, i. 2. Ibid. 26–8.

The Prospects of Medieval History; an inaugural lecture by Z. N. Brooke. *Oxford Magazine*, lxiii. 294–6.

The Study of Modern History, an inaugural lecture by H. Butterfield. Ibid.

The Register of Henry Chichele, Archbishop of Canterbury, 1414–1443, ed. E. F. Jacob, vol. iii. *M.G.* 11 April.

1946

The Economic Motive in Politics. *Econ. Hist. Rev.*, xvi. 85–92.

James Tait 1863–1944. *Proceedings of the British Academy*, xxx, and separately.

REVIEWS: *La Société d'ancien régime: organisation et représentation corporatives*, i, by E. Lousse. *E.H.R.* lxi. 250–2.

A Lincolnshire Assize Roll for 1298, ed. W. S. Thomson. *E.H.R.* lxi. 261–4.

Calendar of the Roll of the Justices on Eyre (1227) for Buckinghamshire, ed. J. G. Jenkins. Ibid. 272–3.

England and the Continent in the Eighth Century, by Wilhelm Levison. *M.G.* 15 May.

1947

KING HENRY III AND THE LORD EDWARD. THE COMMUNITY OF THE REALM IN THE THIRTEENTH CENTURY. In two volumes. C.P.

THREE LECTURES GIVEN IN THE HALL OF BALLIOL COLLEGE, OXFORD, IN MAY 1947. O.U.P.

Research in the Humane Studies. *Handbook to the University of Oxford* [second edition], pp. 173–85. Cf. *supra*, 1932. C.P.

Universities and Scholarship. *The Character of England*, ed. Ernest Barker, pp. 236–51. C.P.

Andrew George Little 1863–1945. *Proceedings of the British Academy*, xxxi, and printed separately.

Three Cambridge Scholars: C. W. Previté-Orton, Z. N. Brooke, and G. G. Coulton. *The Cambridge Historical Journal*, ix. 106–16.

REVIEWS: *The Complete Peerage, or a History of the House of Lords and all its Members from the Earliest Times*, by G. E. C., revised and much enlarged; edited by the late H. A. Doubleday, G. H. White, and the late Lord Howard de Walden, vol. x. *E.H.R.* lxii. 245–50.

'*Le Manuel des Péchés*', *étude de littérature religieuse anglo-normande*, by E. J. Arnould. Ibid. 268–9.

The Hellenistic Civilization and East Rome, by Norman H. Baynes. *Journal of Roman Studies*, xxxvii. 203.

Sir Richard Lodge: a Biography, by Margaret Lodge. *Oxford Magazine*, lxv. 368–9.

The Register of Henry Chichele, Archbishop of Canterbury, 1414–1443, ed. E. F. Jacob, vol. iv. *M.G.* 8 December.

M. TYSON

LIST OF SUBSCRIBERS

R. J. ADAM, Esq., Department of History, The University, Glasgow.

Dr. E. W. AINLEY-WALKER, St. Cuthbert's, Upavon, nr. Marlborough, Wilts.

DENNIS ALLEN, Esq., 'Speldhurst', Villa Road, Stanway, Colchester, Essex.

Miss HOPE EMILY ALLEN, Kenwood Station, Oneida, New York, U.S.A.

Rev. Father AMBROSE, Catholic Church, Raichur, S. India.

Miss MARGARET ARCHER, Department of History, The University, Edmund Street, Birmingham.

C. A. J. ARMSTRONG, Esq., Hertford College, Oxford.

W. H. G. ARMYTAGE, Esq., The University, Sheffield.

Professor A. ASPINALL, 1 Shinfield Road, Reading.

R. L. ATKINSON, Esq., Public Record Office, Chancery Lane, London, W.C. 2.

C. H. COLLINS BAKER, Huntington Library, San Marino, California, U.S.A.

PERCY G. BALES, Esq., Selwyn House, Fakenham, Norfolk.

Miss RUTH BARBOUR, Bodleian Library, Oxford.

Dr. FRANK BARLOW, University College, Exeter.

Professor C. C. BAYLEY, Department of History, McGill University, Montreal, Canada.

Dr. NORMAN H. BAYNES, 4B Abercorn Place, London, N.W. 8.

Professor H. HALE BELLOT, Wayside, Lyndale, London, N.W. 2.

GEORGE F. H. BERKELEY, Esq., Hanwell Castle, nr. Banbury, Oxon.

Dr. BERNHARD BISCHOFF, Ruffini-Allee 27, Planegg bei München 13B, Bavaria, Germany (American Zone).

T. A. M. BISHOP, Esq., St. John's College, Cambridge.

Professor J. B. BLACK, 64 Hamilton Place, Aberdeen.

T. S. R. BOASE, Esq. (The President), Magdalen College, Oxford.

M. F. BOND, Esq., Clerk of the Records, House of Lords, London, S.W. 1.

Mrs. EDITH BRICKELL, 1 Brereton Road, Handforth, Manchester.

Miss SHIRLEY BRIDGES, Goodmans Furze, Headley, nr. Epsom, Surrey.

E. R. C. BRINKWORTH, Esq., Bibury, Horton View, Banbury, Oxon.

Dr. D. M. BRODIE, Newnham College, Cambridge.

F. W. BROOKS, Esq., University College, Hull.

Miss DOROTHY M. BROOME, 37 Ashburn Road, Stockport.

Rev. C. K. FRANCIS BROWN, East Clandon Rectory, Surrey.

Mrs. MARY BROWN, The Foundation, St. Bees School, Cumberland.

Professor ANDREW BROWNING, Westdel, Queen's Place, Glasgow, W. 2.

R. F. I. BUNN, Esq., Manchester Grammar School.

R. W. B. BURTON, Esq., Oriel College, Oxford.

Professor J. R. M. BUTLER, Trinity College, Cambridge.

Professor Sir H. W. B. CAIRNS and Lady B. F. CAIRNS, 29 Charlbury Road, Oxford.

W. M. CALDER, Esq., The Queen's College, Oxford.

Rev. Dr. DANIEL A. P. CALLUS, Blackfriars, Oxford.

Miss HELEN M. CAM, 1 Keble Road, Oxford.

WILLIAM A. CANE, Esq., 169 Parsonage Road, Withington, Manchester.

Professor HARRY CAPLAN, Cornell University, Ithaca, N.Y., U.S.A.

JOSEPH CARRUTHERS, Esq., The Friends' School, Brookfield, Wigton, Cumberland.

Miss E. M. CARUS-WILSON, 14 Lansdowne Road, London, W. 11.

R. H. CARY, Esq., New College, Oxford.

EDWIN CHAPMAN, Esq., 33 Byne Road, Sydenham, London, S.E. 26.

Professor S. CHAPMAN, 43 High Street, Oxford.

LEONARD B. CHARIE, Esq., 7 Lancaster Avenue, Streatley, Luton, Beds.

Miss SUSAN CHENEVIX-TRENCH, 36 Park Town, Oxford.

Professor C. R. CHENEY and Mrs. MARY G. CHENEY, 21 Rathen Road, Withington, Manchester.

MICHAEL CHERNIAVSKY, Esq., 70 London Road, Newcastle-under-Lyme, Staffs.

Dr. S. B. CHRIMES, The University, Glasgow.

Dr. G. N. CLARK (The Provost), Oriel College, Oxford.

WILLIAM D. CLARK, Esq., 1 Lansdowne Walk, London, W. 11.

CHARLES TRAVIS CLAY, Esq., 11 Tite Street, Chelsea, London, S.W. 3.

Miss W. D. COATES, National Register of Archives, Public Record Office, Chancery Lane, London, W.C. 2.

JOHN and THEODORA COATMAN, The Firs, Fallowfield, Manchester.

BERTRAM COLGRAVE, Esq., 56 South Street, Durham.

ROBERT H. COLLIER, Esq., 1 Lark Hill, Worcester.

A. COMERFORD, Esq., Balliol College, Oxford.

Miss G. CONWAY, Department of Education, The University, Manchester.

Mrs. COOKE-HURLE, Kilve Court, Bridgwater.

Very Rev. T. CORBISHLEY (The Master), Campion Hall, Oxford.

KENNETH CHARLES CORSAR, Esq., Mauricewood, Milton Bridge, Midlothian.

A. D. M. COX, Esq., University College, Oxford.

A. H. COXON, Esq., Oriel College, Oxford.

W. LE BLOUNT CROKE, Esq., Research Department, Foreign Office, Princes Street, London, S.W.

JAMES CROMPTON, Esq., Department of History, University College, Gower Street, London, W.C. 1.

Rev. Dr. F. L. CROSS, Christ Church, Oxford.

A. D. CROW, Esq., Oriel College, Oxford.

Professor G. P. CUTTINO, Swarthmore College, Swarthmore, Pennsylvania, U.S.A.

Mlle M. T. D'ALVERNY, Bibliothèque Nationale, Paris, France.

J. ALLAN DARBYSHIRE, Esq., Langland, Middleton Road, Oswestry, Shropshire.

Professor R. R. DARLINGTON, Warrenhurst, Twyford, Reading.

Rev. F. J. T. DAVID, St. David's College, Lampeter, Cards.

RALPH H. C. DAVIS, Esq., Flat 5, 6 Crick Road, Oxford.

Miss RUTH J. DEAN, c/o St. Hugh's College, Oxford.

Rev. H. S. DEIGHTON, Pembroke College, Oxford.

N. DENHOLM-YOUNG, Esq., University College of North Wales, Bangor.

Professor A. P. D'ENTRÈVES, 13 Charlbury Road, Oxford.

Professeur F. JOÜON DES LONGRAIS, Directeur à l'École des Hautes Études (Sorbonne), 4 rue de la Terrasse, Paris 17ème, France.

J. C. DICKINSON, Esq., Emmanuel College, Cambridge.

Miss JOCELYNE G. DICKINSON, 13 Marriner's Drive, Bradford, Yorks.

Professor DAVID DOUGLAS, 4 Henleaze Gardens, Westbury-on-Trym, Bristol.

Miss DECIMA L. DOUIE, 12 Charlbury Road, Oxford.

LESLIE DOW, Esq., Newbourne, Woodbridge, Suffolk.

F. R. H. DU BOULAY, Esq., Bedford College, London, N.W. 1.

Dr. J. F. DUFF, 38 North Bailey, Durham.

H. V. D. DYSON, Esq., Merton College, Oxford.

STANLEY ECKERSLEY, Esq., 'Cotswold', Fakenham, Norfolk.

J. G. EDWARDS, Esq., Jesus College, Oxford.

Miss KATHLEEN EDWARDS, 14 Emsworth Road, Barkingside, Ilford, Essex.

Mrs. M. G. EEUWENS, Avonholm, Offenham, nr. Evesham, Worcs.

J. P. W. EHRMAN, Esq., Trinity College, Cambridge.

Rev. Canon L. E. ELLIOTT-BINNS, Frere House, Kenwyn, Truro.

A. B. EMDEN, Esq. (Principal), St. Edmund Hall, Oxford.

R. C. K. ENSOR, Esq., The Beacon, Sands, High Wycombe, Bucks.

Professor WILLIAM JAMES ENTWISTLE, 12 Fyfield Road, Oxford.

Rev. G. H. FENDICK, 2 College Green, Worcester.

E. FIELD, Esq., 14 The Mount, Churwell, nr. Leeds.

D. G. U. FISHER, Esq., Jesus College, Cambridge.

LINDSAY FLEMING, Esq., Aldwick Grange, Bognor Regis, Sussex.

Rev. JOHN FLITCROFT, St. Thomas's Vicarage, Bury, Lancs.

Sir CYRIL FLOWER, 2 Lammas Park Gardens, Ealing, London, W. 5.

Miss JOYCE M. FODEN, St. Anne's College, St. Anne's-on-Sea, Lancs.

LEVI FOX, Esq., 14 Henley Street, Stratford-on-Avon.

Dr. W. H. C. FREND, c/o Political Division, H.Q. Control Commission (B.E.), Berlin, B.A.O.R. (2).

ALBERT C. FRIEND, 768 Madison Avenue, New York, U.S.A.

E. B. FRYDE, Esq., University College of Wales, Aberystwyth.

Professor V. H. GALBRAITH, Oriel College, Oxford.

Messrs. GALLOWAY & PORTER, Ltd., Sidney Street, Cambridge.

Professor FRANÇOIS L. GANSHOF, 12 Rue Jacques Jordaens, Brussels, Belgium.

Dr. N. H. GIBBS, Merton College, Oxford.

M. S. GIUSEPPI, Esq., 72 Burlington Avenue, Kew Gardens, Surrey.

Miss JOYCE GODBER, Willington Manor, Bedford.

FLORENCE and GEORGE GOODALL, 25 Church Avenue, Ruislip, Middx.

W. HOWARD GOULTY, Esq., Cornbrook, Mortimer Common, Berks.

JOSEPH GRAHAM, Esq., 8 Morland Gardens, Southall, Middx.

Dr. ROSE GRAHAM, 29 Ladbroke Grove, London, W. 11.

Dr. R. W. GREAVES, Bedford College, Regent's Park, London, N.W. 1.

The Very Rev. VICTOR G. GREEN, St. Fidelis Seminary, Herman, Pennsylvania, U.S.A.

Dr. ALYS L. GREGORY, 61 Palatine Road, Withington, Manchester, 20.

JOHN GRUNDY, Esq., Department of Economics, The University, Manchester, 13.

S. A. GUTAUSKAS, Esq., 86 Hinde Street, Moston, Manchester, 10.

H. J. HABAKKUK, Esq., Pembroke College, Cambridge.

Miss ELIZABETH M. HALCROW, 32 Auckland Avenue, South Shields, Co. Durham.

COLIN HARDIE, Esq., Magdalen College, Oxford.

GEORGE HARDING'S BOOKSHOP, Ltd., 64 Great Russell Street, London, W.C. 1.

Miss F. E. HARMER, The University, Manchester, 13.

Dr. W. O. HASSALL, The Manor House, Wheatley, Oxford.

Professor A. F. HATTERSLEY, Natal University College, Pietermaritzburg, South Africa.

DENYS HAY, Esq., Department of History, The University, Edinburgh.

J. R. L. HIGHFIELD, Esq., 83 Rose Hill, Oxford.

Rev. Dr. GILBERT HILL, Greyfriars, Oxford.

J. E. C. HILL, Esq., Balliol College, Oxford.

J. W. F. HILL, Esq., 2 Lindum Terrace, Lincoln.

Miss ROSALIND HILL, Westfield College, London, N.W. 3.

Rev. W. A. HINNEBUSCH, Providence College, Providence, R.I., U.S.A.

R. H. HODGKIN, Esq., Ilmington, Shipston-on-Stour.

J. HOLMES, Esq., 18 Well Street, Exeter.

Miss ANNE HOLT, Oakfield, Penny Lane, Liverpool, 15.

Miss MARGERY L. HOYLE, 150 Copse Hill, Wimbledon, London, S.W. 20.

B. N. HUGHES, Esq., Flat 6, 5 Kensington Park Gardens, London, W. 11.

Professor EDWARD HUGHES, Manor House, Shincliffe, Durham.

Mrs. MARY E. BEGGS HUMPHREYS, Innox Hill House, Frome, Somerset.

Professor R. A. HUMPHREYS, 28 Drayton Gardens, London, S.W. 10.

Dr. R. W. HUNT, 44 Walton Street, Oxford.

Dr. N. D. HURNARD, Lady Margaret Hall, Oxford.

Miss JOAN HUSSEY, Bedford College, Regent's Park, London, N.W. 1.

H. INGRAM, Esq., Lamorbey Park Adult Education Centre, Sidcup, Kent.

Miss BETTY JACKSON, 45 South Street, Durham.

Dr. E. F. JACOB, All Souls College, Oxford.

CHARLES JOHNSON, Esq., 13A Downshire Hill, London, N.W. 3.

Dr. HILDA JOHNSTONE, 20 St. Martin's Square, Chichester, Sussex.

J. E. A. JOLLIFFE, Esq., Keble College, Oxford.

Miss CHRYSTIE M. JENKIN JONES, Moseley Grange, Cheadle Hulme, Cheshire.

Dr. G. P. JONES, Department of Economics, The University, Sheffield, 10.

Professor ERNST H. KANTOROWICZ, Department of History, University of California, Berkeley 4, Cal., U.S.A.

Miss BETTY KEMP, St. Hugh's College, Oxford.

Rev. E. W. KEMP, Exeter College, Oxford.

N. R. KER, Esq., Stonehaven, Kirtlington, Oxon.

R. W. KETTON-CREMER, Esq., Felbrigg Hall, Norwich.

P. I. KING, Esq., 9 North Way, Headington, Oxford.

Professor R. KLIBANSKY, McGill University, Montreal, Canada.

Professor DOUGLAS KNOOP, 25 The Grove, Totley, Sheffield.

ROGER B. KNOTT, Esq., 70 Spring Gardens, Manchester, 2.

Rev. Professor M. D. KNOWLES, Peterhouse, Cambridge.

Dr. H. KOEPPLER, Wilton Park, Beaconsfield, Bucks.

Miss EVA LA BLAY, 71 Parkland Grove, Ashford, Middx.

JOHN L. LAMONTE, University of Pennsylvania, Philadelphia, Pa., U.S.A.

Miss JOAN C. LANCASTER, Institute of Historical Research, London, W.C. 1.

Miss JANE LANG, Frinsted Rectory, Sittingbourne, Kent.

STEPHEN G. LEE, Esq., Talgarth's Well, Rhossilli, Swansea.

L. G. WICKHAM LEGG, Esq., Manor House, Bodicote, Banbury, Oxon.

REGINALD LENNARD, Esq., Paine's Close, Lower Heyford, nr. Oxford.

Professor JOHN LE PATOUREL, 15 Moor Park Avenue, Leeds, 6.

N. B. LEWIS, Esq., 4 Leyfield Road, Dore, Sheffield.

Rev. KENNETH and Mrs. AGNES LEYS, Isel Vicarage, Cockermouth, Cumberland.

KARL LEYSER, Esq., Magdalen College, Oxford.

LIBRAIRIE ENCYCLOPÉDIQUE, 7 Rue du Luxembourg, Brussels, Belgium.

Lord LINDSAY OF BIRKER (The Master), Balliol College, Oxford.

Mrs. A. G. LITTLE, 'Risborough', Vine Court Road, Sevenoaks, Kent.

Miss DORA LITTLE, 16 Fairacres, Roehampton Lane, London, S.W. 15.

Mrs. M. D. LOBEL, 16 Merton Street, Oxford.

Dr. E. A. LOWE, Institute for Advanced Study, Princeton, New Jersey, U.S.A.

JAMES P. R. LYELL, Esq., The Knowl, Abingdon, Berks.

K. B. McFARLANE, Esq., Magdalen College, Oxford.

H. M. McKECHNIE, Esq., The University Press, Manchester, 15.

A. McKERRAL, Esq., Morton, Midcalder.

Miss M. McKISACK, Somerville College, Oxford.

Rev. H. McLACHLAN, 11 Sydenham Road, Liverpool, 17.

M. MACLAGAN, Esq., Trinity College, Oxford.

Professor WILLIAM G. MACLAGAN, 6 The University, Glasgow, W. 2.

Mrs. ANTONIA M. McLEAN, 22 Hill Rise, Colnbrook, Bucks.

Miss KATHLEEN MAJOR, St. Hilda's College, Oxford.

Lt.-Col. G. E. G. MALET, National Register of Archives, Public Record Office, Chancery Lane, London, W.C. 2.

H. M. MARGOLIOUTH, Esq., 14 Bradmore Road, Oxford.

A. F. MARTIN, Esq., 47 Woodstock Road, Oxford.

Rev. C. MARTIN, Campion Hall, Oxford.

J. M. MARTIN, Esq., 25 Pelham Place, London, S.W. 7.

P. D. MARTIN, Esq., 47 Rectory Road, Beckenham, Kent.

Professor KENNETH MASON, 1 Belbroughton Road, Oxford.

Rev. GERVASE MATHEW, Blackfriars, Oxford.

A. G. MATTHEWS, Esq., Farmcote, Oxted, Surrey.

Miss E. M. MAYERS, Woodstock, 5 Dee Hills Park, Chester.

C. A. F. MEEKINGS, Esq., 42 Chipstead Street, London, S.W. 6.

W. T. MELLOWS, Esq., The Vineyard, Minster Precincts, Peterborough.

Miss L. MARGARET MIDGLEY, Crosby Hall, Cheyne Walk, London, S.W. 3.

A. T. MILNE, Esq., 14 Allison Grove, Dulwich Common, London, S.E. 21.

Dr. L. MINIO-PALUELLO, 20 Hernes Road, Oxford.

JOHN MOONEY, Esq., Cromwell Cottage, Kirkwall, Orkney.

Rev. Dr. J. R. H. MOORMAN, The Theological College, Chichester.

Mrs. MORRIS-DAVIES, Graystones, Kingsgate, nr. Broadstairs, Kent.

J. R. MOSS, Esq., Glenmore, Sixty Acres, Prestwood, Great Missenden, Bucks.

Miss HILDA MOYNS, 12 Gordon Avenue, St. Margarets, Twickenham, Middx.

Miss CHRISTINA MULROONEY, 32 Longmead Road, Salford 6, Lancs.

W. F. MUMFORD, Esq., Hillway, Chalk Pit Lane, Oxted, Surrey.

Mrs. KATHLEEN M. MUNN, Brookside, Green Lane, Hucclecote, Gloucester.

Miss ELEANOR MURPHY, St. Anne's Society, Oxford.

Miss AUDREY M. MURRAY, 59 Chaveney Road, Quorn, Leicestershire.

Professor R. A. B. MYNORS, Pembroke College, Cambridge.

J. N. L. MYRES, Esq., Manor House, Kennington, Oxford.

Professor J. E. NEALE, University College, Gower Street, London, W.C. 1.

Professor RICHARD A. NEWHALL, Williams College, Williamstown, Mass., U.S.A.

H. C. OCKENDEN, Esq., 35 Abbotts Road, Aylesbury, Bucks.

H. S. OFFLER, Esq., Durham Castle, Durham.

Miss E. ORFORD, c/o Dr. Williams' School, Dolgelley, Merioneth, N. Wales.

Professor M. D. O'SULLIVAN, University College, Galway, Eire.

Professor SIDNEY R. PACKARD, 45 Ward Avenue, Northampton, Mass., U.S.A.

Mrs. SYLVIA H. PADFIELD (*née* HYDE), 8 Bland Road, Prestwich, Manchester.

Mrs. K. M. PAGE, Bonson, Fiddington, nr. Bridgwater, Somerset.

Professor SIDNEY PAINTER, Johns Hopkins University, Baltimore 18, Maryland, U.S.A.

W. A. PANTIN, Esq., Oriel College, Oxford.

Professor RICHARD PARES, 7 Carlton Terrace, Edinburgh, 7.

PARKER & SON, Ltd., 27 Broad Street, Oxford.

Rev. T. M. PARKER, Pusey House, Oxford.

Miss BETTY J. PARKINSON, Somerville College, Oxford.

Rev. Dr. PETER E. PEACOCK, Greyfriars, Oxford.

Miss HEATHER E. PEEK, The National Register of Archives, The Public Record Office, London, W.C. 2.

Rev. Father FRANCIS PELSTER, S.J., Università Gregoriana, Piazza della Pilotta 4, Roma (101), Italy.

Professor E. PERROY, 9 rue Auguste Angellier, Lille, France.

J. FOSTER PETREE, Esq., 36 Mayfield Road, Sutton, Surrey.

I. G. PHILIP, Esq., 28 Portland Road, Oxford.

G. F. PLANT, Esq., 73 Grove Park Road, London, S.E. 9.

Professor T. F. T. PLUCKNETT, 17 Crescent Road, Wimbledon, London, S.W. 20.

AUSTIN LANE POOLE, Esq. (The President), St. John's College, Oxford.

Professor G. R. POTTER, 21 Slayleigh Lane, Sheffield, 10.

M. R. POWICKE, Esq., 562 Huron Street, Toronto, Ontario, Canada.

J. O. PRESTWICH, Esq., The Queen's College, Oxford.

F. DOUGLAS PRICE, Esq., Department of History, The University, Glasgow, W. 2.

Miss E. S. PROCTER (The Principal), St. Hugh's College, Oxford.

Miss DRUSILLA V. PROSSER, 12 The Rise, Edgware, Middx.

R. B. PUGH, Esq., 11 Lawn Road Flats, London, N.W. 3.

Miss H. J. PYBUS, Newnham College, Cambridge.

Miss DOROTHY MACKAY QUYNN, Frederick (P.O. Box 577), Maryland, U.S.A.

Professor Sir SARVEPALLI RADHAKRISHNAN, All Souls College, Oxford.

H. J. RANDALL, Esq., Erw Craig, Bridgend, Glamorgan.

B. McL. RANFT, Esq., Royal Naval College, Greenwich.

Miss ELEANOR RATHBONE, 4 Squier St., Palmer, Mass., U.S.A.

Miss MARJORIE REEVES, 13 Norham Gardens, Oxford.

HAROLD RICHARDSON, Esq., 18 Elleray Road, Salford, 6.

H. G. RICHARDSON, Esq., 14 Sheridan Road, Merton, London, S.W. 19.

A. H. T. ROBB-SMITH, Esq., 19 St. Giles', Oxford.

H. ROBERTS, Esq., 85 Kings Road, Westcliff-on-Sea.

Sir ROBERT ROBINSON, 117 Banbury Road, Oxford.

Very Rev. MYLES V. RONAN, Presbytery, Halston St., Dublin, Eire.

Dr. JOHN S. ROSKELL, 337 Brandlesholme Road, Bury, Lancashire.

Professor HARRY ROTHWELL, University College, Southampton.

Mrs. MARJORIE P. ROXBY, c/o British Council, 3 Hanover Street, London, W. 1.

N. RUBINSTEIN, Esq., 53 Frognal, London, N.W. 3.

J. F. RUSHBROOK, Esq., 15 Cumnor Road, Lower Wootton, nr. Oxford.

E. RUSSELL, Esq., 'Avoncroft', 34 Shipston Road, Stratford-on-Avon, Warwickshire.

P. E. RUSSELL, Esq., The Queen's College, Oxford.

DAVID C. RUTTER, Esq., Exeter College, Oxford.

W. J. SAINSBURY, Esq., 13 West Eaton Place, London, S.W. 1.

Rev. Dr. H. E. SALTER, Broad Oak, Sturminster Newton, Dorset.

L. F. SALZMAN, Esq., 53 The Avenue, Lewes.

I. J. SANDERS, Esq., 18 South Marine Terrace, Aberystwyth.

Miss E. M. SANFORD, Sweet Briar College, Virginia, U.S.A.

Professor G. O. SAYLES, Aberfoyle, Maryville Park, Belfast, Northern Ireland.

ERIC W. SCORER, Esq., Coombe Hurst, Lincoln.

W. R. SCURFIELD, Esq., Clerk of the County Council, Shirehall, Worcester.

Mrs. E. SEYMOUR, 33 Western Road, Southall, Middx.

Mrs. MARGARET SHARP, 12A Royal York Crescent, Bristol, 8.

Miss MARGARET A. SHATTOCK, Offley Place, Hitchin, Herts.

I. P. SHAW, Esq., King's College, London, W.C. 2.

Dr. R. CUNLIFFE SHAW, Orrysmount, Kirkbride, Isle of Man.

KENNETH SISAM, Esq., 'Yatsden', Boars Hill, Oxford.

Miss M. D. SLATTER, 3 Melcroft Avenue, Western Park, Leicester.

Miss BERYL SMALLEY, St. Hilda's College, Oxford.

E. H. F. SMITH, Esq., St. Peter's Hall, Oxford.

Miss JENNIFER SMITH, 11 Cleeve Lawns, Downend, Bristol.

R. W. SOUTHERN, Esq., Balliol College, Oxford.

R. N. SPANN, Esq., The University, Manchester, 13.

FRANCIS W. STEER, Esq., Patmers, Duton Hill, Great Dunmow, Essex.

Dr. S. H. STEINBERG, 11 Crystal Palace Park Road, Sydenham, London, S.E. 26.

Sir FRANK STENTON, The University, Reading.

ERIC STONE, Esq., Magdalen College, Oxford.

Mr. and Mrs. E. L. G. STONES, 1012 Great Western Road, Glasgow.

J. W. STOYE, Esq., Headington House, Old Headington, Oxford.

Mrs. AMY STRINGER, 56 Parksway, Prestwich, Manchester.

B. H. SUMNER, Esq. (The Warden), All Souls College, Oxford.

Miss HELEN SUTHERLAND, Cockley Moor, Dockray, Penrith, Cumberland.

Miss L. S. SUTHERLAND (The Principal), Lady Margaret Hall, Oxford.

Professor ALFRED H. SWEET, Washington & Jefferson College, Washington, Penn., U.S.A.

Miss MARION SYKES, Newport Vicarage, Brough, E. Yorks.

Rev. Professor NORMAN SYKES, 2 Selwyn Gardens, Cambridge.

A. J. TAYLOR, Esq., Inspector of Ancient Monuments for Wales, Ministry of Works, 76 Onslow Gardens, London, S.W. 7.

Professor S. HARRISON THOMSON, 3939 Broadway, Boulder, Colorado, U.S.A.

Professor S. E. THORNE, Yale University School of Law, New Haven, Conn., U.S.A.

Sir HENRY TIZARD, Keston, Hill Head, Fareham, Hants.

A. TOMKINSON, Esq., 253 Cowley Road, Oxford.

Miss MARGARET E. R. TORRANCE, The Priory, Weston Road, Bath.

Mrs. T. F. TOUT, 10 North Square, London, N.W. 11.

Miss MARGARET TOYNBEE, 22 Park Town, Oxford.

Professor R. F. TREHARNE and Mrs. ELLEN TREHARNE, Hill Side, Bryn-y-Mor Road, Aberystwyth.

T. D. TREMLETT, Esq., Plox House, Bruton, Somerset.

M. H. TROLLOPE, Esq., Holmefield, Hartmore Road, Godalming, Surrey.

Mrs. MABEL TYLECOTE, Heaton Lodge, Heaton Mersey, Stockport, Cheshire.

Dr. MOSES TYSON, The University, Manchester.

Professor B. L. ULLMAN, University of North Carolina, Chapel Hill, N.C., U.S.A.

Mrs. JOAN VARLEY, Diocesan Record Office, Exchequer Gate, Lincoln.

Professor PAUL VAUCHER, 180 rue de Grenelle, Paris 7e, France.

R. B. VERNEY, Esq., Claydon House, Bletchley, Bucks.

Miss JOAN WAKE, The Green Farm, Cosgrove, Bletchley.

Dr. J. WALKER, 'Ashlynne', 33 Heaton Road, Huddersfield.

J. M. WALLACE-HADRILL, Esq., Merton College, Oxford.

R. WALZER, Esq., 39 Portland Road, Oxford.

CYRIL WARD, Esq., City of Worcester Training College, Henwick Grove, Worcester.

Miss P. M. WARD, 46B Edwardes Square, London, W. 8.

W. LEWIS WARREN, Esq., 139 Addison Road, Ashton, Preston, Lancs.

S. H. WATERS, Esq., 5 Belmont Road, Wakefield, Yorks.

Dr. CLEMENT C. J. WEBB, Old Rectory, Pitchcott, Aylesbury, Bucks.

Professor MARTIN A. WEINBAUM, Queens College, Flushing, N.Y., U.S.A.

E. WELBOURNE, Esq., Emmanuel College, Cambridge.

REGINALD D. WHEELER, Esq., 64 Great Russell Street, London, W.C. 1.

STANLEY G. WHEELER, Esq., 64 Great Russell Street, London, W.C. 1.

GEOFFREY H. WHITE, Esq., 321 Upper Richmond Road, Putney, S.W. 15.

Miss DOROTHY WHITELOCK, St. Hilda's College, Oxford.

Dr. GWENETH WHITTERIDGE, Holywell Cottage, Oxford.

Professor B. WILKINSON, The University, Toronto, Ontario, Canada.

J. B. WILLANS, Esq., Dolforgan Kerry, nr. Newtown, Montgomeryshire.

Right Rev. A. T. P. WILLIAMS (Bishop of Durham), Auckland Castle, Bishop Auckland, Co. Durham.

Rev. R. R. WILLIAMS (The Principal), St. John's College, Durham.

Professor F. P. WILSON, Merton College, Oxford.

Professor P. H. WINFIELD, St. John's College, Cambridge.

F. M. WINGATE, Esq., Malcombe, Branksome Park, Bournemouth.

B. P. WOLFFE, Esq., Hertford College, Oxford.

HERBERT WOOD, Esq., c/o Lloyds Bank, Ltd., 72 Lombard Street, London, E.C. 3.

Dr. K. L. WOOD-LEGH, 49 Owlstone Road, Cambridge.

B. L. WOODCOCK, Esq., 'Walton', Rough Common, Canterbury, Kent.

J. M. B. WRIGHT OF AUCHINELLAN, Auchinellan House, Ford, Lochgilphead, Argyll.

LIBRARIES

ABERDEEN: King's College.

ABERYSTWYTH: University College of Wales.

BELFAST: Public Library.

BELFAST: Queen's University.

BIRMINGHAM: Public Library.

BIRMINGHAM UNIVERSITY.

BRISTOL UNIVERSITY.

BRITISH LIBRARY OF POLITICAL AND ECONOMIC SCIENCE.

CAMBRIDGE: Christ's College.

CAMBRIDGE: Emmanuel College.

CAMBRIDGE: Jesus College.

CAMBRIDGE: Newnham College.

CAMBRIDGE: St. John's College.

CHESTER: Public Library.

CHESTER: St. Deiniol's Library.

CHRIST'S HOSPITAL HISTORY GRECIANS.

DOWNSIDE ABBEY, nr. Bath.

DUNDEE: University College.

DURHAM UNIVERSITY.

EDINBURGH: Society of Writers to H.M. Signet.

ENGLEFIELD GREEN: Royal Holloway College.

EXETER: City Library.

GHENT UNIVERSITY.

GLASGOW UNIVERSITY.

HEYTHROP COLLEGE.

HULL: University College.
LEEDS UNIVERSITY.
LEEDS: Yorkshire Archaeological Society.
LEICESTER: University College.
LIVERPOOL: Public Libraries.
LIVERPOOL UNIVERSITY.
LONDON: Birkbeck College.
LONDON: King's College.
LONDON: Queen Mary College.
LONDON: University Library.
LONDON: Warburg Institute.
LONDON: Dr. Williams's Trust.
MANCHESTER: Chetham's Library.
MANCHESTER: John Rylands Library.
MANCHESTER UNIVERSITY.
MANCHESTER UNIVERSITY: Philip Haworth Research Library.
MIRFIELD: House of the Resurrection.
NEWCASTLE-UNDER-LYME: High School.
NEWCASTLE-UPON-TYNE: King's College.
NEWCASTLE-UPON-TYNE: Literary and Philosophical Society.
NORTH CAROLINA UNIVERSITY.
NOTTINGHAM: University College.
OLD STOPFORDIANS ASSOCIATION.
OREGON UNIVERSITY.
OXFORD: Balliol College.
OXFORD: Blackfriars.
OXFORD: Christ Church.
OXFORD: Corpus Christi College.
OXFORD: Faculty of Modern History.
OXFORD: Jesus College.
OXFORD: Lady Margaret Hall.
OXFORD: Magdalen College.
OXFORD: Manchester College.
OXFORD: Mansfield College.
OXFORD: Pusey Memorial Library, Pusey House.
OXFORD: The Queen's College.
OXFORD: St. Anne's Society
OXFORD: St. Hilda's College.
OXFORD: St. John's College.
OXFORD: Somerville College.
OXFORD: Taylor Institution.
OXFORD: Trinity College.

OXFORD: Union Society.
OXFORD: Wadham College.
PENNSYLVANIA UNIVERSITY.
POTCHEFSTROOM: University College.
THE PUBLIC RECORD OFFICE.
ST. ANDREWS UNIVERSITY.
SHEFFIELD UNIVERSITY.
SOUTHAMPTON: University College.
SOUTH WALES & MONMOUTHSHIRE UNIVERSITY COLLEGE.
STELLENBOSCH UNIVERSITY.
SWANSEA: University College.
TORONTO: Pontifical Institute of Mediaeval Studies.
WALLINGTON: Public Library.
WIGAN: Central Public Library.

PRINTED IN GREAT BRITAIN
AT THE UNIVERSITY PRESS, OXFORD
BY CHARLES BATEY, PRINTER TO THE UNIVERSITY